"A welcome and important contribution; moving from tunes to symphonies, indeed! Social marketing has grown in experience, evidence and geography in recent years and this text presents the latest developments in the discipline. Using a mix of case studies, research evidence, practical experience and insight, the reader is presented with the fundamentals of social marketing as well as creative insights for innovation and cutting edge research."

Prof. L. Suzanne Suggs, Head, BeCHANGE Research Group, Institute for Public Communication, Università della Svizzera italiana

"It's hard to imagine a more comprehensive and readable guide to the field, its theory and practice, for both students and practitioners. Everything is explained without pretension and usually illustrated with clear examples and case studies. But *Social Marketing* also emphasises the need for a critical approach and an understanding of social marketing at a systemic level and, in doing so, challenges all of us to re-examine our own role in a globalised consumer economy."

Philip R. Holden, Senior Lecturer, Marketing Communications, Critical Marketing and Social Marketing, The Business School, Old Royal Naval College

"I wish I had had this book when I started but others who want to be effective public health professionals now have the best book there is on the subject and it is hard to believe it but the authors have improved on the first edition."

Ray Lowry, DR Lowry Social Marketing

"Provides leading insights into the tools and frameworks that social marketing practitioners use to shape environments and provide offerings to tempt consumers to make choices for the greater good."

Dr Sharyn Rundle-Thiele, Griffith University, Queensland, Australia

"An empowering read and a remarkable contribution to the field."

François Lagarde, Vice-président, Communications, McGill College, Montreal, Canada

"This is a wonderful book which takes a critical but realistic perspective on commercial marketing. This text will help you better understand the big picture of social forces as well as individual factors that are critical to create social change."

Michael Basil, Professor of Marketing, University of Lethbridge, Canada

"A very good read; more than a classroom missive, it is an engaging treatment of the need for social change and an illustration of social marketing's value to and responsibility for making the world a better place. It is also the only textbook, of which I am aware, that provides a moral compass by which the reader can guide his or her efforts to use their new knowledge."

James Lindenberger, Director of the University of South Florida Social Marketing Group at the College of Public Health, USA

"A powerful new teaching tool for the classroom and a valuable reference guide for social marketing practitioners. Delightful to read."

Carole Bryant, Distinguished USF Health Professor, Florida Prevention Research Center at the University of South Florida, USA

Social Marketing

Second Edition

Social Marketing involves the application of marketing techniques, usually associated with promoting consumption, to social ends. It *critically examines commercial marketing so as to learn from its successes and curb its excesses*, thereby offering an alternative to the standard Western economic model of consumption at all costs.

This popular introductory textbook has been updated to provide greater depth on behaviour change theory, and more on branding and on the increasing importance of digital media. A new chapter examines the need for systemic change to tackle the complex problems, such as global warming, we now face. It explores concepts such as the co-creation of value, Community Based Prevention Marketing (CBPM) and the vital role of partnerships. Another new chapter addresses the subject of Critical Marketing and the need to analyse the impact that business and burgeoning corporate power is having on the health and welfare of us as individuals, our communities and our planet.

These issues are brought to life with the integration of case studies from across the world to provide a textbook which is required reading for undergraduate, postgraduate and advanced level students.

Gerard Hastings is Director of the Institute for Social Marketing at the University of Stirling and Open University, UK.

Christine Domegan is Senior Lecturer in Marketing at the National University of Ireland, Galway.

First published 2007
by Butterworth Heinemann/Elsevier

Second edition published 2014
by Routledge
2 Park Square, Milton Park, Abingdon, Oxon OX14 4RN
and by Routledge
711 Third Avenue, New York, NY 10017

Routledge is an imprint of the Taylor & Francis Group, an informa business

British Library Cataloguing in Publication Data
A catalogue record for this book is available from the British Library

Library of Congress Cataloging in Publication Data
   Hastings, Gerard (Professor)
   Social marketing: from tunes to symphonies / Gerard Hastings and
   Christine Domegan. — Second edition.
      pages cm
   Includes bibliographical references and index.
   1. Social marketing—Handbooks, manuals, etc.   2. Behavior modification.
   I. Domegan, Christine.   II. Title.
   HF5414.H37 2013
   658.8—dc23

                                                              2013007129

ISBN: 978–0–415–68372–2 (hbk)
ISBN: 978–0–415–68373–9 (pbk)
ISBN: 978–0–203–38092–5 (ebk)

Typeset in IowanOldStyle
by RefineCatch Limited, Bungay, Suffolk, UK

Social Marketing

From tunes to symphonies

Second Edition

Gerard Hastings and Christine Domegan

Routledge
Taylor & Francis Group

LONDON AND NEW YORK

Contents

List of illustrations and exercises

Figures

Tables

Boxes

Exercises

Case study contributors

Sharad Agarwal, Hindustan Latex Family Planning Promotion Trust, India

Lucía Aguirre Sánchez, BeCHANGE Research Group. Institute of Public Communication, Faculty of Communication Sciences, Università della Svizzera italiana (USI), Switzerland

Helena Alves, University of Beira Interior and NECE (Business Sciences Research Center), Portugal

Marisa de Andrade, Institute for Social Marketing (ISM), Stirling Management School, University of Stirling, UK

Rafael Araque, Universidad Loyola Andalucía, Spain

Julia Austin, Consultant Midwife, University Hospitals of Leicester NHS Trust, UK

Sara Balonas, Researcher, Communication and Society Research Centre, University of Minho, Social Sciences Institute, Braga; Portugal Strategy Director, b+ communication, Porto, Portugal

Lance Barrie, Centre for Health Initiatives, University of Wollongong, Australia

Abraham Brown, University of Nottingham, Nottingham Business School, UK

Peter Caputi, Centre for Health Initiatives, University of Wollongong, Australia

Katie Collins, Bristol Social Marketing Centre, University of the West of England, UK

Sameer Deshpande, Associate Professor of Marketing, Faculty of Management, University of Lethbridge, Canada

Robert John Donovan, Curtin University, Centre for Behavioural Research in Cancer Control, Perth, Australia

Dr Sinead Duane, National University of Ireland, Galway

Sara Fernandes, 'Querença' Project, Manuel Viegas Guerreiro Foundation, Portugal

Lynda Fielder, Curtin University, Social Marketing Research Unit, Perth, Western Australia

Danielle Gallegos, Faculty of Health, School of Exercise and Nutrition Sciences, Queensland University of Technology, Brisbane, Australia

Karine Gallopel-Morvan, Researcher in Social Marketing, French School of Public Health, Rennes, France

Marie Gendron, Director General of the Lucie and André Chagnon Foundation Early Childhood Project

Robyn Hamilton, Director, Australian Breastfeeding Association

Don Iverson, Centre for Health Initiatives, University of Wollongong

Geoffrey Jalleh, Curtin University, Centre for Behavioural Research in Cancer Control, Perth, Australia

Sandra C. Jones, Centre for Health Initiatives, University of Wollongong, Australia

Keryn Johnson, Centre for Health Initiatives, University of Wollongong, Australia

François Lagarde, Adjunct Professor, Faculty of Medicine at the University of Montreal and Vice-President, Communications at the Lucie and André Chagnon Foundation, Canada

Karen Larsen-Truong Centre for Health Initiatives, University of Wollongong, Australia

Christophe Leroux, Director of Communications, National League Against Cancer, Paris, France

Ray Lowry, Retired Lecturer, Dental Sciences, Newcastle University Dental School, UK

Doug McKenzie-Mohr, McKenzie-Mohr Associates

Lindsay Manning, Bristol Social Marketing Centre, University of the West of England, UK

Susana Marques, Coordinator Professor at the High Institute of Administration and Management, Porto, Portugal

José Montero, Universidad Loyola Andalucía, Spain

Paulo Moreira, Escola Nacional de Saúde Publica, Universidade Nova de Lisboa, Portugal

Melissa Otero, Senior Marketing and Communications Manager

Robyn Ouschan, Curtin University, Social Marketing Research Unit, Perth, Western Australia

Molly Patterson, Research Midwife, University Hospitals of Leicester NHS Trust, UK

Lyn Phillipson, Centre for Health Initiatives, University of Wollongong, Australia

Josephine Previte, UQ Business School, University of Queensland, Brisbane, Australia

Mallely Rangel Garcia, BeCHANGE Research Group, Institute of Public Communication, Faculty of Communication Studies, Università della Svizzera italiana (USI), Switzerland

Natalie Rangelov, BeCHANGE Research Group, Institute of Public Communication, Faculty of Communication Studies, Università della Svizzera italiana (USI), Switzerland

Juan M. Rey, University of Granada, Spain

Rebekah Russell-Bennett, School of Advertising, Marketing & Public Relations, Queensland University of Technology, Brisbane, Australia

Purvi Shah, Hindustan Latex Family Planning Promotion Trust, India

Anne M. Smith, Open University-ISM, UK

Martine Stead, Institute for Social Marketing, University of Stirling, UK

John Strand, Vice President and Director, Social Marketing and Communication Center, Washington DC, USA

L. Suzanne Suggs, BeCHANGE Research Group, Institute of Public Communication, Faculty of Communication Studies, Università della Svizzera italiana (USI), Switzerland

Joanne Telenta, Centre for Health Initiatives, University of Wollongong, Australia

Jeffrey A. Thom, Centre for Health Initiatives, University of Wollongong, Australia

Sanjeev Vyas, Program Director and Communications Advisor, Abt Associates Inc., New Delhi, India

Melinda Williams, Centre for Health Initiatives, University of Wollongong, Australia

Acknowledgements

I would like to give special thanks to Tom and Ruaridh for their help with this book

Gerard

For Catherine, Fiona and Deirdre

Christine

And both of us would like to record our gratitude to Diane and Aileen for their immense support

Foreword

You know you've got a good book in your hands when you open it up, look at the contents and immediately wish you'd written it yourself. I fell in love with the concept straight away: the authors have combined new thinking from a variety of sources in order to blend together the stalwarts of 4Ps, relationships and services marketing, while also introducing new ideas like co-creation. So, a platform is created that allows us to understand that the strength of social marketing lies in its flexibility to change behaviour using a variety of means, and that these are strategic rather than tactical. This is urgently needed: our work with practitioners at the Bristol Social Marketing Centre demonstrates the continuing educational importance of correcting inaccuracies that depict social marketing as being just about posters and adverts.

Reading on, more profound messages emerge. The authors' pioneering work in attacking damaging commercial practices comes to light in the critical marketing chapter. The stories make difficult and disturbing reading for those of us who have worked in commerce. The business sector needs to regain its moral compass; no sign of it happening just yet, and hence all the more need for books like this to shine lights in dark places.

The last chapter really made me sit up straight. In our own work, we have recognized important ecological perspectives in the world of 'behaviour change'. But with their work on 'the system' of social marketing the authors have shown just how cutting edge their thinking is: they understand that the behaviour change world needs multi-disciplinary solutions, and they understand that market orientation gives social marketing a strategic platform for a leading role in this new multi-discipline world.

I hope you enjoy this book as much as I have.

Professor Alan Tapp

December 2012

Preface: Of tunes and symphonies

Tune: 'a melody, esp. one for which harmony is not essential'

Symphony: 'an extended large scale composition usually with several movements'

(*Collins English Dictionary*)

Social Marketing: Why should the Devil have all the best tunes? was published in 2007 and, five years on, we felt it was time for an update. The discipline has progressed, new cases have emerged and thinking has developed – so, like any other textbook, a bit of refreshing was required. On a wider scale, though, bigger changes have led us to undertake a more radical rethink. Specifically, in the last five years, the world of business has suffered seismic shocks. Multiple global banking scandals, the crisis in the Eurozone, burgeoning inequalities, spiralling boardroom pay and the unnerving concept of corporations that are deemed 'too big to fail' have forced on to the front page issues that might once have languished in the finance section. The backdrop to these various detonations is nagging concern about the increasing commercialization of our lives, growing unease about the extent of corporate influence and power, and, underpinning both, a gnawing anxiety about climate change and the planetary impact of an economic model built on perpetual growth and accelerating consumption.

Marketing is heavily implicated in all of this: marketers were the ones, after all, selling the subprime mortgages and multiple credit options; they are also the ones providing the know-how and energy that drives our burgeoning consumption. The rhetoric may be about consumer sovereignty and customer satisfaction, but the reality is all too often about passivity, dependence and damage – especially when the tools and ideas of marketing are wielded by the corporate sector. In this context, it is becoming increasingly apparent that the job of marketing is not to look after the needs of customers, but those of shareholders. Outside the finance sector, this inversion is most obvious with the purveyors of harmful products such as alcohol, tobacco and fast food. For instance, according to the latest Surgeon General's Report (US Department of Health and uman Services 2012), 88 per cent of tobacco users start as children, and Doll *et al.*'s (2004) work shows that half of those who don't manage to quit will be killed by their smoking. The World Health Organization (WHO) estimates that by 2030 this will amount to as many 10 million unnecessary premature deaths a year.

However, the problems with corporate marketing go way beyond bad bankers and dangerous products. Its function is to keep us shopping; its effect is to lionize materialism, engender an unwonted sense of entitlement and dampen down our critical faculties. It has become the means by which corporations retain and extend their power. The banking crisis at one extreme and teen smokers at the other demonstrate the potential malignity of such excess power. And consumption-driven global warming makes it everyone's business.

Business thinkers have recognized the scale and depth of the problem. The *British Journal of Management* speaks of 'a fundamental intellectual failure' (Currie *et al.* 2010), the *Economist* of 'sackcloth and ashes for the world's business schools' (Schumpeter 2009) and business guru Michael Porter, in the hallowed *Harvard Business Review*, of 'the capitalist system' being 'under siege' and 'business increasingly' being 'viewed as a major cause of social, environmental, and economic problems' (Porter and Kramer 2011). All acknowledge the need for fundamental change, although the *Economist* at least is pessimistic about the likelihood of this happening: having 'drawn up blueprints for reform', its Schumpeter column notes 'the giants of management education have laboured mightily to bring forth a molehill'.

We in social marketing also have to recognize that the world has changed; but for us there is cause for optimism. Marketing need not be manipulative. In its pure form, it is a benign and quintessentially human activity. Yes, it has found its way into the MBA syllabus, and has become the corporation's control mechanism of choice, but, in reality, it has a much older and more important role in our lives. Its core principles of mutually beneficial exchange, doing deals and seeking to identify the win-wins that make cooperation pay for multiple parties are the essence of collective living. Marketing oils the wheels of society – it can help a community run more smoothly, improve people's sense of wellbeing and generate new value systems. A key role for social marketers – and this textbook – is, then, to reclaim marketing. It can again be the servant of people and social cohesion, not corporate power and selective enrichment.

To add to the optimism, there is now a well-refined evidence base showing that marketing principles do indeed work well outside the marketplace. Social marketing campaigns on topics as varied as substance misuse, sustainability, weight control and traffic safety have all been shown to work: they not only gain people's attention and appreciation, they also change behaviour – and ultimately they save lives. Furthermore, when Stephen Emmott, Professor of Computational Science at Oxford University and leading climate scientist, points out that the problem is us, and that the only answer to global warming is behavioural change, it is clear that social marketing also has the potential to save the planet (Jack 2012).

This potential intensifies when we move beyond individual campaigns, and start to think more strategically. We need to acknowledge, as the business thinkers quoted above have, that the challenges are great, and that there is a need for fundamental, systemic change. As marketers, we can also appreciate the power and potential of people to bring about change in their own lives, and that the focus of social marketing is not to change people's behaviour for them, but to unlock their potential and power to change it for themselves. This is going to be partly about individual empowerment and enabling people to harness their own internal resources. Equally though, it must look to provide an environment that facilitates both individual and collective action. Thus, we can (and must) accommodate the two complementary viewpoints identified by George Orwell: 'the one, how can you improve human nature until you have changed the system? The other, what is the use of changing the system before you have improved human nature' (1970: 48).

This individual and collective effort needs to be matched by changes in commercial marketing. This is not just a matter of better regulation – though it is clear that, if we are to move beyond Schumpeter's molehills, a degree of compulsion will be needed. Rather, it requires a fundamental rethink of the purpose and values of business. The book *Small is Beautiful* (Schumacher 1993), written in the 1970s, anticipates many of the problems the banking crisis has thrown into relief – problems of size, of power and of greed. It has the subtitle 'A Study of Economics as if People Mattered'. What is needed now is not just a study, but a re-engineering, of marketing as if people (and the planet) mattered. Social marketers have to be at the forefront of this critical debate.

This book then is a second edition in the conventional sense of revising and refreshing the original work. In doing so, it provides an introduction to and an explanation of the basic tools and techniques of social marketing. It also presents new examples and case studies (for which thanks to many colleagues around the world), makes more use of stories and includes many additional interactive features.

In addition, however, this second edition has a more radical aim: to take social marketing to a new level; to show that it can move beyond ameliorative but fragmented campaigns and become a coherent movement for change. And that it can empower and energize people to become the authors of their own fate, while simultaneously encouraging contextual change that will help them to do so. With this in mind, we have introduced new material in two key areas: (a) on critical thinking to help you reflect on the problems of our current business values and practices; and (b) on systems thinking to provide a strategic conception of how beneficial change can be engendered. In this way, we feel social marketing can reach its full potential: to facilitate not just behaviour change, but also far-reaching social change. It is time, we feel, to move from tunes to symphonies.

Given the problems now facing the world, never has this been a more important task.

> ### The Marketing Matrix: How the Corporation gets its power and how we can reclaim it
>
> Interested readers might find this complementary text, which extends the discussion of critical marketing analysis, useful. The Foreword from *The Marketing Matrix* is reproduced at the end of this volume to help you decide.

References

Currie, G., Knights, D. and Starkey, K. (2010) 'Introduction: a post-crisis critical reflection on business schools', *British Journal of Management*, 21(s 1): s1–s5.

Doll, R., Peto, R., Boreham, J. and Sutherland, I. (2004) 'Mortality in relation to smoking: 50 years' observations on male British doctors', *British Medical Journal*, 328: 1519.

Hastings, G. (2012) *The Marketing Matrix: How the Corporation gets its power and how we can reclaim it*. London: Routledge.

Jack, I. (2012) 'The implications of overpopulation are terrifying. But will we listen to them?', *The Guardian*, 3 August 2012. Available at www.guardian.co.uk/commentisfree/2012/aug/03/ian-jack-overpopulation-ten-billion/.

Orwell, G. (1970) *Collected Essays*. 2nd Edition. London: Secker & Warburg.

Porter, M. and Kramer, M. (2011) 'Creating Shared Value', *Harvard Business Review* January 2011.

Schumacher, E.F. (1993) *Small is Beautiful: A Study of Economics as if People Mattered*. London: Vintage.

Schumpeter (2009) *The Economist*. Online: www.economist.com/node/14493183 (accessed 16 May 2013).

Surgeon General, US Department of Health and Human Services. (2012) *Preventing Tobacco Use Among Youth and Young Adults: A Report of the Surgeon General*. Atlanta, GA: US Department of Health and Human Services, Centers for Disease Control and Prevention, National Center for Chronic Disease Prevention and Health Promotion, Office on Smoking and Health.

Chapter **1**

If it works for Coca-Cola . . .

CREATING CHRISTMAS TRADITION

A light flurry of tiny, perfectly formed snowflakes flutter, tumble and drift downwards. Capturing the silver moonlight, they settle softly on the already snow-covered rooftops, street lamps and sidewalks. The clock tower is heard in the near distance tunefully announcing the passing time: one, two, three . . .

There's a relaxed happiness in the air as couples, friends and families meander their way home with the night drawing in. A little girl gazes into the shop window. Snugly wrapped in her warm hat, scarf, gloves and winter coat, she smiles, mesmerized by the magical toy train display and the beautiful, tall, tinsel-laden tree with its sparkling red, green, yellow and blue fairy lights. As the little girl turns, real magic is in the air, for there before her is Santa Claus himself: his familiar red coat, white beard and happy smile show that all is as it should be. A friendly wink completes the enchantment.

It is a timeless Christmas scene. It could be taking place anywhere from Helsinki to Hobart; from Shanghai to San Francisco. It is also a script for a world-famous ad with an equally familiar tagline: 'Holidays are coming, 'tis the season . . . holidays are coming . . .'

Recognize it?

It is one of the many popular Coca-Cola (Coke) Christmas ads we see, hear and experience every year and (assuming you are under 80 years of age) have been doing so since birth. This particular advertisement was aired in 2007 in the UK and Ireland, but the Christmas theme has been a mainstay of Coke's advertising since 1931. The soft, mood-setting music, glittering colour, snow-filled streets and Christmas trees evoke our fondest hopes, dreams and aspirations – and contribute to Coke's status as the number-one global brand.[1] Coke's enormous influence on our lives is even more powerfully illustrated by the fact that the company can seriously lay claim to defining Father Christmas himself. As the company website points out: 'magazine ads for Coca-Cola featured St. Nick as a kind, jolly man in a red suit. Because magazines were so widely viewed, and because this image of Santa appeared for more than three decades, the image of Santa most people have today is largely based on our advertising'.[2] One of the most welcome and reassuring images on earth is actually a Coke trademark.

This book builds on the premise that the immense success of marketing has two sets of implications for anyone interested in behaviour change. First, we should look and learn. If Coke and its commercial marketing colleagues are so good at getting close to us and influencing the way we live our lives, we should study what they are doing and find out what lessons it holds for us.

Second, we should be critical. Such power is daunting and needs checks and balances. The success of companies like Coke in getting people to consume increasing quantities of what nutritionists call 'empty calories' holds important lessons for those who feel our economic system needs better regulation. Specifically, if our concern is with obesity driven by poor diets, perhaps we should seek to put constraints on the fast-food industry; more broadly, if we are anxious about global warming, we should be examining the impact that the marketing of *all* corporate bodies is having on our consumption levels and thereby the planet.

This combination of critically examining commercial marketing so as to *learn from its successes*, on the one hand, and *curb its excesses*, on the other, is the essence of *social marketing*. This book will explain its principles and provide detailed guidance on their practical application to real-life problems. This first chapter discusses the nature of social marketing in more detail, and also explains how to get the most from the rest of the book.

Learning outcomes

By the end of this chapter, you should be able to:

✓ Discuss and explain the power of commercial marketing
✓ Understand the connections between marketing and behaviour
✓ Explain the importance of behaviour change
✓ Outline the linkage between marketing and society

✓ Present the positive and negative effects of marketing

✓ Describe the evolution of social marketing

✓ Define social marketing

✓ Distinguish between social advertising, social media and social marketing.

Key words

commercial marketing – competition – consumption – corporation – critical analysis – exchange – human behaviour – marketing – marketing system – market-place – mutual benefit – relationships – social marketing

THE POWER OF MARKETING

Coke is not alone in influencing us with its marketing. Try doing Exercise 1.1.

EXERCISE 1.1: SHOPPING MATTERS

Consider something you have bought recently – an item of clothing perhaps or a takeaway coffee – or something as big as a car. Anything. Think through why and how you bought it. What made you think of it in the first place? What encouraged or discouraged you? What did you like/dislike about it and the process of buying it? Would you buy it again?

Take a few minutes to do this and jot down some notes.

The exercise demonstrates some of the basic principles of marketing. First, it shows that the process starts not with the marketer, but with you; specifically with something you need or want. This might be for something major, such as a house or food to feed your family; or it could be utterly trivial, such as an impulse to buy a hot drink when a moment previously you had no such desire. Both extremes, though, illustrate a core insight: the customer has to be at the centre of the marketing process. The key lesson from Exercise 1.1 is that when we shop we are seeking satisfaction. The first job of the marketer, then, is to understand us and what we want.

Their second job is to deliver to these needs in the most attractive way possible (or at least in a more attractive way than the competition). What constitutes attractive will vary for different people and needs. An impulse purchaser of a takeaway coffee will prioritize ease of access, and, if they pride themselves on their sophisticated palate, put an emphasis on the quality of the bean and the brewing process. A moderately high price might help to reinforce this high-end positioning. A bit of Italian iconography and American have-a-nice-daying will likely increase the appeal.

A house, by contrast, will involve a much more considered and bespoke purchasing process. But the same four elements will be manipulated to make the process as pleasant as possible: price (perhaps through a financing deal), place (both in the sense of the image and accessibility of the sales agent and the location of the property), promotion (think of the effort that goes into estate agents' property descriptions) and, of course, the product itself – the house has to be the right size and design.

We consumers are also good at learning from experience. If coffee chain X underperforms on any of these dimensions – if the coffee is cold or the service sullen – they will soon lose our custom. Similarly, if the real estate company gets caught cheating, the damage to its good name will make us leery of any future transactions. So, reputation matters, and good ones take time to develop.

Exercise 1.1 then teaches us that consumer orientation is central to good marketing; that the 4Ps of product, price, place and promotion are used to deliver on this promise; that competition in the marketplace hones this process; and that time and experience make it strategic as well as tactical.

Having used this exercise in classes over many years, we can also suggest another lesson: it works. The exercise invariably triggers lots of animated discussion; everyone has a story to tell and they can typically tell it at some length. Marketers have succeeded in making shopping a central and much valued part of our lives. They are, then, masters at getting us to do things – buy their products, visit their shops, attend to their messages, buy their products again . . . They can even get us to do their marketing for them: count how many company names and logos are on the clothing you are wearing; think of the concerns that have been expressed about young people being recruited as 'brand ambassadors' (CAP 2012); remember that the massive recent increases in viral and social networking marketing completely depend on us 'passing on' digital messages or 'liking' particular brands.

What is more, we cooperate with marketers' behaviour change schemes on a voluntary basis. We visit their shops, attend their messages and promote their brands because we want to. We will now explore why this capacity to deliver voluntary behaviour change is such a vital skill in our complex, modern world.

WHY BEHAVIOUR CHANGE MATTERS

EXERCISE 1.2: WHY DOES BEHAVIOUR CHANGE MATTER?

Make a list of what you think are the most pressing problems facing society. Think about the things that have the biggest impact on people's happiness and welfare. Illness and premature death or crime and criminal justice may come to mind, along with conflict and oppression, prejudice and intolerance, and global warming.

Now consider how important human behaviour is to each of these. How in each case these complex and multifaceted problems have our decisions, actions and lifestyles at their heart.

The sense from Exercise 1.2, that how we behave and live our lives has a big impact on both our individual and collective welfare, is amply supported by the evidence. We are now well into an era where chronic, lifestyle-related illnesses are a much greater risk to life and limb than the more familiar communicable killers of yester-year. Two decades ago, a landmark paper in the *Journal of the American Medical Association* concluded that more than half premature deaths, at that time, were attributable to lifestyle diseases such as smoking-related cancer and alcohol-driven cirrhosis (McGinnis and Foege 1993). Since then, the problem of obesity has reached epidemic levels with a combination of poor diet and inactivity bringing an explosion in type 2 diabetes, high blood pressure and heart disease. Experts have raised the real possibility that life expectancy in the US might actually start to decrease as a result – the first such fall since the Wild West was colonized and towns stopped putting up readjusted population figures on a daily basis (Olshansky *et al.* 2005).

The far-reaching impact of tobacco use is an equally alarming threat to public health; as Exercise 1.4 at the end of this chapter states, by 2030, up to 10 million people are likely to be killed by tobacco every year unless we can encourage significant numbers of smokers to quit or youngsters not to start. And, as we write this, rumour has it that the WHO is about to revise upwards its estimates of those who are damaging themselves with drink.

These health behaviours also have a big collateral impact. In Europe, for example, before the implementation of legislation to make public places smoke-free, it was estimated that some 19,000 *non*-smokers were dying from 'second-hand' smoke every year. Alcohol consumption also causes massive damage beyond the individual drinker – think drunk driving (nearly 2,000 deaths a year in the UK alone[3]), and remember that domestic violence and other crime is strongly correlated with inebri-ation. A recent study in the journal *Addiction* suggests that just being in the prox-imity of a heavy drinker damages your health and welfare (Casswell *et al.* 2011).

Then there is our *environmental* behaviour. We seem all too ready to ignore the link between our consumption patterns and environmental degradation (Connolly and Prothero 2003: 289). This goes beyond the purchase of notoriously unsustain-able products such as SUVs or intercontinental holidays, and takes in the collective impact of our shopping habits. As Geels *et al.* point out, 'the lower envi-ronmental impact of a single product may actually be accompanied by higher environmental impact at a more systemic level due to increases in consumption' (2008: 8). This is having an inevitable impact on natural resources: 'Human numbers are growing, forests are shrinking, species are dying, farmland is eroding, freshwater supplies are dwindling, fisheries are collapsing, rivers are constricting, greenhouse gases are accumulating, soot is contaminating the air and lead is contaminating our blood' (Hardin 1968).

Thinking more broadly still, the smooth running of any democratic society depends on people living their lives in a way that serves both individual and collective needs. The criminal justice system, international diplomacy, the democratic process itself all depend on voluntary, cooperative behaviour (Quelch and Jocz 2007).

The capacity to bring about behaviour change, then, is far too valuable to be limited to the marketplace; the wider application of marketing insights has the potential not only to benefit public health but also to make all our lives better, improve social cohesion and even save the planet. This book is all about how to do this. Before proceeding, however, it is also necessary to recognize some less pleasant truths about marketing.

THE DARK SIDE OF MARKETING

At first glance, the implications of Exercise 1.1 and the consumer-centred nature of marketing are very agreeable: marketing, it seems, is ensuring that the economic system is run entirely for our benefit. Whatever we want will be provided for us as efficiently and enjoyably as possible. It is as if we had all migrated to the Sugar Rock Candy Mountain.

The reality, of course, is much less prepossessing: marketers do what they do not for our benefit, but for their own. The perfect Americano in London or condo in Tampa is provided because the seller can make a profit out of it. And this profit motive will ultimately supersede our wishes. If you have any doubts about this, try telling your local coffee shop that you are a bit short of money today so could they let you have your daily coffee for nothing, or try buying that Floridian condo if you are an out-of-work Nicaraguan immigrant. The profit motive effectively excludes the poor from the market.

In this way, marketing, while purporting to meet all our needs, actually both creates and fuels different guises of inequalities. This is what Andreasen (2006) calls 'the dark side of the marketplace'. There are inequalities between those who have and those who don't; the rich and poor; the young and old; male and female; the marginalized, disadvantaged and ethnic minority groups; and between the economic and social needs of our societies. Ronald Paul Hill (2011) picks up the vital concern of inequalities. 'Hill adopts a profoundly ethnographic approach, enabling the poor to tell their own stories and arguing that only when these stories are accorded at least equal value with other narratives will serious progress be made' (Hastings 2011: 11). Cairns *et al.* (2011) take us to another form of inequality: that between developed and developing countries. Whatever form it takes, inequality in a society is harmful to everyone – rich and poor. Reducing consumption, health, environmental and social disparities is a vital global priority; otherwise, social fracture and conflict will continue to dominate our planet (Wilkinson and Pickett 2010).

Meanwhile, for the haves, the blessings of being included in the market can also be distinctly mixed. Commercial marketing is implicated in promoting many of the individually and communally harmful behaviours discussed above. It has now been established, for example, that alcohol, tobacco and food marketing all have a significant impact on our smoking (Lovato *et al.* 2003), drinking (Anderson and Cavanagh 2000) and unhealthy eating behaviour (Hastings *et al.* 2003; McGinnis *et al.* 2006), and this unholy trinity lie at the heart of public ill health.

Thinking more generally, the principal function of marketing is to encourage consumption – which has obvious implications for the sustainability of our lifestyles.

CORPORATE POWER

The contradiction at the heart of commercial marketing – the profit motive disguised as consumer focus – is most apparent in big business. This is dominated by the corporation, for which the prioritizing of profits is enshrined in law through what is called the 'fiduciary imperative' (see Box 1.1 and refer to Chapter 8 for detailed discussion).

BOX 1.1: THE CORPORATION EXPLAINED

The essence of the corporation is that executive decision making is separated from ownership: CEOs spend other people's – shareholders' – money. Because of this, very strict rules are put in place by government to make sure that shareholders' interests (and therefore profits) always come first. This 'fiduciary imperative' ensures that the focus never leaves the bottom line. Even the excessive levels of bonuses and executive pay that we have witnessed in recent years are justified in terms of shareholder returns: 'it's the only way we can get and keep the best people'.

(Source: Hastings 2012: 4)

This single-mindedness has certainly borne fruit. Of the largest 150 economies on our planet, 91 are corporations, not countries, 'with Wal-Mart larger than Sweden or Saudi Arabia and Exxon Mobil larger than Denmark or South Africa. Royal Dutch Shell is larger than Morocco, Vietnam and Slovakia combined' (Bendell 2011: 1). Quite simply, marketing and businesses govern the way we live and preside over our societies and planet to an unprecedented extent.

Thus, the consequences of marketing's power to frame and shape our behaviour goes far beyond the individual consumption of a bottle of Coke or cup of coffee. While commercial marketing can and has contributed to an improved quality of life for individuals (Drucker 1957), it just as often creates new and difficult challenges for society. The true and full extent of marketing's power lies in the often invisible, ignored links our individual consumption behaviours have with our health, environmental, social and societal behaviours. Marketing is a societal process, tightly woven into the fabric of our lives and that of our communities, societies and, in an era of globalization, our planet.

This state of affairs might alarm you. It has brought about a culture of individualism, with all the tensions, power struggles and value differences this produces. It also depends on untrammelled growth and raises unavoidable questions about the extent of consumption in a finite world, and the power and accountability of corporations. However, it cannot be ignored. The critical analysis of our current system is an essential dimension of any attempt to make the world a better place.

ENTER SOCIAL MARKETING

Social marketing pulls these behaviour changes and critical threads together. It is not a new idea. More than 50 years ago, American academic G.D. Wiebe started people thinking in this way when he analysed contemporaneous social advertising campaigns and argued that the best ones were those that mimicked their commercial counterparts. He concluded that it is possible to 'sell brotherhood like you sell soap' (1951: 179). In 1971, Kotler and Zaltman used the term 'social marketing' for the first time in the *Journal of Marketing,* and defined it as 'the design, implementation, and control of programs calculated to influence the acceptability of social ideas and involving considerations of product planning, pricing, communication, distribution, and marketing research' (1971: 5). Prior to the 1970s, 'marketing' was synonymous with economic activities by companies in commercial market settings. Many argued this 'broadening' of marketing from commercial firms into the management of non-profits and social issues was a step too far (Luck 1969).

Bagozzi (1975) brought clarity to the debate, explaining that marketing was about exchanges and that there are different types of marketing exchanges. These range from the restricted exchange of economic goods associated with commercial firms to the more complex, often symbolic, transfer of values seen in social marketing. Figure 1.1 illustrates this process with examples from the commercial, health, safety and waste sectors.

In the health example, the social marketer wants to sell 'non-smoking'. To do this, they too must attempt to satisfy their target group's needs. In the case of young smokers, there may be a need for social status and sophistication, which cigarette smoking is felt to offer. In response, the social marketers can change their messages from ones that, for example, emphasize the carcinogenic properties of tobacco to ones stressing the maturity and strong-mindedness of the non-smoker. In this way, just like the car manufacturer, the social marketers will increase their chances of a sale, of success.

Similarly, in the case of road safety, the social marketer wants to eliminate drunk driving. To make progress, they too must examine, and respond to, their consumers' needs. For example, research in Australia has shown that young people are very dependent on their cars for mobility. This led road-safety advocates to make a compromise, and to change their initial intention of imposing a curfew on young drivers to one of promoting zero blood alcohol levels. This movement towards their consumers again increases the chance of success.

For waste management, social marketers want recycling. Research indicates consumers are willing to recycle, if recycling facilities are local – consumers want

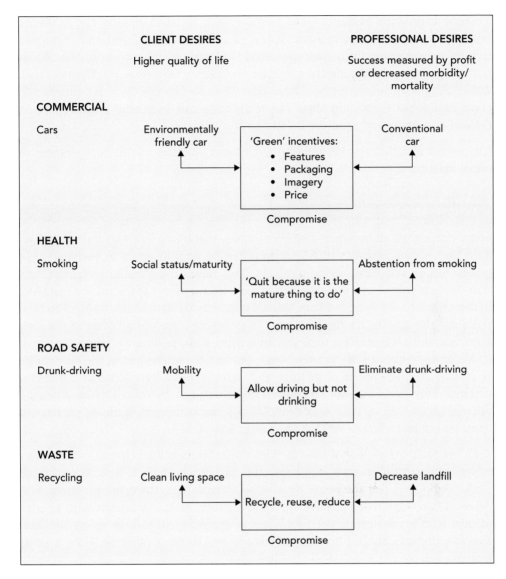

Figure 1.1 The exchange process in marketing
Source: Based on Hastings and Elliott (1993)

convenience and ease. So, local councils and authorities offer mobile Christmas-tree shredding facilities that travel around to communities at convenient times.

Thus, in each case, the marketing idea of compromise, of co-creating exchanges, leads to an increased chance of success. In the social marketing exchange process, 'the consumer in each of us can learn from the citizen, and the citizen can learn from the consumer'. The social marketer must learn from both (Quelch and Jozh 2007: 227).

There is a growing evidence base to show that social marketing can influence multiple behaviours. A systematic review of social marketing initiatives designed to improve nutrition, for instance, showed that, out of 25 interventions, no fewer than 21 had a significant effect on at least one dietary behaviour (McDermott *et al.* 2005). Similar reviews have now been commissioned by the UK Government and show that social marketing ideas and techniques can successfully shift exercise, drinking, smoking and drug-use behaviour.[4]

Chapters 2 to 6 discuss the main principles and practices of this core element of social marketing.

LENGTH AND BREADTH

Social marketers, then, argue that, in essence, marketing is about human behaviour, not money, and that this behaviour can be seen in terms of exchange. We human beings cooperate by doing deals. This raises the question of power; any deal-doing is going to be underpinned by the relative power of the parties involved. In commercial marketing, we have already touched on financial inequalities and the problems this creates for the have-nots in the short term and all of us in the long term. Social marketers have to deal with a wider concept of power; we are none of us in complete control of our own lives – our social circumstances, the availability of choices, the behaviour of siblings and parents will all constrain our decision making. This problem was recognized centuries ago by John Donne when he pointed at out that 'no man is an island'. For social marketers, it means we have to consider not just *which* behaviour to change, but *whose*.

Take the problem of alcohol misuse. This might address the behaviour of the teen who chooses to binge drink; the neglectful parent who fails to intervene; the bar worker who sells her the booze despite being underage; the drink producer who develops alcopops that appeal to juvenile palates; or the politician who fails to control such irresponsibility. This process of analysing the influences on our decision making was dubbed 'moving upstream' by Lawrence Wallack. Have a go at Exercise 1.3.

EXERCISE 1.3: LAWRENCE WALLACK'S RIVER

A man out walking happens across a river in which people are being swept along and in danger of drowning. His immediate desire is to help them and he considers various options – throwing in lifebelts, diving in himself and pulling some to shore or even shouting out instructions on how to swim. And each of these certainly has the potential to help; but it is equally clear that some people will drown – he hasn't got the time or resources to reach them all. He begins to question why this calamity has arisen; why are so many people in the river in the first place? To find out he has to go upstream. When he does so, he finds that a few hundred metres further on there are huge and evocative billboards extolling the virtues of the river – how clean and refreshing it is – and calling on people to 'jump on in; the water's lovely'. A beautiful new diving board has been provided to make the prospect even more enticing, and it costs only 10 cents a go. Kids are daring each other to give it a try.

The man shakes his head and carries on upstream.

After he walks for a few more minutes, the bank begins getting wet, muddy and treacherous. He becomes anxious about falling in the river himself. Then he sees houses built on these poor foundations. They are cheap and dilapidated, more like shacks than houses, and some are clearly in danger of collapse. As he is watching, a small child slips down the bank and only just manages to save itself from falling in the river.

The man is left pondering about how he can best do something about the drowning people: should he help the people who have already fallen in, stop advertisers encouraging others to jump in or move right upstream and change macroeconomic policy so that the poor can afford better housing.

Whose behaviour does he need to change: that of the individual, the marketer or the minister of finance?

(Source: Based on Wallack *et al.* 1993)

The answer is that to be truly successful, a social marketer will need to address the behaviour of all these people. Wallack is compelling us to remember that time and again our individual behaviours are actually intimately related to the system in which we live. Indeed, he is rightly uneasy about approaches that do not recognize this – ones that, in his words, put too much emphasis on the loose threads of the individual, and ignore problems with the fabric of society. Such thinking is not just ineffective, but also unethical.

The idea of systems also introduces the dimension of time to our thinking. As we noted when discussing Exercise 1.1, our behaviour is rarely ad hoc; in particular, we learn from experience. Commercial marketers have recognized this in recent decades and developed the concept of 'relationship marketing' – which has spawned a plethora of reward schemes, loyalty cards and strategic branding efforts – to get and keep our attention. Social marketers have to adopt similar long-term approaches, as we discuss in Chapter 2.

WHY IT'S CRITICAL TO BE CRITICAL

The broader systemic implications of upstream and relational thinking also remind us of the importance of competitive and critical analysis, which we will discuss in detail in Chapters 7 and 8.

The business sector accords great importance to competition, which greatly influences market behaviour – as Exercise 1.1 illustrated. So McDonald's and Pepsi keep a very careful eye on each other, as do Philip Morris and Japan Tobacco. This not only helps them to out-do each other, but it also provides a valuable insight into their customers' behaviour. McDonald's can learn a lot about what people gain from going to a rival fast food outlet, or indeed the broader options they may select in preference to eating a Big Mac, such as having a picnic or eating at home then going to the cinema. Specifically, it tells them more about the needs they are satisfying, and that these can go beyond the obvious one of hunger. This, in turn, helps them hone the service they offer.

All four companies will also be watching those working in public health, nutrition, obesity management and tobacco control – including us in social marketing – closely. We may offer opportunities for collaboration, or threats to their operation in the form of unwelcome criticism or calls for regulation.

Not surprisingly, then, competitive analysis is also very important to social marketers. To start with, we too need to remember that our clients have a choice. Remember, as we've already noted, our interest is in involuntary behaviour change: our clients can choose to go on eating burgers despite their weight problem, or smoking even though their breath is beginning to go. If we cannot compel, we need to take the time and trouble to understand these competing behaviours and learn to outbid them. This approach is sometimes referred to as tackling the 'passive' competition.

There is also 'active' competition in social marketing: we are frequently at odds with parts of the commercial sector. For example, those working in public health want to reduce the consumption of the products marketed by the tobacco, fast food and alcohol industries. Social marketers should therefore use their marketing expertise to deconstruct these activities.

Harking back to Exercise 1.1, for example, it is important to emphasize that advertising and promotion are only part of the picture; we need to think about all the ways that marketers attract customers, including packaging, new product development, price promotions and distribution. In addition, this analysis needs to be backed with careful research to help develop an evidence base that will enable policy makers to act and, where necessary, constrain the activities of commercial marketers. Guiding the development of socially beneficial regulatory systems is a crucial task for social marketers.

Moving beyond the transgressions of individual industries, social marketing can and should contribute to the wider debate about the role and values of commercial marketing in a modern democracy. In a finite world, is a system that works ceaselessly to encourage consumption a desirable one? Should we be concerned about the rise of 'stakeholder marketing' (National Cancer Institute 2008) by the corporate sector, which aims to influence the behaviour of policy makers and politicians just as conventional marketing does that of consumers? And how do we feel about corporate social responsibility (CSR), which, as business texts emphasize, is not driven by philanthropic intent, but commercial interest?

This re-emphasizes the systems thinking we touched on above and locates social marketing in the broader social economy. Following the European tradition of social change, transformation and innovation, social marketing can realign market structures with wider societal values, rather than just applying business models to the day-to-day management of social problems. In this way, it is possible to address the profound question raised by US academics Wilkie and Moore of how to 'facilitate the maximal operations of the system *for the benefit of the host society*' (2003: 118, emphasis added).

Reflecting this broad aim, Figure 1.2 presents a view of the domain of social marketing, which recognizes that the citizen is at the centre of any successful society, and that their empowerment is vital. They need to have the knowledge and skills to make constructive decisions about their lifestyles. Figure 1.2 also recognizes that, as we have noted, this empowerment will be constrained by social context. Building on the work of Bloom and Gundlach concerning the 'paths through which marketing affects societal welfare' (2001: xv), it recognizes the role of three key sets of influences:

- public policy decisions;
- corporate marketing decisions; and
- civil society.

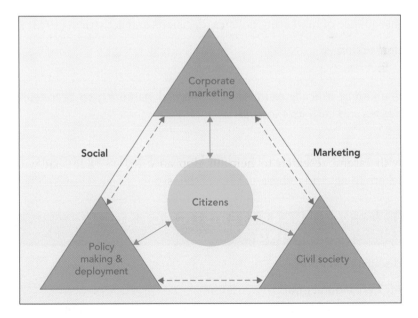

Figure 1.2 The domain of social marketing
Source: Hastings (2011)

This is undoubtedly an ambitious agenda. However, before we get too daunted we should remember the power of our commercial cousins. The Coca-Cola Corporation not only has developed into one of the most successful economic organizations on the planet, but also arguably did more to open up China than Richard Nixon. And, much more ominously, the recent banking crisis, which brought the world economic system to its knees, was largely driven by bright young marketing-literate MBAs. If commercial marketing can do all this, social marketing can foster equitable democratic societies around the world for the betterment of all.

Furthermore, ambitious or not, social marketing has to address these societal issues if it is to continue to be a force to be reckoned with. The alternative is to be relegated to the cleaner-up of other people's messes: whether this be the cancer sufferers created by the tobacco industry or the new poor of a deeply flawed financial sector.

These systemic issues and their ramifications for both society and social marketing are discussed in detail in Chapters 9 and 10.

A DEFINITION

In summary, then, social marketing takes insights from the commercial marketer's efforts to influence our consumption behaviour and applies them to health and social behaviours; it also looks critically at business in order to reduce potential harms being done at both an individual and systemic level. This twin approach was recognized by Lazer and Kelley four decades ago when they stated 'social marketing is concerned with the application of marketing knowledge, concepts and techniques to enhance social as well as economic ends. It is also concerned with analysis of the social consequence of marketing policies, decisions and activities' (1973: ix).

Our briefer version is:

Social marketing critically examines commercial marketing so as to learn from its successes and curb its excesses.

Box 1.2 expands this definition into eight key social marketing precepts.

BOX 1.2: KEY CHARACTERISTICS OF SOCIAL MARKETING

Good social marketing:

1. Sets behavioural goals
2. Creates attractive motivational exchanges with target groups
3. Makes judicious use of theory
4. Thinks beyond communications

5. Thinks beyond the individual
6. Pays careful attention to the competition
7. Looks critically at commercial marketing
8. Thinks systemically

THREE COMMON FALLACIES

Having laid out what social marketing *is*, it is now worth emphasizing what it is *not*.

The word marketing causes perennial problems and considerable confusion. First, it is very familiar to us all both as a term and phenomenon in our daily lives, and the form of marketing with which we are most familiar is advertising – which is unsurprising given that its principal function is to attract attention. This perhaps explains why the literature is full of studies and interventions that are labelled social marketing but turn out to be no more than communications initiatives. Indeed, when Laura McDermott and her colleagues carried out the review on social marketing discussed above, they had to make a deliberate effort to move beyond labels and evaluate interventions that genuinely applied social marketing precepts rather than ones that were simply called social marketing (McDermott *et al.* 2005). So let's deal with our first fallacy: *social marketing is not social advertising*.

Social marketers may make use of communications, or not, depending upon the problem being addressed and, in particular, the needs of the people they are trying to influence. To equate social marketing and social advertising is as misguided as assuming that Coke's dominance of the soft drinks industry has been delivered purely by their advertising campaigns. In reality, advertising is a tiny part of their effort, which also includes getting the right product in the right place at the right price, as well as addressing the needs of key stakeholders, such as suppliers, franchisees and policy makers.

The word marketing also causes emotional problems. For many, it smacks of manipulation. People see it is a twentieth-century invention by business schools simply designed to get us to consume more. It is, in fact, as old as humankind; its core principles of mutually beneficial exchange and doing strategic deals that benefit all those concerned underpin the cooperation at the heart of any successful society. This puts paid to fallacy number 2: while some campaigns are deceitful and misleading, *marketing need not be manipulative*.

Finally, Google the term 'social marketing' and it is easy to conclude that it is a synonym for marketing using social media such as Facebook and Myspace. In reality, as with other forms of communication, social marketing makes use of these channels but it is much more than this. For example, take a look at Case Study 21 on p. 482. Suggs *et al.*'s promotion of a healthy lifestyle among families in a region of Switzerland not only used a variety of online methods to connect with the programme, but also issued personalized letters.

So, to slay our final fallacy: *social marketing is not social media marketing*.

COMING OF AGE

Social marketing has now gained currency around the globe. Many business schools and universities now offer courses in it: the idea that skills learned to push fast-moving consumer goods or financial services can also be used to address pressing social problems such as HIV/AIDS or sustainability is extremely appealing to students.

In addition, the clear need to improve the functioning of our socio-economic system adds to the attraction of a discipline that has insights to share on topics as wide ranging as inequalities, international development and corporate malpractice. In the process, they demonstrate that the discipline has a valuable part to play, not just in tackling micro behavioural problems, such as binge drinking or teen pregnancy, but also in the biggest debates of our time, such as poverty, obesity and global warming (Kotler and Lee 2010).

The case studies featured in the book (see Table 1.1) also demonstrate the real-world impact of social marketing. Some come from the work at the Institute for Social Marketing.[5] The Institute is a collaboration between the University of Stirling in Scotland and The Open University and has over 25 years' experience of conducting research in social marketing with clients such as the World Health Organization, the European Union, Scottish and UK Governments, charities such as Cancer Research UK and Alzheimer's Scotland, and local health bodies. In addition, experienced and respected social marketers from across the world have been kind enough to allow their work to be included. From rural renewal in Portugal (Case Study 2 on p. 311), breastfeeding in Australia (Case Study 5 on p. 334) and HIV prevention in India (Case Study 8 on p. 361) to pharmaceutical regulation in the UK (Case Study 7 on p. 351), it is clear that social marketing is making a difference at both the individual and systemic level.

The case studies also provide tangible evidence of how sophisticated social marketing concepts, tools and techniques have become. A discipline that in the 1980s and '90s (what Andreasen calls its childhood years) focused on ad hoc and individual behaviour change using a limited number of fairly basic tools has developed into a mature and complex one intent on delivering strategic social change.

For example, the role of Relationship Marketing is discussed in 'Blueprint' (Case Study 14 on p. 421) and 'Get Your Life in Gear' (Case Study 9 on p. 369). 'Help Them Grow' (Case Study 12 on p. 409) presents a new public-private social marketing model, while 'Saathiya' (Case Study 17 on p. 444) illustrates the importance of networks and partnerships. We see internal marketing at work in pro-environmental organization and hospital settings, while branding is key to the EU anti-smoking campaign (Case Studies 18 on p. 456, 16 on p. 434 and 6 on p. 344 respectively). Online issues are tackled in 'Breastscreen Queensland' and 'You Kill, You Pay' (Case Studies 4 on p. 326 and 10 on p. 394); while community social marketing is evident in 'Healthy Heroes' and 'Turn it Off' (Case Studies 19 on p. 464 and 15 on p. 434). There are many more cases from renowned social marketing

Table 1.1 The social marketing case studies

No.	Topic	Authors	Key Issues	Country
1	Skin cancer prevention	Jones, S *et al.*	Social Cognitive Theory	Australia
2	Revitalisation of a rural region	Alves, H & Fernandes S	Co-creation; Community social marketing	Portugal
3	Saving lives: involving citizens in the chain of survival	Balonas, S & Marques, S	Placement	Portugal
4	Breast cancer screening	Previte, J *et al.*	New technology	Australia
5	Promotion of breastfeeding	Russell-Bennett, R *et al.*	Internal SM	Australia
6	Tobacco control	Brown, A	Public health brand	EU
7	Strategies used to promote licensed drugs	De Andrade, M	Regulatory system Critical thinking	
8	Promotion of female condoms	Deshpande, S *et al.*	HIV prevention	India
9	Diet and obesity	Duane, S *et al.*	Diet and obesity Behaviour change	Ireland & UK
10	Tobacco control	Gallopel-Morvan, K & Leroux, C	Cancer campaign	France
11	Influenza transmission	Jones, S *et al.*	Infection prevention	Australia
12	Early education	Lagarde, F & Gendron, M	Social advertising	Quebec, Canada
13	Promotion of breastfeeding	Lowry, R *et al.*	Behaviour change	UK
14	Drug use prevention	Marques, S	Drug prevention Relationship marketing	UK
15	Environment	McKenzie-Mohr, D	Environment Community social marketing	Canada
16	Hospital emergency dept overcrowding	Rey, JM, Montero, J & Araque, R	Behaviour change Segmentation	Spain
17	Family planning	Vyas, S	Behaviour change	India
18	Environment	Smith, A	Pro-Environment behaviour; Internal social marketing	UK
19	Healthy lifestyle	Stead, M	Behaviour change	UK
20	Primary health care	Strand, J & Otero, M	Re-branding	Switzerland

(Continued overleaf)

Table 1.1 (Continued)

No.	Topic	Authors	Key Issues	Country
21	Healthy lifestyle	Suggs, S et al.	New technology	USA
22	Alcohol	Collins, K & Manning, L	Co-creation; Research	UK
23	Ethics in SM	Donovan, R et al.	Ethics	Australia
24	Encourage vaccination	Moreira, P	Infection prevention	Angola

Note: The full cases are presented in the Case Studies section.

experts too. All in all, an exciting collection of new and highly informative case studies with stimulating and challenging questions for serious consideration.

WRAP-UP

This first chapter has introduced you to the basic precepts of social marketing. It began by using the example of Coca-Cola to emphasize the power and ubiquity of commercial marketing, which has – time and again – proved its capacity to influence our consumption behaviour. We then explored how important behaviour is to our welfare – whether it be our eating habits, our driving patterns or the sustainability of our lifestyles. Social marketing combines and applies the tools used by commerce to affect our consumption behaviour to address our social and health behaviours. These tools include the need for strategic vision and a recognition of the important influence that social context can have on our behaviour.

In addition, the chapter emphasized the importance of competitive analysis to social marketers. This competition can be either *passive* (we are interested in voluntary behaviour change so by definition our clients have a choice) or *active* (there are obvious commercial vested interests such as tobacco companies pushing in the opposite direction). Thinking more broadly, social marketers need to look critically at the wider economic system to ensure that it too is contributing to welfare of the many.

This led us to define social marketing as a discipline that *critically examines commercial marketing so as to learn from its successes and curb its excesses*. You can remind yourself of its basic precepts by looking again at Box 1.2.

Now try putting the lessons you have learned into practice by doing Exercise 1.4.

EXERCISE 1.4: SOCIAL MARKETING AND TOBACCO

The problem

One in two long-term smokers dies as a result of their habit. Of these, half will die in middle age. This translates to 6.3 million people in the UK since 1950 (Peto *et al.* 2005). Or, in global terms, given present trends in global tobacco consumption, the projected number of deaths by tobacco will grow to 10 million per year by 2030. If prevalence remains unchanged and children start smoking at the expected rates, in 2025, there will be almost 1.9 billion smokers consuming more than 9 trillion cigarettes (Guindon and Boisclair 2003).

The demographics of smoking

The uptake of smoking is a paediatric phenomenon: as we noted in the preface, almost 90 per cent of smokers start as children. Acquiring the habit demands a degree of perseverance and the principal reasons both for trying it and sticking at it are to do with personal image: to look older, more sophisticated and cool. A limited repertoire of premium brands provides the cigarette of choice. Adult smoking is quite different. Most (66 per cent) want to give up (ONS 2004), but cannot. The principal driver of continued consumption is addiction. Nicotine is now known to be as addictive as heroin and cocaine (RCP 2000). Thus, image takes second place to nicotine delivery.

The other principal social demographic at play in tobacco consumption is social class. The further down the social scale you are, the more likely you are to smoke. Only 14 per cent of those in higher professional occupation households smoke compared with 32 per cent of those in semi-routine occupation households (Goddard and Green 2005). Studies of deprived and disadvantaged groups have shown smoking levels among lone parents in receipt of social security benefits in excess of 75 per cent (Marsh and McKay 1994).

The tobacco industry

Until recently, the UK tobacco industry spent around £100 million a year on advertising and promotion. This has now been banned, but the rest of their marketing effort remains: product innovation, distribution, packaging and pricing strategies all play a big part in their effort. Research has shown that this both encourages uptake and discourages cessation.

The economics of smoking

Tobacco is a profitable business. Cigarettes cost pennies to make, particularly with modern production methods, and generate long-term profits. The average UK smoker will smoke a pack a day for 25 years and, at today's prices, spend about £36,000 on tobacco. Governments also do well out of tobacco. In the UK, 80 per cent of the cost of a pack of cigarettes is tax; the Revenue netted £8,093 million in 2003–04 (excluding VAT) (HM Customs & Excise 2005).

Increasing tobacco prices through taxation also has public health benefits. There is a direct, inverse correlation between the price of tobacco and the number of smokers. The one exception to this rule is among the poor, who seem immune to price increases and will carry on smoking regardless, cutting down on essentials in the process.

How would you as a social marketer respond to this problem?

Reflective questions

1. What is marketing?
2. Why is marketing powerful?
3. Describe the three public health problems that have arisen from our consumption behaviours.
4. Explain the relationship between commercial marketing and social marketing.
5. Discuss social marketing's societal role.
6. Bloom and Gundlach maintain social marketers are concerned with three of the 'paths through which marketing affects societal welfare' (2001: xv). Elaborate with illustrations.
7. Delineate the key precepts of social marketing.
8. Differentiate between the concepts of social media, social advertising and social marketing.
9. Elaborate upon Lazer and Kelley's definition: 'Social marketing is concerned with the application of marketing knowledge, concepts and techniques to enhance social as well as economic ends. It is also concerned with analysis of the social consequence of marketing policies, decisions and activities' (1973: ix).

Reflective assignments

1. Conduct an Internet search on social marketing interventions or campaigns.
2. Locate and critique three papers that discuss the characteristics of social marketing.
3. Locate and examine three case studies that display the characteristics of social marketing.
4. Make sure you are comfortable with the content of this chapter by writing a concise paragraph, in your own words, about each of the key words listed at the start of the chapter.

5. You are a social marketer with responsibility for increasing volunteer numbers by 5 per cent for a local meals-on-wheels service. How might you use social marketing to guide your actions and decision making?

6. Your local renewable energy (RE) co-op has employed you to increase the usage of RE within the local area. How might you use social marketing? What other approaches would you consider?

7. In 1868, engineer John Peake Knight invented traffic lights near London's House of Commons for the City of Westminster (BBC 2010).[6] The lights managed horse-drawn carriages and pedestrians at Great George Street and Bridge Street junction in London, to minimize the ever-increasing number of accidents and deaths. Working in railway signalling transportation, Knight borrowed the red and green lights for their associated stop/go behaviour. Red, with its highest wavelength, has the highest visibility from a distance, while green light is the best contrast, with its high wavelength and visibility too – important if you are a train driver and need to stop a 250-ton train!

Make your own traffic lights checklist of the salient points from this chapter where red equals stop (think about this serious issue), amber stands for caution (pause and consider), and green means go (critical lesson). For example, our traffic lights checklist for this chapter are:

Red	Marketing is a very powerful mechanism with no built-in moral compass.
Red	Inequity in society is harmful to everyone – rich as well as poor.
Red	Social marketing is not advertising; not social media and not education.
Amber	Restrictions on business are important but have to be applied with caution.
Green	Social marketing is about human behaviour change.
Green	Social marketing critically examines commercial marketing so as to learn from its successes and curb its excesses.
Green	Social marketers are concerned with three of the 'paths through which marketing affects societal welfare' (Bloom and Gundlach 2001: xv).

Notes

1 www.interbrand.com/en/best-global-brands/2012/Best-Global-Brands-2012-Brand-View.aspx/.
2 www.thecocacolacompany.com/heritage/cokelore_santa.html/.
3 www.dft.gov.uk/statistics/tables/ras51005/.
4 www.nsms.org.uk/.
5 www.ism.stir.ac.uk/.
6 www.bbc.co.uk/nottingham/content/articles/2009/07/16/john_peake_knight_traffic_lights_feature.html/.

References

Anderson, S. and Cavanagh, J. (2000) *Top 200: The Rise of Corporate Global Power*. Washington, DC: Institute for Policy Studies.

Andreasen, A.R. (2006) *Social Marketing in the 21st Century*. Thousand Oaks, CA: Sage Publications.

Bagozzi, R. (1975) 'Marketing and exchange', *Journal of Marketing*, 39(October): 32–39.

Bendell, J. (2011) *Evolving Partnerships: A Guide to Working with Business for Greater Social Change*. Sheffield, UK: Greenleaf Publishing.

Bloom, P.N. and Gundlach, G.T. (2001) *Handbook of Marketing and Society*. Thousand Oaks, CA: Sage Publications.

Cairns, G., Mackay, B. and MacDonald, L. (2011) 'Social marketing and international development', Ch. 22 in G. Hastings, K. Angus and C. Bryant (eds) *The SAGE Handbook of Social Marketing*. London: Sage Publications Ltd.

CAP (2012) *CAP review of the use of children as Brand Ambassadors and in Peer-to-Peer Marketing*. London: Committee of Advertising Practice. Online: www.cap.org.uk/Media-Centre/2012/Ð/media/Files/CAP/Misc/CAP%20Review%20document%20-%20brand%20ambassadors%20%282%29.ashx/.

Casswell, S., You. R.Q. and Huckle T. (2011) 'Alcohol's harm to others: Reduced wellbeing and health status for those with heavy drinkers in their lives', *Addiction*, 106(6): 1087–1094.

Connolly, J. and Prothero, A. (2003) 'Sustainable consumption', *Consumption, Consumers and the Commodity Discourse*, 6(4): 275–291.

Drucker, Peter (1957) *Landmarks of Tomorrow*. New York: Harper & Row.

Geels, F.W., Hekkert, M.P. and Jacobsson, S. (2008) 'The dynamics of sustainable innovation journeys', *Technology Analysis & Strategic Management*, 20(5): 521–536.

Goddard, E. and Green, H. (2005) *Smoking and drinking among adults, 2004*. London: Office for National Statistics: December.

Guindon, G.E. and Boisclair D. (2003) *Past, Current and Future Trends in Tobacco Use*. Health, Nutrition and Population (HNP) Discussion Paper: Economics of Tobacco Control Paper No. 6. Washington, DC: The World Bank, March. ISBN: 193212666X.

Hardin, G. (1968) 'The Tragedy of the Commons', *Science*, 162(3859): 1243–1248.

Hastings, G. (2011) 'Introduction: A movement in social marketing', in G. Hastings, K. Angus and C. Bryant (eds) *The SAGE Handbook of Social Marketing*. London: Sage Publications Ltd.

Hastings, G. (2012) *The Marketing Matrix*. London: Routledge.

Hastings, G. and Elliott, B. (1993) 'Social marketing practice in traffic safety', Ch. III in *Marketing of Traffic Safety*. Paris: OECD, pp. 35–53.

Hastings, G.B., Stead, M., McDermott, L. and Forsyth, A., MacKintosh, A.M., Rayner, M., Godfrey, G., Carahar, M. and Angus, K. (2003) *Review of Research on the Effects of Food Promotion to Children – Final Report and Appendices*. Prepared for the Food Standards Agency, UK. Published on Food Standards Agency website: www.food.gov.uk/healthiereating/advertisingtochildren/promotion/readreview/.

Hill, R.P. (2011) 'Impoverished consumers and social marketing', Ch. 21 in G. Hastings, K. Angus and C. Bryant (eds) *The SAGE Handbook of Social Marketing*. London: Sage Publications Ltd.

HM Customs & Excise (2005) *Tobacco Factsheet (February 2005)*. London: HMCE.

Kotler, P. and Lee, N.R. (2010) *Social Marketing: Influencing Behaviors for Good*. Newbury Park, CA: Sage Publications.

Kotler, P. and Zaltman, G. (1971) 'Social marketing: An approach to planned social change', *Journal of Marketing*, 35(3): 3–12.

Lazer, W. and Kelley, E. (1973) *Social Marketing: Perspectives and Viewpoints*. Homewood, IL: Richard D. Irwin, Inc.

Lovato, C., Linn, G., Stead, L.F. and Best, A. (2003) 'Impact of tobacco advertising and promotion on increasing adolescent smoking behaviours', *Cochrane Database of Systematic Reviews*, (4): CD003439.

Luck, D.J. (1969) 'Broadening the concept of marketing – too far', *Journal of Marketing*, 33(July), 53–55.

McDermott, L., Stead, M. and Hastings, G. (2005), What is and what is not social marketing: The challenge of reviewing the evidence', *Journal of Marketing Management*, 21(5–6): 545–553.

McGinnis, J.M. and Foege, W.H. (1993) 'Actual causes of death in the United States', *Journal of the American Medical Association*, 270(18): 2207–2212.

McGinnis, J.M., Gootman, J.A. and Kraak, V.I. (eds) (2006) *Food Marketing to Children and Youth: Threat or Opportunity?* Committee on Food Marketing and the Diets of Children and Youth; Food and Nutrition Board; Board on Children, Youth, and Families; Institute of Medicine of The National Academies. Washington, DC: The National Academies Press.

Marsh, A. and McKay, S. (1994) *Poor Smokers*. London: Policy Studies Institute.

National Cancer Institute (2008) *The Role of the Media in Promoting and Reducing Tobacco Use*. Tobacco Control Monograph No. 19. Vol. NIH Pub. No. 07-6242. Bethesda, MD: U.S. Department of Health and Human Services, National Institutes of Health, National Cancer Institute.

Office for National Statistics (ONS) (2004) *Proportion of smokers who would like to give up smoking altogether, by sex and number of cigarettes smoked per day: 1992 to 2003: GHS 2003*. London: ONS.

Olshansky, S.J., Passaro, D.J., Hershow, R.C., Layden, J., Carnes, B.A., Brody, J., Hayflick, L., Butler, R.N., Allison, D.B. and Ludwig, D.S. (2005) 'A potential decline in life expectancy in the United States in the 21st century', *The New England Journal of Medicine*, 352(11): 1138–1145.

Peto, R., Lopez, A.D., Boreham, J. and Thun, M. (2005) *Mortality from Smoking in Developed Countries 1950–2000*. 2nd edition. Oxford: Oxford Medical Publications.

Quelch, J.A. and Jocz, K.E. (2007) *Greater Good: How Good Marketing Makes for Better Democracy*. Watertown, MA, Harvard Business Press.

RCP (Royal College of Physicians) (2000) *Nicotine Addiction in Britain*. Report of the Tobacco Advisory Group of the Royal College of Physicians. London: Royal College of Physicians.

Wallack, L., Dorfman, L., Jernigan, D. and Themba, M. (1993) *Media Advocacy and Public Health*. Thousand Oaks, CA: Sage Publications.

Wiebe, G.D. (1951) 'Merchandising commodities and citizenship in television', *Public Opinion Quarterly*, 15(4): 679–691.

Wilkie, W.L. and Moore, E.S. (2003) 'Scholarly research in marketing: Exploring the "Four Eras" of thought development', *Journal of Public Policy & Marketing*, 22(2): 116–146.

Wilkinson, R. and Pickett, K. (2010) *The Spirit Level: Why Equality is Better for Everyone*. London: Penguin Books UK.

Chapter **2**

Social marketing principles

IN-SIGHT

Three old friends had gone to the golf club to have a beer. One, Fred, was an anti-tobacco advocate with many years' experience. The second, Joe, was a successful advertiser, famous for several social campaigns. The third guy, Bill, was a social marketer who had worked on infant mortality in developing countries for many years.

As they drank their beers, they heard a commotion on the golf course and noticed that there was a real fight brewing on the second green. They asked the waiter, 'What's going on?'

'Oh, this happens every Wednesday,' said the waiter. 'The golf course owner's son is blind and he loves to play golf, so the owner opens the course to him and a bunch of his friends to play on Wednesdays. But as you can imagine they are a lot slower than the other players and the sighted guys get angry and often belligerent at the blind guys. We've actually had fist fights, and the blind guys don't always lose.'

Fred said, 'This is easy to fix. Those sighted guys have got to learn to obey the policy. It has got to be clear and then they need to lose their rights to play if they violate the policy which allows these blind guys to play. Somebody's got to stand up for their rights.'

Joe responded, 'You are always looking for bad guys to hurt. I think the sighted guys don't know what the blind guys are going through. I can imagine a campaign with some fabulous images showing how these blind guys navigate the course. Develop some empathy – use emotion to make the sighted guys aware of the blind guys' needs. Empathy and awareness are the deeper answer.'

The debate between Joe and Fred raged for an hour and finally Fred turned to Bill and said, 'You've been awful quiet? Don't you have any ideas at all about how to solve this problem?'

'Oh, sorry,' said Bill, 'I've been making notes about a new service the club could offer: Night-time Golf. Let the blind guys have the whole course when the sun goes down. No electric bill needed. I'd offer a limo to pick them up, but first I'd want to talk to them about what else we could do for them, for a small fee, of course, to cover costs.'

We are indebted to Bill Smith for this story which tells us a lot about social marketing. Specifically, it shows how social marketers see the world (their orientation) and the principal lever (mutually beneficial exchange) that they bring to the challenge of changing the world for the better.

There are four dimensions to a social marketing orientation (see Box 2.1).

BOX 2.1: FOUR SOCIAL MARKETING ORIENTATIONS

Client orientation	Identify people's needs, aspirations, values and priorities
Creative orientation	Find imaginative ways to engage them
Collective orientation	Recognize that the social context matters
Competitive orientation	Reduce the price; critically address the competition

The first is already familiar to us through commercial marketing – the concept of **client orientation** – and is a quintessentially marketing idea. This client orientation is the prime directive for social marketers as successful behaviour change is built through a well-grounded understanding of current behaviour and the people engaged in it. The aim of this understanding is to identify the grail of social marketing, the mutually beneficial exchange.

Social marketing, like commercial marketing, needs to start with a clearly defined behaviour and target group: *what* do you want *who* to do? To deliver effectively to their needs, we have to understand them and their current behaviour very well and this requires a solid grounding in behaviour change theory (Chapter 3) and sophisticated research (Chapter 5). Good social marketing starts by appraising the situation, understanding the problem, assessing the competing forces and only then begins to deduce possible solutions. This process needs to go beyond mere data collection, and incorporate a genuine empathy for the client group. As the Chinese proverb has it, we need to walk a mile in the other person's shoes.

To these insights need to be added vital elements of imagination and innovation to make our approaches as attractive and motivating as possible, always remembering that marketers, whether commercial or social, deal in voluntary behaviour. We cannot compel people to do business with us. Bill Smith's story brilliantly illustrates the value of what Edward De Bono would call lateral thinking – and we use the term **creative orientation** to encapsulate this.

However deep we dig, though, in our bid to understand people, we won't get a full picture unless we also recognize the importance of the *social* determinants of behaviour. All of us are influenced by the circumstances in which we find ourselves: a young person's inclination to smoke is partly a matter of personal volition, but also a function of their local environment (e.g. whether friends smoke and tobacco is readily available in neighbourhood shops) and wider social norms (e.g. whether tobacco advertising or smoking in public places is permitted). Similarly, road accidents are not just a matter of driver and pedestrian behaviour, but also car design (manufacturer behaviour) and road infrastructure (government behaviour).

By the same token, social marketing solutions also have to be multifaceted; often it is as important to think about wider-scale social change as individual behaviours. Effective social marketing therefore has to incorporate a **collective orientation**.

This complex social picture also means that we all have lots of choice. Think about obesity, for instance, and the myriad ways a person can tackle losing weight: buying gym membership to exercise; WeightWatchers dinners to limit calorie intake; lifestyle intervention programmes to rebalance work/life; surgery to shrink the stomach. The individual also has the freedom to choose *not* to deal with obesity, despite what experts might say. The terrain becomes even more contested, because there are other actors – the fast food and soft drinks industries for instance – who have a vested interest in pushing against many obesity interventions.

These multiple choices or decision points for the individual represent competition for the social marketer. By adopting a **competitive orientation**, we can ensure that, as the airlines have taken to saying, we never forget our clients have a choice. It also reminds us that sometimes the best thing we can do for the individual is to protect them from unscrupulous competition. Notwithstanding Bill Smith's story, there are some bad guys out there. Maybe the overweight adult would have avoided becoming fat in the first place if there had been statutory nutritional standards when they were at school – or effective controls on the marketing of energy-dense food.

These four orientations become even more powerful when applied strategically, not just to change ad hoc behaviours, but also to build ongoing relationships. The final part of the chapter discusses how commerce has embraced relationship marketing, and discusses the enormous benefits that can result when social marketers do likewise.

Learning outcomes

By the end of this chapter, you should be able to:

✓ Understand the four key orientations of social marketing and why each is important

✓ Recognize that client orientation, seeing the world as our customers see and value it, is the starting point for good social marketing

✓ Discuss the importance of insight and creativity in ensuring client engagement

✓ Outline the various types of competition faced by the social marketer

✓ Understand the need to address the collective influences on our behaviour

✓ Explain that exchange means both the target population and the social marketer gain something – and why this matters

✓ Understand the value of relationship marketing.

Key words

agency – client orientation – collective orientation – competitive orientation – creative orientation – external and active competition – flexible offerings – internal and passive competition – mutually beneficial exchange – relationship marketing – social context

CLIENT ORIENTATION

Arguably the single most important proposition that marketing has brought to the business process in the last 100 years is that of consumer orientation. It is the simple and unobtrusive idea of putting us at the heart of the business process. As noted in the introductory chapter, this deceptively simple change has revolution-ized how companies work and helped create the enormous corporations that now dominate the globe. This dominance has come about for many reasons, but at its heart is the idea of *putting the customer first*.

Consumer orientation works because, paradoxically, listening to someone and taking care to understand their point of view makes it easier to influence their behaviour. So, in commercial terms, it makes much more sense to work out what people need and want and then set about producing this, rather than developing a product and then putting resources into trying to push people into buying it. This principle is so fundamental to marketing it has been used to define the discipline as 'producing what you can sell', instead of 'selling what you can produce'.

Remember, though, that the marketer's interest in understanding the customer and world is not driven by altruism. As noted before, commercial marketers take an interest in us because listening to us and taking care to understand our point of view makes it easier to sell us things.

Social marketers share the commercial sector's commitment to 'consumer-oriented' thinking and argue that attempts to influence social and health behaviour should also start from an understanding of the people we want to do the changing. The task is to work out why they do what they do at present, their values and motivations, and use this understanding to develop an offering that is equally appealing but with positive personal and/or social outcomes. Given social marketing's focus on voluntary behaviour change, client orientation can be seen as the most important of the four orientations.

The most immediate benefit of this approach is that it allows for the fact that, time and again, the picture is much more complex than mere ignorance of the facts. In public health, for example, most people know that smoking is dangerous or how their diet could be improved. They continue to behave 'badly' because they see some other benefit in doing so, relaxation perhaps or a treat. The secret for the social marketer is to devise a way of enabling them to get the same benefit more healthily. In this sense, social marketing has a great deal in common with good, patient-centred healthcare. The proficiency of experts and other professionals is much more effectively deployed when combined with empathy for the client. Ultimately, better health, a better environment and a better-functioning society has to be a joint endeavour. This process is sometimes referred to as the 'joint creation of value', and we will return to it in Chapter 10.

Social marketers also embrace the idea of mutually beneficial exchange. This brings us to exchange theory, which we will discuss in the next chapter. For the moment, though, it raises two contentious issues:

i) The first concerns motivation, not just on the part of the client group but also the social marketer. The idea that social marketers, just like their commercial counterparts, are looking for some kind of payback has ruffled a few feathers.
ii) The second is the idea of compromise which is at the heart of any mutually beneficial exchange. But can social marketers adjust their offering; aren't they fixed by the evidence base – smoking kills, therefore our non-smoking product is surely set in stone?

We will look at both in more detail.

THE POWER OF PAYBACK

More fundamentally, some commentators have strong reservations about the assumption in exchange theory that the social marketer (safety worker/probation officer/health promoter) as well as the target group is getting something out of the behaviour change process. Buchanan *et al.*, (1994) argue, for example, that such an analysis fundamentally undermines the essentially altruistic basis of health promotion. Exercise 2.1 explores their views in more detail; do you agree with them?

EXERCISE 2.1: IS EXCHANGE UNACCEPTABLE?

We have two concerns with importing the notions of exchange and related concepts into the field of health promotion. By promoting an exchange mentality, social marketing concepts propagate radical transformations in: (i) the types of motivations thought to characterize the health promoter's work and (ii) the ways in which health promoters relate to the public. We wish to explore the implications of such a transformation. To anticipate, our concern is that such a transformation will both undermine the health promoter's commitment to the field and lead to a more antagonistic relationship to the public.

In marketing, the nature of the relationship between the two parties is characterized by the strategic pursuit of self interest. It is an adversarial bargaining relationship. There is mutual antagonism that is captured in the primordial marketing principle: *caveat emptor* (buyer beware). The two parties are drawn together by a cost benefit calculus, and as soon as the costs are perceived to be too high by one or the other, the relationship is terminated.

In contrast, people have traditionally entered the health field out of a sense of caring for others, not to satisfy self interests. The vast majority of health professionals still feel that to be a health professional means to have a vocation, a sense of calling. They strive to create a healthy society in which no one will be handicapped from participating due to unnecessary illness and suffering. The yardstick by which their work is measured is the realisation of a collective good that flows from the elimination of disease, pollution, hunger, poverty and oppression.

A shift to the idea that it would be better to think of the purpose of health promotion in terms of exchange would mark a major transformation. If enough people can be talked around into thinking that the reason for doing health promotion is gains for the health promoter themselves, we believe the field will be sapped of a major source of strength{. . .}We believe the field is better off now, while health promoters draw on inspiration from role models who give freely of themselves without self regard. Under the logic of exchange such people can only be considered suckers.

Finally, if health promoters conceive of their work in marketing terms, then the ways they think about their relationships with the public will also be transformed. The uneasiness many people feel about social marketing is that it constantly threatens to slip into a manipulative relationship.

(Buchanan *et al.* 1994)

How would you respond to Buchanan *et al.*?

● Are the target groups for social marketing inevitably passive?

● Do marketers always seek to manipulate?

● Are all health professionals philanthropists who are answering a vocation?
(Source: Buchanan *et al.* 1994; Hastings and Haywood 1991, 1994)

From a social marketing perspective, there are a number of major problems with Buchanan *et al.*'s view. First, the rejection of exchange seems to suggest that people have nothing of value to offer and health workers can learn nothing from them. But it is only by listening to our clients that we can understand the limitations of our initiatives and the narrowness of our own views. We need their help.

Second, Buchanan *et al.* see exchange as inevitably involving one party trying to get the better of another. They cannot envisage a mutually beneficial system or Lefebvre's 'win-win' (1992). For them, marketing exchange is in reality based on 'mutual antagonism' and 'constantly threatens to collapse into a manipulative relationship'. Of course, there is deceit and manipulation in some marketing exchanges, but this is the exception rather than the rule even in the commercial sector – otherwise, there could be no such thing as repeat purchase, brand loyalty or customer satisfaction.

Third, Buchanan *et al.*'s view of the motivations of health professionals being 'altruism, self-sacrifice and concern for the common welfare' carries with it connotations of superiority: 'we know what's best for you and because we are such good people we are prepared to give you the benefit of our wisdom'. It is a short step from here to imposing our view on the client and condemning their (almost inevitable) ingratitude.

FLEXIBLE OFFERINGS

However, there is another potential snag: client orientation, the mutual benefit it entails and the notion of meaningful relationships raises the thorny issue of flexible offerings. Can social marketers really vary their offerings like their commercial counterparts? Can we really produce what will sell, rather than selling a predetermined offering? Exercise 2.2 presents the views of two commentators who think not.

EXERCISE 2.2: CAN YOU CHANGE THE PRODUCT IN SOCIAL MARKETING?

If a commercial marketer's customers do not like their product, it will be changed. Can a social marketer do the same?

Barry Elliott (1995) argues not. He takes the view that the social marketer's product, often conceived 'outside the market place', is typically an unalterable given, driving the programme manager largely into the business of selling or advocacy. Keith Tones has similar concerns contending that '(i) in general, people do not actually want to be healthy . . . and (ii) health education cannot abandon its product and diversify its interests just because its main product may not be very popular' (1996: 32).

Do you agree with Elliott and Tones? Jot down your thoughts before continuing.

Now consider the following two questions:

1. Does the commercial sector really change its products on a regular basis, even when faced with sustained negative reactions? The tobacco industry provides an example of one that certainly has not. Despite knowing for over 50 years that cigarettes are carcinogenic (Doll *et al.* 2004) and coming under immense political and social pressure as a result, they have steadfastly stuck to their product. On the other hand, they have tried to respond to market concerns by *adjusting* their products – low-tar cigarettes and filters are two examples – but these are relatively minor alterations on the periphery of the product, rather than the full-scale abandonment of it. Neither, for example, makes their products any safer.

2. Second, is not social marketing capable of similar flexibility? In HIV/AIDS education, for example, it has been widely accepted that messages of *absolute* safety and behaviours such as celibacy and complete abstinence from injecting drugs simply will not sell to many potential customers. They have been replaced by offerings of *relative* safety – safer sex and safer drug use.

More fundamentally, keep in mind that an absence of flexibility or the chance to compromise strikes at the heart of social marketing. If social marketers cannot change their offerings, how meaningful are the core marketing concepts of consumer orientation and exchange? Walsh and colleagues encapsulated this point when they concluded their overview of the field with:

social marketing . . . challenges health specialists to think in new ways about consumers and product design. Entering the marketing world requires abandoning the expert's mind-set that the product is intrinsically good, so that if it fails to sell, the defect must reside in uninformed or unmotivated consumers who need shrewder instruction or louder exhortation.

(1993: 117–118)

More fundamentally still, if social marketers cannot change their product or service, how can there be mutually beneficial exchanges? At the end of the day, even the tobacco industry will stop producing cigarettes if no one buys them. Saying that products cannot be changed ignores this ultimate pressure and condemns social marketers to stagnation. They will cease to be valuable and become extinct.

But remember, this is a mutual process. The social marketer needs to be flexible in their offering, but the other side of the coin is that the client is more open to change because of the compromise.

CREATIVE ORIENTATION

Client orientation will not deliver a great deal without insight and innovation. Bill Smith's story beautifully illustrates how an original (but deceptively simple) idea can completely transform our view of a behavioural problem and provide a solution that satisfies everyone. It is surely apocryphal, but the following incident really happened. We know because one of us witnessed it.

Bethany was waiting for her husband, Steve, in my neighbourhood pub and he was late for their rendezvous. As time passed with no sign of her man, Bethany began to get cross. A further half-hour went by and steam began emerging from her ears. When Steve eventually rushed in, he looked hunted; any man reading this who has ever let down his partner will understand precisely how he felt. He knew he was in trouble, and was preparing to take his punishment.

But he had forgotten Mary, the pub landlady, and her acute marketing skills. She had seen what was unfolding and when Steve arrived she drew him across to her at the bar before he could go across the room to Bethany. He was anxious to make his domestic peace, but somehow Mary insisted. She then said one simple phrase to him: 'Remember, Bethany has had her hair done'. Steve's face relaxed and his eyes smiled in gratitude: Mary had provided his 'get-out-of-jail-free' card. He floated across to Bethany and swept aside her irritation with an unanswerable: 'Darling, your hair looks lovely'.

Mary is a consummate marketer. Not only has she worked out what her customers need and provided it just in time, but also her solution is abundantly creative. As a publican, you might expect her offering to be some variation on food or drink – a pint of beer perhaps or a bowl of soup. However, she recognized the need for quick and original thinking and provided a much more valuable alternative: marital harmony. She also recognizes that good marketing has an emotional dimension – it appeals to our hearts as well as our heads. She knows that her adroit move will make Bethany and Steve feel good.

Not that she has forgotten her beer sales; these will surely follow. Her sensitivity and customer focus will result in deep loyalty from Steve (with Bethany also acquiring pleasant associations with the King's Head); as a result, he won't buy her beer just tonight but for weeks and probably years to come. Mary is good not just at marketing but also at relationship marketing, which we will return to later in the chapter.

In social marketing as well, the answer is often not the obvious one as Jones *et al.'s* Case Study 11 'Cold and Flu Affects More than You' (p. 401) shows. The ethos found among younger university staff, through research (Chapter 5) was to 'soldier on' – they didn't want to burden colleagues with extra classes. However, administrative staff, being in greater face-to-face contact with students at reception and service desks, were seriously concerned with all the coughing and sneezing they experienced. Juxtaposed to this, male students did not identify with having a cold or flu as being sick. Instead, they were to be 'coped with' and hence there was no need to stay in bed and away from university!

Social marketers, then, have to put great efforts into understanding and indeed empathizing with clients' behaviour. A very clear fix is needed; not just *what* they do but *why* they do it, what motivates and drives them. And in both the commercial and social sectors this is as much about emotion as rationality. Behaviour is not always the perfect product of rational-deductive reasoning; if it were, no one would smoke and drunk driving would be a distant memory. This is why commercial marketers put such an effort into developing evocative brands. It is also why social marketers put a particular premium on ethnographic, qualitative research and data for good decision making (see Chapter 5).

To illustrate, in the early 1990s, the Institute for Social Marketing conducted a survey of 16–24-year-olds in Dundee. At the time, HIV/AIDS had emerged as a major threat to public health, and sexual transmission by young people was a particular concern – as indeed it still is. The survey therefore concerned sexual habits. The key findings made perplexing reading. Virtually everyone knew that HIV could be passed on during heterosexual encounters; virtually everyone knew this could be prevented by using a condom – *but around a third were continuing to practise unprotected sex.*

Many similar surveys, before and since, have repeated the findings, which beg the question: why is there such a gap between knowledge and behaviour? Social marketers adopt what Taleb (2010) calls the black swan logic: what you don't know is oftentimes more pertinent than what you do. Detailed qualitative research is needed to unpick this riddle, as Box 2.2 notes.

BOX 2.2: THE VALUE OF ETHNOGRAPHY

Marketing is the art of ensuring your offering fits with the needs, emotions and lifestyles of your customer. Quantitative research can only go so far in providing the insights you need. In addition, ethnographic techniques are needed to dig below the surface of socio-demographic statistics and help explain why people behave as they do. There is a need to explain apparent irrationalities, like taking up smoking despite the threat of lung cancer or risking unprotected sex with a stranger. As the psychologist Dick Eiser said, 'just because people do stupid things, it doesn't mean they are stupid'. Ultimately, the social marketer needs to learn to see things from the perspective of their customer – then, and only then, will their world make sense.

Ethnographic or qualitative research typically uses smaller samples than its quantitative cousin and in-depth questioning procedures that enable the researcher to probe deeply and explore the reasons behind people's attitudes and behaviour.

Chapter 5 underlines the value of this sort of research to decision making and explains how it can be done, but in the meantime Exercise 2.3 will help to get you thinking.

EXERCISE 2.3: AN EMBARRASSING ASSIGNMENT

First, remind yourself that using condoms involves talking to your partner about sex before engaging in it, raising issues of previous sexual encounters and the protective steps you did (or did not) take. Then, next time you meet with a friend of the opposite sex, try telling them when you last had sex, whether you used a condom and why you did or did not do so. If your friend has not fled from your presence, ask them to do the same.

Note: In the interests of your mental health and social life, we will keep this exercise hypothetical.

Recall again that the simple injunction to 'use a condom' (how many adverts and posters have you seen this on in the last decade?) demands exactly this behaviour from all its readers. Suddenly, the actions of the young Dundonians do not seem so difficult to understand and the real benefit of empathy becomes clear.

An innovative social marketing research example is seen in operation in Stead's 'Healthy Heroes' Case Study 19 on page 464. The mixed methods research includes regular reflective sessions and interviews with project workers in the development phase to elicit emerging issues and developments. Focus groups and interviews were undertaken with community residents and local partners to discover their experiences and views of participating in the projects. Mini surveys were completed, embracing self-completion questionnaire surveys of participants, primary school-children hands-up survey, and a bus-stop street survey. These were complemented with unstructured observation of several project activities and anecdotal feedback recorded throughout. Insights about actions and processes that would continue beyond the life of the projects and have a longer-term impact on health and well-being in the communities were also gathered.

Ultimately, these two threads of marketing – the client and creative orientations – come together in the idea of partnership working and the joint endeavour. It was Mary's detailed and empathetic insights into her customers' needs that enabled her to come up with such a creative solution – but it would have come to nothing if Steve hadn't immediately grasped her meaning and delivered the cleverly provided compliment to Bethany, who in turn had to accept it with good grace. It was a team effort built on mutual understanding and creative insight.

COLLECTIVE ORIENTATION

Such empowered behaviour, however, is not always possible.

The American philosopher David Foster Wallace (2008) tells the story of two young fish who are swimming along, and they happen to meet an older fish swimming the other way, who nods at them and says, 'Morning, boys, how's the water?' And the two young fish reply, 'It is lovely, thank you.' They swim on for a bit, and then eventually one of them looks over at the other and asks: 'What the heck is water?' Wallace goes on to explain that the point of the story is that the most ubiquitous and powerful influences on our behaviour are those closest to us – the ones we take for granted, do not even realize are there and cannot discuss and describe. Our immediate environment is to us as the water is to the young fish, and has an equally powerful impact on our lives whether we realize it or not. Have a go at Exercise 2.4.

EXERCISE 2.4: TESTING THE WATER

Think about some facet of your own behaviour – your drinking perhaps, or eating habits. Write down all the different influences you can think of that make you behave as you do. These may range from full-on pressure, such as your mate urging you to have another drink because it's your round, to background nudges like a tempting bottle of lager on a supermarket cold shelf. When you have thought of every possible trigger, ask your friends what influences them – and add these to the list.

The exercise typically results in an extensive list.

Recognizing these broader determinants of how we live our lives is important to social marketers for three key reasons:

1. It provides us with a fuller understanding of why our clients behave as they do, so it enhances our client orientation and hence all the benefits of this that are discussed above. In short, it makes our attempts to change behaviour more effective.

2. It avoids the danger of 'victim blaming': pushing someone to change a behaviour that is not – or not entirely – of their own making. This is not only ineffective, but also potentially unethical. The dilemma is most apparent when we consider vulnerable groups: there are obvious problems with a media campaign telling poor sub-Saharan villagers to feed their children better when they can't access food because there has been a drought, their government is corrupt and the world economic system is dysfunctional. The problems are less obvious when people do have good access to food and live in a working democracy. Nonetheless, as the Foster Wallace fish emphasize, it is still necessary to ask how much power any given individual or population has over its own fate. Sociologists refer to such power as 'agency', which has to be balanced against the structures of society that simultaneously constrain and facilitate it. The notion of structuration theory has been conceived to explain the dynamic relationship between agency and structure and social marketers have to be continually aware of this dynamism. Katie Collins and Lindsay Manning from the Bristol Social Marketing Centre capture agency and structure in Case Study 22 on p. 490. They talk of empowerment and engagement and co-creating an alternative to risky drinking in deprived communities where 'high-profile issues like drug abuse and smoking can overshadow the issue of drinking, which is often perceived as a harmless and enjoyable social activity. People with alcohol problems are thought to be in a minority'. The World Health Organization knows better; alcohol, as with tobacco, lies at the core of many global diseases with dire outcomes, such as violence, sexual and mental health problems, chronic liver disease and, ultimately, preventable deaths.

3. Finally, a collective orientation helps us to think properly about genuinely strategic goals. If we consider all the causes of our behaviour, we are compelled to raise our eyes above the detail of individual coping strategies and look at the system. This has fundamental implications for our social marketing efforts because it helps us determine how we can best use the inevitably limited resources at our disposal. In our sub-Saharan example above, it may be that the best thing we can do is to advocate the UN to alter the terms of aid programmes or provide agricultural training for locals so that they can improve crop yield in a dry climate. In social marketing terms, it enables us to make intelligent decisions about *whose* behaviour needs to change and *how* it needs to change.

In essence, then, a collective orientation again puts an emphasis on thinking about the big picture.

COMPETITIVE ORIENTATION

This bigger picture has to include the competition, which for social marketers comes in two forms.

First, there is passive competition. Social marketing recognizes that clients, whether government ministers or teenage tearaways, have choices. They can, and often do, continue with their current behaviour. There are internal barriers to change, which could be in the form of beliefs, feelings, attitudes or intentions. As we have just discussed, such blockages also come from family, friends and the immediate environment.

It is therefore very important to look closely at this 'competition' in order to understand what benefits it is perceived to bring and how alternative behaviour can be made more attractive for a fruitful exchange. For example, it is clear that for some teenagers smoking is felt to hold a range of benefits, including rebellion, weight control and sophistication, which can outstrip health concerns such as lung and heart disease in years to come. Social marketers need to take these perspectives into account if there is to be any hope of winning over young people. The Truth Campaign, a US anti-smoking effort, did precisely this when it adopted the theme of rebellion – not against society but against the manipulative practices of the tobacco industry. It is one of the most successful youth prevention campaigns ever run (Farrelly *et al.* 2002).

Mention of the tobacco industry brings us to the second sense in which social marketers need to address the competition. As well as current behaviours and social systems, there are organizations actively pushing in the opposite direction. This is direct or active competition. Thus, in the case of tobacco, one of the reasons so many young people continue to take up smoking is that the tobacco companies use their marketing to encourage them to do so. And extensive research shows that their efforts are successful, as are those of the alcohol and fast food companies. Box 2.3 discusses why this additional competitive dimension to social marketing, sometimes termed critical marketing, is so important.

BOX 2.3: ACTIVE COMPETITION AND CRITICAL MARKETING: THREE REASONS WHY IT MATTERS

- Understanding the efforts of Philip Morris or Diageo, and consumer response to them, provides us with invaluable intelligence. As advertising guru David Ogilvy once remarked, ignoring this would be like an army general ignoring decodes of enemy signals.
- Commercial activity is a crucial aspect of the environment that we have already accepted is itself an important determinant of behaviour. Ignoring the impact of commercial marketing would open up the discipline to the same criticisms as if it only focused on individual behaviour: ineffectiveness and immorality.
- The success of the tobacco, alcohol and food industries provides a rich seam of evidence that marketing works. If marketing can get us to buy a Ferrari, it can also encourage us to drive it safely.

Collective and competitive orientations come together when we accept that societal progress depends on movement not just by the individual citizen but by community groups and civil society, as Case Study 22 on p. 490 demonstrates. Katie Collins and Lindsay Manning correctly suspected that, even if people wanted to cut down on risky drinking patterns, a combination of social, economic and physical environmental influences blocked them. Some were perplexed by the different advice on offer from professionals, while others were concerned about losing their children, friends, family support or welfare. The issues of passive and active competition are also examined closely in Case Study 4 on p. 326 referring to internal social marketing at BreastScreen Queensland.

This takes us back to the domain of social marketing (Box 1.2) and reminds us that successful social transformation is also influenced by the wider social context and specifically by the actions of other stakeholders, as well as individual citizens. As Marques and Domegan (2011) point out,

social marketers' legitimacy is greater if social marketers are critical about themselves: their own processes and outcomes but especially about their assumptions or taken for granted 'truths'. From a critical perspective, the challenge is to make those assumptions explicit so they can be contested on other grounds than are provided for by the prevailing paradigm.

This last sentiment captures the important role of critical thinking and, indeed, this book, to uncover the taken-for-granted barriers and test it in the courtroom of academic and public debate. And, as Jones (2011), Hoek (2011) and Dewhirst and Lee (2011) make clear, an open and frank debate about the role of commercial marketing is an essential part of this rigour. This book is testament to the power of marketing and its potential to do good if used by the right people in the right way. It would be derelict, and profoundly damaging to social marketing, if we did not also recognize and point out its capacity to do harm. Speaking truth to power is a crucial part of the social marketer's role.

We will continue this discussion of critical and competitive thinking in Chapters 7 and 8.

THE ORIENTATIONS COMBINED

The mandating of smoke-free public places has been one of the great success stories of Scottish public health in recent years. Scotland moved on this ahead of all its UK and European neighbours, with the exception of Ireland, and the success of the measure perfectly illustrates the importance of all four social marketing dimensions:

- **Client orientation**. Smoke-free legislation typifies this first orientation; the measure was almost (see competitive orientation below) universally welcomed. Press speculation about mass disobedience by smokers proved completely groundless. A public opinion survey a few days after the law's introduction showed that no fewer than 84 per cent of 16–24-year-olds not only approved of the measure, but also thought it one 'that Scotland could be proud of' (Cancer Research UK 2006) – a massive endorsement for a patriotic country like Scotland. Realizing smoke-free public places was probably the single most popular achievement of the then McConnell Government.

However, the success was by no means a solo effort by the authorities; the public also played an important role. Their experiences of smoky pubs told them that going smoke-free was a good idea, not so much because it would save them from illness as the ad campaigns maintained, but because it was so unpleasant. The need to wash your hair and clothes after every night out was as influential as the threat of second-hand lung cancer. This policy measure worked because *both* the authorities *and* the public wanted it to. This is a good example of what is sometimes termed 'co-created value' (see Chapter 10).

- **Creative orientation**. Smoke-free was an immensely innovative move. Prior to the legislation Scotland had long been caricatured as the 'sick man of Europe', and Glasgow pubs were a by-word for hard-drinking, unhealthy lifestyles. To make these semi-shebeens the spearhead of a pioneering public health measure was extremely bold. It also presented a perfect opportunity to steal a march on Scotland's proverbial rival England, which took another 18 months to get its smoke-free house in order.

- **Collective orientation**. This success depended on the engagement of multiple stakeholders. The attention of politicians was captured with a carefully marshalled evidence base showing that: (a) second-hand smoke is extremely toxic; and (b) making hospitality venues smoke-free does not harm business. This attention turned to commitment when the Scottish First Minister met with the Irish Minister for Health, Micheál Martin, who had already brought in similar legislation. Reputedly, when asked by Jack McConnell what he would do differently if he had his time over, Martin replied simply: 'I would have done more sooner.' McConnell was won over: he had gone over to Ireland on the Friday night set against going smoke-free and he returned on the Monday all in favour, one of the clearest examples of source effect (see Chapter 6) ever recorded. Other key stakeholders, including the hospitality trade unions, the health and safety professionals and, of course, the medics were recruited to the cause, discussing the benefits both through their professional bodies (more helpful source effects) and concerted press and PR activity.

- **Competitive orientation**. There was, however, also loud and very active competition. Extreme opposition came from the tobacco companies. As persona non grata, they stirred things up from afar. Perhaps the most well-documented evidence of their hostility was revealed in a paper published in the journal *Tobacco Control* (Scollo *et al.* 2003). Of the 97 studies on the economic impact of smoke-free ordinances, 35 showed it had a bad effect on bars and restaurants. However, 31 of the 35 studies had two things in common. First, they were generally of poor quality, e.g. they lacked control groups or objective outcome measures, and, second, every single one was supported in some way by the tobacco industry. (The funding sources for the other four studies were unknown.) The higher-quality independent studies all showed that smoke-free had no negative commercial impact. Despite the revelation of this and other trickery, however, most of the hospitality sector remained adamantly opposed to going smoke-free and an excellent public health intervention had to proceed in spite of their opposition.

Turn again to Stead's 'Healthy Heroes' Case Study 19 on p. 464 to see all four orientations in action. Client orientation is captured in numerous ways: focusing on what communities were already doing 'right' and validating good behaviours of community members was central to community members' needs, as was 'speaking to and sharing with one another' and having fun. 'Community residents were integrally involved, not just as research participants and project beneficiaries, but as decision makers, creative contributors and implementers.' The collective perspective is seen in the variety of resources considered: social assets (statutory organizations, voluntary groups, businesses); cultural assets (schools, colleges, libraries, creative individuals who were invited to donate time to the projects); material assets (community facilities, potential funding or sponsorship sources, the physical environment); and individual assets (the skills, time and enthusiasm of local residents, volunteers and partner organization employees). Competitive orientation plays out in the perceptual and practical barriers identified: most community members did a lot of walking but didn't see this as valuable or 'proper' exercise. Finally, the Case Study's tagline 'Healthy Heroes' reflects its creative orientations where residents 'contributed their creativity in storytelling, cooking, recipe creation, photography, writing and organization'.

Now have a try at Exercise 2.5 to further contemplate the four social marketing orientations in action. The following is an extract from an interview with Kate, a young single mum.

EXERCISE 2.5: KATE

Well I just live up the road really. Eh . . . I've already got two kids, this is ma third. Em I've got a brother, a sister, and a mum . . . em never really knew ma dad. Eh . . . basically a bottle-fed em . . . the two before and I'm not dead against breastfeeding, I just . . . I can't really be doing wi' people like pushing stuff on me so I . . . like breastfeeding's something that . . . it's not really a done thing to do around here . . . I'm not . . . like ma friends just . . . I know none of ma friends do it and a don't really wanna be like gettin', you know, ma boobs out in public an' that, like, I don't wanna have the physical changes and . . . but the main thing is that I just really can't be doing wi' people talking down to me.

I didn't really do well at school, I left school when I was 14, so I really couldn't have, like, a tolerance for people in authority, so you know, an', I've decided that it's just easier if a try make ma mind up myself but you know . . . and speak to midwives and stuff like that . . . they just forcing it an' it's making me like a bit apprehensive and a little bit anxious an' a just can't be doing wi' it to be honest . . . so it's something that I'm a little bit like indecisive about. Eh, Bradley's 4 and Louise is 18 months now. A don't know whether she's doing her job properly or not to be honest because all the information she gives me I just dun't even listen to her because it's the way she says it, it's the . . . she's not asking . . . well she's not advising me, she's like telling me and it's more of a . . . she's saying stuff that . . . what's on her form what she needs to fill out and a don't . . . I just don't like the attitude, so it's probably my own fault really for switching off, but I automatically do cos I don't like somebody talking down to me about something that I feel that is totally my decision an' it makes me a little bit . . . well, not bothered really, so a can't even be bothered. So if, you know, like a say I'm not even against breastfeeding, a just don't like everything that comes with it an' the pressure of being told that breastfeeding is best an' a know that it's best, but you know it's a big responsibility an' . . . bottles just ten times easier and I have got a big social life . . . an' you know, midwives like, 'yeah well you can express and stuff', but I've heard that hurts so . . . she talks down to me a little bit, a just don't like her attitude so I tend to switch off.

What implications do Kate's views on breastfeeding have for the four orientations of social marketing?

Kate's dislike of authority, having stuff pushed on her, being talked down to and being told what to do all seriously detract from any sense of agency and empowerment she might have around breastfeeding. Kate is clearly telling the social marketer there is no client orientation in operation. She is 'switched off' and not open to behaviour change. A collective orientation reinforces this lack of mutuality and compounds her stance, as breastfeeding is not the 'done thing' where she lives or among her friends. Competition-wise, expressing milk is associated with pain, while bottle-feeding is easier, more acceptable with her peers and fits with her social life. So far, three out of the four social marketing orientations are negative from Kate's perspective and she is highly unlikely to engage in any intervention. The fourth and final orientation, a creative dimension, tells the social marketer a significant degree of innovation, empathy, understanding, reform and redesign of numerous issues with many stakeholders would have to occur for Kate to feel empowered to give up bottle-feeding and adopt breastfeeding. The implications arising from Kate's views for the four social marketing orientations call for a strategic and empowered view of behavioural and social change.

RELATIONSHIP MARKETING

The smoke-free success of Scotland is impressive, but on its own it only addresses one element of the smoking epidemic. How much more effective would it be if we were able to build on this success, along with the positive experience of the public and (most of) the stakeholders. How many other problems could be solved? Maybe Scotland could become an international leader not just in the elimination of second-hand smoke, but tobacco control – or public health – as a whole. Given what we have already said about the gravity and complexity of challenges such as global warming, and of the need to empower people and build their agency to engage in change, perhaps this positive energy should be harnessed.

The commercial sector has been thinking along similar lines for several decades and, as a result, has deliberately introduced continuity into the frame. They have progressed from seeking to define and satisfy our needs once, or on an ad hoc basis, to doing it continuously. Their aim is not just to create a one-off transaction, but to build ongoing *relationships* with us. Tesco, for example, does not want us to do our shopping at their stores just once, they want us to go every week; so, if we do, they reward us with a loyalty card and discounts and regularly send us a nice magazine. They try to build a relationship with us. And all the evidence is that, despite the obvious mercenary motivations of their charm offensive, it works: we respond with brand loyalty and regular visits.

This thinking has much to offer social marketing, not least because, just like Tesco and Coca-Cola (Chapter 1), we too want to move beyond the ad hoc. We do not want people to wear a seatbelt once, refrain from hitting their partner every now and then or eat five portions of fruit and vegetables occasionally. We want them to do these things again and again – indeed forever more. Actually our interest is very often in lifestyles rather than isolated behaviours.

Even when target behaviours are apparently ad hoc, such as with one-off immunizations during a sudden outbreak of infectious disease or temporary speed restrictions following a road traffic accident, relationship issues such as source credibility (we will discuss the idea of source credibility in more detail when we consider communications in Chapter 6) and trust are going to be crucial. The scare over the MMR (Measles, Mumps, Rubella) vaccine in the UK, for example, which has bedevilled childhood immunization efforts over the last decade, is driven by a lack of trust in the health authorities among parents (Evans *et al.* 2001). Theory strongly supports this strategic perspective. As we will discuss in Chapter 3, stages of change theory will tell us that changes do not, for the most part, occur overnight. They involve a series of steps from initial contemplation through to reinforcement after the fact, a process that is both dynamic and precarious: the individual can regress or change heart at any point.

Relational thinking also compels us to prioritize client satisfaction, which has fundamental implications for social marketing. It means that Andreasen's (1994) injunction to focus on behaviour change needs to be matched with an equal

Figure 2.1 A strategic vision of social marketing

commitment to service quality. Otherwise, promising programmes that do not result in rapid behaviour change are liable to be written off as failures.

All this suggests that social marketers should combine the four orientations with relational thinking as in Figure 2.1.

Try Exercise 2.6.

EXERCISE 2.6: NE CHOICES – FAILED BEHAVIOUR CHANGE OR INCOMPLETE RELATIONSHIP MARKETING?

NE Choices was a three-year drugs prevention intervention built around a high school drama initiative, with additional community, school governor and parent components. It had four behavioural objectives:

i)   to reduce prevalence of drug use;

ii) to delay the age of onset of drug use;

iii) to reduce the frequency of drug use among those who use drugs;

iv) to reduce mixing of drugs (including with alcohol) by those who use drugs.

The programme adopted a social influences approach, backed by social marketing and was thoroughly researched with all the stakeholder groups using a design that incorporated a two-year pilot, along with formative, process, impact and outcome evaluations. The last comprised a rigorous experimental design.

An action-research model meant that the pilot and formative research informed the initial programme design, and ongoing process and impact findings guided its development. The result was, therefore, extremely consumer oriented, and the young people – as well as other stakeholders – strongly endorsed it. The impact evaluation showed, for example, that the vast majority of children felt the programme was enjoyable (89 per cent), thought-provoking (88 per cent) and credible (84 per cent), and that the drama was realistic (79 per cent) and non-didactic (e.g. 88 per cent agreed that 'it encouraged us to speak our own minds'). In addition, the young people trusted the programme and its brand. For example, the last stage of research had to be conducted by mail, as a proportion of the young people had, by then, left school. The vast majority were prepared to provide contact details, and 70 per cent completed the sensitive and complex (40-minute) questionnaire. However, despite three annual follow-ups, the outcome research showed no changes on any of the four behavioural objectives.

According to social marketing lore, and the programme's own objectives, NE Choices had failed.

From a relationship marketing perspective, is such a judgement justified?

(Source: MacFadyen *et al.* 2002)

NE Choices delivered excellent customer service and built up a marked degree of trust with the young people, as well as other stakeholders, as was demonstrated by the success of the final survey. A valuable database of a vulnerable and normally elusive group was also developed, providing a unique opportunity to develop these putative relationships further. (Indeed, the programme delivery team was approached by more than one commercial operator wanting to buy the database.)

Furthermore, three of NE Choices' impact evaluation successes – reaching a range of stakeholders and settings as well as the core customers (Pentz *et al.* 1997; Fortmann *et al.* 1995; King 1998); the successful use of drama in education to engage the audience (Denman *et al.* 1995; Bouman *et al.* 1998; Orme and Starkey 1998; Blakey and Pullen 1991); and being non-didactic (Allott *et al.* 1999; Blakey and Pullen 1991; Orme and Starkey 1999; ACMD 1993; JRF 1997) – are known to be linked to effective knowledge, attitude and behaviour change. This does suggest that, as well as good relationships being established, the first signs of behaviour change were also emerging.

Arguably, therefore, from a relationship marketing perspective, NE Choices offered a great deal of promise, but transactional thinking cut it off in its prime. As Morgan and Hunt (1994) express it in their analysis of relationship marketing in the commercial sector: 'Understanding relationship marketing requires distinguishing between the discrete transaction, which has a "distinct beginning, short duration, and sharp ending by performance," and relational exchange, which "traces to previous agreements [and] . . . is longer in duration, reflecting an ongoing process".' NE Choices was judged by the former school of thought, but had the potential to deliver the latter (Hastings *et al.* 2002).

Morgan and Hunt's work also identifies two key relational constructs: trust and commitment, both of which have been shown to have particular relevance to social marketing.

TRUST

In an extensive social marketing partnership study, Duane (2012) defines *trust* as the willingness and confidence to depend upon exchange partners. It is this confidence that allows the citizen to assess the dangers of engaging in exchange when the benefits of doing so are often intangible and not immediate; trust then is closely linked to the credibility of the social marketer. In social marketing scenarios where risk and uncertainty are present, for example with infant immunization as we noted above, trust becomes particularly important. Trust, Duane says, can, however, become problematic when concern arises about the motivations of and benefits for the exchange parties. Any perceived conflict of interest, for example, can corrode trust. This happened with MMR in the UK where local doctors were felt to be too closely linked to what some saw as a manipulative government and medical establishment agenda – anxieties that were exacerbated when the then Prime Minister Tony Blair refused to declare whether his own son had been given the vaccine. Note Mr Blair, as most parents would agree, was well within his rights to insist on privacy for his child; the fact that his exercising of this right caused such alarm and despondency is an indicator of how badly damaged trust had become. The effects of this breakdown in trust were very serious: immunizations dropped to dangerously low levels, herd immunity was undermined, and children and parents were badly harmed as a result. And, as history has proved, the concerns about the vaccine were utterly unfounded – the one study raising questions about it has been completely discredited and withdrawn from publication. The problem was not a faulty vaccine, but a faulty relationship.

COMMITMENT

Trust is a precursor of commitment as a party will not commit unless they trust; it is the presence of 'time' that turns trust into commitment (Hastings *et al.* 2003; Donovan and Henley 2010). Duane (2012) explains that commitment in social marketing can manifest itself in different forms, for example, a pledge to undertake and maintain a positive behaviour; a formal contract (Lagarde *et al.* 2005; Donovan and Henley 2010) or access to necessary resources. For example, *safe*food, the promotional body responsible for food safety and healthy eating on the island of Ireland, integrated pledges into their social media strategy whereby citizens could publicly commit to adopting one behaviour into their lifestyles (Duane 2012). Other forms of commitment such as a memorandum of agreement between parties in a social marketing partnership assist in the maintenance of both commitment and trust as the roles and responsibilities of all parties involved are understood and therefore expectations are managed. Once a commitment has been pledged between all parties, it can continue to manifest itself over time: 'after committing oneself to a position, one should be more willing to comply with requests for behaviours that are consistent with that position' (Donovan and Henley 2010: 106). Unfortunately, characteristics such as management styles, loss of ownership and control can cause partners to lose motivation, which can show itself in tension and dilution of the commitment.

COMPLEX RELATIONAL EXCHANGES

Marques and Domegan (2011) point out that 'relationship marketing is based on cooperation with customers, other stakeholders and network partners. This means firms will not view one another from a win-lose perspective but will rather benefit from a win-win situation, where the parties work as partners'. Such relationship building in social marketing is demanding. There is rarely one single entity involved. Consider the typical social marketing scenario – interventions are funded, developed and delivered by different organizations. The delivery, in particular, tends to make use of the existing infrastructures ranging from commercial retail outlets to health and educational pathways, for example, schools, doctors or community partners. Furthermore, conflict and tensions often occur. For instance, delivery agents may not approve or have any allegiance to the funder or the developer, which poses challenges such as the need to define who is responsible for the relationship and for developing the consistency and integration of the 'collective'.

The point is that relational exchanges demand innovative ways of thinking about social issues. As put by Marques and Domegan (2011):

[T]he main contributions of relationship marketing is that it helps to uncover fundamental contradictions in, and challenges to, current social marketing thinking. First and foremost, the collaboration is with the client as a co-creator of value. The organisation starts with the client and where their behaviour is and not where the organisation wants their behaviour to be.

Susana Marques' Case Study 14 on p. 421 illustrates relationship marketing and the importance of processes in practice through the changing needs and wants of parents involved in several drugs prevention programmes. In the beginning, there was a difference between the initial needs of project workers and those of parents. For example, communication skills were not recognized by parents as being important to drugs prevention – many parents just wanted simple reassurance that their children would not be involved in drugs. As project workers and parents progressed, needs became more sophisticated and a great deal of flexibility was necessary. Many parents learned their original perspectives (don't take drugs) were often unrealistic, while project workers realized drug problems don't exist in isolation (peer behaviour is as important as parents). Prevention should not be pursued independently of parenting, family life and wider social issues. Therefore, projects had to be appreciated as a joint or co-learning process allowing both parties to become enthusiastic and willing to go on further with the learning and activities. This further learning was not necessarily related specifically to drugs prevention but rather 'points to the power of dialogue and co-learning to re-contextualise specific problems in wider social issues' (Marques and Domegan 2011).

Thus, the benefits of relational thinking – satisfaction, sustainability and trust – raise the potential for more profound concepts of change; ones that take in the idea of partnership working, popular movements and wide-scale social or 'systemic' change. This type of 'big picture' thinking is of vital importance if we are to tackle complex, multifaceted and highly contended problems such as global warming. We will return to this discussion in Chapter 10.

WRAP-UP

In this chapter, we have examined four social marketing orientations:

1. **Client orientation** – puts a premium on understanding the relevant people and genuinely catering for their needs.
2. **Creative orientation** – emphasizes the need for meaningful insights, innovative thinking and imaginative solutions to problems.
3. **Collective orientation** – a client's behaviour is shaped, moulded and influenced by those around them, such as family and friends, together with the structures and policies of the society they live in. Effective social marketing has to be equally multifaceted.
4. **Competitive orientation** – social marketing is all about voluntary behaviour change: clients have choices – they can ignore, subvert or reject our overtures. The challenge for the social marketer is to understand this 'passive' competition and, whenever possible, transform into cooperation. There is also the need to recognize and address more 'active' competition – the marketing of tobacco companies, for example.

These orientations build on the concept of mutually beneficial exchange and become strategic drivers when combined with relational thinking and recognition of the need to engage with multiple stakeholders.

Ultimately, these ideas make most sense when we see social marketing as a *process* for engaging people in social change, rather than just a means to the end of getting them to behave in a certain way. Complex social problems can only be tackled when we all feel empowered to address them and live in social structures that enable us to do so. In this sense, social marketing is as much about power and agency as it is about smoking cessation services or recycling initiatives.

Reflective questions

1. What are the four orientations of social marketing?
2. Discuss what being client oriented means to the social marketer.
3. 'Behaviours have context' – a core premise of social marketing's collective orientation. Elaborate with examples.
4. Exchange theory underlies client, creative, collective and competitive orientation of social marketing. Explain in detail.
5. How might exchange theory be relevant to social, environmental and welfare issues?
6. What does relationship marketing offer the social marketer?
7. What are the roles of trust and commitment in relationship marketing?

Reflective assignments

1. Locate three social marketing case studies or papers that demonstrate client orientation, creative orientation, competitive orientation and collective orientation.
2. Make sure you are comfortable with the four orientations of social marketing by writing a concise paragraph about each.
3. Based upon the organization you work in, or an organization of your choice, map out its client and competitive orientation.
4. You are social marketing manager with Alcol, a non-profit entity focused on young teenagers in inner cities around the country. You have been tasked with designing an ID card for underage teenagers. How could you use the idea of exchange in your job?
5. How, where and why do the four orientations – client, creative, collective and competitive – integrate with our discussions of social marketing in Chapter 1?
6. Debate with friends or colleagues whether or not social marketers are really just out to satisfy their own ends like commercial marketers, or are they more altruistic? What impact does it have on your argument if we define social marketing outcomes as about engagement and agency rather than just behaviour change?
7. Complete your traffic lights checklist for social marketing principles.

References

ACMD (Advisory Council on the Misuse of Drugs) (1993) *Drug Education in Schools: The Need for a New Impetus.* London: HMSO.

Allott R., Paxton, R. and Leonard, R. (1999) 'Drug education: A review of British Government policy and evidence on effectiveness', *Health Education Research Theory and Practice*, 14(4): 491–505.

Andreasen, A.R. (1994) 'Social marketing: Its definition and domain', *Journal of Public Policy & Marketing*, 13(1), 108–114.

Blakey, V. and Pullen, E. (1991) 'You don't have to say you love me: An evaluation of a drama-based sex education project for schools', *Health Education Journal*, 50(4): 161–165.

Bouman, M., Maas, L. and Kok, G. (1998) 'Health education in television entertainment – "Medisch Centrum West": A Dutch drama serial', *Health Education Research Theory and Practice*, 13(4): 503–518.

Buchanan, D.R., Reddy, S. and Hossain, H. (1994) 'Social marketing: A critical appraisal', *Health Promotion International*, 9(1): 49–57.

Cancer Research UK Press Release (2006) 'Young Scots "most proud" to be smoke-free as iconic image unveiled'. Online: www.cancerresearchuk.org/cancer-info/news/archive/pressrelease/2006-03-14-young-scots-most-proud-to-be-smokefree-as-iconic-image-unveiled (accessed 16 May 2013).

Denman, S., Pearson, J., Moody, D., Davis, P. and Madeley, R. (1995) 'Theatre in education on HIV and AIDS: A controlled study of schoolchildren's knowledge and attitudes', *Health Education Journal*, 54(1): 3–17.

Dewhirst, T. and Lee, W.B. (2011) 'Social marketing and tobacco control', Ch. 26 in G. Hastings, K. Angus and C. Bryant (eds) *The SAGE Handbook of Social Marketing*. London: Sage Publications Ltd.

Doll, R., Peto, R., Boreham, J. and Sutherland, I. (2004) 'Mortality in relation to smoking: 50 years' observations on male British doctors', *British Medical Journal*, 328: 1519.

Donovan, R. and Henley, N. (2010) *Principles and Practice of Social Marketing*. Cambridge: Cambridge University Press, UK.

Duane, S. (2012) *A Social Marketing Partnership Framework: An Extension of Morgan and Hunt's (1994) Commitment – Trust Key Mediating Variable Model*. PhD thesis, National University of Ireland, Galway, Ireland.

Elliott, B.J. (1995) *Marketing's Potential for Traffic Safety: Under or Over Stated?* Presented at the 13th International Conference on Alcohol, Drugs and Traffic Safety (T'95), 13–18 August 1995, Adelaide, Australia. Online: http://casr.adelaide.edu.au/T95/paper/s19p2.html (accessed 16 August 2006).

Evans, M., Stoddart, H., Condon, L., Freeman, E., Grizzell, M. and Mullen R. (2001) 'Parents' perspectives on the MMR immunization: A focus group study', *British Journal of General Practice*, 51: 904–910.

Farrelly, M.C., Healton, C.G, Davis, K.C., Messeri, P., Hersey, J.C. and Haviland, M.L. (2002) 'Getting to the truth: Evaluating national tobacco countermarketing campaigns', *American Journal of Public Health*, 92(6): 901–907.

Fortmann, S.P., Flora, J.A., Winkleby, M.A., Schooler, C., Taylor, C.B. and Farquhar, J.W. (1995) 'Community intervention trials: Reflections on the Stanford Five-City Project experience', *American Journal of Epidemiology*, 142(6): 576–586.

Hastings, G. and Haywood, A. (1991) 'Social marketing and communication in health promotion', *Health Promotion International*, 6: 135–145.

Hastings, G. and Haywood, A.J. (1994) 'Social marketing: A critical response', *Health Promotion International*, 9(1): 59–63.

Hastings G., Stead M. and MacKintosh A.M. (2002) 'Rethinking drugs prevention: Radical thoughts from social marketing', *Health Education Journal*, 61(4): 347–364.

Hastings, G., Stead, M., McDermott, L., Forsyth, A., MacKintosh, A.M., Rayner, M., Godfrey, C., Caraher, M. and Angus, K. (2003) *Review of Research on the Effects of Food Promotion to Children*. Prepared for the Food Standard Agency, 22 September. Stirling: Institute for Social Marketing, University of Stirling.

Hoek, J. (2011) 'Critical marketing: applications', Ch. 22 in G. Hastings, K. Angus and C. Bryant (eds) *The SAGE Handbook of Social Marketing*. London: Sage Publications Ltd.

Jones, S. (2011) 'Social marketing's response to the alcohol problem: Who's conducting the orchestra?', Ch. 17 in G. Hastings, K. Angus and C. Bryant (eds) *The SAGE Handbook of Social Marketing*. London: Sage Publications Ltd.

JRF (Joseph Rowntree Foundation) (1997) *Young People and Drugs – Findings. Social Policy Research*, 133. Online: www.jrf.org.uk/knowledge/findings/socialpolicy/sp133.asp.

King, A.C. (1998) 'How to promote physical activity in a community: Research experiences from the US highlighting different community approaches', *Patient Education and Counselling*, 33(1 Suppl): S3–S12.

Lagarde, F., Doner, L., Donovan, R.J., Charney, S. and Grieser, M. (2005) 'Partnerships from the downstream perspective: The role strategic alliances play in implementing social marketing programs', *Social Marketing Quarterly*, 11(3–4), 38–45.

Lefebvre, C. (1992). 'Social Marketing and health promotion'. Ch. 8 in Bunton R. and MacDonald G. (eds) *Health Promotion: Disciplines and Diversity*. London: Routledge.

MacFadyen, L., Stead, M. and Hastings, G.B. (2002) 'Social marketing', Ch. 27 in M.J. Baker (ed.) *The Marketing Book*, 5th edition. Oxford: Butterworth-Heinemann.

Marques, S. and Domegan, C. (2011) 'Relationship marketing and social marketing', Ch. 3 in G. Hastings, K. Angus and C. Bryant (eds) *The SAGE Handbook of Social Marketing*. London: Sage Publications Ltd.

Morgan, R.M. and Hunt, S.D. (1994) 'The commitment-trust theory of relationship marketing', *Journal of Marketing*, 58(3): 20–38.

Orme, J. and Starkey, F. (1998) *Evaluation of HPS/Bristol Old Vic Primary Drug Drama Project 1997/98*. Full report. Bristol: Faculty of Health and Social Care, UWE.

Orme, J. and Starkey, F. (1999) 'Young people's views on drug education in schools: Implications for health promotion and health education', *Health Education*, 4(July): 142–152.

Pentz, M.A., Mihalic, S.F. and Grotpeter, J.K. (1997) *Blueprints for Violence Prevention: Book One – The Midwestern Prevention Project*. Series editor D.S. Elliott. Boulder, Colorado: University of Colorado.

Scollo, M., Lal, A., Hyland, A. and Glantz, S. (2003) 'Review of the quality of studies on the economic effects of smoke-free policies on the hospitality industry', *Tobacco Control*, 12(1): 13–20.

Taleb, N.N. (2010) *The Black Swan: The Impact of the Highly Improbable*. London: Penguin UK.

Tones, K. (1996) 'Models of mass media: Hypodermic, aerosol or agent provocateur?' *Drugs: Education, Prevention and Policy*, 3(1): 29–37.

Wallace, D.F. (2008) 'Plain old untrendy troubles and emotions', *The Guardian*, 20 September 2008. Online: www.guardian.co.uk/books/2008/sep/20/fiction/.

Walsh, D.C., Rudd, R.E., Moeykens, B.A. and Moloney, T.W. (1993) 'Social marketing for public health', *Health Affairs*, 12(2): 104–109.

Chapter **3**

The shoulders of giants

THEORY: ALWAYS A GOOD BET

Harry likes a flutter on the horses (or, as he puts it, the gee-gees). He has just driven his invalid trike four miles (eight miles there and back) to the next village because the local bookie is closed on a Tuesday. After much pondering, he put 10 Euros on Agamemnon to win in the 3.30 at Wincanton. The odds were 10 to 1, so he stands to make 100 Euros.

He decided on Agamemnon because the filly comes from good stock – her sire (father) won the Grand National in his youth and her dam (mother) was also a well-regarded racer. He also took into account Agamemnon's form to date – one win, and three times placed in the first three. Finally, he thought about 'the going' (the condition of the race course, which is typically rated on a six-point scale: heavy – soft – good to soft – good – good to firm – firm) and calculated that Wincanton's firm all-weather track would suit the young filly.

Harry was now back home with the telly on and waiting eagerly for the outside broadcast from Wincanton to begin.

Harry is an experienced punter and well versed in horse-racing lore. He is rightly proud of his skills. But he would be astonished to discover that he is also an accomplished user of theory. Indeed, his Wincanton punt harnessed three theories: that lineage will influence a horse's performance; that past performance is predictive of future outcomes; and that different horses are suited to different conditions. These theories have emerged because generations of race-goers have observed, recorded and analysed results to try to work out how they can anticipate winners. In short, a legion of past experience has been neatly and economically turned into three predictive models, three theories, with which Harry has been able to improve his chances of winning.

We social marketers do the same thing to improve our chances of changing behaviour. As we've already discovered, this is challenging territory: many things influence how we behave – from individual knowledge, attitudes and agency through collective attributes such as community coherence and family structures to systemic geopolitical factors. With these multiple variables and levels of behavioural influence, where does the social marketer start?

Newton famously remarked that he had achieved so much, not on his own, but by 'standing on the shoulders of giants', a reference to all the hard work done by fellow scientists that formed the basis for his ideas about gravity. So, regardless of whether the behaviour change is sought in the area of health, the environment or safety; whether it is in a conurbation in a wealthy northern country or an impoverished village of sub-Saharan Africa, the starting point for all social marketing is with previous thinking – or what we call theory.

Theory is the distillation of previous endeavours in a particular field. Simply put, theory is a way of learning from other people's work. It enables us to follow suit and codify past efforts so that we too can build on solid foundations. It also helps us avoid the duplication of error and the reinvention of solutions. In addition, theories aim to simplify the world in order to better explain it. Theories model, or provide a systematic generalized framework, of what are typically much more complex phenomena in the real world, and thereby help us to get a grip on them. And it works: 'interventions that are based on social and behavioural science theories are more effective than those lacking a theoretical base' (Glanz and Bishop 2010).

Behavioural scientists have listened and the result is a vast array of theories that can become almost as daunting as the problems to be tackled. In this chapter, we want to introduce you to some of the key theories and look at how they might help solve social marketing problems. In essence, as we have already noted, all social marketers seek to do three things: understand their clients' current behaviour, identify what factors influence this and find a motivational means of triggering change. We will look at how theory can help with all three tasks. In the process, we will discuss seven different theories (see Box 3.1) but even then we will only be scratching the surface.

BOX 3.1: SEVEN USEFUL THEORIES

Theory	Key principles
Stages of Change Theory	Behaviour change is a gradual multi-stage process
Social Cognitive Theory	Social context matters
Social Norms Theory	What other people do around us matters
Social Epistemology Theory	Knowledge has a social as well as a personal dimension
Social Ecological Theory	Everything is connected so the smallest act can have massive repercussions
Social Capital Theory	A sense of belonging to and trust in our communities is vital
Exchange Theory	We look for benefits when considering change

Our aim is not to advocate for particular theories, but to make the more general point that, for social marketers, theory is a valuable tool that is easy to understand and straightforward to use. It will enable you to get to know the principles underlying specific theories and see how helpful they can be, but ultimately we would echo Donovan's (2011) call for 'an eclectic approach to theory, suggesting social marketers should be prepared to trawl a wide selection of models and constructs to select ones that best suit their field of endeavour, always combining this thinking with ethical vigilance'. We are also very cognizant of the Kurt Lewin maxim, 'there is nothing so practical as a good theory' (1951: 169), so the chapter concludes by going beyond principle, and providing an opportunity to put theories to work on a tangible case.

Before we begin, though, a word of caution. Social marketers need to respect theory – but they should also recognize its limitations. Human behaviour is ineffably complex, and almost as difficult to predict as the winner at Wincanton. This means that, on the one hand, we need all the theories and models we can get to help us make sense of it. On the other, we have to recognize that all these theories and models will, inevitably, be gross over-simplifications that will ultimately be found wanting if we set too much store by them. A mathematician friend pointed out that if she were to try to model a cow she would start by assuming it to be spherical; the variability and complexity of a real cow shape is just too much to handle. Her ungulate model might well have been of some help to animal husbandry, but it would fall a long way short of enabling a Martian to recognize a Friesian. Hence, social marketers also adopt a pragmatic perspective on theory, with a keen eye for what works rather than searching for the all-encompassing and unalloyed – but inevitably elusive – perfect theory.

Learning outcomes

By the end of this chapter, you should be able to:

- ✓ Explain why and how theory is important in social marketing
- ✓ Analyse three theories of behaviour change: stages of change theory; social cognitive theory and exchange theory – while recognizing that there are many other useful ones as well
- ✓ Introduce other theories useful for behaviour change
- ✓ Demonstrate how these can help social marketers answer three key questions: where their customers are in relation to a particular behaviour; what factors influence this positioning and how it might be changed
- ✓ Apply the theory to a given social marketing situation
- ✓ List important theoretical considerations in social marketing.

Key words

exchange theory – social capital theory – social cognitive theory – social ecology theory – social epistemology theory – social norms theory – stages of change theory

THREE QUESTIONS TO GET YOU STARTED

In essence, a social marketer's focus on behaviour change begs three questions:

1. Where are people in relation to a particular behaviour?
2. What factors cause this positioning?
3. How can they be moved in the desired direction?

Theory can help answer these questions. The first and third are relatively straightforward and we discuss just two theories under these headings. Stages of change or the Transtheoretical Model helps us examine people's proximity to a particular behaviour, and recognize that this varies between individuals, behaviours and over time. Exchange theory, a quintessentially marketing contribution, addresses the third question and brings dynamism to the process. As Kurt Lewin advises, it focuses our attention on the practicalities of change.

The second question, what factors influence our relationship to change is more complex. It picks up all the issues we have already acknowledged about the social drivers of behaviour. We start by discussing social cognitive theory, a sort of catch-all that maps out this social space, but then pick up on the four other theories that populate it with specific ideas about the forces at play.

Just to emphasize what we said above, this is not to suggest that these are the only theories that social marketers should use. There are also many other useful ones you can call upon. The Food Dudes Programme, for example, combined taste acquisition theory (repeatedly tasting different foods) with reinforcement theory (rewards and positive role models) and exchange theory (behaviour change) for increased consumption of fruit and vegetables among school-age children in the UK, Ireland, Italy and now the USA (Food Dudes 2012).

STAGES OF CHANGE THEORY

The stages of change theory is more formally known as the Transtheoretical Model of Behaviour Change. This rather clunky name belies the beautiful simplicity underlying Prochaska and DiClemente's (1983) basic idea: that we do not make and carry through decisions, especially complex behavioural ones, in a simple binary fashion. So the smoker does not just wake up one morning and think, 'OK, I'll quit', then do so and sit down to breakfast as a non-smoker. It is much more likely they will spend a long time considering the possibility of giving up, think about ways of doing it, give quitting a go and then spend weeks or months adjusting to the change. Indeed, the accepted definition of a non-smoker is someone who has been smoke-free for at least 12 months.

Prochaska and DiClemente noticed this foot-dragging phenomenon and began to study it in detail. It occurs not just with smoking but also with a whole series of addiction-related and other health behaviours. Prochaska and DiClemente suggest that we move through five stages, from ignorance of or indifference towards the idea of changing through trial to becoming committed to the new behaviour:

- **Precontemplation**: you may be aware of the new behaviour (e.g. quitting smoking or obeying the speed limit) but are not interested in it, at least at this point in your life.
- **Contemplation**: you are consciously evaluating the personal relevance of the new behaviour.
- **Preparation**: you have decided to act and are trying to put in place measures needed to carry out the new behaviour.
- **Action**: you give it a go.
- **Confirmation (or maintenance)**: you are committed to the behaviour and have no desire or intention to regress.

The Transtheoretical Model has undergone considerable field testing. Since 1983, Prochaska and his colleagues have validated it for 12 types of behaviour, including smoking cessation, condom use, quitting cocaine, using sunscreen and weight control (Prochaska and Velicer 1997).

Current smokers	Precontemplation:
Q1 During the **past 12 months** have you, **on purpose**, given up smoking for one day or more? (Please tick one box only) Yes ☐ No ☐ I'm not sure ☐	'No' to Qs 1, 2 & 3.
	Contemplation: 'No' to Q1 & 'Yes' to Q2. *Or* 'No' to Q2 & 'Yes' to Q3.
Q2 Do you plan to give up smoking in the next 30 days? (Please tick one box only) Yes ☐ No ☐ I'm not sure ☐	
IF 'YES' GO TO Q4 **OTHERWISE CONTINUE WITH Q3**	**Preparation:** 'Yes' to both Qs 1 & 2.
Q3 Do you think you will **try to give up smoking** in the next 6 months? (Please tick one box only) Yes ☐ No ☐ I'm not sure ☐	**Action:** Abstinent for less than 6 months [Answers 4 (a) – (c)].
Past smokers	
Q4 When did you give up smoking cigarettes? (Please tick one box only) (a) Within the last week ☐ (b) Within the last month ☐ (c) Within the last 6 months ☐ (d) Within the last year ☐ (e) Within the last 3 years ☐ (f) Within the last 5 years ☐ (g) Within the last 10 years ☐ (h) More than 10 years ago ☐ (i) I'm not sure ☐	**Maintenance:** Abstinent for 6 months or more [Answers 4 (d) – (h)]

Figure 3.1 Assessing people's stage of change

Alan Andreasen argues that, from a social marketing standpoint, three features of this model are significant. First, Prochaska and DiClemente have been able to show that it is relatively straightforward to separate consumers into these five stages by asking them a few simple questions. Figure 3.1 shows a questionnaire based on their work, which was used in Scotland to map low-income smokers across the stages, along with definitions of how respondents should be allocated to the various stages.

Second, they found that the appropriate intervention strategy depends on position in the process. For example, it is important to emphasize benefits in the early stages and costs in later stages. Finally, they recognized that a social marketer's goal should not be to propel the consumer to the Confirmation Stage in one step, but to move the consumer to the next stage. Only through a series of steps will the consumer reach the social marketer's goal of sustained behaviour change (Andreasen 1995). Have a try at Exercise 3.1.

EXERCISE 3.1: MEASURING STAGE OF CHANGE

Try out the questionnaire in Figure 3.1 on your colleagues. If you wish, you can adjust it to deal with another behaviour such as speeding or diet.

Does it work? Are you convinced by the idea that decisions to change these behaviours are indeed multi-stage?

This all seems very plausible and agreeably practical: the social marketing practitioner has a nice simple rubric for enacting behaviour change. At which point, we should beware; as we have already noted, nothing is that simple with human behaviour. The UK Smoking Cessation Service (SCS) adopted stages of change with great gusto and applied it much as Andreasen recommends. The result was that precontemplators were ignored and only those in the action stage were referred to the service. This assumes that the model is spot on (and we know no model ever is) and that our measurement procedures are perfect (which, as we will discuss in Chapter 5, they never are).

Predictably, therefore, the model has come under criticism on a number of fronts. First, it has been challenged for assuming people move in a linear fashion through the stages (Davidson 1992). Although it was initially proposed that people would progress linearly, behaviour change is now recognized as a 'spiral' where the individual may relapse back to a previous stage, but through experiential learning may eventually reach maintenance (Basler 1995).

Second, the model has been criticized for not considering those who change their behaviour without consciously going through all five predefined stages (Davidson 1992). This point is refuted by the authors who suggest that consumers may pass through some stages more rapidly than others (Prochaska *et al.* 1992). Later versions of the model recognize these dynamics and variations (see Figure 3.2).

These refinements of the model (seen in Figure 3.3), however, still fall a long way short of providing a complete representation of our behaviour. To muddy the waters further, for instance, complex and challenging behaviours typically take several attempts to change – as the anonymous wit pointed out, 'Giving up smoking is easy – I've done it hundreds of times'. Some of these attempts will, undoubtedly, be spur of the moment. Heavy drinkers will spontaneously forswear booze and dieters cake on a regular basis. Indeed, Robert West points out that the evidence suggests that *most* smokers kick the habit in this apparently instantaneous manner (West 2005). This seemingly damning failing – West goes on to argue that the model should be laid to rest – does not fatally undermine the theory, however; spur of the moment quitters may well have gone through all the stages of change in their previous attempts.

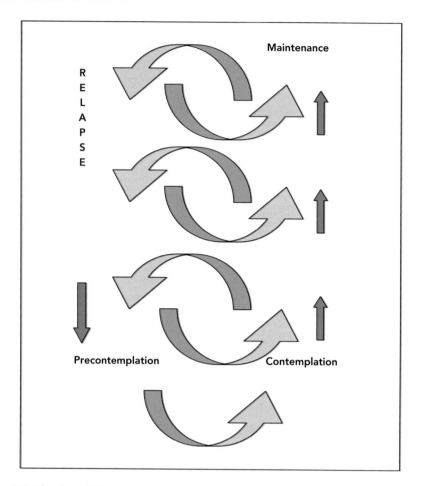

Figure 3.2 The 'Spiral' Model
Source: Adapted from Buxton *et al.* (1996)

The theoreticians will go on arguing about the validity of this model. From a social marketer's point of view, however, the discussion becomes increasingly redundant. Theories will never model human behaviour perfectly, but they can help us think about it more systematically. Stages of change brings a useful and plausible idea to the table: that behaviour change is a process rather than an on/off switch, and it is a good idea for those interested in enacting change to start by finding out how far people have progressed along this process.

The problems that Robert West identified are real enough, but they stem more from how the theory is being applied than from flaws in its basic precept. It does not provide a rigid manual on how to proceed; nor should it be used in the inflexible way it was by the UK Smoking Cessation Service. As DiClemente (2005) himself recently put it, it is a mistake to treat 'the model as a religion and not a heuristic to explore the change process'. The model simply provides

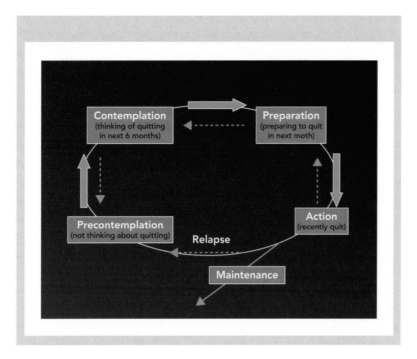

Figure 3.3 Stages of change Mark 2

an intelligent way of thinking about how close our clients are to a particular behaviour.

We need to turn elsewhere to understand why people arrive at a particular stage and what moves them on to the next (Buxton *et al.* 1996).

SOCIAL COGNITIVE THEORY (SCT)

Social cognitive theory postulates that human behaviour is reciprocally determined by internal personal factors (such as knowledge and self-efficacy) and environmental factors (such as levels of deprivation or availability of facilities in the local community) (Bandura 1986; Maibach and Cotton 1995). As social marketers, then, our view of behaviour should take into account the influence not only of the individual, but also of their environment. The latter can be further divided into two domains. First, there is the relatively direct influence of friends, family and the local community, which has been termed the 'immediate environment'. Second, there is the more indirect influence of social mores, economic conditions and cultural norms, which we have called the 'wider social context', that is, the structures and systems surrounding their lives. Figure 3.4 illustrates how these different influences interact.

In this way, social cognitive theory recognizes the two-way relationship that exists between personal and environmental factors: environments shape people and their

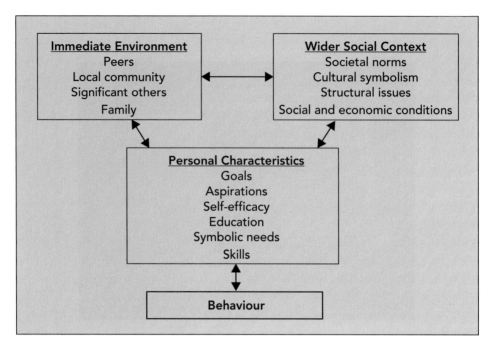

Figure 3.4 The wider determinants of health behaviour
Source: Adapted from MacFadyen *et al.* (1998)

behaviours, who in turn shape their environments through their behaviour and expectations (Maibach and Cotton 1995). Try applying this thinking by doing Exercise 3.2.

EXERCISE 3.2: EXTERNAL INFLUENCES ON OUR BEHAVIOUR

Think of a social problem with which you are familiar – maybe youth smoking, obesity or some aspect of non-ecological behaviour. Try to complete your own version of Figure 3.4 using this as an example.

In the case of youth smoking, for instance, the immediate environment might include shops that sell age-limited goods to minors, the wider social context, ubiquitous tobacco advertising, personal characteristics and extensive ignorance of the dangers of smoking.

The people/structure nature of social cognitive theory echoes our discussion of structuration and agency in Chapter 2 and underlines the need for social marketers to address both dimensions or risk failure. Simply telling people in poor communities to eat more fruit and vegetables if none is available in local shops is going to do little for public health. Arguably, as we noted in Chapter 2, it is also an unethical case of victim blaming – putting an unfair degree of responsibility for their own predicament on people who are already suffering and disempowered.

This thinking also underpins the idea of 'denormalization' – that if we can adjust people's perceptions of how common and normal a particular behaviour is we will also be able to influence their inclination to engage in this behaviour (Hansen 1990; Sussman 1989). For example, young people's perceptions of the prevalence and acceptability of smoking in both their immediate peer and family group, and in society as a whole, are key predictors of their tendency to take up smoking. Accordingly, smoking uptake will be reduced if pro-smoking norms are challenged and anti-smoking norms strengthened. Normative education, or denormalization programmes, therefore, correct 'erroneous perceptions of the prevalence and acceptability of drug and alcohol use and establish conservative group norms . . . [they] are postulated to operate through lowering expectations about prevalence and acceptability of use and the reduced availability of substances in peer-oriented social settings' (Hansen 1992). Evidence reviews suggest this is a useful insight and that normative education is a valuable ingredient of effective substance use prevention (e.g. Donaldson *et al.* 1994; MacKinnon *et al.* 1991; Coggans *et al.* 2003).

Social norms, social epistemology, social ecology and social capital theories can help social marketers to unpick and respond to this phenomenon.

SOCIAL NORMS THEORY

Social norms theory builds on the established phenomenon that our behaviour is partly derived from what other people do or say (descriptive norms), and what are approved behaviours (injunctive norms). This is the herd instinct at work – conforming to and wanting to be accepted by others in one's group, such as family members, friends, work and society. Rewards (e.g. acceptance, status, power) are provided for conformity, while punishments (e.g. exclusion, fines and jail) can occur for non-compliance. Social norms are pervasive: Kenny and Hastings (2011) list social norms studies in areas as varied as smoking; littering and environmental protection; sexual behaviour; gambling; tax compliance; eating and dieting behaviours; video pirating; opinion formation in childhood; pre-marital counselling; voting intentions; workplace health and safety; the purchase of luxury products; subject enrolment choices in schools and parenting approaches.

The 'lead by example' principle lies at the core of descriptive norms. We are influenced by our perceptions of what others do because those who are similar to us provide behavioural cues and triggers. This is particularly important in new situations such as a first-year college student in the university student bar or a child arriving at her new secondary school. In contrast, a trans-situational effect defines injunctive norms as they reflect societal values. That's to say injunctive norms 'communicate generalized values and indicate what is generally socially acceptable within a particular culture', whereas 'descriptive norms seem to communicate effective behaviour in a particular setting' (Kenny and Hastings 2011: 66).

Social norm campaigns work (Hastings *et al.* 2010). Enacting strong regulations (i.e. clean indoor air regulations and laws prohibiting sales to youths) in Massachusetts significantly affected adults' and youths' perceived community norms to be more anti-smoking (Hamilton *et al.* 2008). In Scotland and the rest of the UK, support for smoke-free legislation pre-ban significantly increased perceptions of non-smoking norms (Brown *et al.* 2009). Now have a go at Exercise 3.3.

EXERCISE 3.3: SOCIAL NORMS APPROACH TO PREVENTING BINGE DRINKING

You are employed as a social marketer by a non-governmental organization to design a social marketing campaign to discourage first-year university students from binge drinking. Consider how you could use a social norms approach to plan an intervention to decrease binge drinking on campus.

What are the limitations of this approach to your campaign?

(Source: Brown *et al.* 2009)

As the success of most social norms campaigns is grounded in a sound understanding of the majority attitudes and/or behaviours, you could start by doing a survey to gather reliable data about first-year students. This would need to establish how many students actually drink and to what extent, as well as their perceptions of their peers' drinking habits. Any tendency for the latter to be exaggerated would suggest a need for a campaign correcting these misperceptions. The evidence suggests that repeated exposure to a variety of positive, credible data-based norms messages can correct misperceptions and assist in reducing binge drinking.

Although social norms campaigns hold great promise for behaviour change, some campaigns have failed, as shown in Box 3.2.

BOX 3.2: A FAILED NORMS SOCIAL MARKETING CAMPAIGN

Clapp *et al.* (2003) tested the efficacy of an intensive norms social marketing campaign to reduce heavy drinking among college students living in a residence hall. They employed a pre-test/post-test non-equivalent comparison group design, conducted in two (experimental and comparison) comparable residence halls located in a large urban public university. The campaign successfully corrected students' misperceptions of drinking norms but had no effects on actual drinking behaviours. They concluded that, despite the popularity of such norms interventions, universities would be prudent to proceed with care before adopting social norms wholesale.

(Source: Clapp *et al.* 2003)

This last point, proceed with care when utilizing social norms, is reinforced by social epistemology.

SOCIAL EPISTEMOLOGY THEORY

Social epistemology (Hastings *et al.* 2010) focuses on the social aspects of knowledge – how groups acquire and justify knowledge and not just knowledge as a personal, individual concern. For example, social marketers involved in campaigns to inform smokers in the precontemplation stage about the health consequences of smoking would benefit from having an informed idea about how their target group – as a group – acquire and justify knowledge. If the informational campaign does not take account of how the target group thinks, reasons and puts emphasis on knowledge, it is unlikely to succeed. Social epistemology is useful because it shifts the SCT focus on knowledge as an internal, personal phenomenon to an external, contextual one. Social epistemology asks 'how did the client arrive at and justify their beliefs?', while SCT asks 'what does the client know?' (Hastings *et al.* 2010). Exercise 3.4 explores how useful this distinction is.

EXERCISE 3.4: SOCIAL EPISTEMOLOGY AND INFORMATIONAL CAMPAIGNS

You are a social marketer faced with developing an informational campaign to improve the dietary choices of a group of people that (a) is predominantly vegan, (b) distrusts official public advice on health and relies heavily on 'alternative, non-scientific, spiritual experts', (c) frequently takes yoga classes and (d) is subject to malnutrition, because their diet contains too few proteins.

Social epistemology emphasizes how social groups acquire knowledge and whom they trust as reliable sources of information.

Why is this perspective important to your campaign?

To design an effective campaign, it is crucial for the social marketer to understand how the target group acquires knowledge, and what sources of knowledge it particularly values. If your target group, for instance teenagers, distrust public experts, an informational campaign that quite clearly originates from a public health department is going to be a significant disadvantage. To get your message across, you will need to tap into a knowledge source that the target group respects and trusts – a celebrity perhaps, or community leader. In Exercise 3.4, a partnership with yoga instructors might be an effective way to support and strengthen your social marketing communications. In this way, social epistemology strengthens the marketer's power of persuasion through encouraging an exploration and analysis of the target group's idea of reliable knowledge and harnessing the power of source effect (a point picked up again in Chapter 6).

SOCIAL ECOLOGICAL THEORY (SET)

Social ecological theory adopts an even wider perspective on change, looking at whole social systems. It recognizes what is called 'the butterfly effect', a phrase coined by meteorologist Edward Lorenz to convey how tiny seemingly unrelated events, such as butterfly wings flapping in Brazil, could become magnified by the world's essential interconnectedness and have potentially huge effects on the other side of the world – causing, for instance, tornado weather in Texas. In essence, the butterfly effect describes the *co-ordinated* and *interactive* links; individuals and groups are loosely bonded in the system, permitting it to operate as a whole, while at the same time allowing for alterations and modifications in parts by some of those individuals or groups (Alderson 1957). It explains individual/environment interactions as dynamic and active processes.

To this end, McHugh (2013) in her work demonstrates how social ecological theory moves us towards an understanding of multiple group behaviours from a networked stance. Whole network behaviour integrates *multi-structural, multi-factorial* and *multi-institutional* influences and co-ordinates the cross-level interrelationships in a system. Applied to obesity, for example, this challenges us to think not just about the child's eating behaviour, but also about parents' cooking skills, as well as school lunch policies, food advertising and production methods, in addition to government regulations and how they all affect the child. Advocating more fruit and vegetable consumption may be meaningless until our highly processed and sugary food production methods are dramatically transformed.

Another pressing example of these effects in action is global warming: the tiny butterfly-wing consumption acts of the individual in Paris are linked with the activities of multinationals, the decisions of governments and the degradation of the planet – and across the world in Bangladesh fishing villages are disappearing under the sea. Figure 3.5 provides a graphic illustration of SET.

We will return to these complex, interconnected problems and how to deal with them in later chapters. For the moment, let us just note that they need equally sophisticated and far-reaching solutions – SET helps us to appreciate this complexity.

SOCIAL CAPITAL THEORY

Social capital theory addresses the patterns and configurations of connections between people. The World Bank defines social capital as the relationships that shape societal interactions, while organizations such as the Organisation for Economic Co-operation and Development (OECD) and WHO acknowledge that social capital influences education, social justice, health, civic engagement and hence the quality of life in a society.

Importantly for social marketing, social capital highlights the importance of *structural* and *relational* embeddedness within and among individuals in a society; that is our sense of belonging to and trust in our communities. The structural aspect looks

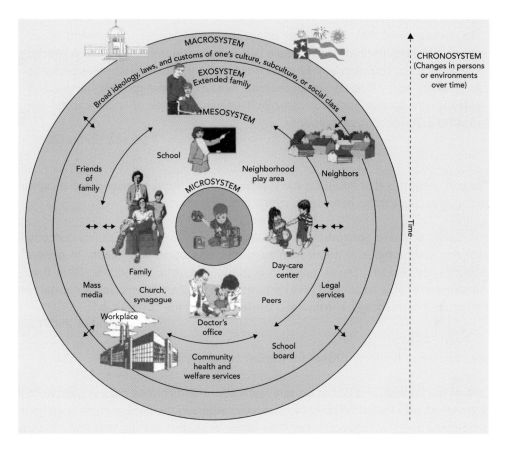

Figure 3.5 A Social Ecological Model

Source: Brofenbrenner (1988)

at networks and their ties; their connectivity; density and form. The relational element concerns values, trust, norms, identity and expectations, reflected in shared narratives, meanings and language. Together, these shape the quantity and quality of a society's social interactions.

There are three different kinds of social capital: bonding, bridging and linking as captured by Jones in Box 3.3.

BOX 3.3: BONDING, BRIDGING AND LINKING

'Bonding, bridging and linking have to be carefully balanced if society is to function effectively. Bonding refers to the networks that exist among "people like us" or people who share the same values. . . . In extreme cases bonding can lead to terrorism. . . . The OECD refers to this as the "ties that bind turning into ties that blind". Bridging social capital is the relationships with "people not like us" such as those from different faith or ethnic groups . . .

the vertical links that go up and down the social ladder. . . . Linking social capital refers to the networks people use to leverage resources from powerful institutions. . . . I suspect bonding has increased considerably whereas bridging and linking social capital has decreased because of the growing mistrust of citizens. . . . Broken societies can result unless all types of social capital are present in roughly equal amounts.'

Source: Jones (2011)

The core insight is that social capital is about relationships. Increased social capital encourages cooperative behaviour, which is vital. In fact,

the quality of these networks can help explain variations in key policy outcomes between communities in areas such as crime, education and health. In general, higher levels of social capital result in communities, and individuals within them, that are better able to act and take responsibility for themselves. Social capital can also assist in spreading behavioural change amongst the community'.

(Hyndman et al. 2007: 25)

We can turn to Lefebvre (2011) for further social marketing insights:

One of the implications is that people learn about and choose among behavioural options not only based on directly observing others in their social circle engage in behaviours and the consequences they experience, but also by who their friends and associates also connect with outside that proximal network and then transmit that information or those practices back to the immediate network.

We return to this last point again in Chapter 6 and in discussions about engagement, communication and participatory media. But Lefebvre also warns us, as with all theory, that, while social capital theory has become popular in social science and public health, it's not without its detractors. In particular, there are concerns that social capital theory does not deal adequately with issues of power and conflict – and yet these are inherent to relationships. This concern about relative power will re-emerge when we discuss exchange theory.

In summary, social cognitive theory adds a helpful social perspective to the understanding of behaviour change. Social norms, social epistemology, social ecology and social capital make it easier for social marketers to apply this insight. Specifically, they shed light on why people have a given positioning with regard to a particular behaviour; why a working-class teenager may be more inclined to smoke than a middle-class one, for example, or why quitting tobacco may be more of a challenge to a resident of inner-city Glasgow than it is to their affluent peer in the suburbs. The theories also begin to identify possible social marketing interventions that might alter this positioning.

Exchange theory can also help here.

EXCHANGE THEORY

Exchange theory is central to social marketing, which is why we have already touched on it in the two previous chapters. To recapitulate, the theory posits that, given behavioural options, people will ascribe values to the alternatives and select the one that offers greatest benefit – or enhancement – to themselves. This process assumes that we are need-directed beings with a built-in inclination to try to improve our lot. Richard Layard takes this thinking way back to the origins of our species, arguing that cooperation and mutually beneficial exchange were key to our success on the African savannah:

If human beings had not been able to co-operate in this way they would probably not have survived the rigours of the savannah – or subsequently of regions much colder. At best our lives would have been, as Thomas Hobbes put it, solitary, poor, nasty, brutish and short. We survived because our genes gave us the ability to co-operate.

(Layard 2005: 98)

He goes on to point out that 'the result of this co-operation is not a zero sum game; it is a win-win activity'. Crucially, Craig Lefebvre (1992) argues that social marketing is in essence this same process of seeking win-wins.

In order to increase consumer readiness to change, therefore, social marketers must provide them with something beneficial in return. In this sense, exchange and the notion of value co-creation (where the client and social marketer jointly deter- mine what values matter) involves the transfer of tangible or intangible items between two or more social actors (Bagozzi 1979). Kotler (2000) suggests five prerequisites are required for exchange to take place:

1. There are at least two parties
2. Each party has something that might be of value to the other party
3. Each party is capable of communication and delivery
4. Each party is free to accept or reject the offer
5. Each party believes it is appropriate or desirable to deal with the other party.

Central to these assumptions is the notion that the exchange must be mutually beneficial. Exchange theory postulates that, if social marketers can 'demonstrate that the perceived benefits . . . outweigh the perceived costs of its purchase, volun- tary adoption by the consumer is most likely' (Maibach 1993). A tobacco advertiser put the same point more baldly when he pointed out that: 'If a brand of cigarettes does not convey much in the way of image values, there may well be little reason for a young adult smoker to persist with or adopt the brand' (Rothmans UK 1998, cited in Hastings and MacFadyen 2000: 12).

It might seem that exchange is a difficult idea to apply in social marketing, where the benefits customers can derive are often more ambiguous than in commercial marketing. In the latter sphere, goods or services with a tangible purpose are exchanged for money; a prawn sandwich that satisfies our hunger in exchange for an agreed amount of cash, for example. What Bagozzi calls 'utilitarian exchange' (1975: 38). By contrast, he argues social marketing usually involves the mutual transfer of psychological, social or other intangible entities – what can be termed 'symbolic exchange'. So, he goes on to state, while 'there is most definitely an [mutually beneficial] exchange in social marketing relationships ... the exchange is not the simple quid pro quo notion characteristic of most economic exchanges'.

This suggests that the job of the social marketer – forever selling unseen benefits such as not getting cancer or avoiding a traffic accident – is particularly challenging.

However, further consideration reveals that commercial marketers also spend a great deal of time selling intangibility. They offer us *services* such as restaurant meals, the enjoyment of which depends on much more than the simple quality of the food or the satisfaction of hunger; insurance from which (for the most part) we hope never to get any tangible return; and lifestyle benefits such as weight control. Even with straight *products*, we happily pay more for branded goods because we trust them, feel more fashionable consuming them or want to be seen to belong to a particular social group. The tobacco advertiser quoted above is offering the young smoker ephemeral emotional and psycho-social benefits. Charles Revlon famously argued that, while his factories made cosmetics, the shops sold hope!

It seems then that commercial marketers do not see 'symbolic exchange' as a problem, but very much as an opportunity. Social marketers should do so too.

There is also plenty of evidence that people respond to incentives to change their behaviour. In their book *Freakonomics*, Levitt and Dubner (2005) show how school teachers were motivated to defy years of training and professionalism and cheat in school tests in order to gain financial rewards for good results. In the same book, he points out that inadequate rewards or penalties can actually be counter-productive. He tells the story of a nursery that instituted a system of fines for parents who were late picking up their offspring. The fines were set so low that parents saw it as a cheap form of additional child minding! Even so, the example demonstrates how susceptible our behaviour is to an incentive; it just adds in a reminder that we need to consult the target group if we want to make it an effective one.

Two other criticisms have been directed at exchange theory and its applicability to social marketing. The first concerns the suitability of the idea of mutual benefit for a discipline focused on doing good and was discussed in Chapter 2. The second is more profound and echoes our discussion of SCT. It concerns Kotler's third and fourth prerequisites: social marketers face problems in ensuring that people are capable of communication and delivery and also have the ability to accept or reject the offer. It assumes a balance of power that is often no more than a chimera; many groups in society lack the knowledge, articulacy and power to ensure that a genuine compromise is reached. For example, those living in disadvantaged communities may not have either the money or the access necessary to eat fresh fruit and vegetables. This re-emphasizes the need to maintain a collective as well as an individual perspective in social marketing; there is a continuous need to be cognizant of both the individual and social determinants of behaviour – and all the theories about this discussed above. It also underlines the importance of thinking critically about how people's lives are constrained by those with power. We will return to this theme in Chapters 7 and 8.

FROM THEORY TO PRACTICE

At the beginning of this chapter, we noted the adage that 'there is nothing so practical as a good theory', so we will now have a go at using the theories we have explored.

EXERCISE 3.5: THE CASE OF GREENVILLE

Greenville is a town of 100,000 people with awful dental health. Children as young as five years old have significant caries and are in need of fillings. By the age of ten, 50 per cent have fillings, and many also have had to have teeth extracted. Because their teeth are associated with so much pain and discomfort, many of these extractions take place under general anaesthetic with, inevitably, a small risk of serious side effects – and even death. Widespread dental disease progresses into adulthood and, by the age of 40, a third of the population have lost all their natural teeth, a proportion that rises to two-thirds by the age of 60.

You are a social marketing consultant who has been retained by the local health authority to tackle this problem. What additional information would you seek about the people of Greenville in order to guide your efforts? Jot down your thoughts before continuing.

The theories suggest that three additional types of information would be helpful to address Greenville's problems.

Where are Greenville's people with regard to dental health? (Stages of change)

The people of Greenville know little about the principles of dental health, and do not feel it to be a very important issue. Toothbrushes and toothpaste are familiar items to them but they are considered to be expensive and non-essential. Other oral health products, such as floss and fluoride drops, are unfamiliar to them.

Fillings, extractions and false teeth are seen as a normal and acceptable part of everyday life. Indeed, false teeth are felt to have many advantages over natural ones – not least the absence of pain and discomfort. Sugary food is also very popular in Greenville: it provides a cheap and tasty way of getting calories into the diet.

This suggests that they are very early on in the process of improving their own dental health. They are what Prochaska and DiClemente would term precontemplators, and this has obvious implications for any direct approaches you might make. It also begs questions about why the people of Greenville are so distant from the ideas of dental health.

Why are they in this position? (Social cognitive theory plus SNT, SET and SCT)

The people of Greenville are very poor, and dental health inevitably has a low priority compared with basics such as food, clothing and housing. The local health professionals are concerned about oral hygiene in Greenville, but feel they are fighting a losing battle. Their bosses in the nearby city are more concerned with issues of community safety and crime, which have a greater political priority. The oral hygiene product manufacturers see Greenville as a lost cause with little demand for their products, so take no interest in it. Their products are not promoted or widely distributed in Greenville. The sugar industry, on the other hand, sees it as a lucrative market opportunity. High-sugar products, such as candy, cakes and cookies, are relatively cheap, readily available and heavily promoted as nutritious and fun. After all, it is well known by all in Greenville that children love sweets and good parents regularly give treats to reward good behaviour. Journalists, doctors and scientists are seen as authoritarian and mistrusted, while friends and family are more reliable and dependable.

This insight forces us to think beyond the individual and recognize the social determinants of health, reinforcing the importance of the broader perspectives encapsulated in the social sciences school of thought. However, it leaves you wondering about how things might be improved.

How can change be encouraged? (Exchange theory)

There are some shafts of light. The young people of Greenville put a priority on their appearance and a good smile, with clean white teeth, is an important part of this. There are also centrally funded welfare schemes that could allow activity at no cost to the people of Greenville. Competition in the oral hygiene market is fierce and new markets are badly needed. At the same time, the sugar industry is coming under increasing scrutiny for its marketing practices.

The mists are now beginning to clear and a series of mutually beneficial exchanges can be planned with both people and stakeholders alike. Only the sugar industry looks like it may remain an obstacle to progress – but any marketer worthy of the name has to learn to best the competition.

CHOOSING YOUR THEORY

As we explained at the outset, the aim in this chapter is not to present an exhaustive list of the 60-plus models discussed in the social marketing literature (Darnton 2008; French *et al.* 2010; Jackson 2005). Instead, we simply wanted to demonstrate that theory is helpful – and will continually become more so: theory is constantly being tested and amended, giving the ability to explain more. With more explanatory and diagnostic power comes greater capability and capacity to achieve innovation and transformation. So, having established that theory matters, the key skill is that of selecting the particular theory that will help you with your social marketing challenge. To this end, we suggest the following six rules:

1. Theory is essential
   There has to be a theoretical basis to any social marketing strategy. Without theory, there is no reliable basis upon which to explain or predict human behaviour. Without theory, there's no building on past experience or past knowledge.
2. Exchange is at the core of social marketing
   Exchange theory lies at the heart of social marketing. Exchange theory does not replace or supersede other behavioural theories, but its premise of mutually beneficial rewards is central to social marketing's change agenda. Without exchange theory, there is no social marketing.
3. Combine theories
   Behavioural theories that explain human actions/inactions together with theories of behaviour change are utilized to complement exchange theory in social marketing. As Darnton explains in his overview of behaviour change models, behaviour theories and behaviour change theories 'are highly complementary; understanding both is essential in order to develop effective interventions' (2008: 1). Donovan (2011: x) agrees and points out there are now some generally agreed principles of behaviour change (see Box 3.4).
4. Include social perspectives
   Horses are renowned for their herd instincts. Survival in the wild for an individual horse is exceptionally rare. As a result, all horses have strong instincts to be with other horses. There is safety in numbers and horses are, inherently, social animals. In a similar manner, people don't live their lives in isolation (OK, except for hermits – but how many can you name?); the importance in our lives of exchange, values, networks and relationships all testify to this. That is why models like social cognitive theory and so many others recognize this collective dimension; and why this chapter has given it so much emphasis.

5. Think about the change domain

   In examining social marketing principles and exchange, there's been much discussion about changing the individual. Social marketing also considers altering the environment or situation to free or unblock the person to change their behaviour – think of the point of sale (POS) ban on cigarettes. Would-be non-smokers are reporting that the lack of POS helps them in their fight to give up cigarettes (Galvin 2011). The point is people behaviours are often situation behaviours. Therefore, choose the theory domain according to the appropriate level, be that downstream, midstream, upstream – or all three together, as we will see when we revisit systems thinking later on.

6. Recognize the limits of theory

   Remember what we said at the beginning of the chapter. Theory is an attempt to model the complexities of the real world and will inevitably fall short in this task. It pays, therefore, to be sceptical and to question. As for other aspects of social marketing, theories are no substitute for critical thinking.

   Now have a read of Box 3.5, which describes a complex and ongoing social marketing exercise and think about how the different theories and rules we have discussed in this chapter apply.

BOX 3.4: DONOVAN'S CONSENSUS

Social marketer Rob Donovan argues that 'behavioural scientists have now generally come to the following set of principles with respect to an individual performing a recommended behaviour:

1. There are no physical or structural environmental constraints that prevent the behaviour being performed.

2. The individual has the skills and equipment necessary to perform the behaviour.

3. The individual perceives themselves to be capable of performing the behaviour.

4. The individual considers that the rewards/benefits of performing the behaviour outweigh the costs/disbenefits.

5. Social normative pressure to perform the behaviour is perceived to be greater than social normative pressure not to perform the behaviour.

6. The individual perceives the behaviour to be consistent with their self-image and internalised values (i.e., morally acceptable).

7. The individual perceives the behaviour to be consistent with their social roles and

8. The individual's emotional reaction (or expectation) in performing the behaviour is more positive than negative.'

Source: Donovan (2011)

BOX 3.5: BEHAVIOUR CHANGE TECHNIQUES USED BY THE NATIONAL LANDCARE PROGRAMME

Influencing landholders to adopt more sustainable natural resource management practices is complex because it's not one decision (as, for example, deciding to give up smoking is one decision, albeit a difficult one) but a large number of different decisions – big and small, easy and complex – every week. It requires ongoing commitment, considerable knowledge, skill and at times considerable investment in capital equipment.

Despite this complexity, progress has been good because:

- They target the landholders most ready for exchange. Because Landcare and other landholder groups are voluntary – they usually comprise landholders who are either at the contemplation stage (beginning to think about change) or actively involved in change.
- They increase landholders' self-efficacy by providing them with the skills and knowledge to adopt natural resource management measures. They provide feedback, ongoing advice and assistance for those in the process of adopting new techniques, that is, 'farmers teaching farmers'.
- They utilize peer pressure and peer support to influence members to adopt natural resource management measures. Landholders delivered project outcomes partly because they did not want to let the other landholders down.
- They reduce the risk of adopting new methods because landholders can observe if the new methods work in their local conditions by visiting and observing other members who have already adopted the new methods. This also helps to overcome the fear of change barrier.

The bottom-up, local nature of the projects funded under the National Landcare Programme enables landholders to feel a strong sense of ownership of projects. In addition, this approach, by reflecting local priorities, enables landholders to see more easily the benefits to them and their local area of adopting new natural resource management methods.

Source: Hyndman *et al.* (2007: 25)

WRAP-UP

Ultimately, social marketers are interested in people – in understanding and responding to their needs. Theories are one important way of helping us think about them and how we might engage in the co-creation of value. They do this by explaining some of the behaviour we see or don't see. They also direct us to possible change options. Theories are guides but that is all they are. Theories don't design programmes or interventions. Theories don't do the co-listening or co-learning needed for mutually beneficial exchanges. Theories are no substitute for research and planning, critical reflection or creative thinking. They can inform our decision making about the needed exchange processes – about the plans we devise and the activities we engage in – but as we see in the remaining chapters, so do other tools and techniques.

Against this background and by way of example, this chapter introduced you to the more popular theories of behaviour change that are of potential value to social marketers:

1. Stages of change, which shows that decisions about complex behaviour are often protracted, ranging from first beginning to considering the possibility of change through to trying to reinforce permanent change.
2. Social cognitive theory, which emphasizes the social as well as the individual causes of behaviour, particularly when extended by social norms, social epistemology, social ecology and social capital theories.
3. Exchange theory (combined with relational thinking), which helps us think about how people can be encouraged to change.

This chapter is not – nor is it intended to be – an exhaustive list of theories. Its primary goal is to illustrate the enormous potential for theory to help, and hopefully in the process has removed some of the negative connotations the word can have. Finally, remember theory is only as useful as it is practical; in the next few chapters, we turn to these more applied considerations, starting with the social marketing toolbox.

Reflective questions

1. What is theory? What are its strengths and weaknesses?
2. How and why is theory relevant and useful to the social marketer?
3. Model and explain the stages of change theory.
4. 'Social cognitive theory postulates that human behaviour is reciprocally determined by internal personal factors and environmental factors.' Discuss with examples.
5. Social cognitive theory has a number of limitations with which social norms, social epistemology, social ecology and social capital theory can assist. Explain.
6. Define social capital theory, its components and relationships to health, education and quality of life.
7. Explain how exchange theory is foundational to social marketing.
8. 'What's more poignant and theoretically illuminating for the social marketer is the aptitude to select and use theories, rather than an in-depth descriptive knowledge of numerous models'. Discuss with examples.

Reflective assignments

1. Visit www.peecworks.org/PEEC/PEEC_Gen/S01796129-01796169 and read about the uses of theory in social marketing. In particular, work your way through the appendices where behaviour is matched to theories and areas of application are mapped to models.

2. Locate and critique a social marketing intervention or programme that includes a theory section.

3. Download scholarly papers in relation to the Food Dudes case study. Describe how exchange theory is combined with theories from other fields, such as taste acquisition theory, to change children's behaviour about trying new fruits and vegetables.

4. Identify one behavioural theory and one behaviour change theory that could be applied to an issue facing an organization of your choice. Outline the behaviour change implications of these theories for this organization.

5. You are the social marketing manager for the WHO's Healthy Cities in your area. Choose one aspect of Healthy Cities, such as gardening, cycling, waste management or drunk driving, and develop a theory grid to identify relevant behavioural and behaviour change theories that could potentially underlie a social marketing initiative. The more specific you can be about the particular intervention, the better to guide the selection of theories.

6. Construct your traffic lights checklist for theories in social marketing.

References

Alderson, W. (1957) *Marketing Behaviour and Executive Action: A Functionalist Approach to Marketing Theory*. Illinois, US: Richard D. Irwin Inc.

Andreasen, A.R. (1995) *Marketing social change – Changing behavior to promote health, social development, and the environment*. San Francisco, CA: Jossey-Bass.

Bagozzi, R. (1975) 'Marketing and exchange', *Journal of Marketing*, October 39(4): 32–39.

Bagozzi, R. (1979) 'Toward a formal theory of marketing exchanges', in O.C. Ferrell, S.W. Brown and C.W. Lamb Jr (eds) *Conceptual and Theoretical Developments in Marketing*. Chicago, IL: American Marketing Association, pp.431–447.

Bandura, A. (1986) *Social Foundations of Thought and Action: A Social Cognitive Approach*. Englewood Cliffs, NJ: Prentice Hall.

Basler, H.D. (1995) 'Patient education with reference to the process of behavioral change', *Patient Education and Counseling*, 26: 93–98.

Bronfenbrenner, U. (1988) 'Interacting systems in human development', in N. Bolger, C. Caspi, G. Downey and Moorehouse, M. (Eds). *Persons in Context: Developmental Processes*. Cambridge, UK: Cambridge University Press, pp 25–30. Also see www.des.emory.edu/mfp/302/302bron.PDF accessed July 19th 2012.

Brown, A., Moodie, C. and Hastings, G. (2009) 'A longitudinal study of policy effect (smoke-free legislation) on smoking norms: ITC Scotland/United Kingdom', *Nicotine and Tobacco Research*, 11(8): 924–932.

Buxton, K., Wyse, J. and Mercer, T. (1996) 'How applicable is the stages of change model to exercise behaviour?' *Health Education Journal*, 55: 239–257.

Clapp, J.D., Lange, J.E., Russell, C., Shillington, A. and Voas, R. (2003) 'A failed norms social marketing campaign', *Journal of Study of Alcohol*, 64: 409–414.

Coggans, N., Cheyne, B. and McKellar, S. (2003) *The Life Skills Training Drug Education Programme: A review of research*. Edinburgh: Scottish Executive Drug Misuse Research Programme, Effective Interventions Unit.

Darnton, A. (2008) *GSR Behaviour Change Knowledge Review. Reference Report: An overview of behaviour change models and their uses*. London: Government Social Research (GSR). Online: www.civilservice.gov.uk/wp-content/uploads/2011/09/Behaviour_change_reference_report_tcm6-9697.pdf.

Davidson, R. (1992) 'Prochaska and DiClemente's model of change: A case study (Editorial)', *British Journal of Addiction*, 87(6): 821–822.

DiClemente, C.C. (2005) 'A premature obituary for the transtheoretical model: A response to West (2005)', *Addiction*, 100(8): 1046–1048.

Donaldson, S.I., Graham, J.W. and Hansen, W.B. (1994) 'Testing the generalizability of intervening mechanism theories: Understanding the effects of adolescent drug use prevention interventions', *Journal of Behavioral Medicine*, 17(2): 195–216.

Donovan, R. (2011) 'Theoretical models of behaviour change', Ch. 1 in G. Hastings, K. Angus and C. Bryant (eds) *The SAGE Handbook of Social Marketing*. London: Sage Publications Ltd.

Food Dudes (2012) *Food Dudes Around the World*. Online: www.fooddudes.co.uk/en/fda-around-the-world/ (accessed 5 September 2012).

French, J., Blair-Stevens, C., McVey, D. and Merritt, R. (2010) *Social Marketing and Public Health: Theory and Practice*. Oxford: Oxford University Press.

Galvin, C. (2011) *The Ban on the Display and Promotion of Tobacco at Point of Sale in Ireland*. MSc thesis, National University of Ireland, Galway.

Glanz, K. and Bishop, D.B. (2010) 'The role of behavioral science theory in development and implementation of public health interventions', *Public Health*, 31: 399.

Hamilton, W., Biener, L. and Brennan, R. (2008) 'Do local tobacco regulations influence perceived smoking norms? Evidence from adult and youth surveys in Massachusetts', *Health Education Research*, 3(4): 709–722.

Hansen, W.B. (1990) 'Theory and implementation of the social influence model of primary prevention', in K. Rey, C. Faegre and P. Lowery (eds) *Prevention Research Findings: 1988, OSAP Prevention Monograph Number 3*. Rockville, Md: OSAP.

Hansen, W.B. (1992) 'School-based substance abuse prevention: A review of the state of the art in curriculum', *Health Education Research*, 7(3):411.

Hastings, G., Brown, A.K. and Anker, T. (2010) 'Theory in social marketing,' in M.J. Baker and M. Saren (eds) *Marketing Theory: A Student Text*. 2nd edition. Sage: London, pp. 330–344. ISBN 9781849204651.

Hyndman, D., Hodges, A. and Goldie, N. (2007) *National Landcare Programme Evaluation 2003–06*, p. 25

Jackson, T. (2005) *Motivating Sustainable Consumption: A Review of Evidence on Consumer Behaviour and Behaviour Change*. London: Sustainable Development Research Network (SDRN). Online: www.sd-research.org.uk/wp-content/uploads/motivatingscfinal_000.pdf

Jones, J. (2011) 'Lessons learned from the London riots', *The Irish Times*, Tuesday, 30 August, p.20.

Kenny, P. and Hastings, G. (2011) 'Understanding social norms: Upstream and downstream applications for social marketers', Ch. 4 in G. Hastings, K. Angus and C. Bryant (eds) *The SAGE Handbook of Social Marketing*. London: Sage Publications Ltd.

Kotler, P. (2000) *Marketing Management – Analysis, Planning, Implementation and Control*. 10th Edition. London: Prentice Hall International.

Layard, R. (2005) *Happiness: Lessons from a New Science*. London: Allen Lane.

Lefebvre, R.C. (1992) 'Social marketing and health promotion',Ch. 8 in R. Bunton and G. MacDonald (eds) *Health Promotion: Disciplines and Diversity*. London: Routledge.

Lefebvre, R.C. (2011) 'Social models for social marketing', Ch. 2 in G. Hastings, K. Angus and C. Bryant (eds) *The SAGE Handbook of Social Marketing*. London: Sage Publications Ltd.

Levitt, S. and Dubner, S.J. (2005) *Freakonomics: A Rogue Economist Explores the Hidden Side of Everything*. London: Allen Lane.

Lewin, K. (1951) *Field Theory in Social Science; Selected Theoretical Papers*. Cartwright D. (ed). New York: Harper & Row.

MacFadyen, L., Hastings, G.B., MacKintosh, A.M. and Lowry, R.J. (1998). 'Tobacco marketing and children's smoking: moving the debate beyond advertising and sponsorship'. Paper presented at the 27th EMAC Conference, Stockholm, Sweden, 20—23 May. In *Track 3 'Marketing Strategy and Organization': Proceedings, 27th EMAC Conference – Marketing Research and Practice*, pp 431–456. Stockholm: European Marketing Academy.

McHugh, P. (2013) *The Use of Social Marketing and Innovation Theory for the Development of Process Indicators for Science Communication*. PhD thesis, National University of Ireland, Galway, Ireland.

McHugh, P. and Domegan, C. (2013) 'From reductionism to holism: How social marketing captures the bigger picture through system indicators', in K. Kubacki and S. Rundle-Thiele (eds) *Contemporary Issues in Social Marketing*, Newcastle, UK: Cambridge Scholars Publishing Ltd.

MacKinnon, D.P., Johnson, C.A., Pentz, M., and Dwyer, J.H. (1991) 'Mediating mechanisms in a school-based drug prevention program: First year effects of the Midwestern Prevention Project', *Health Psychology*, 10(3): 164–172.

Maibach, E.W. (1993) 'Social marketing for the environment: Using information campaigns to promote environmental awareness and behavior change', *Health Promotion International*, 3(8): 211.

Maibach, E.W. and Cotton, D. (1995) 'Moving people to behaviour change: A staged social cognitive approach to message design', Ch. 3 in E.W. Maibach and R.L. Parrott (eds) *Designing Health Messages. Approaches From Communication Theory and Public Health Practice*. Newbury Park, CA: Sage Publications, pp.41–64.

Prochaska, J.O., and DiClemente, C.C. (1983) 'Stages and processes of self-change of smoking: Toward an integrative model of change', *Journal of Consulting and Clinical Psychology*, 51(3): 390–395.

Prochaska, J.O., Velicer, W.F. (1997) 'The transtheoretical model of health behavior change', *American Journal of Health Promotion*, 12(1): 38–48.

Prochaska, J.O., DiClemente, C.C. and Norcross, J.C. (1992) 'In search of how people change', *American Psychologist*, 47: 1102–1114.

Rothmans UK (1998) 'Young Adult Smokers', *Smoking Behaviour and Lifestyles 1994–1997*. The Rothmans (UK) Marketing Services, October. Cited in G.B. Hastings and L. MacFadyen (2000) *Keep Smiling: No one's going to die. An analysis of internal documents from the tobacco industry's main UK advertising agencies*. The Centre for Tobacco Control Research and the Tobacco Control Resource Centre. London: British Medical Association. ISBN 0727916009.

Sussman, S. (1989) 'Two social influence perspectives of tobacco use development and prevention', *Health Education Research*, 4: 213–223.

West, R. (2005) 'Time for a change: putting the Transtheoretical (Stages of Change) Model to rest', *Addiction*, 100(8): 1036–1039.

Chapter **4**

Making it happen – the toolbox

THE IMPORTANCE OF VISION

I say to you today, my friends, so even though we face the difficulties of today and tomorrow, I still have a dream. It is a dream deeply rooted in the American dream.

I have a dream that one day this nation will rise up and live out the true meaning of its creed: 'We hold these truths to be self-evident: that all men are created equal.'

I have a dream that one day on the red hills of Georgia the sons of former slaves and the sons of former slave owners will be able to sit down together at the table of brotherhood.

I have a dream that one day even the state of Mississippi, a state sweltering with the heat of injustice, sweltering with the heat of oppression, will be transformed into an oasis of freedom and justice.

I have a dream that my four little children will one day live in a nation where they will not be judged by the color of their skin but by the content of their character.

> I have a dream today.
>
> I have a dream that one day, down in Alabama, with its vicious racists, with its governor having his lips dripping with the words of interposition and nullification; one day right there in Alabama, little black boys and black girls will be able to join hands with little white boys and white girls as sisters and brothers.
>
> I have a dream today.
>
> Martin Luther King Jr, August 28, 1963

Martin Luther King's ringing words remind us that any enterprise needs a vision; a clear declaration of what its authors seek to achieve. King calls it a dream rather than a vision, perhaps reflecting the obvious challenges that stood in the way of racial harmony at that point in US history, but spelling out his destination – however distant – in this way put the foundations for success in place. First, it put all his followers and colleagues on the same page: they could agree, argue or even leave the movement – but they knew where they stood. Second, it expressed the vision in a deeply engaging way: a perfect example of the creative orientation we discussed in Chapter 2. King connected with his listeners' hearts as well as their minds. Third, and most importantly, he laid the basis for action. Having identified the destination, the journey could now be planned.

In this chapter, we take up his cue and move on from theories and principles to examine the practicalities of changing behaviour. Like him, we need a vision; like him, we must remember that our efforts depend on voluntary cooperation; like him, we need to think long term. Tactics have to be bedded in strategy, transactions built into relationships.

We begin with the vital importance of strategic planning, which helps map out a route towards our equivalent of King's dream. The social marketing planning process (see Figure 4.1) starts by appraising the situation, defining the problem and assessing the competing forces. This avoids the danger of making assumptions about the challenge at hand or how we should consider addressing it. Specifically, it helps answer the three crucial strategic questions that lie at the heart of any social marketing endeavour: *who* we would like to do *what*, and how we can *best encourage them to do it*.

King's speech suggests there were multiple possible answers to these questions for the Civil Rights movement in 1963. The *who* could have been the ancestors of both sides of the slave trade; state and federal political leaders or the next generation. The *what* could, respectively, have been to come together in mutual understanding; to pass enlightened race relations policies or to carry on the struggle. The third strand, encouragement, comes from his inspirational presentation. The job of the social marketing planner is to assess these alternatives and chart them against the current situation to decide which show most promise and how they can best be implemented.

More specifically, the *who* question leads us to 'segmentation and targeting', which helps improve our understanding of our customers, and lays the ground work for helping to meet their needs more effectively. Similarly, the *what* question makes us think about our objectives – the milestones en route to our vision – a crucial first step in both identifying our direction of travel and, later on, determining whether or not we have arrived.

These preparations bring us to the crux of the matter: how do we devise an offering that will encourage the target group to engage in an exchange with us not just once but repeatedly? What is our equivalent of Martin Luther King's inspiration? To approach this task, marketers like to think about getting the right product to the right people in the right place at the right price – 'right' being that which best satisfies their customers. Social marketing adopts a similar mix of tools, recognizing that in the arena of voluntary behaviour change it is vital to make your offerings as appealing, accessible, available and appreciated as possible.

Finally, to cement in the strategic progress being made, marketers pull this thinking together with the idea of positioning. King made sure his followers understood the full power and potential of his offer – nothing short of a new dawn. Social marketers need to be equally far sighted – and indeed equally ambitious.

This chapter will provide a detailed explanation of all these concepts and processes.

Learning outcomes

By the end of this chapter, you should be able to:
- ✓ Explain that planning guides strategic as well as tactical decision making, and ensures that our efforts take account of the social context
- ✓ Undertake a stakeholder and harm chain analysis
- ✓ Discuss why segmentation and targeting are important, and how to do them
- ✓ Outline the importance of setting measurable and realistic objectives
- ✓ Use the social marketing mix (the 4Ps) as a tool for devising appealing, accessible, available and appreciated (the 4As) offerings
- ✓ Demonstrate the practical application of positioning in social marketing.

Key words

harm chain analysis – intervention mix – objectives – place – positioning – price – product – promotion – segmentation – situation analysis – stakeholder analysis – strategic planning – targeting

STRATEGIC PLANNING

Constructing a successful programme to change behaviour is like climbing a Himalayan peak. You need to acquire or devise a map, take careful compass bearings, check your equipment and ensure you have the skills and resources to reach the top. Marketing therefore puts great emphasis on planning and any marketing enterprise worthy of the name begins with a marketing plan. Figure 4.1 presents a typical schema for one.

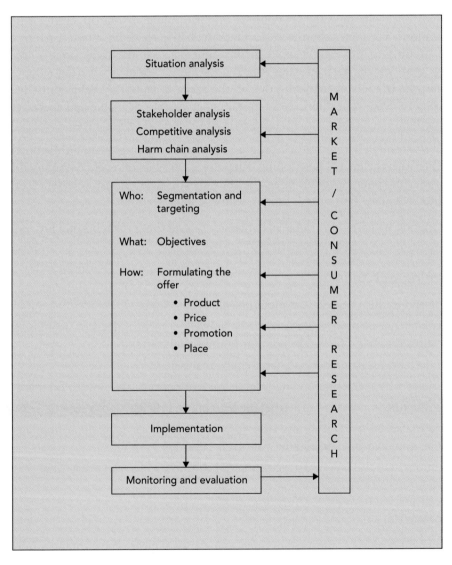

Figure 4.1 A social marketing plan

Source: Adapted from Hastings and Elliott (1993)

As can be seen, it comprises a number of standard steps that guide the marketer through accepted best practice from an analysis of the operating environment through to outcome evaluation. Before discussing the detail of these steps, three general points should be noted.

The first reflects what might be called the gestalt of marketing planning. Seen in the whole, the plan becomes more than the sum of its parts. It provides a progressive process of learning about the market and its particular exchanges. This learning takes place within particular initiatives. For example, a systematically produced and carefully researched cycling proficiency initiative for schoolchildren will enable social marketers to improve their understanding of schoolchildren and their desires, and thereby to enhance the initiative.

Second, the learning process also takes place between initiatives. The social marketer will be able to use the lessons learned from one initiative as a basis for future projects. Thus, the process is not just progressive but also cyclical; hence, the 'return arrow' in Figure 4.1. Furthermore, the development of understanding is not restricted to repeated cycling proficiency initiatives; social marketing efforts in quite different areas, such as pedestrian safety or sexual health may well provide useful insights. The link between cycling and sex may seem tenuous, but both are social behaviours that are heavily influenced by perceptions and imagery. Both also have to address the competing interests of safety and social acceptability. Condoms and cycling helmets, in fact, have a lot in common: adolescent behaviour.

In this way, when marketing planning is seen in the whole and as an ongoing process, it can maximize the chance of success both for a particular initiative and, more importantly in the longer term, for health, safety and the environment in general. Thus, as well as providing the tactical support through various marketing tools, planning also guides strategic thinking. This idea of *progressive and continuous learning* is absolutely fundamental to social marketing. We've seen it in relationship marketing in Chapter 3 and we will return to it when we discuss research in Chapter 6, communications in Chapter 7 and systems thinking in Chapter 10.

A SITUATION ANALYSIS

Strategic vision requires breadth as well as length, and the third general lesson we should draw from marketing planning concerns the importance of setting our actions within a broader context. To return to our Himalayan metaphor, before choosing your mountaineers and getting them equipped, you need to check out some bigger issues: has the mountain been climbed before? What are the weather conditions at different times of the year? Do you have to get permission from the necessary authorities to undertake the expedition? Without this advance thinking, you are not only less likely to succeed, but you will also put your sponsor's resources and the lives of your team in unnecessary jeopardy – you will be behaving unethically as well as unprofessionally.

The business community has long recognized that economic success is dependent not only on their own 'micro level' marketing, but also on the macro political and economic environment within which the company operates. Standard marketing texts (Jobber 2004; Kotler and Armstrong 2004; Wilson and Gilligan 2005) typically divide this macroenvironment into four forces: political/legal, economic, social and technological (PEST) (Figure 4.2).

Effective business planning includes careful monitoring of these forces. In many instances – such as the weather conditions on our Himalayan peak – they are largely uncontrollable. Technological developments, for example, or social mores cannot typically be manipulated at will. However, companies still need to know about them so that they can respond to the threats and opportunities they present. And these forces can have a fundamental impact on decisions about marketing strategies. For example, in the United States in the early 1970s, tobacco companies were required to fund health promotion messages at a similar level to their own expenditure on television advertising. After just a few years of this, they elected to withdraw from television altogether, transferring their promotional budgets to other, unfettered media (US Department of Health and Human Services 1989). Similarly, in the UK, television advertising for cigarettes was banned in 1965, but the decade saw a steady increase in advertising spend reflecting the move to other media (ASH 2006).

In other instances, however, there is at least the potential for business to exert influence. Thus, the tightening of tobacco control policy in Europe over the last 20 years has greatly influenced the tobacco industry's marketing to both consumers

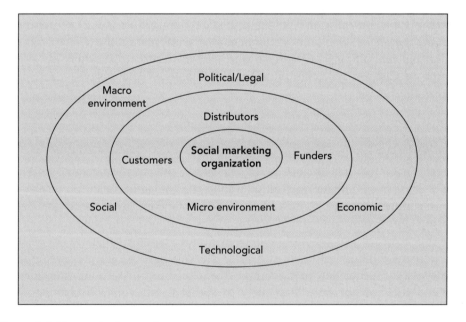

Figure 4.2 The marketing environment

and stakeholders – in the latter case spawning numerous campaigns to stave off legislation in such areas as smoke-free provisions and advertising bans (Hastings and Angus 2004).

This can include marketing to the final consumer, or it may not. For example, a UK brewer conducting a situation analysis in the late 1980s would have identified a major threat to their business in the form of the Government Monopolies and Mergers Commission undertaking a review of the industry. This ultimately forced brewers to sell off their retail outlets, but careful and sustained marketing to politicians (rather than consumers) mitigated the extent of the changes (Stokes 1997).

Exactly the same thinking applies in social marketing. Sticking with the same sector, anyone trying to respond intelligently to the UK problem of binge drinking would need to do a careful assessment of licensing laws, which have made alcohol more available than at any time since the First World War, taxation policy, which has brought prices to their lowest level in 30 years, and technologies that have delivered a range of new products on to the market – before considering consumer-directed efforts.

Decisions about how to respond to environmental forces are made by mapping the analysis against the strengths and weaknesses of the marketing organization. This is often referred to as a SWOT analysis – the Strengths and Weaknesses of the organizations are laid alongside the Opportunities and Threats of the environment. In this way, thinking is influenced not just by what is out there, but also by the capacity of the marketer to respond. To stick with our Himalayan metaphor, the weather conditions, physical environment and sheer scale of the peaks have been tackled in two distinct ways over the years. Some have chosen to invest enormous funds in very large parties of climbers and porters who effectively lay siege to the mountain. They succeed almost by a process of attrition. Others, who lack – or disapprove of using – such extensive resources opt for a much quicker in and out approach with a small, lightly equipped team. It is not that either is intrinsically wrong or right, just that two sets of factors – the external and the internal – need to be taken into account.

In the case of binge drinking, the social marketer needs to think about their capacity to influence policy makers or the market. This may well be considerable, and an 'upstream' approach can be contemplated. Alternatively, they may conclude that their power in this domain is actually very limited and the only thing they can do is produce downstream efforts targeting teenagers, however challenging this might be in an unsympathetic environment.

Furthermore, many social marketers are faced with a 'done deal'; they respond to a tender to do a specific task, to reduce binge drinking or some other behaviour in a particular population, and the approach is already defined – perhaps specifying a public education campaign or schools-based initiative. They have to take on trust that someone else has done the necessary strategic analysis.

In both instances, it still makes sense to at least do some of this thinking themselves: at the very least, it will give them a realistic idea of the task they face, as well as potentially useful insights into any shortfalls in their performance. It will also enable them to engage constructively with the funder and help them to think more carefully in the future. Gradually, the result will be a very desirable increase in the strategic emphasis of all our work. Exercise 4.1 illustrates the point.

EXERCISE 4.1: SOCIAL MARKETING AND HIV IN INDIA

Go to Case Study 8 by Sameer Deshpande *et al.* on p. 361 where you will read about *Swayam* – a peer educators' intervention to increase female condom usage. You are a social marketing consultant working for a major NGO and have been charged with developing a marketing plan to tackle HIV/AIDS in India. What will your SWOT (Strengths, Weaknesses, Opportunities and Threats) analysis look like?

If you are daunted by the result (and you should be), just imagine what it would be like trying to tackle the HIV problems of India without these insights.

A STAKEHOLDER ANALYSIS

The planning process continues by assessing what is currently happening in the marketplace (or the macro environment in Figure 4.2). We need to establish who the key stakeholders are and what they are doing or might do. Stakeholders are 'all of those groups and individuals that can affect, or are affected by' the social marketer's behaviour change proposal (Freeman 1984). They may control assets, information, communications, networks and markets, as will be seen in Chapters 6 and 10. In many cases, their support is needed to implement behaviour change and, occasionally, they are the problem, the dark side of the marketplace. In other cases, as we discussed in Chapter 2, they can represent direct opposition to change.

Stakeholder analysis is the systematic mapping of these potentially influential actors, which might include suppliers, trade unions, charities, policy makers, commercial firms, special interest groups, governments, banks, the media and many others. Translating this into practice, the Australian Red Cross Blood Service (ARCBS) identified 11 key (or primary) stakeholder groups for its work as shown in Box 4.1.

BOX 4.1: KEY STAKEHOLDER GROUPS FOR THE ARCBS

1. The Commonwealth Government of Australia
2. The parent non-profit organization
3. State and territory governments
4. Union representatives (including some ARCBS employees)
5. The health sector (including end users in hospitals)
6. Regulators
7. Suppliers
8. Major commercial stakeholders
9. Blood donors
10. R&D institutions
11. The media

(Source: Fletcher *et al.* 2003: 513)

Next, there is a need to recognize that different stakeholders have different levels and types of interest. The key consideration is how power is dispersed among the stakeholders. Does power reside within a few stakeholders (making them more influential) or is power spread out (making them less influential)? The ARCBS deemed all 11 stakeholders to be powerful and highly influential to their performance.

The Australian Red Cross Blood Service used stakeholder identification and analysis to identify the Key Performance Areas they needed to pay attention to for strategic deployment and management of their resources (human, structural and relational). They achieved this through stakeholder workshops and interviews where product safety and sufficiency emerged as the top two priorities (Box 4.2) for ARCBS to deliver a valued public service and fulfil their raison d'être.

BOX 4.2: STAKEHOLDER ANALYSIS AND KEY PERFORMANCE AREAS

1. Safe product   All matters relating to the safety of products
2. Product sufficiency   Availability of products as and where required
3. R&D & other services   Provision of specialist services & R&D initiatives
4. External management   All aspects of governance and compliance

(Source: Fletcher *et al.* 2003: 525)

Stakeholder analysis then leads to a scrutiny of possible behaviour change strategies, if any, with each stakeholder. Stakeholders can be helpful in changing behaviours, such as schools, or they can hinder change, causing harm. If helpful, there is opportunity for social marketers to collaborate with them in the social marketing exchange, through greater co-ordination, interaction and integration of efforts. This normally happens when there are many stakeholders with dispersed power and a win-win is possible for all.

If stakeholders are quintessentially harm-causing, such as tobacco firms, the only option for the social marketer is a *competitive strategy*, where the social marketing norm of a win-win can become a win-lose. We will discuss this dimension of social marketing in greater detail in Chapter 7.

This analysis can take on a much broader system-wide form if we think about complex, multifactorial issues such as inequalities, conflict resolution or global warming. The extent of change needed in these instances can generate opposition from stakeholders who have a vested interest in the status quo. As we will discuss in Chapter 8, this is especially true of the corporate sector, which, because of past marketing investments (especially in brand-building), along with its commitment to growth and increasing shareholder value, is, at best, going to consider only minor *improvements or redesigns* to an imperfect system. Radical change, however necessary, is simply too threatening.

Stakeholder analysis involves three broad steps:

1. Identify, map and prioritize stakeholder power
2. Establish stakeholder propensity for good or harm
3. Choose your stakeholder strategy: collaborate or compete.

For examples of stakeholder analysis in action, look at Case Study 16 on p. 434 by Juan Rey and colleagues as well as Case Study 10 on p. 394 from Karine Gallopel-Morvan and Christophe Leroux as well as trying Exercise 4.2.

EXERCISE 4.2: CONDUCT A STAKEHOLDER ANALYSIS

Take the three steps to stakeholder analysis and apply to a behaviour change option of your choice. When you have done this, take a look at Case Studies 10 and 16 and use them to reassess your work.

When stakeholders matter, Case Studies 16 and 10 illustrate how useful stakeholder mapping is to the social marketer to address the social ill at hand. Power can be gauged as high or low, active or passive and presented in grids as shown in the cases. This will also suggest the relevant strategies (cooperate/compete) for the social marketer to pursue when designing their offering.

HARM CHAIN ANALYSIS

The notion of stakeholders causing good or harm can be expanded by a harm chain analysis. It connects who is affected and who is affecting the problem. A harm chain analysis addresses the interconnections between a person's behaviour, the context of that behaviour and how other actors fit within that setting. It identifies gatekeepers within society, such as the media and community groups, who influence the affected and affecting stakeholders. It gives us further insight into the forces to be contended with and the pathways to the root of the problem. Harm chain analysis builds on stakeholder analysis and investigates stakeholders from a co-ordinated group behaviour perspective, as opposed to from a single organizational perspective. In this way, harm chain analysis reduces the risk of defining behaviour change too narrowly because it identifies 'all those involved not just those who are directly suffering the effects of the harmful situation' (Noble 2006: 3).

This is achieved by structuring organizations according to whether they (1) cause harm; (2) are harmed; or (3) regulate harm throughout the different stages of an exchange. Figure 4.3 provides some examples of how it might be applied to tobacco.

It shows how harm chain analysis steers the social marketer towards the *interconnections* in what might be termed dark exchanges, given that many social ills being tackled by the social marketer arise due to circumstances beyond that individual's

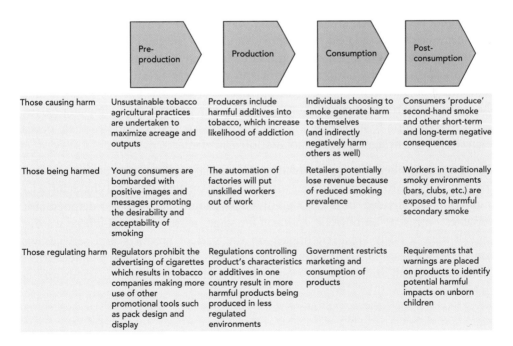

	Pre-production	Production	Consumption	Post-consumption
Those causing harm	Unsustainable tobacco agricultural practices are undertaken to maximize acreage and outputs	Producers include harmful additives into tobacco, which increase likelihood of addiction	Individuals choosing to smoke generate harm to themselves (and indirectly negatively harm others as well)	Consumers 'produce' second-hand smoke and other short-term and long-term negative consequences
Those being harmed	Young consumers are bombarded with positive images and messages promoting the desirability and acceptability of smoking	The automation of factories will put unskilled workers out of work	Retailers potentially lose revenue because of reduced smoking prevalence	Workers in traditionally smoky environments (bars, clubs, etc.) are exposed to harmful secondary smoke
Those regulating harm	Regulators prohibit the advertising of cigarettes which results in tobacco companies making more use of other promotional tools such as pack design and display	Regulations controlling product's characteristics or additives in one country result in more harmful products being produced in less regulated environments	Government restricts marketing and consumption of products	Requirements that warnings are placed on products to identify potential harmful impacts on unborn children

Figure 4.3 The Tobacco Harm Chain

Source: Polonsky *et al.* (2003)

control. This is not threatening, however, because there can be *positive* chains too, where exchange activities encourage new social norms. For example, designated-driver initiatives can create positive community attitudes towards socially acceptable drinking behaviour.

In summary, stakeholder and harm chain analysis reveal two powerful ideas: malign systems (harm chains) and benign systems (positive chains), which social marketing should both map and then respond to using the rest of the planning process.

THE REST OF THE PLANNING PROCESS

Once these macro and micro environments have been examined and factored in, social marketing planning focuses down on the nitty-gritty of *who* needs to do *what*, and *how* they can be encouraged to do it. Or more formally: segmentation and targeting, setting objectives and devising an offering, each of which is discussed next. The notion of 'positioning' – how their offering sits in a client's mind and with competing offerings – which helps marketers to think through these decisions, is also considered here.

Segmentation and targeting

Marketers recognize that we are all unique: we all have different make ups and experiences and live in varied circumstances. This means we will also have diverse needs, and, because marketing is all about meeting these needs as well as possible, the ideal marketer would offer a bespoke service – a unique offering for each and every one of us. This is clearly impractical in most instances. A few (typically expensive) operators – such as tailors and architects – can offer this level of customization, but, in most cases, a compromise is necessary. This involves dividing the population into reasonably homogenous segments and then choosing partic-ular target groups to approach with an offering that better matches their needs than would one designed for the population as a whole.

There are a number of criteria which a commercial marketer can use to segment the population into potential target markets (see Box 4.3). Personal characteristics – typically subdivided into demographic, psychographic and geo-demographic variables – present an obvious option. Life stage, personality and where we live can all have a fairly apparent impact on the sort of products and services we consume. For example, a car manufacturer might consider offering people carriers to families, small runabouts to single women and sports cars to testosterone-charged men.

BOX 4.3: THREE COMMONLY USED SEGMENTATION CRITERIA

1. *Personal characteristics*: demographic, psychographic and geo-demographic variables can all have an important link to behaviour.
2. *Past behaviour*: in commercial terms, for example, previous purchasing can provide important insights; in social marketing, proximity to the desired behaviour (perhaps measured using Stages of Change) can be useful.
3. *Benefits sought*: why people do as they do at present – and how these motives vary – can be a sensible way of subdividing the population.

Previous purchase behaviour – usage of a particular product category, loyalty to a brand and related attitudes – also provide a helpful tool for sorting potential customers. Someone who has bought a BMW before is a likely prospect for another one – and a better prospect for a Mercedes than, say, a Ford customer. The benefits different customer groups are seeking can also help with categorization. As we have already alluded to, cars actually offer far more than a means of transportation: they can represent modern family living, independence or machismo.

From a social marketing perspective, all these segmentation approaches offer potential, but they often need extending and developing. Try Exercise 4.3 before proceeding.

EXERCISE 4.3: DIETARY SEGMENTATION

You have been charged with developing a strategy for improving the dietary health of the Scottish population. As a first step, you are considering the task of segmentation. How might the three approaches we have discussed here – personal, behavioural and benefit – help? Can you see ways in which they should be developed or extended for use in a social marketing context?

Demographic characteristics have obvious implications for health. Gender, for example, provides a sensible starting point for many screening programmes; age and ethnicity are related to specific conditions such as Alzheimer's disease and sickle cell anaemia; and in Exercise 4.3 schoolchildren have particular dietary needs, as do the elderly and nursing mothers. Health status itself provides a useful extension to the personal characteristics we might consider – you might want to target specific efforts at people who are obese or have type 2 diabetes.

Psychographic methods also show potential, particularly if we think back to social cognitive theory (Chapter 3), which shows that characteristics such as self-efficacy are an important determinant of behaviour.

In both Chapters 1 and 3, we noted that inequalities are linked to damaging health, social and environmental behaviours, such as smoking, unhealthy diet, crime and recycling rates. Perhaps not surprisingly, they are also linked to greater illness and earlier death. In the UK, for example, men in the deprived inner-city area of Calton in Glasgow have a life expectancy of just under 54 years – that is 13 years lower than their peers in Baghdad and a full 22 years lower than the UK average (Gillan 2006). This suggests that degree of disadvantage/inequality is a very useful extension to geo-demographic segmentation, particularly because it does tend to cluster in well-defined localities such as inner-city housing schemes.

Social marketing's focus on behaviour also suggests that **behavioural** segmentation has potential. Furthermore, again thinking back to Chapter 3, it can be linked into stages of change and social norms theories. Populations can be segmented according to their proximity to a particular behaviour or perceptions thereof – with precontemplators being approached differently from contemplators for instance. In our exercise, this might involve plotting the population in terms of their readiness to change their eating habits.

The final approach to segmentation, the *benefit* different customer groups are seeking, might also help with improving diet. Food is much more than fuel and provides many psycho-social benefits, which could generate useful segmentation variables. For example, people who are more inclined than most to use food as a means of treating themselves might need to be approached with different offerings than other segments of the population. Box 4.4 shows how benefit segmentation worked for social marketers who were trying to encourage more active lifestyles.

BOX 4.4: THE BENEFITS OF EXERCISE

A comparative study into younger and older people's perceptions of exercise found that different sub-groups perceived different benefits in the product 'physical activity': some, typically younger men, wanted to compete against an opponent, while others aimed to better their own personal targets – to run faster or swim further for example. A third group was most concerned with body image and a fourth enjoyed the prospect of meeting new people, maintaining friendships and just 'getting out'.

These benefit segments formed the basis of a targeted strategy to encourage physical activity.

(Source: Stead *et al.* 1997)

Choosing the target

Having chosen the segmentation variables and divided the population into groups, the next task is to decide which segments will become targets. Three principles guide this decision. First, the target should be big enough to warrant attention – it should be **viable**. In commercial terms, it must be capable of generating sufficient profit; in a social context, it must have the potential to make an impact on the problem being tackled. This will be determined by the size of the group and their level of need. Picking up the example of disadvantaged groups, these are likely to score highly on this criterion. Second, it must be **accessible**. Usable channels of communication and service delivery must exist. Again, low-income groups are likely to meet this condition – as noted above, they are frequently geographically clustered, and if we focused down further to women or teenagers then community groups and schools offer obvious channels to access them.

Third, the target should be one that the marketer is capable of serving; it should be, at least potentially, **responsive** to their efforts. There is no point in having a big and accessible target if there is nothing to offer them or they are likely to be impervious to any initiatives. Past research and the statistics of inequality suggest that low-income groups are typically unresponsive, at least in the public health arena. Arguably, however, this just emphasizes the crucial need, which we will discuss later on in this chapter, to design an offering that genuinely meets the need of the target group. Certainly, Box 4.5 shows how targeting was success-fully used to improve cancer screening rates among disadvantaged groups in the West of Scotland.

BOX 4.5: REACHING DISADVANTAGED GROUPS

There has traditionally been low awareness of both bowel (24 per cent) and mouth (6 per cent) cancer in the West of Scotland, particularly among working-class groups. Knowledge of the signs and symptoms of these cancers is also poor despite the fact that presenting early to the NHS can greatly improve survival outcomes and quality of life. The West of Scotland Cancer Awareness Project aimed to tackle this. The segmentation was geo-demographic, and the key target working-class, over-50-year-olds of both sexes. These were both numerous enough and sufficiently reluctant to present to the NHS to comprise a *viable* target group. *Accessing* them was also straightforward: this group are more likely than most to watch television (ITC data shows that in 2001 C2DEs watched an average of four hours of TV per day compared with three hours among ABC1s). Focusing on the correct age group was done by ensuring that the messages were delivered by people in their fifties. Furthermore, local services could be geared up to ensure that it was easy for people to act on the messages. And they were *responsive*: a high proportion of patients that were aware of the campaigns admitted that seeing them had encouraged them to seek advice more quickly (62 per cent for bowel cancer and 68 per cent for mouth cancer), and those who attended were genuinely symptomatic.

(Source: WoSCAP 2005; ITC 2002)

Thinking beyond the final client

The tendency in discussing segmentation and targeting is to assume we are concerned only with grouping our end clients. But, in many instances, social marketers are thinking about stakeholders as well – or even instead, as we outlined above. Remember what social cognitive and social ecology theory tells us about the impact that social context (and its levels) has on people's behaviour. Remember, therefore, that we should always ask ourselves which stakeholder groups can have an impact on the relevant parts of this social context.

As we discussed in Chapter 1, Wallack *et al.* (1993) described this as a process of moving 'upstream'. Moreira's 'H1N1 2009 Pandemic flu and the promotion of vaccines' Case Study 24 on p. 512 provides a nice illustration of how this type of thinking might have assisted global vaccination rates.

Obstacles to segmentation and targeting

Two potential problems with segmentation and targeting may have already occurred to you.

First, there is an assumption in the process that our potential clients want what we are offering, and we just have to split them into groups who will want it even more. But, as Tones (1996) pointed out (refer back to Exercise 2.2), this is not always the case in social marketing. Exercise 4.4 describes such a situation, where the key target is actually least likely to take up the offering. Before proceeding, consider how this impacts on our discussion so far.

EXERCISE 4.4: RELUCTANCE TO ATTEND FOR CERVICAL SCREENING

A public health department wishes to encourage women within a certain age range in the health authority area to attend for cervical screening. There are a number of possible ways in which this population can be segmented, including:

● Personal – for example, socio-demographic (social class, education, income, employment) or psychographic (beliefs about preventive health, fatalism, attitudes towards health services);

- Behavioural – health behaviour (smokers/non-smokers, etc.); previous usage behaviour (attendance for screening);
- Benefits – health protection; reassurance.

From available secondary research into the characteristics of attenders and non-attenders for cervical and other screening (Thorogood *et al.* 1993; Austoker *et al.* 1997; Skinner *et al.* 1994), the public health department could make certain assumptions about the women most likely to respond positively to the programme: they will be ABC1, well educated, in work, have positive beliefs about their ability to protect themselves from cancer, favourable attitudes towards health services, and so on. If the screening programme were to be run as a profit-making service, this would be the segment to target. The screening agency could develop messages consonant with these women's beliefs, deliver them through workplaces at which the women are most likely to be employed, utilize media most likely to be consumed by them, and so forth. However, the health authority's objective is not to run the most profitable screening service but to make the biggest possible impact on public health by reducing incidence of cervical cancer. To do this, the screening programme needs to reach those groups with the highest risk of cancer – the groups who, the same research shows, are the least likely to attend for screening.

How does this impact on our discussion of segmentation? Specifically:

- How practical is it when our clients do not want our offerings?
- How acceptable is it when our offerings are life-saving?

Despite initial appearances, this does not undermine the principles of segmentation and targeting – indeed, it presents a nice example of how all the variables we discussed above can be used in concert – but it does suggest that, as well as benefits, social marketers should look to perceived *barriers* as a differentiating tool. The research is not just telling us that there will be problems in reaching our target, but also how we can overcome them. As we will discuss below, making our approach more appealing is not just a matter of increasing its perceived benefits, but also of reducing its costs.

The second potential obstacle is philosophical, and focuses on the fact that social marketers are typically addressing more serious issues, such as cervical screening services, clean water or needle exchanges, than people in commerce. Making segmentation and targeting decisions can be especially fraught as a result. Deciding which group will get life-saving services (and, by extension, which will not) is much more contentious than who will get a new brand of chocolate bar.

How would you respond to this concern? Jot down your ideas before you continue; thinking about inequalities might help. You can remain focused on cervical screening or pick another example.

Lefebvre *et al.* (Box 4.6) argue that, because people vary, they will, in any case, respond differently to generalized offers. Segmentation and targeting, they point out, is an inevitable product of human diversity. If our behaviour change efforts omit to manage it, they will simply fall victim to it.

BOX 4.6: THE INEVITABILITY OF SEGMENTATION

'This [segmentation and targeting] often raises the concern among some public health professionals that by focusing so narrowly on certain segments of the population, others will be missed. The reality, however, is that – depending on how the health message is executed and distributed – certain groups will always be reached and others will not. The only issue is whether the targeting is done based on research and strategic analysis or by happenstance and default.'

(Source: Lefebvre *et al.* 1995: 222)

Although they are talking specifically about communications, their view dovetails with the inequalities literature. This shows, as we have already noted, that health behaviours and outcomes are strongly linked to relative wealth. In the UK, for instance, these differentials have emerged and remain despite decades of population-wide health promotion and a universally available free health service. The most highly resourced, educated and motivated sections of society – and the least in need – seem to be best able to avail themselves of standardized provision. Thus, it seems that an egalitarian, level playing field might make the provider feel morally satisfied but does relatively little for the most in need.

The inequalities experience also suggests that past efforts have, albeit inadvertently, actually been of most benefit to the better-off, and thereby *increased* social divisions. Arguably, segmentation and targeting can help us do a bit of systematic and overdue positive discrimination.

Objectives: measurability and realism

Once the target(s) has (have) been determined, the next step is to clarify exactly what we would like them to do: to set our behavioural objectives. These objectives can be to avoid, modify or adopt behaviours. There can be a primary objective – an overarching main behavioural goal supported by secondary objectives or aims, which break the primary goal into more manageable aims, or a management number of main objectives. This thinking should, of course, be informed by the strategic planning process.

Setting clear objectives brings two important benefits (see Box 4.7). First, they ensure that a clear understanding and consensus about the intent of the intervention is developed by all those involved. This includes people both within the organization and outside it. For example, if an advertising agency is being used, well-defined and agreed objectives can ensure that they are absolutely clear about what their advertising has to achieve from the outset. Similarly good objectives facilitate communication with superiors and controlling bodies. This can be particularly important in social marketing where funding agencies or politicians may have to be convinced of the value of an intervention.

Second, objectives provide an excellent measurement tool. They give a clear focus to intervention design and make it possible to monitor progress and ultimately assess effectiveness.

BOX 4.7: GOOD OBJECTIVES

Clear objectives bring two benefits:

- *Improved communications* between the stakeholders in the initiative. Everyone knows what they are trying to do.
- *Enhanced evaluation*: if you know exactly where you are trying to reach, it is much easier to confirm whether or not you have arrived.

To provide these benefits, objectives need two qualities:

- *Measurability*: there must be an agreed way of calibrating whether or not they have been achieved – or at least a suitable proxy.
- *Achievability*: you need a realistic hope of success.

It follows, therefore, that good objectives are **measurable**. It may be very desirable, for instance, to run an initiative with the objective of making people happier, as Richard Layard (2005) suggests, but actually calibrating this will present great challenges. Measurability is also a function of resources. As we will discuss in Chapter 6, determining whether a particular programme has brought about a change in a population demands a complex and expensive research design that would probably swamp the budget of most small interventions. This raises the challenging question of whether or not we should set objectives – however desirable – that cannot be measured. One solution is to do so, but only if you can agree reasonable proxy measures to peg progress. Have a try at Exercise 4.5.

EXERCISE 4.5: PROMOTING SAFER SEX

You have been awarded a contract to improve the sexual health of Brownton's teenagers. You have six months, a modest budget and a large supply of free condoms. What objectives might you set for the programme?

Direct, attributable measures of changes in the sexual health of Brownton's teen sexual health is going to be beyond your means; so setting this as an objective will not be very helpful. Indeed, measuring any change in the population is going to be very challenging, unless there just happen to be existing surveys going on from which you can benefit. Assuming not, it makes much more sense to set more modest but measurable objectives – such as encouraging a specified minimum proportion of Brownton's teenagers to access the free condoms, and do so in a way that they find empowering and acceptable.

The need for measurability leads naturally to the second key attribute of good objectives: that they are **achievable**. That is, they should be within the capability of the organization and the programme budget. Again, the strategic planning process helps here, especially the process of matching external threats and opportunities with internal strengths and weaknesses. The temptation in social marketing is to be over-ambitious. This may be because the jobs we are trying to do are so obviously desirable and worthy. Giving people the support they need to quit tobacco or get their baby immunized are quite literally matters of life and death; and the rewards for success are truly mind blowing. If we really could get all the UK's 12 million smokers to give up overnight, Doll *et al.*'s (2004) work shows we would save around *six million* lives.

However, as we noted in Chapter 3 when discussing theories of human behaviour, changes are usually hard won. This is particularly true of the sort of engrained lifestyle behaviours we tend to focus on, which often have an element of addiction thrown in for good measure. So, it behoves us to cut our cloth accordingly. In time, this may also help, as we noted in our discussion of strategic planning, to educate funders and policy makers about the long-term and systemic work that is usually needed to generate real improvements in health and environmental status.

The ultimate arbiter

Ultimately, objectives, as with all aspects of effective marketing depend on the target group. They have crucial insights into a particular behaviour and can be studied to uncover valuable antecedents. Research published in the *Harvard Business Review* shows that consumer satisfaction is an absolutely vital measure of both current and future success in the business sector (Reichheld 2003). This only emerged through research with customers. To complete the circle, Reichheld also produced a reliable and straightforward way of measuring his construct: Would you recommend this product/service to a friend? Furthermore, not only does this reveal how well you are doing now, but it also predicts how fast you will grow by identifying not just satisfied, but 'delighted customers'. These *will* recommend the service to a friend. Indeed, Reichheld suggests that, on average, they will tell four other people of their pleasure, effectively becoming the company's marketing department.

This takes us back to our discussions of relationship marketing in Chapter 2. Box 4.8 shows how this thinking might be applied to the smoking cessation services, which enable some 15 per cent of their clients to successfully give up smoking. (If you are not convinced that giving up smoking is an extremely positive experience flick forward to Box 7.3 on 205)

BOX 4.8: RELATIONAL THINKING IN SMOKING CESSATION

'Let us think for a moment about the 15 per cent of users who quit success-fully. They will be delighted with both themselves and the service. Just suppose we did not lose interest in these people, but, like Tesco, gave them a loyalty card, kept in touch, and built relationships with them. They would persuade friends and family to use cessation services (they are living, breathing testimonials) and could be encouraged to think about their other health behaviours. From a marketing point of view, there is an obvious oppor-tunity to build on success. It comes back to the basic point of marketing – and indeed medicine – that progress is made by co-operation and partnership. The doctor has the medical expertise, but it is the patient's behaviour.'

(Source: Hastings and McDermott 2006)

FORMULATING THE OFFER

In this section, we will get down to the nitty-gritty of how a marketer goes about designing and deploying an offering to a particular target segment to meet the agreed objectives. The starting point has to be the client. We need to understand why they are currently behaving as they are (e.g. speeding or binge drinking or not recycling), the perceived attractiveness of behaving differently (e.g. driving safely or drinking sensibly or recycling) and how the latter might be enhanced.

The targets themselves will undoubtedly have valuable insights in all these areas. For example, teenagers will be able to shed light on the challenges of practising safer sex, and will have ideas about how these might be overcome. They will also be able to tell you how it feels to be faced with the task of discussing safer sex with a potential partner or how empowered they feel by a poster simply telling them to use a condom. However, there are also very real limitations to their insights into their behaviour. A smoker might not really know why they took up smoking, or whether addiction, peer pressure or tobacco advertising are playing a role in rein-forcing the habit. This is no surprise – they are smokers not social scientists, and answering such questions requires more complex research procedures.

Similarly, your client group may know the answers to your questions, but be unwilling to divulge them. To take an upstream example, a politician may be reluc-tant to let on that their disinclination to legislate on smoking in public places is caused by a fear of electoral harm because many of their constituents smoke – that they are, in effect, putting their own interests ahead of the public's health.

So, yes, the offering is designed around the needs of the client, but the task of divining these must be approached in a subtle and sophisticated way. We will return to this topic in Chapter 5 when we talk about research.

The intervention mix

Marketers do not just think about the customer with respect to their core offering; consumer perceptions also influence decisions about what the offer will cost, where it will be made available and how they should talk about it. As Cannon succinctly puts it: 'commercial marketing is essentially about getting the right product, at the right time, in the right place, with the right price and presented in the right way that succeeds in satisfying buyer needs' (1992: 46).

These four variables – **p**roduct, **p**rice, **p**romotion and **p**lace – are, for some, the core tools of marketing that need to be manipulated carefully to produce the most effective 'mix'. This construct, however, has also been criticized in marketing literature over the last ten years for being too mechanistic and naive to handle complex marketing situations, such as service provision, business to business networking – or, indeed, the challenging behaviours typically being addressed by social marketers. The 4Ps managerial approach of 'green products for green consumers has had little or no impact on reducing carbon emissions or consumption' in the call for sustainability (Walsh *et al.* 2012).

The criticism of the mix is justified, but does not mean that it should be completely abandoned. As with behavioural theory (Chapter 3), it just needs to be used with care and subtlety. It offers a way of thinking about a behaviour change challenge and how resources should be allocated to maximize the potential for success. It is not a pastry cutter, forcing every social marketing effort into the shape of the 4Ps.

The marketer is seeking the best combination of variables to offer their consumers (Kotler *et al.* 1999) and this is the one that comes closest to satisfying their needs – this is what Cannon means by the term 'right' in the quote above. Hence, it is essential to monitor the marketing mix continually so it can be designed and developed to meet these needs. For example research may show that a particular population is unaware of the benefits of safer sex, and so the promotional element of the mix may be given greatest emphasis. However, as the campaign proceeds, awareness may become widespread and the main problem changes to one of condom availability. This is likely to increase the importance of the product and place elements of the mix.

In essence, therefore, the marketing mix is a multifaceted and flexible means of responding to client needs. Exercise 4.6 gives some illustrations of the marketing mix and gives you a chance to try it out for yourself. While doing this, it will help to take a look at Rebekah Russell-Bennett and colleagues' work in Australia, where the marketing mix helped inform their MumBubConnect (MBC) programme pro-breastfeeding initiative (Case Study 5 on p. 334). The MBC programme was designed with a pricing strategy that reduced the 'social and emotional' cost of breastfeeding to the mother and a place strategy that increased access to breast-feeding services and reduced embarrassment.

The acid test for the much poked and prodded marketing mix is whether or not you find it useful. If you do, use it. If not, find another way of thinking through how you will make your offer as appealing, accessible, available and appreciated as possible. These 4As are the important issues to focus on, because they force us to think about what we are doing from the perspective of our clients.

Product

Social marketing products are frequently intangible and complex behaviours, which makes it difficult to formulate simple, meaningful product concepts (MacFadyen *et al.* 2002). To take an example, 'reducing one's fat intake' involves a change in food choice, menu design, shopping behaviour, food preparation, personal habits, family routines, wider social values and so on. Furthermore, it is a behaviour which needs to be practised not just once but repeated and sustained over a long period of time.

EXERCISE 4.6: THE SOCIAL MARKETING INTERVENTION MIX

Tool	Definition	Examples	Key marketing question
Product	The behavioural offer made to target adopters	Adoption of idea (belief, attitude, value) Adoption of behaviour (one-off, sustained) Distance from current behaviour Non-adoption of future behaviour	How appealing is the offer? Or What behaviour does the product enable?
Price	The costs that target adopters have to bear and barriers they have to overcome	Psychological, Emotional, Cultural, Social, Behavioural, Temporal, Practical, Physical, Financial	How affordable is it? Or On what basis is the client empowered?
Place	The channels by which the change is promoted and places in which the change is supported and encouraged	Media channels Distribution channels Interpersonal channels Physical places Non-physical places (e.g. social and cultural climate)	How readily available is it? Or Where does engagement occur?

Tool	Definition	Examples	Key marketing question
Promotion	The means by which the change is promoted to the target	Advertising Public relations Media Advocacy Direct Mail Interpersonal	How well known and appreciated is it? Or How is the desired behaviour exemplified?

Your task: choose a behaviour change challenge – speeding in your town for instance, or teen antisocial behaviour – and design a marketing mix for it. Consider how useful the various Ps, As and Es are and how they might vary given another project or the same project at a different stage.

(Source: Adapted from MacFadyen et al. 2002)

As a first step towards formulating product concepts, social marketers need to identify and clarify their product attributes. In commercial marketing, these range from the tangible (colour, taste, shape, size, packaging, performance) to the intangible (brand, image, status). Social marketing product attributes are largely situated at the intangible end of this continuum. Some potential classifications of product attributes are suggested in Box 4.9.

BOX 4.9: SOCIAL MARKETING PRODUCT ATTRIBUTES

Trialability: Can the behaviour be tried out beforehand before permanent or full adoption (wearing a cycling helmet)?

Ease: How easy or difficult is it to adopt the behaviour (wearing a seatbelt versus giving up smoking)?

Risks: What are the risks of adopting the behaviour?

Image: Is the behaviour attractive or unattractive?

Acceptability: Is the behaviour socially acceptable?

Duration: Is the behaviour to be practised once or repeatedly? Is it to be sustained over the short or long term?

Cost: Does the behaviour have a financial cost or not (eating a healthier diet may involve more expense; drinking less alcohol does not)?

(Source: MacFadyen et al. 2002)

Analysing product attributes in this way helps social marketers to formulate meaningful and communicable offerings. For example, in addressing teen smoking, research may suggest that image is a key issue, rather than the avoidance of health risks. The social marketer can then put particular emphasis on producing non-smoking options that are cool and trendy – such as self-empowerment and independence – rather than ones that major on the health benefits of quitting.

Kotler *et al.* (1999) provided another way for social marketers to think about their products when he distinguished the *actual* product (the behaviour change), the *core* product (the benefits it brings) and the *augmented* product (tangible objects and services to support the behaviour change). Again, it helps us think coherently about what we are offering from the perspective of the client group.

Price

Only a few of social marketing's products have a monetary price, and, given all we have said about inequalities, this might seem to be a good thing. If the poor are in most need of our products, it seems crazy to start charging for them; this will surely be regressive. However, marketers remind us that price and value are closely inter-related: the value of a Rolls-Royce is reinforced by its exclusive price tag, and, at the other extreme, freebies are often – figuratively as well as literally – taken for granted. Condom social marketing in developing countries provides instructive lessons here. Initial efforts to encourage contraception in India involved shipping out large quantities of free condoms. However, because they were free, neither the distributors nor the would-be users treated them with much respect. The product ended up mouldering in warehouses, sell-by and storage instructions were not respected and the products acquired a poor public reputation.

By contrast, it was very apparent that commercial products such as soft drinks were doing much better. They were well distributed (even the poorest village seemed to have a Coke machine), properly stored and readily consumed. Brand value was also very much in evidence. Success was due to commercialization: everyone in the supply chain stood to make money out of effective distribution. Even the final customer gained because the product offering had added brand value, to which price contributed. The condom social marketers decided to follow suit and charge (a very modest) amount for their products. The result has been a vastly increased condom usage and much wider availability (Harvey 1997; Dahl *et al.* 1997).

This does not suggest that we should rush to commercialize all social marketing efforts. But it does warn us to think carefully about what free actually means – and ensure that it does not just result in second-rate product or service offerings.

Price also has a wider meaning in social marketing; there are almost always costs associated with behaviour change. These may be to do with time, embarrassment, effort, inertia, pain, perceived social stigma, among other variables. Thus, the speeding driver thinks he is going to be late if he obeys the speed limit; the teenager has to overcome embarrassment to acquire a condom. These costs are balanced against the benefits of engaging in the behaviour – and both costs and benefits vary for different behaviours. Exercise 4.7 suggests a systematic way of thinking about these variations.

EXERCISE 4.7: THINKING SYSTEMATICALLY ABOUT PRICE

	Tangible	Intangible
Low cost	Personal benefits e.g. Wearing seatbelts	Societal benefits e.g. Recycling programmes
High cost	Personal benefits e.g. Smoking cessation	Societal benefits e.g. Avoiding use of cars

Which combination will be the toughest for social marketing to address? Which the easiest? What are the strategic implications of your answers?

(Source: Based on Rangun et al. 1996)

i)   *Low cost and tangible, personal benefits,* e.g. seatbelt wearing.

In this case, the target perceives clear, direct benefits to themselves, and change is easy (assuming reliable seatbelts are fitted as standard) relative to the four other types of initiative. Communication is likely to be a key element of the social marketing strategy.

ii)   *Low cost and intangible, societal benefits,* e.g. recycling programmes.

Here the behaviour change is relatively easy to adopt, but the benefits are not perceived to be as relevant to the individual. Kash Rangun and colleagues argue that convenience is the key to this type of programme and the ultimate benefit to the recycler and to society should be stressed.

iii)   *High cost and tangible, personal benefits,* e.g. smoking cessation programmes.

In this case, there is a very clear personal benefit to adopting the suggested behaviour, but the costs associated with doing so are high. Here the authors advocate the adoption of what they call 'push marketing' approaches: providing support services and augmented products that will reduce the cost.

iv)   *High cost and intangible, societal benefits,* e.g. avoiding car use

This is the hardest type of behaviour change to induce as the costs are high and the benefits are hard to personalize and quantify. In this case, it may be necessary to adopt de-marketing approaches, use moral persuasion or social influence. In addition, increasing the cost of the current behaviour (e.g. by increasing fuel tax) may help.

Place

Kotler and Zaltman suggest that place in social marketing covers both distribution and response channels, and 'clear action outlets for those motivated to acquire the product' (1971: 9). Thus, where there is a communications element to a social marketing initiative, place applies to the media channels through which messages are to be delivered, but it can also apply to distribution channels for tangible products or services, such as clean needles or smoking cessation groups.

In both instances, place variables such as channel, coverage, cost, timing (Kotler and Roberto 1989), location, transport (Woodruffe 1995) and accessibility (Cowell 1994) are all relevant. For example, an initiative to increase uptake of cervical screening could reduce the costs of attending by manipulating the place variables of distance, time and convenience (offering screening at flexible times and in varied locations).

In addition, many social marketing initiatives depend on intermediaries, such as health professionals, pharmacists, teachers, and community workers, to act as distribution channels for media materials or as retailers for a particular behaviour change product. For example, GPs are often given responsibility for changing smoking and drinking behaviour. Where intermediaries are to act primarily as distribution agents for media products, key variables such as accessibility and appropriateness should be considered. When these intermediaries have a more complex role (e.g. youth workers and teachers delivering a sex education curriculum), place variables such as source visibility, credibility, attractiveness and power (Percy 1983; Hastings and Stead 1999) should guide the selection of appropriate agents and inform the sort of support and training that is offered to them. For example, the drugs prevention literature has examined the relative merits of teachers, youth workers, police and peers as delivery channels for drugs prevention messages (Bandy and President 1983; Shiner and Newburn 1996).

Social marketers are often dependent on the goodwill and cooperation of intermediaries for access to their end targets. This is particularly the case when dealing with sensitive health issues or with vulnerable groups such as young people, where there is usually a need to communicate not only with young people themselves but also with key groups such as parents, teachers and politicians. These groups may act as gatekeepers, controlling or influencing the distribution of a message to a target group, or as stakeholders, taking an interest in and scrutinizing the activities of the prevention agency (McGrath 1995). If an initiative is to be effective, it needs to satisfy the information and other needs of these two groups and to maintain their support.

In Case Study 3 on p. 318, Sara Balonas and Susana Marques provide an example of how schools and workplaces were identified as key channels for cardiac arrest survival interventions in Portugal, and how physical placement is complemented by virtual placement in a well-thought-through marketing mix, to get citizens involved in saving lives.

Promotion

The final P is promotion, and this is discussed in Chapter 6.

> ### Positioning

This chapter has introduced us to the marketing toolbox, but the danger with toolboxes is that they get us too focused on the minutiae and in the process crowd out the big picture – not being able to see the woods for the trees. Commercial marketers help to avoid this with the idea of 'positioning' their products. Mullins *et al.* (2004), for example, in their textbook *Marketing Management*, describe how French wine was successfully repositioned in the US market from an elitist option for the cognoscente to something you can quaff at your barbecue. A combination of well-targeted, down-to-earth advertising, accessible point of sale material, a pocket guide with supporting website and a helpline all succeeded in achieving their objective of making the product less exclusive and thereby widening appeal.

Positioning is guided by two things: how the consumer sees the product and how it measures up to the competition. In the case of French wine, it was seen as high quality, but too exclusive for ordinary occasions. In terms of the competition, it was losing out to more mundane alternatives such as a can of casbeer; indeed, the effort to reposition it was characterized as 'trying to make Americans as comfortable with fumé blanc as they are with a Bud'.

Social marketers can do likewise. It simply provides a reminder that, in using the tools we have examined in this chapter, we have to retain a strategic view of where we want to be in our client's mind and relative to the competition. Rob Donovan and colleagues give a great illustration of how this can work in their review of the 'Act-Belong-Commit' Mentally Healthy Campaign in Western Australia (Donovan *et al.* 2006). In this instance, the aim was to reposition mental health from its current focus on illness and symptoms to a much more positive one; or as they express it: 'to reframe people's perceptions of mental health away from the absence of mental illness, to the belief that people can (and should) act proactively to protect and strengthen their mental health'. Careful market research was used to understand how people currently framed mental illness, and how this related to more positive concepts of mental health.

As Box 4.10 illustrates, being active, socially engaged and feeling in control of your circumstances were widely accepted prerequisites for good mental health. The 'Act-Belong-Commit' Campaign shows how Donovan and colleagues used the social marketing toolbox both to reinforce this positive construction and deliver to the resulting needs.

BOX 4.10: REPOSITIONING MENTAL HEALTH

'There was near universal support for the concepts that remaining active (physically, socially and mentally), having good friends, being a member of various groups in the community, and feeling in control of one's circumstances were necessary for good mental health.'

(Source: Donovan *et al.* 2006)

The social marketing planning process and associated tools can be observed in action in Duane and Domegan's 'Get Your Life in Gear', Case Study 9 on p. 369 'Get Your Life in Gear' was a 12-week pilot intervention developed by *safe*food (promotional body responsible for food safety and healthy eating on the island of Ireland) using social marketing principles and processes to think through complex exchange issues surrounding obesity and workplace behaviour change. The specific problem addressed is burgeoning male obesity in truck drivers. The case study describes how the intervention has been positioned as an exercise rather than a dietary intervention, because the men found this more appealing. Note, however, this does not mean that diet was ignored, just that it was covered within this male-oriented framing – just as Lucozade is positioned as a sports drink but its contents remain unchanged. The intervention's tagline, which also came from the truck drivers, Get Your Life in Gear, reinforced this positioning for the men.

WRAP-UP

This chapter began by evoking one of the twentieth century's greatest exponents of social change, Martin Luther King. From his lead, we have examined how a clear strategic vision enables us to put together an effective strategic plan. We then examined how environmental and competitive analysis set the context for the deployment of three key marketing tools: segmentation and targeting help us to get a better fix on whose behaviour we want to change; objective setting helps us pin down precisely what we want them to do; and the marketing mix provides a systematic way of thinking about how we will encourage people to engage with the idea of empowered change. Specifically we want to make our offer appealing, accessible, available and appreciated. This tactical activity is guided by the strategic idea of positioning.

We will continue this practical theme in the next chapter when we discuss the use of research and storytelling in social marketing.

Reflective questions

1. What is strategic planning? What are the steps in strategic social marketing planning?
2. Critically discuss how the principles of social marketing are reflected in the social marketing planning process.
3. 'We run to awareness and education like an alcoholic runs towards his next drink. We have got to "get on the wagon," and identify those interventions that really do determine behaviour' (Newton-Ward 2011: personal communication). Discuss with examples.
4. Define a situation analysis. Explain its role and function in the strategic social marketing planning process.
5. Outline what a stakeholder analysis is and is not.

6. Harm chain analysis is about those affected and those doing the affecting. Elaborate.

7. What should a social marketer consider when setting objectives?

8. Segmentation is central to the strategic social marketing planning process. Discuss with examples.

9. Explain how the marketing mix (4Ps or 4As) helps the social marketer respond to their client's needs.

10. 'Positioning is guided by two things: how the consumer sees the product and how it measures up to the competition.' Elaborate.

Reflective assignments

1. Conduct an Internet search on social marketing planning.

2. Locate and review a strategic social marketing plan.

3. Model a harm chain analysis for one of the following: drug addiction, caffeine addiction, a drink addiction or a sugar addiction.

4. A renowned university in the top 100 has approached you to use your behaviour change skills in tackling campus student binge drinking which is now considered out of control. How might you use a strategic focus and social marketing planning process?

5. Devise a strategic plan for a local community who wish to increase the number of community members who harvest rainwater.

6. Develop a one-page summary of a segmentation and targeting strategy you recommend for a social marketing topic of your choice.

7. Apply the theory about positioning to a behaviour change strategy of your choice.

8. Complete your traffic lights checklist for the social marketing planning process.

9. Angola[1] suffers from recurrent outbreaks of infectious diseases in different parts of its territory including the capital city, Luanda. The sources of the outbreaks are a combination of several factors including lack of sanitary structures, access to clean water and personal hygiene measures. The country is becoming an important oil producer and the governmental budget for intervention towards developing public infrastructures is rapidly growing. The major infectious diseases identified in Angola are very high risk and can be organized into exposure categories including the following specific infectious diseases:

    Food or waterborne diseases acquired through eating or drinking on the local economy: Hepatitis A – viral disease that interferes with the functioning of the liver; spread through consumption of contaminated food or water in areas of poor sanitation; patients will exhibit fever and diarrhoea; vaccines are available. **Typhoid fever** – bacterial disease spread through contact with contaminated food or water; patients exhibit sustained high fevers and, if not treated, mortality rates can reach 20 per cent.

Vectorborne diseases acquired through the bite of an infected arthropod: **Malaria** – transmitted to humans via the bite of the female Anopheles mosquito; parasites multiply in the liver attacking red blood cells resulting in cycles of fever, chills and sweats, accompanied by anaemia possibly leading to death due to damage to vital organs and interruption of blood supply to the brain; this is endemic in most tropical countries with over two million estimated annual deaths occurring in sub-Saharan Africa. **Dengue fever** – mosquito-borne (*Aedes aegypti*) viral disease associated with urban environments; manifests as sudden onset of fever and severe headache; occasionally produces shock and haemorrhage leading to death in 5 per cent of cases. **African Trypanosomiasis** – caused by the parasitic protozoa *Trypanosoma*; transmitted to humans via the bite of bloodsucking Tsetse flies; infection leads to malaise and irregular fevers and, in advanced cases when the parasites invade the central nervous system, coma and death; endemic in 36 countries of sub-Saharan Africa; cattle and wild animals act as reservoir hosts for the parasites. **Crimean-Congo haemorrhagic fever** – tick-borne viral disease; infection may also result from exposure to infected animal blood or tissue; geographic distribution includes Africa, Asia, the Middle East and Eastern Europe; sudden onset of fever, headache and muscle aches followed by haemorrhaging in the bowels, urine, nose and gums; mortality rate is approximately 30 per cent. **Chikungunya** – mosquito-borne (*Aedes aegypti*) viral disease associated with urban environments, similar to dengue fever; characterized by sudden onset of fever, rash and severe joint pain usually lasting three to seven days, some cases result in persistent arthritis.

Water contact diseases acquired through swimming or wading in freshwater lakes, streams and rivers: **Leptospirosis** – bacterial disease that affects animals and humans; infection occurs through contact with water, food or soil contaminated by animal urine; symptoms include high fever, severe headache, vomiting, jaundice and diarrhoea; untreated, the disease can result in kidney damage, liver failure, meningitis or respiratory distress; fatality rates are low, but left untreated recovery can take months. **Lassa fever** – viral disease carried by rats of the genus *Mastomys*; endemic in portions of West Africa; infection occurs through direct contact with or consumption of food contaminated by rodent urine or faecal matter containing virus particles; fatality rate can reach 50 per cent in epidemic outbreaks.

Respiratory disease acquired through close contact with an infectious person: **Meningococcal meningitis** – bacterial disease causing an inflammation of the lining of the brain and spinal cord; one of the most important bacterial pathogens is *Neisseria meningitidis* because of its potential to cause epidemics; symptoms include stiff neck, high fever, headaches and vomiting; bacteria are transmitted from person to person by respiratory droplets and facilitated by close and prolonged contact resulting from crowded living conditions, often with a seasonal distribution; death occurs in 5–15 per cent of cases, typically within 24–48 hours of onset of symptoms; highest burden of meningococcal disease occurs in the hyperendemic region of sub-Saharan Africa known as the 'Meningitis Belt', which stretches from Senegal east to Ethiopia.

Animal contact disease acquired through direct contact with local animals: Rabies – viral disease of mammals usually transmitted through the bite of an infected animal, most commonly dogs; virus affects the central nervous system causing brain alteration and death; symptoms initially are non-specific fever and headache progressing to neurological symptoms; death occurs within days of the onset of symptoms.

Keeping in mind the country data below and the specifics of the diseases above, discuss the key elements for intervention to prevent the dramatic impact of the infectious diseases recurrent outbreaks within the framework of a five-year Social Marketing Plan.

Data on the Country (2011)

Population: 18,056,072 (July 2011 est.)

Age structure:

   0–14 years: 43.2% (male 2,910,981/female 2,856,527)

   15–64 years: 54.1% (male 3,663,400/female 3,549,896)

   65 years and over: 2.7% (male 157,778/female 199,959) (2011 est.)

Population growth rate: 2.784% (2011 est.)

Birth rate: 39.36 births/1,000 population

Death rate: 12.06 deaths/1,000 population (July 2011 est.)

Net migration rate: 0.55 migrant(s)/1,000 population (2011 est.)

Urbanization population: 59% of total population (2010)

Rate of urbanization: 4% annual rate of change (2010–15 est.)

Major cities – population: Luanda (capital) 4.511 million; Huambo 979,000 (2009)

Infant mortality rate:

   total: 83.53 deaths/1,000 live births

   male: 87.39 deaths/1,000 live births

   female: 79.47 deaths/1,000 live births

Life expectancy at birth:

   total population: 54.59 years

male: 53.49 years

female: 55.73 years

Total fertility rate: 5.54 children born/woman

HIV/AIDS – adult prevalence rate: 2% (2009 est.)

HIV/AIDS – people living with HIV/AIDS: 200,000 (2009 est.)

HIV/AIDS – deaths: 11,000 (2009 est.)

Major infectious diseases degree: very high

food or waterborne diseases: bacterial and protozoal diarrhoea, hepatitis A, typhoid fever

vectorborne diseases: malaria, African trypanosomiasis (sleeping sickness)

water contact disease: schistosomiasis (2009)

Nationality: Angolan(s)

Ethnic groups: Ovimbundu 37%, Kimbundu 25%, Bakongo 13%, mestico (mixed European and native African) 2%, European 1%, other 22%

Religions: indigenous beliefs 47%, Roman Catholic 38%, Protestant 15% (1998 est.)

Language: Portuguese

Literacy definition: age 15 and over can read and write:

total population: 67.4%

male: 82.9%

female: 54.2%

School life expectancy (primary to tertiary education) total: 9 years (2006)

Education expenditures: 2.6% of GDP (2006)

Maternal mortality rate: 610 deaths/100,000 live births (2008)

Children under the age of 5 years underweight: 27.5% (2001)

Health expenditures: 4.6% of GDP (2009)

Physicians density: 0.08 physicians/1,000 population (2004)

Hospital bed density: 0.8 beds/1,000 population (2005)

Note

1   Written by Prof. Paulo Moreira, Escola Nacional de Saúde Publica, Universidade Nova de Lisboa.

References

ASH (2006) *Tobacco Advertising and Promotion, Factsheet No: 19.* London: Action on Smoking and Health (ASH). Online: www.ash.org.uk/files/documents/ASH_temp_7160.pdf/.

Austoker, J., Davey, C. and Jansen, C. (1997) *Improving the quality of the written information sent to women about cervical screening. NHS Cervical Screening Programme Publication No 6.* London: NHSCSP Publications.

Bandy, P. and President, P.A. (1983) 'Recent literature on drug abuse prevention and mass media: Focusing on youth, parents and the elderly', *Journal of Drug Education,* 13(3): 255–271.

Cannon, T. (1992) *Basic Marketing. Principles and Practice.* 3rd Edition. London: Cassell.

Cowell, D.W. (1994) 'Marketing of Services', Ch. 29 in Baker M. (ed) *The Marketing Book.* 3rd edition. Oxford: Butterworth Heinemann.

Dahl, D.W., Gorn, G.J. and Weinberg, C.B. (1997) 'Marketing, safer sex and condom acquisition', Ch. 11 in M.E. Goldberg, M. Fishbein and S.E. Middlestadt (eds) *Social Marketing: Theoretical and Practical Perspectives.* Mahwah, NJ: Lawrence Erlbaum Associates.

Doll, R., Peto, R., Boreham, J. and Sutherland, I. (2004) 'Mortality in relation to smoking: 50 years' observations on male British doctors', *British Medical Journal,* 328: 1519.

Donovan, R.J., James, R., Jalleh, G. and Sidebottom, C. (2006) 'Implementing mental health promotion: The "Act-Belong-Commit" Mentally Healthy WA campaign in Western Australia', *International Journal of Mental Health Promotion,* 8(1):29–38.

Fletcher, A., Guthrie, J., Steane, P., Roos, G and Pike, S. (2003) 'Mapping stakeholder perceptions for a third sector organisation', *Journal of Intellectual Capital,* 4(4): 513.

Freeman, R.E. (1984) *Strategic Management: A Stakeholder Approach.* Boston: Pitman.

Gillan, A. (2006) 'In Iraq, life expectancy is 67. Minutes from Glasgow city centre, it's 54', *The Guardian,* 21 January.

Harvey, P.D. (1997) 'Advertising affordable contraceptives: The social marketing experience', Ch. 10 in M.E. Goldberg, M. Fishbein and S.E. Middlestadt (eds) *Social Marketing: Theoretical and Practical Perspectives.* Mahwah, NJ: Lawrence Erlbaum Associates.

Hastings, G. and Angus K. (2004) 'The influence of the tobacco industry on European tobacco-control policy', in The ASPECT Consortium (ed) *Tobacco or Health in the European Union Past, Present and Future.* Prepared with financing from the EC Directorate-General for Health and Consumer Protection. Luxembourg: Office for Official Publications of the European Communities.

Hastings, G. and Elliott, B. (1993) 'Social marketing practice in traffic safety', Ch. III in *Marketing of Traffic Safety.* Paris: OECD, pp.35–53.

Hastings, G. and McDermott, L. (2006) 'Putting social marketing into practice', *British Medical Journal;* 332; 1210–1121.

Hastings, G.B. and Stead, M. (1999) *Using the media in drugs prevention*. Drugs Prevention Initiative Green Paper. London: Home Office Central Drugs Prevention Initiative, Paper 19.

ITC (2002) Developments in the UK Television Market. London: Independent Television Commission (ITC). Online at: www.ofcom.org.uk/static/archive/itc/research/industry_info_march02.pdf

Jobber, D. (2004) *Principles and Practice of Marketing*. 4th Edition. Maidenhead: McGraw-Hill International.

King Jr., M.L. (1963) *Address at March on Washington for Jobs and Freedom*, 28 August, Lincoln Memorial, Washington, D.C.

Kotler, P. and Armstrong, G. (2004) *Principles of Marketing*. 10th Edition [International Edition]. London: Pearson/Prentice Hall.

Kotler, P. and Roberto, E.L. (1989) *Social Marketing: Strategies for Changing Public Behaviour*. New York, NY: The Free Press.

Kotler, P. and Zaltman, G. (1971) 'Social marketing: An approach to planned social change', *Journal of Marketing*, 35(3): 3–12.

Kotler, P., Armstrong, G., Saunders, J. and Wong, V. (1999) *Principles of Marketing*, 2nd European edition. Prentice Hall Europe.

Layard, R. (2005) *Happiness: Lessons from a New Science*. London: Allen Lane.

Lefebvre, R.C., Doner, L., Johnston, C., Loughrey, K., Balch, G.I. and Sutton, S.M. (1995) 'Use of database marketing and consumer-based health communication in message design: An example from the office of cancer communications' "5 A Day for Better Health" program', in E. Maibach and R.L. Parrott (eds) *Designing Health Messages. Approaches From Communication Theory and Public Health Practice*. Thousand Oaks, CA: Sage Publications.

MacFadyen, L., Stead, M. and Hastings, GB. (2002) 'Social marketing', Ch. 27 in M.J. Baker (ed) *The Marketing Book*, 5th edition. Oxford: Butterworth-Heinemann.

McGrath, J. (1995) 'The gatekeeping process: The right combinations to unlock the gates', Ch. 11 in E. Maibach and R.C. Parrott (eds) *Designing Health Messages. Approaches From Communication Theory and Public Health Practice*. Thousand Oaks, CA: Sage Publications.

Mullins, J.W., Boyd, H.W., Walker, O.C. and Larreche, J.-C. (2004) *Marketing Management* (Intl Edition), UK: McGraw-Hill.

Noble, G. (2006) 'Maintaining Social Marketing's Relevance: A Dualistic Approach', ANZMAC Conference, Brisbane, Australia.

Percy, L. (1983) 'A review of the effect of specific advertising elements upon overall communication response', *Current Issues and Research in Advertising*. University of Michigan.

Polonsky, M.J., Carlson, L. and Fry, M.-L. (2003) 'The harm chain: A public policy development and stakeholder perspective', *Marketing Theory*, 3 (3): 345–64.

Rangun, V.K., Karim, S. and Sandberg, S.K. (1996) 'Do better at doing good', *Harvard Business Review*, 74(3): 42–54.

Reichheld, F.F. (2003) 'The one number you need to grow', *Harvard Business Review*, 81(12): 46–54.

Shiner, M. and Newburn, T. (1996) *Young People, Drugs and Peer Education: An Evaluation of the Youth Awareness Programme (YAP)*. London: DPI, Home Office.

Skinner, S.C., Strecher, V.J. and Hospers, H. (1994) 'Physicians' recommendations for mammography: Do tailored messages make a difference?' *American Journal of Public Health*, 84(1): 43–49.

Stead, M., Wimbush, E., Eadie, D.R. and Teer, P. (1997) 'A qualitative study of older people's perceptions of ageing and exercise: The implications for health promotion', *Health Education Journal*, 56(1): 3–16.

Stokes, D.R. (ed) (1997) *Marketing: A Case Study Approach*. 2nd Edition. London: Letts Educational.

Thorogood, M., Coulter, A., Jones, L., Yudkin, P., Muir, J. and Mant, D. (1993) 'Factors affecting response to an invitation to attend for a health check', *Journal of Epidemiology and Community Health*, 47(3): 224–228.

US Department of Health and Human Services (1989) 'Reducing the Health Consequences of Smoking', Report of the Surgeon General.

Wallack, L., Dorfman, L., Jernigan, D. and Themba, M. (1993) *Media Advocacy and Public Health*. Newbury Park, CA: Sage.

Walsh, A., Domegan, C. and Fleming, D. (2012) 'Marketing response to environmental decline and the call for sustainability', *Social Business*, 2(2): 121–143.

Wilson, R.M.S. and Gilligan, C. (2005) *Strategic Marketing Management: Planning, Implementation and Control*. 3rd Edition. Oxford: Elsevier Butterworth-Heinemann.

Woodruffe, H. (1995) *Services Marketing*. London: M&E Pitman.

WoSCAP (2005) West of Scotland Cancer Awareness Project 2002–2005. Final Report. UK Institute for Social Marketing.

Chapter **5**

Research and the art of storytelling

Holidays and birthdays during their first year on welfare were particularly traumatic for them. For months prior to [Christmas], the television paraded an endless series of programs and commercials before her children's eyes that showed Santa Claus and loving families enjoying the holiday season. These scenes typically contained beautifully adorned trees, brightly coloured seasonal decorations, and individually selected gifts that demonstrated either their love for one another or the fact that they had been good all year long. Anita's children anxiously asked for her reassurance that they had behaved properly during the year so that Santa would come to their house with his bag full of toys. They also were concerned that the small tree and meagre decorations in their home didn't display the proper Christmas spirit. Anita told them they were all good boys and that Santa Claus came without regard for the quality of the decor in a home.

Inevitably the day was a disappointment for everybody. All three children rose early, with her eldest son leading the charge. As they looked at the meagre gifts under the tree, Anita could sense the drop in their enthusiasm level. The children had two items each to open, but neither gift was very exciting or desirable. The holiday meal was similarly uninspiring, with few additions beyond their ordinary evening meals. As Anita expected, her eldest son asked what happened and why Santa Claus had ignored the Christmas list he had so carefully prepared and mailed to the North Pole. She responded that Santa wasn't able to make it to their apartment this year, but he promised to bring them extra gifts next time around. This reply satisfied his curiosity for the moment, but Anita wondered what she would tell him if things failed to improve by the following holiday season.

(Source: Hill 2011: 325)

Remember the magic of Christmas and our little girl, snugly wrapped in her warm hat and scarf, awaiting her special presents from Santa Claus from the first page of the opening chapter. The contrast with Anita's family is stark. Anita's dilemma of needing to trim fantasies without damaging her children's evolving sense of self and Coca-Cola's images of family joy, abundance and happiness are two very different Christmas narratives. However, they have in common an important quality: they both illustrate the power of the story. The Coke Christmas has been carefully crafted by ad agency creatives to evoke feelings of comfort and plenty and link these with a commercial product. However synthetic it is, it has been immensely powerful, moulding our understanding and appreciation of one of humankind's most important festivals. A festival, incidentally, that is supposed to be about religion, new beginnings, renewal and not the consumption of sugary drinks.

Anita's story brings us down to earth with a bump by reminding us that many people will never have a 'Coke Christmas', just a painful awareness of its unaffordability. Again, it evokes emotions, but very different ones: sadness perhaps, or anger about injustice. Together, the stories tell us a great deal about our society: about the extent of materialism, about inequalities, about vulnerability. They connect individual behaviour to social context and give each of us an identity; we all have our own story to tell. As a result, they resonate and offer insight and wisdom that facts and figures alone cannot provide. This makes them invaluable to social marketing: they are the bedrock of our core social marketing orientations – client, creative, collective and competitive – we discussed in Chapter 2.

At the same time, however, while stories take us beyond the data, they must emerge from and be grounded in it. Anita's story depends for its power on detailed facts and figures about the extent of inequalities in our society. This is how we know that her family's predicament is not an aberration or even an exception – it is commonplace. Likewise, the glitzy and seductive image of Coke is put into proper perspective by the same data showing that many are excluded by a system that depends on money for participation. And carefully conducted public health studies remind us that the much-lauded product actually makes you fat and rots your teeth (a dentist friend refers to all such sugary sodas as 'liquid chainsaws').

Stories, then, depend on the science of research, while research becomes the art of storytelling. For these reasons, social marketing has an 'abiding and very adult relationship with research – which recognises that it should act as neither an over-bearing judge nor a blunt substitute for decision making, but as a facilitator of intelligent action' (Hastings 2011).

Against this background, we examine research in this chapter. The intention is to look at research through a social marketing lens: the thinking that underpins it; the purpose it serves; the potential and pitfalls it presents. In the process, we discuss methodology, but only insofar as it serves our main purpose. We start by arguing that research should be seen as (a) a navigational aid, to guide progress and aid decision making; and (b) a way of learning about people and empathizing with them. We then consider what decisions we, as social marketers, have to make and examine the qualitative and quantitative research methodologies that can be used to inform them.

The chapter concludes by warning about the potential downsides of research if it is misused or overused. It can, for example, become a way of avoiding hard choices or smothering intuitive thinking. It can also encourage what might be termed the 'intervention mentality', which focuses efforts on perfecting materials and mechanisms for intervening, rather than the more important task of improving our understanding of people, their lifestyles and how they make sense of the world.

This brings us full circle. Arguably, the job of social marketing research is to uncover and map the development of people's individual and collective stories so that social marketers can then work with them to enable progressive and empowered change.

Learning outcomes

By the end of this chapter, you should be able to:
- ✓ Discuss the importance of research in social marketing
- ✓ Explain the navigational and empathic roles of research
- ✓ Discuss the role of the story in social marketing research
- ✓ Outline the research decisions social marketers have to make
- ✓ Model the research steps and methodologies that can help guide them
- ✓ Outline the dangers of an over-reliance on research, stultifying decision making and hindering progress.

Key words

decision making – empathy – evaluation – formative research – individual/group interviews – Internet research - navigational aid – problem definition – qualitative research – quantitative methods – research – research methodology – secondary data – storytelling

THE PURPOSE OF LEARNING IN SOCIAL MARKETING

In social marketing, research is a strategic tool: it guides the planning process (Chapter 4) and helps maintain the creative, competitive, collective and (all-important) client orientations (Chapter 2).

Strategic planning As we discussed in Chapter 4, building successful behaviour change programmes is like climbing a Himalayan peak – with a resulting need for maps, compasses and careful route planning. Research fulfils the role of these **navigational aids**. It helps us get our bearings, establish achievable objectives and staging posts towards these, check on progress, adjust our route and determine when we have reached the summit. Furthermore, because our ultimate goal is relative rather than absolute (improved, rather than perfect health; a better society, not an idyll); our Everest is infinitely high and our planning has to be continuous. This may sound grandiose, but it merely reflects what happens in commercial marketing: Coke has been realigning our conceptions of Christmas for the best part of a century.

This long-term perspective emphasizes the need for progressive learning not just within but also between initiatives, and ties in with our discussion of social marketing planning in Chapter 4 and communications in Chapter 6. The implications for methodology feedback to the work of Kurt Lewin, who coined the term 'action research' and emphasized the need for empirical study to go beyond the production of books and articles, and help us take action on social phenomena. This is the same man whose much-quoted aphorism 'there is nothing so practical as a good theory' we noted in Chapter 3.

Lewin emphasized the notion of incremental learning using a range of methodologies and expressed this as a cyclical research process (Figure 5.1).

This feeds into a plan of action that will define ultimate goals/objectives as well as immediate and intermediate steps, all of which will be honed and adapted as the plan is implemented. At the same time, however, the sequential model should not be applied too rigidly; because social phenomena are complex and subtle, the researcher has to be both flexible and sensitive. All these lessons transfer neatly into social marketing thinking, which sees research as a process that provides progressive learning, not just about how we should intervene, but about the people with whom we want to intervene.

Client orientation This brings us to the primary orientation of (refer back to Chapter 2) social marketing, the drive to see the world through the eyes of our clients and stakeholders. As we have already noted, clients, stakeholders and even competitors are all free to choose whether or not they do business with us. The decisions we make about constructing our marketing plan, therefore, have to be

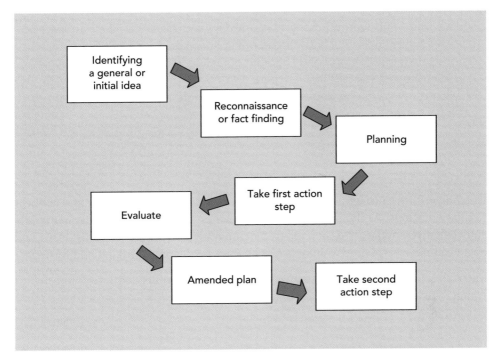

Figure 5.1 Action research
Source: Adapted from Lewin (1951)

driven by an understanding of these actors, their motives and lifestyles. This is sometimes referred to as adopting an *'experiential'* view taking in the thinking, feeling and doing or head, heart and hands of potential exchanges.

In *To Kill a Mockingbird* (see Box 5.1) Harper Lee suggests that to really understand why people behave as they do you have to 'get inside their skin'; she is making the point that you need to be able to empathize with them.

BOX 5.1: EMPATHY – A SIMPLE BUT CRUCIAL TRICK

Atticus (the father) is explaining to his daughter (Scout) how she can get on better with her new teacher:

Atticus stood up and walked to the end of the porch. When he completed his examination of the wisteria vine he strolled back to me.

'First of all,' he said, 'if you can learn a simple trick, Scout, you'll get along a lot better with all kinds of folks. You never really understand a person until you consider things from his point of view – "Sir?" – until you climb into his skin and walk around in it.'

Atticus said I had learned many things today, and Miss Caroline had learned several things herself. She had learned not to hand something to a Cunningham, for one thing, but if Walter and I had put ourselves in her shoes we'd have seen it was an honest mistake on her part. We could not expect her to learn all Maycomb's ways in one day, and we could not hold her responsible when she knew no better.

(Source: Harper Lee, *To Kill a Mockingbird* 1960)

One powerful way to empathize with others is to listen to their story and connect to their emotions. At the beginning of this chapter, hearing about Anita, her family and their lives makes it easier for us to empathize with their circumstances and begin to understand how welfare is altering her behaviour, thinking and feelings.

Exercise 5.1 explores how Nelson Mandela used a similar approach to connect with young African men.

EXERCISE 5.1: NELSON MANDELA AND TOBACCO CONTROL

When Nelson Mandela was serving his sentence in the prison on Robben Island, he took on the task of briefing each new intake of prisoners. These were young men whose lives had been turned upside down; a few weeks previously they had been fighting the hated Apartheid regime with Molotov cocktails and stones, now they were prisoners of this same brutal system. They were angry and frustrated. Mandela's talk was designed to help them adjust and survive in what were very difficult circumstances.

Perhaps surprisingly, he found time to touch on tobacco. However, he was far too wise to wag the finger or invoke horror stories about premature death. Instead, he simply remarked that he had noticed some of the new prisoners were smoking, and reminded them that tobacco is dependence-inducing. He also noted that the guards were well aware of this and would on occasion supply prisoners with tobacco. In return, of course they would ask favours of the prisoners. Sometimes, he continued, the inmate's need for tobacco would be small, and the favours small; but sometimes the need would be big and the favour would grow accordingly . . .

That is all Mandela said; he left his audience to complete the story.

Put yourself in the shoes of one of these the young men. How would you react? How would it make you feel about your smoking? What would you do?

Now think about how you would have reacted if Mandela had taken a more traditional approach, telling you that smoking causes lung cancer – and anyway was prohibited by the prison's new smoke-free ordinances.

Mandela used the power of the story to both connect with these angry young prisoners, and provide them with a constructive way forward. He knows they are united by a hatred of the Apartheid regime and he aligns tobacco use with this regime – an indictment that easily surpasses its carcinogenic properties. He then presents the rejection of tobacco as an act of rebellion against the regime, as a means of undermining the guards. Thus, tobacco becomes part of their political struggle, their fight for justice, freedom and status, of their story – and quitting smoking enables them to become heroes in this story.

But the lesson here is not that we all have to become Nelson Mandelas; it is that we all have a story to tell, a narrative that encapsulates what we think is important in our lives past, present and future. Harnessing these stories is a potentially invaluable social marketing tool, but doing so requires careful research and systematic methods. Even Mandela's efforts were in a sense research based. Not that he had done surveys of the young prisoners, or interviewed them – but he certainly knew them, their values and their aspirations intimately and these insights were vital.

Richard Krueger (2010) reminds us that there are three key steps in what he terms storytelling research. Having identified the practice or behaviour of concern you have to (a) capture the story of those engaged in it using pictures, words and dialogue; (b) present that story by identifying themes, patterns or contradictions; and (c) uncover a lesson or moral. These correspond perfectly with the three core stages of any research project: data collection, analysis and presentation.

Try it for yourself with Exercise 5.2.

EXERCISE 5.2: TELLING A POLISHED STORY

From your experience or reading, choose a behaviour that is known to be risky and needs to change, and a target group which is involved with it. It might be binge drinking among teenage girls or football hooliganism by young men. Now follow Krueger's three steps:

1. Capture the story (through quotes, pictures, words, dialogue).
2. Present the story (as told or re-scripted?). What are the main themes, patterns and differences?
3. End with the message (the moral, point being made, lesson).

(Source: Krueger 2010)

Krueger goes on to present a beautiful example of how insightful this can be (see Box 5.2).

BOX 5.2: STORY EXAMPLE: MEDICAL MISTAKES

We were conducting an evaluation of patient safety in a large medical system. Our goal was to uncover the barriers that deterred the hospital staff from disclosing mistakes. It was a sensitive topic. With some frequency, frontline staff contended that hospital management sent mixed signals. One participant told this story:

'I enjoy hang gliding. We've got some terrific places to hang glide in this area. When we do it, we do it as a group. We gather at the top of a mountain and then one person sails off alone while the others watch. We call this person the 'wind dummy'. Everyone's eyes are on this first person. We watch how the updrafts and crosswinds affect the glide. We are attentive to the turbulence and watch for any difficulties encountered by the wind dummy. When this first person has completed the sail, then the rest of us take off, incorporating the lessons we learned from watching the wind dummy. The same is true here at the hospital. We watch what happens when someone reports a medical mistake. If they crash and burn, then the rest of us change our behaviour accordingly.'

(Source: Krueger 2010)

Stories then have huge potential to enrich all social marketing research.

A MIX OF METHODOLOGIES

This strategic purpose, combining long-term planning with empathy for people's stories, encourages social marketers to draw on both *positivist* and *humanist* research traditions. The first builds on the notion that there is an objective reality out there that we are trying to measure and influence. This pushes us towards quantitative methods, theory to build on previous insights, establishing cause and effect and hypothesis testing. The second recognizes that the world – or at least the social and behavioural bits of it in which we are interested – is actually much messier than this, and will not succumb to scientific analysis, however rigorous and highly powered. As a result, social marketers, like their commercial cousins, adopt a pragmatic mix of methodologies that they feel will best aid decision making and help them get a better (though always imperfect) understanding of what makes people do what they do.

Case Studies 8 (p. 361), 13 (p. 414), 18 (p. 456) and 19 (p. 464) all provide good illustrations of action-oriented, empathetic social marketing research.

All too often with behaviour change, however, the focus is on testing the *intervention*, which pushes things towards a more positivist research approach. In public health, for example, such thinking is exemplified in the randomized controlled trial (RCT). The RCT adopts the classic experimental design, randomly ascribing subjects to either an experimental or a matched control group. The first group is exposed to the intervention and both are monitored before and after the trial. Inferential statistics are then used to determine whether or not the intervention had any effect. The overriding aim is to separate out the effects of the intervention from any other possible change agents – most notably there is a need to discount the impact of the characteristics of the different populations.

This makes very good sense when the problem at hand is to determine whether or not a new drug therapy is effective. In these circumstances, it is vital that we determine what impact a new substance has, not least – as thalidomide (see Box 5.3) will always remind us – because it can do all too apparent harm as well as good. As the UK's Medical Research Council (MRC) makes clear, the great virtue of the RCT is that it helps to separate out the 'active ingredients' in an intervention. We can find out precisely what the drug is doing by using placebos and double-blind procedures to factor out any contribution from the human beings involved (MRC 2000).

BOX 5.3: THE THALIDOMIDE DISASTER

Thalidomide was developed in the 1950s by the West German pharmaceutical company Chemie Grünenthal GmbH to expand the company's product range beyond antibiotics. It was an anticonvulsive drug, but instead it made users sleepy and relaxed. It seemed a perfect example of newly fashionable tranquilisers . . .

Animal tests did not include tests looking at the effects of the drug during pregnancy. The apparently harmless thalidomide was licensed in July 1956 for prescription-free over-the-counter sale in Germany and most European countries. The drug also reduced morning sickness, so it became popular with pregnant women . . .

There was an increase in births of thalidomide-impaired children in Germany and elsewhere. However, no link with thalidomide was made until 1961. The drug was only taken off the market after the German Widukind Lenz and the Australian William McBride independently suggested the link. Over 10,000 children were born with thalidomide-related disabilities worldwide.

There was a long criminal trial in Germany and a British newspaper campaign. They forced Grünenthal and its British licensee, the Distillers Company, to financially support victims of the drug. Thalidomide led to tougher testing and drug approval procedures in many countries, including the United States and the United Kingdom.

(Source: Science Museum)

However, social marketers, as do many in health promotion, get uneasy when the same methods are advocated as the 'optimal study design' for 'complex interventions to improve health', which includes 'media-delivered health promotion campaigns' (MRC 2000: 2). In similar vein, the US Department of Education argues that 'well-designed and implemented randomized controlled trials are considered the "gold standard" for evaluating an intervention's effectiveness, in fields such as medicine, welfare and employment policy, and psychology' (2003: 1).

It is not that we can be less cautious about our offerings than a surgeon or pharmacist. A badly conceived drug prevention programme that hectors and patronizes might actually increase the attractiveness of illicit substances. In addition, the programme will typically use public money, so it is important to know this is being well spent. Furthermore, as we will discuss in Chapter 9, there are serious ethical issues to consider in behaviour change. All of this demands that we treat our offerings with great care.

On the other hand, the Hippocratic principle, advising us first and foremost to do no harm, can be too limiting a guide when inactivity is also dangerous.

We should also recognize that caution and precision are not the same thing. Focusing in on testing the intervention before we proceed underrates the importance of the target group in the behaviour change process. Think back for a moment to our discussion of relationship marketing in Chapter 2 and pick up the idea that satisfaction, trust and commitment are key outcomes. How people feel about what we are doing will help determine what behaviour change results. Add to this the idea that our clients are not just recipients, but co-designers of improved health or community safety. From these perspectives, limiting our studies to the isolated influence of the intervention seems perverse to the social marketer. Or, as Stead *et al.* put it, 'the traditional biomedical approach to evaluation, with the randomised controlled trial as its gold standard, has limited relevance for the analysis of complex health promotion interventions' (2002: 354).

RCTs are also extremely expensive and time-consuming. They typically cost hundreds of thousands of pounds and several years to complete. As a result, the research process becomes distorted and decision making ponderous. The question 'did it work?' dominates all. Yet, even in this arena, the findings will be of limited value; they may tell us that intervention A worked with population B at time C – when we need to intervene with population D at time E and, in any case, would find it very difficult to replicate intervention A because the world has changed. Then imagine our desired outcomes are long term; suppose we want to intervene with primary schoolchildren so we can pre-empt adult obesity or drug use. We need an RCT lasting 25 years. Or suppose we want to reduce global warming; we now need an intergalactic control group.

Think back to Nelson Mandela in Exercise 5.1. To prove his intervention worked, we would need to establish another prison, on a duplicate Robben Island with a cloned Mandela and compare the smoking prevalence outcomes with and without his pep-talk. In reality, another story can tell us much more. The Mandela story was used by one of us in a talk in Nablus on the Palestinian West Bank. Afterwards, a member of the audience said the story echoed his own experience. He explained that he had fought during the First Intifada in the late 1980s, and been arrested by the Israeli army. He was strip-searched and put in a cell on his own and, as a heavy smoker, his need for nicotine added significantly to the privation. After three days, a guard came into his cell and put four cigarettes down on his bed. Four cigarettes, but no lighter. 'That', he said emphatically, 'was the day I gave up smoking.'

The story beats the RCT not just with its practicality, but because it tells us about people. (Think back to our discussion of client and creative orientations of social marketing in Chapter 2.) The danger with an overly positivist approach is that the people we want to persuade, influence and build relationships with become marginalized, which both limits our effectiveness and causes alienation. As the songwriter Jez Lowe expresses it:

So you people in power and position I tell you beware
I tell you beware
Of your facts and your figures to tell you what, when and where
'Cos your facts and your figures are the likes of me
And don't try and tell me how me life should be
– or you won't make old bones.

(J. Lowe / Lowe Life Music 1985)

The lyrics have a sweet symmetry about them, as the last line turns the threat, so beloved of public health and safety campaigns, back on us. We will discuss the pros and cons of fear messaging again in Chapter 6.

LESSONS FROM COMMERCE

A myopic focus on the intervention also undermines the great opportunity to learn on the hoof. The dominant brands in our lives – Marlboro, Coca-Cola, Nike, McDonald's – have an enormous impact on our behaviour. We know, for example, that tobacco and alcohol brands are among the key drivers of youth smoking (Grant *et al.* 2008) and drinking (Hastings *et al.* 2010), and a recent study in California among three- to five-year-olds showed that children's food preferences are being moulded by McDonald's branding even before they have learned to tie their shoe-laces (Robinson *et al.* 2007). But these brands do not emerge from randomized control trials. They come from a mixture of happenstance, intuition and bright ideas, which are guided by a variety of different research exercises and traditions, ranging from the ethnographic to the heavily quantitative.

It is not that commercial marketers reject RCTs and experimental designs. In the guise of pharmaceutical companies, they probably do more of them than most – as the thalidomide case we discussed above graphically underlines. It is just that they don't limit themselves to this research methodology, or see it as the Gold Standard, the Rolls-Royce approach. Perhaps they remember that the Gold Standard had to be abandoned and Rolls-Royce cars went bust!

Figure 5.2, for example, shows how, having used RCTs to develop them, pharmaceutical companies go about selling their new drugs in the UK. This gives us a useful glimpse of how a marketer sees the task of behaviour change. Bear in mind that, as this document concerns prescription medicines in the UK, the marketing is aimed at doctors not patients.[1] It seems that even when trying to influence the behaviour of highly trained professionals, whom it might be thought would be susceptible to hard-nosed, positivist arguments, softer, more flexible appeals are needed. They want to engage 'emotional' as well as 'rational drivers' and determine how 'using the brand makes the customer feel' and 'how others would see the users of the brand'. This is one of a number of internal documents that go on to talk about the need to make doctors feel 'reassured', 'fashionable' and even 'sexy' about prescribing particular drugs.

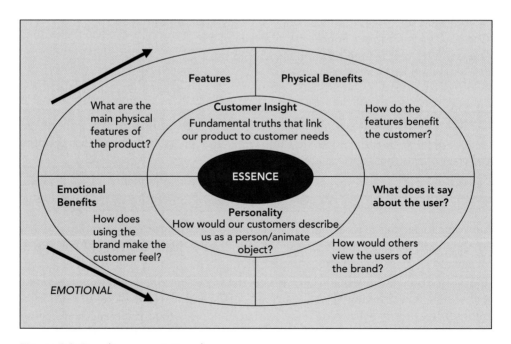

Figure 5.2 Branding prescription drugs
Source: Devlin et al. (2007)

RCTs are unlikely to help here. They might be able to disentangle cause and effect, but they will say little about the personality of a brand. More flexible methods are needed to do this.

Figure 5.2 also illustrates a more basic truth: human behaviour is just too complex to succumb to the RCT. The MRC's comments extolling their virtues for public health researchers overlook a crucial point for social marketers: that, when it comes to behaviour change, the most important 'active ingredients' are people. Or as Jez Lowe puts it: 'your facts and your figures are the likes of me'.

In the final analysis, for the social marketer, using RCTs to guide our efforts at behaviour change feels a bit like using a ruler to measure the circumference on an orange.

RESEARCH METHODOLOGY

Social marketers then will do all sorts of research at every juncture of the marketing planning process. The point is to get the best possible grip on the client's perspective (both rational and emotional) so that we can make intelligent decisions about how to build and maintain good relationships with them. The trick is to work out *what* sort of information we need *when* to guide our decision making and actions.

Before looking at these issues in detail, however, we need to know more about methodology. This section will touch briefly on secondary research (the use of existing research data), and then qualitative and quantitative interviewing. It is not intended to provide a comprehensive discussion of methodology or a do-it-yourself guide; there are other sources for this (Kent 2007; Domegan and Fleming 2007). Rather, we just want to demonstrate that there are a range of techniques available, each of which has its strengths and weaknesses – and that the best social marketing uses them in conjunction with one another.

Secondary research

Any research exercise should begin by seeking out and analysing existing relevant studies. This can be done with great rigour and precision using the systematic review (SR) procedures or more flexibly using more conventional narrative reviews (NR) (see Box 5.4).

BOX 5.4: SYSTEMATIC AND NARRATIVE REVIEWS

'A review of a clearly formulated question that uses systematic and explicit methods to identify, select, and critically appraise relevant research, and to collect and analyse data from the studies that are included in the review. Statistical methods (meta-analysis) may or may not be used to analyse and summarise the results of the included studies.'

(Source: The Cochrane Collaboration 2005)

The rigour and precision SR provides are invaluable when we need to resolve specific issues of cause and effect (e.g. does tobacco advertising encourage teen smoking?), which are likely to be hotly contested – and can even finish up in the courtroom. The same qualities are also useful when trying to establish whether a particular behaviour change approach produces results. For example, ISM has recently undertaken a series of SRs looking at whether social marketing works in three specific fields: nutrition, exercise and substance misuse. Because the reviews were systematic, the (positive) results are much more credible than they would have been had we conducted standard reviews. The principal aim is to disentangle cause and effect, so SR is again the best solution.

However, SR can be less helpful when we are trying to answer broader questions of not just what works, but in what circumstances, how and why. Like RCTs, they can be too inflexible for the task. This is perhaps not surprising: the rigorous quality controls that SR applies mean that they frequently limit inclusion to RCTs.

For example, the UK's Advisory Council on the Misuse of Drugs summarizes the evidence from SRs on schools-based substance misuse as follows:

While many of the evaluations were poorly designed, those that were conducted to an acceptable standard found that even carefully designed, resourced and implemented programmes resulted in, at best, small and short-lived delays in the use of tobacco, alcohol or other drugs by pupils. Indeed many studies showed no effect at all, and some programmes were found to be counter-productive.

(ACMD 2005)

One is left feeling that nothing works.

Reassuringly, the same report goes on to wholeheartedly recommend the much broader and strategic idea of health-promoting schools, despite the absence of RCT standard data to support it. The absence of such evidence is not a surprise; as the ACMD says earlier in its report: 'the reviewers underlined the difficulties in evaluating community-wide programmes. The unique nature of each community also makes it difficult to know how readily even a successful intervention could be translated to other areas or countries' (ibid.: 75). And a school is essentially a small community.

There *is* evidence to support school-wide initiatives – research in the West of Scotland (Henderson 2006; West 2004)has shown that levels of substance misuse in schools is closely related to the policies in place for supporting both staff and pupils and rewarding good behaviour in the latter – it is just that the evidence is not rigorous enough to meet RCT or SR standards. Furthermore, it is worth noting that a key component of a health-promoting school is (again, not surprisingly) an active health education and substance misuse programme – the very activity that systematic reviews are so pessimistic about.

In this arena, a narrative review is a more flexible and practical option. The focus can move beyond identifying what previous efforts have worked, and towards helping us define the problem and identify potential solutions. Thus, secondary sources can help answer crucial questions about the prevalence and prominence of a particular social or health problem. They can shed light on the extent of the drugs or youth disorder problems in a particular locality, for instance, and show how these stack up against other issues. They may show that drugs are indeed a problem, but that alcohol is much more of one, suggesting that funders are less comfortable with addressing this issue head on (perhaps because of industry interests).

Using a narrative review, secondary sources can also reveal how previous campaigns and initiatives have fared, providing valuable clues about the best way forward. Note we are not now talking simply about whether previous interventions worked, but the broader questions we identified above about how they were received and why.

Thus, both systematic and narrative reviews have a role to play in social marketing research: the rigour of the first helps identify cause and effect; the flexibility and pragmatism of the latter helps us move forward. Furthermore, it is wasteful and risky to start on primary research until existing secondary sources have been exhausted. However, primary research is usually essential once we need to know about how today's target group will respond to a specific intervention, the objectives it can realistically fulfil and how it should set about doing so.

Broadly speaking, primary research comes in two forms: qualitative and quantitative.

Qualitative methods

Qualitative methods can cover a range of techniques such as ethnography, grounded theory, case studies and participatory research, as highlighted in Box 5.5.

BOX 5.5: PARTICIPATORY RESEARCH

What makes participatory research participatory? Typically, participatory research involves a process of learning and reflection, followed by action, and then by more learning and reflection, and so on. Crucially, though, the research is carried out *with* people rather than *on* them; ordinary people who would normally be 'subjects' of research are given the power to help define the research problem, collect and analyse the data, interpret its meaning and communicate it to others. They – not the research team or the funder – own the findings and the goal is to take action, rather than simply to create knowledge.

Paulo Freire maintained 'the silenced are not just incidental to the curiosity of the researcher but are the masters of inquiry into the underlying causes of the events in their world' (1982: 30–31). This illustrates the core principle of participatory research: that people who wouldn't usually have a great deal of power or influence are empowered, through research, to change things for themselves and their communities. So, the participatory researcher becomes a catalyst and facilitator of the process, rather than the sole seeker, interpreter and owner of knowledge.

This section now concentrates on the ever-popular observational and interviewing qualitative procedures. (For a detailed discussion of ethnography, grounded theory and case studies, see Pettigrew and Roberts 2011. If you want to know more about observation and other methods, consult with standard market research textbooks, e.g. Churchill *et al.* 2009; Kent 2007; Domegan and Fleming 2007: 37.)

Qualitative interviewing is typically done in-depth with small samples that have been selected through non-random procedures; it can take various forms including individual in-depth interviews, paired interviews, small group interviews and focus groups. Detailed questionnaires are not used, although interviews may be guided by a schedule of 'points to be covered' or 'questions to be asked' or a 'script'. Respondents can be interviewed individually or in 'focus' groups of 4–12 people.

The main advantage of qualitative interviewing comes from the depth or quality of the data that it provides. It enables the researcher to approach a subject in a completely open-ended manner, starting from the perspective of the respondent; using their language and concepts to develop the discussion and relying on their experiences to illustrate it. Thus, in contrast to questionnaire-based research, there is no need to make assumptions about what the important issues are, how to label these or the type of responses that might be expected.

Qualitative interviewing procedures also allow a range of responses to be examined. For example (Chapter 6), in checking reactions to media materials, fairly straightforward matters, such as understanding of the language used, or its ability to communicate clearly, can be assessed, as well as more complex issues, such as likes and dislikes, audience identification and other emotional responses. For instance, in examining response to fear-inducing anti-AIDS advertising (Hastings *et al.* 1990), qualitative research revealed a tendency for people to distance themselves from the message that only became apparent after detailed probing. Similarly, researching material that aims to promote images as well as facts is very difficult without the flexibility of qualitative interviewing.

Thinking back to the pharmaceutical marketing discussed in Figure 5.2, how would we go about exploring brand image, and how prescribing particular medicines would make a doctor feel? What is the best way to approach elusive phenomena such as reassurance, fashion and sexiness? Try Exercise 5.3.

EXERCISE 5.3: MEASURING HOPES AND DREAMS

In Figure 5.2, we saw the complex and subtle ways in which pharmaceutical companies promote their prescription medicines to doctors. We noted that branding, and the capacity of a particular product to make a GP feel reassured, fashionable and even sexy, introduces elusive constructs and ideas that are not susceptible to rigorous positive methodologies such as the RCT. Indeed, even qualitative methodologies struggle to plumb these depths. How might you go about doing research to provide these insights? What questions might you ask and how? What obstacles might you meet?

One option would be to address the issues directly and simply ask GPs how they feel about prescribing different medicines, and how this varies depending on whether it is a branded or generic product. The problem you will face, however, is that GPs may be reluctant to admit their prescribing is influenced by anything other than the best science. It is also possible, of course, that this behaviour is unconscious; that they do not realize their prescribing is affected by something as subjective as brand image. You would likely meet the same problem if you asked most men why they bought a particular car. They would tell you about engine size and performance, not the feeling of superiority they get from piloting a four-wheel-drive BMW, which is perfectly capable of crossing the Serengeti, to the local supermarket.

We therefore have to approach our GPs in a more indirect way, probably using some sort of 'projective' technique, where the answer is projected away from the respondent to a third party. This makes it both safer and easier to answer. So you might like to ask a GP, 'What sort of doctor would prescribe medicine A?' or 'How would they feel in doing so?' Taking it a step further, you might try showing them pictures of doctors who just happen to be prescribing generic or branded versions of a particular drug, and ask them to describe the scene. Box 5.6 presents some other examples of projective techniques.

BOX 5.6: FIVE USEFUL PROJECTIVE TECHNIQUES

1. *Personification*: e.g. if the product (image/slogan) were a person, how would you describe him or her / what kind of life would they lead / how would they be different from each other, etc. (adaptable and easy to use).
2. *Choice ordering*: e.g. place these products (images/slogans) in order from the one you like best to the one you like least (provides a way of

understanding the factors that differentiate subjects or items – straight-forward to use).

3. *Mapping*: e.g. position each product (image/slogan) on the two-dimensional grid to indicate how much you like each product and how popular each is (more sophisticated version of choice ordering, allows you to explore the relationship between different attributes – more difficult to administer).

4. *Clustering*: e.g. position the products (images/slogans) according to how closely related they are to each other (useful way of understanding the dimensions people use to judge products – can be difficult to administer).

5. *Completion*: e.g. so . . . ? / what springs to mind . . . ? / what about that one . . .? (useful way of understanding the factors that shape a person's view about a subject (product / image / slogan) – naturalistic form of enquiry, simple and extremely adaptable).

(Source: Douglas Eadie, Institute for Social Marketing)

The quality of the data produced by these methods is also enhanced by the fact that they enable the interviewer to delve into the motivations and reasons underlying responses. They make it possible to ask 'why?'. This point is illustrated by a Scottish anti-smoking campaign which was misinterpreted by its 10–14-year-old target audience (see Box 5.7). They assumed that bogus products such as a hairspray called 'Ashtré' and an aftershave called 'Stub', which were intended to highlight the drawbacks of smoking, were actually real. Focus groups revealed that this was not because they lacked intelligence or were unsophisticated, but because they could see real benefits in the bogus products. In particular they seemed to be offering a good means of smoking surreptitiously. From the audience's perspective, this was the *sensible way* to interpret the ads. It is difficult to imagine quantitative procedures uncovering this explanation.

BOX 5.7: STUB AND ASHTRÉ

A television advertising campaign aimed at 10–14-year-olds aimed to emphasize the benefits of not smoking by promoting a number of bogus products, including an aftershave called 'Stub' and a hairspray called 'Ashtré', both of which made the user smell of cigarettes and thereby much less attractive to the opposite sex. Qualitative research with 10–14-year-olds revealed problems. When they saw the commercials, the anti-smoking message was lost. They believed the products would be real and available in shops.

To understand why they reacted in this way, it was necessary to understand what it is like to be an underage smoker. The research showed that, for them, smoking is: forbidden by parents, teachers and other adults, expensive and a difficult habit to acquire. Initially, it is unpleasant – youngsters complained that their first cigarettes had caused sore throats and sickness – and only after considerable perseverance does it become enjoyable. The bogus products in the anti-smoking commercials would overcome these problems. For the respondents, the products offered obvious benefits that justified their existence; and the strap-line for the ads *'all the fun of cigarettes, without the drag of smoking'* inadvertently confirmed this.

(Source: Hastings 1990)

Qualitative procedures also improve the quality of the data collected by enabling the researcher to monitor *how* things are said. Tone of voice, context and non-verbal cues can all be important here. For example, when researching the potential for using the female condom as a contraceptive among Glasgow women, their hilarity at the idea spoke very articulately about how awkward the product made them feel and how unlikely they were to use it without a considerable amount of persuasion. Again, it is difficult for quantitative methods to provide this kind of insight.

Finally, in terms of data quality – as the last example illustrates – qualitative procedures permit the examination of delicate and embarrassing topics because they enable the researcher to build a rapport with the respondent. This makes it possible to discuss topics that are socially unacceptable – or even criminal – such as shoplifting or vandalism; as well as very personal ones such as sexual behaviour. It is difficult to delve into areas like these without the trust that in-depth interviewing can generate. However, as we will discuss in Chapter 9, the licence these methods give also raises serious ethical issues.

As well as the quality of the data it provides, qualitative interviewing also has at least three important practical advantages. First, because it is flexible, a range of unfinished materials can be researched. Everything, from rough drawings and concept boards through to polished television commercials, can be used to stimulate response. This makes qualitative interviewing particularly suitable for developmental research on new initiatives. For example, focus groups to guide the development of an initiative to promote fruit and vegetable consumption in a major Scottish city (Anderson *et al.* 2005) tested out the idea of distributing these through primary schools. Initial reactions were favourable. Only when a storyboard depicting a small child carrying the fruit and veg home did the parents hit on the sheer impracticality of the idea: visions quickly emerged of veggies being thrown around the school bus, bananas getting squashed and tomatoes sat on! Second, research projects can be conducted quickly – within a week if necessary. Third, because small samples are involved, qualitative research is often relatively cheap.

The main disadvantages of qualitative research concern its statistical validity. In statistical terms, both the sampling and interviewing procedures are flawed. The former is typically too small and selected incorrectly to be representative and the latter is not standardized, thereby precluding the summation of responses. Consequently, it is not possible to use qualitative methods to produce estimates of population prevalence to any calculable degree of accuracy.

Qualitative procedures are also criticized because they put respondents in an artificial situation. For example, in asking them to respond in great detail to a particular leaflet or service, you are probably asking them to do something they would not normally do. However, this criticism is true of any research procedure – qualitative or quantitative – that examines response to an initiative by prompting the subject with examples. It does not invalidate such methods; it just means findings have to be interpreted with caution.

A final criticism commonly levelled at qualitative interviewing is that it is very dependent on the researcher conducting the interview well and analysing the data correctly. All too often, it is argued, excessive subjectivity contaminates the process. In the case of data analysis, for example, the fact that qualitative researchers rely on their own selection and interpretation of the findings is contrasted with the quantitative researchers' production of apparently independent and hard statistics (see below). These problems are most apparent with projective techniques. How do we interpret people's responses to the pictures? How reliable is word association as a means of revealing underlying and unconscious associations? And how do we begin to calibrate the influence of such associations on decision making?

Two points can be made in response to this criticism. First, the objectivity of statistical data is often more illusory than real. Just as with qualitative data, they are greatly influenced by the researcher – they design the questions, attribute meanings to the answers and numbers to the meanings. Second, it is questionable whether researcher influence is a bad thing. Researchers are typically highly qualified, skilled and intelligent – surely we should be encouraging rather than discouraging their deep involvement in every aspect of the research process. A bit like with extreme positivism, we end up so distrusting the subjectivity of humankind that we overlook its benefits.

However, the main point to note here is not that there is an overall conclusion to be drawn for or against qualitative research. It is that qualitative procedures have both strengths and weaknesses. The former make them a valuable tool for certain research tasks, but the latter should always be kept in mind.

Individual versus group interviews

Exactly the same 'horses for courses' point applies when choosing between individual and group interviewing. Both approaches have strengths and weaknesses. Individual in-depth interviews provide a clear and longitudinal view of each person's perspective, avoid the problems of peer and group pressure, and permit the discussion of extremely intimate issues.

The strengths of focus groups, on the other hand, stem from the interaction that takes place between respondents. This can take many forms. Respondents can question each other's claims. A group member might remind a fellow respondent that, although he claims to have given up smoking, he accepted a cigarette immediately prior to the group. Respondents might also seek information and guidance from each other – 'What is that new doctor like?' and 'How do you find using condoms?' are both questions asked by one respondent of another in groups we have moderated.

They can also provide reassurance and group identity that facilitates the discussion of otherwise difficult topics. For example, groups on drunk driving only came to life when one respondent admitted committing a serious drunk-driving offence. The other members of the group then felt able to admit to similar behaviour. In these instances, the respondents are essentially interviewing each other. It is this dynamic process that contributes to the 'gestalt' of group discussions – the tendency for the whole to amount to more than the sum of the parts. It has a number of benefits – for example, it generates data, avoids respondent intimidation, and makes it possible to exploit differences in opinion and examine peer interaction.

So, again, individual and group interviews each have strengths and should be used as appropriate. Indeed, in many instances, a combination of the two approaches may be the best option. Exactly the same points apply when considering quantitative methods.

Quantitative methods

Quantitative methods put a great emphasis on *sample selection* and *questioning procedures*.

Sample selection – Samples have to be collected in a way that ensures they are representative of a particular population. Ideally, random selection procedures should be used, because this ensures that each potential respondent has an equal chance of being included in the study. Quota sampling methods sidestep this issue by identifying the key variables (e.g. gender or ethnic origin) and ensuring that these are adequately represented in the final sample. As a result, they lack a certain degree of statistical rigour, but provide a pragmatic way through. As with RCTs, marketers tend to veer to the pragmatic end of the argument and will readily use quota sampling methods.

Representative sampling also usually requires large numbers. Whereas a qualitative study might typically measure its sample in dozens, a quantitative one will do so in hundreds or thousands.

This can be a complex and expensive process; at the very least, it assumes you have an accurate 'sampling frame' or list of the population in question – which may not be too difficult to find if your interest is in all adults or schoolchildren, but if you want to sample sex workers and their clients, or illegal immigrants, it becomes much more difficult. Fiona Harris (2011) explains that, as well as accessing sampling frames, the process can be difficult when we need to engage with vulnerable (e.g. young children, older people) or under-represented groups (e.g. religious or ethnic minorities), recruit around sensitive issues (e.g. underage drinking, teenage pregnancy, drug usage) and, if we are conducting longitudinal research, find replenishment samples (i.e. respondents to replace any drop-outs between research stages). Try Exercise 5.4.

EXERCISE 5.4: SOCIAL MARKETING SAMPLING CHALLENGES

You are working as part of a Healthy Cities initiative to improve mental health among young adults in your city. You need a sample of individuals to interview.

How would you define your population of interest? What list, if any, will you use as your sampling frame? What sampling method will you use and Why? How many individuals will you recruit? How will you ensure full representation from young adults? How will you incentivize young adults to participate in your research?

You could begin by defining your population as all 18–24-year-olds within the geographical area of your city. For a sample list, you could use the local registrar of electors. This is a direct sample frame. You could use quota sampling to reflect the mixture of 18–24-year-old male and females, from lower and higher social classes, employed and unemployed, who had or are experiencing mental health difficulties for full representation. This will need a large sample size (100+) to ensure all quota categories (male/female, etc.) are filled. These people could be incentivized, depending on budgets, with USBs, phone credit or other music, clothes and festival vouchers.

Questioning procedures – The second key quantitative challenge is with the standardization of questioning. It is vital that each respondent is asked exactly the same set of questions, in the same order and, as far as possible, in the same way. Hence, we move from the free-flowing interview sequences of focus groups and depth interviews designed to gather unique data, to carefully constructed and piloted questionnaires, combined with detailed interviewer instructions, to collect common data. Standardization is so important because answers will be summed. If we want to know how many people use a particular service, or exactly how pleased they are with it, we have to be able to add up the answers to our questions. The questions and answers therefore have to mean the same thing – otherwise, we are adding up apples and oranges.

Again, it is worth emphasizing that the purpose here is just to give a flavour of quantitative research that will enable our discussions about the purpose of social marketing research. Readers who want to go into more depth on quantitative research and sampling should consult Harris's (2011) comprehensive discussion of measurement in quantitative methods. Other questionnaire design or sampling dimensions can be consulted in standard market research texts (e.g. Churchill and Iacobucci 2010; Kent 2007).

Internet research

It would be remiss of us to talk about research in social marketing without examining the role for and potential of Internet research.

Internet research is the use of the Internet and computer networks in any phase of the social marketing research process, including the development of the problem, research design, data gathering, analysis, and report writing and distribution. Internet research 'is transforming the way research is conducted at virtually every level. It is the single most significant change affecting research today' (Pettigrew and Roberts 2011).

In secondary data research, 'online data collection, storage, and retrieval systems deliver volumes of secondary data on trends and the competitive environment' (Domegan and Fleming 2007). Whether one is doing systematic or narrative reviews, the Internet facilitates speedy access to and management of numerous databases, directories, government sources and professional reports. And Internet research also goes far beyond library and database access. In the words of Pettigrew and Roberts,

[C]hat rooms, bulletin boards, and social networking sites contain massive quantities of information across almost limitless topics, exposing researchers to the array of variables associated with the phenomenon of interest and the colloquial terms used by the target segment to refer to these variables (Merchant, 2001). Interactions between online actors can demonstrate meaning in the making, allowing analysis of the nature of the interactions and how consensus is, or is not, achieved (Sandlin, 2007). Such interactions can be a valuable source of data relating to issues that are inappropriate to raise directly with certain populations. For example, discussing recreational drug use or sexual activity with young teens in a research context may unintentionally normalize this behaviour (Williams and Fitzsimons, 2005).

(2011: 215)

Turning to primary research, the Internet can provide detailed access to many community groups and population segments through email, web or panel surveys. Interactive storytelling and experiential insights are possible and valuable outputs from Internet research, as Grindle (2004) explains:

[B]y combining interactivity and reward structures – as evolved by the computer games industry – with storytelling and emotional structuring – as evolved by commercial cinema – Social marketing can help clients experiment outside of their local, real world familial and peer group milieu. Social marketers can collaborate with and help to co-create identities, environments, behaviours and lifestyles.

(We pick up this point again in Chapter 10.)

As a result, the Internet is facilitating more and more qualitative research with online focus groups offering advantages over the traditional face-to-face group interviews.

The researcher can access hard-to-reach target audiences such as doctors, professional people and working mothers. Online focus groups can cost less money and save time. For the same reasons, in-depth interviews and projective techniques are also popular Internet research techniques.

The task of analysing marketing data is no longer relegated to research specialists. Increasingly, managers are using networked desktop computers, data analysis and data mining software, and Internet search engines to access and process marketing research information.

(Domegan and Fleming 2007: 37)

The advantages of internet research are self evident; for example the task of data entry, a costly and time consuming process involved in traditional offline research, is avoided as data is collected automatically, saving time and money while eliminating coding errors and interviewer bias. Also, respondents can feel more comfortable in answering sensitive questions with their anonymity ensured. (Kotler 2005). Fieldwork can be validated in real time enabling greater levels of quality control (consistency checks, item response checks) and the ability to fine tune surveys as they are being executed. Survey questions can be randomised, eliminating a potential source of response bias. In the online environment there are fewer of the conventional research constraints such as the difficulties in accessing multiple, geographically disparate physical sites. The sheer quantity of data that can be collected using electronic methods is unprecedented. For example, web based surveys can be programmed to reject improper data entry.

(Domegan and Fleming 2007: 37)

But Internet research has its own pitfalls; some groups, such as over 55s, do not use the Internet to the same degree as those who are 20 or 30 years old. Countries have varying degrees of Internet coverage affecting the social marketer's ability to utilize it, particularly in primary research. Furthermore, there are ethical issues of trust and privacy to consider (discussed in Chapter 9). Remember, Internet research is another case of horses for courses.

WHEN TO DO WHAT SORT OF RESEARCH

Social marketers, then, have a range of methodologies to choose from. To select the right one – or, more likely, the right combination – is going to depend on the decisions we have to make. Exercise 5.5 will help you think through what these decisions might be.

EXERCISE 5.5: SOCIAL MARKETING RESEARCH QUESTIONS

You are a consultant who has been commissioned to use social marketing to try to reverse the rise in antisocial behaviour among the adolescent boys of Brownesville, a small industrial town in a deprived part of the country. You will be working with the local social work department and an advertising agency. The initial proposal is to use a combination of youth outreach, mass media activity and police liaison, but nothing has yet been firmly agreed.

How will you use research to guide your decision making? Specifically: WHEN during the campaign will you want to answer WHICH QUESTIONS, and WHAT METHODOLOGIES will provide the best insights?

Figure 5.3 presents the answer to Exercise 5.5 as a diagram, which we will now explore step by step.

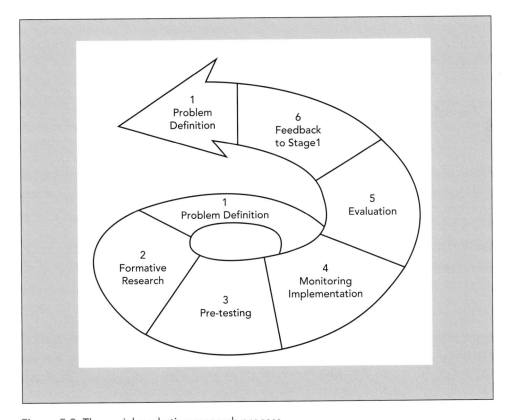

Figure 5.3 The social marketing research process

Problem definition

In the first place, research can help define the problem (Box 1 in Figure 5.3) from the target group's perspective, exploring their perceptions of the particular issues being considered, such as smoking, sex or cancer – or, in this case, antisocial behaviour. More specifically, it examines what role, if any, a particular intervention might perform, and, assuming it has a role, campaign objectives can be clarified and a precise brief be given to the production and delivery teams.

Problem definition research can also clarify who the key target and stakeholder groups are. In Exercise 5.5, for instance, the latter may include parents, youth workers, civic leaders and neighbours of the proposed youth centre, all of whom may have useful insights to offer at each decision-making stage.

Methodologically, the first stop here is with secondary research (see above) to check what is already known from past studies and official statistics about the problem. For example, in our case, it might tell us something about the extent of the problem, the age and demographic background of offenders and whether previous research tells us anything about their motives or patterns of behaviour. Equally, it might inform us about past efforts to tackle the problem, and how the target groups responded.

If existing sources are inadequate new primary research might need to be commissioned: qualitative to give us ideas about the target group's perceptions and quantitative to reveal more statistical data, such as the prevalence of particular behaviours.

Formative and pre-testing research

Assuming this problem definition research suggests the need for an intervention, further primary research can guide its development. Figure 5.3 divides this into formative and decision-making research, but this is perhaps overly neat and tidy. In reality, several stages of research – typically qualitative – may be needed to perfect and hone the campaign. Essentially, the need is to identify key intervention ideas and work out how they can best be executed.

For example, qualitative research could be used to compare the potential of two different ideas for a youth outreach service, on the one hand, or a more conventional communications effort designed to encourage young people to be more considerate, on the other. These methods would enable you to show examples of materials and visuals of potential services. They would also make it possible to assess complex emotional reactions. A youth club might seem a plausible option, and make sense on a rational level – if the kids are playing five-a-side, they are not fighting in the town square – but it may be more valuable to determine what sort of youngster would actually use the service. Would they be middle-class 'goody-goodies' or those with street cred? This type of issue typically calls for not just qualitative methods, but also projective techniques.

This same research approach can be used to guide decisions about both the nature of the initiative (youth service or media effort) and how it should be executed. Thus, if the youth service shows most potential, it can help us determine what form it should take, where it should be located and how it should be promoted. There may also be some demand for quantitative research at this stage to determine the extent of demand or the prevalence of opinions.

We will revisit these formative and decision-making stages of research in the next chapter when we discuss communications.

Monitoring implementation

During implementation (Stage 4 in Figure 5.3), our questions concern *what* is being delivered (how many training courses were run or leaflets handed out) and the extent to which it matches the programme objectives and expectations (Flora *et al.* 1993). It also assesses the extent to which implementation is internally consistent across different sites and over the duration of the intervention period, and identifies the factors that can aid or hinder delivery. This is particularly important where there are many contextual and other factors that can affect how a programme is run – and, in turn, how effective it is. Box 5.8 illustrates some of the benefits of what is also called process evaluation, using a drugs prevention initiative as an example. It also illustrates how the monitoring of implementation fits in with both formative and evaluation research.

BOX 5.8: THE BENEFITS OF MONITORING IMPLEMENTATION

Think, for example, about a drug education package designed to be taught by classroom teachers in 20 different schools, by 50 different teachers. Even if teachers are supplied with exactly the same package, the same written instructions on how to use it and the same training in its methods, how they teach the package is likely to vary widely depending on how confident they feel about drug education, whether they agree philosophically with the approach taken in the package, whether they volunteered to teach the package or are doing it unwillingly, whether their classroom space is suitable for the activities, whether their head teacher values drug education and makes them feel it is worthwhile, whether parents support or oppose teaching their children about drugs, and many other factors.

Process evaluation of programme implementation is an essential part of any social marketing research study, not only because it yields valuable learning in itself (for example, about the challenges of doing drug education in schools) but also because it can help explain the final results of a research study. Supposing our drug education research study finds that the package does not seem to have produced any changes in pupils' attitudes towards drugs: without process evaluation, we cannot know whether this is because the package was a bad package or whether it was just poorly implemented.

(Source: Stead et al. 2002)

All the points made in the figure apply to our youth initiative. Monitoring implementation will, for instance, help us establish whether the youth centre has been successfully set up, is being used and matching the requirements established in the formative research. It can also give feedback on the sort of young people using the club and their experiences of doing so.

In terms of methodology, both qualitative and quantitative research can be used. In addition, a technique we mentioned briefly under methodology, observation, can also be useful. For example, the process evaluation in Box 5.8 included systematic classroom observation of lessons taking place.

Evaluation

Evaluation research occurs before, during and after a programme. Stead and McDermott (2011) explain how evaluation 'shapes programme content and quality; examines the delivery process and the immediate outcomes and subsequent long-term impact. In short, it tells one whether the programme has made a difference'. The starting point for any evaluation of effectiveness must be our objectives, as the social marketing planning process teaches us (Chapter 4). It is not possible to measure achievements without clear original intentions. This reinforces the importance of clearly defining objectives at the problem definition stage.

There are essentially two kinds of objectives. First, there are those concerned with the target's reactions to an initiative – whether they are aware of it, have participated in it, understood it and so on. Second, there are objectives concerned with changes in the target population – whether, for example, there are fewer accidents as a result of an initiative, or whether, following a seatbelt promotion campaign, the target population has become more aware of the value of seatbelts, more in favour of them or more likely to actually use them. These two types of objectives require different evaluation procedures.

Measuring reactions to an initiative is fairly straightforward. Once the initiative is complete, the target audience simply has to be asked the relevant questions (e.g. have they seen the relevant advertising, or visited the youth club). Provided that the research methodology is sound, reliable data will result. However, it may be argued that objectives and evaluations that are restricted purely to response are too limited. Furthermore, if social marketing aims to bring about social change, then, arguably, change is what should be measured when evaluating its effectiveness. Surely we need to know whether antisocial behaviour has reduced?

However, measuring effect is much more difficult than measuring response. Done properly, it demands a full-blown RCT, with all the drawbacks and distortions we discussed earlier. These problems of attribution and measuring change become most prevalent when we are trying to judge the success or failure of an individual initiative. In reality, the evaluation of effectiveness should, as in Figure 5.3, be seen as only one part of a research function that takes place throughout the development and implementation of a given programme of change.

THE BIG PICTURE AGAIN

As we noted at the beginning of this chapter, social marketing should look beyond these one-off judgements in research, and adopt a strategic perspective combining *long-term planning* with *empathy* for the client. To this we have now added the idea of the *integrated* research model, which, like the strategic planning process described in Chapter 4, is action oriented and progressive.

The Swiss response to the challenge of HIV/AIDS provides a good example of the value of this type of integrative, strategic research model. In 1987, they were faced with an urgent problem of having the highest prevalence of HIV/AIDS in Europe. A wide-ranging prevention programme was instigated, and, after an initial assessment of the first wave of publicity, a comprehensive and ongoing evaluation approach was adopted. They describe this as a 'comprehensive, utilization-focused evaluation' that 'seeks to produce results of immediate value to the development of the prevention strategy, and includes a continual process of questioning and feedback between the strategy makers and other potential users of the findings and the evaluators' (Dubois-Arber *et al.* 1999: 2573). They conclude that this approach to research 'allows for a "real world" verification of strategic choices that in turn can guide further resource allocation and, last but not least, can help to maintain a high level of commitment of the different stakeholders' (ibid.: 2580).

Social marketing suggests that this thinking can be applied not just to HIV/AIDS prevention programmes as in Switzerland, but to behaviour change more generally. However, to do so, we need to engage all four social marketing orientations – client, creative, collective and competitive (see Chapter 2). The stories we have examined in this chapter reinforce the need for this comprehensive approach.

Think of the power of Anita's tale with which we began this chapter, or Mandela's intervention on Robben Island, and its follow-up in Nablus. These stories help us see through the eyes of others and to recognize that agency and empowerment are essential precursors to any significant change programme. Mandela's young men seemed to be in an utterly parlous situation, but Mandela's creative approach gave them the power to walk away from tobacco. The stories also remind us of the value of a collective orientation. Ultimately, the young Africans' lives were transformed not by tobacco control but by wholesale political changes in South Africa: the Apartheid system was swept away. Anita needs a similar political transformation if her place at the bottom of the heap is to change. Such change will undoubtedly encounter both passive and active competition, which will need to be addressed (refer back to Chapter 2 and on to Chapters 7 and 8).

In this way, ad hoc behaviour change can develop into comprehensive social change. We will develop this thinking in Chapter 10.

THE DANGERS OF OVERDOING IT

Given what we have agreed about the importance of doing plenty of research in social marketing, it is perhaps surprising to have a section warning against becoming too dependent on it. But there are such dangers, and they stem from misunderstanding about: (a) how research and decision making fit together; and (b) the strategic purpose of research.

RESEARCH AND DECISION MAKING

As we have seen, a mix of research methodologies is used to guide decision making in social marketing. However, it is important to recognize that research does not make decisions for us; it is not a matter of delegating the tough choices to the focus group or the questionnaire. The target group's expertise is in responding, not social marketing or intervention design. For example, as we will discuss in Chapter 6, fear campaigns are frequently justified on the grounds that target audiences ask for them, opting for some variant on the blackened, cancerous lung or bloody car smash – the gorier the better. This misses the point of pre-testing. Smokers and drivers have a great deal to tell us about what it is like to be on the receiving end of our interventions, but they do not know which ones are most effective. They are clients, *not* consultants.

In other closely related spheres, we readily accept this argument. We recognize, for instance, that most people are not experts in human behaviour, not even their own. So we would not simply ask smokers why they smoke, and take their answers at face value. Indeed, in the 1980s, when the tobacco industry did precisely this to try to show that advertising had no effect on children's smoking (Jenkins 1988), their research was rightly dismissed.

Indeed, there are times when decisions have to be made without any research. Good marketing has to cope when there is no data available and good marketers leave space for imagination, lateral thinking and educated guesses even when there are no data. For the truth is all research can do is lessen the risk that we get things wrong. It can reduce uncertainty; it cannot produce certainty.

Malcolm Gladwell, in his book *Blink* (2005), reminds us of the power of intuition. He tells the story of a Kuoros, an ancient Cretan statue that was offered to the John Paul Getty Museum in California. The museum subjected the potential exhibit to 14 months of very careful and high-powered scientific analysis to try to ascertain whether it was genuine. Their research provided reassurance, and they were on the verge of buying the Kuoros when a visiting expert looked at it and immediately warned against the purchase. He had done no research, no science, but just felt the statue was dubious. Other experts then responded in a similar negative way, again on the basis of intuition.

The statue was a fake.

Gladwell does not conclude that we should therefore abandon science and go back to guess work. Indeed, he points out that gut feel can be just as misleading, and in any case the experts will have educated their instincts with years of scientific rigour. He simply argues that we should leave space for intuition in our decision making. Marketers agree.

WRAP-UP

In this chapter, we have examined the two key roles of research in social marketing:

i)   **As a navigational aid in the strategic planning**. Here, its job is to guide our decision making from project inception through to completion, and illuminate the strategic fit between initiatives. We have also looked at the strengths and weaknesses of qualitative and quantitative methods, and how they complement each other. Both have a role in guiding social marketing decision making. We also acknowledged the dangers of being over-dependent on research. It guides but does not replace decision making, and should not preclude intuition.

ii) **As an experiential tool**. Here the challenge is to provide an empathetic perspective on our clients' lives. The Chinese proverb argues that to understand a person you have to first walk a mile in their shoes; only when we use research to do the same thing can we hope to really understand why people behave as they do – and have any hope of negotiating change. More profoundly, these insights enable us to start building relationships that make the ideas of co-creation we will discuss in Chapter 10 a realistic possibility.

Pulling these ideas together we concluded that systematic research acting as the servant of social marketing helps to improve our understanding not just of our marketing tools and techniques, but also of our target groups and their behaviours. Like good carpenters, we come to understand the wood as well as the chisels. In this way, it can move us beyond the stop-start of interventions and towards a process of continuous health, environmental and welfare improvement.

Or, in the language of storytelling: the function of research is to uncover and examine the stories we all have to tell so that social marketing can enable us to become heroes in these stories. When we can begin to develop coherent collective stories, we will be able to tackle not just behaviour change but also systemic change; the sort of change that will make Anita's story, with which we began this chapter, a historical curiosity; the sort of change we need to address complex, 'wicked' (see Chapter 10) problems such as obesity, inequalities and climate change.

Reflective questions

1. What is the purpose of research in social marketing?
2. Secondary research lends itself to systematic or narrative review. Explain.
3. Discuss the two types of primary research: qualitative and quantitative and when they might be used in research.
4. Discuss the navigational and empathetic benefits of research.
5. Quantitative research is concerned with sampling and questioning in a way qualitative research is not. Discuss.
6. Explain evaluation research.
7. The Internet is influencing social marketing research. In what ways? Why?
8. 'Research is the art of storytelling' Discuss with examples.
9. What are the research pitfalls for the social marketer?
10. The 'best' social marketing research combines rigour with pragmatic flexibility. Discuss with short illustrations.

Reflective assignments

1. Conduct an Internet search on storytelling tips and suggestions.
2. Locate and critique a social marketing example that includes a story.
3. Locate and review a social marketing systematic review study.
4. Locate and evaluate a social marketing RCT.
5. Select secondary research about a behaviour change topic of your choice and locate a story that supports the data.
6. Locate and present a story of a behaviour change experience in the health or environmental field.
7. Locate a large-scale social marketing survey and develop three success stories around the data.[2]
8. You are a team comprising of (a) social marketing consultants, (b) a local city council and (c) a PR agency. You have been charged with developing and running an initiative to encourage rainwater collection. How will you use research to help you to develop and evaluate your initiative? What research methods would you use?

9. Reconsider how your answers to question 8 above might change if you were just using Internet research?

10. Complete your traffic lights checklist for social marketing research and storytelling.

Notes

1   In the UK, prescription medicines cannot be promoted directly to the public.
2   Adapted from Kruger's Course Syllabus EdPA: 5080 Special Topics: Using Stories as a Research Procedure, Spring Semester 2011 Section: 003. 22 January 2011 Version.

References

ACMD (2005) Pathways to Problems. Online: www.drugs.gov.uk/publication-search/acmd/pathways-to-problems/Pathwaystoproblems.pdf.

Anderson, A.S., Porteous, L.E.G., Foster, E., Higgins, C., Stead, M., Hetherington, M., Ha, M.-A. and Adamson, A.J. (2005) 'The impact of a school-based nutrition education intervention on dietary intake and cognitive and attitudinal variables relating to fruits and vegetables', *Public Health Nutrition*, 8(6): 650–656.

Churchill, G.A. and Iacobucci, D. (2010) *Marketing Research: Methodological Foundations*. Ohio, USA: Cengage Learning.

Churchill, G.A., Brown, T.J. and Suter, T. (2009) *Basic Marketing Research*. Ohio, USA: Cengage Learning.

Devlin, E., Hastings, G., Smith A., McDermott, L. and Noble, G. (2007) 'Pharmaceutical marketing: a question of regulation', *Journal of Public Affairs*, 7(2): 135–147.

Domegan, C. and Fleming, D. (2007) *Marketing Research in Ireland, Theory and Practice*. Dublin, Ireland: Gill and Macmillan.

Dubois-Arber, F., Jeannin, A. and Spencer, B. (1999) 'Long-term global evaluation of a national AIDS prevention strategy: The case of Switzerland', *AIDS*, 13(18): 2571–2582.

Flora, J.A., Lefebvre, R.C., Murray, D.M., Stone, E.J., and Assaf, A. (1993) 'A community education monitoring system: Methods from the Stanford Five-City Project, the Minnesota Heart Health Program and the Pawtucket Heart Health Program', *Health Education Research Theory and Practice*, 8(1): 81–95.

Freire, P. (1982) 'Creating alternative research methods. Learning to do it by doing it', in Budd Hall, Arthur Gillette and Rajesh Tandon (eds) *Creating Knowledge: A Monopoly*. New Delhi: Society for Participatory Research in Asia, pp.30–31.

Gladwell, M. (2005) *Blink: The Power of Thinking Without Thinking*. London: Allen Lane

Grant, I.C., Hassan, L., Hastings, G., MacKintosh, A.M. and Eadie, D. (2008) 'The influence of branding on adolescent smoking behaviour: Exploring the mediating role of image and attitudes', *International Journal of Nonprofit and Voluntary Sector Marketing*, 13(3): 275–285.

Grindle, M. (2004) 'At what stage is our understanding of the interactive entertainment development industry in Scotland?', paper presented at *The Scottish Media and Communication Association Annual Conference*, 3 December, Dundee: University of Abertay.

Lee, H. (1960) *To Kill a Mockingbird*. New York: HarperCollins Publishers Inc.

Harris, F. (2011) 'Measurement in quantitative methods', Ch. 15 in G. Hastings, K. Angus and C. Bryant (eds) *The SAGE Handbook of Social Marketing*. London: Sage Publications Ltd.

Hastings, G. (2011) 'Introduction: A movement in social marketing', in G. Hastings, K. Angus and C. Bryant (eds) *The SAGE Handbook of Social Marketing*. London: Sage Publications Ltd.

Hastings, G., Brooks, O., Stead, M., Angus K., Anker, T. and Farrell, T. (2010) 'Alcohol advertising: The last chance saloon', *British Medical Journal*, 340: b5550, doi: 10.1135/bmj.b5550.

Hastings, G.B. (1990) 'Qualitative research in health education', *Journal of the Institute of Health Education*, 28(4): 118–127.

Hastings, G.B., Eadie, D.R. and Scott, A.C. (1990) 'Two years of AIDS publicity: A review of progress', *Health Education Research*, 5(1): 17–25.

Henderson, M. (2006) *School effects on adolescent pupils' health behaviours and school processes associated with these effects*. Glasgow: MRC Social & Public Health Sciences Unit, University of Glasgow.

Hill, R.P. (2011) 'Impoverished consumers and social marketing', Ch. 21 in G. Hastings, K. Angus and C. Bryant (eds) *The SAGE Handbook of Social Marketing*. London: Sage Publications Ltd.

Jenkins, J. (1988) 'Tobacco advertising and children: Some Canadian findings', *International Journal of Advertising*, 7(4): 357–357.

Kent, R. (2007) *Marketing Research: Approaches, Methods and Applications*. London: Thomson Learning.

Krueger, Richard A. (2010) 'Using stories in evaluation,' in Joseph S. Wholey, Harry P. Hatry and Kathryn E. Newcomer (eds) *Handbook of Practical Program Evaluation*. San Francisco: Jossey Bass, pp.404–424.

Lewin, K. (1951) *Field Theory in Social Science: Selected Theoretical Papers*, Cartwright D. (ed). New York: Harper & Row.

Lowe, Jez (1985) Extract from the song 'Old Bones', published by Lowe Life Music.

MRC (2000) *A Framework for Development and Evaluation of RCTs for Complex Interventions to Improve Health*. London: Medical Research Council, April.

Pettigrew, S. and Roberts, M. (2011) 'Qualitative research methods in social marketing', Ch. 14 in G. Hastings, K. Angus and C. Bryant (eds) *The SAGE Handbook of Social Marketing*. London: Sage Publications Ltd.

Robinson, T.N., Borzekowski, D.L., Matheson, D.M. and Kraemer, H.C. (2007) 'Effects of fast food branding on young children's taste preferences', *Archives of Pediatrics & Adolescent Medicine*, 161(8): 792–797.

Science Museum 'Thalidomide'. Online: www.sciencemuseum.org.uk/broughttolife/themes/controversies/thalidomide.aspx

Stead, M. and McDermott, R., (2011) 'Evaluation in Social Marketing', Ch. 13 in G. Hastings, K. Angus and C. Bryant (eds) *The SAGE Handbook of Social Marketing*. London: Sage Publications Ltd.

Stead, M., Hastings, G. and Eadie, D. (2002) 'The challenge of evaluating complex interventions: A framework for evaluating media advocacy', *Health Education Research Theory and Practice*, 17(3): 351–364.

The Cochrane Collaboration (2005) *Glossary of Terms in The Cochrane Collaboration*. Version 4.2.5. Online: www.cochrane.org/sites/default/files/uploads/glossary.pdf (accessed 16 August 2012).

US Department of Education (2003) *Identifying and Implementing Educational Practices Supported by Rigorous Evidence: A User Friendly Guide*. Prepared for the Institute of Education Sciences. Washington, DC: Coalition for Evidence-Based Policy, December 2003.

West, R. (2004) *Stop Smoking Service Quality and Delivery Indicators and Targets*. A briefing for the Healthcare Commission, July. Online: www.ash.org.uk/html/cessation/smqtargetsbrief.pdf.

Chapter **6**

Only connect

Four score and seven years ago our fathers brought forth on this continent a new nation, conceived in liberty, and dedicated to the proposition that all men are created equal.

Now we are engaged in a great civil war, testing whether that nation, or any nation, so conceived and so dedicated, can long endure. We are met on a great battle-field of that war. We have come to dedicate a portion of that field, as a final resting place for those who here gave their lives that that nation might live. It is altogether fitting and proper that we should do this.

But, in a larger sense, we cannot dedicate . . ., we cannot consecrate . . ., we cannot hallow this ground. The brave men, living and dead, who struggled here, have consecrated it, far above our poor power to add or detract. The world will little note, nor long remember what we say here, but it can never forget what they did here. It is for us the living, rather, to be dedicated here to the unfinished work which they who fought here have thus far so nobly advanced. It is rather for us to be here dedicated to the great task remaining before us – that from these honored dead we take increased devotion to that cause for which they gave the last full measure of devotion – that we here highly resolve that these dead shall not have died in vain – that this nation, under God, shall have a new birth of freedom – and that government of the people, by the people, for the people, shall not perish from the earth.

(Source: Abraham Lincoln, *The Gettysburg Address*, 1863)[1]

Lincoln's speech on the battlefield of Gettysburg is a brilliant piece of oration, and, 150 years after its delivery, it can still teach us much about how to communicate. First, he had a clear **aim**: he very much needed to steady a wavering public in the northern states to ensure their continuing support for what was proving to be a very costly war against the South. More specifically, he needed to keep the electorate's vote in the upcoming presidential elections. Second, he **understood his audience**. Speaking as he was on the remnants of a battlefield, with half the dead still unburied, he was careful to invoke the heroism of the soldier, and he used this powerful symbolism to reframe the war as an historic struggle for freedom and emancipation (refer back to the discussion of positioning in Chapter 4). In the process, he took a third step and aligned his need to be re-elected with his audience's need for an enlightened and responsive political system – government of the people, by the people, for the people. He was putting them in charge and beautifully illustrates the principle of **co-creation** (Chapter 10). Fourth, he was **focused** on the job in hand: the iconic address took less than two minutes to deliver.

Fifth, he took his chance. You may be surprised to learn that Lincoln was not the main presenter at the Gettysburg dedication; that honour went to Edward Everett, another eminent politician and renowned public speaker. Everett spoke for over two hours, but few now remember him or what he said. He was humble enough to acknowledge Lincoln's accomplishment: 'I should be glad if I could flatter myself that I came as near to the central idea of the occasion, in two hours, as you did in two minutes.'[2]

Clear aims, understanding your audience, co-creation, focus and pragmatic opportunism: all characteristics of great social marketing communications. In the century and a half since Gettysburg, our understanding of how mass communications work has been honed through decades of academic and applied research – and this understanding reinforces the same social marketing insights manifested in the Gettysburg Address. In particular, it is now clear that the audience is actively involved in the communication process: what we understand from and how we react to a particular message is as much a function of us and our experiences as it is of the characteristics of the message. It is therefore crucial for would-be communicators to use careful audience research to guide the development and monitor the impact of their efforts. We will discuss these research challenges in this chapter.

Looking more carefully at communications also shows that Lincoln was right to get emotional. Much public health and social change activity adopts a positivist perspective, assuming that, if we are told that behaviour A has negative consequences, we will respond by changing to behaviour B; that we will logically weigh up the pros and cons and do the sensible, healthy and safe thing. In reality, life is more complex than this; I will continue to eat chocolate and drink beer despite the health risks because they make me feel good – and for me feeling good is an important part of being healthy. Similarly, my friend has bought himself a gas-guzzling SUV despite the damage he knows it is doing to the planet because it makes him feel successful and rugged, and he will speed in it on his way to work because, even though this will not get him there much faster (all the other SUVs on the road will see to that), it gives him the reassuring illusion of being in control. Life is imperfect and emotion plays a big part in the strategies we deploy to cope with it. Attempts to encourage us to change our behaviour for the better must take this into account.

If we think about road safety or public health campaigns, however, where emotion is considered at all, it tends to revolve around only one sentiment: fear. And yet the evidence supporting the use of fear is chequered at best. Over-reliance on it also means that we miss out on opportunities to engage with our clients using other, more positive, emotions and puts serious limitations on our long-term efforts at behaviour, lifestyle and social change. The commercial sector is not so self-limiting. It uses branding to get across a sustained array of attractive and reassuring associations and images. Lincoln was equally positive, evoking powerful emotions of validation and empowerment.

These themes of active audience involvement, positive emotion and empowerment have been reinforced and energized by digital communications. Facebook, blogs, apps and other mobile and social media innovations might seem like revolutionary developments, but in reality they just confirm not only the lessons from the Gettysburg address, but also the ensuing communications research – and indeed the discussions we have had throughout this book about the importance of relational thinking and partnership working. Social marketers need to think beyond hackneyed ideas of doing things *to* people and instead start conceiving of ways of doing things *with* people. One phenomenon of the digital era – user-generated content – neatly demonstrates the impossibility of any other course of action.

This focus on people also reminds us that this chapter is about communications, not media. The Gettysburg Address was delivered in person, and face-to-face engagement is also important in social marketing. This is most apparent when we think about what might be termed social marketing sales force: the staff in the clinic, classroom or on the street who have direct contact with the target group. The commercial sector invests heavily in front-line staff selection and their training, so should social marketers. Refer to Ray Lowry's Case Study 13 on p. 414 which highlights the importance of front-line staff training and empowerment to improve breastfeeding rates in low socio-economic groups.

Before we jump in, though, let us return to Abraham Lincoln and the final crucial lesson he provides. His speech reminds us that communication – however well crafted – is but a small part of what is needed to successfully bring about social change. Remember, as well as making a great oration, he also had to get re-elected, win a war and abolish slavery! So it is with social marketing. Communications can form an important part of our work, but, as we noted in Chapter 4, they are only one element of the marketing mix – which, in turn, is but one step in the strategic planning process. More importantly, Lincoln reminds us that social change will only be achieved when people are fully engaged in the process: government of the people, by the people, for the people. By the same token, we need social marketing of the people, by the people, for the people.

Learning outcomes

By the end of this chapter, you should be able to:

✓ Explain that social marketers have to recognize that the message sent is not necessarily the same as the message received – and that it is the latter that matters

✓ Recognize that this underpins the need for careful developmental, process and outcome research to guide and monitor campaigns

✓ Critique fear-based messages from a marketing perspective

✓ Understand the potential of positive emotion and branding in social marketing

✓ Discuss the role of participatory media in social marketing

✓ Present the case for and model internal social marketing, because employee behaviour (internal customers) affects client behaviours (external customers)

✓ Explain that communications are only part of the social marketing process.

Key words

communication – two-step communication model – opinion leaders – research – problem definition – medium – language – images – links – fear-based messages – branding – new media – participatory media – Gen C – internal marketing – internal and external clients

HOW COMMUNICATION WORKS

When Orson Welles broadcast his radio production of *The War of the Worlds* in 1938 (*Guardian* 1938) (see Figure 6.1), the effect was dramatic. Around a million Americans actually believed that the science-fiction story was true, and little green men from Mars were invading Earth and about to march on New York. The result was extensive public panic, people actually getting killed in the ensuing rush to avoid the invaders and the US rules of public broadcasting being changed for ever.

From our perspective, the events also had a more subtle impact: they engrained a perception that the mass media are extremely powerful, and that all that is needed to get people to do as you want is to design a suitably clever message. The contemporaneous rise of the Nazi party in Germany, and the central role played by Goebbels' infamous Ministry of Propaganda, served to reinforce this omnipotent reputation.

A wireless dramatisation of Mr. H. G. Wells's fantasy, *The War of the Worlds* – a work that was written at the end of last century – caused a remarkable wave of panic in the United States during and immediately after its broadcast last night at eight o'clock. Listeners throughout the country believed that it was an account of an actual invasion of the earth by warriors from Mars. The play, presented by Mr. Orson Welles, a successful theatrical producer and actor, gave a vivid account of the Martian invasion just as the wireless would if Mr. Wells's dream came true.	The programme began with music by a New York City hotel dance band, which was interrupted suddenly by a news announcer who reported that violent flashes on Mars had been observed by Princeton University astronomers. The music was soon interrupted again for a report that a meteor had struck New Jersey. Then there was an account of how the meteor opened and Martian warriors emerged and began killing local citizens with mysterious death-rays. Martians were also observed moving towards New York with the intention of destroying the city.	Many people tuning in to the middle of the broadcast jumped to the conclusion that there was a real invasion. Thousands of telephone calls poured into the wireless station and police headquarters. Residents of New Jersey covered their faces with wet cloths as a protection against poisonous gases and fled from their homes. Roads leading to a village where a Martian ship was supposed to have landed were jammed with motorists prepared to repel attackers. Panic evacuations were also reported around the New York area. In some cases people told the police and newspapers that they had seen the 'invasion'.	Mr. Jacques Chambrun, Mr. H.G. Wells's representative, stated today that Mr Wells was 'deeply concerned' that last night's wireless dramatisation should have caused such alarm. Mr. Wells added that the dramatisation was made 'with a liberty that amounts to complete rewriting and made the novel an entirely different story'. Today nerves are steadier and it is recalled that in England some years ago there was a similar reaction to the famous 'spoof broadcast' by Father Ronald Knox. Many listeners took his parodied description of a riot in London seriously.

Figure 6.1 Report of a radio broadcast of *The War of the Worlds* from *The Guardian*, 1 November 1938

Source: *The Guardian* (Copyright Guardian News and Media Limited 2002)

However, the seven decades of research done since Goebbels' demise suggest that this picture is actually very misleading. Early models in communication theory did characterize the process as a one-way phenomenon, involving an active message sender and a completely passive recipient. Analogies are often drawn between this model and a hypodermic syringe: just as the doctor injects the drug into the patient so the communicator injects the message into the audience. In both cases, the effects are both predictable and easily measured.

This analysis presents the communicator as powerful and directly manipulative, with dramatic effects being relatively easy to achieve. The media, particularly television and radio, as channels of mass communication, come to be seen as a means of controlling the population. These ideas were given added credibility when commentators like Vance Packard (2007) applied them to commercial advertising, the influence of which he exaggerated and over-simplified.

The limitations on the manipulative power of advertising can be illustrated by a couple of examples. It is estimated that 80–90 per cent of new food products fail within one year of introduction (Rudolph 1995). If advertising were as powerful as Packard suggests, this could never be. Similarly, given the frequency of mass media efforts to dissuade people from taking up smoking (and in many countries a complete ban on pro-tobacco advertising), one would have expected an all-powerful media to have resolved the problem – and yet thousands of young people still take up smoking every year in Europe alone.

It is not that advertising lacks influence – it is immensely powerful – it is just that more complex explanations were needed and these duly emerged. They included the two-, or more, step model initially proposed by Katz and Lazarsfeld (1955), involving opinion leaders in the process of communication; the use and gratification approaches (McQuail *et al.* 1962; Rosengren and Windahl 1962),which depict the consumer as deliberately using the media rather than vice versa, and, more recently, cultural effects models, which place the media in a cultural context and see its effects as indirect and long term (Tudor 1996).

Interestingly, thinking in communication theory matches that in advertising. Early models of advertising conceptualized the process as a hierarchy of effects on consumers – typically cognitive (e.g. product awareness), affective (e.g. product liking) and then conative (e.g. product purchase). However, these 'linear sequential models' have also been heavily criticized (Barry and Howard 1990). As with early communication theory, they assume a passive audience, ignore the effects of significant others and present an overly tidy picture of how communication actually works. Indeed, it has become increasingly apparent that it is at least as relevant to ask 'What do people do to advertising?' as 'What does advertising do to people?' (Hedges 1982). English health promoters have been all too aware of this since the mid-1980s, when teenagers were found to be stealing supposedly off-putting 'Heroin Screws You Up' posters and hanging them on their bedroom walls (see Box 6.1).

BOX 6.1: HEROIN SCREWS YOU UP

'In the mid-1980s, the Government responded to a surge in heroin use with a television and poster campaign featuring a wasted youth with the caption: "Heroin Screws You Up." Dozens of posters went missing as the boy in them became a teenage pin-up. Within months "heroin chic" appeared on the catwalks.'

(Source: Burke and Thompson 2002)

Linear sequential models also overlook all the thinking that has emerged from postmodernism and what it tells us about the importance of symbolism and cultural meaning to consumption, whether of products or messages (Elliott and Wattanasuwan 1998). We now know that audiences, especially young ones, are extremely sophisticated consumers of the media and that meaning has to be negotiated, not imposed.

Thus, many plausible theories of how the mass media and advertising work have emerged. Much as with behaviour change theory (Chapter 3), social marketing does not get too hung up about which of these theories is right (they are probably all a bit right). Rather, it uses the insights that result to progress campaigns; and the key insight that links all these theories is that *the audience is actively involved in the communications process*. As our colleague Douglas Leathar used to express it: communication, like beauty, is in the eye of the beholder. Whether in the form of opinion leaders, self-gratifiers or postmodern cynics, the audience is as important as the communicator in the process of getting the message across.

John Redmond is talking about poetry when he argues:

as sparks fly up when flint meets rock, so meanings fly up when reader meets poem. Sparks are contained neither by flint nor rocks but arise from their relationship. In the same way, meanings are contained neither by the reader or the poem but arise from their relationship.

(2006: 7)

He could just as easily have been talking about advertising; the only difference is that a poem is a purely creative exercise, whereas an ad is deliberately produced to get across a particular message. The ad developer therefore has to be particularly careful to take account of the active nature of the audience as they go about their business.

Exercise 6.1 is a chance to explore the two-way nature of communication in advertising.

> ### EXERCISE 6.1: ADVERTISING AND WHAT IT DOES
>
> Next time you are watching television, sit through a commercial break and ask yourself the following questions:
>
> 1. What factual information do the ads provide?
> 2. What other messages are communicated?
> 3. Do any appeal to you? Why/Why not?
> 4. How do the ads compare or contrast with others you have seen?
> 5. What might you do as a result of seeing them?

It will illustrate that adverts – certainly television commercials – communicate a vast array of messages, many of them emotional rather than factual; that some work for you, but some do not; and, if you are watching with other people, that preferences vary from person to person who will each bring different experiences and priorities to the communication process. This variation in response will also be accentuated if you watch commercials at different times of the day.

THE CRUCIAL ROLE OF RESEARCH

Exercise 6.1 and the conclusions we have drawn about the two-way nature of communication demonstrate that the only certain way of knowing what is being communicated by a particular media effort is to ask the intended audience. The more obvious manifestations of this conclusion are unlikely to be disputed. Thus, the need to check that an audience understands the language in a leaflet or that the images on a poster are decipherable needs little justification.

However, the implications are more fundamental than this. An active audience means more than testing understanding of particular words or passing verdicts on completed posters. It implies a need to design communications, from inception to dissemination and beyond, with the intended audience's needs and perspectives clearly in mind. To do this, social marketers must maintain continuous contact with the target audience – ideally through formal consumer research. This contact will provide invaluable insights at every stage and on all aspects of a campaign.

This need for continuous research is fundamental to the whole social marketing process, as Chapter 5 demonstrated, discussing its whys and hows. At this point, focusing on communications, we will look at the sort of pitfalls research can help us avoid. This naturally leads us first to formative research which can help us decide whether the media can help resolve a particular social marketing problem, and, if so, what task it can perform, as well as guiding decision making about all aspects of message design. These include problem definition; medium; language; images and links discussed below.

Problem definition

At the very beginning of a project, research with the target group can help define the nature of the problem to be tackled, determine whether the media has a role to play and, if so, what objectives it might fulfil. Let's assume we are considering the possibility of developing an ad campaign for 15–16-year-olds to tell them about the dangers of STDs. As a first step, research could examine teenagers' perceptions about sexual health and explore what, if any, information they feel they need. This might show that teenagers know of the risks and that condoms afford the best protection, but that they feel extremely disempowered about using them – suggesting that the campaign needs to focus on safer sexual skills development rather than simply warning about the dangers.

Arguably, in the process, it might suggest that this is not principally a communication problem and, hence, a media campaign is not the best solution here. That, in fact, something more engaging and better able to develop skills is needed – maybe a combination of school-curriculum development, outreach work and condom distribution. Thus, audience research can help to define not only advertising objectives, but also whether media activity is needed at all.

Assuming initial contact with the consumer does define a role for the mass media, further research can help determine the relative merits of different creative ideas or approaches on which to base a campaign. For instance, the sexual health campaign could approach the subject with a conventionally negative emphasis on the drawbacks of *not* practising safer sex – unwanted pregnancy and disease. Alternatively, it could be more positive, emphasizing the benefits of safer sex in terms of enjoying more adult and fulfilled relationships. Interestingly, when these alternative ideas were presented to young people and their views sought, an initial preference for the more familiar, negative approach rapidly changed to a preference for the positive one. In particular, teenage girls were much more able and willing to associate themselves with the benefits of using contraception than the drawbacks of not doing so (Hastings and Leathar 1986).

Research with the consumer can also provide invaluable feedback on all aspects of campaign design, including the choice of medium, language, images and links with non-media campaign elements.

Medium

'Judge Dredd' is a cartoon character (Figure 6.2), with his own comic or magazine, which is read by teenagers. A few years ago, it was proposed to use him and his comic as a vehicle for drug education material, but the idea had to be abandoned when teenagers were consulted. Many had never read the comic and saw it as puerile, assuming it to be for young children. Those who did read it rejected its use as a vehicle for such a serious topic. 'Judge Dredd' was, for them, a fantasy character whose rather ridiculous escapades were not intended to be taken literally. He had no basis in reality, no existence off the page or outside the reader's mind.

Using him as a way of transmitting a very serious and literal message about drugs completely contradicts this. It suggests that they believe 'Judge Dredd' to be real, much as a child might believe in Superman. It implies that they defer to him and are likely to do as he tells them. As a result, it is grossly patronizing.

A similar instance of the medium being the message – or at least greatly influencing the effectiveness of it – is provided by 'advertorials'. These are jointly written and produced by the social marketer and the producer of the host publication. When a Scottish health agency was looking for a more reliable means of delivering information-rich messages capable of engaging its audience, research showed that people were far more likely to read and attend to content that was endorsed by and written in the style of their favourite magazine. The agency went on to use this approach to deliver health messages requiring detailed information to groups who were regular readers of news and entertainment magazines – dietary advice emerged as just one area to benefit from this approach.

Ray Lowry and colleagues (2000) make a similar point in their work to encourage the use of sugar-free medicines, showing how the choice of communication

Figure 6.2 The medium is the message
Source: *2000AD* (1998)

channel – in this case, a sales person with customized materials – was a key dimension of their success.

Language

The language used in media material must be understandable to the intended audience. Reading-age tests can help in this respect, but the only certain check is to expose the material to your audience and ask for their reactions. This assesses not only comprehension, but also equally important issues such as acceptability. For example, draft material on the safer sex campaign discussed above used the term 'bonking' for making love, in an attempt to be fashionable. Teenagers took great exception to this. They felt it implied a totally amoral and cynical attitude to sex that they rejected and found insulting.

The Foolsspeed road safety campaign illustrates a similar point. A pre-test using storyboards and narrative audiotapes helped avoid the inappropriate use of language and gesture. In one version of the proposed ads, road users were portrayed tapping their heads to show their disapproval of the (speeding) central character, and to encourage him to 'use his head' and slow down (see Figure 6.3a). Unfortunately, the gesture was interpreted as an act of aggression more likely to elicit a violent response than to encourage more responsible driving, or as one male respondent put it, *'it doesnae mean "use your head" it means "you're a nutter!" – it's a threatening gesture.'* This problem was subsequently resolved by focusing the story-line exclusively on the driver where he was challenged to drive more slowly by his alter ego, talking to him in his rear-view mirror (see Figure 6.3b).

Images

Similar strictures apply to the visual elements of media materials. They must be decipherable and acceptable. In 2005, as part of a sexual health initiative targeting young people in deprived communities in the east of Scotland, the Scottish Government funded[3] a campaign promoting respect for others and acceptance of difference.

One approach tested was to superimpose the wigs worn by court judges onto young people to signify inappropriate judgemental behaviour (see Figure 6.4a). While the target audience understood the imagery and could relate this to their behaviour, the creative approach was ultimately rejected because it was seen as childish and failed to deliver a credible challenge. A different creative route was therefore adopted, which set out to challenge young people in public spaces (such as at bus stops and on board public transport) where they might be encouraged to make inappropriate judgements about people based on appearance alone (see Figure 6.4b).

In passing, it is worth noting that the quality of the graphics in Figure 6.4a is quite low. This is because we are not looking at finished material, but an image produced purely for research purposes.

Links

As we have noted numerous times, social marketing thinking suggests that the mass media is most likely to work if it is used in conjunction with other initiatives. Target group opinion can help determine the nature of these other elements and how they should be linked to the media activity. This takes us naturally to wider social marketing research, which was discussed in Chapter 5. Issues of campaign evaluation are also discussed in this chapter.

In addition, these examples illustrate another point that we already noted during our discussion of planning in Chapter 4 and research in Chapter 5. Target audience

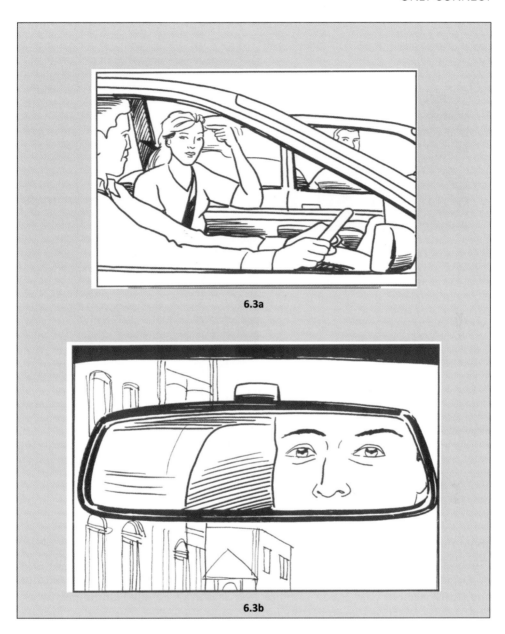

6.3a

6.3b

Figure 6.3 The hazards of using sign language
Source: The Foolsspeed road safety campaign (From the Scottish Road Safety Campaign)

research does not just help improve individual media campaigns; because it requires continuous contact between communicator and audience throughout and between initiatives, it also enables us to increase our understanding of our clients. Some of the examples quoted above illustrate this point. The research on 'Judge Dredd' revealed as much about teenagers and how they read comics as it did

Figure 6.4 Images have many levels of meaning

Source: Campaign promoting respect for others. Reproduced with permission from 1576 Ltd and Healthy Respect (a Scottish Executive funded national health demonstration project for young people and sexual health) (2001–2008), www.healthyrespect.co.uk.

about the actual material. Similarly, young people's reaction to the word 'bonking' provides a valuable insight into their sexual feelings and attitudes. This type of target audience understanding is fundamental to effective communication and clearly seen in Case Study 17 on p. 444, Saathiya's Family Planning Network. The communication strategy, including radio, in-clinic materials, posters, flyers and billboards, focuses on understanding the behaviours and barriers around sexually active young married couples to guide communication decision making.

We also have noted a number of times now that social marketing is, in essence, a process of exchanging values. Likewise, communication is a form of exchange – it requires shared experiences, mutual understanding and empathy. If, as social marketers, we do not take the trouble to try to understand our clients, to take their ideas seriously and, at least to some extent, accept their view of the world, how can we expect them to accept ours?

FEAR MESSAGES IN MARKETING

Given what we have agreed about the two-way nature of communication and the need for empathy and shared understanding, it seems inappropriate to ask generic questions about whether certain sorts of messages work better than others. The answer is bound to be 'it depends' – on circumstances, past communications, available channels and so on. Above all, it depends on the audience. And yet precisely this question has been asked again and again about fear messages.

Thus, several attempts have been made to develop a theory to explain and predict how fear works, but the results are inconclusive. Three alternative models have emerged. First, the curvilinear model posits that fear *can* persuade up to a threshold of tolerance, beyond which it becomes counter-productive.

Second, Leventhal's (1960) parallel response model proposes that emotional and cognitive factors act independently to mediate behaviour, with emotional factors affecting internal attempts to cope with the threat (e.g. by rationalizing or rejecting it), while cognitive factors will determine the behaviour change.

Finally, Rogers' (1965) expectancy-valence model states that the effectiveness of a fear-arousing communication is a function of three variables: the magnitude of the threat; the probability of its occurrence; and the efficacy of the advocated protective response. It is proposed that these three variables will interact to produce a level of 'protection motivation' within an individual and that this will determine the level of change.

The research into the effectiveness of fear appeal is inconclusive, but the majority of studies show a positive relationship between fear arousal and persuasion (Higbee 1969). More specifically, the following conclusions have been drawn:

- Fear appeals can raise awareness of an issue and bring it to the forefront of people's thoughts.
- Fear appeals can make people re-evaluate and change their attitudes.
- Fear may be successful in stimulating an intention to change behaviour sometime in the future.
- In some cases, *immediate* behaviour change takes place shortly after exposure to a fear communication.

In summary, therefore, while the findings do vary considerably between studies, broadly speaking, it is true to say that the research supports the use of fear appeals. The problem, however, is that the research has been very narrowly focused, typically using experiments in laboratory settings, to ask very specific and short-term questions. As we have seen, the resulting answers can, with some difficulty, be resolved into a coherent picture, but many other questions are left begging. Most importantly, it is not clear what happens outside the laboratory where there is much less control, nor what the long-term and wider effects of fear appeals are.

Marketing provides a rubric for asking these bigger questions. Have a try at Exercise 6.2.

> ### EXERCISE 6.2: FEAR IN TRAFFIC SAFETY
>
> You have just been appointed as Head of Communications at the Transport Accident Commission in Victoria, Australia. They have used fear messages consistently for the last 15 years. Log on to their website (www.tacsafety. com.au) and click on CAMPAIGNS followed by any of the campaign topics to view some of the road safety ads. As a social marketer, what questions does their approach raise?
>
> You might, for example, like to consider the following:
>
> a) What will our clients do with these messages?
>
> b) What benefits will they get from them?
>
> c) How will it affect our brand name?
>
> d) How will it affect their feelings for our other products?
>
> e) What about our non-targets who will also see the message?
>
> f) What are our competitors doing?
>
> g) Where do we go from here?
>
> h) What about alternative approaches?
>
> i) Are our messages ethically acceptable?

a) *What will our customers do with the message?*

Outside the laboratory, audiences can choose whether or not to accept our messages; they cannot be compelled to pay attention any more than they can be compelled to drive safely or give up smoking. This creates several potential barriers: the audience may not look at the message at all; they may look at it, but ignore it; they may look at it, accept it, but misunderstand it; or they may look at it, understand it, but rationalize it (e.g. 'that couldn't happen to me', 'there are other greater risks' or simply 'life is risky'). All of these barriers – especially the last – can be accentuated by fear appeals – look at point 1 in Box 6.2. In a world where mass media messages are an optional extra, it may make more sense to use subtlety and compromise than brute force.

At a more fundamental level, it is arguable that campaigns employing extreme fear appeals, such as those used in Victoria by the Road Safety Commission (Exercise 6.2), undermine the whole notion of voluntary behaviour. The ads literally say accept our message or *'you're a bloody idiot'*. The danger is that people will reject such uncompromising approaches, or, like characters in the movie

Crash, even do the opposite of what is proposed. This latter response is not as far-fetched as it may sound. Focus groups conducted at ISM suggested that certain young men enjoy gory road safety ads in the same way as horror movies: *'that was a cracker that one'*, *'that's brilliant that, when you saw her face get smashed up'*, *'really clever'*, *'and you hear it go bang, crack!'*. Social change practitioners would no doubt be appalled to discover they are competing with violent pornographers!

b) *What benefits will they get from them?*
Voluntary behaviour is benefit driven, so paying attention to mass media messages, just like buying Coke or driving safely, must provide the target with something they want. As Barry Day, vice-chairman of McCann-Erickson Worldwide, expressed it, 'I believe an ad should be a reward' (Foote 1981). The question then is: 'What reward does a fear appeal offer?', and, by extension, is being upset, scared and/or discomfited much of a reward?

c) *How will it affect our brand name?*
Coca-Cola, Nike and Marlboro will all be very careful to ensure that any ads they produce not only work effectively in their own right, but also enhance or (at the very least) do no damage to the company and the product's good name – typically encapsulated in the brand. Most successful brands are the result of decades of careful effort and design.

Social marketing organizations have their equivalents of brands; they have an image and reputation with the public. The question then is how do fear appeals affect this reputation? Do claims that are felt to be exaggerated, or at least not to reflect people's everyday experience, discredit the communicator? Do messages that cause short-term offence, but which might be justified by high awareness figures, do long-term damage to the sender's good name? The issue of how damaging fear appeals can be is illustrated well in Case Study 23 on p. 498, Donovan *et al.*'s evaluation of the 'White Ribbon Day' campaign in Australia, 2006.

d) *How will it affect their feelings for our other products?*
Fear messages say something about the absolute risk of the behaviour being addressed, but also imply things about the relative risk of other behaviours. Take traffic safety as an example: a very fearful anti-drink campaign may lead audiences to assume that other driving behaviours, such as speeding, are less dangerous. Focus groups with young drivers conducted at the University of Wollongong in New South Wales (see Box 6.2) showed that, while drunk driving and speeding were recognized as risky behaviours, others, such as driving at night and driving while under the influence of marijuana, were not. Indeed, some respondents interpreted the constant messaging on drunk driving as implicitly endorsing the alternative of marijuana use. The option of extending the traffic topics addressed by fear messages to cover all potential risks is equally problematic. It would likely lead to overload and rationalization: *'I know the roads are dangerous, but I have to get on with my life'*.

It is also worth remembering that road use is only one source of danger in people's life (and danger is only one source of problems). For example, tobacco use kills more people in Europe than traffic, crime and accidents in the home and workplace combined.

Fear messages need to reflect this reality, if only for ethical reasons.

BOX 6.2: YOUNG AUSTRALIAN DRIVERS AND THE USE OF FEAR

Focus groups with young (18–24-year-old) drivers conducted recently at the University of Wollongong in New South Wales revealed worrying tendencies in their response to fear-based messages. The discussions examined responses to ads they had seen on television in the last few months and years, which had been dominated by hard-hitting messages on drunk driving and speeding. Three findings stand out:

1. The young drivers were becoming inured to fear messages and numerous comments were made about being tired of being told what to do and that speeding and drunk driving are dangerous.

   'the ads are all the same, can't speed, can't drink and drive or you will crash – so what? Everyone knows that . . . they don't stop me' (Eric, 18)

   'ever since I can remember the ads have been about what happens when you speed . . . I stopped taking any notice of them ages ago' (Jenny, 21)

   'the ads are silly, the latest ad shows a guy crashing this big powerful car after speeding and killing people, then right after is an ad for the same car showing these young guys enjoying themselves in it . . . I just turn off from the anti-speeding ads now' (Dean, 23)

2. Other risky driving behaviours such as driving at night or with lots of friends in the car were not even on their radar. As long as they did not speed or drink they felt they were OK.

   'I guess other things are dangerous but not as bad as speeding and drink driving' (Tim, 16)

   'I don't think there is a problem if you have four or five of your mates in the car with you' (Michael, 18)

   'No one has said that driving at night is more dangerous than driving at daytime . . . have they?' (Samantha, 22)

3. Dysfunctional solutions emerged from the narrow focus on alcohol; most notably the less well educated of the young people were inclined to see

no problem with marijuana use and driving. The broader idea of mind-altering substances in general impairing driving had been lost.

'smoking some weed then driving home isn't as dangerous as having a heap of beers at a party' (Tiffany, 16)

'when I go out and if I'm driving and I had a choice between dope and alcohol then it's a no brainer . . . you're safer with the dope' (Adam, 20)

'I have a friend and he thinks his driving improves when he has had some herb' (Sam, 24)

(Source: Noble *et al.* 2006)

e) *What about our non-targets who will also see the message?*
   Targeting is an important aspect of marketing: only well-targeted products and messages can really satisfy customer needs. However, messages transmitted in the mass media will inevitably reach other people as well as the intended target. Sticking with road safety, TV ads aimed at 18–24-year-old 'boy racers' will also reach older drivers. The use of fear in these circumstances can have two untoward effects. First, it may breed complacency among older speeding drivers by implying that deaths on the roads are the fault of other inexperienced and unskilled drivers. Second, it may cause unwarranted anxiety among other road users, perhaps discouraging parents from letting their children play outside or walk to school.

f) *What are our competitors doing?*
   As we will discuss in Chapter 7, social marketers frequently have to compete with commerce. Tobacco, alcohol, fast food, car producers – among others – frequently push in the opposite direction. Even a cursory look at their advertising shows that they make relatively little use of fear.

g) *Where do we go from here?*
   Fear appeals present both creative and strategic problems. On the creative front, once fear has been used, there is a need to increase it on each subsequent occasion to have the same impact. At what point does this cross the threshold of acceptability? On the other hand, is there a point at which people become inured? (Have another look at Box 6.2.) On this point, Henley and Donovan remind us of 'an unintended consequence of the frequent use of fear-arousal in social marketing may be the creation of a sense of helplessness both in the target market and in unintended markets' (1999: 1).

   Turning to strategy, if marketing tells us that success is dependent on building long-term relationships with the customer, the strategic question becomes: is fear a good basis for a relationship? Even parents rapidly abandon it as a pedagogical option as their offspring leave early childhood.

h) *What about alternative approaches?*

It is clear then that fear approaches present considerable costs to social marketers. The main benefit it offers is high profile: strong emotional messages attract a lot of attention. But other approaches can also have a strong emotional pull – love, excitement, sex, hope, humour and sophistication are all used successfully by commercial advertisers. The key issue therefore is not 'Should fear appeals be used?' but 'Will they do the job better and more efficiently than alternative approaches?'

i) *Are our messages ethically acceptable?*

The final question a marketer will ask (or be compelled to ask by the relevant regulatory authorities) is: 'Do our messages meet normal ethical standards?' Will people be hurt or damaged by them? The fact that we social marketers tend to fight on the side of the angels does not absolve us from this responsibility. The end cannot be used to justify the means as shown in the 'White Ribbon Day' campaign Case Study 23 on p. 498.

EMOTION AND BRANDING

From a social marketer's perspective, then, fear messages leave many questions unanswered. However, the one thing they do confirm for us is that our behaviour is driven by both rational and emotional factors (the head and heart concept again). As Joan Bakewell put it: 'for many people reasoned argument is not the final arbiter of how they choose to live their lives. They are swayed by feelings, moved by loyalties, willing to set logic aside for the sake of psychic comfort' (2006: 7). Their recognition of this encourages commercial marketers' to produce lots of advertising that focuses on feelings, promotes a product's or a company's image, generates positive associations and generally makes the potential customer feel good.

Research suggests that three other factors make emotional messages particularly persuasive:

- they are better able to gain consumers' attention than factual messages. Audiences are under pressure from an increasing clutter of advertising and promotional messages, and it becomes impossible to cognitively process them. They therefore attend selectively to those messages which are relevant, comprehendible and congruent with their *values* (Hawkins and Mothersbaugh 2010);
- they encourage deeper processing of the message and as a result tend to be remembered better;
- people buy products (and engage in behaviours) to satisfy not only objective, functional needs, but also symbolic and emotional ones, such as self-enhancement and group identification. The most obvious example of this is cigarette smoking. When they first take up the habit, the prospective smoker does not have an objective need for nicotine, but rather a symbolic need to display independence or rebellion (Barton *et al.* 1982).

Lefebvre *et al.* (1995) also remind us that all social marketing communications have an emotional dimension – a 'personality' or 'tonality' – whether the sender intends it or not. They caution that we – just like our commercial counterparts – must use research, design and careful targeting to ensure that the tonality matches the needs of their target audience. Leathar (1980) and Monahan (1995) go a step further and argue that we should actively promote positive images about health: 'Positive affect can be used to stress the benefits of healthy behaviour, to give individuals a sense of control, and to reduce anxiety or fear. All of these tactics are likely to enhance the success of a communication campaign' Monahan (1995).

On a more specific level, qualitative research conducted by the Health Education Authority in England with pregnant women (Bolling and Owen 1996) also emphasizes the importance of emotional communication, concluding that messages have to be sympathetic, supportive and non-judgemental. The primary need, the research suggested, is to establish a sense of trust. This resonates with the discussions of relationship marketing in Chapters 2 and 4 and value co-creation in Chapter 10.

BRANDING

The brand is the marketers' most advanced emotional tool. It combines and reinforces the functional and emotional benefits of the offering (Murphy 1986; de Chernatony 1993) and so adds value, encouraging consumption and loyalty. In essence, a good marque facilitates recognition, makes a promise and, provided the full marketing back-up is in place, delivers satisfaction. This last point is vital: promise without delivery is extremely damaging. To paraphrase Wally Olins, it is like painting the toilet door when the cistern is broken. Inevitably, therefore, the brand is developed using not just communications, but the whole marketing mix (see Chapter 4).

The process also needs care and time, and to be driven by customer needs – which will be both individual and social. At an individual level, a brand will be chosen because it is liked and matches the person's self-image. At a social level, brands can be used by consumers to tell other people more about themselves, particularly with conspicuously consumed products. Moreover brands can also provide very practical benefits, making consumption easier. They can act as guarantees of quality or reduce risks by confirming that 'this product is for you'. For example, for young people, quick and clear brand identification can make both the buying and smoking of forbidden products such as cigarettes much less risky.

Over time, brands become a fast and powerful way of confirming the synergy – the relationship – between marketer and customer. Indeed, it can be argued that successful brands are only part-owned by the company – the customer also has a share. When Coca-Cola changed their formulation a few years ago, its ultimate failure and the need to scurry back to Coca-Cola Classic was partly put down to consumer displeasure at *their* brand being adulterated.

There is also evidence that branding may be a particularly effective way to reach people in deprived communities. Research into how working-class populations use cultural symbols in advertising found that these groups are often poorly informed about the objective merits of different products and therefore tend to rely more heavily than other groups on 'implicit meanings' – context, price, image – to judge products (Durgee 1986). Similarly, de Chernatony (1993) and Cacioppo and Petty (1989) found that people in deprived communities are less likely to evaluate products on a rational, objective basis, but look for clues as to the product's value in terms of its price or its image. They argued that the symbolic appeal of brands is particularly effective in targeting those individuals who do not have the time, skills or motivation to evaluate the objective attributes and benefits of a particular campaign.

The use of such a powerful emotional tool by commercial operators, and its particular influence over vulnerable groups raises obvious concerns. We touched on these in Chapter 1, when we noted that branding is implicated in the uptake of smoking, drinking and unhealthy diets in young people, and will give them a full airing in the next two chapters. For the moment, though, let us focus on the more positive implication – that branding might be a useful tool for social marketers. A review, conducted on behalf of the UK's National Institute for Health and Clinical Excellence (NICE), for example, suggests that brands may be an effective way of reaching information-deprived communities with social marketing messages (McDermott *et al.* 2005). Exercise 6.3 explores the possibilities.

EXERCISE 6.3: BRANDING IN SOCIAL MARKETING

The Scottish Health Education group (SHEG) was the government body responsible for health education in Scotland in the 1980s and early 1990s. Over a number of years, they commissioned a full range of research on their mass media activity, from basic problem definition work, through concept and pre-testing to evaluation. This began to reveal a number of recurrent problems, including a tendency for the advertising to be:

- Negative rather than positive. Smoking campaigns emphasized the dangers of smoking, not the benefits of non-smoking; contraception advice threatened people with unwanted pregnancies, rather than stressing the advantages of safer sex.

- Authoritarian rather than empathetic. Material seemed to be telling people what to do and how to run their lives, rather than enabling and encouraging them to make their own informed health decisions.

- Long-term rather than short-term focused. Anti-smoking material emphasized the health risks of cigarettes, many of which are very long term and probabilistic.

- Fragmented from other non-media activity. It did not connect with other types of intervention such as local services or policy changes – there was only one P in the marketing mix.
- Topic-based rather than whole-person orientated. Separate campaigns were run on drinking, smoking and contraception, seemingly ignoring the fact that these activities can overlap and often reflect the individual's overall lifestyle.

How might branding help resolve these problems?

(Source: Hastings and Leathar 1986)

While some of the weaknesses highlighted by SHEG's research could be removed during pre-testing of individual campaigns, it is branding that can communicate a general lifestyle message of empowerment – 'promoting good health in much the same way as a marketing company would promote its corporate identity' (Hastings and Leathar 1986). Branding links positive imagery to clear solutions and real health problems by, for instance, providing branded health products.

Abraham Brown's Case Study 6, the EU 'Help' anti-smoking campaign, on p. 344, which aimed to prevent smoking uptake among young Europeans, shows how. First, branding is about the needs and values of the target audience. Qualitative research showed European youths were amenable to getting help with quitting or avoiding smoking. But, for them, it was more about tobacco than smoking – as well as smoking prevention and cessation, they were concerned about second-hand smoke. Second, branding has to reflect these needs and values through the brand attributes of packaging, positioning and framing. In EU Help, this was achieved with a web-driven social media campaign with the tagline 'a life without tobacco' rather than 'a life without smoking'. And all of this has worked – 2010 campaign evaluation results report 43 per cent of respondents recalling a minimum of one ad and 90 per cent understood the tobacco control message. Furthermore, smokers reported using this awareness to quit smoking.

Box 6.3 explores the birth and development of a social marketing brand to address problem gambling. It provides a fascinating insight into the complexities, pitfalls and potential of branding in social marketing. Read it through and then have a try at Exercise 6.4.

BOX 6.3: DEVELOPING A 'COMMUNITY BRAND' – 'CHOICE NOT CHANCE'

In 2006 the Health Sponsorship Council (HSC) was tasked with developing a national social marketing strategy to address gambling harms. The strategy included significant national communications activities and HSC decided that a brand would assist positioning, collective action and coherence.

Part of HSC's operating philosophy is that social brands need to be community brands. By this we mean that instead of operating to commercial brand management practice which sees brands centrally and rigidly managed to maintain their identity and integrity, the brand is designed for the community and is 'given away'. The identity and integrity of the brand grows and develops because it is used by the communities that want to act on the issue being addressed – social marketing and community development blend. Control is not required, permission isn't needed (though some friendly advice and usable tools help with consistency). Success is measured by how often it is used by others as well as to what extent it is embraced and understood by the intended audiences. This had been a very successful approach with other HSC brands such as 'Smokefree' and 'SunSmart'.

In considering how to provide what was hoped would be an enduring brand to carry many years of messages and themes the HSC analysed existing terms and names used by the gambling harm minimisation sector. 'Problem Gambling' was the almost universally used descriptor by the key organisations and for communications activities, etc. HSC also considered a number of other possibilities but none worked well and therefore a 'Problem Gambling' brand was launched with phase one of the campaign.

Over the first few years of the programme concerns were raised by the problem gambling sector about the brand – primarily that it focused on the problem, not the solution. Many within the sector commented that it was difficult to usefully use the brand as part of their public health work because the public immediately turned away from it. Unlike other HSC community brands, the sector were not actively utilising the brand as part of their work and therefore the ideal of having a single image being used to carry messages and themes nationally was not being achieved.

At the implementation level it failed the 'tee-shirt test'. Would you want to wear a tee shirt that boldly proclaimed 'Problem Gambling'? Would you visit a marquee at a community event that was branded 'Problem Gambling' – might as well put up a sign – herpes sufferers line up here! It was not engaging, it was not offering a solution.

So, HSC undertook an extensive exercise with the sector to identify the values that they believed were inherent in their work and therefore that a brand should reflect. A creative process was then entered into – and not surprisingly it proved very difficult to find a solution. However – out of a very exhausting process emerged the thought – 'Choice Not Chance'. The sector believed that it met their needs – empowering, speaks to individuals, families and communities, and can be related to various campaign messages over time. At a community level, this could mean making a choice to end harmful gambling, rather than leaving the effects of gambling in your community to chance. On a personal level, it might mean making a choice to reach out and help someone or as a gambler to choose more positive and certain options rather than the chance associated with gambling.

A question mark was whether the name would be immediately understood as it could be about any number of things. However, it was agreed that the visuals and core messages provided alongside it would provide the context. In addition, a strapline such as 'let's choose to end harmful gambling' would be added to help support the brand, particularly in the first few years.

The 'Choice Not Chance' brand has been a success in that it has been embraced by the sector and is enthusiastically used and displayed as part of the many community based activities undertaken by people interested in minimising gambling harms. It passed the 'tee-shirt' test and is being used to promote individual behaviour change, help seeking and societal change. It has assisted collective effort and coherence.

Iain Potter
Former CEO Health Sponsorship Council
August 2012

EXERCISE 6.4: BUILDING A WINNING BRAND

When you have read through the case, try to answer Iain Potter's three questions:

1. Why wasn't the 'Problem Gambling' brand working?
2. What traits should a brand carry?
3. How could a community brand be supported and encouraged?

Iain answered his own questions for us. The brand failed, he explains, because 'the people who should be using it – the community – did not feel comfortable with it, it was problem oriented not solution focussed, it did not represent the values the sector believed were inherent in their work. As a result they didn't like it and it didn't encourage public engagement'. Turning to key characteristics, he argues that 'a brand should carry the personality traits that you believe are central to your offering – in this case these included empowerment, community, caring, aspiration'. Finally, addressing the issue of support, he emphasizes the key notion of involvement, collaboration and co-creation: 'the development process could include sector involvement, it should be used on all national promotional materials, an offering of branded resources could be made available to the sector, merchandise could be offered to sector workers – meeting the "tee-shirt" test – sector personnel could be invited to suggest resources that could be developed'.

Ultimately, the case illustrates beautifully how branding can help us think collectively and coherently about the problems we are trying to tackle, making sure that the needs of all stakeholders are being met. It also provides a refreshing illustration of social marketers being prepared to talk about and learn from their mistakes.

[Note: readers who want to look further into the role of branding in social marketing might want to consult the book *Public Health Branding* (Evans and Hastings 2008).]

The potential of branding in social marketing is unsurprising. It sits comfortably with ideas of active engagement and partnership working. Recent technical innovations in communications have reinforced this empowering approach to behavioural and social change. Traditional mass media are essentially unidirectional, and messages are predetermined – you cannot have a dialogue with a poster or a TV ad. As we noted above, it this that makes developmental research so important. Digital media takes things to a new level: blogs, Twitter and Facebook have made the theory of jointly created meaning a practical reality. They also provide a whole new arena for research.

PARTICIPATORY MEDIA

Social marketing has embraced these possibilities (see Box 6.4 for example).

BOX 6.4: NEW MEDIA, COMMUNICATION AND RESEARCH COME TOGETHER

The Internet is a resource available to an increasing number of European citizens, especially health consumers and health professionals on the web. The profile of online health consumers can be broadly defined as patients, patients' friends/relatives and citizens in general. Health information-seeking behaviour varies depending on type of information sought, reasons for, and experience of, searching.

Women are more likely than men to search for health information, and online health consumers tend to be more educated, earn more and have high-speed Internet access at home and at work. Internet-based health information is accessed from a variety of sources, including websites run by organizations, homepages run by individuals and online support groups where people actively exchange health information and blogs.

Health professionals' use of the Internet to obtain health and medical information has increased. Eighty per cent of physicians reported experience of patients
presenting printed Internet-sourced health information at visits. Thus, the traditional doctor–patient relationship is being challenged as 'nothing has changed
clinical practice more fundamentally than one recent innovation: the Internet'.
However, the wealth of information available means that 'healthcare professionals are increasingly finding that they have more information available than
they can handle with confidence in their busy time schedules' and 'the hardest
task now is to actually locate the information required from the flood of information received'. The literature also highlights the difficulty of identifying and
filtering the most useful, accurate and credible sources while searching online
for health information.

As more people use the Internet as a source of health information, the issue of
source credibility and trust in websites becomes important. A lack of research
in the European context means that the potential of the Internet as a source of
health information may not be fully understood. Nevertheless, the Internet
would appear to provide the ideal medium for the provision of information
targeted at the prevention and control of communicable disease for both health
consumers and health professionals in Europe.

(Source: Adapted from Higgins *et al.* 2011)

Arguably it is the active, empowered engagement in digital media of Gen C (those
born between 1974 and 1994) – a phenomenon that has led researcher Mark
Grindle (2004) to rename them 'participatory media' – that has the most fundamental implications for social marketing. It provides an electronic and ubiquitous
platform for the grassroots activism of social change and community engagement
(see Chapter 10). This has the power to transform ordinary people and community
groups from passive message recipients into fellow storytellers, network builders
and co-creators of value. They are now able to search for, or 'pull', information they
want, instead of waiting for it to be 'pushed' to them (ibid.). As Lefebvre notes,
mobile technologies provide:

More than a communication device – they can become marketing tools that address
all elements of the marketing mix when strategically considered in the context of
how people use them. Cell phones are an always-on, two-way communication
channel, a signal or cue for action, a resource of instant access to health information, a tool for social support and the development of social capital, a production
tool, a way to engage audiences, and a data collection and feedback device.

(Lefebvre 2009)

And it's not just Gen C. All segments of society, rich, poor, young and old, are
adopting participatory media, admittedly at different rates. Resonating with Grindle

(2004), Mays *et al.* (2011: 188) also demonstrate that participatory media changes 'the ways consumers communicate, share, and seek information, facilitating more active participation in the information exchange process' and 'understanding their potential for content interactivity and constant connectivity with large, diverse populations is critically important' for the social marketer.

Participatory media help make value co-creation and relationship marketing possible as 'individuals can actively acquire, prioritize, and interpret information when, where, how, and from whom they want' (ibid.: 183). The dialogue and inter-actions needed for partnership working can occur and be shared in real-time two-way conversations and engagements through connected storytelling of experiences and lived lives. Pictures, videos, games, words, music, sounds, events – a collage of communication tools and channels can be simultaneously shared between the client, partners, stakeholders and social marketers. Interestingly, though, this progress is dependent on traditional constructs such as trust, likeability, language, source reputation and source credibility (see Mays *et al.* 2011, and refer back to our discussion of relationship marketing in Chapter 2).

In this way, digital media can again be seen as an extension to current thinking. In particular, echoing our discussions of planning in Chapter 4, it raises a series of strategic and operational questions about the target audience, the organizational resources and the social marketing strategy/intervention (see Box 6.1). *Plus ça change, plus c'est la même chose!*

The commercial sector is also embracing digital media and learning lessons about the rules of engagement – in particular, that the agency of digital participants has to be given due respect. People use participatory media for their own purposes – to meet like-minded people, help each other, develop themselves and gain status (Gossieaux and Moran 2010). They adopt a healthy and critical distance from commerce and its products, even if it's simply at the level of pointing their peers towards better deals – and/or behaviours elsewhere. Moreover, significant rewards are made available in the form of peer approval and social status to those who do. Commerce is learning quickly that participatory media grows and speaks from the bottom up; it allows marketers to come alongside customers, listen to them, under-stand *their* motives and desires – and then helps *them* to co-create *their own* new products, processes, behaviours and lifestyles. This reminds us that digital media present research as well as intervention possibilities (see Chapter 5).

The prospects of participatory media for social marketers are indeed exciting, and the greatest potential will come, Grindle (2010) argues, when we move beyond a focus on technological wizardry and begin to absorb some of the storytelling skills of traditional media (perhaps best exemplified by commercial cinema). Interactive storytelling allows people not just to participate but also to perform in a journey of their own making. Cinematic storytelling has the ability to structure and evoke powerful emotions – pride, self-worth, identity, belonging, status and validation: it will make it possible for people to experiment with whole new lifestyles in safe and self-asserting, life-affirming contexts. Refusing a cigarette from your mate can be

Table 6.1 Strategic and operational questions for use of participatory media

Target Audience Characteristics	Can the needs of the population of interest be addressed by using new media?
	What are the media use behaviours among those in the population of interest?
	Can the population be broken down and segmented based on their use of new media?
	What members of the population use new media the most? Is it best suited to target a certain segment of the population?
	Is access to the media a barrier to achieving programme objectives? If so, what prevents access within the population of interest?
	Do members of the population of interest prefer to use the media and are they comfortable doing so? Do they have the knowledge and skills needed to use the media?
	Is the new media accepted by members of the target population?
	Are there costs that may result from using new media, such as loss of support, trust, or credibility in the population of interest?
Organisational Resource Issues	Is there substantial monetary cost associated with the use of the media? Are these costs justifiable relative to the potential benefits?
	What proportion of programmatic resources (e.g. time, financial) is needed to invest in this media? Will that divert resources from other important aspects of the programme?
	Are key programme stakeholders aware of the new media and the relevance within the population of interest?
Social Marketing Strategy and Intervention	Does the medium augment the proposed strategy in some way in order to achieve programme objectives?
	Does the application of new media help reduce costs involved for members of the target population to access the social marketing message(s)/product(s)?
	Is it possible to evaluate the impact of the new media on the health and social outcome(s) of interest?

Source: Adapted from: Mays *et al.* (2011)

very challenging in real life – and it is unlikely to deliver any greater status or rewards – but as an avatar such possibilities can be tried out, tested and rewarded:

By combining interactivity and reward structures – as evolved by the computer games industry – with storytelling and emotional structuring – as evolved by commercial cinema – Social Marketing can help clients to experiment outside of their local, real world familial and peer group milieu – as many young people around the world are beginning to do and enjoy. By embracing participatory media and emergent storytelling forms, Social Marketers can collaborate with and help to co-create identities, environments, behaviours and life styles. It can help

participants rehearse real-life challenges, take on real-life antagonists and experience rewards and emotions unavailable anywhere else. We can be heroes.

(Grindle 2004, quoted in Hastings 2011: 11)

The last sentiment was recognized fully by game designer Jane McGonigal who, in collaboration with World Bank, ran an initiative last year called *Evoke: A crash course in changing the world* (Hawkins 2010).[4] Participants were given the opportunity to take on the role of hero and experiment with the challenges of real-world development scenarios played out online. Real-world financial rewards and opportunities were given to those who were able to empower others and collaborate to collect real-world evidence. No formal evaluation has been released at the time of writing, but the weblogs are certainly very positive. It's also seen in *Operation Transformation* – an Irish lifestyle behaviour change programme. The television show, created by VIP Productions and airing on RTÉ (Ireland's national TV broadcaster), challenges five overweight or obese individuals – or 'leaders' as they are called on the show – to change their weight, health and lifestyle in general. They receive assistance from a fitness instructor, nutritionist and psychologist. The general public are encouraged to adopt and follow one of the leaders in order to achieve the same behaviour change goals. The *Operation Transformation* Facebook page has over 65,000 fans. These 65,000 fans participate and co-create stories with one another, offering support, motivation, tips and camaraderie for those trying to reach behaviour change goals.[5]

Participatory media clearly have much social marketing potential, giving more power to the people and pushing towards a further rebalancing between expert and citizen.

DIGITAL DOWNSIDES

However, before we get carried away, the digital domain is not a magic bullet. Nor is it revolutionary – it just extends and reinforces what good social marketing should already be doing: listening, empowering and partnering to bring about beneficial behavioural and social change. There are also three specific concerns to consider:

1. **Unhealthy marketing** – As we noted, commerce is increasingly active in hyperspace and this activity is frequently antithetical to social marketing efforts. For example, last year, Facebook and Diageo announced a link-up. We will look in more detail in Chapter 8 (see Figure 8.2), but, at this point, it is sufficient to note the drinks company will benefit from Facebook's SWAT team of marketing (a term that originates from the Los Angeles police force and refers to the 'Special Weapons And Tactics' needed to control dangerous criminals); that this team will enable them not just to sell their drinks to young people but also recruit them as brand advocates; and that the particular interest is in developing countries. Have a try at Exercise 6.5.

EXERCISE 6.5: 'HEINEKEN MAKES DEAL WITH GOOGLE IN SOCIAL-MEDIA PUSH'

Why would Heineken want to link up with Google in this way? Imagine you work for Balance North East (www.balancenortheast.co.uk) an NGO focused on reducing the harm caused by alcohol, especially to young people. What implications does this development have for your work? How would you respond? If you had two minutes with the Minister of Health for England what would you ask him to do about it, if anything?

http://online.wsj.com/article/SB10001424052702304584004576417301681
632980.html

2. **Corporatization** – The operating platforms for many digital media are becoming corporatized. In his recent book *The Master Switch* (2011), Timothy Wu shows how each new generation of communications technology – telephone, radio, television – began as a grassroots and open free for all, but then rapidly was taken over and controlled by the corporate sector. The same, he argues, is now happening to digital media.

3. **The digital divide** – Getting and building a presence online costs money. Doing this in a sophisticated way is even more expensive. The result is that a digital divide has opened up between those with resources who can exploit the Internet, and those without who may even struggle to access it. Go back to Exercise 6.5 and imagine you are Head of Campaigns at Balance North East and one of your key tasks concerns 'Educating and informing – giving you all the information and support you need to make you aware of and understand the issues related to alcohol so you can make informed choices'. How might you use digital communications to achieve this? How would your efforts compare with those of Diageo and Heineken?

There is, then, as with other aspects of marketing, a need to adopt a critical perspective when assessing the contribution of digital media. We will return to this topic in the next two chapters.

INTERNAL SOCIAL MARKETING

So far in this chapter, we have focused on the media, but remember our topic is communication – and as Lincoln demonstrated from the outset face-to-face interactions can be the most powerful. Ann Smith (2011) reminds us that this is particularly so when we want to connect with the social marketing 'sales force', whether they be classroom teachers, health and safety officers or smoking cessation workers. She explains that such internal communications with employees is just as important to the social marketer as external communication. Ann also brings to us an innovative application of internal social marketing in Case Study 18 on p. 456, which shows how the workplace can become the locale for creating sustainable pro-environmental behaviours to reduce an organization's carbon emissions though 'change champions'. This is accomplished through three elements of internal social marketing: objectives, barriers and behaviours and their impact on workplace pro-environmental behaviours.

Essentially, social marketers have to connect with employees (internal customers) as their behaviour can have major consequences for the behaviour of clients (external customers). In health areas, social marketing services cover, for example, smoking cessation, family planning/sexual health, alcohol reduction and cancer screening. For pro-environmental behaviours, services are important for waste disposal, water conservation, energy effectiveness, forest conservation and transportation. In all such scenarios, the service providers' and clients' interactions are woven together as co-creators of behaviour change. In Smith's words:

> The service encounter provides the stage for role players to enact performances which will impact on their service satisfaction and quality evaluations as well as emotional reactions. Employee behaviour may differ from that expected by customers as a result of many factors including, lack of understanding of customer requirements; role ambiguity/conflict; low self-efficacy and low levels of perceived control. Alternatively, employees may 'delight' customers, exceeding customers' expectations.
>
> (2011: 309)

For this form of double engagement, internal and external clients, Smith recommends internal marketing to highlight 'gaps' in organizational processes, which can give rise to a breakdown between value design and delivery, e.g. poor service, customer dissatisfaction and client complaints. One such gap can be the lack of relationships between 'front-stage' and 'back-stage' employees. Smith's model for this double or internal/external client engagement process is captured in Figure 6.5.

Effectively, shared values, leadership and internal communications result in employees forming perceptions about the service/product. In turn, these employee perceptions shape and influence *their* behaviours around the design, delivery, experience and interactions concerning the service/product. Employee behaviour *affects* and *effects* that of the clients, which we measure as service quality, client satisfaction levels and ultimately behaviour change.

WRAP-UP

Communication, whether in traditional or new media, is a complex process in which both communicator and audience are actively involved. This means that careful audience research is needed to decide whether, how and with what combination of other marketing activity it should be used. When designing a communication approach, social marketers have to decide whether the media can help resolve a particular social marketing problem, and, if so, what task it can perform, as well as guiding decision making about all aspects of message design.

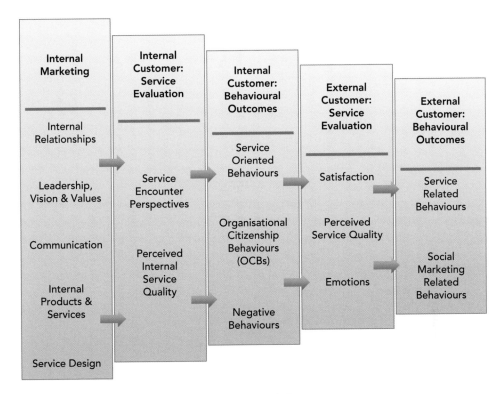

Figure 6.5 Engaging internal clients with external clients
Source: Smith (2011)

Relevant communication activities include problem definition; medium choice; language selection; images and links.

The communication job becomes more complex when the vagaries of human decision making are factored in – especially our tendency to decide things on emotional as well as rational bases. It's disappointing that the principal acknowledgement of this emotional dimension of our lives in the health and safety sector comes in the form of fear-based communications, which raise many marketing questions. A more interesting line of thought is that other emotions, such as wellbeing, vitality, happiness, coolness and validation, could be engaged more effectively through branding and relational approaches with much greater strategic change potential.

The rise of digital media has reinforced this need to embrace the role of individual agency and empowerment to bring about change. It is more true than ever that social marketers have to think in terms of doing things with, rather than to, their clients. This, however, reignites the questions about relative power we discussed in Chapter 1, and the need not just for individual but also systemic change. To return to the Gettysburg Address, Lincoln warns us that the soldier's struggle, however brave, will amount to nothing without a proper democratic system – in his words, 'government of the people, by the people, for the people'. We will turn a critical eye onto these broader issues in the next three chapters.

Table 6.2 Descriptions, characteristics and examples of new media

Technology	Description	Characteristics	Example(s)
Social network websites	Interactive websites in which users are able to create a profile, which might contain personal information, photos, blogs, music, messages from other users, and a list of 'friends'	Users interact with their friends by sharing information through public or private messages, posting photos, writing and commenting on personal blogs, and giving gifts	www.myspace.com www.facebook.com www.bebo.com
Personal wireless devices	Portable devices that allow consumers to connect with information and others	Portable wireless devices enable consumers to have voice conversations, send and receive text messages, access email, the Internet, and a host of other activities	Cellular/mobile phones Smartphones Personal digital assistants Portable media players
Blogs	Blogs provide commentary on various topics, report on news, relay information and/or share personal experiences	Bloggers generally write on a particular subject. Blogs typically include hyperlinks to related blogs, news articles and other online information. Most blogs have a comments section following each blog post, in which readers and bloggers can share comments	http://blog.aids.gov www.cdc.gov/ healthmarketing/blog.htm http://getreadyforflu. blogspot.com/
Wikis	A wiki is an online collaboration tool allowing multiple users to post and edit content about a particular subject	Users can post information about a topic, which can subsequently be added to, changed or deleted by other users. An effective tool for asynchronous online information sharing	www.wikipedia.com www.healthwikinews.com
Sharing sites	Interactive websites where users can share information with others in many different formats	Users can share web links, news clips, photographs, video, audio, and other content	www.youtube.com www.flickr.com www.digg.com
Virtual worlds	A virtual world is an Internet site where users, or residents, interact with one another through avatars. An avatar is a virtual representation of an individual	Avatars act much as people do in the real world, living, working, playing, building structures, attending events, and travelling throughout the Second Life environment. The action is controlled by users	www.secondlife.com www.whyville.com
eGames	Electronic games, or eGames, are interactive games that are played through an electronic application such as the Internet, a videogame console or a mobile phone	eGames provide users with opportunities for training on a specific topic, to build new skills and knowledge, and to engage in physical activities	CDC eGames BAM and Choose Respect Dance, Dance Revolution

Source: Adapted from Mays et al. (2011: 188)

Reflective questions

1. What is meant by the two-way communication process? Why is it important to the social marketer?

2. Define, in your own words in two or three sentences, each of the key words at the beginning of this chapter.

3. Explain the function of problem definition; medium; language; images and links in the communication process.

4. 'The research into the effectiveness of fear appeal is inconclusive.' Elaborate with illustrations.

5. Branding represents an alternative to fear campaigns. How? When? Where and Why?

6. What is new media? What should the social marketer consider when looking to use participatory media?

7. Model and explain internal marketing as it applies to social marketing.

Reflective assignments

1. Conduct an Internet search and describe two common marketing communication models.

2. Locate and critique a social marketing communication example that includes a fear-based message.

3. Locate and review a social marketing example of good and poor branding.

4. Locate and document social marketing examples of the use of each of the new media technologies in Table 6.2.

Write a short paragraph on the how and why each of the following: (a) communication; (b) branding; (c) fear appeals; (d) participatory media; and (e) internal social marketing. *Cross reference* with (1) the four orientation principles of social marketing in Chapter 2; (2) research in Chapter 5; and (3) relationship marketing in Chapter 3.

1. Model and explain how internal marketing works, or does not work, in an organization of your choice.

2. Draw up your Connect traffic lights checklist.

Notes

1 Lincoln A (1863). *The Gettysburg Address*, 19th November, Soldiers' National Cemetery, Gettysburg, P.A.

2 http://en.wikipedia.org/wiki/Edward_Everett#cite_note-Simon41-7/.

3 Healthy Respect is a Scottish Government-funded national health demonstration project for young people and sexual health (2001–2008). For further

information, contact Healthy Respect at NHS Lothian, Deaconess House, 148 Pleasance, Edinburgh. www.healthyrespect.co.uk/.

4 The EVOKE game is available online at: www.urgentevoke.com/.

5 Niamh Gately, Social Marketing Research Fellow with *safe*food, 2012.

References

2000AD (1998) Program 1112, Cover Judge Dredd by Kevin Walker. 23–29 September.

Bakewell, J. (2006) *The Guardian* Review, 23 September.

Barry, T.E. and Howard, D.J. (1990) 'Review and critique of the hierarchy of effects in advertising', *International Journal of Advertising*, 9(2): 121–135.

Barton, J., Chassin, L., Presson, C.C. and Sherman, S.J. (1982) 'Social image factors as motivators of smoking initiation in early and middle adolescence', *Child Development*, 53: 1499–1511.

Bolling, K. and Owen, L. (1996) *Smoking and Pregnancy: A Survey of Knowledge, Attitudes and Behaviour*. London: Health Education Authority.

Burke, J. and Thompson, T. (2000) 'Rachel: Shock photo backed by boyfriend', *The Observer*, 3 March: 10.

Cacioppo, J.T. and Petty, R.E. (1989) 'The elaboration likelihood model: The role of effect and affect laden information processing in persuasion', in Cafferata P. and Tybout, A. (eds) *Cognitive and Affective Responses to Advertising*. Lexington, MA: Lexington Books, pp.69–90.

de Chernatony, L. (1993) 'Categorizing brands: Evolutionary processes underpinned by two key dimensions', *Journal of Marketing Management*, 9(2): 163–188.

Durgee, J.F. (1986) 'How consumer sub-cultures code reality: A look at some code types', *Advances in Consumer Research*, 13: 332–336.

Elliott, R. and Wattanasuwan, K. (1998) 'Brands as symbolic resources for the construction of identity', *International Journal of Advertising*, 16(2): 131–144.

Evans, D.W. and Hastings, G.B. (2008) *Public Health Branding: Applying Marketing for Social Change*. Oxford: Oxford University Press.

Foote, E. (1981) 'Advertising and tobacco', *Journal of the American Medical Association*, 245: 1667–1668.

Gossieaux, F. and Moran, E. (2010) *The Hyper-Social Organization: Eclipse Your Competition by Leveraging Social Media*. New York: McGraw-Hill.

Grindle, M. (2004) 'At what stage is our understanding of the interactive entertainment development industry in Scotland?', paper presented at *The Scottish Media and Communication Association Annual Conference*, 3 December, Dundee: University of Abertay.

Grindle, M. (2010) 'Can computer games save the planet? The role interactive entertainment might play in marketing sustainable consumption', paper presented at the *ISM-Open Conference Changing Times, New Challenges*, 3 November. Milton Keynes: The Open University.

The Guardian (1938) From the Archives: Report of a Radio Broadcast of *The War of the Worlds* from *The Guardian*, November 1, 1938. Online version: www.guardian.

co.uk/fromthearchive/story/0,12269,1075343,00.html. *The Guardian*. Copyright Guardian News and Media Limited 2002.

Hastings, G.B. and Leathar, D.S. (1986) 'Anti-smoking publicity in Scotland: A decade of progress', *New York State Journal of Medicine*, 86(9): 480–484.

Hawkins, D. and Mothersbaugh, D. (2010) *Consumer Behaviour: Building Marketing Strategy*. 11th edition. Maidenhead: McGraw-Hill International.

Hawkins, R. (2010) 'EVOKE – a crash course in changing the world', EduTech A World Bank Blog on ICT use in Education (Weblog), Online: http://blogs. worldbank.org/edutech/evoke-a-crash-course-in-changing-the-world (accessed 27 January 2011).

Hedges, A. (1982) *Testing to Destruction: A Fresh and Critical Look at the Uses of Research in Advertising*. London: Institute of Practitioners in Advertising.

Henley, N. and Donovan, R. (1999) *Unintended consequences of arousing fear in social marketing*, Australian and New Zealand Marketing Academy Conference, Sydney, Australia. Available online at: http://ro.ecu.edu.au/smatl_pubs/14/.

Higbee, K.L. (1969) 'Fifteen years of fear arousal: Research on threat appeals', *Psychological Bulletin*, 62(6): 426–444.

Higgins, O., Sixsmith, J., Barry, M.M. and Domegan, C. (2011) 'A literature review on health information seeking behaviour on the web: A health consumer and health professional perspective'. Stockholm: ECDC.

Katz, E. and Lazarsfeld, P. (1955) *Personal Influence*. New York: The Free Press.

Leathar, D.S. (1980) 'Images in health education advertising', *Health Education Journal*, 39(4): 123–128.

Lefebvre, R.C. (2009) 'The change we need: New ways of thinking about social issues', *On Social Marketing and Social Change*, 29 January 2009. Available from: http://socialmarketing.blogs.com/r_craig_lefebvres_social/2009/01/index. html/.

Lefebvre, R.C., Doner, L., Johnston, C., Loughrey, K., Balch, GI. and Sutton, S.M. (1995) 'Use of database marketing and consumer-based health communication in message design: An example from the office of cancer communications' "5 A Day for Better Health" program', in E. Maibach and R.L. Parrott (eds) *Designing Health Messages. Approaches From Communication Theory and Public Health Practice*. Thousand Oaks, CA: Sage Publications, pp.216–246.

Leventhal, H. (1960) 'Findings and theory in the study of fear communications', *Advances in Experimental Social Psychology*, 5: 119–186.

Lowry, R. (2000) Social Marketing and Communication: Persuading GPs to prescribe sugar-free medicines. Open Wide Summer, Oral Health Promotion Research Group, London

McDermott, L., Stead, M. and Hastings, G. (2005) 'What is and what is not social marketing: The challenge of reviewing the evidence', *Journal of Marketing Management*, 21(5–6): 545–553.

McQuail, D., Blumer, J.G. and Brown, J.R. (1962) 'The television audience, a revised perspective', in D. McQuail (ed.) *Sociology of Mass Communications*. Harmondsworth: Penguin.

Mays, D., Weaver, J.B. and Bernhardt, J.M., (2011) 'New media in social marketing', Ch. 12 in G. Hastings, K. Angus and C. Bryant (eds) *The SAGE Handbook of Social Marketing*. London: Sage Publications Ltd.

Monahan, J.L. (1995) 'Thinking positively: using positive affect when designing messages', in E. Maibach and R.L. Parrott (eds) *Designing Health Messages. Approaches From Communication Theory and Public Health Practice*. Newbury Park, CA: Sage Publications.

Murphy, J. (ed.) (1986) *Branding: A Key Marketing Tool*. New York: McGraw-Hill.

Noble, K.G., Farah, M.J., and McCandliss, B.M. (2006) 'Socioeconomic background modulates cognition–achievement relationships in reading', *Cognitive Development*, 21 (3): 349–368.

Packard, V. (2007) *The Hidden Persuaders*. Brooklyn, New York: IG Publishing.

Redmond, J. (2006) *How to Write a Poem*. UK: Blackwell Publishing, p.7.

Rogers, R.W. (1965) 'A protection motivation theory of fear appeals and attitude change', *Journal of Psychology*, 91: 93–114.

Rosengren, K.E and Windahl, S. (1962) 'Mass media consumption as a functional alternative', in D. McQuail (ed.) *Sociology of Mass Communications*. Harmondsworth: Penguin, pp.166–194.

Rudolph, M.J. (1995) 'The food product development process', *British Food Journal*, 96(3): 3–11.

Smith, A.M. (2011) 'Internal social marketing: Lessons for the field of services marketing', Ch. 20 in G. Hastings, K. Angus and C. Bryant (eds) *The SAGE Handbook of Social Marketing*. London: Sage Publications Ltd.

Tudor, A. (1996) 'On alcohol and the mystique of media effects', in T. O'Sullivan and Y. Jewkes (eds) *The Media Studies Reader*. London: Edward Arnold, pp.164–180.

Wu, Timothy (2011) *The Master Switch: The Rise and Fall of Information Empires*, New York: Vintage Books.

Chapter **7**

Competitive analysis

LOOK AND LEARN . . .

Uggina had woken up with a simple but brilliant idea in her head.

Her man Ugg was the strong silent type. He had once killed a grizzly bear with only his hands, but he did not have Uggina's skill for tracking animals. Nor had he mastered the spear, like Nugg who lived nearby. As a result, they had not eaten meat for nearly three weeks. Uggina set about preparing another breakfast of unappetizing wild millet porridge and, predictably enough, Ugg returned soon after, empty-handed from yet another unsuccessful hunting trip.

She had noticed that the tribe at the other side of the valley did things differently; they hunted in groups. It was this that had given her the brilliant idea, which she now put to Ugg. She suggested that they combine their talents: she would track the animals and Ugg could use his strength to kill them. Now for the tricky bit she thought, as she continued: 'But if the animal we track is a deer or a wild ox, it will run away before you can get your great hands and powerful arms on it.' Ugg glowed with pride at this reference to his strength. 'So why don't we approach Nugg and see if he will help us with his spear'.

'Why should he?' asked Ugg, who didn't like Nugg much and envied his weapon-handling skills. 'And anyway who would get the meat?' 'He might do it because he needs my tracking skills to find the deer, and your strength to protect him from any roving bears,' she replied – 'and we can all share the meat.'

Ugg thought hard about Uggina's idea; thinking was not his forte but he could see the sense in it. No one was taking advantage of anyone else – this was a fair exchange from which all three of them would benefit. Furthermore, the alternative was another day of the awful millet porridge, which Uggina managed to burn every time she made it. Maybe he should suggest to her another exchange: he would do the cooking if she would stick to thinking and see if she could come up with some more revolutionary ideas.

As we noted in Chapter 1, marketing is as old as human society. Uggina's story shows how its key principles of cooperation and mutually beneficial exchange were deployed by our earliest ancestors to overcome the disadvantages of being relatively weak and ill protected from both the weather and our fellow creatures. Our key superiority as a species – our large brains – enabled us to work out, as Uggina did, that our chances of survival are greatly enhanced if we pool our resources and operate collectively; if we can find win-wins. So, marketing is not something that emerged from the US business schools in the middle of the last century, but a timeless protocol for cooperation, mutual benefit and advancement. This book is all about reclaiming this wider purpose.

Uggina's story also tells us a great deal about the benefits of critically analysing the competition. We noted in Chapter 4 that the crucial function of strategic planning starts by looking internally, at our own personal or organizational strengths and weaknesses. Paradoxically, however, our appreciation of these is honed by looking around us at what our rivals are doing. Uggina's analysis of her local community helps her to identify the importance of her own tracking ability and Ugg's strength. It also revealed a crucial gap in spear-throwing ability – the benefits of which were apparent from Nugg's successes. In a sense, the whole discipline of social marketing bears witness to the relevance of this lesson – as we noted in Chapter 1, it originated from attempts to imitate commercial marketing.

Assessing the competition can also sharpen our overall performance: it was Uggina's observation of the competing tribe that gave her her revolutionary idea for cooperation. We social marketers can also learn from the competing marketers around us – even when, as with the fast food, alcohol and tobacco industries, their activities are inimical to ours. As we discuss below, branding is a particularly good example here.

Third, the story tells us something about relative power and its impact on our lives. The trio can track antelope, and defend themselves from bears, but supposing a woolly mammoth happens along? Or one of the large roaming wolf packs frighten off all the available game? Their only recourse is to make regular sacrifices to their deities to protect them from these calamities. We social marketers also face potent competition, but luckily don't have to rely on superstition to defend us: we can make intelligent, informed decisions about how to proceed.

Unfortunately, though, our competition is more intelligent than the average mammoth, and has learned that size and wealth gives it immense power. This power imbalance can make life difficult for social marketers, and hard decisions have to be made about how we respond to it. As we began to explore in Chapters 2 and 4, do we compete and challenge, despite our relative weakness, or do we cooperate? In this chapter, we take the discussion further and examine the concept of corporate social responsibility (CSR), and the extent to which it represents a genuine solution or is just an evasive practice that reinforces the original problem. Does the much greater power of one party inevitably result in exploitation?

And where does regulation come into the picture? How and when should it be instigated?

Inevitably, these questions of power pull us into broader issues of how corporate capitalism works, and the need to move beyond ad hoc competitive analysis and start making judgements at a systemic level. We will pick this up at the end of the chapter, showing how it underlines the value of independent critical thinking.

Learning outcomes

By the end of this chapter, you should be familiar with the idea of competitive analysis and the benefits it can bring to social marketing. Specifically, you should understand:

✓ That we in social marketing can learn from the strengths of others – even when those others are operating in direct competition to us

✓ The pros and cons of cooperation and competition

✓ The role of regulation and the need for evidence

✓ For social marketers, the competition is both immensely powerful and systemic, and this raises much broader issues that are addressed by critical marketing.

Key words

client power – competitive analysis – competitive strategy – cooperate or compete – CSR – direct and indirect competition – Porter's Four Forces – sustainable change

IT'S A COMPETITIVE BUSINESS

As we noted in Chapter 2, competitive analysis underpins one of the four defining orientations of social marketing. This reflects its pivotal role in business. Burger

King and McDonald's, Nike and Adidas, Coca-Cola and Pepsi are proverbial rivals; stock market ratings are the equivalent of sports leagues, with takeovers and company failures the obvious results for the winners and losers in this jockeying for position. By contrast, among us gentle herbivores of the social marketing world, such rivalry seems counter-intuitive. Surely social marketers are all on the same side, trying to do good – not put each other down? In reality, however, competitive analysis can be a useful tool.

Marketing is concerned with profitably addressing needs, and we have already examined how this operates as far as the company and the customer are concerned, but there is a third 'C' in the equation: the competition. Like the natural world, business is also driven by the law governing the survival of the fittest. However, in this case, the forces are not hidden Darwinian genes, but an overt managerial process guided by deliberate planning. Marketers seek to understand the behaviours of their competitors, just as they do those of their customers, so that they can control, influence or at least adapt to the resulting forces.

The ultimate aim is to establish sustainable competitive advantage, with the emphasis on sustainable. Above all else, studying your rivals informs your strategic planning; it helps define where you want to be not just in the next year, but in the next decade. And this long-term vision is invaluable. Rumour has it that one Japanese car manufacturer is more than happy to show its competitors around its factories, and give them as much information as they want about its production methods. By the time they have copied them, its erstwhile host will have moved on, made improvements and left them far behind. The story is apocryphal, but its thrust is correct.

Good competitive analysis, as with so much else in marketing, starts by looking at the world through the eyes of the customer. What need are *they* trying to satisfy? What products do *they* use to satisfy the same need? What do *they* buy instead? Who do *they* see as the competition? Box 7.1 presents a simple competitive analysis for McDonald's.

BOX 7.1: WHAT CUSTOMER NEEDS DOES MCDONALD'S MEET?

Think for a few moments about what needs the fast food outlet is satisfying for a father and his two small children. As a good marketer, you would seek to answer this question with a bit of market research asking the father and his children why they have come to the Golden Arches.

The obvious answer you are likely to get is food; McDonald's has to satisfy their hunger – but it is very likely that this is only part of the picture. Competitive analysis suggests questions specifically about what they consider to be the alternative – *the competing* – options can usefully extend your research. Questions like:

(i)   Where might you have gone today if not to McDonald's?

(ii) What other places do you like going together?

(iii) How good are these alternative offerings?

The answers may produce predictable responses such as KFC or Burger King (because they have better free toys). A little more unsettlingly, but still reasonably predictably, the answer may be the new juice bar (because the food is healthier). However, the father and his children may also suggest less obvious alternatives, like a picnic in the park (because you can also feed the ducks and try out the swings) or a trip to the cinema to see the latest Disney (because it has been trailed on children's television and all their friends have seen it).

This simple exercise has two great benefits for McDonald's: it helps them think more incisively both about their rivals and (more importantly) their customers. As far as their rivals are concerned, the answers in Box 7.1 will enable McDonald's executives to see who they are up against – Burger King, the juice bar or the cinema. They can then think through how they should respond. Is it straight 'them or us' rivalry or are there also cooperative opportunities? For example, in the case of the juice bar, direct competition is probably needed, perhaps by adding healthier options to the menu; the picnic option, on the other hand, may suggest that opening a franchise in the park has potential. Similarly, in the case of the cinema, the best strategy may not be to compete head on, but to form an alliance and begin serving McDonald's meals to theatre-goers.

As far as their customers are concerned, the answers in Box 7.1 start to give McDonald's a much better fix on the precise customer need they are seeking to meet. It becomes clear, for example, that this is about much more than food and hunger. Fun, entertainment and a child-friendly atmosphere are all also in there as exchange benefits. Indeed, some people actually patronize McDonald's *despite* the food: a nutritionist friend living in Geneva takes her children there, although she has grave reservations about the menu, because it is one of the few child-friendly restaurants in town. Creating and delivering value, such as fun and a child-friendly atmosphere, is, as we discuss in Chapter 10, at the core of mutually beneficial marketing exchanges.

SOLUTIONS NOT PROBLEMS

Thus, our small competitive analysis has helped us uncover a valuable marketing insight: the distinction between the offering made (in this case, ostensibly at least, a meal) and the need satisfied (child-oriented entertainment). This is a vital distinction. Have a try at Exercise 7.1.

EXERCISE 7.1: CARLING STARLINGS

You work for Sensible Limits, an NGO concerned with youth alcohol problems. You are very much aware that the brewers of Carling lager are successfully reaching young people in your area and you want to learn more about how they are doing this. You have two opportunities to do so. First, you are familiar with a very successful cinema ad they produced featuring a flock of starlings that gradually came together to reveal the word 'BELONG' dressed up as the Carling logo (Google 'carlingstarlings' and follow the link to YouTube).

Second, a recently commissioned Memorandum for the UK Parliament Health Select Committee (www.publications.parliament.uk/pa/cm/cmhealth.htm) took an inside look at all the industry's marketing, and highlighted the starlings campaign (which had caused some disquiet among regulators when it appeared). Two quotes about this stand out:

1. 'Carling celebrates, initiates and promotes the togetherness of the pack, their passions and their pint because Carling understands that things are better together,' this is then split into '3 Aspects of Belonging: <u>Initiation</u>: Expressions of the moment when an individual joins a group and finds a happy home in the pack – the moment of belonging <u>Celebration</u>: An expression of the sheer joy of belonging <u>Contagion</u>: An expression of the magnetic power of the group – the power of belonging.'
2. 'Broadly speaking each piece of communication will either celebrate "Join Us" by championing the benefit of togetherness or facilitate "Join Us" by providing and enhancing experiences where togetherness is key.'

List some of the lessons for Sensible Limits.

The interesting issue for Sensible Limits is how far the Carling marketing is from overtly selling beer – nothing is said about hops, brewing skills or even thirst. The pitch is to do with mates and social connectedness, not about beer as such. Given the skill and success of Carling, this provides a useful insight into the priorities of your target group. Unless you tread very carefully, messages about not drinking or drinking less risk being interpreted as a recipe for loneliness and social isolation. Perhaps Sensible Limits should be looking at healthier, non-alcohol-related ways of belonging?

It's a timely reminder that marketers – whether commercial or social – don't sell products or services, they sell solutions. Consider for a minute this question inspired by Theodore Levitt (1960) 'what do Black and Decker make?' Jot down your answer(s).

The obvious response is perhaps drills, or, more broadly, do-it-yourself equipment or tools. But a marketer would say no, the company doesn't sell drills, it sell holes. Drills just happen to be the best way of making them, but it may not always be so. New technology may, for instance, produce a laser-driven machine that can do the job better. Unless Black and Decker realize they are in the hole business rather than the drill business, they will be as vulnerable to the competition as buggy-whip manufacturers were to the new technology of the internal combustion engine.

Robert Browning's poem about three heroic horsemen bringing good news from Ghent to Aix helps reinforce this point. In the poem, three riders set out to deliver 'the news which alone could save Aix from her fate'; two of their horses die during the gallop and Roland – our hero's mount – expires on the streets of Aix as the tidings are delivered. Have a try at Exercise 7.2.

EXERCISE 7.2: HOW THEY BROUGHT THE GOOD NEWS FROM GHENT TO AIX

1	2
I SPRANG to the stirrup, and Joris, and he; I galloped, Dirck galloped, we galloped all three; 'God speed!' cried the watch, as the gate-bolts undrew; 'Speed!' echoed the wall to us galloping through; Behind shut the postern, the lights sank to rest, And into the midnight we galloped abreast.	. . . By Hasselt, Dirck groaned; and cried Joris, 'Stay spur! Your Roos galloped bravely, the fault's not in her, We'll remember at Aix' – for one heard the quick wheeze Of her chest, saw the stretched neck and staggering knees, And sunk tail, and horrible heave of the flank, As down on her haunches she shuddered and sank.
3	4
. . . 'How they'll greet us!' – and all in a moment his roan Rolled neck and croup over, lay dead as a stone; And there was my Roland to bear the whole weight Of the news which alone could save Aix from her fate, With his nostrils like pits full of blood to the brim, And with circles of red for his eye-sockets' rim.	. . . And all I remember is, friends flocking round As I sat with his head 'twixt my knees on the ground; And no voice but was praising this Roland of mine, As I poured down his throat our last measure of wine, Which (the burgesses voted by common consent) Was no more than his due who brought good news from Ghent.

In Browning's famous poem (abridged here) what did Joris, Dirck and our nameless hero really need?

What sales opportunity would you, an entrepreneurial marketer living in nineteenth-century Ghent, have been able to exploit? What would you have sold them?

The obvious answer is better horses. Or even a motorbike. But what they really needed – and any marketer worthy of the name would recognize this – was a telephone. Joris, Dirck and co were not looking for a means of transport at all, but a means of communication. Competitive analysis aids this type of lateral thinking. McDonald's analysis of the competition stops them becoming obsessed with the product and keeps them focused on the need they are satisfying.

A BROADER AGENDA

Competitive analysis also broadens beyond commercial rivals. McDonald's, for instance, will take careful readings of how their customers see the current obesity debate. Do they have any sympathy with the New York teenagers who tried to sue the company for making them fat, or support a ban on fast food advertising? This will help inform their consumer marketing – perhaps they should employ celebrity chefs or include healthier options on the menu. It also guides their stakeholder marketing. The rise in public concern about obesity has pushed the fast food industry to engage much more actively with policy makers.

This is even more apparent in the tobacco business. We noted in Chapter 4 when discussing strategic analysis that, as David Jobber, a leading business academic, explains, 'close relationships with politicians are often cultivated by organizations both to monitor political moods and also to influence them' (2004: 145). The importance of doing this is increased by the activities of tobacco control NGOs, as Jobber goes on to note: 'the cigarette industry, for example, has a vested interest in maintaining close ties with government to counter proposals from pressure groups such as ASH'. In this sense, competitive analysis is a natural progression from environmental scanning, as discussed in social marketing planning in Chapter 4.

Exercise 7.3 applies this thinking to a social marketing example.

EXERCISE 7.3: SCHOOL DINNERS: IDENTIFYING THE COMPETITION

Imagine that you are a social marketer and have been asked for help by Oldsville High School. Only about a third of their pupils eat school dinners; the others make alternative arrangements, either bringing their own or going out of school to local cafés. The school want you to make their new healthier lunches more popular.

Competitive analysis suggests that questions like these may be revealing:

(i)   Where do the two-thirds of non-school diners eat at the moment?

(ii) What do they like about these alternatives?

(iii) Why do the one-third remain loyal?

As with our McDonald's and Carling examples – and Browning's poem – you may well find that the answers take you well beyond food and hunger. Local cafés, for instance, may offer a chance to rebel, to hang around with friends in an unstructured environment or simply to save money on the allowance disbursed by parents. On the other hand, the third who remain loyal are presumably rejecting the competitors' offerings, so asking them why they do so may uncover some hidden strengths in the school's dinners.

PORTER'S COMPETITIVE FORCES

The nature of the competition is influenced not just by what other companies do, but also by more fundamental forces in the marketplace. Michael Porter (2004) divides these into four categories (see Box 7.2).

BOX 7.2: PORTER'S COMPETITIVE FORCES

1. The power of the *buyer* or customer is, of course, crucial. Do they have access to alternative offerings that will satisfy their needs?
2. The *power of suppliers* and the extent to which they can control what the marketer does. The room for manoeuvre of BP, for example, may be significantly constrained by OPEC.
3. The degree to which offerings can be *substituted*. Generic, easily produced commodities, such as potatoes or paper, are much more vulnerable to competition than are branded snacks or a unique piece of software.
4. Finally, *new entrants* to the market can also increase competition, and the number of these will depend on how difficult it is to start up in a particular business. Setting up a new pharmaceutical company is, for example, much more challenging than a new beauty salon.

(Source: Adapted from Jobber 2004: 678–680)

First, as you would expect, the buyer or customer has potential power. We have already explored this in some detail, but Porter reminds us that the amount of power the buyer has will vary according to market conditions. In a monopoly situation or a time of shortage, for instance, their power can shrink dramatically. The second force, the power of suppliers, is essentially the corollary of the first. The third force concerns the potential for substitution: are there alternative products or services available that can do the same job? In the commercial sector, branding is used to capture this sort of power – a trainer is a trainer, but a Nike Air Max is unique.

Finally, Porter considers the threat from new entrants to the market. The extent of this will be determined by how easy it is for others to move in and start satisfying the same consumer needs. In some sectors, such as pharmaceuticals and nuclear energy, the barriers are very high. In others, such as the small businesses service sector (e.g. hairdressers and cafés), entry is much easier and competition much more widespread – with a resulting tendency for businesses to appear and disappear on a regular basis.

As with other strategic decisions, a company's options for engaging with and tackling competition are going to be influenced by its internal capacity. What skills and resources can they call on? What strategic approaches can they realistically adopt? Can they compete on price, for example, or will differentiation (offering a valued alternative), focus (servicing a particular area or group), pre-emption (offering some innovation) or synergy (exploiting particular strengths) be feasible? This capacity will ultimately depend on the potential to develop a workable and effective marketing mix.

Porter's analysis is relevant to social marketing.

Buyer power in social marketing

The fact that social marketers deal with *voluntary* behaviour means that their clients always have a choice – they have 'buyer power' (see Box 7.2) – and, hence, there is always *passive* or *indirect* competition (refer back to Chapter 2). Client power is a valuable concept in a discipline that also competes professionally with expert-driven approaches such as public health and road safety, and reminds us of the need to satisfy our target's inherent self-interest by providing *real* benefits. In this context, *real* must incorporate both the objective (technical benefits such as symptom relief or greater safety) and the subjective (what the recipient feels about consuming the offering).

In competitive terms, there is what seems to be a natural tendency for social marketing offerings to be worthy, hard work, and, as a consequence, inherently unattractive compared with our clients' alternative options. Thus, a bad diet is fun and indulgent, a good one Spartan and dissatisfying; a sedentary life is restful and relaxing, exercise hard work and tiring. Furthermore, we always seem to be asking people to give things up – chocolate, cigarettes, the rugged manliness that comes with driving an SUV. But, as Richard Layard (2005) points out, we put a greater premium on loss than gain: we get more upset from an £80 bill than we get happiness from an £80 windfall. This suggests the Health Promotion Board of Singapore was right to turn the negative offering of anti-smoking into a positive in its Pro-Quitting campaign (Ogilvy & Mather 2012).

Similarly, social marketing seems doomed to offer long-term, probabilistic benefits (or often the absence of awful repercussions), whereas the competition brings short-term, definite ones. The immediate pleasure of chocolate competes all too effectively with the deferred (and often elusive) advantage of weight loss; more dramatically, today's nicotine fix competes easily with the possibility of a heart attack in a couple of decades. 'Discounting' exacerbates this problem: rewards lose their value and costs are less onerous in the future.

This again compels us to think about what we are offering and the extent to which it meets people's real needs. If deferred gratification is such a weak product, why do we focus on it? Especially when a little consideration shows that it is far from being the only benefit of a healthy lifestyle. Have a look at Figure 7.1, for example, which presents the results of research with prisoners and people on low income who have successfully given up smoking.

It shows the immense sense of achievement that successfully giving up smoking can bring to the most disadvantaged populations. Similarly, back in Box 4.4 we saw that exercise is not by definition unpleasant – whole swathes of the population get a variety of (short-term) benefits as a result.

This takes us back to the discussion of fear messages and positive branding in the previous chapter. It also helps explain the World Health Organization's (1946) definition of health – 'a state of complete physical, mental and social well-being and not merely the absence of disease or infirmity' – which pushes us in a very positive direction.

Furthermore, if people want an enjoyable life today rather than the probability of more life tomorrow (and it is hardly surprising that they do), should we not be making sure that our products deliver this? Competitive analysis and customer power, just as with McDonald's, must lead us to think about our core business: is

Figure 7.1 The delights of quitting

Source: MacAskill et al. (2002); MacAskill and Eadie (2002)

it just freedom from physical illness or a more fulfilled and rewarding life, as WHO indicates? Is public health and safety about avoiding threats or realizing opportunities; about drills or holes?

Competitive analysis reminds us, if we do not get this right, others surely will. Exercise 7.4 shows how the tobacco industry is working hard to provide attractive short-term offerings to potential new smokers. As we noted above, there is a Darwinian discipline at play here – we social marketers have to compete successfully or we will not survive.

EXERCISE 7.4: THE IMPORTANCE OF COMPETITIVE ANALYSIS IN SMOKING PREVENTION

Market research from the UK tobacco industry makes it clear the young are a key target and that image and emotion are vital appeals:

'To smoke Marlboro Lights represents having passed a rite of passage.'

'Young adult smokers are looking for reassurance that they are doing the right thing, and cigarettes are no exception. Any break with a brand's heritage must be carefully considered in order not to throw doubt into the minds of young adult smokers.'

'Young adult smokers are also searching for an identity. Cigarettes have a key role to play as they are an ever-present statement of identity.'

'Smoking for these people (young smokers) is still a badge. A sign of maturity, discernment and independence.'

'Younger smokers give more weight to the imagery of cigarettes and pay more attention and are open to fashionable brands and up-to-date designs.'

Successful brands exploit these emotional needs and insecurities:

'The success of Marlboro Lights derives from its being the aspirational lifestyle brand . . . The Diet Coke of cigarettes.'

'To be successful any Gallaher brand will have to tackle Marlboro's coolness of image – smokers do smoke the image as well as the taste.'

'We want to engage their aspirations and fantasies – "I'd like to be there, do that, own that".'

How well will long-term, probabilistic health warnings compete here? Are there more attractive offers we could make?

(Source: House of Commons Health Select Committee 2000)

Ray Lowry's work on breastfeeding among low socio-economic groups (Case Study 13 on p. 414) demonstrates how careful and empathetic research can provide the sort of insights needed to devise offerings that meet psycho-social needs. Only when midwives were exposed to role-playing actors did they appreciate the sensitivity that was needed to approach this issue with low-income women. In a similar way, using reflection and action research methods, colleagues Katie Collins and Lindsay Manning, from the Bristol Social Marketing Centre, UWE, highlighted that risky drinking was often a consequence of other situational factors rather than a problem. Improvements in self-esteem, feelings of competence and community engagement needed to be tackled if any inroads were to be made in risky drinking patterns (Case Study 22 on p. 490). In this context, simple fear inducement seems, at best, a limited response, as discussed in Chapter 6.

As we noted when discussing exchange theory in Chapter 3, insurance companies, like social marketers, have the problem of deferred gratification; they offer a benefit tomorrow that is both probabilistic and inherently unattractive. Very few of us want to actually claim on our household insurance because it assumes some misfortune has visited us first. The same is even more true of life insurance. The benefit that insurance companies push, then, is not so much financial payback later, but peace of mind now. They do not sell *insurance*; they sell *reas*surance.

Substitution, suppliers and new entrants

Porter's other three forces (Box 7.2) also have something of interest to offer, as Exercise 7.5 explores.

EXERCISE 7.5: APPLYING PORTER'S FORCES IN SOCIAL MARKETING

Have another look at Box 7.2. How well do Porter's other three forces – *substitution*, the *power of suppliers* and *new entrants* – help us think about social marketing problems? Jot down some ideas under each heading before continuing.

Substitution is an obvious development of client power. There are many easily substituted products for ours on offer. Celebrity diets present an attractive alternative to lifestyle change, and cleverly promoted four-wheel-drives can deflect us from more ecologically sound modes of transport. Similarly, almost any other television channel is preferable to the one showing yet another tediously graphic speeding or drunk-driving ad.

More broadly, our issues compete for attention. Tobacco control, alcohol safety and HIV/AIDS are all competing for the same health dollars. Furthermore, as lifestyle illnesses proliferate, resources become more stretched. For example, obesity has only emerged as a public health concern in the last 20 years, but it is estimated that in the US by 2018 it will be absorbing 344 billion dollars a year – which is more than a fifth of the entire health budget (Lang and Rayner 2012).

In social marketing, the **supplier** is, in many instances, very powerful – often more so than in the commercial sector. There are two reasons for this. First, the supplier is frequently also the funder, with a resulting inclination to call the tune. Second, they do not have the laws of the market breathing down their neck as a commercial company does. They will not go bust if they get things wrong. As a result, in social marketing, the demands of the supplier can sometimes supersede the needs of the client. For example, speed cameras might be imposed on a community despite the public's suspicions about the purity of the motives behind them or morning-after contraception discouraged because of the supplier's religious beliefs.

The absence of a profit motive means suppliers can not just buck the market, but actually create it. Thus, governments will often decide what the priorities are for social marketers. This, of course, is no bad thing in a democracy, but serious problems can result. Recall how, in the UK, during the 1980s, the Conservative Government of Margaret Thatcher refused to accept any connection between inequalities and ill health; or more recently George Bush's focus on the 'war on terror' pulled in resources that might otherwise have been used in more conventional public-safety initiatives.

These pressures put an additional onus on social marketers. There is a need to question and, if necessary, challenge the social marketing agenda being set by suppliers. This can be difficult to do, but is essential for the discipline's long-term survival. It also reinforces the points made in Chapter 2 about the importance of building relationships with suppliers. We will return to this need for bigger thinking below.

Porter's fourth force – **New Entrants** – brings us to a perhaps uncomfortably selfish notion of competition. Social marketers do compete with each other and other behaviour change specialists for funding and work. The recent upsurge of interest in the subject has brought a range of new providers into the market. This presents real threats, not just in terms of work, but also to the discipline itself. If anyone can set up in business as a social marketer – if, in Porter's terms, the barriers are too low – there is a risk that prices, and then standards, will plummet. When medicine faced this threat a century or so ago, it responded by setting up very considerable barriers to entry. We would not advocate such a strategy in social marketing, but we do need to set professional standards and agree reasonable criteria for qualifications.

More direct competition comes from a corporate sector that is coming under attack for the collateral harm that it causes. A bit of do-gooding social marketing can help avert criticism and burnish the brand image – so tobacco companies run youth smoking prevention campaigns, the alcohol industry establishes health initiatives such as the Drink Aware Trust in the UK[1] and Bedrinkaware in Australia[2] and Coke, in the wake of concerns about its ecological performance in India, links up with the WWF.

This raises concerns about effectiveness – are Philip Morris or Diageo really the best people to run public health initiatives? Is Coke actually more devoted to the planet or to its profits? The evidence suggests that the concerns are well founded; for example, a review of tobacco industry youth prevention found that not only do they fail to prevent the onset of smoking – they actually make things worse (Wakefield *et al.* 2006).

This shape-shifting also triggers questions about transparency. Have a go at Exercise 7.6.

EXERCISE 7.6: COKE AND WWF

'We have built our partnership on targets, very specific targets for achieving growth at Coke while maintaining no growth in the CO_2 emissions. Pursuing the best practices in sustainable agriculture, and the partnership brings together two of the biggest brands in the world. We have two great networks that are coming together in places around the world, and it's interesting, business leaders I've talked to, they've commented on the importance of businesses becoming leaders in addressing the world's problems because the best and the brightest don't just want to achieve more market share they also want to be leaders in solving the biggest problems that face the world'.[3]

Who said this?

You might guess that the speaker in Exercise 7.6 is Muhtar Kent, the $24m-a-year CEO of Coke, or maybe the company's marketing manager; but it is actually Carter Roberts who runs WWF in the US. How helpful do you think it is to have the leader of an NGO devoted to conservation and sustainability speaking up so enthusiastically about the Coca-Cola Corporation's potential for growth? Would he have done so if Coke had not given WWF so much financial support?

From the perspective of the social marketing discipline, though, the greatest potential harm is more insidious. If these ineffective and ambiguous campaigns are presented to the world as examples of social marketing, the work of all social marketers will be diminished.

LEVELS OF COMPETITION

Noble and Basil (2011) develop our thinking about competition, and show that it is useful to divide it into four levels:

● **Generic level competition** – this is the broadest level relating to the issue, rather than the service or product. For example, a computer-recycling initiative is, in its most macro sense, about waste management and indirectly competes with energy, education, health and other social concerns for funding, support and space. At this level, our situational analysis from Chapter 4, with its SWOT and environmental scanning as well as Harm Chain Analysis, is important. It assists in identifying those broad cultural, technological, legal, economic, social and political drives that, strategically, may act as barriers or benefits to our behaviour change programme.

- **Enterprise level competition** – still at the macro level, this is one stage less than generic. For computer recycling, there are also the options of reuse (give to children, donate to schools, ship to Africa) or reduce (keep computer for another year; use computer in work and don't purchase for home). This correlates to the traditional 'market' or 'business'. Substitutions and new entrants are significant threats here as they often create and script new markets, out-manoeuvring established organizations.

- **Product level competition** – refers to other known recycling facilities, such as the local dump, that are a viable and direct alternative, presenting real barriers to your recycling offering. In Porter's terminology, this is about present suppliers.

- **Brand level competition** – other recycling organizations, profit and non-profit, directly seeking your clients to engage in a computer-recycling exchange with them as opposed to you, i.e. other firms, charities and entities in the same industry/business with the same offering as you, head-to-head competition. Piercy succinctly summarizes the levels of competition when he says: 'the truth is customers just do not fit traditional industry definitions of markets: you think you make crisps, the retailer thinks that the category is salty snacks but the customer-defined market is lunch' (2009: 271). Thus, there's serious food for thought in a competition-level analysis for the social marketer because it explodes the mental market box that can limit our thinking. It also puts the spotlight on direct competitors.

EXERCISE 7.7: FOUR LEVELS OF COMPETITION

Think of a field of social marketing endeavour – tobacco control perhaps or energy conservation – and analyse it using Basil and Noble's (2011) framework.

Utilizing Basil and Noble's framework in energy conservation has us identify, at the brand competition level, Carey Glass as an example of a leading triple-glazed window supplier and exporter in the UK and Ireland. They compete against 'window' products such as double glazing and UPVC. At the enterprise level, competition moves past windows into loft and cavity wall insulation as well as solar panels, more efficient light bulbs and wood pellet burners. This brings us to our broadest type of competition – the generic level – where we have all products and suppliers concerned with all facets of energy conservation and energy-saving products and suppliers, including novel, innovative wind, solar and water devices.

Active competition

There is, of course, also a very direct way that we can think about competition in social marketing: in some instances, other organizations – typically companies selling unhealthy products such as tobacco, alcohol and energy-dense foods – push in completely the opposite direction. WHO dubbed them the 'hazard merchants' a few years ago. Thus, one simple and compelling answer to the question of why so many people take up and continue smoking is because a raft of large and extremely powerful multinational tobacco corporations encourage them to do so. And they undoubtedly succeed, as study after study has demonstrated. Box 7.3 presents one fragment of this evidence base, the conclusion of a systematic literature review on the impact of tobacco advertising and promotion by the world-renowned Cochrane Collaboration.

BOX 7.3: TOBACCO ADVERTISING DOES HAVE AN EFFECT

'Longitudinal studies consistently suggest that exposure to tobacco advertising and promotion is associated with the likelihood that adolescents will start to smoke. Based on the strength of this association, the consistency of findings across numerous observational studies, temporality of exposure and smoking behaviours observed, as well as the theoretical plausibility regarding the impact of advertising, we conclude that tobacco advertising and promotion increases the likelihood that adolescents will start to smoke.'

(Source: Lovato *et al.* 2003: 1)

Similar evidence bases are emerging for the promotion of energy-dense food and alcohol. Reviews conducted by ISM for the Food Standards Agency (Hastings *et al.* 2003) and the World Health Organization (Hastings *et al.* 2005) have concluded that, in each market, commercial promotion is contributing to the public health burden.

Thinking beyond WHO's hazard merchants, other industries may also present obstacles to social marketers. Car manufacturers can encourage speeding, as discussed above – and certainly have a vested interest in encouraging ecologically damaging forms of travel. The toy and entertainment markets may contribute to the sedentary lifestyles of young people. The armaments business has a role in human conflict. The evidence base in these fields may be less well formed than for tobacco, alcohol and food, but social marketers involved in ecological transportation, exercise promotion and conflict resolution would be unwise to ignore their potential influence.

So, how should social marketers respond to this competitive activity?

First, let us note that competitive analysis confirms that it is perfectly legitimate – indeed, necessary – for us to respond. This reinforces our discussion in Chapter 2 that commercial marketing is part of the social context and that we not only *can* but actually *have* to make this context our business. Indeed, our insights into marketing make our role in this arena particularly valuable. We understand the forces at work here, that there is, for example, so much more than advertising involved. It is the whole of the marketing mix – the products being developed, the pricing strategies used and the well-resourced distribution network that makes commercial marketing so successful.

For example, while it is known that alcohol advertising contributes to youth drinking, product innovation is probably an equally important driver (Jackson *et al.* 2000). The advent of alcopops, heavily branded 'FABs' (flavoured alcoholic beverages such as Bacardi Breezer) and shots has undoubtedly had an impact on drinking. A recent paper in the *American Journal of Public Health*, for instance, argues that it has transformed the youth alcohol market in the US. The author provides a forensic case study of Smirnoff Ice, a leading brand of alcopops, and explains how

Diageo developed a sophisticated marketing strategy to reenergize its Smirnoff Vodka brand using 3 key components:

1. Develop a beverage that tasted like soft drinks.
2. Use the Smirnoff Vodka brand name but market the product as a malt beverage to compete effectively with beer in terms of price, availability, and advertising in electronic media.
3. Reorient Smirnoff Vodka itself as a young person's brand by adding new fruit flavors and using other marketing innovations.

(Mosher 2012: 57)

Similarly, tobacco, alcohol and energy-dense foods are available at every turn. Figure 7.2 gives one illustration of this; it shows posters offering special deals on snack food at an Australian cinema. It is worth bearing in mind that in its investigation into obesity, the UK Government's Health Select Committee pointed out that a king-size Mars bar has as many calories as a three course meal.

The most immediate response to this unhealthy marketing is to recognize, as we have already noted, that we social marketers have to match our competitor's game: we too need ubiquity, convenience and seductive branding.

Another response for the social marketer is to address the client and warn them about the activities of the hazard merchants. The Truth campaign in the US, as we noted in Chapter 2, did exactly this for tobacco companies, highlighting their unscrupulous business practices and deliberate attempts to attract youngsters to the habit. The ads were completely uncompromising – showing, for example, body bags being delivered to tobacco corporation headquarters to represent the numbers killed by smoking and ambushing executives with embarrassing questions. The

Figure 7.2 Promoting obesity? The ubiquity of obesity: calories galore being hawked to cinema goers. And the film at the top of the bill? *Super Size Me!*

result was a very high-profile social marketing campaign that worked: it brought about a marked reduction in youth smoking rates (Farrelly *et al.* 2002). So we can compete and win.

To compete or cooperate?

When faced with a direct competitor like this, however, some form of cooperative response is also a possibility – as we noted in our McDonald's example. This is sometimes rather clumsily called 'co-opetition'. Some commentators suggest that this is the way forward for tobacco control: a tobacco industry-funded academic quoted in the journal *Science* argued that 'the real enemy' in tobacco control 'is the death and disease smokers suffer', not the tobacco industry (Grimm 2005). Given the insights of competitive analysis, this is a simplistic argument – a bit akin to suggesting that the mosquito is a distraction in the fight against malaria. The problem is that, for cooperation to work, as with relationship marketing, two conditions have to be present:

1. There must be some capacity to find mutual benefit.
2. The partners must have at least roughly equal power.

Neither is present with tobacco.

This is an instance where the competitive analysis throws up the conclusion that a head-to-head fight is the only solution: as long as we have tobacco corporations, we will have smoking, along with its toll on life expectancy and inequalities – as illustrated in Case Study 10 'You Kill, You Pay' on p. 394.

This sort of competitive analysis has led public health researchers to conclude that tobacco companies will have to be bought out and replaced by social enterprises who will continue to ensure a supply of tobacco to dependent smokers, but will do so with a clear public health agenda (Borland 2003; Callard *et al.* 2005). Instead of the current system, where tobacco companies are required by law to maximize returns to their shareholders – and, hence, to increase sales of tobacco, they would have the specific remit of reducing the public health burden from smoking. Thus, they would procure only tobacco products that meet stringent public health goals (e.g. of reduced nitrosamines or with specified nicotine content) and produce generic cigarettes that meet only the nicotine needs of smokers. They will not be incentivized, as corporations are, to produce evocative brands or try to meet any of the psycho-social needs of smokers discussed in Exercise 7.4.

Other competitors present a more complex picture, however. There is a convincing evidence base to show that both food and alcohol marketing have a significant and unhealthy impact, especially on the young, as the Food Standards Agency and the World Health Organization reviews discussed above show.

At the same time, however, the issues are less black and white than for tobacco. Taking alcohol as an example, most public health professionals would accept that this is not an irredeemably bad product. While it is becoming increasingly apparent that any level of consumption is risky, there are potential social and hedonistic benefits. And, if, as we noted above, health is indeed more than the absence of illness, these broader benefits deserve to be considered. Similarly, while we should always remember that the majority of the world's population does not use alcohol, in many societies, it is an acceptable and normal part of life. The problem is more one of abuse rather than use. This suggests that one of our two criteria for cooperation is being met: most alcohol manufacturers would argue that they share public health's interest in the safe use of their product.

There are complications, however. The evidence base shows that the most effective public health response is to reduce per capita consumption, a measure that an alcohol corporation, driven as it is by a need to increase returns to shareholders, will find very difficult to accept. So, while public health and the alcohol producers might have some shared understanding of the problem, they differ on the solution.

The second criterion, of equal power, presents even greater problems. The alcohol industry is very big business and the main producers such as Diageo are among the wealthiest of our global corporations. We therefore need to proceed with caution.

Exercise 7.8 describes a collaborative project between a social marketer and Miller Brewing. How do you feel about this? What are the strengths and weaknesses of the collaboration?

EXERCISE 7.8: TO COMPETE OR COOPERATE?

In a rural, blue-collar community in the Northern US, drunk driving among young men is common practice. Forty per cent of 21–34-year-olds drive themselves home after an average of seven drinks at least twice a week. The competition has a monopoly; there is no other way of getting home; and its leading brand 'I can drive myself home' has huge market share. This is reinforced by the fact that brand consumption typically does not result in the negative consequences threatened by social marketers. Most of the men, on most occasions, do manage to drive home without mishap.

However, the brand also has at least one weakness. They know they are taking unreasonable risks, and feel guilty about it. An alternative offering might have potential, provided it did not come at too high a cost or interfere with their self-interest in having a good night at their local bar. The offering made was a free ride service, customized to each community and promising 'no hassles, no worries, more fun'. It succeeded. Some 20,000 rides have now been given. Analysing the competition, and the target's perception of the competition, enabled the build-up of sustainable competitive advantage.

The case emphasizes the need for social marketing to offer 'unique meaningful benefits', which both present better value than the competition and accommodate the customer's self-interest more effectively. Specifically, it underlines the value of emphasizing the short-term benefits and reducing short-term costs in this process.

But did it also create problems?

(Source: Rothschild *et al.* 2006)

The example provides a good illustration of the dilemma. On the one hand, it could be seen as a great example of the effective use of competitive analysis to deliver a simple and powerful intervention, and a major threat to public health – drunk driving – was reduced. On the other, we might have concerns about the potential repercussions of a collaboration that effectively reinforced drunkenness – and actively delivered these drunks home to their families. From a competitive perspective, it also enables the brewery to promote its products as actively as ever, with an undesirable implication that getting drunk is both acceptable and fun. This theme would ordinarily get them into trouble, but, in this case, they actually stand to get very positive public relations benefits from it.

Thinking more strategically, as we noted above, we have to ask questions about the impact these sorts of collaborations have on the standing of social marketing. Any company entering such an agreement would think very carefully about the impact it might have on its brand image; so should social marketing. This is not necessarily an argument against the Miller collaboration; just a reminder that we need to think strategically about relationships with business, on the one hand, and civil society, on the other. And, in the case of alcohol, this thinking has to be particularly careful, because the division made above, between use and abuse, is simplistic. The evidence shows that the two are in fact intimately related: the wider the availability and use of alcohol in a given jurisdiction, the greater the abuse that will result (Edwards *et al.* 2004, 2005).

THE LIMITS OF CORPORATE SOCIAL RESPONSIBILITY

The idea for cooperation with industry has its most obvious manifestation in corporate social responsibility (CSR): the principle that companies should not just keep an eye on their financial bottom line, but also monitor and control their impact on health and social welfare. This is an attractive-sounding option; business is causing problems so it is right that it should be responsible for limiting these and cleaning up any mess that results. At first glance, it seems like a pleasing variant on 'the Polluter Pays' principle.

CSR is indeed a good thing. There is no doubting the genuine motives of many business leaders in this area. Furthermore, business is probably in the best position to self-regulate the minutiae of its activities. Advertising content, for example, or selling methods need technical and professional insight to guide control. However, CSR also has very real limitations. First of all, it can only deal with the specific, not the general. Thus, while it can identify and remove an alcohol ad that transgresses a code of conduct, it can do nothing about the fact that there is simply too much alcohol advertising.

Second, and more fundamentally, corporations are required by law to put the interests of their shareholders – not society – first (see the 'fiduciary imperative', Box 1.1 in Chapter 1). The social bottom line will always be trumped by the fiscal one. As Niall FitzGerald, former CEO of Unilever, succinctly put it: 'Corporate social responsibility is a hard-edged business decision'. We do it 'not because it is a nice thing to do or because people are forcing us to do it' but 'because it is good for our business' (Elliott 2003). As we discuss in Chapter 8, business textbooks are completely transparent about this ulterior motive.

So, if you are a social marketer and a company offers to fund your campaigns as part of its CSR programme, you have to accept that you are signing up to work on their marketing team. If this makes you uncomfortable, perhaps you should think again. As we will discuss in the next chapter, it has certainly been the cause of concern in international development and ecological sectors. CSR also raises much bigger questions about the functioning of corporate capitalism to which we will also return.

REGULATION

Thus, cooperation then may get us so far, but it has very real limitations. The alternative is to seek to contain – or at least constrain – the competition through regulation. This takes us back to the importance of stakeholder marketing; social marketers have to build relationships with policy makers and politicians that will encourage them to take action. The hazard merchants – as Jobber reminded us above – certainly put a great deal of effort and resource into such lobbying.

Regulation can take many forms from self-regulatory codes of conduct to mandatory rules with clear and enforceable penalties for transgressions. The regulation of advertising in the UK comes into the first category; have a go at Exercise 7.9.

EXERCISE 7.9: CATCHING STARLINGS

Refer back to Exercise 7.1.

The self-regulatory codes on UK television advertising state that alcohol cannot be linked to the social acceptance or social success of individuals, events or occasions. More specifically, advertisements must not imply that drinking can enhance an individual's popularity, confidence, mood, physical performance, personal qualities, attractiveness or sexual success.

Does the Carling starling ad breach this code? Were the Advertising Standards Authority (ASA) right to reject complaints?

There is no clear-cut answer. Advertising has become so subtle and creative that making judgements about the nature of particular messages is remarkably difficult. Furthermore, as we noted in Chapter 6, different audiences are likely to have different interpretations, so who decides when a breach has occurred – the middle-aged, middle-class adman on the ASA panel or the 15-year-old binger? The result is confusion and this confusion can and will be exploited. The real problem is not the complexity of the code, though this surely does not help, it is that these types of self-regulatory procedures are built on the assumption that public health and big business are both on the same side. As we have rehearsed several times already in this chapter, all too often they are not because they have different priorities – the first that of reducing unnecessary sickness and early death, the second that of boosting shareholder value.

BUILDING THE EVIDENCE BASE

In these circumstances, statutory regulation has to play a central role. A comparison with health and safety is useful here. When the industrial revolution first took hold and mass production began in earnest, factories were dangerous places where worker safety was given little consideration. Children were employed as a matter of course, and death and injury were commonplace. Box 7.4 gives an evocative illustration of working practices.

BOX 7.4: 'COMING BACK BROCKENS'

In the early days of the Durham coalfields in the Northeast of England, the pits comprised a central vertical shaft which, as it was sunk, passed through horizontal seams of coal. The miners worked out along these seams leaving in place columns of coal to hold up the roof. Once they reached the limits of the seam they returned to the central shaft, removing the columns as they came, because the mine owners wanted every scrap of coal they could get. This was called 'coming back brockens' The miners' great skill was to judge just how much pillar they could remove without the roof collapsing. The dangers involved are demonstrated by the fact that 'coming back brockens' was only practised in coalfields with no habitation up above.

(Source: Holden 1994)

The official response to this hazardous state of affairs was not to encourage factory owners to produce comforting codes of conduct; it was to pass hard-nosed legislation such as the Factories Acts, which, for example, made it illegal to employ children. Now that we know that marketing in the hands of a tobacco company is just as dangerous as a machine tool or overly harsh shift regime, we also need to look to firm regulatory measures.

Statutory regulation needs a solid evidence base. Policy makers will not act unless they are confident that they can bring about genuine improvements; regulation necessarily means the infringement of liberty and there has to be credible justification for doing this. This high principle is reinforced by vested interest. We have already noted how companies actively cultivate policy makers, and their approaches become more energetic when regulation is on the cards. Indeed, in the case of tobacco, it has resulted in litigation: the tobacco industry recently took the UK Department of Health to court arguing that its new regulation on point of sale (POS) advertising was disproportionate. They lost because there is a rigorous and convincing evidence base to show that POS advertising does influence young people to smoke.

Building this evidence base involves both primary and secondary research. The International Tobacco Control Policy Evaluation Project,[4] for example, is a longitudinal research programme designed to assess the impact of different tobacco control policy options such as advertising bans, on-pack warnings and price increases. It uses a multi-country design – originally four countries were involved (the UK, the

US, Canada and Australia) but has now been extended to more than a dozen – and natural experiments to track policy impact. For example, it has been possible to show how the ban on tobacco advertising in the UK has resulted in significant public health improvements that are not evident in the US, where no such ban has been enacted (Harris *et al.* 2006).

An alternative approach to building the evidence base is to analyse secondary research, which, because of the degree of contention involved, presents particular challenges. The medical community, which also has to make challenging, consensual decisions about a contested evidence base, has responded by developing the concept of 'evidence-based decision making' (Mulrow 1994). This is built around the 'systematic review' (SR), which strengthens traditional literature reviewing by making it comprehensive, rigorous and transparent (refer back to Chapter 5). The process starts by laying down a clear protocol for searching all relevant databases, the content and quality criteria that will be used to determine inclusion in the review and the methods used to assess the relative quality of the included studies and their synthesis into conclusions. The contents of this protocol are included in the completed review and can therefore be subjected to detailed scrutiny and, if necessary, replicated by other researchers.

The technical paper prepared for WHO in 2006 by Hastings *et al.* (2006) describes how SR methods were, for the first time, applied to a marketing problem: the impact that food promotion may or may not be having on childhood obesity. Have a read of the report and consider how the SR procedures used made the work proof against criticism and helped it have a considerable influence on stakeholders.

Two factors were important in strengthening the review. SR procedures backed by consistent peer review made it largely unassailable by criticism. In particular, the transparency about the methods used meant that critics have to point out precise flaws or omissions; blanket disagreement or dismissal is untenable. Second, there was a clear acceptance that no final proof is possible. As with all social science research, we can only reduce uncertainty by testing hypothesies and judging the balance of probabilities. More recently, the same procedures have been used to assess the value of mandating the plain packaging of cigarettes. In this case, the review became part of the UK Government's official consultation on the subject.[5]

SR, then, provides a useful and robust way of building the regulatory evidence base. It is, however, very resource intensive. The plain packaging review, for instance, took two teams of researchers nearly 12 months to complete. In addition, it is inherently conservative. Only the most obvious and well-proven effects will be acknowledged. These are useful qualities in a public policy debate, where the stakes are high. As we noted in the introduction to the book, business is the engine of wealth creation, which means it effectively funds all our health and social services – and indeed social marketing. Checks and balances need to be applied with considerable caution.

However, as we discussed in Chapter 5, social marketers would argue that the value of SR in other areas, such as intervention design, is more limited. Furthermore, in the area of regulation, it proceeds with grindingly slow caution. An alternative approach to the plain packaging of tobacco, for instance, is to adopt what is sometimes termed the 'precautionary principle': we know tobacco is really dangerous so why would we take the chance of letting tobacco companies do anything that *might* encourage consumption – far better to play safe. This, in essence, is what the Australian Government has done: it did not conduct an SR; it just acted to mandate plain packaging.

WRAP-UP

In this chapter, we have examined how competition, which is a defining characteristic of business, also has resonance for social marketers. Competitive analysis can help us think more effectively about our clients' needs, the vital strategic importance of relationships with our suppliers and the very nature of the discipline.

It has also brought us into the crucial area of direct competition: social marketers can and must address the activities of the hazard merchants if they are serious about facilitating beneficial social change. This does not preclude collaboration with commercial partners, but it does warn us to proceed with great caution.

We have also seen how competitive analysis links with a range of much bigger questions: if tobacco industry marketing is wrecking our lungs by encouraging us to consume tobacco, to what extent is all marketing damaging our planet by encouraging us to consume a massive array of carbon-rich products and services; if corporations are legally required to prioritize their shareholders' interest, how can we ever expect them to prioritize the public interest; why do regulators mandate hard hats but go soft on television ads? This raises a much wider debate about how business and civil society interrelate, and pulls us inevitably into the field of critical marketing – which we will discuss further in the next chapter.

Reflective questions

1. What is meant by competitive analysis? Why is this important to the social marketer?

2. Model and discuss the role of competitive analysis in the social marketing planning process (from Chapter 4).

3. Explain how competitive analysis informs your social marketing positioning choices.

4. Discuss the two types of competition: direct and indirect, and when they might emerge in social marketing.

5. Model and delineate Porter's Four Forces for social marketing.

6. The social marketer's competitive strategy, following competitive analysis, is either to cooperate or compete. Discuss with illustrations.

7. Provide examples of when and how the social marketer would adopt a 'cooperate' competition strategy in the food and drinks industry.

8. Provide examples of when and how the social marketer should adopt a direct competition strategy in the food and drinks industry.

9. What is CSR? What are its advantages? What are its disadvantages? What are the implications of CSR for the social marketer?

10. What is the role of regulation in social marketing?

Reflective assignments

1. Find three social marketing case studies or papers that demonstrate competition in action.

2. Locate and assess a social marketing competitive analysis example.

3. You are a team comprising of (a) social marketing consultants, (b) a local City Council and (c) an advertising agency. You have been charged with developing and running an initiative to encourage waste avoidance. How will you use competitive analysis to help you to develop and evaluate your initiative? What strategy would you use?

4. You are a social marketer working with the National Roads Authority in your country. How might you use competitive analysis to assess your present behaviour change performance in relation to (a) policy makers and regulatory modifications to laws about drunk driving, speeding and drug usage; (b) speeding drivers due to alcohol, drugs or tiredness; (c) non-use of seatbelts and child safety restraints; and (d) unsafe driving endangering vulnerable road users such as pedestrians, motorcyclists, cyclists and young children?

5. You have recently joined a multi-disciplinary team considering man's impact upon the oceans. Specifically, you are examining different stakeholders concerned with food supply; human health; transport; energy and leisure and tourism and their demands upon our seas. How might a competitive analysis assist you?

6. Select one competitor of a social marketing organization you are familiar with. Based upon your existing knowledge of this competitor, along with an analysis of readily available data, write down what type and level of competition they represent to your chosen organization. How would you recommend your organization proceed?

7. Complete your traffic lights checklist for competitive analysis.

Notes

1   www.drinkaware.co.uk/.
2   www.bedrinkaware.com.au/.
3   www.youtube.com/watch?v=lkR0WDvFK1Q/.
4   http://itcproject.org/.
5   http://phrc.lshtm.ac.uk/project_2011-2016_006.html/.

References

Borland, R. (2003) 'A strategy for controlling the marketing of tobacco products: A regulated market model', *Tobacco Control*, 12(4): 374–382.

Browning, R. 'How they brought the good news from Ghent to Aix'. Online: 'The Project Gutenberg EBook of Browning's Shorter Poems, by Robert Browning', www.gutenberg.org/files/16376/16376-h/16376-h.htm (accessed 23 November 2012).

Callard, C., Thompson, D. and Collishaw, N. (2005) *Curing the Addiction to Profits: A Supply-side Approach to Phasing OUT Tobacco*, Ottawa, ON: Canadian Centre for Policy Alternatives and Physicians for a Smoke-Free Canada.

Edwards, G., West, R., Babor, T.F., Hall, W. and Marsden, J. (2004) 'An invitation to an alcohol industry lobby to help decide public funding of alcohol research and professional training: A decision that should be reversed', *Addiction* 99(10): 1235–1236.

Edwards, G., West, R., Babor, T.F., Hall, W. and Marsden, J. (2005) 'The integrity of the science base: A test case', *Addiction*, 100(5): 581–584.

Elliott, L. (2003) 'Cleaning agent'. Interview with Niall FitzGerald, Co-Chairman and Chief Executive, Unilever, *The Guardian*, 5 July.

Farrelly, M.C., Healton, C.G, Davis, K.C., Messeri, P., Hersey, J.C. and Haviland, M.L. (2002) 'Getting to the truth: Evaluating national tobacco countermarketing campaigns', *American Journal of Public Health*, 92(6): 901–907.

Grimm, D. (2005) 'Is tobacco research turning over a new leaf?' *Science*, 307:36–37.

Harris, F., MacKintosh, A.M., Anderson, S., Hastings, G., Borland, R., Fong, G.T., Hammond, D. and Cummings, K.M., for the ITCPES Research Team (2006) 'Effects of the 2003 advertising/promotion ban in the United Kingdom on awareness of tobacco marketing: Findings from the International Tobacco Control Four Country Survey', *Tobacco Control*, 15(Suppl 3): iii26–iii33.

Hastings, G., Stead, M., McDermott L., Forsyth, A., MacKintosh, A., Rayner M., Godfrey C., Caraher M. and Angus K. (2003) *Review of Research on the Effects of Food Promotion to Children – Final Report and Appendices*. Prepared for the Food Standards Agency. Stirling: Institute for Social Marketing.

Hastings, G., Anderson, S., Cooke, E. and Gordon, R. (2005) 'Alcohol marketing and young people's drinking: A review of the research', *Journal of Public Health Policy*, 26(3): 296–311.

Hastings, G., McDermott, L., Angus K., Stead, M. and Thomson, S. (2006) *The Extent, Nature and Effects of Food Promotion to Children: A Review of the Evidence.*

Technical Paper prepared for the World Health Organization, July 2006. Geneva: World Health Organization. Online: www.who.int/dietphysicalactivity/publications/Hastings_paper_marketing.pdf.

Holden, M. (1994) *Coming Back Brockens: A Year in a Mining Village*. London: Jonathan Cape (as quoted in *The Marketing Matrix*).

House of Commons Health Select Committee (2000) *Second Report – The Tobacco Industry and the Health Risks of Smoking*. Volume II, *Minutes of Evidence and Appendices* (October 2000), London: The Stationery Office.

Jackson, K.M., Sher, J.K. and Wood, P.K. (2000) 'Prospective analysis of comorbidity: Tobacco and alcohol use disorders', *Journal of Abnormal Psychology*, 109(4):679–94.

Jobber, D. (2004) *Principles and Practice of Marketing*. 4th Edition. Maidenhead: McGraw-Hill International.

Lang, T. and Rayner, G. (2012) 'Ecological public health: The 21st century's big idea?' *British Medical Journal*, 345: e5466.

Layard, R. (2005) *Happiness: Lessons from a New Science*. London: Allen Lane.

Levitt, T. (1960) 'Marketing Myopia', *Harvard Business Review* July/August.

Lovato, C., Linn, G., Stead, L.F. and Best, A. (2003) 'Impact of tobacco advertising and promotion on increasing adolescent smoking behaviours', *Cochrane Database of Systematic Reviews*, (4): CD003439.

MacAskill, S. and Eadie, D. (2002) *Evaluation of a Pilot Project on Smoking Cessation in Prisons*. Glasgow: University of Strathclyde, Centre for Social Marketing.

MacAskill, S., Stead, M., MacKintosh, A.M. and Hastings, GB. (2002) ' "You cannae just take cigarettes away from somebody and no' gie them something back": Can social marketing help solve the problem of low income smoking?' *Social Marketing Quarterly*, VIII(1): 19–34.

Mosher, J.F. (2012) 'Joe Camel in a Bottle: Diageo, the Smirnoff Brand, and the Transformation of the Youth Alcohol Market', *American Journal of Public Health*, January 102(1): 56–63.

Mulrow, C.D. (1994) 'Rationale for systematic reviews', *British Medical Journal*, 309: 597–599.

Noble, G. and Basil, D. (2011) 'Competition and positioning', Ch. 9 in G. Hastings, K. Angus and C. Bryant (eds) *The SAGE Handbook of Social Marketing*. London: Sage Publications Ltd.

Ogilvy & Mather (2012) 'From Anti-Smoking to Pro-Quitting', National Smoking Control Campaign, 2011, IPA Effectiveness Awards, Health Promotion Board of Singapore.

Piercy, N.F. (2009) *Market-Led Strategic Change, Transforming the Process of Going to Market*, 4th edition. Oxford, UK: Elsevier Ltd.

Porter, M.E. (2004) 'The Five Competitive Forces that Shape Strategy', *Harvard Business Review*, January 2008, pp.86–104.

Rothschild, M.L., Mastin, B. and Miller, T.W. (2006) 'Reducing alcohol-impaired driving crashes through the use of social marketing', *Accident Analysis and Prevention*, 38(6): 1218–1230.

Wakefield, M., Terry-McElrath, Y., Emery, S., Saffer, H., Chaloupka, F.J., Szczypka, G., Flay, B., O'Malley, P.M. and Johnston, L.D. (2006) 'Effect of televised, tobacco company-funded smoking prevention advertising on youth smoking-related beliefs, intentions, and behavior', *American Journal of Public Health*, 96(12): 2154–2164.

WHO (1946) Preamble to the Constitution of the World Health Organization as adopted by the International Health Conference, New York, 19–22 June, 1946; signed on 22 July 1946 by the representatives of 61 States (Official Records of the World Health Organization, no. 2, p. 100) and entered into force on 7 April 1948.

Chapter **8**

Critical marketing[1]

STONE WALLS DO NOT A PRISON MAKE

Barney crept out of his hole and ventured once more into the wide world. In the seven weeks since his mother's sudden and unexplained disappearance, the young white mouse had gradually learned to fend for himself. He now knew where to find food; the dead-ends to avoid and the misleading scents to ignore. His first efforts had been halting and inadequate and he hadn't eaten at all for the first two days. Now he not only dined whenever he wanted, but he had also worked out how to quench his thirst. The water, which he could so enticingly smell, could be accessed if he climbed on top of the yellow pebble and stood on his hind legs against the wall. It had all been very scary at first, doing everything for himself, but now he had got to like it. It was an adventure and a challenge all in one; a test that he was passing more successfully every day. It might not be as comfortable and easy as when his mother had provided for him, but Barney had come to the conclusion that he preferred being his own mouse. Independence and self-empowerment, he thought to himself, you can't do better.

Then he heard the white-coats talking and scurried back to his hole.

'Peter, that's me leaving now. Please can you make sure you fill the water bottle in the mouse cage before you go home.'

Barney is happy but utterly deluded. He thinks he is free, self-empowered and successfully making his way in the world, when, in fact, he is a laboratory mouse being manipulated and controlled at will by the white-coated scientists. It is tempting to sneer at his naivety, but we are all at risk of being just as gullible as Barney if we fail to question and challenge the world around us. If we simply accept things at face value, omit to scrutinize the rights and wrongs of the system we live in or recognize that our seemingly independent decision making about how we live our lives is, on the one hand, actually greatly influenced by our social context and, on the other, having a profound impact beyond us as individuals.

Nowhere is this critical consciousness more important than in the world of marketing. As we explained in earlier chapters, social marketing came into being because it was recognized that marketing's well-established capacity to influence our behaviour might be useful outwith the marketplace. That which so successfully gets us to eat burgers and drink vodka might also be used to encourage healthy eating and moderate drinking – or even abstinence. This power transfer makes sense, but it also begs enormous questions about the influence of commercial marketing, and the legitimacy this has. Who decides which behaviours commercial marketers are to change and how they go about it? When does justifiable encouragement become inappropriate manipulation? Is it ever acceptable to trick the unwary, hoodwink the naive or exploit the vulnerable by simply invoking the fig leaf of *caveat emptor*?[2] Above all, who is checking whether the inevitably narrow focus of the business strategy is in conflict with the (hopefully) broad inclusivity of government strategy?

This chapter, then, will introduce and stress the importance of this principle of independent critical thought. It calls on us all to ask questions, challenge the status quo, look underneath the surface and expose assumptions to the harsh light of day.

It starts by reminding us that such thinking is not new to marketing; it dates back to the very origins of the discipline. It then points out that the need to be critical puts us all on the spot: we have to take responsibility for our behaviour and its impact on others. However, we are not alone; we revisit Foster Wallace (Chapter 2) and add a systemic view to our analysis. Specifically, the dominance of marketing and the resulting drive for ever-greater consumption has to be addressed. Ideas of strategic planning, ubiquity and the deployment of multiple tools, which we have seen to be valuable insights for social marketing in earlier chapters, become a threat when we think about materialism, inequalities and global warming. Next we move upstream, revisiting CSR and linking it to corporate attacks on political power.

This brings us back to the need for regulation, but takes us beyond the control of ad hoc malpractice by the hazard merchants we discussed in Chapter 7. Rather, we explore the need for strategic regulation, guided by more enlightened aims than profits and shareholder returns – values such as physical, mental, social and planetary wellbeing. Finally, though, we recognize that top-down solutions cannot work alone; they must be combined with the critical engagement of us all in the process of change.

This may seem like an ambitious agenda, but in reality it is just core business for a discipline which *'critically examines commercial marketing so as to learn from its successes and curb its excesses'* (see Chapter 1). It is also an essential first step if we want to move away from ad hoc amelioration to tackling the major issues that face the world. Issues such as inequalities, conflict and climate change. How can we start to put things right if we haven't taken the time and trouble to work out what is wrong; if we haven't undertaken some intelligent critical marketing?

Learning outcomes

By the end of this chapter, you should be much more sceptical about the world of marketing. Specifically you should be able to:

✓ Define and explain the fiduciary imperative and the dangers of corporate power
✓ See why a leading psychiatrist diagnosed the corporation with psychopathy
✓ Recognize the inequalities inherent in a system that perpetually chases money to the exclusion of other values
✓ Understand some of the individual and collective harms that can be done by corporate marketing, and how these come about
✓ Appreciate that corporate social responsibility is just as much marketing as are brand management and advertising
✓ Understand why these critical insights are so important to social marketing.

Key words

cause-related marketing – consumption – corporate social responsibility (CSR) – critical thought – fiduciary imperative – individual and collective harm – inequalities

A CENTURY OF CRITICAL MARKETING

The idea of addressing the social consequences of business is far from being a new issue for marketing. It takes us back to the origins not just of social marketing thought, but also of marketing thought. An extensive review of the field published in the *Journal of Public Policy & Marketing* points out that what the authors Wilkie and Moore call 'marketing and society' has been a key part of marketing since it first became a distinct discipline at the turn of the twentieth century. They go on to note that well before the Second World War marketers were not limiting themselves to studying managerial issues, but addressing much wider social questions, such as whether advertising is desirable or certain industries should exist at all (see Box 8.1). They were interested in how the relationship between consumers, marketers and government could 'facilitate the maximal operations of the system *for the benefit of the host society*' (Wilkie and Moore 2003: 118).

> ### BOX 8.1: MARKETING AND SOCIETY
>
> Wider social Issues have always been a concern of marketing thought, as Wilkie and Moore's summary of the broader questions early marketers were addressing shows:
>
> - Are there too many middlemen? Does distribution cost too much?
> - Does advertising raise or lower prices?
> - What control, if any, should be exerted over new combinations in distribution?
> - Of the total costs paid by consumers, which elements are desirable?
> - Indispensable?
> - What about 'non-essential' services such as credit availability; should these be eliminated?
>
> (Source: Wilkie and Moore 2003)

Wilkie and Moore's review goes on to conclude that this interest in the social impact of marketing needs to continue and indeed strengthen, a call reinforced by the discipline's premier *Journal of Marketing* in its millennium edition.

Social marketing has a crucial role to play in this renaissance. Just as our knowledge of marketing can help us deconstruct the practices of the hazard merchants (Chapter 7), so we can contribute to the wider debate about the role and values of commercial marketing in a modern democracy. Naomi Klein (2001) and Joel Bakan (2004) have led an onslaught of commentators pointing out the deficiencies of corporate capitalism, from sweatshops to inflationary branding. Indeed, Bakan concludes that the modern corporation is nothing more or less than a psychopath (see Excercise 8.2). Others have responded defensively, pointing out that corporations do a lot of good, not least by underpinning much of the wealth that funds modern medicine, social services and education. They also point out that, while Bakan and Klein make a great job of flagging up deficiencies, they do not present much in the way of solutions; good box office, but light on direction.

Social marketing can help plug this gap with its combination of balance and practical solutions. In terms of balance, this whole book points out that the marketing used by corporations and so despised by its critics is not intrinsically harmful. On the contrary, it can be used to great social benefit, as the Case Studies at the end of the book show. Helping disadvantaged smokers to quit, combating racism and making our roads safer are all very desirable social outcomes. Social marketing demonstrates that marketing is an amoral technology that, provided it is controlled properly and deployed ethically, can bring about great good.

We all then have to think carefully about our use of and relationship with marketing. This raises the idea of individual responsibility, and hence that of critical thinking (see Box 8.3).

INDIVIDUAL RESPONSIBILITY

When we discussed social cognitive theory in Chapter 3, we emphasized the dangers of victim blaming. None of us has complete control of our behaviour – environmental influences, such as social norms or the absence of resources, inevitably influence our options – so it is both wrong and ineffective to put the onus for change entirely on the individual.

The founding story of public health epitomizes this view. In 1854, John Snow, a doctor working in London, found convincing evidence that a cholera epidemic in the district of Soho was being caused not by bad air as contemporary wisdom had it, but by polluted water. When the authorities refused to listen, he took matters into his own hands and had the handle removed from the public pump that was delivering up sewerage-contaminated drinking water. In this way, he proved his point and resolved the problem all in one. He also hard-wired the public health discipline's focus on intervening upstream. The danger otherwise is that you end up blaming people for a predicament in which they find themselves through no fault of their own. There was, for instance, little the individual Soho inhabitant could do about their poor-quality water, even had they known it was toxic.

Social marketing respects Dr Snow's insights, and shares the public health aversion to victim blaming. We too need to ask what we can do to make the system better so that healthy – and ecological, socially enhancing, politically intelligent, ethical – choices become the obvious and easy ones. But equally social marketers recognize systemic change is not enough; a degree of personal responsibility is essential. We are all perfectly capable of being miserable in paradise if we don't have internal balance. Kropotkin was right when he lauded the human capacity to cooperate and work together, but that collective instinct is also dependent on robust individuals. Barney the white mouse, hapless though his circumstances are, has his own strengths to bring to the party. And even in situations where the individual seems utterly parlous – the drug addict, the third or Majority World indigenous farmer facing starvation, the dying cancer patient – it is vital to recognize they still have immensely valuable resources to bring to the behaviour change table. Box 8.2 shows how a development agency made great progress because they benefited from the strengths of the local Quechua Indians. Their language will have brought all the learning from a thousand years of culture, their labour made projects possible, their intelligence and entrepreneurialism provided the essence of the Kamayoqs. The result is sustainable change based on genuine partnership between actors who all have something of value to offer.

BOX 8.2: KAMAYOQS

A development NGO called Intermediate Technology Development Group (Practical Action) working in Peru has recognized the value that indigenous citizens provide and has moved away from the conventional practice of drafting in external experts with one of training up local people as Kamayoqs, which in the local Quechua tongue means knowledge bearers.

The process 'began by simply talking to the local people'. These conversations were in Quechua, which is typically disparaged by officialdom, and the development workers put 'great emphasis on local culture' because, they argue, change 'has to be rooted in campesino institutions otherwise it won't be sustainable'. Nonetheless, 'to begin with, people were mistrustful. They were used to a vertical relationship with state agencies, even with development agencies. For them, a vet was someone who turns up in a car wearing good boots and a new jacket and says: "This is what we're going to do" '.

But cultural sensitivity combined with partnership working succeeded in removing these barriers. For example, the irrigation system, which dated back to the Incas, was renovated with due deference to its powerful religious significance and by teamwork: Practical Action provided the materials and 'the campesinos did the work, they invested their labour' and so 'now they're managing the irrigation system themselves. They've made it their own – that's what makes it sustainable'.

Practical Action took the same approach to agriculture. Rather than parachuting in expensive external experts, they helped local people access training in animal husbandry. The resulting system of Kamayoqs has three major advantages: it avoids expensive consultants' wages; it is sustainable because the Kamayoqs are and will remain locally based; and it sets in train a process of self-improvement. To use a well-worn metaphor, this was not a matter of providing people with fish, but enabling them to fish for themselves. The last word should go to one of the Kamayoqs, a woman called Vicenta Cahuana: 'I used to take orders from my husband and sometimes he was violent. In the past women didn't have rights. I began to think this has to change. I started to respect myself more. My husband got very uncomfortable. He said: "Whatever you're learning, it's no good for this household because you're answering me back. You're not respectful any more since you've been running around." In a friendly way, I told him I'm taking better care of the animals. I don't waste money getting them cured. Now he says carry on."

(Source: Open University and BBC 2000)

George Orwell squares the circle between John Snow and the Kamayoqs by pointing out that 'two viewpoints are tenable' (social marketing would say essential): 'the one, how can you improve human nature until you have changed the system? The other, what is the use of changing the system before you have improved human nature' (Orwell 1970: 48). Any recipe for change, then, has to address the individual as well as the systemic.

Try Exercise 8.1.

EXERCISE 8.1: THE FREEDOM TO SMOKE?

The latest Surgeon General's (2012) report shows that 88 per cent of US smokers take up the habit before the age of 18, and most of the other 12 per cent have joined in before they are 21. Adults, then, do not start smoking. It seems once we are mature enough to appreciate the downside of the cigarette – a lifetime's expensive addiction followed by a one in two chance of a painful premature death – we turn on our heels at the mere sight of a tobacco marketer. Furthermore, three-quarters of the adults who made a bad call in childhood and took up smoking now regret it and would prefer to quit – but their dependence on nicotine ties them to tobacco. Unless they manage to break this dependence they have a 50 per cent chance of becoming one of the estimated five million who are killed globally each year by tobacco (WHO 2008).

On the other hand, FOREST, the tobacco industry-funded lobby group, argue that tobacco use is about freedom of choice and free markets, and rail against the interference of the nanny state and over-weaning 'health fascists' meddling in a legal and productive business. Tobacco marketing is a legitimate way for a long-established industry to go about its business.

Think through the arguments on both sides. Who do you agree with? Does the fact that the trade in tobacco is legal make it right? Is freedom a reasonable concept to use for a product that is only chosen by the immature and contains a highly addictive drug? Would you take a job in a tobacco company? Would you advocate banning tobacco?

There are no right or wrong answers to the exercise. It is there to stimulate questions; to remind us that we have a duty to challenge and be sceptical – to think critically (see Box 8.3). Only in this way will we identify problems, generate original solutions and change the world for the better

BOX 8.3: CRITICAL THINKING

Critical thinking is the search for objective truth; it questions the assumptions underpinning what we think to be true, to uncover what we can objectively state to be true.

Defining qualities: analysis, questioning assumptions, search for objective truth.

OUR CORPORATE WORLD

Turning now to Orwell's point about the system, think back to Chapter 2 and David Foster Wallace's (2008) story of the two young fishes who don't even realize that they are swimming in water, let alone that it is vital to their survival. He is reminding us that normalcy and familiarity can render the environmental influences on our lives almost invisible. Furthermore, the unobtrusiveness of these stimuli makes them all the more powerful; effects can simply slip under our radar.

Marketing is one of these very powerful influences. The increasing commercialization of our lives – of the water we swim in – has profound effects on how we think, feel and behave. Thinking again about Exercise 8.1, the continued marketing of tobacco, even where this has been limited by legislation,[3] makes it more difficult to remember that nicotine is as addictive as heroin and that tobacco killed more First World War soldiers than did the bullets. Similarly, the massive budgets spent on promoting alcohol in Europe and North America encourage us to forget that worldwide most people are teetotal; in a statistical sense, at least, drinking alcohol is abnormal. Or consider obesity: given that in the US, Australia and the UK around two-thirds of people are either obese or overweight, how much sense does it make to have Coke and McDonald's as principal sponsors of the Olympic Games?

Furthermore, our analysis of the water we swim in has to move beyond individual products and examine the system more generally. Most of us now live in capitalist, free market economies, which are increasingly dominated by multinational corporations. Corporations depend on shareholders (also known as the stockholders in North America) to invest their money with them; in return, shareholders get to share the profits of the business. Corporations, then, spend other people's money and, in order to guard against corruption, their obligation to look after the investors' interests above and beyond all others has been enshrined in law. As we noted in Chapter 1, this is known as the 'fiduciary imperative' and has become the driving force of the modern corporation (see Box 8.4).

BOX 8.4: 'RESISTANCE IS FUTILE, YOU WILL BE ASSIMILATED'

For the *Star Trek* fans among us, the Borg are known as the ultimate invasion threat to mankind – a pseudo race with immense and awesome adaptability who savagely kidnap different species from all over the universe to serve as cybernetic implanted drones of the collective hive with their Borg Queen. The Borg relentlessly pursue one goal – total dominance – through central control and forced assimilation with no individuality, freedom or equality tolerated. One could argue the Borg Principle at its finest – 'resistance is futile, you will be assimilated' – is operating in many of the corporations around the planet today.

THERE IS BUSINESS AND THERE IS CORPORATE BUSINESS

The ability to do business is one of the things that separates us from other animals. Barter, trade and the doing of deals is at the core of our capacity to operate collectively. This cooperation is also essential for our survival. We cannot possibly cater for all our worldly needs without the help of others, so we need a way of harnessing this help. Friends and family may well contribute voluntarily, but in a complex world their efforts will not suffice: strangers have to be brought into the equation. Business provides a mechanism for doing this.

Michael, the greengrocer in my Scottish hometown, epitomizes the benefits of business. He provides a good range of the foods we need – from apples to zucchini – and, if asked, will happily try to source items he doesn't normally stock. His prices are competitive, although most people would probably guess (incorrectly) that he charges more than the local supermarket. Michael also provides a pleasant service, expertly modulated to his customers. The dowager ladies from up the hill get the personal touch and their bags packed, the children are handled with kindness and respect, and those customers who show a taste for it get a fine line in Scots wit and repartee. He even offers a home delivery service. Michael's business acumen is matched only by his unerring diplomacy: he never risks offending his customers. His adroit fencing of the inevitable anti-English jokes (many of his best customers come from south of the Tweed) is a joy to behold. When he retires from the shop, a job at the United Nations beckons.

What is more, Michael has succeeded in moving across the commercial border and becoming a real friend. He surely likes what we do for his bottom line, but he also genuinely likes us – and we him. Being his customer not only keeps our store cupboard well stocked, it also makes us feel good.

Contrast this small-town bliss with another Scottish business: the Royal Bank of Scotland (RBS). Superlatives and invective have been worn out describing the harm Fred Goodwin[4] and his colleagues caused: cupidity and insane greed brought the bank to the brink of ruin – and came close to taking the whole country with it. It is tempting to see this as an anomaly, driven by particularly toxic business models in a temporarily out-of-control financial sector.

However, the problem is neither new nor a one-off. Steinbeck wrestled with exactly the same issues back in 1939 when writing about the predations of the banks on dustbowl farmers. He characterized the bank as a monster which 'needs – wants – insists – must have'; 'those creatures don't breathe air, don't eat side-meat. They breathe profits; they eat the interest on money' (1939: 39). Thirty years later, Republican President, and former soldier, Dwight D. Eisenhower warned of the immense dangers of the 'Military Industrial Complex' and its 'unwarranted influence – economic, political, even spiritual' being 'felt in every city, every Statehouse, every office of the Federal government', warning that 'we must not fail to comprehend its grave implications. Our toil, resources, and livelihood are all involved. So is the very structure of our society.' (You can listen to his whole speech on YouTube.)[5]

Move forward another 30 years and this time a professor of marketing, Michael Thomas, provides the admonishment:

We have unleashed a monster that no one can control, even that minority that profits from it. Unashamed self-interest is a vice, not a virtue. We must recognise that the usefulness of an activity is not necessarily measured by its profitability, and that what someone earns is not an indicator of their talents and abilities, still less of their moral stature.

(Thomas 1999)

The essential difference between Michael the greengrocer and RBS is one of power: Michael is a vulnerable small business; RBS is a too-big-to-fail corporation. As social marketers, we have to recognize that such power matters, and, unless we are prepared to analyse its impacts and challenge its harmful effects, our work is unlikely to be effective.

ADDING CHARM

This begs the question as to why any of us would want to do business with an organization ruthlessly focused on its own interests and making money out of others' needs. Why would anyone willingly engage with such a body? This is where marketing comes in, adding an all-important charm to the mix. As we have already noted, marketing long predates the corporation, but it has been adopted by the corporate marketer to help make the organization's selfish intent less apparent.

Branding is a perfect illustration of this. Joel Bakan (2004), in his book *The Corporation*, points out that one of the first brands was developed by the giant US corporation General Electric to try to give a human face to what was in reality a monolithic conglomerate focused on delivering maximum returns to its shareholders and management. Since these early days, the brand has become a commonplace in the commercial sector, softening the image of corporate bodies, from Coca-Cola to Diageo.

Branding is, of course, just part of a much broader marketing effort, which deploys new product development, packaging, distribution, pricing and multifaceted communications to win our hearts and minds. Equally energetic efforts, in the form of corporate social responsibility, public relations and corporate affairs, are used to court stakeholders, policy makers and politicians. All to ensure that we love the corporation (or at least don't criticize it too much). We will return to these different marketing tools, and their potential problems, later in the chapter.

Such was Bakan's concern about the nature of the corporation that he consulted a leading psychiatrist, Dr Hare, to find out what he would make of a person with this combination of a single-minded focus on their own interests, along with the superficial charm provided by marketing. Dr Hare's diagnosis is presented in Exercise 8.2.

EXERCISE 8.2: THE CORPORATION AS PSYCHOPATH

'[W]hen we asked Dr. Hare to apply his diagnostic checklist of psychopathic traits (italicized below) to the corporation's institutional character, he found there was a close match. The corporation is *irresponsible*, Dr. Hare said, because "in an attempt to satisfy the corporate goal, everybody else is put at risk." Corporations try to "*manipulate* everything, including public opinion," and they are *grandiose*, always insisting "that we're number one, we're the best." A *lack of empathy* and *asocial tendencies* are also key characteristics of the corporation, says Hare – "their behaviour indicates they don't really concern themselves with their victims"; and corporations often *refuse to accept responsibility for their own actions and are unable to feel remorse* . . . Finally . . . corporations relate to others *superficially* – "their whole goal is to present themselves to the public in a way that is appealing to the public [but] in fact may not be representative of what th[e] organisation is really like"'. (Bakan 2004: 56–57)

Do you agree with Dr Hare's diagnosis? What, if anything, do you think could or should be done to make the corporation less selfish?

Whether you agree with his conclusion or not, it is clear there is an odd mismatch between the corporation, with its definitively selfish focus, and marketing, which is supposed to be all about customer needs. Corporate marketing would seem to be a contradiction in terms, like 'military intelligence' or 'free trade'.

THE HARM DONE BY CORPORATE MARKETING

Certainly a great deal of harm is done by corporate marketing. We have already touched on the ill health and personal damage inflicted by tobacco, alcohol and an excess of fast food. More broadly, we should also note the potential for psychological harm that comes with a system that promises to meet our every need. A core function of marketing is continuously to scan and research our wants and preferences, so as to cater for them as effectively as possible. But doesn't this risk making us all overly materialistic? Isn't there a danger that we resort too much to retail therapy and get misled into thinking we can buy happiness? Might it not lead us to become spoilt and self-centred?

David Foster Wallace (2008) reminds us that we have a natural tendency to see the world in an egocentric way. What we see, hear, understand and experience is filtered through our own senses – through what he terms the 'lens of self'; everyone else's views and experiences come to us second-hand; they have to be communicated to us. This creates a default position of perceiving everything as revolving around ourselves.

He goes on to highlight the dangers of this perspective. When things go wrong – the train doesn't arrive or the computer crashes – we take it as a personal affront, and give no allowance to the fact that other perfectly legitimate – indeed, more important – priorities than our own might exist. We behave like over-indulged children.

Buddhists would agree with Wallace about the dangers of such an egocentric perspective, and the need to avoid it: 'to conquer oneself is a greater victory than to conquer thousands in a battle'.[6] The alternative, Wallace (2008) warns, is fruitless and self-destructive: 'worship your own body and beauty and sexual allure and you will always feel ugly, and when time and age start showing, you will die a million deaths before they finally plant you'.

Think for a minute how the cosmetics marketer overlooks these stark warnings. Oil of Olay, for instance, offers the opportunity of 'achieving younger-looking skin at any age' and the chance to 'fight 7 signs of aging' with a 'fragrance- and color-free daily facial moisturizer', which 'moisturizes to create visibly younger-looking skin'.[7] L'Oréal promises even more: 'Visible Lift' is their '1st anti-wrinkle foundation with a serum inside' so you can have 'instantly younger-looking skin' – no need to even wait for your eternal youthfulness to be created.[8] (Notice, incidentally, the use of the word 'daily' by Oil of Olay – the promises may be fulsome, but you will need to make a long-term commitment.)

Wallace (2008) takes his argument much further and argues that 'pretty much anything else you worship will eat you alive. If you worship money and things – if they are where you tap real meaning in life – then you will never have enough'. He is alerting us to a fundamental contradiction at the heart of corporate marketing: the offer of perpetual satisfaction to a species who can never be satisfied. The problem is we are seeking happiness not stuff; and stuff brings us about as close to happiness as Christmas tinsel does to redemption. To quote the Dalai Lama again: 'happiness is not something ready-made. It comes from your own actions'. You cannot buy it any more than you can buy youth.

Or, as the graffiti artist put it (Figure 8.1), what if the best things in life aren't things?

Figure 8.1 The limits of materialism

Corporate marketing also raises concerns about inequalities. The perpetual quest to satisfy our every need comes at a price, both literally and figuratively. Do Exercise 8.3.

EXERCISE 8.3: THE PRICE OF ETERNAL YOUTH

Go online or visit a shop and work out how much it would cost, over a one-year period, to 'achieve younger-looking skin' and 'fight 7 signs of aging' using Oil of Olay's daily facial moisturizer.

Work out how long it would take someone on your country's minimum wage to earn this amount. (Don't forget to take deductions such as income tax into account.)

The exercise demonstrates that we have a system that caters for our needs provided we have the resources to pay. As an MBA student recently remarked to a colleague: 'Why should marketers worry about the poor, they have no money?'[9] The result is a continuous accentuation of the gulf between the haves and the have-nots.

But the MBA student is missing a crucial point: we are all damaged by inequalities. As we noted in Chapter 1, it has now been well demonstrated that the best societies to live in are those with the smallest divisions between rich and poor. This is because even the richest people depend on communally provided resources such as roads, an educated workforce and an independent criminal justice system. Many important benefits in life, then, depend on our working together, rather than fragmenting into groups and individuals (remember Uggina's lesson from Chapter 7). Arguably, the classic marketing tools of targeting and segmentation push in the opposite direction and so serve to accentuate inequalities (see Exercise 8.4).

EXERCISE 8.4: THE DIVISIVE PERILS OF SEGMENTATION

'[T]here is also a big social cost to segmentation and targeting: it divides us into exclusive groups. I find myself feeling superior because I drive a certain car, or sneering at someone for buying what I see as a second rate clothing brand. I hate this condescending tendency, but somehow it insinuates itself. . . . The observation that we are all different is axiomatic, and indeed to be welcomed and celebrated. I just think that having a phenomenon as powerful and effective as corporate marketing focused on accentuating these differences is dangerous – especially when the only motive for doing so is to get us consuming more.

The second major problem with segmentation and targeting is that it institutionalizes the notion that being able to afford something justifies its consumption. The ludicrous wealth of corporate CEOs leads seamlessly to Lear jets; bonus-happy city traders take us to jeroboams of vintage champagne; bejewelled despots provide the rationale for arms sales. Thus the pocket book preempts moral judgement or intelligent debate.

Third, and most fundamentally, segmentation and targeting hone and perfect the aim of the corporate marketer. It makes everything he or she does more powerful, just as a magnifying glass concentrates the power of sunlight. So everything we have been discussing in this book becomes turbo-charged; it accelerates and gains even more influence. And so we shop.' (Hastings 2012)

Think about the points being made. Do you agree with them?

THE SELFISH SYSTEM

The discussion so far suggests that, when seen from an individual's perspective, our system of corporate marketing can be selfish and flawed. From a global perspective, the problems become even more worrying. Have a try at Exercise 8.5.

EXERCISE 8.5: THE LIFEBOAT

It was just over half an hour since the passenger ship had gone down and the eight strangers found themselves shocked but safe in a lifeboat. Their condition was better than might be expected, after all the boat was designed for 14, so they had plenty of blankets and supplies to go round. Then someone noticed that there were still people clinging to wreckage near where the ship had sunk and suggested they row over to pick them up. This caused a lively debate. It was pointed out that, while this would certainly be a nice thing to do, it would make things more difficult and dangerous for them all. At the moment they were warm and well catered for, but if others got into the boat there would be less to go round. And if there were a lot of newcomers they might even swamp the boat. After some toing and froing, it was decided to keep well away from the other survivors and concentrate on enjoying the energy-dense biscuits and really rather good medicinal rum.

(Source: Adapted from Baggini 2005)

Discuss the pros and cons of the passengers' decision.

Would you have done the same or behaved differently?

The behaviour of the passengers seems at best hard-hearted and at worst down-right disgraceful. How could they so callously disregard the plight of their fellow human beings? However, before we get too indignant, we should note that the story is taken from a book of moral philosophy by Julian Baggini and the lifeboat is actually a metaphor for our planet. We in the rich north – the 'Minority World' – are behaving just as selfishly as the folk in the lifeboat. How did this come to be?

Textbooks date the modern business era back to the days of Henry Ford, when demand greatly outstripped supply, and all that mattered was mass production. As long as you could make it, people would buy it, and the maxim 'any colour you want as long as it's black' was not arrogant (though it sounds it now), it was just a simple statement of reality. Then, after the Second World War, the economic balance changed, supply increased and began to outstrip demand. In the case of food, for example, historian Clive Ponting (2000:790) points out; 'After the mid twentieth century there was, for the first time in world history, enough food in the world to feed everybody adequately. The problem was that it was very unequally distributed.' This might have been a good point at which to rethink the model. Instead, as Ponting continues; 'By the late twentieth century the people of the industrialised countries of western Europe, Japan and north America ate half the world's food though they constituted only a quarter of the world's population. Much of the problem was caused by the fact that land in Asia, Africa and South America was devoted to growing crops for export to the major industrialised countries. A large proportion of this trade was simply to provide greater variety in the diet for people who were already well fed... in the second half of the twentieth century a domestic cat in the US ate more meat than people living in Africa and Latin America.' The 1950s, when supply began to outstrip demand in our bit of the globe, marked the time when we in the rich minority countries rowed away from our planetary fellow passengers.

Instead of wrestling with problems of redistribution and inequalities, the emphasis of business simply switched from production to selling. As one marketing textbook explains: 'faced with stagnant markets and the spectre of price competition, producers sought to stimulate demand through increased selling efforts' (Baker 2003: 5). A generation of sales reps stepped up to the plate and the growth of mass advertising gave them enormous reach. Vance Packard (2007) famously tore the mask off this world in *The Hidden Persuaders*, uncovering a vast array of in-depth 'psychological' market research methods and correspondingly unscrupulous selling techniques. However, his book was rightly criticized for being piecemeal, descriptive and lacking insight into the fundamental economic and political forces underlying marketing: 'His critique has no systematic basis. Packard sees the problem of covert "persuasion" as a mere unsettling fad within the marketing establishment, and not as an inevitable outgrowth of the economic system' (Miller 2007: 19). Sixty years later, with the benefit of hindsight, these systemic problems are all too apparent.

Not so in the 1950s: the textbook continues, the 'spectre of price competition' remained:

if all the products are perceived as being the same then price becomes the distinguishing feature and the supplier becomes a price taker, thus having to relinquish the important managerial function of exercising control. Faced with such an impasse the real manager recognizes that salvation (and control) will be achieved through a policy of product differentiation.

(Baker 2003: 5)

The marketer's version of history continues with the decline and fall of this flawed era of high-pressure selling, and the dawn of the enlightened age of marketing. Business came to see the benefits of replacing the old system of selling what could be produced with one of producing what could be sold. This has saved them from ruin and transformed what were dinosaur-like monoliths into consumer-focused modern companies. All because, the comforting narrative continues, marketing puts the consumer at the apex of the pyramid and focuses the whole business effort – from receptionist to CEO – on the Holy Grail of their complete satisfaction. We, the consumers, are now in charge. From this perspective, marketing begins to seem like an enlightened, almost democratic business model.

Except that, as we have already noted, the corporate structure gives this the lie – we are not in charge; the shareholder is. And seeking perpetual satisfaction is as futile as it is corrosive. And, while we live in almost farcical plenty (a large UK supermarket, for example, has no fewer than 40,000 different product offerings), the Majority World continues to live in grinding need. Just one statistic: almost half the world's population, around three billion people, live on less than two Euros a day (Shah 2010). Referring back to Exercise 8.3, calculate how much Oil of Olay moisturizer someone living on this income could afford, were they reckless enough to spend their money in this way.

So we end up as part of an extremely selfish system. We are behaving just like the people in the lifeboat. Do Exercise 8.6.

EXERCISE 8.6: WHAT MAKES US SELFISH?

We are all behaving like the people in the lifeboat. How has this come to be? Take a little time to think through how we have all been pulled into this morally questionable position.

Write down your thoughts.

THE METHODS OF CORPORATE MARKETING

There are many answers to Exercise 8.6, but corporate marketing has to be a big part of them. It seduces and entices us into consuming more and more. This power comes from the three characteristics that we have explored in early chapters: strategic planning, ubiquitous deployment and a mix of tools.

> ### Strategic planning

Time is the key dimension of strategic planning: doing something today in the knowledge that it will bear fruit tomorrow; analysing future possibilities and emerging trends; recognizing that building trust and loyalty are long-term endeavours. Nowhere is the corporate marketers' commitment to the long term more apparent than in their attitude to children.

The textbook *Consumer Psychology for Marketing* tells us that

Children are important to marketers for three fundamental reasons:

1. They represent a large market in themselves because they have their own money to spend.
2. They influence their parents' selection of products and brands.
3. They will grow up to be consumers of everything; hence marketers need to start building up their brand consciousness and loyalty as early as possible.

(Foxall and Goldsmith 1994: 203)

Do Exercise 8.7a.

EXERCISE 8.7A: SUFFER THE LITTLE CHILDREN

Consider the quotation from *Consumer Psychology for Marketing* and think through what implications this has for society as a whole. You might like to think about:

a) child development and the stage at which youngsters can fully understand the persuasive intent of marketing;

b) family relationships and the concept of 'pester power';

c) how sensible it is, in a finite world, to encourage new generations to become 'consumers of everything'.

In 2007, the UK got a wake-up call when a UNICEF[10] report ('Report Card 7') (UNICEF 2007) put it bottom among 21 developed countries for child wellbeing. It was a shocking judgement and the resulting furore encouraged UNICEF to commission a follow-up study (UNICEF 2010) looking behind the statistics to understand why British kids are so badly off. This was an extremely thorough, in-depth exercise, which involved talking to and observing around 250 children and parents in the UK, as well as Sweden and Spain.

Do Exercise 8.7b.

EXERCISE 8.7B: CHILDREN'S WELLBEING IN THE UK, SWEDEN AND SPAIN

Access the UNICEF Report 'Children's Wellbeing in the UK, Sweden and Spain: The Role of Inequality and Materialism' (UNICEF 2011).

Read the Executive Summary and consider its main conclusions.

To what extent do you think marketing is responsible for the UK's woeful showing in Report Card 7?

The UNICEF report reveals problems with all three of the levels of 'importance' that *Consumer Psychology for Marketing* ascribes to children. First, it shows children are wise enough to be deeply ambivalent about material possessions, pointing out that: 'the message from them all was simple, clear and unanimous: their well-being centres on time with a happy, stable family, having good friends and plenty of things to do, especially outdoors' (Nairn 2011: 1). They don't want to be seen merely as 'a large market in themselves'. Furthermore, they don't have any obvious sense of entitlement – they are disparaging about what they see as 'spoiled kids', who don't have to wait, save up for and earn their rewards. A sensible reticence about the real potential benefits of consumption will, then, need to be overcome to access the child pound. Corporate marketers have to make children more materialistic to generate profits.

This brings us to the second level of marketing importance. Conduits work in two directions: if children give you access to parents, parents (especially insecure and vulnerable ones) give you access to children. This undermines family relationships. In particular, UK parents almost compulsively resorted to buying stuff in a failing attempt to compensate for the absence of quality time with their kids. The report speaks evocatively of 'boxes and boxes of toys, broken presents and unused electronics' being 'witness to this drive to acquire new possessions, which in reality were not really wanted or treasured' (ibid.: 2). The irony that the need to earn the money to buy these products costs parents the very time that their children crave seems to have been missed (or neutralized by relentless marketing).

On a more positive note, one might see the children's wisdom relative to their parents as boding well for the future – they are, after all, the next generation of parents and they will get the priorities right. Not if the marketers have their way. Remember, their third level of importance is that 'they will grow up to be consumers of everything; hence marketers need to start building up their brand consciousness and loyalty as early as possible'. That awful phrase 'consumers of everything' is a chilling distillation of the impact of over-consumption on our planet. Nonetheless, the marketer eyes not threats to the planet, but opportunities for long-term sales. It is vital to get the next generation trooping into the malls.

Go back to Exercise 8.7a and re-examine your notes. Has the UNICEF research changed your mind in any way? Now consider what protections, if any, you think young people need from marketing. In particular, should we move to a much more controlled system as in Sweden, which does not allow any advertising to children up to the age of 12? (Note: Sweden came top for child welfare in the original UNICEF (2007) analysis.)

The UNICEF case underlines the strategic impact of corporate marketing. In his novel *Brave New World*, Aldous Huxley talks about propaganda acting

not so much like drops of water, though water, it is true, can wear holes in the hardest granite; rather drops of liquid sealing-wax, drops that adhere, incrust, incorporate themselves with what they fall on, till finally the rock is all one scarlet blob. Till at last the child's mind is these suggestions and the sum of these suggestions is the child's mind. And not the child's mind only. The adult's mind too – all his life long. The mind that judges and desires and decides – made up of these suggestions.

(Huxley 1958)

Some might argue that corporate marketing is equally insidious; would you agree?

Ubiquitous deployment

Have you noticed how difficult it has become to buy a garment – even underwear – without a brand name? These logos are now integral to our clothes, so anonymizing them is impossible; we are all becoming mobile billboards. As well as providing free advertising, corporate marketers also benefit in two additional ways from this: (a) they gain access to our credibility as a source of marketing messages; we are not only displaying but actively endorsing their brand names; and (b) we are doing this voluntarily, with no gain, so there is no apparent sales pitch. Both these phenomena increase the power of their marketing.

The depth and breadth of corporate marketing's reach is powerfully illustrated by the Olympic Games. This is the ultimate global celebration of the power of amateurism, of humankind coming together to share our sporting accomplishments. As the International Olympic Committee's (IOC) first Fundamental Principle puts it:

Olympism is a philosophy of life, exalting and combining in a balanced whole the qualities of body, will and mind. Blending sport with culture and education, Olympism seeks to create a way of life based on the joy of effort, the educational value of good example, social responsibility and respect for universal fundamental ethical principles.

But, if you click on the IOC sponsorship site,[11] you will also discover that 'The Olympic Games are one of the most effective international marketing platforms in the world, reaching billions of people in over 200 countries and territories throughout the world'. You will also learn that Coke has been a major sponsor since in 1928, and it has been joined by McDonald's for the last three and half decades – though sugar and fat are hardly at the core of a successful athlete's diet. Do Exercise 8.8.

EXERCISE 8.8: OLYMPIC SPONSORSHIP

Do you think that Coke and McDonald's should be allowed to sponsor the Olympics? Consider issues of public health, inequalities and the marketing messages such link-ups promote. Visit the Coke, McDonald's and IOC websites to help you decide.

The IOC site explains that the TOP, or 'Olympic Partners' worldwide sponsorship programme', was instigated in 1985 'to develop a diversified revenue base for the Olympic Games and to establish long-term corporate partnerships that would benefit the Olympic Movement as a whole'. In cash terms at least, it has paid off: IOC's Olympic Marketing File, available on the same site, boasts how revenues increased from US$96 million in 1985/88 to US$866 million in 2005/08. In return, 'the TOP programme provides each Worldwide Olympic Partner with exclusive global marketing rights and opportunities within a designated product or service category'. 'The TOP Partners may exercise these rights worldwide and may activate marketing initiatives with all the members of the Olympic Movement that participate in the TOP programme.'

It is clear then that sponsorship is about business, not philanthropy. Corporations become TOPs for the same reason that they engage in all their other marketing activity, because it will enhance their bottom lines in a number of ways. One leading marketing text lists five of these: 'gaining publicity', 'creating entertainment opportunities', 'fostering favourable brand and company associations', 'improving community relations' and 'creating promotional opportunities'. Specifically, it notes, sports sponsorship provides the 'transferred values to the sponsor' of 'healthy', 'young', 'energetic', 'fast', 'vibrant' and 'masculine'. As the text observes: 'the audience, finding the sponsor's name, logo and other symbols threaded through the event, learn to associate sponsor and activity with one another' (Jobber 2004: 506).

So, the IOC takes money from Coke and McDonald's in return for their association with its core Olympic values and imbuing them with a healthy image. Do you think Coke and McDonald's deserve this healthy image? If not, how does this fit with 'the educational value of good example' in its first Fundamental Principle?

More widely, how does the strategy of selling the Olympic Games to corporate brand-building fit with the IOC's fifth Fundamental Principle that 'the Olympic

Movement shall have the rights and obligations of autonomy'? To what extent do you think freedom ceases to be freedom when it has a price tag?

So, from our most personal garments to our treasured global icons, the brand is omnipresent. It colours the very water we swim in. Nowhere is this more apparent than in hyperspace.

Late in 2011, Facebook and Diageo announced that they had entered into a partnership; the social networking site is going to help the drinks multinational strengthen its marketing by giving them access to a '"SWAT team" from its marketing, research and product engineering groups' (see Figure 8.2, and access the announcement in the *Financial Times* (Bradshaw 2011)). The military language is interesting in an era that emphasizes relationship marketing and customer service, and for a channel that is supposed to be principally about making friends and meeting people.

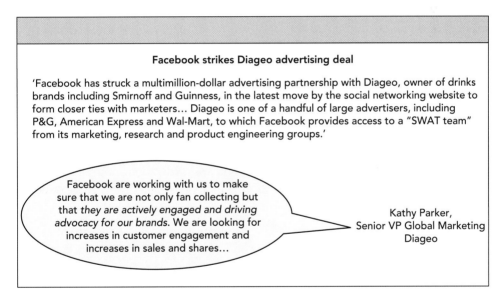

Facebook strikes Diageo advertising deal

'Facebook has struck a multimillion-dollar advertising partnership with Diageo, owner of drinks brands including Smirnoff and Guinness, in the latest move by the social networking website to form closer ties with marketers... Diageo is one of a handful of large advertisers, including P&G, American Express and Wal-Mart, to which Facebook provides access to a "SWAT team" from its marketing, research and product engineering groups.'

Facebook are working with us to make sure that we are not only fan collecting but that *they are actively engaged and driving advocacy for our brands*. We are looking for increases in customer engagement and increases in sales and shares...

Kathy Parker,
Senior VP Global Marketing
Diageo

Figure 8.2 Social networking or selling booze?
Source: Adapted from Bradshaw (2011)

EXERCISE 8.9: WHEN FRIENDS START TO SELL

Read Figure 8.2. Consider how the Diageo/Facebook link-up blurs the edges between friendship and marketing. Is this desirable? Would you feel deceived? Is it reasonable for friends to market to friends?

Figure 8.3 Facebook and you

This cartoon presents one perspective; do you agree with it?

A mix of tools

So far, we have focused on the corporate marketers' attempts to influence us through different forms of communication. Three additional marketing tools also need to be considered: the price (the amount of money we can be persuaded to part with in return for a given product or service); the place (the distribution network and point of sale activity); and the product or service itself. The task of the marketer is to ensure that the 'right' decisions are made about each of these: the 'right' price is set, the 'right' outlet is located and/or designed, the 'right' product or service is made.

The definition of 'right' takes us back to the discussion we had earlier in the chapter and the core marketing idea of consumer orientation. On the face of it, this means ensuring all three elements – price, place and product – are pitched so as to best satisfy us customers, which sounds most agreeable. However, a little thought throws up an inherent contradiction: as customers we would favour cheap prices, ready accessibility and high quality; but the marketer wants to make money. Specifically, as we have noted, the corporate marketer has an over-riding need to deliver increased shareholder value through higher profits, which, in turn, requires maximized margins and (especially) greater sales. Our consumption needs to be encouraged and accelerated. We have to be kept in the shops.

This reality can easily get lost in the rhetoric about customer satisfaction and consumer orientation, but is nonetheless clearly recognized in business textbooks: 'the key principle of the optimum marketing mix is that which maximises share-holder value' (Doyle 2003: 291), thereby putting it in the frontline of the corporate mission. On this, Doyle agrees with *Business Week* that 'the fundamental task of today's CEO is simplicity itself: get the stock price up. Period.' He goes on to quote, in turn, the mission statements of Coca-Cola, the Disney Corporation and Cadbury Schweppes – each emphasizing the primacy of shareholder value.

Then, to reassure us, lest we take fright at such transparency, he adds: 'these shareholders are not the bloated capitalists of socialist propaganda, but rather the pension funds and insurance companies responsible for managing the savings of ordinary people'. To be fair, he was writing before the banks had imploded, causing mass bankruptcy and home repossession. Before the scandal of profligate boardroom remuneration had been fully exposed. Before the socialists had been joined by the 99 per cent in decrying the 1 per cent of 'bloated capitalists'. And before Nobel Laureate Joseph Stiglitz, writing in *Vanity Fair*, warned about the corrosive impact of the current levels of inequality in the USA:

[I]n our own democracy, 1% of the people take nearly a quarter of the nation's income . . . In terms of wealth rather than income, the top 1% control 40% . . . [as a result] the top 1% have the best houses, the best educations, the best doctors, and the best lifestyles, but there is one thing that money doesn't seem to have bought: an understanding that their fate is bound up with how the other 99% live. Throughout history, this is something that the top 1% eventually do learn. Too late.

(Stiglitz 2011)

Interestingly, when it comes to the application of the marketing mix, the language becomes more direct. Thus, rather than a route to our satisfaction, it now becomes the set of 'controllable demand-impinging elements (instruments) that can be combined into a marketing programme used by a firm to achieve a certain level and type of response from its target market' (Baker and Saren 2010: 189). These instruments 'influence demand to a greater or lesser extent'. Or, as our blunt business academic puts it: 'the marketing mix is the main way management seeks increases in sales' (Doyle 2003: 295).

Demand-impinging, achieving response, influence demand, increases in sales – there is no hiding the forceful purpose. The aim is to get us consuming, to boost sales and thereby corporate growth.

Each of the three marketing tools is, therefore, designed to stimulate our consumption: pricing is carefully calculated to maximize both the price we will pay and the number of us who will pay it; place, both in the sense of the distribution network and the configuration of each outlet, is designed to get us in with our wallets out; and the product itself is developed and tweaked to ensure it tempts us as seductively as possible.

EXERCISE 8.10: MARKETING AND CONSUMPTION

Consider how marketers use the marketing mix to get us to consume. Discuss how desirable this is, given the problems of global warming and a clear need for us to use less stuff. Is there a compromise to be had if marketers focus their efforts on reduced carbon options? If so, how would you ensure this happens?

MARKETING TO (GET) POWER

Corporate marketers understand the lessons of Foster Wallace about our social context having a big influence on our individual behaviour. So, as we noted in Chapter 7, just as they put enormous effort into influencing us, so they also target those with the power to change the social context. Politicians, policy makers and other stakeholders can make life easier for the corporate marketer by, for instance, introducing laws, by liberalizing regulation, or by lobbying for such changes.

The more blatant attempts to get these groups onside – overt lobbying, donations to campaign funds, revolving-door employment practices – already get considerable attention. For example, Box 8.5 shows the financial services sector was recently revealed to be donating large sums to the ruling Conservative Party in the UK, just as the government was debating the thorny issue of bank regulation. Do you think there is any connection between this funding and the gentle pace with which new controls are being introduced or David Cameron's use of the UK's EU veto, which some argue (Curtis 2011) has protected the City of London from tighter European regulation?

BOX 8.5: BUYING POLITICAL INFLUENCE?

Revealed: 50% of Tory funds come from City

Donations from the financial sector have risen steeply since David Cameron became leader of the Conservative Party

When Cameron became Tory leader; the City gave the party £2.7m, or 25% of its funds.

That figure rose to £11.4m in 2010.

'Financiers in the City of London provided more than 50% of the funding for the Tories last year, new research has revealed, prompting claims that the party is in thrall to the banks. A study by the Bureau for Investigative Journalism has found that the City accounted for £11.4m of Tory funding – 50.79% of its total haul – in 2010, a general election year. This compared with £2.7m, or 25% of its funding, in 2005, when David Cameron became party leader. The research also shows that nearly 60 donors gave more than £50,000 to the Tories last year, entitling each of them to a face-to-face meeting with leading members of the party up to and including Cameron.'

(Source: Watt and Treanor 2011)

However, the work of the corporate marketer in this arena is less widely discussed. 'Stakeholder marketing' uses the same techniques as consumer marketing, but now the target is those who have power. The aim is to build and burnish corporate reputations; in stakeholder marketing, corporate identity is as important as the brand is in consumer marketing.

The two favoured and linked techniques are 'cause-related marketing', where the corporation links up to a personable and self-evidently worthy issue such as child literacy and makes sure this apparent good deed is well publicized; and 'corporate social responsibility' (CSR), which, as we discussed in Chapter 7, links this specific act with longer-term commitments to good practice. Corporate marketers are open about the self-serving nature of this activity and clearly state that this is business not altruism. According to one text, for instance, it is good at

enhancing reputation, building image and brands, creating relationships and loyalty among customers and stakeholders, adding value, generating awareness and PR, driving trial and traffic, providing product and service differentiation, developing emotional engagement with the consumer and other stakeholders, and obviously increasing sales, income and volume.

(Adkins 2003: 674)

The same author underlines this quid pro quo agenda: 'whatever cause-related marketing is, it certainly is not philanthropy or altruism' (ibid.: 670).

The charity Christian Aid, however, is extremely critical of CSR and uses the notorious case of Shell in Nigeria to illustrate its concerns. Have a try at Exercise 8.11 before continuing.

EXERCISE 8.11: DOING WELL BY DOING GOOD

Read Christian Aid (2004) *Behind the Mask: The Real Face of Corporate Social Responsibility*, which is available at www.st-andrews.ac.uk/media/csear/app2practice-docs/CSEAR_behind-the-mask.pdf. Discuss the pros and cons of CSR as used by Shell in the Niger Delta.

Then update yourself by consulting Amnesty International's more recent *The True Tragedy: Delays and Failures in Tackling Oil Spills in the Niger Delta*, which is available at www.amnesty.ca/files/afr440182011en.pdf (Amnesty International and CEHRD 2011). Revisit your pros and cons.

In the early 1990s, the oil giant wanted to quell discontent among the local Ogoni people, whose land in the Niger Delta it was despoiling, and called on Nigeria's military dictatorship for help. This resulted in savage repression, dozens of people being shot down and the subsequent execution of Ogoni leader Ken Saro-Wiwa. Shell's response to the resulting outcry was to invest heavily in CSR. It was the first major company to do so, and arguably is responsible for taking the strategy into the mainstream of business thinking.

However, the good deeds and fine promises have done little to improve the lot of the Ogoni people; over a decade later, the Christian Aid (2004) report documented their continued suffering at the hands of Shell. And, in 2011, a report by Amnesty International noted further extensive harm to the Ogoni. Two oil spills happened in the Niger Delta in 2008, which between them were as big as the Exxon Valdez disaster. In both cases, no clean-up has happened and there were extensive delays before any remedial action was taken:

Eight months later, Shell finally appeared to recognize that people's food sources had been affected. On 2 May 2009, Shell staff brought food relief to the community. It included 50 bags of rice, 50 bags of beans, 50 bags of garri (a cassava product), 50 cartons of sugar, 50 cartons of milk powder, 50 cartons of tea, 50 cartons of tomatoes and 50 tins of groundnut oil.

(Amnesty International and CEHRD 2011: 11)

By contrast, in the quarter July – September 2011, the company posted profits of $7.2 billion (Rowley 2011).

The marketing of infant formula provides another worrying example of the failure of CSR and voluntary corporate action. These are the words of Jasmine Whitbread, Chief Executive Officer, Save the Children UK:

I shouldn't be standing in front of you, on the 25 year anniversary of the Code, telling you so little has changed and that companies continue to encourage mothers to spend money they don't have on manufactured food most of them don't need. I shouldn't be standing in front of you because it shouldn't still be happening. But it is, because the voluntary code clearly isn't working, and children are dying as a result.

(Save the Children and The Corporate Responsibility Coalition 2007: 3)

It is perhaps little wonder, then, that Christian Aid concludes that what we need is not more voluntary responsibility from corporations; but accountability and statutory regulation. Unfortunately, as it also notes, a key function of CSR is to fend off regulation. John Hilary, Director of Campaigns and Policy at War on Want, confirms this view describing the Corporate Responsibility agenda as having been 'created explicitly in order to get away from corporate accountability and regulation' (Worth 2007: 7). Revisit your answers to Exercise 8.11; decide whether or not you agree. Then reread Box 8.4; is CSR a classic example of the Borg Principle in action?

FINDING SOLUTIONS

Christian Aid and War on Want bring us back to the discussion in Chapter 7: the need for more robust and independent regulation, but this time not just for a minority of hazard merchants, but for the whole corporate system. This certainly makes sense. If, as we noted in the last chapter, moves can be made to constrain tobacco marketing because it damages our lungs, it is simple logic to constrain marketing more generally because the excessive consumption it encourages is damaging our planet.

And the problems are fundamental so this regulatory process needs to be equally deep-seated. Arundhati Roy, for instance, calls for 'another imagination – an imagination outside of capitalism as well as communism' (2011), 'an imagination that has an altogether different understanding of what constitutes happiness and fulfilment' (Arundhati Roy, quoted in *New Internationalist*, October 2011, p.30). Wallace would surely agree; the materialism inherent in our current system often falls far short of offering anything that could genuinely be called happiness and fulfilment. This suggests a need for controls on business, which encourage enlightened strategic intent; something more than the ad hoc control of bad practice we discussed in Chapter 7. Perhaps we should be thinking of a regulatory system that addresses priorities beyond those of the fiduciary imperative – instead of profits and shareholder returns, the focus could be on physical, mental, social, and planetary wellbeing.

Radical and contentious, and on its own doomed to failure. As Orwell reminded us, top-down system change has limited value if the individual is overlooked. And, as we noted at the outset of the chapter, progress depends on us all taking our own share of responsibility and becoming critically engaged. Change has to come from the bottom up as well as the top down; it has to be systemic. This is immensely challenging, but vital if we are to tackle complex and contended problems such as climate change.

WRAP-UP

This chapter has looked at the dark side of marketing, and you might have found this shocking. But the purpose is not to shock, it is to reinforce the importance of independent critical thought. Just as corporations sometimes have a vested interest in behaving badly, so they have a vested interest in covering this up. It is our responsibility as social marketers – and as citizens – to look beneath the surface and ask questions.

The Nazis were possibly the worst example of moral degeneracy in the twentieth century. Yet *New York Times* journalist Charles Higham, in his forensically researched book *Trading with the Enemy* (1983), shows that leading corporations like Ford, ITT and the Chase Manhattan Bank worked with the regime throughout the war. ITT literally helped Hitler's regime to perfect the doodlebugs that so devastated London. This extreme example of keeping the focus on the bottom line was, he explains, hidden behind 'an ice cream mountain of public relations'. Our job is to look behind the ice cream.

Failing to do so is not just ethically unacceptable, but it also damages us personally. We run the risk of leading our lives in the sort of fool's paradise inhabited by

Barney the white laboratory mouse who we met at the start of the chapter. So, critical thinking makes us better, more fulfilled people. More importantly, though, it is an essential prerequisite for tackling the major, multifaceted and contested problems now facing humankind – the most profound of which is global warming. The solutions are surely elusive and challenging, but the first step is to take a thorough and critical look at our current ways of doing things. In Chapter 10, we will then go on to examine how systems thinking can help us build on these insights and so start to meet these massive challenges.

First, though, we need to consider ethics.

Reflective questions

1. What is 'fiduciary imperative'? Why is it important to marketing? What is its connection to social marketing?
2. Discuss what critical thought means to the social marketer.
3. The dark side of marketing results from an imbalance of power in the marketplace giving rise to individual and collective harm. Explain in detail.
4. Does marketing make us selfish? Answer with reference to the work of David Foster Wallace.
5. Social marketers should be 'concerned with analysis of the social consequence of marketing policies, decisions and activities' (Lazer and Kelly 1973). Elaborate with examples.
6. Is marketing driving unsustainable consumption? If yes, what would you do about it?
7. Is corporate social responsibility going to save the planet? If yes, how; if not, why not?
8. How is CSR linked to cause-related marketing?

Reflective assignments

1. Make sure you are comfortable with the concept of critical thought by writing a concise paragraph, in your own words, about it.
2. Locate three social marketing case studies or papers that illustrate inequalities or the dark side of marketing.
3. You are social marketing manager with Jigsaw, a non-profit entity focused on mental health in young adults (18–35-year-olds) in inner cities around the country. You have been tasked with designing a mental health intervention specifically targeting suicide. How could you use critical thinking in your social marketing job?
4. How, where and why does critical thought integrate with our discussions of social marketing in Chapters 1 and 2?

5. Find a CSR or cause-related marketing example and, using critical thinking, assess its advantages and disadvantages.

6. Revisit your debate with friends or colleagues from Chapter 2 as to whether or not social marketers are really just out to satisfy their own ends like commercial marketers, or are they more altruistic. Applying critical thought, does your opinion alter? If so, how?

7. Complete your traffic lights checklist for critical thinking.

Notes

1 This Chapter builds on *The Marketing Matrix: How the Corporation gets its power and how we can reclaim it*, (Hastings 2012) Routledge, which you may want to consult. The Foreword from *The Marketing Matrix* is reproduced at the end of this book to help you decide.

2 *Caveat emptor*: 'buyer beware'.

3 Tobacco advertising has been banned in many countries. In the UK, for example, it disappeared in 2005, but marketing in a broader sense continues in the form of ubiquitous distribution, evocative packaging and carefully honed brands.

4 Fred Goodwin was CEO of RBS and his calamitous leadership epitomizes the worst of the 2008 financial crisis: macho management, hubris and excessive greed. His crude attempts to destroy evidence about the mistakes made on his watch earned him the sobriquet 'Fred the Shred'.

5 D.D. Eisenhower (1961), www.youtube.com/watch?v=8y06NSBBRtY (accessed 06/11/2012).

6 The Dalai Lama (and many other Buddhists).

7 www.olay.com/skin-care-products/total-effects/fragrance-free-daily-moisturiz er?pid=075609001772/.

8 www.loreal-paris.co.uk/skincare/face-care/revitalift/anti-wrinkle-plus-firming-day-cream.aspx (accessed 06/11/2012).

9 With thanks to Professor Mike Saren.

10 The United Nations Children's Fund which was created by the United Nations General Assembly in 1946 to provide emergency food and healthcare to children in countries that had been devastated by the Second World War. It has continued ever since to provide long-term humanitarian and developmental assistance to children and mothers across the world.

11 www.olympic.org/sponsorship/.

References

Adkins, S. (2003) 'Cause-related marketing: Who cares wins', in M.J. Baker (ed.) *The Marketing Book*. 5th Edition. Oxford: Butterworth-Heinemann.

Amnesty International and CEHRD (2011) *The True 'Tragedy': Delays and Failures in Tackling Oil Spills in the Niger Delta*, 10 November 2011. London: Amnesty International

Ltd. Online: www.amnesty.org/sites/impact.amnesty.org/files/PUBLIC/Niger%20 Delta%20True%20Tragedy%20EMBARGOED10Nov.pdf.

Arundhati Roy (2011) Interview, *The Guardian*. Online: www.guardian.co.uk/ world/2011/nov/30/arundhati-roy-interview, 30 November (accessed 9 December 2011).

Baggini, J. (2005) *The Pig That wants to be Eaten: And Ninety-Nine Other Thought Experiments*. London, UK: Granta Publishing.

Bakan, J. (2004) *The Corporation: The Pathological Pursuit of Profit and Power*. Toronto: The Penguin Group (Canada).

Baker, M. (2003) 'One more time – what is marketing?' M.J. Baker (ed.) *The Marketing Book*. 5th Edition. Oxford: Butterworth-Heinemann.

Baker, M. and Saren, M. (2010) *Marketing Theory*: *A Student Text*. Sage Publications.

Bradshaw, T. (2011) 'Facebook Strikes Diageo Advertising Deal', *Financial Times*, 18 September. Online: www.ft.com/intl/cms/s/2/d044ea24-e203-11e0-9915-00144feabdc0.html#axzz1irtgC58l/.

Christian Aid (2004) *Behind the Mask: The Real Face of Corporate Social Responsibility*. Online: www.st-andrews.ac.uk/media/csear/app2practice-docs/CSEAR_behind-the-mask.pdf.

Curtis, P. (2011) 'Will David Cameron's veto protect the City?', *The Guardian*, 12 December 2011. Online: www.guardian.co.uk/politics/reality-check-with-polly-curtis/2011/dec/12/debt-crisis-conservatives/.

Doyle, P. (2003) 'Managing the marketing mix', in M.J. Baker (ed.) *The Marketing Book*. 5th Edition. Oxford: Butterworth-Heinemann.

Foxall, G.R. and Goldsmith, R.E. (1994) *Consumer Psychology for Marketers*. London: Routledge.

Hastings, G. (2012) *The Marketing Matrix: How the Corporation gets its power and how we can reclaim it*. London: Routledge.

Higham, C. (1983) *Trading with the Enemy: An Exposé of the Nazi-American Money Plot, 1933-1949*. New York, NY: Delacorte Press.

Huxley, A. (1958) *Brave New World Revisited*. New York: HarperCollins.

Jobber, D. (2004) *Principles and Practice of Marketing*. 4th Edition. Maidenhead: McGraw-Hill International.

Klein, N. (2001) *No Logo*. London: Flamingo.

Lazer, W. and Kelley, E. (1973) *Social Marketing: Perspectives and Viewpoints*. Homewood, Illinois: Richard D. Irwin.

Miller, M.C. (2007) 'Introduction', in V. Packard, *The Hidden Persuaders*. Brooklyn, New York: IG Publishing.

Nairn, A. (2011) *Children's Wellbeing in the UK, Sweden and Spain: The Role of Inequality and Materialism*. Ipsos MORI.

Open University and BBC (2000) 'Looking for a Future: Sustainability and Change in the Andes', in *U213 International Development: Challenges for a World in Transition* (DVD recording). Milton Keynes: The Open University.

Orwell, G. (1970) *Collected Essays*. 2nd Edition. London: Secker & Warburg.

Packard, V. (2007) *The Hidden Persuaders*. Brooklyn, New York: IG Publishing.

Ponting, C. (2000) *World History – a new perspective*. London, UK: Chatto and Windus, p. 790.

Rowley, E. (2011) 'Never Mind the Euro Bailout, Worry About Growth, Says Shell', *The Telegraph*, 27 October 2011. Online: www.telegraph.co.uk/finance/newsbysector/energy/oilandgas/8852496/Never-mind-the-euro-bailout-worry-about-growth-says-Shell.html (accessed 28 November 2011).

Save the Children & The Corporate Responsibility Coalition (2007) *Why Corporate Social Responsibility is Failing Children*. London: Save the Children & CORE. Online: www.savethechildren.org.uk/sites/default/files/docs/Why_CSR_is_failing_children_1.pdf (accessed 30 November 2011).

Shah, A. (2010) 'Poverty Facts and Stats', in *Global Issues*, 20 September 2010. Online: www.globalissues.org/article/26/poverty-facts-and-stats/.

Steinbeck, J. (1939) *The Grapes of Wrath* London: Everyman's Library.

Stiglitz, J. (2011) 'Of the 1%, by the 1%, for the 1%', *Vanity Fair*. Online: www.vanityfair.com/society/features/2011/05/top-one-percent-201105/.

Surgeon General (2012) *Preventing Tobacco Use Among Youth and Young Adults: A Report of the Surgeon General*. Atlanta, GA: US Department of Health and Human Services, Centers for Disease Control and Prevention, National Center for Chronic Disease Prevention and Health Promotion, Office on Smoking and Health.

Thomas, M.J. (1999), *Thoughts on Building a Just and Stakeholding Society*, 20th Anniversary Conference, Alliance of Universities for Democracy, Budapest (Hungary), 7 November.

UNICEF (2007) Report Card 7. Online: www.unicef.org.uk/Documents/Publications/rc7_eng.pdf.

UNICEF (2010) Report Card 9. Online: www.unicef.org.uk/Documents/Publications/rc9.pdf.

UNICEF (2011) Report 'Children's Wellbeing in the UK, Sweden and Spain: The Role of Inequality and Materialism'. Online: www.unicef.org.uk/Documents/Publications/IPSOS_UNICEF_ChildWellBeingreport.pdf.

Wallace, D.F. (2008) 'Plain old untrendy troubles and emotions', *The Guardian*, 20 September 2008. Online: www.guardian.co.uk/books/2008/sep/20/fiction/.

Watt, N. and Treanor, J. (2011) 'Revealed: 50% of Tory funds come from City', *The Guardian*, 8 February 2011. Online: www.guardian.co.uk/politics/2011/feb/08/tory-funds-half-city-banks-financial-sector (accessed 30 August 2012). Link to full study: www.thebureauinvestigates.com/2011/10/25/city-financing-of-the-conservative-party-doubles-under-cameron/.

WHO (2008) Report on the Global Tobacco Epidemic. Online: www.who.int/tobacco/mpower/mpower_report_tobacco_crisis_2008.pdf.

Wilkie, W.L. and Moore, E.S. (2003) 'Scholarly research in marketing: Exploring the "Four Eras" of thought development', *Journal of Public Policy & Marketing*, 22(2):116–146.

Worth, J. (2007) 'Corporate responsibility: Companies who care?' *New Internationalist*, December 2007, pp.5–6.

Chapter **9**

Ethical issues

LAURA'S DILEMMA

Laura has been going out with Daniel for three weeks now. He is a lovely boy – blonde hair, tall and quick-witted. He also captains the school football team and is the first boyfriend she has had who has made her feel really valued. They laugh a lot together. He doesn't criticize or try to change her; just accepts – likes her – for what she is rather than what she might be. She does not consider herself to be pretty or particularly accomplished, but she is 'comfortable in her own body' and Daniel has a gentle way of reinforcing this. The word love has begun to enter their conversations.

But Laura is anxious about sex. Fond though she is of Daniel, she does not feel ready to go this far. At 15, she isn't even sure it is legal, and she is anxious about possible repercussions – most especially pregnancy. Her friend Allison had to leave school early last year when she and Tommy Harlow 'had an accident'; the school did an assembly about it. And the Social and Personal Development class on STDs had alarmed her.

But Daniel is clearly keen.

Now the Local Authority's new health promotion strategy has resulted in condom machines appearing in the school toilets. Daniel said this shows it is

all right. Some of the other boys use the now readily available contraceptives to tease and embarrass the girls.

Her girlfriends are supportive but also uncertain. The teen magazines they all read seem to assume they will have sex – agony aunts, social workers, even doctors – offering advice on how best to do it. One magazine goes so far as to feature a 'position of the month', which had shocked Laura – though she pretended it didn't.

Against all this, Laura's parents are very religious and conservative. They barely mention sex, change the subject or the channel if the topic crops up and believe fervently in the sanctity of marriage. But Laura's elder sister had rebelled and recently left home to live with her boyfriend in a nearby town. Her name has not been mentioned by her father since.

Laura reminds us that people's lives are complex, and the problems they face both agonizing and multifaceted. She also shows how social marketing – however well meaning – can have unforeseen repercussions, create discord with other influences and inadvertently undermine important support networks. Condoms may prevent unwanted pregnancy but they can also cause unwonted discomfort.

We social marketers are perennially interfering in people's lives, and this raises many moral dilemmas. We decide what behaviour is desirable, devise strategies to encourage it, choose who should get the benefits of our efforts (and who should not), criticize other people's campaigns and conduct endless research. All of these steps present ethical issues that have to be recognized, acknowledged and addressed.

This chapter starts by discussing why ethics are so important in social marketing and examines the principal dilemmas we face. Inevitably, there are no simple solutions – as we saw in our discussion of theory (Chapter 3) and will note again when discussing systems social marketing in the next chapter – but the chapter goes on to show how practical and theoretical approaches reinforce each other and help us to pick our way through the maze.

Learning outcomes

By the end of this chapter, you should be able to:

✓ Recognize that there are many important ethical dilemmas facing the social marketer

✓ Understand some basic points about ethical theory

✓ Explain the difference between *deontological theory* and *teleological theory*

✓ Address practical ethical problems.

Key words

deontological theory – ethical challenges – ethics – inequalities – morality – teleological theory – theories of rights

WHY WE NEED ETHICS IN SOCIAL MARKETING

Ethical dilemmas arise because we deal with people and try to change what they do: our target customers, stakeholders, competitors and wider society are all impacted by our efforts. Furthermore, we focus on behaviours that are illegal, taboo or culturally sensitive – just over the last couple of years, our work in the Institute for Social Marketing has covered illicit drug use, sex, addiction, speeding, domestic violence, prisoner health and childhood immunization.

As a result, the social marketing solution often requires difficult and stressful behaviour change options of people. For example, giving up addictive substances carries severe physiological and psychological repercussions, while encouraging increased fruit and vegetable consumption can have implications for the cost of a family's weekly shopping basket and for family relationships, particularly with fussy children.

As a result of concerns about inequalities, social marketers also tend to work with particularly vulnerable and hard-to-reach target groups. These groups include those in poverty, ethnic minorities, children and those with disabilities or pressing health needs. This poses challenges for research, segmentation and targeting.

However, the most fundamental reason that social marketers should be concerned with ethics is because ultimately their business is 'messing with people's lives'. It is imperative that we take time out and consider the morality and relevance of our values for others, and the effects (intended or otherwise) our campaigns have on those who engage with them.

One example of such a campaign that was compounded by difficult ethical dilemmas was a social marketing initiative to fluoridate the water supply of northeast England. Fluoridation is a remarkably simple and effective public health measure; it involves adding a small amount of fluoride to the water, the technology is foolproof and the benefits immense. Most strikingly, it ensures virtually perfect dental health for everyone, regardless of social background. But it also raises concerns about mass medication and 'nannying'. Box 9.1 gives a flavour of exactly how strongly some people feel about these issues.

BOX 9.1: SOCIAL MARKETING CAN RAISE VERY SERIOUS MORAL CONCERNS

During a campaign to fluoridate the public water supply, a letter was received from an old soldier expressing very grave reservations:

'we believe that neither you nor anyone else has the right to tell us what to consume – would you like us to tell you what to consume? Of course you wouldn't! Don't try to hijack the democratic system and individual rights in pursuit of ideological goals. Never try to deny consumers the right of choice in anything, choice also comes with democracy. Those rights were hard won on the battlefields of Europe, would you condemn those sacrifices to oblivion in your pursuit of self-gratification?'

However there are no easy answers; the option of not fluoridating also presents moral dilemmas. Is it right to deprive a community of known public health benefits, especially one that has a proven effect on inequalities?

And all this assumes our social marketing efforts are successful. What happens when things don't work – do we just reinforce the negative behaviour, creating bad social marketing which makes the original problem worse? Do, for example, fearful messages about the side effects of smoking just provide teenage boys with a better prop for demonstrating how tough and rebellious they are? Is it unethical to make less than optimal use of limited government resources or charitable funds?

So, yes, we need to address ethical considerations. In the commercial field, this forms an integral part of strategic thinking – good ethics are ultimately good business. The same thinking should apply in social marketing. But the first task is to pin down the ethical issues we face.

THE KEY ETHICAL CHALLENGES FACING SOCIAL MARKETERS

EXERCISE 9.1: ETHICAL CHALLENGES IN SEXUAL HEALTH

You are a social marketing consultant who has been commissioned to undertake and evaluate an initiative on teenage sexual health in Dundee. You already know that there are above-average levels of teenage pregnancy and sexually transmitted infections among 14–16-year-olds in the area.

What ethical dilemmas will you face with this project?

Looking back at the discussion of marketing planning in Chapter 4 will help.

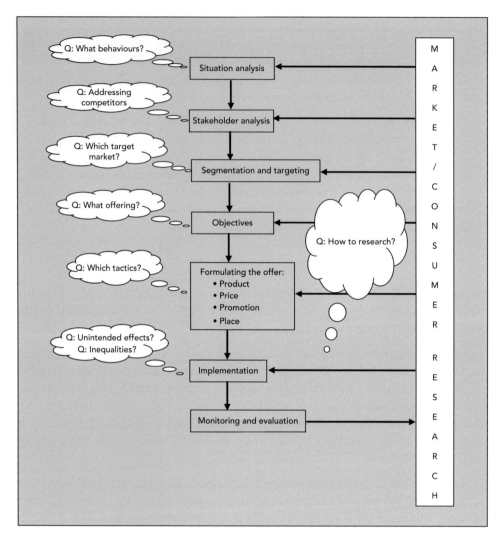

Figure 9.1 Ethical dilemmas in social marketing planning

Source: Adapted from MacFadyen and Hastings (2001)

In essence, every stage of the marketing planning process discussed in Chapter 4 raises ethical as well as managerial challenges. As Figure 9.1 shows, we need to address six questions:

1) Which behaviours to address?
2) Are there potential competitors and how should we deal with them?
3) Which consumer groups to target?
4) What products/services to offer in their exchange?
5) How to use the marketing mix to make this offering?
6) How to conduct research to inform this process?

Each of these ethical questions is now addressed.

What behaviour?

Social marketers must make informed judgements about what problems to address or what behaviour to influence. These decisions have clear moral dimensions – should restricted budgets be spent on encouraging behaviours that are likely to improve the health and wellbeing of small numbers of people (e.g. intensive cessation counselling), or on large campaigns that reach large populations but with uncertain results (e.g. mass media anti-smoking campaigns)?

More fundamentally, social marketers must make moral judgements about what behaviours are important to endorse or discourage, and for which groups of society particular behaviours are appropriate. Legislation provides obvious guidelines, but in other areas matters are less clear-cut. For instance, in Exercise 9.1, addressing the sexual behaviour of teenagers below the age of consent, or to young people of certain religious backgrounds, presents particular problems.

It is important not to be arrogant and assume that we social marketers ('experts') know best. There may, for example, be situations where, on balance, certain 'dangerous' or undesirable behaviours may be permissible. Who determines that the best and only correct life choices should be that we all become: non-smoking, moderate-drinking, blood-donating, vegetarian recyclers who live to become centenarians? Perhaps people do have the right to decide to take risks. It is important that, as social marketers, we avoid the easy trap of assuming that ours are the only legitimate priorities.

The letter in Box 9.1 actually gives a glance into a small but typically well-organized anti-fluoridation movement. The reality is that any fluoridation programme, at least in the UK, is going to have to be progressed in the teeth of this opposition group. Difficult judgements have to be made about the legitimacy of their objections – are they based on sound science, for example, or just prejudice and emotion? Then there are questions about how we deal with the competition – do we try to ally with them, as in the Miller Brewing-funded drunk-driving initiative (see Exercise 7.8 on p. 209), or oppose and defeat them?

In Exercise 9.1, the Catholic Church may well represent serious opposition to, say, the promotion of condoms. As a social marketer, you will need to think through how you respond to this.

Which target market?

Segmentation in the social marketing marketplace poses unique ethical problems. Despite the superiority of segmented versus undifferentiated campaigns, the decision to target (i.e. help) certain social groups to the exclusion of others can be extremely difficult. There may be an important trade-off between reaching less needy, but easy-to-reach groups (geographically or strategically) and very needy, but hard-to-reach groups. For example, consumers in geographically isolated islands, very low-income communities or convicted prisoners may be difficult to 'reach' with mainstream initiatives, but can you really afford to ignore their needs?

Testing the efficacy of social marketing initiatives using an experimental research design shares this problem. The initiative is administered to one group but not another. Arguably, the control group participants sacrifice the opportunity for better health or safety to benefit others.

On the other hand, being targeted by a social marketing campaign may have deleterious consequences. Being publicly singled out for special support because of gender, poverty, disability, race, etc. may leave consumers open to stigmatization. For example, a government drugs prevention initiative in the northeast of England was unable to target young drug users for fear of stigmatization. The programme had developed a range of intervention components for young people already using drugs. However, it would have been impossible to secure the necessary cooperation of schools, communities and parents, who would not have wished their children labelled as drug users (Stead *et al.* 1997). A partial solution was found by combining blanket targeting with self-selection, where young people with similar interests (and, presumably, similar attitudes/experiences of drugs) could opt in to certain components (Home Office Drugs Prevention Initiative 1998).

In Exercise 9.1, there are similar dilemmas; will youngsters targeted by sexual health clinics suffer embarrassment or worse? Do girls come under pressure to have sex if boys are targeted with safer sex programmes?

What offering?

Ethical questions are also likely to occur when making decisions about the social marketing offering. As we have noted, social marketing is based on the principle of 'exchange'. A common point of understanding and fulfilment of needs must be reached for an exchange to take place. This ultimately results in some form of compromise between the principal actors. Because the behaviours involved are often deep rooted, this may result in adopting more modest objectives or advocating behaviour that, while reducing risk, does still have negative repercussions. This level of compromise may seem defeatist and unethical.

For example, in Exercise 9.1, Dundee is not exceptional; the UK as a whole has one of the highest rates of teenage pregnancy in Europe (United Nations Statistics Division 2011). Because so many young people are already sexually active, many would advocate that it is more important to prioritize safer sex than complete abstinence. This, and other harm minimization campaigns, including the safer or more informed use of illegal drugs, raise key dilemmas in social marketing. Is it more important to have fewer people engaging in an undesirable behaviour, or to have more people doing it, but doing it more safely? Also, does it help to remember that, in both cases, we are running against the spirit, if not the letter, of the law?

Another ethical question that may arise when deciding on a suitable offering is the level of involvement required on the part of the consumer. Some solutions, such as practising safer sex or going for cancer screening, require very active participation. Others do not require the consumer to do much, or indeed anything at all: a fluoridated water supply delivers better dental health without any action on the part of you or me. Indeed, most people do not even know whether or not their water is fluoridated. This raises a crucial ethical issue: informed consent. Regardless of how much active participation a given programme demands, people have a right to know what is being done to them. This right applies, however well intentioned and benevolent the programme.

Which marketing tactics?

In Chapter 4, we considered the value of the marketing mix as a management tool, helping us think through the effectiveness of different value co-creation tactics: of getting the right product in the right place at the right time – and saying supportive things about it. We emphasized that right in this context means in close alignment with consumer needs; but here we are concerned with it in an ethical sense – and there can be conflicts between these two perspectives. For example, in Exercise 9.1, a distribution strategy of putting condoms in school toilets may well encourage boys to think more seriously about using them, but at the cost of putting pressure on girls to have sex.

A closely related problem is that of ends and means. Because social marketers are typically involved in doing good, there is a temptation to assume that otherwise unacceptable tactics are justified. This type of thinking is most apparent in communications. Fear-based messages, whether they work or not, depend for their effectiveness in portraying alarming repercussions from a particular behaviour. Paradoxically, problems can then arise if these outcomes are not upsetting enough.

The anti-smoking campaign 'Every Cigarette is Doing You Harm' is a classic example. Developmental research showed that the target audience of young smokers did not find the prospect of disease and death in later life particularly disturbing; like many people under 40, they were inured by a combination of perceived immortality and short-termism. The campaign designers overcame this problem by emphasizing the short-term health consequences of smoking using graphic images to illustrate the campaign's evocative strapline.

The problem is, it is not true. Doll et al.'s (2004) ground-breaking research on health consequences, which followed British doctors for fifty years, shows that people who quit by the age of 35 (as Doll himself actually did) show no long-term ill effects.

This tendency for 'risk proliferation' may suggest a deeper ethical issue. Is the underlying assumption that our customers are ignorant, reckless and irrational children behaving in dangerous and unhealthy ways, and our job is to goad or trick them into behaving better? The additional danger here is that, in our rush to put them right, we forget that behaviour is not just caused by the individual, but – as we noted when we discussed social cognitive theory – by their social circumstances. In this way, an over-reliance on threatening messages may simply be adding to consumers' feelings of stress and disempowerment. Whether it changes a particular behaviour or not, this is a serious moral concern.

Unintended effects

As we noted in Chapter 5, it can be difficult enough to establish whether your campaign has done what you wanted with the intended target group. From an ethical perspective, though, it is equally important to think about people who may respond to your campaign because they misunderstand it, or are simply the wrong target. For example, in Scotland, a smoking helpline established to assist adult smokers to quit was unexpectedly popular with underage smokers (Network Scotland 1997). This was not problematic in itself, but the system was not equipped to deal with the very particular needs of young smokers; as a consequence, a demand had been created that could not be met.

Mission creep of this type can have very unfortunate results. The early attempts to warn people of the dangers of HIV resulted in a phenomenon dubbed 'the worried well', with people such as children and the elderly, who could not possibly be at risk, becoming alarmed. Similarly, in Exercise 9.1, having wrestled with your conscience and decided that it is justified for 13-year-olds to receive a programme on safer sex, how comfortable would you be if 11- and 12-year-olds were also exposed to it?

There is a related issue here about keeping stakeholders informed and involved in your work. If you have indeed had to wrestle with your conscience to make decisions about the ethics of your campaign, are there other groups – such as parents or teachers – who have a right to be consulted or at least informed of developments?

Upstream interventions can also have unforeseen outcomes. Increasing the tax on – and thereby the price of – cigarettes has played an important role in reducing the UK's smoking prevalence (Townsend 1987). However, this proved a regressive policy, having most impact among the more privileged social groups, whose circumstances mean that they have found it easiest to quit. The least well-off continue to smoke and the policy just makes them poorer (Marsh and McKay 1994).

Research issues

Conducting research into the sensitive, taboo and, at times, illegal behaviours of social marketing business requires careful consideration. The research process, particularly qualitative methods, which depend on the intensive involvement of participants, may enhance fears, whether justified (e.g. discussion of cervical screening among those with experience of disease) or not (e.g. other respondents in a focus group hyping unreal risks) or cause embarrassment. It can also prompt risky behaviour, by, for instance, creating the impression that everyone is smoking tobacco or using drugs, encouraging impressionable participants to subscribe to a spurious norm. This is particularly problematic when the behaviour being researched is illegal, such as drug use, drunk driving or underage sex.

On the other hand, research is certainly necessary, as we have discussed throughout this book, and it would present equal if not greater ethical dilemmas if we were to proceed without conducting it at all. By the same token, research has to be as reliable and rigorous as possible. This means researchers do have to probe, put respondents under pressure and check their answers for veracity.

In this sense, research ethics is a microcosm of all the ethical dilemmas social marketers face: a tension between individual vulnerability and overall effectiveness; a balance between means and ends.

HOW DO WE RESPOND?

Let us leave aside complex issues of social marketing for a moment. How would you decide on a more everyday ethical problem? Try Exercise 9.2.

EXERCISE 9.2: A SWEET DILEMMA

You are in your local newsagent when you see a small child of eight or nine steal some sweets. Do you intervene? And, if so, how – by telling the shopkeeper or the parent, or by confronting the child directly?

The chances are you will have used a combination of two ways of thinking about the dilemma: whether the action itself is right or wrong and whether the results of the action (intended or not) are desirable or not. You may also have considered the idea of human rights. Interestingly, these echo the principal strands of ethical theory that we will discuss in a moment. We would say this with some confidence because that's typically what happens in the classroom.

In addition, you probably looked for clues in the actions of others – what would your friends or peers do in the same situation? Or, more generally, are there any codes of conduct or rules that give us some guidance about the correct course of action? Again, you are not alone. Our responses to ethical dilemmas – just like our behaviour more generally – is influenced by our environment and social norms. This lies behind the increasing inclination in business, medicine and research to lay down formal rules and procedures to guide practice.

THE THEORY

As with human behaviour (Chapter 3), there are many theories in the study of ethics. We will focus on the three that are of most immediate use: deontological theory, teleological theory and theories of rights.

Deontological theory

This view of ethical conduct is based on *the principle of duty* – the actual behaviour is emphasized, rather than its consequences. It institutes rules of good behaviour by focusing on motives rather than outcomes and assumes that a good intention is likely to produce good results. Kant expressed this in his 'categorical imperative': 'I ought never to act except in such a way that I can also will that my maxim should become a universal law' (2002). Kant argues that we should act in ways that we hope all others would do.

Deontologists have been criticized for not focusing on the consequences of actions and ignoring the situational context of particular courses of action. For example, most would agree that it is in many instances wrong to lie, but can easily imagine circumstances when such a transgression would be justified – and many more where, while an outright lie is unacceptable, avoiding telling the whole truth would be.

It is important not to lie to consumers in social marketing, but there may be decisions to make regarding which truth to tell. For example, research to inform an initiative to encourage older men to climb stairs instead of taking the escalator found that the key message for this target was weight loss, rather than disease prevention. In cases such as this, social marketers have to choose between a traditional public health message (to take exercise to avoid a heart attack) and a more superficial, but motivating message (take some exercise to be more slim and attractive).

Teleological theory

Teleological theory (or utilitarianism) describes the morality of a particular decision in terms of its consequences, rather than its motives (Mill 1978). An action or decision is argued to be ethically correct if it delivers the greatest good to the greatest number. This perspective rests on the assumption that morality is to promote human welfare by maximizing benefits and minimizing harm. To assess the consequences of actions, it is necessary to conduct a social cost-benefit analysis.

However, this perspective begs the question 'who decides what is good?' For example, there are some who believe that only pleasure and happiness are intrinsically good, while others believe that there are other 'good' values, such as friendship, knowledge, health and beauty (Beauchamp and Bowie 1988).

Furthermore, the drive to maximize total good may produce morally doubtful consequences. For example, in the UK, the greatest health benefits can be delivered most easily to those not in poverty. The health divide between rich and poor would likely be exacerbated if we relied only on teleological reasoning.

Theories of rights

Alternatively, decision making can be framed in terms of its duty to ensure human rights (Waldron 1984). Theories of rights assume that there exist some universal human rights, to which we should all have equal access. These rights include: rights to life, safety, truthfulness, privacy, freedom of conscience, freedom of speech and private property. Arguably, social marketers have a corresponding duty to ensure these rights are not infringed.

This perspective may offer some clarity in the resolution of ethical questions. Take, for instance, the case of access to a database of children's contact details, which would be of great use for research on health behaviours, such as smoking or drug use. Should this database be given to researchers to conduct research that will allow them to construct a random sample and produce new data that would contribute to evidence-based public policy? Or is this unethical use of confidential information? Deontological and teleological theories offer competing resolutions. Teleological theory would suggest that in the interests of the greater good – in this case, the better public policy to protect children – access to the database should be agreed. Deontological reasoning, however, would focus on the wrong being done to those on the database, and therefore militate against access. Human rights thinking provides a way through this impasse. If we accept that everyone has equal rights to privacy, then a system of informed consent emerges as a solution.

THE PRACTICE

This theory needs to be backed up by systems. As we noted in Exercise 9.2, we depend on social cues and guidance from those around us when making and carrying through ethical judgements as captured by the moral maxims for marketing in Exercise 9.3.

EXERCISE 9.3: MORAL MAXIMS FOR MARKETING

Listed below are a number of moral maxims for marketing that ask for some truthful soul searching. For each one, see if you can identify a work situation (even if it's not social marketing) where you have used the rule.

Contemplate the why, where, when and how. Are there any maxims you have not applied? Why?

The Golden Rule: Act in a way that you would hope others would act towards you.

The Professional Ethic: Take only actions that would be viewed as proper by an objective panel of your professional colleagues.

The TV/Newspaper Test: Always ask: 'Would I feel comfortable explaining this action on TV or on the front page of the local newspaper to the general public?' (The *Wall Street Journal* or *Financial Times* Test).

When In Doubt, Don't: If you feel uneasy in your mind, heart or gut about a decision, there is probably reason to question it. The individual should probably seek guidance from a trusted person before proceeding with the decision.

Slippery Slope: This maxim suggests that organizations must be careful not to engage in debatable practices that may serve as a precedent for undertaking other even more questionable strategies later (e.g. recent scandals that plagued several financial firms and the accounting profession are classic illustrations of the slippery slope.)

Mother/Founder On Your Shoulder: Would your mother or the company founder be comfortable with the ethical decisions being made? Could you explain it to them in common-sense terms they would understand?

Never Knowingly Do Harm: This asserts that a manager would not consciously make or sell a product not deemed to be safe. Called the 'Silver Rule' because it does not hold marketers to as high a standard as the Golden Rule does.

Examine How Results Are Achieved: This statement focuses on the means rather than the ends in the selling of products. If attention is devoted to ethically accomplishing results, they are likely to be justly achieved.

Ethics Is Others: This comment implies that ethical individuals will always consider others in making decisions. It goes against the egoistic conception of individuals that always place themselves first.

(Source: Adapted from Murphy *et al.* 2012)

These systems are being developed and increasingly it is difficult to get very far with a social marketing idea before you trip over not just ethical issues, but also requirements to address these issues. Most typically, this is driven by research ethics that has now become a mainstream aspect of any modern study. Prior to even starting, ethical approval by a formally constituted Ethics Committee is a prerequisite for funding. As yet, interventions themselves do not have to be scrutinized in this way – ethical systems are not in place – and so require careful thought on behalf of the social marketer.

Without systems, it is easy to get lost. The case of Bill Mitchell illustrates how.

Bill Mitchell, a newly hired sales rep for Phalkirk Pharmaceuticals, was surprised to learn that there was a very extensive expense sheet to fill out after trips on the road. He spent almost an hour reading the instructions and filling out the first form after he finished training and made his first 'solo' trip through his territory. He realized that there were some expense categories that did not appear on the form. These included laundry. In his first draft of the expense account, he put laundry under miscellaneous.

His sales manager examined the report and suggested that, rather than a large miscellaneous total, it would be better to classify laundry under meal expenses, because individual receipts were not required and he was under the daily meal allowance. Bill was told that, while miscellaneous charges were usually examined very carefully, as long as meal totals were below the allowed limit, management never examined them.

Was Bill right? What would you have done?

A few months later, Bill was on the road dealing with the introduction of a new product when a good customer asked if he would like to attend a Premiership football match. Bill offered, because of his relationship with the customer, to obtain tickets and host a total of three customers from the same firm to the game. Upon returning from the trip, he asked about how he should deal with the match tickets and was again told to find a category in which he had not exceeded the limit. By this time, he understood the process and felt comfortable about doing so.

Was Bill right? What would you have done?

Several months later, he called in from a long road trip and explained to his sales manager that, because of the difficulty in making appointments, he was going to miss his wife's birthday. The sales manager told him he should do something really special for his wife to make it up to her. After talking with his wife on the telephone, he felt worse than ever. He sent her €80 worth of flowers and claimed extra on his meals (which were still well under the limit) to cover the cost.

Was Bill right? What would you have done?

Several days after returning from the road trip, he was called into the marketing manager's office and asked about the flower expense. Bill explained that he felt justified to have the company pay for the flowers. The marketing manager listened carefully while Bill told the story of his wife's birthday. He went on to explain how it was commonly accepted practice among the sales force and sales managers.

Was Bill right? What would you have done?

Bill was fired for fraud on his expense account. Moral: ethical issues are very important and addressing them is most challenging when they are neglected by the systems in which we operate.

WRAP-UP

Every step of the social marketing process raises ethical dilemmas, but marketing itself is amoral. As we have seen throughout this book, it can be used as readily to encourage consumption of lethal and addictive drugs as it can to promote road safety. Social marketers, therefore, have to engage actively with ethics.

Theory and practice unite to help with this task. Thus, we are naturally inclined to think about both the inherent rights and wrongs of a particular action and about the relative merits of its outcomes, thereby, even if unwittingly, picking up on the thinking of both Immanuel Kant and John Stuart Mill. An increasing sense that we all have certain basic human rights also helps us make progress. None of these philosophies provides the whole answer, but between them they can certainly help us analyse the challenges. The context in which we make our judgements, the views of our colleagues and peers, and formal systems, such as Research Ethics Committees, help us carry this thinking into practice.

There are no easy or clear-cut answers. We will make mistakes, people will get hurt – but, as long as we try to apply ethical thinking to our work, there is a better chance of doing good than harm. And, by way of consolation, if doing social marketing presents ethical dilemmas; not doing it presents more.

Reflective questions

1. What are ethics? Why are ethics important to the social marketer?
2. Model and explain how the social marketing planning process can guide one's thinking about ethics when designing a social marketing intervention.
3. 'Social Marketing faces distinctive ethical challenges which are not faced by commercial marketing' (Brenkert 2002: 14). Elaborate.
4. Compare and contrast deontological and teleological theories of ethics.
5. Provide examples of deontological theory at work in social marketing practice.
6. Provide examples of teleological theory at work in social marketing practice.
7. How can deontological and teleological theories together with the theories of rights assist the social marketer?

Reflective assignments

1. Locate and examine three social marketing interventions from an ethical perspective.
2. How, where and why do ethics integrate with our discussions of research in social marketing in Chapter 5?
3. Apply deontological and teleological theory to a fear-based social marketing strategy of your choice.

4. Take the Theories of Human Rights and use it to evaluate a social marketing intervention of your choice.

5. You are marketing manager with the Chief Science Officer with responsibility for more young people choosing science as a career option. Specifically, you want to target young female teenagers, 16–18 years old, and design an intervention whereby they select science degree offerings at university over and above art or business programmes. Address the following six ethical questions in designing your intervention: 1) which behaviours to address?; 2) are there potential competitors and how should we deal with them?; 3) which 16–18-year-old girl groups to target?; 4) what products/services to offer in their exchange?; 5) how to use the marketing mix to make this offering?; and 6) how to conduct research to inform this process?

References

Beauchamp, T.L. and Bowie, N.E. (1988) *Ethical Theory and Business*. 3rd Edition. New Jersey: Englewood Cliffs.

Brenkert, G. (2002) 'Ethical challenges of social marketing', *Journal of Public Policy & Marketing*, 21(1): 14–25.

Doll, R., Peto, R., Boreham, J. and Sutherland, I. (2004) 'Mortality in relation to smoking: 50 years' observations on male British doctors', *British Medical Journal*, 328: 1519.

Home Office Drugs Prevention Initiative (1998) *Managing a drugs prevention initiative: The experience of NE Choices 1996–98*. Newcastle-upon-Tyne: Northumbria Drugs Prevention Team.

Kant, I. (2002) *Groundwork for the Metaphysics of Morals* [1785], edited and translated by Allen W. Wood. London: Yale University Press.

MacFadyen, L. and Hastings, G.B. (2001) 'First do no harm: The case for ethical considerations in social marketing'. Presented at: Academy of Marketing Science 10th Biennial World Marketing Congress – *Global Marketing Issues at the Turn of the Millennium*, jointly organised with Cardiff University, 30 May–2 June.

Marsh, A. and McKay, S. (1994) *Poor Smokers*. London: Policy Studies Institute.

Mill, J.S. (1978) *On Liberty* [1859]. Indianapolis: Hackett Publishing Co.

Murphy, P., Laczniak, G.R. and Prothero, A. (2012) *Ethics in Marketing: International Cases and Perspectives*. London, UK: Routledge.

Network Scotland (1997) *Calls to Smokeline: Weekly Report 267*. Unpublished.

Peto, D. (1994) 'Smoking and death: The past 40 years and the next 40', *British Medical Journal*, 309(6959): 937–939.

Stead, M., Mackintosh, A.M., Hastings, G., Eadie, D.R., Young, F. and Regan, T. (1997) 'Preventing adolescent drug use: design, implementation and evaluation design of NE Choices'. Paper presented at Home Office, DPI Research Conference, Liverpool, 3–5 December.

Townsend, J.L. (1987) 'Cigarette tax, economic welfare and social class patterns of smoking', *Applied Economics*, 19(3): 355–365.

United Nations Statistics Division (2011) Table 10: Live births by age of mother and sex of child, general and age–specific fertility rates: latest available year, 2000–2009, in *Demographic Yearbook 2009–2010*. New York: United Nations, pp. 399–420. Online: http://unstats.un.org/unsd/demographic/products/dyb/dybsets/2009-2010.pdf (accessed 5 September 2012).

Waldron, J. (1984) *Theories of Rights*. Oxford: Oxford University Press.

10

The big picture

Systems social marketing

Beethoven's Fifth Symphony opens with a dramatic flourish, the famous four-note motif, short-short-short long, which provides the theme for the first movement. As it weaves in and out, the tune is picked up by different instruments with 'pithy imitations tumbling over each other with such rhythmic regularity that they appear to form a single, flowing melody'. With echoes of the theme drifting through the third and fourth movements, the symphony merges into a coherent whole.

Each instrument contributes its own unique sound, each musician his or her particular skill, but the music only gains its real power in being scored for orchestra. The conductor's job is to keep the orchestra together and release their potential. Today, over 200 years since its composition, the ground-breaking theme of Beethoven's Fifth is still among the best-known classical melodies. Revolutionary for its time in technicality and emotion, it has inspired generations of composers and given immeasurable pleasure to audiences. Indeed, its momentous influence can be traced through art and literature and far beyond the musical realm. The scene from *The Simpsons* where Clancy Wiggum leaves a performance of the work after the opening bars declaring the rest is 'just filler' perhaps best exemplifies its diffusion beyond the hallowed walls of the concert hall into popular culture.

A key element of Beethoven's genius was his capacity to see the bigger picture, to combine notes, melodies and instruments in a way that enhances the value of individual contributions. In fact, in its creation of a whole greater than the sum of its parts, his symphony defies the laws of physics and in the process changed the world.

Social marketers need to master this craft if they too want to want to change the world.

This chapter, then, is about thinking big. It builds on the key ideas we have already discussed – the individual and collective determinants of health and wellbeing; the need for co-ordinated approaches to behaviour change; and the benefits of long-term, strategic, critical thinking. It argues that, because we are social beings who live in mutually dependent groups, behaviour change is inextricably linked to societal change.

This interconnectedness is present even for quite trivial and seemingly individual actions, such as buying a piece of fruit. On the surface, this is a simple transaction between customer and shopkeeper – two Euros in exchange for, say, a pineapple. But closer analysis reveals complexities. If the pineapple comes from Costa Rica, where press reports make clear farmers are being very badly treated (see Box 10.1), your purchase may well reinforce this brutality.

BOX 10.1: THE COSTA RICAN PINEAPPLE INDUSTRY IN 2011

'[T]his is an industry built on environmental degradation and poverty wages. Moreover, price cuts appear to have led to an immediate, sometimes brutal deterioration in conditions that were already poor. . . I heard repeated allegations of chemical contamination, wage cuts, union-breaking involving mass sackings and accidental poisonings. Like many other local experts, Ramirez, who is the country's coordinator for the Pesticide Action Network fears that the pineapple boom has outpaced the government's ability to regulate it. "The fight now is against pineapples because there's been an explosion in production, but it's difficult because the owners of the plantations have very big political and economic influence." By now, the sprayer was bearing down on us and we reached for our masks. Then, out of nowhere, an armed guard rode up on his motorbike to inspect us. Costa Rica, with a population of just over 4m, has only 12,000 or so policemen and no army, but an estimated 17,000 gun-carrying security guards employed by private companies.'

(Source: Lawrence 2010)

Unless you happen to live in Costa Rica, the fruit will also have been transported many, perhaps thousands of, miles using fossil fuels, thereby contributing to global warming. While the World Trade Organization (WTO) has regulatory oversight of this market, it is dominated by wealthy developed countries and prioritizes economic over other values. Thus, your purchase makes a small contribution to WTO's debatable legitimacy.

The power of the individual shopper is limited to refusing the pineapple, but, taken to scale, this small decision could have considerable ramifications. If everyone turned their backs on unfair and unsustainable fruit-producing systems, the entire organizational structure – farming practices, logistics, WTO regulation – would have to change. And these changes would help not just Ramirez, not just Costa Rica, but all third world farmers. It is this leverage, this potential for full-scale social change, that makes thinking about how our society operates and the geopolitical structures that govern it so important for social marketers. This is what is meant by 'systems thinking'.

The need for systems thinking becomes even more apparent when we move from small decisions about shopping to large-scale problems with multiple stakeholders such as global warming. These sorts of problems are not only complex, but also typically conflicted because differing interests have to be accommodated. The oil industry will have one perspective, Friends of the Earth another and car-owners a third – with politicians caught in the middle trying to please multiple constituencies while also hoping to get re-elected. These problems become so intractable they are sometimes termed 'wicked' and the temptation is to ignore them. It is much easier and more pleasant to focus on simpler actions – a bit of recycling here and litter-picking there. But, when, as with planetary degradation, the problems are systemic, the solutions have to be equally wide ranging.

Systems are built on value and values: the value we put on things and processes; and the values that hold our societies together. This chapter starts by exploring these concepts, showing how subjective, changeable and profoundly important they are. In essence, no significant social change is possible without a change in values. The chapter then goes on to examine how we can set about changing values to ones that will form the basis of a better system. Given the voluntary principles at the heart of social marketing, it will come as no surprise that the idea of value co-creation – working in partnership to develop a consensus about what really matters – is a vital part of this process. This recognizes the importance of people becoming directly and actively involved in the process of change, one which can be broken down into three related functions:

1. value co-discovery (uncovering and exploring new types of value);
2. value co-design (designing valued products and services); and
3. value co-delivery (taking 1 and 2 to scale) in a collectively co-ordinated strategy. (Think back to our discussion of client and collective orientations of social marketing in Chapter 2.)

The chapter then moves into practical mode and examines how the central theme of value co-creation has been put into practice, first in community social marketing, which melds social marketing and community development into a value-creating network, and, second, in international development, which reminds us of the importance of respecting indigenous wisdom. Finally, the practical and theoretical aspects of conducting social marketing strategies for societal change are drawn together in a concluding discussion about systems social marketing.

The result may not be as melodious as Beethoven's Fifth, but hopefully it can be as influential.

Learning outcomes

By the end of this chapter, you should be able to:

✓ Discuss value and values in social marketing
✓ Model and describe value co-creation
✓ Delineate community social marketing
✓ List the dominant community social marketing models
✓ Outline what Kamayoqs are and why they matter
✓ Discuss systems thinking social marketing
✓ Define the role and functions of partnerships
✓ Name the emerging indicators for systems social marketing.

Key words

value – value co-creation –value co-discovery – value co-design – value co-delivery – community social marketing (CSM) – Kamayoqs – systems social marketing (SSM) – co-ordinated networks of shared values – partnerships – indicators for systems social marketing

VALUE IS IN THE EYE OF THE BEHOLDER

When talking about value, we discuss what we value and don't value. We equate value with money, price, quality and cost. In the plural, 'values' take in high-minded principles – as in 'the values of a civilized society'.

We know value is individualized and subjective, based upon experiences, actual and perceived. As Hastings and Lowry remind us 'values ascribed to the marketer's offering during an exchange may be tangible (e.g. monetary) or psychological (e.g. status), immediate (e.g. nicotine now) or deferred (e.g. better health later), but they will always be subjective' (2010: 15). For example, the subjective nature of value is reflected when social marketers talk about physical activity as fun for young children, exercise for the 30+s, fitness for the 40+s and wellness for the 50+s.

Value cannot and does not have a single meaning. Value also presents complexity for the social marketer because clients, policy makers, stakeholders and funders all have different values. Moreover, these diverse outlooks can seem like chalk and cheese. Think of the doctor who sees non-smoking as a valuable health advantage and the teenager who uses smoking to control weight, to impress, to be accepted and to 'be cool' or as a way to rebel against the establishment and parents. This highlights one last important aspect of value – its collective generation within families, friendship groups, communities and societies (Alderson 1957).

Tie the notion of value/values to systems thinking and we are saying people need to get directly involved in their own futures. This ties back to our discussion of agency and empowerment in earlier chapters. The values we hold and put on things are vital to this process. It will come as no surprise that social marketers need to understand these existing values from the client's perspective, and then work with clients to develop mutually acceptable new values and ways of realizing these. The social marketer must also avoid this degenerating into manipulation. Finally, the social marketer has to engage in the same processes with stakeholders, co-ordinating values the way a conductor directs the orchestra to reflect and develop a bigger and more harmonious picture.

As with Beethoven's symphony, all of this begins with a simple tune and its three-note motif: value co-discovery, value co-design and value co-delivery.

AN EMPOWERING START

Read through Box 10.2 to and think through the different values that are being displayed by Monica, Tom and Fred.

BOX 10.2: CO-CREATING VALUES

Monica is a 35-year-old with strawberry blonde hair, unusual green eyes, a great sense of fun and a deep belly laugh, all rolled into a neat five feet eight inch frame. She's a mother, housewife, part-time shop assistant and volunteer with the local basketball team, and has serious multitasking skills. Now and then, especially when it is raining, she finds it hard to get parking near the local bank for the few minutes she needs to do her business. On such occasions, Monica borrows her mother's disabled driving badge to park in the reserved parking bay outside the bank.

Monica is not alone.

Tom also parks there for a few minutes every Monday and Wednesday morning to offload his delivery of bread to the café that is next door to the bank. And there's Fred, a retired teacher who attends the bridge club every

Thursday afternoon for an hour or so, four doors down from the bank. Neither has a disabled parking badge.

Monica, Tom and Fred are violating the law; they are parking in a disabled parking space illegally. They are not the only ones complicit in this behaviour. Monica's mother lent her the disabled permit, while a traffic warden overlooks Fred's infringement, just as Tom's boss does, when he says, 'Sure it's only a few minutes.' All of them would be dismayed to think they are adding hardship to the lives of other community members. None of them would argue that their need is greater than a disabled person's; and each would agree that the policy of priority parking places for the disabled is enlightened and desirable.

Different values are evident in Monica, Tom and Fred's behaviours. For behaviour change to occur, the social marketer should engage with all three in 'value co-discovery' to understand them and their lived experiences, analysing their subjective values through attitudes, beliefs, knowledge, motivations and current behaviours (recall research in Chapter 5). Together, they carry out 'value co-design' to capture new meanings relevant to the problem through jointly devised product, service, price, place and promotion offerings (the marketing mix from Chapter 4). In 'value co-delivery', both clients and the social marketer factor in the system's role in the new potential behaviours. The system either blocks or empowers Monica, Tom and Fred to alter their behaviours. When this three-note motif of value co-discovery, co-design and co-delivery is played (Figure 10.1), we have the central theme of our symphony, value co-creation.

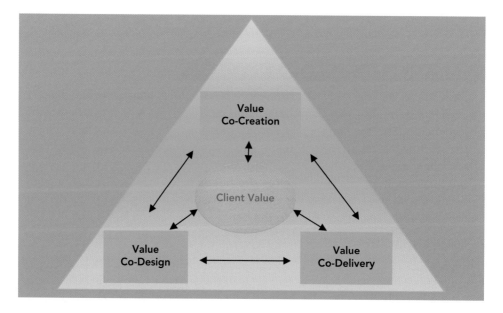

Figure 10.1 Value in social marketing

Each of these value processes are now explained.

Value co-discovery

Value co-discovery, as the first note in our tune, is about genuine in-depth relationships with clients and goes significantly beyond just asking people for their opinions or what might be called 'participation by consultation'. It gives people a voice, ownership and responsibility to influence their welfare, through direct interactive participation. Research is 'with' and not 'on' the client. Increasingly, the evidence shows that third sector programmes, 'designed and directed by community members, are far more likely to succeed than those planned and executed exclusively by outsiders' (Bryant *et al.* 2000: 61).

EXERCISE 10.1: HOW EMPOWERED ARE YOU?

Identify and compare situations in your life where you have experienced (a) passive participation/participation by consultation; and (b) interactive participation or self-mobilization.

Using critical thought (refer back to Box 8.3), question the how, why, where and when of these two forms of participation.

Which is more empowering? Why do you think so?

Active, versus passive, participation is more empowering because it reflects our values and gives us control. Value co-discovery empowers individuals in the same way as the client and social marketer are **co-storytellers** of improved wellbeing. Clients and the social marketer become dynamic *and* equal in developing a deep understanding of experiences. Consider Monica, our multitasking part-time volunteer with the local basketball team. Her mother leaves all the banking to her so she feels entitled to use the parking badge. She (Monica) had never really stopped to think about other disabled drivers and their needs to use the disabled parking space until one of the basketball parents commented on the difficulties of getting their wheelchair out of the car. Monica did have a short conversation about such parking difficulties with the parent while waiting for the children to put away the basketball equipment. She walks to the bank on dry days. Monica resolves in her own mind not to park in front of the bank again, but is worried about the next time it rains and she is in a hurry. Will she be tempted to use the parking space? Perhaps there could be paid parking meters in front of the bank or she could consider Internet banking?

Other value co-discovery examples include the Truth campaign, which we discussed in Chapter 2, where non-smoking was presented as an alternative way to rebel (against tobacco industry manipulations), driven by symbolic and emotional values versus the traditional health-focused values. In a similar manner, Hill (2011) adopts a profoundly ethnographic approach to value co-discovery, enabling the poor to tell their own stories and arguing that *only* when these stories are accorded at least *equal value* with other narratives will serious progress be made.

Value co-discovery's essence lies in relationship marketing, which we first discussed in Chapter 2, which provides the necessary dialogue, interaction and mutual learning. As Marques and Domegan (2011) explain, the intent is to build 'shared meanings' and gain insight into *what the parties can do together and for one another*. Our parking hero Tom is a good example. The café manager and Tom's boss argue the City Council has a responsibility to them. They pay rates and, if the Council don't provide adequate unloading bays, they are within their rights to use the disabled parking bay to make a living. Meanwhile, the City Council has to contend with traffic wardens who report threatening and abusive behaviour from drivers given traffic tickets for illegal parking.

Value co-discovery's drive towards this fuller understanding of clients is also evident in the work from Katie Collins and Lindsay Manning at the Bristol Social Marketing Centre in Lauren's story in Exercise 10.2.

EXERCISE 10.2 LAUREN'S STORY

- Lauren is 21 years old and she lives in a two-bed flat with her ten-month-old daughter.
- Her partner left her six weeks after she gave birth – he still provides some financial support but lives outside Gloucester.
- Her mum lives in Barnwood and her brother and his family are in Gloucester – neither can provide much help due to time / mobility restrictions.
- Lauren has a good relationship with her Health Visitor, who is concerned about Lauren and encourages her to go and meet other mums.
- Lauren feels really isolated and lonely – she has lost touch with her old group of friends since she gave birth. Ever since the age of 12 she used to go out drinking with them regularly, but now every evening she has to stay in the house to look after the baby. She feels trapped, so she often has a drink on her own when she is watching TV.
- She feels nervous accessing local services for mums as she doesn't want to be criticized for being young and single.
- She has met some mums in her street who have started inviting her to their flats during the day. However, they often get their kids together in the afternoon and then start drinking. Lauren wants their company but knows that drinking so much is not good for her or her child. She also wants their friendship because they could cause a lot of trouble for her if they turned against her.
- Lauren worries that she is a bad mum because she sometimes blames her daughter for the fact that she is so lonely. She also worries that if she tells anyone about the amount she drinks that they will take her daughter away.

How would you go about value co-discovery in conjunction with Lauren?

Storyboard created by Uscreates (www.uscreates.com)

Dialogue, empathy, interactions and mutual respect are core to working with Lauren because value co-discovery is essentially about an 'experiential' understanding of her and her values, i.e. knowing Lauren as a 'feeler', 'thinker' and 'doer'. Lauren *feels* lonely, isolated and afraid. She *thinks* drinking too much can be harmful and she *drinks* while *watching* TV. Monica also shows us this. She hadn't *thought* about other disabled drivers, she *felt* entitled to use her mother's parking badge as she was on her mother's business and *did walk* to the bank when it was dry. (Revisit our client orientation head, heart and hands discussion in Chapter 5.)

Value co-design

Value co-design, the second note in our tune, takes this full and intensely deep understanding of clients, worked out in partnership with them, and captures it in jointly designed products and services. Four types of value can potentially be co-developed within the social marketer and client partnership (Smith and Colgate 2007). These are:

- Functional value
- Emotional value
- Social value
- Cost/sacrifice value.

Functional value tends to be straightforward – it's the value derived from an object that performs a function or delivers an outcome, e.g. a watch tells the time, a car gets you from A to B or the scanner technology scans car registrations for traffic wardens. *Emotional value* designates sensory feelings, experiences and/or emotional worth, e.g. the sounds and smells of a dentists' office, the mood of a restaurant, how one is treated by a service provider such as a cancer screening nurse or the feeling of mobility given with the ownership of a disabled parking permit. *Social value* translates into self-identity, self-esteem and the psycho-social meaning of the exchange. For example, people who choose Fairtrade products perceive themselves to be responsible or ethical, while people who recycle, reuse or reduce might gain satisfaction from the notion of being environmentally friendly and community conscious. Fred sees himself as an outgoing and intellectual person – hence his involvement in the bridge club instead of hill walking.

Marques and Domegan (2011) maintain that, if the client's feelings of 'self-esteem and personal comfort are threatened by fear messages it is likely that they will not be receptive to building relationships' with the social marketer and 'if they do, that it will probably be a patronizing relationship rather than one of mutual respect'. (Think back to our discussion of fear messages in Chapter 6.)

Lastly, there is the *cost/sacrifice value*. This is the economic and/or psychological cost or risk associated with the purchase of an item or service. For Monica, Tom and Fred, the cost of a parking fine is simply not enough to deter them from using disabled parking spaces.

EXERCISE 10.3: VALUE CO-DESIGN WITH LAUREN

Revisit Lauren's story above – how would you go about value co-design with Lauren now? Think in terms of social marketing planning.

Value co-design with Lauren embraces the 4Ps – product (service), price, place and promotion – within social marketing planning. As part of the value co-design process, the social marketer and Lauren consider the appeal, affordability, availability and appreciation of the offer and, together, they must work out where engagement is to occur, the basis for client empowerment, as well as ways to exemplify and enable the desired behaviour. These ideas of co-production, co-packaging, co-promotion and co-pricing recognize the important role of the client in what would traditionally be seen as very much the preserve of the marketer, as discussed in Chapter 4.

Two examples help illustrate the benefits of this thinking. First, in a public health-care service quality study, co-designing values improved confidence, trust and engagement as well as knowledge, choice, initiative and commitment – all significant to the perception of high service quality (Gill *et al.* 2011). Second, in a breast cancer screening service in Queensland, the service provider and women co-designed activities such as reminder letters for the client. This interactive process results in a better experience for the consumer as the service provision is participant generated, delivering benefits for the service client, the service organization, and the wider community (Zainuddin *et al.* 2011).

Value co-delivery

With value co-delivery, the final note in our motif, the co-ordinating system around shared values comes into operation, which means front-line staff are important at this point. Public policy, technology, infrastructure, and media are relevant too. The system has to facilitate the manifestation of the new values or they cannot come into being. For example, value co-delivery for Monica, Tom and Fred means the disabled parking bay physically has to be free when they want to use it. Furthermore, for Tom, the café also has to be open to take stock to complete this cycle of value co-creation for him. For Fred, the traffic warden has to ignore his behaviour and not issue a parking violation ticket. If the traffic warden had written a fine, it would have been an entirely different value co-delivery experience for Fred! To see the parking system at work in value co-delivery, read about deterring parking abuse in Box 10.3.

BOX 10.3: VALUE CO-DELIVERY: DECRIMINALIZED PARKING IN EDINBURGH

'In Edinburgh, a large proportion of off-street car parks are managed by either National Car Parks Ltd (NCP) or Central Parking System Ltd (CPS). At Castle Terrace, a 750-space facility which is mostly used by tourists and office workers, abuse of reserved spaces is deterred by the following measures:

- An on-site kiosk which is manned 24 hours a day, seven days a week
- Staff members make periodic checks around the car park
- The car park is monitored by CCTV cameras

> - *If the driver is present, they are politely requested to move; if not, a £50 fine is issued*
> - *Disabled people are obliged to pay the same rates as non-disabled people*
> - *Electronic barriers to ensure all drivers purchase a parking ticket*
>
> When there are instances of abuse of disabled people's parking spaces, NCP's policy is to issue a Penalty Charge Notice. However compliance with the payment of fines is reported to be low. The site manager preferred to ask motorists to move their car rather than to issue fines. In the majority of cases, this more low-key approach, using direct face-to-face contact, was thought to be very effective. When motorists are approached by car park attendants, they are often embarrassed and move their car. Furthermore, the fact that many of the bays reserved for disabled people are located near to the attendant's kiosk means that they can be readily overseen.'
>
> (Source: Scottish Government Social Research 2007: 54)

In its simplest form, value co-delivery is about the instruments in the orchestra – the system factors beyond the control of the client that block or facilitate the materialization of new shared values. You will hear the terminology 'barriers or benefits' used by social marketers to denote this bigger picture thinking. Health services often bear witness to this. Take young adults (18–35-year-olds) with type 1 diabetes who are notorious for missing vital annual health checks. Think about the 'value barriers' the health system presents – waiting rooms that smell like operating theatres, no free wi-fi access and no privacy for people with distressing symptoms.

EXERCISE 10.4: VALUE CO-DELIVERY WITH LAUREN

Revisit Lauren's story once more – how would you go about value co-delivery with Lauren now? Think about the 'system' in question.

Value co-delivery means Lauren and the social marketer need to talk about the ways the health system assists and hinders her as a young single mother of a ten-month-old baby. While she is comfortable with her Health Visitor, she is wary of other health professionals. Under these circumstances, health checks may prove more successful in her flat than at a hospital. Alternatively, hospital staff could schedule mother and baby clinics in a manner that enables young single mothers to socialize together. Alternatively, staff could receive training in how to deal with hard-to-reach populations. Lauren and the social marketer could also explore facilities such as the local library or swimming pool for outings better suited to meeting Lauren's needs for friendship and wellbeing. This takes them into the educational or local community sub-systems, which could offer attractive alternatives to using the health service.

To cement these insights about value co-creation (co-discovery, co-design and co-delivery), turn to Case Study 22 on p. 490 from Katie Collins and Lindsay Manning from the Bristol Social Marketing Centre. There you will read how participatory action and individual empowerment can bring about a positive outcome, by jointly tackling risky drinking in deprived communities in a sustainable manner.

Now, contemplate our theme of value co-creation and its three-note motif with stakeholders as well as clients – that is, scaling up value co-discovery, co-design and co-delivery to manifest 'value communities'. This is akin to the string or wood instruments, musical families in the orchestra, playing variations and progressions of the central tune in harmony to create our first symphony movement.

COMMUNITY SOCIAL MARKETING

This is exactly what is happening in community social marketing (CSM) – variations on the central tune played by different instruments – multiple value co-creations *with* different stakeholders such as local residents, college students, hoteliers, businesses, local police, youth organizations and local authorities. CSM is about community development and building participation with social marketing tools. It takes a values-based barriers and benefits approach to behaviour change linking the environment to the person in the way a symphony expresses the relationship between its theme and movements. Anker and Kappel (2011) maintain CSM's framework allows members from the affected community to select the complex social problems they want to tackle, set programme goals and participate in the research, strategy development, and programme activities used to reach those goals. (Again, think back to our discussion of client and creative orientations of social marketing in Chapter 2.)

Read Doug McKenzie-Mohr's Case Study 15 'Turn it Off' on p. 429 to understand how CSM facilitates behaviour change by emphasizing personal contact and communications. It also shows how, in contrast to traditional mass media environmental campaigns, CSM functions as an effective alternative. Then reflect upon a minor digression of our community value co-creation melody and find out about the small rural the village of Querença in Portugal, brought to us by Helena Alves and Sara Fernandes in Case Study 2 on p. 311. This involved identifying the community barriers to sustainable living, designing a strategy to overcome these barriers using knowledge from the social sciences, piloting the strategy to ensure that it is successful, and then implementing it on a broader scale.

One of CSM's distinguishing characteristics is the partnerships created between social marketers and community members. Communities are networks based on locality, ethnicity, sexual orientation, occupation, or shared interests. When based on geographic bounded localities, community boards or coalitions are formed that typically include local public health professionals, lay leaders and activists, representatives of local businesses, churches, voluntary organizations, and residents. Thus, in addition to enhancing the long-lasting success of social marketing interventions, CSM enhances community organizing efforts by giving its members a more effective planning process (Bryant *et al.* 2000), as displayed in the dominant CSM models in Table 10.1.

Another distinguishing feature hinted at in the CSM models in Table 10.1 is CSM's goal to build the community's capacity to solve local problems by teaching them social marketing principles and skills. Unlike other community organizing models, community members are taught to analyse the competition, select target behaviours and priority population segments to optimize their return on investment, and use consumer research to develop a strategic plan based on marketing's 4Ps or 4As. Through direct participation in all phases of the planning and implementation process, some community members gain the social marketing skills needed to address other issues and work together to sustain and institutionalize solutions.

Table 10.1 Dominant community social marketing models

Model	Description	Key Features	Applications
Community Preventative Social Marketing	Community directed framework where social marketers teach and work with community partners	Community learning, participation, ownership and empowerment	Initiation of tobacco and alcohol use; promote physical activity; obesity prevention and prevention of eye-related injuries
Community-based Social Marketing	Focuses upon the barriers to behaviour change at the community level	Barriers and benefits analysis	Environmental issues such as waste and pollution, water, energy, transportation, agriculture and conservation
Community Readiness Social Marketing	Community change used for assessing the level of readiness of a community to develop and implement prevention	Readiness assessment	Drug and alcohol use, domestic and sexual violence, HIV/AIDS and environmental issues
Community-led Assets-based Social Marketing	Based on the concept that the client is the most important participant in the change process	Audience insight, consumer solution generation	Used in health inequalities issues

Source: Fitzgerald (2012)

EXERCISE 10.5: COMMUNITY CATERING SERVICES

Confronted with a tough economic climate, diminished funding and increased demand, community health services, such as Meals on Wheels, are currently facing challenging times. In Ireland, the UK and globally, Meals on Wheels are evolving from a traditional charity-dependent, expert-led system, to a public–private partnership concept, supporting a client-orientated and information-led approach. A successful transition to this new approach is dependent on the collaboration of stakeholders in the provision of Meals on Wheels.

(Source: Fitzgerald 2012)

What is the role for community social marketing in community catering services?

Community social marketing's role is to understand how community stakeholders' behaviours and values can act as benefits (value consensus) or barriers (value dissensus) to change. Using value co-creation processes with community stakeholders will uncover information about local problems and the assets available to resolve them. This enhances the fit between programme strategies and local institutions and customs. By stakeholders working together, network ties (recall social capital theory, Chapter 3) may be strengthened and new problem-solving and critical thinking skills acquired, thereby enhancing the community's capacity to tackle new issues. Most importantly, communities are treated as change agents and active partners.

Look at the 'Anti-Smoking to Pro-Quitting 2011 Campaign' from the Health Promotion Board of Singapore Campaign (Ogilvy & Mather 2012). Traditionally, complex problems such as smoking have been approached through a reductionist view of community value co-creation – the top-down way where experts, e.g. health authorities and doctors, know best. But knowing what appears to be right (smoking kills and is bad for you, stop smoking) closes the door to learning and gives rise to value dissensus. Instead, tools such as Facebook and mobile apps can be used to empower community co-ordination and collaborative efforts to generate new value consensus, such as pro-quitting. This gets us beyond simple promotion and communication and into the interrelationships and interconnections between individuals and other community members. A good place and space to be in!

Experience in several settings has demonstrated that CSM is effective in teaching communities to use social marketing approaches for designing new public health and environmental interventions, tailoring evidence-based interventions for application in new settings, and creating local programmes to capitalize on the brand equity of national media campaigns (Bryant *et al.* 2009). It has also increased community coalitions' capacity to use marketing principles for policy advocacy, and service delivery improvements.

KAMAYOQS

Similar thinking has been applied around the world. In the Netherlands, the Eigen Kracht Centrale (Family Group Conferencing) is 'striving for a society based on participation and mutual self-reliance of citizens, where citizens remain in charge of their own life, especially when dealing with organisations and government bodies' (Eigen Kracht Centrale 2011). Amnesty International's work in the Northern Territory of Australia shows that giving aboriginal communities greater control of their own health services enhances outcomes (Marland 2010). Across the Pacific in Peru, as we saw in Chapter 8, a development NGO called Practical Action has also recognized the value of indigenous wisdom. (Reread Figure 8.2: Kamayoqs.)

The Kamoyoq example reminds us that CSM gains much of its success from the synergy between community organization, community mobilization and social marketing principles. By leveraging the wisdom of local groups and nurturing ownership of the problem-solving process, CSM increases the likelihood of interventions being successful and changes being sustained. Social learning and participatory problem-solving come together for better segmentation, targeting, audience research, and intervention mix, design and delivery. Community participation also enhances the validity of formative research results, strengthens participants' sense of social connectedness, control over their lives and ability to change.

Like all community approaches, CSM is also challenging. Community participation and self-determination can be difficult and time-consuming. Trust and cooperation between 'outsiders' – i.e. social marketing experts and community members – can be difficult to establish, especially in disenfranchised populations. Moreover, the time required to reach consensus on major programme decisions can extend the planning process and delay programme implementation. In addition, CSM is not appropriate for all communities and all problems: the social marketing expertise and/or community leadership and commitment may simply be unavailable or an inappropriate CSM could be misguidedly applied. Nonetheless, CSM is an extremely promising and archetypal social marketing approach, which takes the core notion of client and collective orientations and establishes a broad social agenda for the discipline.

Just as Beethoven's four-note theme resounds between different members of the orchestra to create harmony, so too in community social marketing, where our three-pronged tune is taken up by other players to produce an integrated model. In a similar manner, CSM's stakeholder-network perspective and client-empowered outlook can be expanded to other communities, groups and networks, other musical families. It engages local governments in health development through a process of political commitment, institutional change, capacity-building, partnership-based planning and innovative projects. About 90 cities are members of the WHO European Healthy Cities Network.'[1] This is systems social marketing. Like the symphony conductor whose job it is to synchronize the principal divisions of the orchestra and become part of the orchestra they conduct, systems social marketing uses value co-ordination and partnerships, within and across networks of communities, to inspire comprehensive transformational change strategies. When value co-creation comes together for individuals, communities and society in a unified whole, like Beethoven's music, sweet social change is the result.

SYSTEMS SOCIAL MARKETING (SSM)

To follow in Beethoven's footsteps and create a whole that is greater than the sum of its parts – a full-bodied 'symphony' rather than a flimsy 'tune' – we must ensure co-ordinated, harmonized critical action. By bringing on board a variety of public, private and third sector stakeholders, we create an atmosphere in which ideas can be introduced and developed in a democratic and holistic way, reflecting the four principles (client, creative, collective and competitive orientations) in Chapter 2. Systems social marketing strategies must be sufficiently robust to manage and meet the requirements of multiple stakeholders. With various stakeholders interacting at different levels, and aspects of value reflecting the interdependency of social systems, contexts, content and actors, systems social marketing therefore demands greater:

1. Co-ordinated networks of shared values co-creation
2. Transformational partnerships
3. Indicators of those relationships.

The final part of this chapter tackles each of these systems social marketing issues in turn.

Co-ordinated networks of shared values co-creation

Systems social marketing, drawing upon the social cognitive and social ecological theories explained in Chapter 3, sees networks of value co-creation communities co-ordinated across four levels: micro, group, macro and planet level. This is outlined in Table 10.2.

By conducting communities of value co-creations across and between levels, systems social marketing links the individual to the collective, the consumer to the citizen and vice versa. Such communities of empowered change allow no 'opt out' or 'hand over' by upstream stakeholders, e.g. by government to the commercial or non-profit sectors. Similarly, we as individual citizens cannot avoid our own responsibilities, especially those that flow from our consumption behaviours.

Table 10.2 Systems social marketing and co-ordinated value co-creations

Change	Micro level (individual)	Group level (group/ community/ organization)	Macro level (society/nation)	Planet level (global)
Short-term example:	*Behaviour change* Attendance at stop-smoking clinic	*Changes in norms/ Administrative change* Removal of tobacco advertising from outside a school	*Policy change* Banning of all forms of tobacco marketing in the UK or EU	*Policy change* Banning of all forms of tobacco marketing in all countries
Long-term example:	*Lifestyle change* Smoking cessation	*Organizational change* Deter retailers from selling cigarettes to minors	*Socio-cultural evolution* Eradication of all tobacco-related disease in the UK or EU	*Socio-cultural evolution across societies* Eradication of all tobacco-related disease in the world

Source: Adapted from MacFadyen *et al.* (1999: 4)

EXERCISE 10.6: DIFFERENT SHADES OF OPTING IN AND OUT

Read this piece by Bob Doppelt (2011) and consider who is opting in and out of reform and redesign.

'Increasing the recycling rate of cans and glass bottles is a positive step. Increasing the recycling rate of plastic bottles can be considered "first order" change. Such changes attempt to tweak and improve existing business models and products, while leaving their underlying goals and structures intact. Yet if those business models and products are inherently harmful, making them more efficient or changing their ingredients will, at best, only make their negative impacts a little less bad. Many plastics found in our bedding, clothing, carpets, cookware, food containers, cosmetics and other products include chemicals that can harm nature and people. Manufacturers claim the chemicals found in plastic will not leach or transfer into our food, air, water or skin. But as plastic ages or is exposed to stress or heat, it can transmit some of its ingredients. Bisphenol-A, known as BPA, is found in hundreds of household items, including baby bottles – and it is one of the chemicals known to leach. While toxic leaching from plastic bottles is hard to see, they obviously produce a massive amount of trash. Studies estimate that nationwide, more than 30 billion of them are thrown away each year. That's the reason legislators want to increase their recycling rate.

A more sustainable option would be to ban most plastic bottles. Outlawing the majority of plastics made of fossil fuels would be an even better sustainable choice. A mandatory phase-out of all products, plastic or not, that cannot be continually reused in their current form, "up-cycled" into similar or high-quality products, or returned to nature to serve as nutrients for new growth would be the most truly sustainable approach of all. The latter system is "second-order" change – transformative shifts in assumptions and goals that produce fundamentally different types of business models, products, and policies. Such change eliminates impacts, or even helps restore the environment.

This type of second-order change is not that far-fetched. Many European nations have closed their landfills and now require manufacturers, importers and sellers to take back their packaging, electronics, and many other products when they are no longer of use. A profound shift in thinking and design has resulted.'

Now, think about our health system and obesity. Do you see first or second order change?

You would be correct in arguing that singular interventions have been successful as first order change, e.g. targeting young children to exercise and/or to eat fruit and vegetables. Systems social marketing, through networks of value co-creating communities, seeks second order change to eliminate obesity. Its purpose is to set and co-ordinate agendas between clients, social marketers and stakeholders from down-, mid- and upstreams, in order to bring about meaningful change. Communities of shared values reinforce the need for, and importance of, co-ordinated change strategies. For example, *Healthy Cities* sees health and change 'as the business of all sectors'. 'It engages local governments in health development through a process of political commitment, institutional change, capacity building, partnership-based planning and innovative projects. About 90 cities are members of the WHO European Healthy Cities Network, and 30 national Healthy Cities networks across the WHO European Region have a membership of more than 1400.'[1] The phrase whole-systems-in-the-room has been coined to signal this bigger harmonious systems picture, as Box 10.4 explains.

BOX 10.4: WHOLE-SYSTEMS-IN-THE-ROOM

'Finland will base its economy on forms of production that increase national wealth and well-being without depleting biodiversity or exceeding the carrying capacity of natural systems through their environmental impacts . . . New eco-efficient, product-service systems, sustainable high-quality products and social innovations will encourage a shift away from the accumulation of material goods to more *service-based* consumer cultures . . . A society with sustainable consumption and production patterns will also involve *intensified networking* and *dialogue* between different sectors, with environmental and social innovations effectively promoted.'

(Source: Committee of Sustainable Consumption and Production, Finland, 2005)

In this sense, systems social marketing moves clients, stakeholders and change agents into '*we*' co-created exchanges, thereby ensuring that the social marketer goes further than their commercial counterpart in considering economic, ecological and social values for all. We've already seen from CSM that *co-ordination* presents significant advantages because assets from one organization can augment and embellish assets of another. The focus is shifted from the linear and top-down approach to a co-ordinated, adaptive, value consensus process. Co-ordination of *shared values* brings outliers as well as established system actors together in mutually beneficial ways (Geels *et al.* 2008). In Case Study 17 on p. 444, Saathiya's Family Planning, co-ordination is a key element to their success. The Saathiya network of 3,000 healthcare providers, including traditional doctors (alternative practitioners), family doctors, specialists and chemists successfully built confidence and increased trust among clients leading to increased use of family planning methods via co-ordinated communication strategies. Effective collaboration of community leaders, corporate sector and media, as gatekeepers of public opinion, connect people in the circulation of ideas and experience, thereby extending relationships across boundaries and groups. Take The Heart Truth example – the National Heart, Lung and Blood Institute initiative to create awareness about women and heart disease. Cooperation with America's fashion industry was essential to access the 'considerable promotional and communication capabilities and distribution channels of the fashion industry . . . and [to] opening doors to opportunities with the corporate and media sectors' (Temple *et al.* 2008: 68).

Similarly, in Abraham Brown's EU Help Branding Case Study 6 on p. 344, he explains:

the overall 'Help' campaign was an example of unique cooperation, designed and conducted in partnership with stakeholders such as youth organizations across the EU, comprising:

- *European Medical Student Association (EMSA)*
- *International Federation of Medical Students' Association (IFSMA)*
- *European Youth Forum/Forum Jeunesse*
- *communication experts such as tobacco control professionals from the European Network for Smoking Prevention (ENSP) and the European Network of Quitlines (ENQ)*
- *students from over 50 youth organizations and medical student organizations.*

All this requires *co-learning* (progressive learning from Chapter 5) that encourages stakeholders to engage active trust instead of hierarchical ownership. Susana Marques' Blueprint Relationship Marketing Case Study 14 on p. 421 shows how, for youth drug usage, this sharing of knowledge resulted in stakeholders (youth, families, schools and community) accepting the lack of recreational activities as a contributory element to drug use. In such situations, a potential intervention could be to train community members in grant writing. A further learning example is evident at *safe*-food, The Food Safety Promotion Board of Ireland, and their use of systematic reviews. The rigorous standards of systematic reviews (refer back to Box 5.4) assisted in building trust, cooperation and commitment between social marketing researchers and policy makers. The interactive process of the systematic review changed the role of the stakeholders from being isolated, passive and unaware to being strategically connected, active and engaged. It enabled a common language and negotiated understanding to emerge about the problem (McHugh and Domegan 2010).

EXERCISE 10.7: SHARED VALUES – 'OPERATION TRANSFORMATION'

Operation Transformation, as we saw in Chapter 6, is a novel concept on television screens not alone in the fact that lifestyle changes serves as the programme's 'plot', but also because of the innovative network effects. The programme has transcended the traditional television format to adopt a cross-media broadcasting platform via television, radio (RTÉ Radio 1) and Internet (www.rte.ie). For the most recent series of the programme, an interactive mobile site, MyOT.ie, was developed to enable the audience to chart their progress, obtain daily recipes and exercise videos, and assist them in reaching their lifestyle goals. This mobile site proved highly popular, and was supported by the food and leisure industries.

Policy change is a key area of the show, with the latest series focusing on a proposed legislation of calorie counts on menus across Ireland. Perhaps the most novel outcome of the television show, however, is the community that has emerged both online and offline. The show's Facebook account has over 65,000 fans, who frequently engage with one another offering helpful support and reinforcement management. The show openly calls for local towns and villages, workplaces and clubs to come together and become one of the numerous 'Operation Transformation' support groups.

Early evidence supports the hypothesis that systems social marketing is unrivalled in its effectiveness at generating behaviour and social change around social ills.

What potential 'shared values' around healthy eating and exercise are emerging through *Operation Transformation*? 'Who' is involved in creating these shared values?

(Source: Gately 2012)

Shared values networks or systems social marketing are witnessed in the *Healthy Cities network* around Europe, the *Food Dudes Programme* now in Iceland, the EU and USA, and the community-based FAN project which Suzanne Suggs and colleagues present in Case Study 21 on p. 482. Targeting children (6–12 years) and their parents, FAN was successful at engaging policy makers, teachers, health practitioners, parents and children to participate in developing an effective healthy body weight programme, tailored to the needs and wishes of all stakeholders. FAN facilitated positive attitudes and behaviours and the community becoming 'Fans of FAN', promoting healthy nutrition and physical activity among children, while encouraging parents and children to work together.

With community social marketing as the first movement of our symphony and networks of value co-creating communities as the second movement, we now turn our ear to our third symphony movement, Partnerships.

Partnerships

Partnerships are central to, and closely aligned with, networks of value co-creating communities and are widely accepted as the 5th 'P' in the social marketing mix. However, confusion prevails as to the precise meaning of the term.

EXERCISE 10.8: PARTNERSHIP TERMINOLOGY

The word partnership has many connotations. Jot down synonyms for the word 'partnership'.

In a landmark social marketing partnership study drawing on over 50 years of writings, case studies and research, Sinead Duane (2012) documented relevant partnership terminology. She found over 15 terms to describe social marketing partnerships. More importantly, however, she notes two key forms of partnership. The first is operational or intervention-led – the more traditional alliance where organizations liaise to supply a product or service or open communication/distribution channels to a target audience for the social marketing intervention. The second type is a systems-led partnership, reflecting community relationship networks and shared values, seen in Figure 10.2.

Since relational partnerships epitomize the emphasis on the strategic long-term development of sustainable co-ordinated relationships between stakeholders, how do social marketers develop a systems partnership mindset? The answer takes us back to Chapter 2 and our initial discussion of relationship marketing: good relationships depend on the two core constructs of trust and commitment. For these to grow mutual benefit, shared values and communication are necessary. Mutual benefit signals tangible and intangible gains from participating in the partnership.

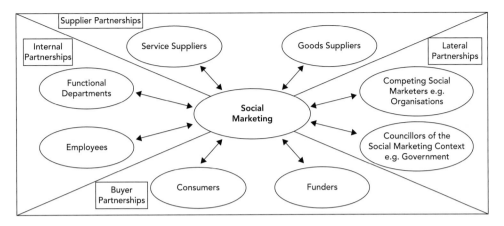

Figure 10.2 A multi-partnership model of social marketing
Source: Hastings *et al*. 2003.

Partners sharing similar goals and values agree on how the problem is defined. Where shared values exist, organizational values are also thought to be similar leading to partners adopting the same perspective on the problem. As evident from Chapter 6, communication, a two-way process incorporating formality, frequency and quality of communications, is associated with trust as an open dialogue process. All of this is displayed in Figure 10.3.

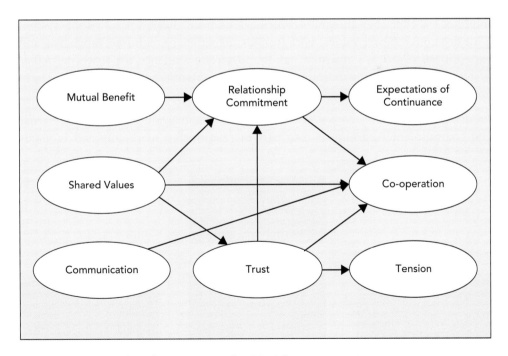

Figure 10.3 A Social Marketing Partnership Model
Source: Duane (2012)

Three outcomes of trust and commitment also exist: expectation of continuance, cooperation and tension. Expectation of continuance is the likelihood of switching between problems and the future development of the relationship. As the focus of social marketing partnerships moves from the short to long term, there are higher levels of commitment and lower likelihoods of partnership termination. Cooperation is the sharing and co-leveraging of resources, while tensions are manifestations of negative relationships. Unmanaged tensions erode trust.

Turn to Duane and Domegan's Case Study 9, 'Get Your Life in Gear', on p. 369 and read about the dynamics of partnership, from selection to management.

Within community networks of shared values, such transformational partnerships represent new and uncharted melodies in terms of meeting human needs and bringing about significant change.

INDICATORS FOR SYSTEMS SOCIAL MARKETING

In the way a would-be composer muses on how to conclude the symphony through its fourth movement, the Systems Social Marketer must ponder about how new values, communities, networks and partnerships can spring from the old, flawed industrial and economic views of our world.

To accentuate our fourth and final movement, Patricia McHugh (2013) explains indicators are useful in reducing broad concepts, such as 'trust' and 'networks' to measurable forms, while maintaining the bonds between them. The advantage of indicators is that they integrate contributions from diverse parts of the system with dissimilar views, values, backgrounds, experiences, cultures, languages and expectations. Patricia's research has found strong evidence for three particular systems social marketing indicators: knowledge, networks and relationships. These are displayed and categorized in Figure 10.4.

Relationship indicators, as we saw in Chapter 2 and again above, include trust and commitment. Learning is also part of relationship marketing and is about

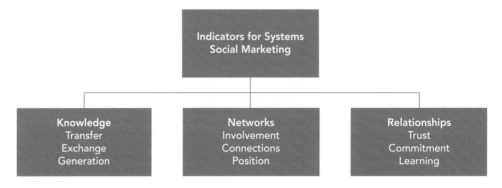

Figure 10.4 Indicators for Systems Social Marketing
Source: McHugh (2013)

information acquisition, information dissemination and shared interpretation. Without learning, there can be no value co-creation with clients or stakeholders.

Network involvement is about the identities, status, resources, access and other stakeholder characteristics. In 'Get Your Life in Gear' (GYLIG), Case Study 9 on p. 369, *safe*food traditionally defines their network as a food network, but, to achieve behaviour change for truck drivers, they had to redefine this particular network as Men's Health. This opened doors to working with organizations such as The Irish Heart Foundation, the national Men's Health Forum and service stations, all of whom had a vested interest in and experience of men and their well-being. *Network* ties represent the connections between people. These will be weak or strong depending on frequency, intensity, intimacy and reciprocity of interaction. Initially, the GYLIG network ties were weak but grew over the duration of the study based on face-to-face meetings and communications. Network positions are the degree an organization directly and indirectly connects to other organizations. In this case, *safe*food held a central network position, acting as the hub for the study. The Irish Heart Foundation also had a strong position emanating from its immense experience of working with men. In contrast, the service stations had more peripheral positions, being indirectly connected to other networks and actors. *Knowledge* indicators are about co-learning and include knowledge transfer as the flow of information from knowledge producers to knowledge users, for example, from researchers and scholars to policy makers and professionals. Knowledge exchange is shared learning and communication between problem-solvers with a propensity to act as seen in Healthy Cities where local police, hospitals, health agencies, retailers and resident communities work together to tackle college binge drinking. Knowledge generation denotes the tacit and explicit knowledge shared continuously by all actors, i.e. the experiential insights from value discovery we discussed at the beginning of this chapter.

As social marketers, what is important for us to remember is that our and the client's struggle to change is never isolated from society's effort to transform. Indicators are our reminder and measurement of this big picture and how well the conductor is fulfilling their role with the whole orchestra.

WRAP-UP

Listening to and learning from the people we want to work with, whether we term them consumers, clients, target groups or citizens, is the *sine qua non* of social marketing (Hastings, 2011). Nowhere is this better reflected than in *social marketing which sees both the individual and wider society as the client*. We call this systems social marketing, and values lie at the heart of the endeavour.

Values are subjective and encompass many meanings. The value rationale invites the social marketer and client to work together to understand each other as 'feelers', 'thinkers' and 'doers' within the context of their lives and social structures. This has been termed value co-creation, and involves value co-discovery, co-design and co-delivery. It acknowledges individual behaviour change as an essential part of broader social change.

For any large-scale change to happen, there needs to be a cooperative system of values in place – people need to work together to agree on 'what really matters'. This is community social marketing at work, with its capacity to solve local problems by teaching community stakeholders social marketing principles and skills.

Systems social marketing expands this joint behavioural change agenda beyond the client and organization to networks of stakeholders. In this way, and propelled by networked partnerships of shared values, systems social marketing strategies can genuinely start to address the broad challenges of societal change. It deals with George Orwell's conundrum (see Chapter 8) and addresses both the individual and the systemic. Above all, it provides the necessary complexity and sophistication we need to tackle the great multifactorial problems – most notably global warming – that humankind now faces.

Reflective questions

1. Define in two or three sentences, and in your own words, each of the key words at the beginning of this chapter.
2. What has value differences to do with behaviour change?
3. Model and explain value co-creation.
4. Explain the key characteristics of community social marketing.
5. Model and explain social marketing partnerships.
6. What is the role and function of networks and partnerships in systems social marketing?
7. Define the term indicator. How might indicators be useful to the social marketer? List three systems social marketing indicators.

Reflective assignments

1. Make sure you are comfortable with the content of this chapter by writing a concise paragraph, in your own words, about community social marketing and partnerships.
2. Using the framework in Table 10.2, identify the co-creation of value activities that an organization of your choice successfully completes. Also outline the value co-creation activities that the organization does not perform well and consider why.
3. Locate and critique social marketing examples that include community social marketing.
4. Locate and critique social marketing examples that include partnerships.

5. You have been hired by the Alzheimer's Society to design a behavioural intervention aimed at farmers over the age of 65 with no family history of dementia.
Specifically, the society wishes such individuals to undertake self-checks for
dementia and for farmers to be more proactive in seeking help/medical advice,
if required. What might be the pitfalls facing you?

6. For each of the three client value co-creation processes of discovery, design
and delivery, take all the stages of the social marketing planning process and
map the various tools and techniques onto the value co-creation processes.

7. Go to www.euro.who.int/en/what-we-do/health-topics/environment-and-health/
urban-health/activities/healthy-cities and investigate Healthy Cities. What
hallmarks of systems social marketing does Healthy Cities display?

8. Develop your own traffic lights checklist for systems social marketing.

Note

1   www.euro.who.int/en/what-we-do/health-topics/environment-and-health/urban-
health/activities/healthy-cities (accessed 8 August 2012).

References

Alderson, W. (1957) *Marketing Behaviour and Executive Action: A Functionalist Approach
to Marketing Theory*. Illinois, US: Richard D. Irwin Inc.

Anker, T. and Kappel, K. (2011) 'Ethical challenges in commercial social marketing',
in G. Hastings, K. Angus and C. Bryant (eds) *The SAGE Handbook of Social
Marketing*. London: Sage Publications Ltd., pp. 284–297.

Bryant, C.A., Forthofer, M., McCormack Brown, K., Landis, D. and McDermott,
R.J. (2000) 'Community-based prevention marketing: The next steps in
disseminating behavior change', *American Journal of Health Behavior*, 24(1):
61–68.

Bryant, C.A., McCormack Brown, K., McDermott, R.J., Debate, R.D., Alfonso,
M.A., Baldwin, J. L., Monaghan, P., and Phillips, L.M. (2009) 'Community-based
prevention marketing: A new planning framework for designing and tailoring
health promotion interventions', in R. DiClemente, R.A. Crosby, M.C. Kegler
(eds) *Emerging Theories in Health Promotion Practice and Research: Strategies for
Improving Public Health*, 2nd edition, San Francisco, CA: Jossey-Bass.

Committee of Sustainable Consumption and Production, Finland (June 2005)
'Getting more from less', www.ymparisto.fi/default.asp?content:d=62075&
lan=en (accessed 07/08/2013).

Doppelt, Bob (2011) 'Making products "less bad" isn't sustainable', *The Register-
Guard*, Thursday, 2 June.

Duane, S. (2012) 'A Social Marketing Partnership Framework: An Extension of
Morgan and Hunt's (1994) Commitment – Trust Key Mediating Variable Model',
PhD thesis, National University of Ireland, Galway, Ireland.

Eigen Kracht Centrale (2011) 'Eigen Kracht: The first decade in the Netherlands'. Online: www.eigen-kracht.nl/sites/default/files/2011%20Eigen%20Kracht,%20 the%20first%20decade%20in%20The%20Netherlands%20(okt%202011).pdf/.

Fitzgerald, C. (2012) 'Community Catering and the Community Readiness Model', Presentation to the Graduate Research Committee, NUI Galway, 19 June.

Gately, N. (2012) 'Social Marketing Sponsorship – A Conceptual Model', Presentation to the Graduate Research Committee, NUI Galway, 19 June.

Geels, F.W., Hekkert, M.P. and Jacobsson, S. (2008) 'The dynamics of sustainable innovation journeys', *Technology Analysis & Strategic Management*, 20(5): 521–536.

Gill, L., White, L. and Cameron I. (2011) 'Service co-creation in community-based aged healthcare', *Managing Service Quality*, 21(2): 152–177.

Hastings, G. and Lowry, R. (2010) 'Social marketing: A tale of beer, marriage and public health', in A. Steptoe (ed.) *Handbook of Behavioral Medicine*, New York: Springer Science & Business Media.

Hastings, G., Stead, M., McDermott, L., Forsyth, A., MacKintosh, A.M., Rayner, M., Godfrey, C., Caraher, M. and Angus K. (2003) *Review of Research on the Effects of Food Promotion to Children*. Prepared for the Food Standard Agency, 22 September. Stirling: Institute for Social Marketing, University of Stirling.

Hill, R.P. (2011) 'Impoverished consumers and social marketing', Ch. 21 in G. Hastings, K. Angus and C. Bryant (eds) *The SAGE Handbook of Social Marketing*. London: Sage Publications Ltd.

Lawrence, F. (2010) 'Bitter fruit: The truth about supermarket pineapple', *The Guardian*, 2 October 2010. www.guardian.co.uk/business/2010/oct/02/ truth-about-pineapple-production/.

MacFadyen, L., Stead, M. and Hastings, G. (1999) *A Synopsis of Social Marketing*. Online: www.social-marketing.com.html.

McHugh, P. (2013) 'The Use of Social Marketing and Innovation Theory for the Development of Process Indicators for Science Communication'. PhD thesis, National University of Ireland, Galway, Ireland.

McHugh, P. and Domegan, C. (2010) 'Systematic Reviews: Their emerging role in the co-creation of social marketing value'. 9th International Congress of the International Association on Public and Nonprofit Marketing. Bucharest, Romania: Conference Paper

Marland, S. (2010) 'Healthy homelands', Amnesty International. Online: www. amnesty.org.au/poverty/comments/22681/.

Marques, S. and Domegan, C. (2011) 'Relationship marketing and social marketing', Ch. 3 in G. Hastings, K. Angus and C. Bryant (eds) *The SAGE Handbook of Social Marketing*. London: Sage Publications Ltd.

Ogilvy and Mather (2012) 'From Anti-Smoking to Pro-Quitting', National Smoking Control Campaign, 2011, IPA Effectiveness Awards, Health Promotion Board of Singapore.

Scottish Government Social Research (2007) 'Tackling the abuse of off-street parking for people with disabilities in Scotland'.

Smith, J.B. and Colgate, M. (2007) 'Customer value creation: A practical framework', *Journal of Marketing Theory and Practice*, 15(1): 7–23.

Temple, S., Long, T., Wayman, J., Taubenheim, A.M. and Patterson, J. (2008) 'Alliance building: Mobilizing partners to share the heart truth with American women', *Social Marketing Quarterly*, 14: 68–79.

Zainuddin, N., Previte, J. and Russell-Bennett, R. (2011) 'A social marketing approach to value creation in a well-women's health service', *Journal of Marketing Management*, 27: 3–4, 361–385.

Afterword: A call to action

AFTERWORD: A CALL TO ACTION

6 March was a day of two meetings.

The first was with Coca-Cola, and took place over an excellent lunch of wild mushroom risotto at the 5-star Scotsman Hotel in the centre of Edinburgh. A small group of public health researchers and practitioners had been invited along to hear about the corporation's response to the obesity epidemic. The head of corporate affairs for Coca-Cola Enterprises welcomed us with a reminder that Coke is the world's leading supplier of sparkling (not, he stressed, fizzy) drinks and that, as such, it is taking the obesity crisis seriously. There followed a well-honed PowerPoint presentation explaining the company's latest initiatives. These included a new two-minute television ad, to be screened nationally that same night, presenting a community-wide call to action against obesity. It was an upbeat and infectious manifesto for change. The emphasis was on exercise rather than diet, and a second, standard-length commercial explained to Coke drinkers some enjoyable ways in which they could use up the sugared beverage calories they consumed. The presentation was extremely professional and the production values of the ads simply stunning.

The second meeting took place the same evening in an anteroom of the Scottish Parliament. It was between volunteers, academics and parliamentarians, and concerned fair trade. Scotland had just achieved Fair Trade Nation status (joining Wales) and two Malawian farmers were present to explain how this was helping them. There was no wild mushroom risotto, no TV advertising or PowerPoint presentation; but there was an uplifting message. Howard and Henry each had smallholdings on which they grew rice; they planted, tended and harvested their crops by hand. The additional money forthcoming from getting a fair price for their produce was enabling them to educate their children, access healthcare and (very gradually) improve their agricultural methods. The principal point of their short talk was to thank the volunteers at the meeting for all their hard work and campaigning.

The two meetings illustrate what this book is all about.

Coke's anti-obesity push demonstrates the potential power of marketing to engage and mobilize. It can turn a threat (weight gain) into an opportunity (an active lifestyle). Furthermore, Coke has immense resources, so the campaign would have tremendous reach; airing a two-minute ad about obesity on prime-time TV was probably a first anywhere in the world. In times of austerity, public health budgets cannot possibly match this expenditure.

Furthermore, Coke went on to explain that the communications effort was being combined with other initiatives such as product redesign (replacing sugar with low-calorie sweeteners) and serving-size reductions. Alternative low-calorie offers such as flavoured water and Diet Coke were also being marketed. And the company recognized this was a long-term issue that it had been working on for decades and would continue to do so for decades into the future. All good social marketing stuff: multifaceted, pragmatic and strategic.

It may seem odd then that the response of the public health representatives was muted. It seemed wrong to be critical of our hosts – they were being so polite and had provided a very nice lunch. After some non-committal initial remarks, however, concerns began to emerge. The question of dosage was raised: how much Coke would the company recommend a parent to give a five-year-old child? This caused some havering: 'it's up to the mother'; 'we don't make that sort of recommendation'; 'it's about having a balanced diet'. Then one of the invited dieticians volunteered an answer. Her department had done some calculations on what constituted a balanced diet and this showed that an adult should drink no more than one 330ml can (whether sugared or not) per week. They hadn't done the equivalent calculation for a five-year-old.

The issue of 'empty calories' was also raised. The problem with the calories from sweet beverages like Coke is that they are nutritionally useless and the body does not even recognize that they have been ingested. In other words, we consume them as well as, not instead of, our other dietary intake. Then 'sweet tooth syndrome' was raised: the danger that eating and drinking very sweet things (whether sugared or sweetened) trains our palates to want more of the same.

It began to seem like the best thing Coke could do for public health would be to reduce its sales, or shut up shop altogether!

The new exercise commercial added to the unease.[1] Rather than apologizing for Coke's fattening sugar, or warning of its unhealthiness, it boasts that each can of Coke provides '139 happy calories to spend on extra happy activities' – such as '25 minutes of letting your dog be your GPS', '10 minutes of letting your body do the talking' (aka dancing) or just '75 seconds of laughing out loud'. Covering all the bases, the ad continues: 'but if today you don't feel like doing it . . . have a Coke with zero calories' (accompanied by an image of the company's Coke Zero product). Finally, the end-frame comprises a picture of the iconic Coke bottle along with the words 'open happiness' (Coke's corporate slogan since 1999).

It was difficult to avoid the conclusion that the ad was not so much addressing the public health problem of obesity as turning it into a marketing opportunity for Coke. It is quite brilliant, but unnerving given the clear need for people to drink less of such products. We have to pinch ourselves and remember that two-thirds of the US population is now overweight, half of these (around 100 million people) are clinically obese and sugary drinks like Coke are, on average, supplying every American with an annual dose of 3,700 teaspoons of sugar – which amounts to 60,000 calories (Moss 2013:109).

The evening meeting on fair trade provided a refreshing change of mood. After the cheers for Scotland's fair trade success had died down, a detailed discussion about future possibilities began. Thanks to the fair trade premium, the farmers said they and their colleagues were planning on setting up a seed bank to improve their stock and their yields. This would also enable them to improve quality, something that their customers had complained about in the past. In addition, they were thinking about reputation management and branding, which would help enhance customer relationships. All of this promised to deliver even more resources for education, healthcare and reinvestment.

In other words, Howard and Henry are beginning to hone their marketing skills and this is benefiting both them and their communities. Note, though, this has not come about as a result of some top-down initiative, but by partnership working and co-creation. The strength of fair trade comes from the fact it is a social movement built on mutual respect and empowerment. In this way, it can, when necessary, begin to change the system. By contrast, Coke's anti-obesity efforts may bring about some minor adjustments but are essentially designed to perpetuate it.

The importance of this systemic approach was reinforced when someone asked the farmers about global warming and whether it was affecting them. The reply was both steely and sobering.

'Do not believe', Howard said, 'that climate change is not happening. It is. We see it in our daily lives all the time. Our parents could predict the start of the rains so accurately they planted the crops before the rain even began to fall. Now we have to wait for the second or even third start before risking planting, because we cannot be sure it is not a false start.' False starts to the rain are catastrophic – the seed germinates but then dies, and the Malawians have no spare seed. He went on to explain that floods and soil leaching from abnormally heavy rains were becoming common. Denial of global warming, he concluded, is as foolish as it is futile.

The Malawians' plea reminds us that the problems we face are massive and multi-faceted. They require not just ad hoc interventions but individual and community empowerment; not just one but many social movements to bring about multifac-eted systemic change. Used well, social marketing can help all this to happen. We hope this book has convinced you of the urgency of the task and given you the skills and understanding to start addressing it.

Note

1   www.brandchannel.com/home/post/Coca-Cola-Be-OK-Obesity-Commercial–
    011613.aspx/.

Reference

Moss, M. (2013) *Salt, Sugar, Fat: How the food giants hooked us*. UK: Random House.

Appendix: Foreword to *The Marketing Matrix*

THE MARKETING MATRIX: HOW THE CORPORATION GETS ITS POWER – AND HOW WE CAN RECLAIM IT

BY GERARD HASTINGS

Preface

Power and manipulation

This book is not an attack on business; on the contrary, it respects and applauds business. It is an attack on power and manipulation: the power that business acquires when it gets too big; and the manipulation modern marketing makes possible. When a supermarket chain attains such dominance that it covers every corner of a country the size of the UK, threatens farmers' livelihoods with its procurement practices, undercuts local shops and bullies planners into submission, it becomes reasonable to ask: does every little really help? Once the 100 billionth burger has been flipped and yet another trouser button popped, it is sensible to wonder: are we still lovin' it? As the planet heats up in response to our ever-increasing and utterly unsustainable levels of consumption, it is fair to question: are we really worth it?

This book raises these and many more questions about the use by the corporate sector of the powerful and ubiquitous behaviour change tools of modern marketing; what I have termed 'the marketing matrix'. Given the impact that our consumption behaviour has on ourselves, our fellow human beings and our planet, it argues that there is a need for much greater vigilance. In the seventy years since Steinbeck castigated the banks for their treatment of dustbowl farmers, and the fifty since Eisenhower warned us of the growing power of the military industrial complex, things have got steadily worse. Corporations have grown ever bigger, transcending national boundaries and dwarfing regulatory institutions. In one sense, this is unsurprising: as many commentators, from Joel Bakan to Naomi Klein, have noted, a ruthless regard for the shareholder, corporate wealth and the bottom line is written into corporate DNA, and this, in turn, makes continuous growth a necessity.

What is surprising is that we have all remained so unruffled about this catastrophic state of affairs. As boardroom salaries rocket, companies outgrow countries and these largely undemocratic organizations become some of the most powerful on the planet, we have remained remarkably quiescent. In recent times, the financial crisis and the obvious outrages perpetrated by financial institutions have generated some protests – Occupy is a welcome case in point – but, given the transgressions of corporate capitalism, they are not nearly as widespread as might be expected. Also, vociferous and refreshing though Occupy might be, remember that, each day protesters camped out in Wall Street or in front of St Paul's, Tesco was turning over around 268 million dollars, McDonalds 65 million and L'Oréal 72 million.[1] Meanwhile the much-reviled Royal Bank of Scotland has 40 million customers (that's several million more than the population of Canada).

Such is the success of the marketing matrix in selling the depredations of the 1% to us, the 99%, that we don't just fail to protest; we continually give them our money, and, with it, massive power.

If, for example, an unelected government were to kill millions of people, there would be an outcry, UN resolutions and serious talk of military intervention; yet the world's five big tobacco companies have been doing this for half a century and no one talks of invading Philip Morris International or arraigning the CEO of British American Tobacco in The Hague. On the contrary, we show them tolerance and treat them as civilized entities. We live comfortably with their brands in our corner shops where our kids spend their pocket money; we are accepting of the reality that these same children, our children, will deliver up the next generation of smokers for them to exploit; we make no demur as they continue to make massive profits from addicting and killing those who are credulous enough to fall into their clutches.

Now if we pan out and think not just of the harm that the consumption of tobacco products does to smokers' lungs, but the harm that the consumption of all products is doing to the planet, the full import of corporate power becomes clear.

The secret of this corporate impunity is the remorseless – yet soft – power of the marketing matrix. We are won over by the faux charm of witty ads, seductive bargains, captivating ubiquity and an Aladdin's cave of choice – all wrapped up in the opiate of the brand. We buy their products, however damaging they might be to us or our planet; we buy their empty rhetoric of consumer sovereignty. And, because corporate marketers recognize that context matters, our political leaders are also seduced by glitzy corporate social responsibility and cause-related marketing campaigns, the easy option of voluntary codes and the attraction of being associated with those same evocative brands. Meanwhile, statutory regulation and proper corporate accountability are quietly forgotten. More prosaically, our leaders are all too often wrong-footed and pre-empted by the single-minded focus, massive resources and sheer nerve of the corporate marketer – who then turns on the charm to magic away any unease.

It brings to mind a scene from *Watership Down*, Richard Adams's parable about a community of rabbits forced by developers to find a new place to live. At one point, the homeless rabbits arrive at an attractive warren with plentiful supplies of fresh food – lettuce, carrots and parsnips appear near their holes every morning seemingly by benign magic. The new arrivals feel in their water that something is wrong, but cannot work out what it is; the current inhabitants are close-lipped. Then it emerges that the food is being left by men, to tempt the rabbits into their snares.

For us too something is badly wrong and we have to start looking beyond the tempting offerings and heeding what are now time-honoured warnings. We already know that consumption does not bring satisfaction and material possessions do not deliver happiness, even without the countless studies proving this to be so. We know our lifestyles are foolishly unsustainable. But we keep on walking into the corporate marketers' snares and carry on shopping. It is time to fight back against the marketing matrix.

Fighting back

To find solutions, we have to look both internally and externally. First, it is necessary to examine our own behaviour and question why we consume so much; why we persistently fall for the tricks of modern marketing; and why we use the one remaining power many of us have – our purchasing power – with such profligacy and lack of thought. So *caveat emptor*, let the buyer beware, but not in the traditional sense of looking after our own interests, which for most of us in the rich countries are already being all too well met, but in the interests of our fellow human beings, our species and our planet. This will take resolve and determination – the marketing matrix perpetually pushes us to stay in our role of passive, spoilt consumers – but, as we will see, there is ample evidence that we have more than enough strength to resist.

Nonetheless, we also need to recognize the power that marketing has and respond in two complementary ways. First, as some 'social marketers' have begun to realize; a discipline focused on behaviour change has the potential to do much good. Most human problems can be traced back to our behaviour – eating, exercise and substance use are the three pillars of public health. Just persuading smokers to stop killing themselves would save millions from a premature demise. More broadly, our respect for the law, treatment of other people and contribution to the common-wealth are all major determinants of social welfare. From self-harm, through intol-erance to full-on violence, how we behave collectively defines the line between a society's success and failure. If marketing can really influence behaviour (and commerce shows all too well it can), we should invest in it properly, not to enrich already wealthy shareholders and CEOs, but to make the world a better place.

This social marketing, however, will surely fail if it becomes a top-down attempt at social engineering; a sort of well-intentioned version of the corporate marketing matrix. Rather it should harness the traditional wisdom of ordinary people and our innate capacity to improve our own lot. Both Steinbeck and Eisenhower recognized that salvation resides at a grassroots level; so should we. Indeed, marketing itself can be seen as part of this traditional wisdom; in its purest form it is all about doing the deals that enable human cooperation – which depends on reciprocation and mutual understanding. Corporations did not invent it; they just co-opted and corrupted it.

But all the social marketing in the world will get nowhere until we tackle the excesses of the marketing matrix which underpins corporate power and drives our unsustainable lifestyles. This matrix has to be re-engineered so that, instead of incessantly boosting sales, it deliberately reduces them, and actively encourages responsible – that is ethical and sustainable – consumption. This will require statu-tory measures; the corporation's relationship with the idea of market shrinkage is identical to that of the turkey with Christmas. If I can mix my poultry metaphors a little, the 1% will not like the idea of the 99% gaining control of their golden goose. But ultimately it is in everyone's interest to change course in this way: even the wealthiest merchant banker needs a planet to live on.

These three strands of change – personal reflection, the harnessing and empower-ment of existing wisdom through social marketing and the containment and redi-rection of commercial marketing – will begin a much-needed process of transformation. To reach its full potential, we have to come together as a species and think through how we want to organize a world that recognizes the vital distinction between being a consumer and being a citizen. The former is an occasional necessity in a complex post-industrial world, the latter is a birth right in a civilized world – and maintaining the distinction is essential if we are ever to realize a sustainable world.

Note

1   2010 data taken from annual reports.

Don't let the sun get under your skin: Targeting adolescent sun protection with a novel social marketing campaign

Sandra C. Jones, Keryn Johnson, Joanne Telenta, Jeffrey A. Thom, Melinda Williams, Don Iverson and Peter Caputi

INTRODUCTION

The adolescent demographic is significantly different in how it perceives and performs sun protection; it therefore needs interventions which acknowledge this difference, developing messages and strategies to minimize the barriers to sun protection and providing salient benefits that can be realized in the short rather than long term.

PROBLEM DEFINITION

Australia has the highest incidence of skin cancer in the world, with incidence rates outnumbering all other forms of cancer by more than three to one. Childhood and adolescence are recognized as the most vulnerable periods for increasing skin cancer risk (NSW Health & The Cancer Council NSW 2001; Australian Institute of Health and Welfare 2008). However, despite 25 years of mass media and programmes aimed at sun-protective behaviours in the Australian community, adolescents generally engage in fewer sun-protective strategies than adults (Dobbinson and Hill 2004) and sun-protection practices among Australian adolescents have continued to decline (Beckmann and Conor 2004; Livingston *et al.* 2003).

This decline begins in pre-adolescence, troughs around 15 to 17 years of age, and appears to improve as adolescents move into young adulthood (Schofield and Freeman 2001; Sjoberg *et al.* 2004). However, US data from national surveys conducted between the years 2000 and 2010 indicate no change in the percentage of persons aged 18–29 years who experience sunburns, with two in three persons reporting at least one sunburn in the last year. In addition, use of sunscreen always or most of the time is reported by only a minority of females (37.1 per cent) and males (15.6 per cent) (Hartman *et al.* 2012).

COMPETITIVE ANALYSIS

Pro-tan attitudes are the strongest competition to sun protection among most adolescents and young adults (Lazovich and Foster 2005; Nicol *et al.* 2007; Wichstrom 1994). Previous research (including 14 focus groups with Year 9 and 10 students and surveys of 2,332 adolescents) and the development of evidence-based guidelines resulted in clear recommendations for the development of social marketing interventions to address sun protection in this demographic (Johnson *et al.* 2009).

Formative research highlighted that many adolescents are aware of the need for sun protection and have mostly positive intentions to protect themselves from the sun, but also perceive a number of barriers to 'adequate' sun protection. These barriers include those related to issues of *self-efficacy*, such as forgetfulness, unpreparedness or laziness; and those related to the *social norms* surrounding sun protection and the perceived benefits of tanned skin, such as peer group attitudes regarding the need for a tan and the 'uncool' image associated with wearing sun-protective clothing (Lynch *et al.* 2007).

STAKEHOLDER ANALYSIS

In developing the intervention, extensive community consultation was undertaken – incorporating school administrators, local and State government agencies, youth services (such as youth centres and the Police Citizen Youth Clubs), private shopping centre and mall management teams, and council staff responsible for community services at beaches, pools, parks and sporting grounds. Information was sought on locations in which young people would be likely to congregate, and particularly those where they would be likely to spend extended periods exposed to the sun.

AIMS AND OBJECTIVES

The purpose of the current project was to target a defined segment of the adolescent population with a sun protection 'offering' that positioned sun protection as beneficial and addressed identified barriers, particularly inconvenience and image. The target group was Year 9 and 10 students (aged 14–16 years) who are aware of the need for sun protection but often don't protect themselves as they forget, are unprepared or are lazy; may sometimes want to get a bit of a tan, and so limit their sun protection or do not reapply sunscreen; know about the risks of skin cancer but see this risk as a long way off, and do not realize how much damage they have already done to their skin; and feel it is too difficult to protect properly all the time.

RESEARCH

Previous project research (Lynch and Jones 2007) identified different adolescent audience segments and labeled this group the 'Forgetful Attempters'.

A commercial advertising agency was contacted to develop a set of advertisements for the adolescent sun-protection programme, providing them with a detailed brief based on published literature, social marketing guidelines, and the findings from the formative research. The brief emphasized the need for messages to target immediate appearance concerns (rather than cancer), and to address social norms and self-efficacy. The agency developed a campaign using UV-photos, with multiple components including print advertisements/posters, brochures, ambient advertising, photo booths and a website. Advertisements were created using male and female models, with each showing (on the left-hand side) a photo of a young person taken using a regular camera and (on the right-hand side) a photo of the same young person taken using a UV-camera (see example of final advertisements in Figure CS1.1).

The advertisements were pre-tested with 10 groups of young people (a male-only and a female-only group from each of Years 8 to 11; n =104) and two teachers from a local secondary school. Trained facilitators led the discussions and asked the students to comment and provide suggestions/alternatives on the taglines, images and text of the posters developed by the agency. They also asked where the materials should be displayed and whether students thought a UV-camera would be a useful and interesting activity for their peers.

Revisions were made to the materials based on the results of the group discussions, and the final advertisements were retested with groups of young people and teachers from the same secondary school to ensure that the messages and images reflected the feedback from the target group.

FORMULATION OF STRATEGY

The intervention was conducted in one community (Illawarra region of New South Wales, which is primarily coastal, with a number of beaches) over the 2009/2010 summer school holidays. The aim of the intervention was to position sun protec-

Figure CS1.1 (i, ii) What you can't see

tion as an appearance- and health-enhancing behaviour that can fit easily within the lifestyle of adolescents, and the objectives were to:

- promote awareness of the need for sun protection at the 'point of decision'
- communicate the key campaign messages in a fun and interactive format
- engage young people in co-creation of the intervention, and provide 'cues to action'.

The underlying theoretical framework, which drove both the development of advertising messages and the suite of campaign activities, was social cognitive theory (SCT) (Bandura 2011), which explains human behaviour in terms of a dynamic model, where factors of behaviour, personal and environmental influences all interact simultaneously; and a change in any one component has implications for the others (Baranowski *et al.* 2002). This theory was viewed as particularly useful in explaining the sun-protection behaviours of 'Forgetful Attempters', recognizing that at any time the sun-protective behaviour that is performed by this segment is a consequence of a moment-to-moment weighing of benefit and cost ratios, which are influenced by mood, time and physical and social environments.

Using SCT as a guide, the intervention sought to influence young people's anticipated outcomes for sun protection (expectations) and the value that they place on these outcomes (expectancies) through the use of the visual images of the UV-photographed models (observational learning), and the offering of UV-photographs of young people as a visual reinforcement of the normally unseen effect of sun exposure on their skin. The SCT constructs of behavioural capability and self-efficacy also suggested strategies that attempted to make sun protection fit more easily into the lives of young people, as well as build knowledge and skills in sun protection. This was achieved through the use of tangible products targeting the image and convenience of sun protection, as well as information and 'cues to action'.

As well as the *actual product* (reduction in sun damage), the intervention provided *augmented products* that were designed to address the identified barriers: 'image' (by making sun protection 'cool'); 'efficacy' (by making sun protection 'easy'); and 'forgetfulness' (by providing a constant reminder). These tangible products included sunscreen samples, UV-wristbands, glow-in-the-dark wristbands, bookmarks and laptop stickers. The sunscreen sample sachets, donated by several manufacturers, were used to provide immediate and demonstrable efficacy in reducing immediate sun damage and reinforcing longer-term sun-protection behaviours; and the laptop stickers, bookmarks and silicon wrist straps were used to address 'forgetfulness' and 'image' barriers.

The community intervention consisted of two main components. First, the distribution of collectable materials (described above) conveying the key intervention messages. Second, concurrent with the distribution, free UV-photographs were offered to young people in local shopping areas on Thursday nights (late-night trading) and weekends. These components were supported by competitions for secondary school students (entry forms distributed with intervention materials), a Facebook page and a website, which enabled young people to develop their own sun-protection messages.

DISCUSSION

Getting the message right

Social marketing theory stresses the importance of pre-testing messages with the target audience to reduce the likelihood of counter-productive or unintended effects (e.g. Weinreich 1999). The messages were developed by a leading advertising agency with decades of experience in crafting messages for specific target groups; however, pre-testing resulted in a substantial change to the wording and presentation of the messages in the campaign materials. While this initial evaluation collected data from only a small number of respondents, recall of sun-protection messages in general was substantially higher in the intervention community; and one in eight respondents in that community who reported exposure to any sun-protection message were able to recall (unprompted) the main message of our campaign. Importantly, virtually all of those who recalled the message reported that it was relevant to them and that it had made them more likely to protect themselves from the sun.

Getting the delivery right

A number of unanticipated barriers and difficulties were experienced that impacted on the delivery of the intervention – including some (unseasonal) overcast, windy and cold days, resulting in very low numbers of contacts on those days; barriers to the flexibility of our photo booth intervention due to the requirements of the shopping centres in which the photo activities took place; and problems due to the very tendencies of young people that limit their sun protection (such as throwing away the items that weren't immediately useful).

However, the process evaluation suggests that the intervention was popular and well received among adolescents. Importantly, feedback from the target group suggests we were successful in rebranding sun protection as an appearance-enhancing (rather than cancer-preventing) behaviour; and that the intervention was seen as 'cool' and salient to adolescents (rather than to children and parents). While the intervention was conducted in a single geographic region, it is likely to resonate with other young people from similar populations and with similar social and identity concerns. For example, the Health Sponsorship Council in New Zealand recently announced the commencement of its adolescents-targeted campaign, which is based on the messages and approach developed in this research project.[1]

Note

1   http://sunsmart.org.nz/media/adolescent-education-programme/.

References

Australian Institute of Health and Welfare (2008) *Number of new cases and age-specific rates by year, sex and 5-year age groups, Australia, 1982–2004.* Cancer Incidence Data Cubes. Retrieved from: www.aihw.gov.au/cognos/cgi-bin/ppdscgi.exe?DC=Q&E&=/Cancer/australia_age_specific_1982_2004.

Bandura, A. (2011) 'Social Cognitive Theory: An Agentic Perspective', *Annual Review Psychol.*, 52: 1–26.

Baranowski, T., Perry, C.L., and Parcel, G.S. (2002) 'How Individuals, Environments, and Health Behavior Interact', in Glanz, K., Rimer, B.K., and Lewis, F.M. (eds) *Health Behavior and Health Education: Theory, Research, and Practice.* 3rd edn. San Francisco, CA: Jossey-Bass. p.165–184.

Beckmann, K. and Conor, P. (2004) *Sun protection practices among South Australian adolescents in 2002: Results of the 2002 ASSAD survey.* Adelaide: The Cancer Council of South Australia.

Dobbinson, S. and Hill, D. (2004) 'Patterns and causes of sun exposing and sun protecting behaviour', in D. Hill, J.M. Elwood, and D.R. English (eds) *Prevention of Skin Cancer.* Dordrecht: Kluwer Academic Publishers, pp.211–240.

Hartman, A.M., Perna, F.M., Holman, D.M., Berkowitz, Z., Guy Jr, G.P., Saraiya, M. and Plescia, M. (2012) 'Sunburn and sun protective behaviors among adults aged 18–29 years – United States, 2000–2010', *Morbidity and Mortality Weekly Report*, 61(18): 317–322.

Johnson, K.M., Jones, S.C. and Iverson, D. (2009) 'Guidelines for the development of social marketing programs for adolescents' and young adults' sun protection', *Public Health*, 123(Suppl 1): e6–10.

Lazovich, D. and Foster, J. (2005) 'Indoor tanning by adolescents: Prevalence, practices and policies', *European Journal of Cancer*, 41: 20–27.

Livingston, P.M., White, V., Hayman, J. and Dobbinson, S. (2003) 'Sun exposure and sun protection among Australian adolescents: Trends over time', *Preventive Medicine*, 37: 577–584.

Lynch, M. and Jones, S.C. (2007) 'Divide and conquer: Adolescents, sun protection and brand loyalty segmentation', Proceedings of the Social entrepreneurship, social change and sustainability: International Nonprofit and Social Marketing Conference, Brisbane, 27–28 September.

Lynch, M., Jones, S.C. and Phillipson, L. (2007) 'Branding: An adolescent sun protection perspective', Proceedings of the Australian and New Zealand Marketing Academy (ANZMAC) Conference, 1662–1670.

Nicol, I., Gaudy, C., Gouvernet, J., Richard, M.A. and Grob, J.J. (2007) 'Skin protection by sunscreens is improved by explicit labeling and providing free sunscreen', *Journal of Investigative Dermatology*, 127: 41–48.

NSW Health and The Cancer Council NSW (2001) *Sun protection: a guide to develop better practice in skin cancer prevention in NSW*. Sydney, Australia: NSW Health.

Schofield, P.E. and Freeman, J.L. (2001) 'Trends in sun protection behavior among Australian young adults', *Australian and New Zealand Journal of Public Health*, 25: 62–65.

Sjoberg, L., Holm, L.-E., Ullen, H. and Brandberg, Y. (2004) 'Tanning and risk perception in adolescents', *Health, Risk & Society*, 6: 81–94.

Weinreich N. (1999) *Hands-on Social Marketing: A Step-by-step Guide*. Thousand Oaks, California: Sage Publications.

Wichstrom, L. (1994) 'Predictors of Norwegian adolescents' sunbathing and use of sunscreen', *Health Psychology*, 13: 412–420.

Case study questions

1. How did the intervention use observational learning to address the target audience's expectations and expectancies?

2. Using social cognitive theory as a framework, define the personal, environmental and behavioural factors that are important in addressing adolescent sun protection, and describe how they were addressed in this intervention.

3. The case study refers to pro-tanning attitudes as the strongest competition to sun protection for adolescents and young adults. What does this mean? What other competitors exist for sun protection in this audience?

4. This was a pilot study on a limited budget. If you were scaling this up for a population intervention, what materials, media and distribution channels would you use? What strategies could you put into place to address the barriers identified in the implementation of this pilot intervention (such as the target audience not keeping materials, unseasonal weather, inflexibility of shopping centre management processes)?

Case Study **2**

'From theory to action: Co-creation in the rural world' – the Querença Project

Helena Alves and Sara Fernandes

INTRODUCTION

This case study demonstrates how, through the co-creation of activities in conjunction with the local population, innovative solutions may be generated for dealing with social problems. The 'Querença Project' was founded with the objectives of recovering and revitalizing the village of Querença, through enhancing the value of its natural, cultural and social resources, and attracting educated, young persons to live and engage in sustainable initiatives in the community for nine-month periods.

Figure CS2.1 Querença Project logo

PROBLEM DEFINITION

The village of Querença belongs to the council of Loulé located in the Algarve region of Portugal. This village has experienced a progressive decline in its population at the annual rate of 9.3 per cent (INE – Portuguese National Institute of Statistics 2006). This region is experiencing a generational crisis with one of the highest levels of ageing in Loulé council, compounded by a dispersed population, including 154 individuals living in complete isolation (INE 2006). The majority of its active population works either in the city of Loulé or on the coast. In Querença itself, in addition to craftsmanship, traditional agriculture prevails, even though it is perceived as a complementary activity that generates only small surpluses for sale (Vicente 2006). There is, correspondingly, a sense of loneliness and insecurity prevalent in the village.

Faced by the progressive exodus out of rural communities, the loss of cultural values and the scarce employment opportunities alongside a profound disconnect with inland Portugal among both the young and university establishments, there emerged the associated need to combat this situation, and hence the Querença Project.

AIMS AND OBJECTIVES

The main objective was to revitalize the village of Querença using its natural, cultural and social resources which included the need to:

1. Reverse the process of rural desertification, especially of the younger generation.
2. Combat the social inertia prevailing throughout inland regions of the Algarve.
3. Boost the local economy.
4. Raise the level of awareness in society as to the potential of lowly populated rural areas with longstanding knowledge, customs, and powerful heritage legacies.
5. Disseminate positive values to boost the willingness of persons to actively contribute towards the development of the rural environment.

COMPETITOR AND STAKEHOLDER ANALYSIS

Barrier identification:

- Majority of the active population do not work in Querença itself
- Aged and dispersed population
- Traditional agriculture main source of income, but not meeting optimum potential
- Disconnection from mainland Portugal resulting in isolation and insular culture
- Lack of employment opportunities for the young and educated.

Stakeholder identification:

- Portuguese Institute of Employment
- University of Algarve
- Manuel Viegas Guerreiro foundation (private body)
- Local businesses and landowners
- Local population of Querença.

RESEARCH

Despite the aforementioned challenges, the parish of Querença is actually rich in resources: it falls entirely within the Nature 2000 Network,[1] is home to the Fonte da Benémola Protected Local Landscape, with hydric resources, some local business initiatives in terms of the production of fortified spirits, jams and preserves, and ice-creams, and it hosts a large diversity of indigenous species nurtured by the respective qualities of this region. Hence, there was a clear need for a solution to reverse the process of rural desertification and leverage the activities ongoing in the village within a framework of long-term sustainability.

To make this happen, such products and actions needed a new approach involving an effective and efficient image aligned with a communication strategy able to attain positive marketplace discrimination. Consequently, this drives the attention of the different public and private sector entities and their interest in rendering project logistical and/or financial support through partnership and sponsorship.

FORMULATION OF STRATEGY

The pilot project sought to act through establishing a multi-disciplinary team of young persons from across a range of different but complementary educational and professional backgrounds: marketing, management, design, landscape architecture, ecotourism, biological engineering, environmental engineering and agronomy.

The process

In mid-2011, following prior evaluation of the regional potential in terms of its natural, agricultural, cultural, social, landscape and tourist resources, as well as its support infrastructures and housing and accommodation stock, an advert was placed in the University of the Algarve. This process resulted in 75 applications, from which a team was recruited that took up residence in Querença for a 9-month period in the first phase. These young persons signed up to this professional internship that received support from the Portuguese Institute of Employment and Professional Training within the scope of the application made by the Manuel Viegas Guerreiro Foundation. In September 2011, work began.

The ongoing project

Each team member was charged with a task or key objective. These tasks were mutually interlinked and complementary to each other. Thus, and to provide but one example, while some got on with agricultural production, others studied the market potential, brand image, target consumers and design of communication and retail strategies. Creativity, innovation and experimentation were constants throughout the project structure. Meanwhile, other team members evaluated the success of the actions and initiatives and set out business plans to produce a range of viable proposals that would enable the establishment of small companies or other means of attaining project continuity.

In keeping with the resources present, the Querença Project decided to focus on three areas crucial to leverage village life in both economic and social terms:

1. Agriculture

   The project focused on getting existing fertile land back into production after having been abandoned by the elderly community unable to maintain the fields as previously. They launched a revitalization process designed to boost local agricultural production through the incorporation of efficient product distribution channels able to generate added value.

   A local producers club was founded, the 'Local Farmers Club', which established partnerships with local hotels who bought surplus production. Local hotels signed up to this initiative through incorporating local products into their menus. Cooperation between various entities proved possible and was critical to the implementation of this action project. Correspondingly, important agricultural equipment and organic compost was provided by commercial suppliers. Querença Parish Council mediated throughout the entire process between the project team and the local population, which loaned the abandoned lands.

   Another of the areas focused on was innovation in the agro-food chain seeking out new utilizations for local products such as carob, arbutus and fig. This action line was undertaken by the Biological Engineering degree at the laboratories of the University of the Algarve engaged in such research work. One of the results, for example, was an energy bar, produced from fig, almond, honey and carob and high in calorific value that is due for public launch in the near future, targeting sporting-related outlets.

In terms of the landscape and sustainable gardening, the work has consisted of collecting seeds from the many indigenous species with the objective of founding a breeding centre able to provide the plants necessary for public and private gardening projects as well as reforesting initiatives. A sustainable garden is already under construction and that provides an area of leisure, recreation and a venue for a diverse range of activities.

2. Ecotourism

Products and tourism services are under development and designed to capitalize on the natural resources existing in the territory and mostly within the framework of the Nature 2000 Network. Among the projects under implementation is a pioneering project on the Iberian Peninsula to observe and identify different species of dragonfly with support from the University of the Algarve, and a network of pathways for exploring and discovering the landscapes and countryside and experiences in close proximity to the local community.

3. Events, marketing and communication

This action line sought to come up with a distinctive brand that gave credibility to the products and services linked up with Querença and thereby adding value. Hence, the project staged local events, set up a local distribution network and strongly backed an online website and a strong social network presence.

One of the most high-profile events is the 'Querença market', held monthly and now able to attract hundreds of visitors on a regular basis. This event is designed to provide the conditions for target markets to live out an experience through the provision of a diverse range of products and cultural, ecotourism and sensorial activities. Throughout recent markets, the team raised substantial levels of funding for the local community and raised awareness about over 50 agricultural, gastronomic and handicraft products. In addition, it raised the level of social acceptance of the pilot project among local stakeholders and residents that proved motivational in their entering into the ongoing projects. This event would not have existed without the involvement and engagement of the local population. Thus, the population takes on the creation and production, and in the process revitalizes existing traditions, of the products they wish to sell at the Querença market.

The innovation factor inherent in the project immediately proved able to attract the attention of the media that provided continuous and sustained reporting and coverage of the project alongside its respective events and developments. Indeed, this media coverage led other locations to seek to replicate the success of the Querença Project with this national scale of interest confirmed by regular contact with the respective levels of government in Portugal.

OUTCOMES

This project demonstrated that there are feasible innovative solutions to social problems. As recognised by Vargo and Lusch (2008) and Edvardsson *et al.* (2011), whenever organizations combine to co-create solutions with their clients, this enables the creation of genuine value.

In this specific case, the implementation of the co-creation methodology in conjunction with the local population resulted in the development of solutions both incorporating and expanding citizen resources through integrating them into their social context. Thus, citizen involvement, joint project design and leveraging the knowledge and capacities for problem solving – activities considered by Prahalad (2004) as drivers of value – proved able to generate value both for individuals and the community as a whole. The union of the various stakeholders around a single objective eased bureaucratic procedures, broke down institutional barriers and freed up project implementation processes.

Young persons with high educational qualifications immersed themselves in the rural community through residing there and becoming engaged in the day-to-day activities of its residents, absorbing its knowledge and fostering its practices and interactions. The dissemination of positive values boosted the willingness of persons to actively contribute towards the development of the rural environment whether through community cleaning of protected areas, the cultivation of abandoned agricultural land, participation in ecotourism activities or even simply opting in favour of purchasing the traditional local gastronomic and/or handcrafted products.

Effective responses to serious social issues require innovative solutions and as such are frequently only attainable through the development of approaches that involve service users from the very outset and from service design right through to provision and hence through the co-creation of value for both of the parties involved.

Note

1   An EU-wide network of nature protection areas established under the 1992 Habitats Directive. The aim of the network is to assure the long-term survival of Europe's most valuable and threatened species and habitats.

References

Edvardsson, B., Tronvoll, B. and Gruber, T. (2011) 'Expanding understanding of service exchange and value co-creation: A social construction approach', *Journal of the Academy of Marketing Science*, 39: 327–339.

Instituto Nacional de Estatística (INE) (2006) O País em Números – Informação Estatística 1991–2004, Lisboa.

Prahalad, C.K. (2004) 'The co-creation of value, in invited commentaries on "Evolving to a New Dominant Logic for Marketing"', *Journal of Marketing*, 68 (January) : 18–27.

Vargo, S.L. and Lusch, R.F. (2008) 'Service-dominant logic: Continuing the evolution', *Journal of the Academy of Marketing Science*, 36: 1–10.

Vicente, L. and Silva, L. (2006) Carta Educativa do Concelho de Loulé, Loulé.

Case study questions

1. What social needs are encountered here?

2. In this case, how did the co-creation of value generate benefits both for individuals and for the community?

3. Identify the co-creation activities in effect in this case study and how they contributed to this value creation process.

4. If you were part of the project development team, what other activities would you develop?

Case Study **3**

Saving lives – Involving citizens in the chain of survival: The critical role of placement

Sara Balonas and Susana Marques

INTRODUCTION

Cardiac arrests are the main cause of death not only in Portugal but also in the world (Nolan *et al.* 2010). The majority of those deaths occur outside hospitals and 60–80 per cent of them happen at home. Survival decreases by 7–10 per cent for every minute of delayed intervention (Fullerton 2011).

Managed by a group of experienced doctors, the Portuguese Resuscitation Council (PRC) is a non-profit organization launched to disseminate the best practices in resuscitation in Portugal. Based upon the scientific guidelines of the European Resuscitation Council (ERC), in the UK, the PRC is dedicated to research on death due to cardiac arrest and how to raise survival rates. Importance is given to the

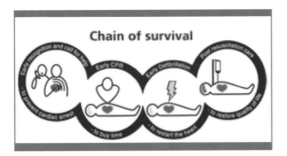

Figure CS3.1 Chain of survival

teaching of Extend Life Support (ELS) to all citizens, because it is not always possible to start defibrillation (Automatic External Defibrillator – AED) within the first 4–5 minutes after the cardiac arrest (Nolan *et al.* 2010) (see Figure CS3.1).

PROBLEM DEFINITION

In Portugal, according to the PRC, citizens are not aware of the medical emergency issues around ELS. There is a common thinking that this kind of practice is for doctors and other medical professionals. The survival chain is not well known among citizens. Furthermore, there are no awareness campaigns about the ELS theme, only episodic campaigns to 'call 112 (911)' or first aid courses.

FORMULATION OF STRATEGY

In order to promote an effective social change, in 2011, the PRC decided to launch a citizen awareness program towards a higher involvement in the survival chain, informing, teaching and promoting active behaviors in an emergency (Figure CS3.2). In order to enable this program, the PRC invited a marketing and communication company to develop a program, according to the social marketing principles, with the following objectives:

- widespread interest about knowing what the survival chain means;
- proactive search for information and training;
- individual feeling of responsibility; and
- social corporate responsibility of each organization.

At a second stage of the project, the objective will extend to another topic – to influence the agenda-setting and the government in order to adopt ELS practices in schools.

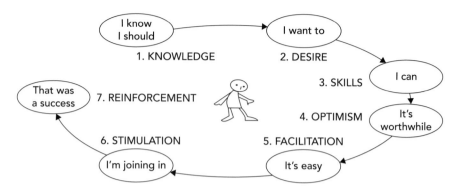

Figure CS3.2 PRC citizen awareness program towards a higher involvement in the survival chain

The program

To achieve the defined purposes, strategic marketing decisions were taken. Concerning the segmentation and targeting process, a specific marketing program was designed for each client or segment:

a) **for citizens:**

In order to make the ELS practices more tangible, a roadshow was conceived making the mass training available and closer to people.

b) **for schools:**

A specific school program with educational material for teachers was designed to support them and also to ensure that the correct key messages were communicated. For this target, it was proposed to include a special day in the school calendar named 'The Day to Save Lives'. In that day, the roadshow would be at the front of the school that has accepted the visit and a mass training session would be available for all students. This program was planned to start in the school year September 2012.

c) **for organizations:**

In the specific case of corporations, the strategic team took into account that, presently, companies seek social responsibility programs. So it was decided that major organizations, with a considerable number of employees, should be part of the program, focusing the service in ELS practices as an internal team-building action and also as a volunteering opportunity.

Once the segmentation and targeting processes were designed, other decisions became more clear concerning service and pricing. For citizens in general, the PRC decided to design a free demonstration and access to mass training. As a non-profit organization, with no resources to hire specialized monitors, the PRC started to recruit volunteers with expertise in ELS practices, through their professional links and through the Facebook official page.

To create a tangible effect of the 'product', at the end of each mass training all participants receive a diploma in ELS, signed by the president of the PRC. Finally, the 'product' ELS practices became available on the official website[1] through two tutorials, on a free basis, as well as the roadshow.

Organizations interested in developing internal ELS sessions had to pay for it, contacting the network of trainer entities recommended by the PRC – an exception was made for those invited to be pioneer partners of this program, giving their support with the products directly linked to their activity. Two companies immediately joined the program: an automotive national company lent a truck for one year; and Portugal's oil and natural gas integrated operator offered 5,000 euros in fuel, making the roadshow able to reach the whole country.

Branding and promotion were another part of the social marketing program. The first step was to find a name and a logo that could immediately reveal the program purpose. Once an approved and appropriate positioning solution was worked out, this was recorded in a similar process to trademarks (Figure CS3.3). The official website address was also protected.

An integrated offline and online campaign was conceived to promote the key messages and contribute to an effective change in behavior. Several professionals offered their services – photographers, film producers, media planners, website programmers, and printing companies. Eight public figures participated in a testimonial campaign.

The placement factor

Despite the importance of the marketing variables mentioned above, the key focus was on the placement issue. This variable was particularly critical because there was a need to demonstrate, and to bring the training closer to the people, showing that it is easy to learn. In other words, making an intangible mission more tangible, by offering an ELS training with monitors and proper equipment and, at the end, awarding a qualified diploma. It is expected that these procedures can influence behavioral change, from ignorance and indifference to action and confirmation, as defined by Prochaska and Di Clemente (1983, cited in Andreasen 1995).

The program has defined two major places: the virtual dimension – creating the official website and Facebook – and the physical dimension, providing real sites to

Figure CS3.3 Branding and a new logo as part of the social marketing program

reach people, mass training in schools and organizations, and a roadshow throughout the country. Finally, one of the crucial strategic decisions was based on the fact that the 'product' should be available and accessible in places where people are, rather than inviting people to seek out the 'product'. Therefore, all the places chosen must guarantee that people are already there for any sort of reasons (e.g. entertainment, shopping, etc.) (Figures CS3.4 and CS3.5).

The first phase of this program started at the end of November 2011 and continued until September 2012. It focused on citizens, in order to improve awareness and to stimulate a proactive search for information and training. The program started with a mass training in a hotel, involving several professional groups very used to relating and interacting with people. According to the PRC, around 100 participants filled the room: together with civilians, there were police officers, *guard maritime*, personal trainers, teachers, boy scouts and journalists. This first mass training was spread via Facebook. Since then, and up to April 2012, the Facebook page has reached 7,000 fans.

During December 2011, the campaign was launched, through an offline campaign (TV, press, radio, posters and flyers) and online (website, Facebook). A second media effort started March 2012, to raise more awareness of the theme and support the first roadshow action in the open, in a shopping center. However, the focus of

Figure CS3.4 Bringing the roadshow to the people

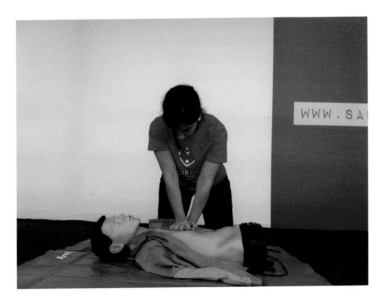

Figure CS3.5 Mass training program in accessible places

this campaign was not to specifically promote the first mass training; the purpose was to emphasize the general key messages. On 31 March, it started the first open-air initiative of the program, which is intended to reach the country through the roadshow, including schools, universities, student festivals and the main summer mass events. This decision to start in March and not sooner is based on the fact that those mass training sessions took place in open areas, with the truck giving the physical support, with a stage, microphones, videos and the monitors. Therefore, the roadshow calendar – available on the website – was designed for spring and summer, with less risk of bad weather conditions.

Concerning the first mass training opened to all citizens, some procedures were activated:

- the PRC asked for ELS monitors for volunteering that day, via Facebook; 40 professionals responded, a sufficient number to support the 100 participants expected.[2] It also got volunteers to promote the action in the shopping center during the day;
- promotional material requested by the shopping center marketing management team was specifically created to be used in the shopping center internal media (e.g. Corporate TV) focusing on the theme, action and day;
- a press release was sent to main media, by the shopping center marketing management team; and
- finally, the shopping center volunteered to receive the registrations, via the information desk staff.

Contrary to what happened on the first mass training at the hotel, this open-air event for citizens was not a strong success. Few people participated – less than 50. Many of the shopping center clients that arrived 'felt fear as we approached to publicize the action and try to associate it to the event. Our volunteers tried to invite people to the event, but people feared it that it was a paid event or sale of any product,' said Anabela Moreira, PRC training manager.

Despite the procedures described above, the campaign was not running on internal media and the press release did not get any coverage. This event also showed that communicating in shopping centers is challenging and difficult. There are many stimuli trying to influence and get consumers' attention.

DISCUSSION

With the program still running, some success has already been achieved:

- the program was raised in a *pro bono* way. Most of the companies and professionals invited to contribute their expertise or their service have immediately accepted, recognizing its importance;
- public figures, including athletes, popular entertainment figures, TV stars, musicians and chefs, have participated for free;
- the main media players (such as the public TV) have agreed to give free space;
- so far, the program has 317 registered volunteers to help spread the initiative;
- all the institutions that have been contacted to be part of the roadshow – crucial for the placement strategy – immediately agreed (universities, schools, local public institutions, entertainment companies, students organizations and shopping centers);
- people's comments on Facebook show how citizens confirm the positive response to the program. Some examples: 'Congratulations on your project! The successful rescue depends on the integration of all in the integrated medical emergency. The citizen is undoubtedly the first link in the acting chain of survival and must have knowledge to act quickly and effectively' (António Rodrigues, firefighter). 'I always thought schools should be trained in basic life support . . . try to occupy students with courses that are useless and they forget that there are things that should be familiar with all. Congratulations for your initiative' (Ana Batata, student); and
- through Facebook and via mail, the PRC notes that professional groups seek this kind of training, asking when and where will be the next mass training or where they can find a training course.

LESSONS LEARNED

- To transform an intangible product into a tangible benefit, it is crucial to develop an appropriate physical structure – e.g. truck, stage, training models.

- Despite the importance of the physical structure, this is not sufficient – an integrated online/offline strategy will maximize the program, e.g. registrations, access to the roadshow calendar, and ELS monitors way of volunteering for mass trainings.
- Intermediates are a key success factor.
- Although place is traditionally an expensive variable, it is possible to raise a *pro bono* network in a sustainable way.
- When it comes to choosing the specific places to implement the mass training sessions, the process can become more complex due to environmental and less controllable factors.
- Promotion and placement must be integrated and this has strong implications in the way responsibilities are allocated to the different actors of the program.

Notes

1   www.salvarvidas.com.pt/.
2   It is assumed that a proper training demands one monitor per group of four participants.

References

Andreasen, A. (1995) *Marketing Social Change: Changing Behavior to Promote Health, Social, Development, and the Environment*, Jossey-Bass Publishers: San Francisco.
Fullerton, J. (2011) International Resuscitation Conference, Porto, November.
Nolan, J. *et al.* (2010) *European Resuscitation Council Guidelines for Resuscitation 2010*, (Portuguese version), Ed. Paula Grácio, revista Saúde Infantil ASIC: Coimbra.

Case study questions

1. For this kind of program what are the advantages and disadvantages of shopping centers as channels?

2. How would you design the management model, concerning different responsibilities and tasks when implementing the mass training?

3. How can this program articulate and balance offline and online placement?

Case Study **4**

The need for Internal Social Marketing (ISM): Extending the people focus to service employees

Josephine Previte and Rebekah Russell-Bennett

BreastScreen Queensland (BSQ) is a government-based health service that provides free breast cancer screening services to eligible women using digital mammography technology.[1] In 2007, BSQ launched its first social marketing campaign[2] aimed at achieving a 30 per cent increase in women's programme participation by addressing the barriers to regular screening and by dispelling myths about breast cancer (Tornabene 2010). 'The Facts' mass media social marketing campaign used a credible spokesperson, Australian journalist Jana Wendt, to deliver the call to action – 'Don't make excuses. Make an appointment'.

During the implementation of campaign activities, additional marketing challenges were identified. Specific issues included: low levels of acceptance and understanding of social marketing by key service delivery staff within BSQ service centres (i.e. administrative staff and radiographers); service centre managers' lack of social marketing knowledge; and the limited experience of health promotion staff in implementing localized social marketing tactics. Furthermore, additional barriers, including a radiographer shortage in Queensland during 2007–2010, influenced the delivery of screening in some service centres, and the target audience's outdated knowledge about screening and the BSQ programme (ibid.) also hampered achievement of campaign goals. Combined, these internal and external service problems indicated a need for BSQ to adopt a 'people' orientation so they could better produce good-quality service and customer satisfaction.

Adopting a 'people' orientation focuses on satisfying the needs of external health customers – women being screened *and* internal customers, that is BSQ staff; particularly staff who have a service touch-point with women being screened. The proposed solution to aligning the needs of internal and external customers, as well as addressing the identified challenges, was the implementation of an internal social marketing (ISM) approach. The underlying premise of internal social marketing is that, to satisfy external customers, it is desirable, and in most circumstances necessary, to have satisfied internal customers – namely employees. The internal customer concept is well established in marketing thinking and was originally proposed over 30 years ago as a solution to the problem of delivering consistently high-quality service (Berry *et al.* 1976). The contribution of ISM thinking is that it has more to offer than purely improving the HR function within social marketing services. It also calls for designing initiatives that aim to motivate employees towards service-mindedness and customer-oriented performance through active marketing-like tactics (Gronroos 1990).

PROBLEM DEFINITION

Many marketing scholars have spoken of the need for organizations to focus efforts on developing and sustaining an organizational culture that emphasizes internal customer wellbeing (e.g. staff morale and self-esteem) as a means to attract and retain external customer commitment (see Bansal *et al.* 2001). However, few have considered the influence of internal marketing on social marketing outcomes (see Smith 2011). In BSQ, there were four distinct social marketing changes that needed to be considered to encourage staff motivation and alignment with customer service thinking. These were:

1. **Social marketing strategy had limited influence**. Within BSQ, the responsibility for the implementation of social marketing localized activities was considered the sole responsibility of Health Promotion Officers (HPOs). Typically, these staff coordinate awareness-raising activities such as breast screening information workshops, promotions at public events (e.g. participating in

community events), and distributing local service information at invited presentations.

2. **Social marketing was implemented as advertising and promotion**. The social marketing campaign introduced in 2007 focused on one of the four marketing mix Ps (mass media communication), reflecting the strong general perception in health services that social marketing is limited to advertising and promotion activities (Grier and Bryant 2005).

3. **BSQ service staff did not embrace a whole-of-service philosophy to providing customer care**. Health workers primarily focused on their role responsibilities. For example, radiographers focused on the technical quality and clarity of the mammogram service provided.

4. **Limited marketing experience in service centres**. BSQ services are predominantly managed by decision-makers with a clinical health background. As a result, there was limited service marketing experience and interest in marketing-like tactics focused on improving internal and external customer satisfaction.

STAKEHOLDER AND COMPETITIVE ANALYSIS

Individuals and groups who have a 'stake' in BSQ services include:

- Employees
- Customers
- Service managers
- Politicians
- Health funders
- Resource suppliers (including advertising and research agencies)
- The wider community.

Each stakeholder potentially has an active or passive role (Mahoney 1994) in influencing the BSQ services provided to women. Active stakeholders are those who seek to participate in BSQ's activities. Stakeholders do not necessarily have to be part of an organization's formal structure. Service management and staff are active stakeholders, but this group can be extended to include groups outside of BSQ, such as professional health bodies, and government funders who show an active interest in the standard of healthcare provided to women. Passive stakeholders, on the other hand, are those individuals and groups who do not seek to participate in an organization's policymaking, which does not mean that they lack interest or power. Rather, in the public sector, passive stakeholders, such as the wider community and media, have a legitimate interest in the services provided by BSQ.

The adoption of ISM thinking in the endeavour to change staff marketing-like behaviours also considers alternative types of competitors. Traditionally, within social marketing practice, competitors include the client's choices between one or more existing behaviours or habits. A significant challenge for social marketing when dealing with competing behaviours is that the rewards from behaviour change are typically not immediate, nor do they provide short-term gratification (Hastings 2007). In implementing an ISM process in BSQ, there are two forms of competition (Kotler and Lee 2008: 164) that require consideration to motivate staff towards the adoption of marketing-like activities:

- **Behaviours target audience would prefer over the ones being promoted.** Evidence from the data collection and social marketing literature indicate that some health professionals and clinicians are resistant to embracing marketing-like activities as these are seen to potentially redirect health funding to inconsequential service features. Health professionals are also resistant to the use of marketing terminology, such as the term 'customer', and require more evidence to rationalize the adoption of marketing-like activities in areas beyond healthcare itself, such as attending to elements such as waiting-room comfort.

- **Behaviours that encumber target audience and lead to service inefficiencies.** Specific service groups, such as radiographers and nurses, feel a strong commitment to maintaining health practices because of health service accreditation requirements and other service policy protocols. This is particularly so in relation to the amount of time taken to complete the breast screening service. As a result, health professionals can be resistant to the introduction of service-scripts that encourage interpersonal communication, or aim to deliver standardized messages that encourage women to repeat the breast screening experience.

AIMS AND OBJECTIVES

- To adopt a 'whole of service' philosophy to customer care
- To extend social marketing strategy so it has broader influence
- To adopt ISM thinking in the endeavour to change staff marketing-like behaviours.

RESEARCH AND EVALUATION

Focus groups and interviews were conducted with staff (n=60) from all service locations (n=12) to document the factors that impact upon staff knowledge, service role behaviour and the successful implementation of social marketing-like activities. Drawing from the established internal marketing (IM) literature (see Lings and Greenley 2005), staff members were asked questions that explored four key IM dimensions: formal information generation (written and face-to-face); informal information generation; information dissemination; and responsiveness. The IM dimensions were adapted for the BSQ context and additional questions were also asked concerning staff knowledge and attitudes to social marketing; intelligence generation about external customers' breast screening behaviours; and employees' service responses to managing women's needs.

The research data from staff focus groups and interviews revealed interesting insights into staff behaviours. Key insights included:

- Limited knowledge of social marketing processes. There was a prevailing belief that social marketing is primarily used in promoting health behaviours via mass media communication. While some staff had concerns about using funding for social marketing activities, most held positive attitudes towards the department's investment in marketing BSQ goals and the screening programme.
- Health promotion officers (HPOs) expressed the view that service managers were generally not interested in social marketing activities. In essence, HPOs believed managers were 'happy' that community and media responses to the campaign were positive.
- Some staff felt negatively about information generation and internal communication. They claimed they were excluded from service and marketing decision-making (e.g. no consultation with them about branding or campaign messages). On the other hand, some HPOs used the launch of 'The Facts' campaign to engage managers in more open discussion of marketing-like activities and the use of service resources to promote the programme.
- Communication within disciplinary areas was generally positive. For example, HPOs reported good information-sharing activities among the HPOs. However, within the service centre, HPOs sometimes said they had limited voice and influence over service issues (such as influencing opening hours and appointment scheduling, which was directed by radiographers and managers). There was also limited evidence of formal communication across different service roles and positions (e.g. administration roles – i.e. client data managers and receptionists; radiographers and nurses), which impacted upon the sharing of service experiences among the various professional groups.
- For some service centres, the external focus on women, while caring, was driven more by staff needs rather than the service needs of women.

During this exploratory research, new social marketing ideas were generated for future internal and external approaches, which focused on aligning internal and external social marketing-like activities. Thus, the goal of the project's research phase was also to generate new ideas to encourage and increase staff participation in marketing-like activities that focused on improving service outcomes and client satisfaction.

DISCUSSION

Service-focused thinking benefits social marketing programmes, which rely on service employees to communicate with target audiences, distribute social marketing product ideas (e.g. the need to repeat the behaviour) and tangible objects, and create a pleasant and accessible environment in which target customers feel comfortable and at ease. As a result, the quality of service impacts upon consumers' behaviour, which is particularly true of health-related behaviours (Smith 2011). For example, in health treatment services such as cancer care, the exchange process facilitated through the employee–customer interaction is likely to significantly influence the individual's quality of life (Dagger and Sweeney 2006). In extending the IM service perspective to BSQ's social marketing programme, three main building blocks were introduced to the preventative health process:

(a)   The view of healthcare employees as an internal customer;

(b)   Staff acceptance of the idea that each BSQ service role was critical to creating a 'whole-of-service' approach to engaging sustainable behaviour change among both internal and external customers; and

(c)   Decision-makers needed to train and satisfy all internal customers so that they were prepared and skilled in serving external customer needs. The key social marketing outcome from focusing on service quality and customer satisfaction is achieving sustainable behaviour change in the target population of women called to attend a breast screen every two years.

Notes

1   BreastScreen Queensland (2012), About Us, www.health.qld.gov.au/breast-screen/about-us.asp. Accessed 1 June 2012.
2   In Queensland, the participation rate for the target age group in the period 2006–2007 was 56.4 per cent, which is below the state and national target participation rate. BreastScreen Queensland (2009): Finding out about breast cancer. Online: www.uq.edu.au/shared/resources/personnel/UQWellness/Breast Screen QLDworkplace Talk.pdf.

References

Bansal, H.S., Mendelson, M.B. and Sharma, B. (2001) 'The impact of internal activities on external marketing outcomes', *Journal of Quality Management*, 6: 61–76.

Berry, L.L., Hensel, J.S. and Burke, M.C. (1976) 'Improving retailer capability for effective consumerism response', *Journal of Retailing*, 52(3): 3–14.

Dagger, T. and Sweeney, J.C. (2006) 'The effect of service evaluations on behavioural intentions and quality-of-life', *Journal of Service Research*, 9(1): 3–18.

Grier, S. and Bryant, C. A. (2005) 'Social marketing in public health', *Annual Review of Public Health*, 26: 319–339.

Gronroos, C. (1990) *Service Management and Marketing: Managing the Moments of Truth in Service Competition*. Lexington, MA: Lexington Books.

Hastings, G. (2007) *Social Marketing: Why should the devil have all the best tunes?*. Elsevier: Amsterdam.

Kotler, P. and Lee, N.R. (2008) *Social Marketing: Influencing behaviours for good*. 3rd Edition. Thousand Oaks, CA: Sage Publications.

Lings, I. and Greenley, G. (2005) 'Measuring internal market orientation', *Journal of Service Research*, 7(3): 290–305.

Mahoney, J. (1994) 'Stakeholder responsibilities: Turning the ethical tables', *Business Ethics – A European View*, 3(4): 212–218.

Smith, A. (2011) 'Internal social marketing: Lessons from the field of services', in G. Hastings, K. Angus and C. Bryant (eds) *The SAGE Handbook of Social Marketing*, London: Sage Publications Ltd, pp. 298–316.

Tornabene, M. (2010) 'BreastScreen Queensland: Breaking Down the Barriers', 2010 International Nonprofit & Social Marketing Conference (INSM) Conference Proceedings, 15–16 July 2010 Brisbane. Access: http://icebergevents.com/uploads/File/2010%20INSM/2010-INSM-Conference-Proccedings.pdf.

Case study questions

1. What marketing aspects do you believe make it difficult, or challenging, for health professionals to adopt social marketing practices? What approaches can social marketers take to challenge the limited views some health professionals have towards using social marketing methods in health services?

2. BSQ is a preventative health service for well-woman. It is a voluntary service, offered for free to eligible women. Using Table CS4.1, list the various internal and external stakeholders who might influence the adoption of marketing-like activities in a health service. Consider the stakeholder's interest in the health service provided, and the type of power each stakeholder has over an organization's marketing and service activities.

Table CS4.1 Internal and external stakeholders who might influence the adoption of marketing-like activities in a health service

Stakeholder	Type of Stakeholder *External* or *Internal*	Stakeholder interests	Influence *Passive* or *Active* power

3. Think about the different stakeholders involved in delivering social marketing services in a breast cancer screening service. Outline each stakeholder and think about the value each contributes to achieving individual and societal change in Table CS4.2. What role might 'relationship marketing' play in creating stakeholder value?

Table CS4.2 Value each stakeholder contributes to achieving individual and societal change

Stakeholder	Value created for the Individual	Value created for society	Potential problems or role conflict

4. How would you go about assessing the various levels of stakeholder satisfaction with the social marketing activities used in a breast cancer screening service?

Case Study **5**

MumBubConnect: Using SMS to engage new mothers

Rebekah Russell-Bennett, Danielle Gallegos, Josephine Previte and Robyn Hamilton

INTRODUCTION

Breastfeeding is considered the optimal method of infant feeding as it directly reduces the incidence of infant mortality and morbidity (Australian Health Ministers' Conference 2009; Australian Institute of Health and Welfare 2011; Horta *et al*. 2007; Kramer and Kakuma 2009). Breastfeeding helps to prevent infectious diseases and allergies in young children, and decreases the risk of overweight and obesity among infants, children and adolescents and of chronic disease later in life (Horta *et al*. 2007; Kramer and Kakuma 2009). For women, breastfeeding results in decreased postpartum bleeding and increased rates of recovery after birth (Kramer and Kakuma 2009). For this reason, the World Health Organization (WHO) recommends exclusive breastfeeding for the first six months of life (Kramer and Kakuma 2009; Butte *et al*. 2002; World Health Organization 2003).

The advantages of breastfeeding are dose dependent, with exclusive breastfeeding providing greater benefits.

While breastfeeding initiation rates are high in Australia (over 95 per cent), the level of sustained breastfeeding at six months is well below the international, national and state targets (Australian Health Ministers' Conference 2009; Australian Institute of Health and Welfare 2011; Australian Institute of Family Studies 2008). It is for this reason that this project focuses on maintaining breastfeeding rather than initiation. The current literature on breastfeeding campaigns globally reveals that one of the areas showing promise for maintaining breastfeeding behaviour is access to peer and professional support services (Dennis 2002; McInnes *et al*. 2000; Dennis 2002; Hoddinott *et al*. 2006). However, conventional support, relying on face-to-face or telephone encounters, is highly labour intensive and costly and is therefore often limited to first-time mothers or for a limited time post-partum. With the ubiquitous spread of the Internet and mobile devices across all demographics, the need to examine technology-enabled support for breastfeeding has arisen. Despite the interest in using SMS technology, governments are typically reluctant to digress from traditional approaches such as mass media without an evidence base to justify any innovative approaches. This case reports on the world's first two-way automated social marketing SMS project: MumBubConnect.

PROBLEM DEFINITION

For the purpose of this project, breastfeeding consists of several different levels; exclusive breastfeeding, predominant or 'full' breastfeeding, and complementary or partial breastfeeding (Australian Health Ministers' Conference 2009). While exclusive breastfeeding for six months is optimal, breastfeeding for even a few weeks, or partially, is beneficial and has definite advantages over not breastfeeding at all (Kramer and Kakuma 2009). In Australia, breastfeeding duration declines rapidly after three months. A total of 47 per cent of infants were predominantly (fully) breastfed to three months (less than four months), reducing to 21 per cent to five months (less than six months) (Australian Institute of Health and Welfare 2011). Some groups breastfeed less than others and there are indications that breastfeeding rates are lower in mothers who are younger, less educated and on low incomes (Mitra *et al*. 2004; Australian Bureau of Statistics 2009; Amir and Donath 2008).

The critical nature of promoting breastfeeding behaviour is exemplified with the release of the Australian National Breastfeeding Strategy (Australian Health Ministers' Conference 2009), which aims to improve the health of infants, young children and mothers by protecting, promoting, supporting and monitoring breastfeeding. Failure to address low breastfeeding rates could result in increased infectious and chronic diseases. The determinants of breastfeeding are complex but have been classified into seven main factors: socio-demographic characteristics of the mother and family; social support and structures; health of the mother and infant; mother's knowledge, attitudes and skills; aspects of feeding practices; health services organization; and social, cultural and environmental factors (Hector *et al*. 2004).

To date, there have been a range of interventions designed to increase both breast-feeding initiation and duration (Guise *et al.* 2003). There is recognition that stand-alone information (pamphlets, posters) is ineffective in influencing breastfeeding duration (Kukla 2006). Rather, interventions that leverage education with support from professionals, trained peers and significant others are recommended under the Australian National Breastfeeding Strategy (Australian Health Ministers' Conference 2009).

COMPETITION ANALYSIS

Competition in social marketing can be defined as the current or non-desired behaviour of the target market (Kotler and Lee 2008) or combative firms who provide alternative or opposing products/services (Ritchie and Weinberg 2000). Using Andreasen's (2002) classification framework, competition for breastfeeding behaviour operates within the general 'product category' of infant feeding.

Table CS5.1 Classification of competition for infant feeding

	Definition	Examples
Subject-market competition	Other key social issues that 'compete' for share of mind/ wallet with infant feeding	Vaccination, mental health of mothers, childhood obesity, childhood illnesses, early childhood education, return to paid employment, environmental concerns
Generic competition	Different types of competing solutions for infant feeding	Exclusive breastfeeding, full breastfeeding, partial breastfeeding, formula, water
Product competition	Infant-feeding behaviour in the community that can be targeted though education, marketing and law	Local government agencies creating competing messages (e.g. Queensland Government agency message: 'happy, healthy, normal'); medical professionals (midwives, doctors, nurses) who influence women's breastfeeding confidence (positively or negatively); professionals who might offer conflicting advice about breastfeeding duration
Branding competition	Other organizations that also seek to enact infant-feeding behaviour	Commercial suppliers of formula (e.g. Nestle, Heinz, Karicare, Wyeth); government agencies such as health departments, non-government agencies, such as the Australian Breastfeeding Association (ABA)
Intervention level	Different societal levels that believe infant-feeding behaviours must be targeted	Individuals, couples, families, community groups, NGOs, government agencies, health practitioners

Breastfeeding 'brands' of exclusive, full, and partial or complementary account for the majority of infant feeding until four months of age, when formula has been adopted as the primary infant food by more than 50 per cent of mothers. The competitive advantage of breastfeeding is protection for the infant against illness and infection, and against a higher risk of allergy, juvenile diabetes, heart disease and SIDS (Sudden Infant Death Syndrome). The competitive advantage of breastfeeding also includes benefits to the mother – reduced financial cost, reduced risk of breast and ovarian cancer, heart disease and osteoporosis, and, for some women, delayed return of menstruation and fertility. The competitive advantage of formula is that feeding can be readily shared with other carers, and that consumption can be visibly measured.

Given that many women do not breastfeed for the recommended time, the barriers need to be identified and lowered to improve breastfeeding rates. The determinants identified as key to influencing breastfeeding are low levels of education and income, being a younger mother, levels of self-efficacy (including the ability to be able to problem solve and empowerment), social support and supportive environments (Dennis 2006; Blyth *et al.* 2002; Kools *et al.* 2006; Mossman *et al.* 2008). The MumBubConnect (MBC) program was therefore designed with a pricing strategy that reduced the 'social and emotional' cost of breastfeeding to the mother and a place strategy that increased access to breastfeeding services and reduced embarrassment.

STAKEHOLDER ANALYSIS

MBC stakeholders share the common goal of encouraging the initiation of breastfeeding and providing support to mothers to encourage extending breastfeeding duration. At the micro-level, there are stakeholder such as partners/husbands, women's mothers, and other family and friends who offer emotional support. Additionally, the Australian Breastfeeding Association (ABA)[1] and its staff members provide counselling support and services to women seeking assistance with breastfeeding, and government agencies who act as secondary influences via the promotion of breastfeeding as a desirable action that achieves broader health and nutrition goals. At the macro-level, external stakeholders such as health agencies, the general public and the media are persuasive stakeholders who influence the maintenance of women's sustainable breastfeeding behaviour. Table CS5.2 outlines the needs, benefits and roles performed by major breastfeeding stakeholders.

AIMS AND OBJECTIVES

The overall aim of the program was to develop an SMS program that had the primary aim of being mother-oriented, personalized, digital, providing positive support and limiting guilt. The theories that underpinned the program development were: self-efficacy (Bandura 1977) and coping theory – specifically seeking-social-support (Vitaliano *et al.* 1985). The program objectives were:

1. Increase self-efficacy and social-support-seeking coping behaviours;
2. Maintain breastfeeding rates;
3. Identify women's reactions to the use of an SMS support program.

Table CS5.2 Needs, benefits and roles of primary stakeholders

Stakeholder	Needs	Benefits from increasing breastfeeding	Potential role in MumBubConnect
ABA not-for-profit organization ABA volunteers	Delivery of effective counselling service for mothers and the promotion of breastfeeding (BF)	Meeting the ABA's vision to educate and support mothers to BF their baby exclusively for six months, with continuing BF for two years and beyond	Connecting directly with mothers who are experiencing BF problems
Baby	Sustenance, nutritional health and bonding with mother	Optimal nutrition. Reduction in chronic disease risk and health protection against childhood illnesses	The focal beneficiary of the BF behaviour
Mother	Bonding with infant; reinforcement of 'good' mother; physical, mental and emotional health	Mothers – psychological reinforcement of their maternal choices (i.e. continuation of their behaviour) Continuation of family norms and tradition	Primary recipient
Husbands/partners	Have healthy happy baby; seeking information from credible sources (i.e. ABA) about BF issues and challenges	Being a supportive partner/husband, participating in decisions about a new baby in the family and feeling connected with the family	Encouraging wife/partner to access support services when they are needed Talking about and sharing information about BF challenges
Family and friends	Other family/friends: Being involved in extended-family decisions	Other family/friends: psychological and emotional benefits	Advocates for BF behaviours and for the ABA brand
Macro-level stakeholder			
Health agencies	To promote the benefits of BF to society, where BF rates are in decline	Potential improvement in population health statistics and reduced population-wide health costs	Providing government grants and funding opportunities to support ABA services and training programs

| Public | Perceived quality of life and good standard of healthcare in society | Reduced health burden attributed to the good nutritional practices learned through BF knowledge and behaviour | Receptive to ABA fundraising events Offering support to BF women in society |
| Media | Reporting health and lifestyle stories focused on a public health interest | Being identified within the community as a credible source of information on important issues and lifestyle practices | Providing objectives reporting on people's BF experiences |

RESEARCH

Consumer insight is a critical part of developing an effective social marketing program (Andreasen 2002; French and Blair-Stevens 2006), and, as such, secondary and primary research was conducted. The secondary research indicated that often an education-only approach was used to promote breastfeeding rates where posters and mass media were the typical tools. When breastfeeding support services were offered, success rates were higher, but these tended to be restricted to in-hospital or when the baby was less than six weeks old. There was a distinct lack of social marketing campaigns with exceptions being the 'Be A Star' UK campaign and the 'Get Closer' USA Campaign. Given that information-based or education campaigns are ineffective when awareness or knowledge is high (French and Blair-Stevens 2006; Rothschild 1999), there was a need for an in-home support service that made women feel supported and confident. While the ABA provides telephone counselling and peer support to thousands of women in Australia, there is persistent negative opinion towards the pro-breastfeeding association, in line with negative representation in the media (Bridges 2010). This poor perception of the ABA creates a barrier for women seeking advice using its Breastfeeding Helpline. In addition, the ABA is faced with a dwindling number of trained volunteer breastfeeding counsellors to maintain its telephone services, creating the need to investigate alternative solutions.

To identify attitudes towards infant feeding among new mothers and responses to a proposed SMS program, 5 focus groups were conducted with 29 women in South-East Queensland. Information was also collected on mobile phone experiences and opinions towards specific SMS information that was being considered (Gallegos et al. 2011; Russell-Bennett et al. 2012).

MUMBUBCONNECT

The program developed was a two-way automated SMS program piloted for 8 weeks with 120 new mothers in Australia. While the program was collaboratively developed between the ABA, Queensland University of Technology and University of Queensland, the role of the ABA was publicly minor to avoid negative perceptions of the ABA and

Figure CS5.1 MumBubConnect brand and website

to test MBC as a stand-alone brand. The mothers were recruited through a Facebook site, webpage[2] and media publicity (Figure CS5.1). Women were sent an SMS every week enquiring about their breastfeeding and they responded using a keyword selected from a list on a card. These keywords were developed by the ABA based on issues identified through their telephone counselling and adapted for use on a mobile phone by the creative consultant hired for the project. The SMS system then replied to the women's response with advice, tips or support. If a mother was identified as struggling, she also received an outbound counselling call from the ABA.

OUTCOMES

Recruited women were required to complete an online survey that identified their attitudes and behaviours towards breastfeeding, intentions and support structures before they commenced the program and at the completion of the eight weeks. Almost all the women stayed in the program with 95 per cent completing the second survey. The data showed significant increases in self-efficacy and social-support-seeking coping behaviour, which indicated that the theoretical underpinnings of the program design had been effective. Importantly, breastfeeding rates were maintained with only 4 per cent of women stopping full breastfeeding compared to 16 per cent nationally (Australian Institute of Family Studies 2008).

The qualitative feedback was overwhelmingly positive with women indicating that they 'looked forward' to receiving the texts each week and felt as though 'someone was listening'. The women did not perceive their text replies as a cry for help in the same way as a phone call and believed the SMS to be non-intrusive and private. The perception of the ABA also increased as a by-product of the program and women who might not have otherwise done so contacted the ABA.

CONCLUSION

MBC as a concept has been proven to positively influence women's coping behaviours and self-efficacy in a way that minimizes feelings of failure and guilt, effectively reducing the social 'price' of undertaking the behaviour. In light of the positive results of the MBC project, the ABA is exploring the possibility of adding MBC to its current service offerings, adopting it as adjunct to their currently available Breastfeeding Helpline and email counselling service.

The implementation of MBC is a new venture for ABA, and required changes to its business model. The advantages, however, have been identified as threefold. First, MBC's mobile platform catapults ABA further into its target market, using the technology with which that market is most familiar. Second, the ABA brand has a distinct image, which can polarize the market, so the separate branding of MBC provides an opportunity to connect with and help mothers who may not otherwise approach ABA. Finally, the introduction of MBC technology, while challenging to integrate, has been used to facilitate IT change management.

From the results of the MBC trial, we are confident that the concept of a two-way SMS service supports and empowers women to maintain their breastfeeding behaviour. The qualitative results also indicate that the mode of delivery is effective and suits the lifestyles of women. The next phase of MBC will identify whether the provision of a two-way SMS service independently increases self-efficacy and positive coping rather than this being related to other factors such as partner support or experience. The concept will also be trialled in some of those more difficult-to-reach groups, such as very young mothers, mothers on low incomes and those from indigenous backgrounds.

MBC as a technological adjunct to peer and professional support currently available has exemplified the advantages of a joint social marketing and health promotion approach to identify solutions to promoting a complex behaviour.

Notes

1   Australian Breastfeeding Association, About Us. Online: www.breastfeeding. asn.au/aboutaba/purpose (accessed 22 March 2012).
2   www.mumbubconnect.com.au/.

References

Amir, L.H. and S. Donath, M. (2008) 'Socioeconomic status and rates of breast-feeding in Australia: Evidence from three recent national health surveys', *Medical Journal of Australia*, 189(5): 254.

Andreason, A.R. (2002) 'Marketing social marketing in the social change market-place', *Journal of Public Policy and Marketing*, 3–13.

Australian Bureau of Statistics (2009) *Australian Social Trends.* Australian Bureau of Statistics: Canberra.

Australian Health Ministers' Conference (2009) *The Australian National Breastfeeding Strategy 2010–2015,* Australian Government Department of Health and Ageing: Canberra.

Australian Institute of Family Studies (2008) *Growing Up In Australia: The Longitudinal Study of Australian Children, Annual Report 2006–07.* Canberra.

Australian Institute of Health and Welfare (2011) *2010 Australian National Infant Feeding Survey: Indicator Results,* AIHW: Canberra.

Bandura, A. (1977) 'Self-efficacy: Toward a unifying theory of behavioral change', *Psychology Reviews,* 84(2): 191–215.

Blyth, R., Creedy, D.K., Dennis, C.L., Moyle, W., Pratt, J., and De Vries, S.M. (2002) 'Effect of maternal confidence on breastfeeding duration: An application of breastfeeding self-efficacy theory', *Birth,* 29(4): 278–284.

Bridges, N. (2010) 'Breastfeeding in the Australian media', *Essence,* pp. 35–36.

Butte, N.F., Lopez-Alarcon, M.G. and Garza, C. (2002) *Nutritional adequacy of exclusive breastfeeding for the term infant during the first six months of life.* World Health Organization: Geneva.

Dennis, C.L. (2002) 'Breastfeeding initiation and duration: A 1990–2000 literature review', *Journal Obstetric Gynaecological Neonatal Nursing,* 31: 12–32.

Dennis, C.L. (2002) 'Breastfeeding peer support: Maternal and volunteer perceptions from a randomised controlled trial', *Birth,* 29: 169–176.

Dennis, C.L. (2006) 'Identifying predictors of breastfeeding self-efficacy in the immediate postpartum period', *Research in Nursing & Health,* 29(4): 256–268.

French, J. and Blair-Stevens, C. (2006) *Social Marketing: National Benchmark Criteria.* National Social Marketing Centre: United Kingdom.

Gallegos, D., Russell-Bennett, R. and Previte, J. (2011) 'An innovative approach to reducing risks associated with infant feeding: The use of technology', *Journal of Nonprofit and Public Sector Marketing,* 23(4):327–347.

Guise, J.-M., Palda, V., Westhoff, C., Chan, B.K.S., Helfand, M., and Lieu, T.A. (2003) 'The effectiveness of primary care-based interventions to promote breastfeeding: Systematic evidence review and meta-analysis for the US Preventive Services Task Force', *Annals of Family Medicine,* 1(2): 70–78.

Hector, D., King, L. and Webb, K. (2004) *Overview of recent reviews of interventions to promote and support breastfeeding.* NSW Centre for Public Health Nutrition and NSW Department of Health: Sydney.

Hoddinott, P., Chalmers, M. and Pill, R. (2006) 'One-to-one or group-based peer support for breastfeeding? Women's perceptions of a breastfeeding peer coaching intervention', *Birth,* 33(2): 139–146.

Horta, B. L., Bahl, R., Martinés, J.C., and Victora, C.G. (2007) 'Evidence on the long-term effects of breastfeeding', in *Systematic Reviews and Meta-Analyses.* World Health Organization: Geneva.

Kools, E.J., Thijs, C., Kester, A.D., and de Vries, H. (2006) 'The motivational determinants of breast-feeding: Predictors for the continuation of breast-feeding', *Preventive Medicine,* 43(5): 394–401.

Kotler, P. and Lee, N.R. (2008) *Social Marketing: Influencing Behaviors for Good.* 3rd ed. Thousand Oaks, California: Sage Publications.

Kramer, M.S. and Kakuma, R. (2009) '*Optimal duration of exclusive breastfeeding*' *Cochrane Database of Systematic Reviews* 2002, Issue 1. Art. No.: CD 003517.uk.

Kukla, R. (2006) 'Ethics and ideology in breastfeeding advocacy campaigns', *Hypatia*, 21(1): 157–180.

McInnes, R.J., Love, J.G. and Stone, D.H. (2000) 'Evaluation of a community-based intervention to increase breastfeeding prevalence', *Journal of Public Health Medicine*, 22: 138–145.

Mitra, A.K., Khoury, A.J., Hinton, A.W., and Carothers, C. (2004) 'Predictors of breastfeeding intention among low-income women', *Maternal and Child Health Journal*, 8(2): 65–70.

Mossman, M., Heaman, M., Dennis, C. L., and Morris, M. (2008) 'The influence of adolescent mothers' breastfeeding confidence and attitudes on breastfeeding initiation and duration', *Journal of Human Lactation*, 24(3): 268–277.

Ritchie, R.J.B. and Weinberg, C.B. (2000) 'A typology of nonprofit competition: Insights for social marketers', *Social Marketing Quarterly*, 6(3): 63–71.

Rothschild, M.L. (1999) 'Carrots, sticks and promises: A conceptual framework for the management of public health and social issue behaviors', *Journal of Marketing*, 63: 24–37.

Russell-Bennett, R., Gallegos, D. and Previte, J. (2012) *Overcoming barriers through new technology: Support via text message*, in *Mother Support: The 10th Step*, V. Thorley and M. Vickers, Editors. Hale Publishing: Texas, USA.

Vitaliano, P.P., Russo, J., Carr, J.E., Maiuro, R.D. and Becker, J. (1985) 'The ways of coping checklist: Revision and psychometric properties', *Multivariate Behavioral Research*, 20: p. 3–26.

World Health Organization (2003) *Global Strategy for Infant and Young Child Feeding.* WHO: Geneva.

Case study questions

1. Why did the MumBubConnect program achieve its outcomes?

2. Why is breastfeeding such an emotional issue that often polarizes public opinion?

3. The SMS technology overcame barriers of time and personal embarrassment. The benefit of the technology was that it was convenient and non-intrusive, as well as providing credible advice and reassurance from a non-judgemental source on breastfeeding. What other social issues do you think could benefit from the use of a two-way SMS system as part of the social marketing mix?

Case Study **6**

'Help – For a life without tobacco': Public health branding campaign

Abraham Brown

INTRODUCTION

This case examines how the strategic application of marketing principles can provide health advocates with a unique opportunity to effect changes in health behaviour and societal settings by developing successful public health brands.

The case of the European Union (EU) 'Help' anti-smoking campaign, designed to prevent smoking uptake and cessation among young people is a clear demonstration of the effective application of the notion of branding to fulfil the primary goal of any public health brand, i.e. creating brand salience, engagement and adoption of the health behaviour.

PROBLEM DEFINITION

Drawing on the EU 'Help' anti-smoking campaign to examine the salient features of branding, three questions needed consideration:

1. What does the target audience want from a health brand?
2. How do health practitioners define this brand?
3. How can we effectively package, position and frame the public health brand to create a long-term communicative relationship with the audience?

COMPETITIVE ANALYSIS

Two key forces come into play in considering how to effectively package and position a public health brand. These are:

1. The tobacco industry and its marketing activities.
2. The target consumers' alternative desires, i.e. what your audience forgoes in opting for your product (adoption of a socially desirable behaviour). With respect to smoking in the EU, the tobacco industry and its marketing activities were a major source of competition to tobacco control efforts to prevent tobacco use. Public health practitioners have recognized this fact, and have subsequently organized its social marketing activities, policy and intervention activities to thwart industry tactics.

STAKEHOLDER ANALYSIS

Stakeholder analysis informed the 'Help' campaign about key people, groups and institutions whose interests might influence the success of the brand. Thus, the overall 'Help' campaign was an example of unique cooperation, designed and conducted in partnership with stakeholders such as youth organizations across the EU, comprising:

- European Medical Student Association (EMSA)
- International Federation of Medical Students' Association (IFSMA)
- European Youth Forum/Forum Jeunesse
- communication experts such as tobacco control professionals from the European Network for Smoking Prevention (ENSP) and the European Network of Quitlines (ENQ)
- students from over 50 youth organizations and medical student organizations.

AIMS AND OBJECTIVES

1. To develop the EU 'Help' anti-smoking campaign as a successful brand.

2. To communicate a distinctive message to the youth audience, i.e. to encourage a move towards tobacco de-normalization.

3. To empower young people to take control of their health and lifestyles, as opposed to their being the subject of media objectification.

4. To challenge the image of smoking as fun and socially acceptable.

5. To reinforce awareness and comprehension of the dangers of smoking and to provide young people with the requisite tools to take charge of their lives.

FORMULATION OF STRATEGY

The identification and understanding of consumer preferences is paramount to ensuring product effectiveness and sustained demand (McDivitt 2003). A major challenge for health advocates is to avoid the traditional marketing approach that seeks to design a product or promote a behaviour that they wish the target audience to purchase and/or practise (e.g. contraceptive use, monogamy, healthy eating or smoking cessation) only to find that the audience has little or no desire for the product/behavioural change message. A core tenet of public health branding is therefore to define the product based on the real needs and desires of the audience, rather than on the beliefs, thoughts and instincts of the public health practitioner (Andreasen 1995).

In the case of the EU 'Help' brand, this was clearly defined by undertaking several initiatives **to learn about the target audience** and their views on smoking, as well as to learn from past anti-smoking campaigns:

1. Rather than communicate a one-off message, the intent was **to understand the specific cultural and environmental factors** that drive young people to smoke so as to develop a brand that conveys a uniform product identity and allows consumers to relate directly to it (Hastings 2003).

2. Recognition that **no single message can be effective** because there is no universal message, i.e. smokers smoke for different reasons.

3. Campaign planners also resolved that public health campaigns targeting youth need to be linked to the origins of youth **normative beliefs and culture**.[1]

4. A **systematic review of existing literature** was conducted to understand the success of previous health brands by appraising the impact of mass media anti-smoking campaigns on youth smoking and societal norms.

5. A **qualitative research project** (focus group study) was conducted in 20 EU member states to explore young people's reaction to, and understanding of, the 'Help' campaign creative concept. This was crucial to the success of the EU 'Help' campaign as the meanings and values attached to the concept determined whether or not favourable attributes and positive social image would be associated with the brand. The group study provided insights into consumers' thoughts and beliefs about what they desired from the 'Help' brand.

Pre-testing of draft campaign materials was conducted first in 2005 and throughout the next five years of the campaign. Hence, any significant changes in youth perceptions and cultural beliefs were integrated into the 'Help' brand in successive campaigns.

Given the cluttered health product market in the EU, both traditional and new social media were used to communicate the unique brand attributes to the target audience. Thus, the campaign was web-driven, aimed to draw young Europeans to the 'Help' website where they could find information on the dangers of smoking, as well as linking them to other tobacco control organizations, youth organizations and partner organizations in their respective countries. The website focused on awareness-raising around tobacco issues, engaging young people in the social sites via participation in viral campaigns in order to encourage a move towards tobacco de-normalization in Europe. The website was available in 23 languages, and the online presence and media campaign were complemented by a series of European and national public and press relations events.

By using social media (including digital ads), the 'Help' campaign engaged the youth with the brand and, in so doing, fulfilled the primary goal of increasing brand awareness of the dangers of smoking and encouraging non-smoking as a socially acceptable behaviour. While there had been a few public health anti-smoking campaigns prior to this campaign, these focused on a few of the EU member states and/or employed either traditional or digital media.

RESEARCH AND EVALUATION

To appreciate campaign impact, process evaluation of the 'Help' campaign was done by measuring media delivery versus goals:

- the number of impressions for all digital ads;
- number of video views;
- visits to the 'Help' websites and to the mini-sites, including duration of visits and degree of engagement (number of pages and videos clicked);
- visits to 'Help' pages or places on other social network sites; and
- attendance at events.

Likewise, ongoing post-evaluation of the 'Help' campaign was conducted via telephone surveys which commenced in 2005. Each wave included more than 1,000 respondents – a representative sample of the national population aged 15 and over in each country (except in Malta and Cyprus where only 500 interviews were conducted). In total, over 26,300 respondents were interviewed.

Results from the 2010 survey indicated that awareness of the 'Help' campaign was high across Europe, with 43 per cent of respondents being aware of at least one 'Help' television advertisement, an increase of 14 percentage points over the 2005 level of 29 per cent. The increased awareness was even more pronounced among smokers and people aged under 25. Eight out of ten respondents who recalled the ads in 2010 found them interesting, and 90 per cent found their tobacco control message easy to understand.

Additionally, 85 per cent of respondents who recalled the ads in 2010 agreed that they conveyed the availability of help to face smoking-related problems, and 81 per cent agreed that the campaign communicated the fact that a website and/or telephone support was available. Most smokers (69 per cent) said the campaign was an incentive to look for information/help and a third of the respondents thought that the campaign was from a credible source as they correctly identified the European Union as being behind the campaign.

More importantly, smokers from countries with relatively low tobacco regulation, such as Germany and Greece, reported that awareness of the cessation and passive smoking campaign positively affected their attempts to quit. Those from Denmark and Lithuania associated knowledge of the dangers of smoking with their comprehension of the 'Help' campaign, which also impacted their attempts to quit smoking. Smokers from countries with high tobacco regulation, such as the UK, said that awareness of the cessation campaign positively affected their intentions to quit. UK smokers also reported that campaign comprehension positively affected their knowledge of the health dangers of smoking and intention to quit.

DISCUSSION

Overall, the EU 'Help' brand was successful due to the following strategies:

1. It was **effective in getting the attention of the target audience** and motivating them to look for assistance in avoiding tobacco and second-hand smoke. As mentioned above, the campaign not only had solid recall among young adults and smokers, but also the majority of smokers said the campaign was an incentive to seek information or help.

2. It **demonstrated that a target audience of 'young Europeans' existed**, and that, despite national and cultural differences and specificities, young people across Europe have similar needs and responses. Thus, the 'Help' campaign could apply the same messages across member states.

3. **Use of social media facilitated youth's 'owning' of the campaign** and made it more participative. In the initial phase of the 'Help' campaign, working with youth organizations was not easy due to their unwillingness to be 'used' by a cause. But, gradually, they took over the message themselves and organized youth meetings in Brussels as well as in their respective member states. They also used social media to boost 'Help's' visibility (in terms of numbers of Facebook fans, etc.). The organization of 1,800 events and high youth participation levels would not have been possible if social media had been unavailable or had not been widely used.

4. **Branding as a communicative strategy** offered health practitioners a viable pathway to **develop a relationship between a public health campaign and its target audience**. This has become even more important as a consequence of the multiple messages from simultaneously functional public health campaigns and other competing sources attempting to persuade consumers to change or modify lifestyles (Randolph and Viswanath 2004). As such, health advocates not only have to capture the attention of their audience amid competition, but also have to motivate them to adopt new lifestyles and/or initiate habits that may be new (Hornick 2002).

5. **Branding created a unique identity for a health product** and helped the audience cultivate the desired healthy lifestyle. Achieving this in a cluttered health market required consumer insight into why people choose one product over other competing products, what unique benefit the product has to offer, and the costs involved in engaging long term with the product/health campaign.

6. **Engaging the audience in a collaborative relationship with the product** was vital as it determined the pathways to communicate a health message to counter powerful but unhealthy brands like 'Marlboro Man' and sustained use of tobacco products.

CONCLUSION

Branding as a communicative strategy can ensure that brand salience is followed by adoption and long-term use. The 'Help' campaign showed that this can be accomplished by utilizing social media sites alongside conventional media to promote a reciprocal relationship that actively engages people.

Note

1   http://ec.europa.eu/health/tobacco/events/ev_20031113_en.htm/.

Bibliography

Aaker, J. (1997) 'Dimensions of brand personality', *Journal of Marketing Research*, 34: 347–356.

Andreasen, A.R. (1995) *Marketing Social Change: Changing behaviour to promote health, social development, and the environment.* San Francisco: Jossey Bass.

Eisenberg, M., Ringwalt, C., Driscoll, D., Vallee, M. and Gullette, G. (2004) 'Learning from the truth: Youth participation in field marketing techniques to counter tobacco advertising', *Journal of Health Communication*, 9: 223–231.

Evans, W.D., Price, S. and Blahut, S. (2005) 'Evaluating the truth@Brand', *Journal of Health Communication*, 10: 181–192.

Evans, W.D., Renaud, J., Blitstein, J., Hersey, J., Ray, S., Schieber, B. and Willett, J. (2007) 'Prevention effects of an anti-tobacco brand on adolescent smoking initiation', *Social Marketing Quarterly*, 13: 2–20.

Hastings, G. (2003) 'Social marketers of the world unite, you have nothing to lose but your shame', *Social Marketing Quarterly*, 9: 14–21.

Holt, D.B. (2003) *Brands and Branding*. Boston, MA: Harvard Business School.

Holt, D.B. (2004) *How Brands Become Icons: The Principles of Cultural Branding*. Watertown, MA: Harvard Business Press.

Hornick, R.C. (2002) *Public Health Communication: Evidence For Behavior Change*. Mahwah, NJ: Erlbaum.

Keller, K.L. (2007) *Strategic Brand Management: Building, Measuring, and Managing Brand Equity*, 3rd ed. Upper Saddle River, NJ: Prentice Hall.

Lefebvre, R.C. and Flora, J.A. (1988) 'Social marketing and public health intervention', *Health Education Quarterly*, 15: 299–315.

McDivitt, J. (2003) 'Is there a role for branding in social marketing?', *Social Marketing Quarterly*, 11: 11–17.

Randolph, W. and Viswanath, K. (2004) 'Lessons learned from public health mass media campaigns: Marketing health in a crowded media world', *Annual Review of Public Health*, 25: 419–437.

Case study question

The case of the European Union 'Help' anti-smoking campaign discussed above clearly highlights the fact that branded campaigns position the desired health behaviour by creating positive associations that can transcend any promotional activity. Drawing from the present study, (a) which distinct feature of branding might be particularly important for the success of a branded anti-smoking campaign and (b) how do you ensure effective communication?

Case Study **7**

A case of critical thinking: Marketing strategies used to promote licensed drugs

Marisa de Andrade

INTRODUCTION

The UK Government has stressed the need to question and challenge the actions of drug companies and the effect they may have on patients. A report by the House of Commons (HoC) Health Select Committee on *The Influence of the Pharmaceutical Industry* noted that it was important 'to examine critically the industry's impact on health to guard against excessive and damaging dependencies' (HoC 2005: 97). Given 'profit-maximization' is drug companies' main purpose, while patients strive for the 'optimisation of drugs' benefit-risk ratios' (Abraham 2008: 869), this called for a case of critical thinking.

PROBLEM DEFINITION

Regulatory failures are of great concern to public health, whether inefficiencies in pharmaceutical regulation are attributed to corporate bias (Middlemas 1979;

Abraham 2008; Lewis and Abraham 2001) or regulatory capture (Abraham 2008). If patients take licensed drugs that, for whatever reason, should not be on the market, death may be the end result.

This is obviously a problem. But who should be accountable when health regulatory systems fail to protect patients or when drug companies use illegal or unethical marketing practices to promote their products and are not sufficiently sanctioned? If regulators are to fulfil their mission of protecting and promoting public health, then they have a duty to act as dependable decision-making bodies. However, sometimes this trust is misplaced (Davies 2007; Farrar 2000; McGoey and Jackson 2009; Smith 2005).

If regulators cannot be trusted to protect public health, then perhaps patients should place their trust in the doctors who take an oath to put their interests first? But, here again, the academic literature proves it unwise to place blind faith in such authority. Indeed, research indicates that medical practitioners are partly responsible for the 'medicalization of society' and its dependency on pharmaceuticals (Conrad 2007; Illich 1975). There is also evidence that physicians' behaviours are influenced by drug company promotions (Goodman 2001) and that many doctors are 'on the take' (Kassirer 2005).

Furthermore, pharmaceutical research departments in academic institutions have been accused of promoting 'science in the private interest' (Krimsky 2004), while esteemed 'independent' scientists working for universities, and on the pharmaceutical industry's payroll, have been the source of much controversy (McHenry 2010).

Elsewhere, the media has been accused of scaremongering and propagating health scandals (Coombes 2009). There are documented examples of public relations (PR) practitioners, lobbyists and research institutions being hired by drug companies to influence policymaking (Abraham 2002; Burton and Rowell 2003; Miller and de Andrade 2010) and patient advocacy groups (PAGs) and charities increasingly collaborating with industry (Moynihan and Cassels 2005).

Clearly, patients do not immediately know who to trust when licensed drugs are illegally or unethically marketed. Neither do they know who must be held responsible when things go wrong. The following case explores the importance of independent critical thought in the context of public health.

STAKEHOLDER ANALYSIS

The main identified stakeholders[1] from a review of the literature are:

- patient advocacy groups (PAGs);
- medical communication companies/medical education firms;
- academics (and educational institutions);
- regulators;

- medical practitioners;
- PR firms;
- the media; and
- lobbyists.

AIMS AND OBJECTIVES

This case study identifies which of these stakeholders collaborated during the promotion of a selected licensed drug. It highlights some of the strategies used to promote the drug off-label[2] due to these affiliations, and helps to determine who may be accountable for ineffective pharmaceutical regulation. Finally, it considers why this is important for critical marketers.

RESEARCH AND EVALUATION

A documentary analysis was conducted of internal industry documents pertaining to olanzapine (or Zyprexa), which became publicly available during legal proceedings in the US. Eli Lilly's atypical antipsychotic agent was licensed in the UK and the US in 1996 to treat schizophrenia, bipolar I disorder and agitation associated with these conditions (Lader 1999; Spielmans 2009; Spielmans and Parry 2010; United States Department of Justice (USDJ) 2009).

From September 1999 until at least November 2003, its manufacturer was accused of promoting the drug off-label for the treatment of agitation, aggression, hostility, dementia, Alzheimer's dementia, depression and generalized sleep disorder (Berenson 2006; Goldstein 2007; USDJ 2009). In 2009, Lilly conceded that it had promoted the drug's use for the treatment of dementia and 'plead[ed] guilty to a misdemeanor criminal charge of misbranding' (Spielmans 2009; USDJ 2009).

Olanzapine was also linked to side effects including weight gain, the onset of diabetes mellitus and hyperglycaemia, which manufacturers neglected to inform patients of (Berenson 2006; Guo *et al.* 2006, 2007; Bogenschutz and Nurnberg 2004; Robinson *et al.* 2006).

In excess of 300 internal documents were reviewed for a larger study (from which selected findings are presented here). These documents entered the public domain in 2006, when they were leaked to a *New York Times* reporter and articles subsequently published. US court proceedings ruled in favour of allowing original litigation documents to be disseminated on various websites and the entire dataset is available on *Furious Seasons*.[3] All documents, dated from 2000 to 2005, were reviewed and analysed thematically, according to relevant stakeholders. They have also been used in the academic literature to illustrate how olanzapine was marketed in primary care settings in the US, and how there is a trend towards 'marketing-based medicine' (Spielmans 2009; Spielmans and Parry 2010). Quotes presented in the case study have been drawn from internal industry documents.

FORMULATION OF STRATEGY

A series of promotional strategies were implemented among the following groups:

- medics
- academics and medical education firms
- patient advocacy groups
- PR firms
- regulators.

Promotional strategies with medical practitioners

Following a lengthy study by the US brand team, the drug company decided to 'actively promote Zyprexa to selected primary care prescriber [PCP] targets' as the 'potential in this arena' was 'virtually untapped' (Eli Lilly 2000).

Specific messages were developed, market research conducted and a training calendar created to direct the strategy to PCP targets. The project additionally involved a 'communications plan', 'customer targeting and direct-to-physician initiatives' and 'additional pre-launch activities', such as 'sales force integration' and 'sales support items' (Eli Lilly 2000).

The brand team 'focused on two key points of emphasis': 'peer-to-peer activity and competitive differentiation'. To achieve this, Lilly 'completed the second of two speaker training programs' and 'unleashed more than 130 psychs [psychiatrists] and PCPs' who were 'chomping at the bit to help you [sales representatives] sell Zyprexa' (Eli Lilly 2001b).

Lilly also outlined its intention to create effective PR strategies to disseminate key messages related to diabetes and weight gain. The 'Zyprexa Infonet' was set up with online links to the latest product information, positioning statements, strategies, tactics and best practices. Tactical resources made available to company representatives included medical letters, standby statements, sales force verbatim, sales force training materials, publications and studies and slide sets and posters (Eli Lilly 2002a).

Promotional strategies with academics and medical education firms

Internal emails indicated that some Lilly representatives felt uneasy about the drug's associated link to weight gain and diabetes. A poster presentation at a conference, for example, caused much distress as it assessed the risk of antipsychotic-induced diabetes among schizophrenics and concluded that olanzapine was among the drugs 'associated with a significant risk of developing type 2 diabetes when compared to typical antipsychotics'. It was brought up by a Lilly representative as it would almost undoubtedly be published and 'raise noise around diabetes and olanzapine' (Eli Lilly 2002d).

Attention turned to how the company could minimize the impact of the manuscript both locally and globally. Representatives were asked to consider where the paper would be published and if it would be possible to halt or postpone publication. It was suggested that the latter would be problematic unless a company scientist could demonstrate that the entire methodology was defective. The notion that it may be possible to influence the author was raised, even though the danger of this was acknowledged as it was deemed an unethical action. Similarly, representatives were asked to consider whether it may be possible to shape the decisions of those on the selected journal's editorial board and if high-ranking referees should be contacted and made aware of methodological restrictions (Eli Lilly 2002d).

It was proposed that Lilly immediately start penning a 'landmark' paper, which would be published in a high-profile journal and written by a 'credible' individual who was sympathetic towards the company's position. One representative asked about the company's collaborations with medical education firms and whether these stakeholders could rapidly step in to assist (Eli Lilly 2002e).

The drug company decided to identify an external 'Consultant Panel' to examine the issue of hyperglycaemia, and hire someone who would appear to be 'independent' (Eli Lilly 2002b). A consultant, who was familiar with the data, was considered; an academic who served on the Lilly board was a doubtful candidate as he was 'too close'; and a specialist employed by another pharmaceutical company was not supported. One Lilly representative reiterated the importance of not selecting a chairperson with a 'pre-existing' and 'longstanding relationship' with the company (Eli Lilly 2002b).

Promotional strategies with patient advocacy groups

Lilly built strong relationships with influential patient advocacy groups such as the American Diabetes Association (ADA), a PAG that 'aims to prevent and cure diabetes and to improve the lives of all people affected by diabetes' (ADA 2011). In 2004, the group announced that there was a link between Zyprexa and diabetes (ADA 2004).

Internal email exchanges illustrate how the drug company conducted an 'after action review' of the ADA's recommendation. The review process was considered to be extremely advantageous as it could be applied 'to the broader long term Neuroscience influence agenda' (Eli Lilly 2004). A Lilly representative stated that the company was aware of 'ADA influence' and therefore 'should have had a greater influence early on before it was a done deal'. This had occurred as the drug company had 'underestimated the players' and 'didn't really understand [the] role & approach [the] competition would take'. Consequently, it had 'inadequately influenced key players on decision [making]'; made a presentation to America's health regulator, the Food and Drug Administration, which 'was not as strong as it could have been to influence [the] group (particularly [in] the response to the weight-gain question); and responded in the 'press' 'at a point [which was] too late to fundamentally influence the outcome' (Eli Lilly 2004).

Promotional strategies with PR firms

A Zyprexa management team was set up with representatives from the company's medical, regulatory, corporate affairs, health outcomes and marketing divisions. Two representatives from the PR firm Cohn & Wolfe were also enlisted (Eli Lilly 2002a).

Promotional strategies with regulators

To manage its relations with regulators, the company planned 'pre-emptive actions' to manage 'critical external issues' such as 'regulatory environment uncertainties'. It recognized the importance of building 'flexibility' into its business strategy 'to allow for fulfilment of unexpected requirements from regulatory authorities' and 'to shape regulatory decisions and requirements' (Eli Lilly 2001a).

DISCUSSION

The case shows that marketing olanzapine for approved and off-label uses was a priority for Eli Lilly and the product team vigorously pursued this objective by devising strategies to promote the drug. This they did through collaboration with several stakeholders, including medical practitioners, regulators, medical communication companies, PAGs and PR firms.

Building and maintaining strong relationships with respected academics, key opinion leaders, PAGs and medical practitioners was a priority, as was working with PR firms to disseminate positive messages about the product and adapting strategies to shape regulation.

This case illustrates the necessity of understanding that marketing strategies are implemented with other players in the pharma-sphere – the stakeholder network comprised of individuals or groups collaborating with the pharmaceutical industry during licensed product promotion – and that these stakeholders help shape and define the messages disseminated to the public through the media and other channels. In this way, they consciously or unconsciously facilitate the industry's pursuit of profit. Relations in the stakeholder network also make it difficult to apportion blame to specific stakeholders. By exploring the nature of the relationships between elite stakeholders who collaborate with the pharmaceutical industry during the promotion of licensed drugs, it may therefore be possible to understand how pharmaceutical regulation is ineffective due to systemic problems (de Andrade, forthcoming).

Undoubtedly, many drugs produced by the pharmaceutical industry are beneficial to society. But, when licensed drugs are misbranded and marketing strategies used to promote products that may be harmful to patients, the consequences of an inefficient pharmaceutical regulatory system become all the more apparent. It is therefore imperative for consumers to be aware of the 'dark side of marketing' in the public health arena and think critically about the ways in which other stakeholders may be inadvertently or deliberately facilitating corporate motivations.

Notes

1   Isolated criticisms of the pharmaceutical industry arising from its affiliations with these stakeholders have been consolidated as a model of intra-elite communication in pharmaceutical regulation called *pharmaffiliation*. By focusing on the nature of relationships between these affiliated stakeholders, the model facilitates an understanding of why pharmaceutical regulation may be ineffective (de Andrade, forthcoming).
2   This is when a pharmaceutical product is prescribed for an unapproved indication.
3   www.furiousseasons.com/.

Bibliography

Abraham, J. (2002) 'The pharmaceutical industry as a political player', *The Lancet*, 360: 1498–1502.
Abraham, J. (2008) 'Sociology of pharmaceuticals development and regulation: A realist empirical research programme', *Sociology of Health & Illness*, 30(6): 869–885.
American Diabetes Association (ADA) (2004) Antipsychotic Drugs Raise Obesity, Diabetes and Heart Disease Risks: Joint Panel Urges Increased Screening, Monitoring of Side Effects, January 27, 2004, ZY201386949.
American Diabetes Association (ADA) (2011) 11/11/2011-last update, About Us: American Diabetes Association [Homepage of ADA], [online] Available at: www.diabetes.org/about-us/?=rednav> [Accessed 21 November 2011].
Berenson, A. (2006) 'Eli Lilly Said to Play Down Risk of Top Pill', *The New York Times*, [online] (Last updated 17th December 2006) Available at: www.nytimes.com/2006/12/17/business/17drug.html> [Accessed 17 October 2009].
Bogenschutz, M.P. and Nurnberg, H.G. (2004) 'Olanzapine versus placebo in the treatment of borderline personality disorder', *Journal of Clinical Psychiatry*, 65: 104–109.
Burton, B. and Rowell, A. (2003) 'Unhealthy Spin', *British Medical Journal*, 326(7400): 1205–1207.
Conrad, P. (2007) *The Medicalization of Society: On the Transformation of Human Conditions into Treatable Disorders*. Baltimore: The Johns Hopkins University Press.
Coombes, R. (2009) *Cervarix: definitely not the new MMR*. Available at: www.bmj.com/content/339/bmj.b4124.full edn> [Accessed 13 June 2010].

Davies, M. (2007) *Medical Self-Regulation: Crisis and Change*. Hampshire: Ashgate Publishing Limited.

Eli Lilly (2000) Zyprexa – Primary Care Strategy and Implementation Overview, August 2000, ZY100589868.

Eli Lilly (2001a) 2001 Integrated Product Plan Zyprexa Product Team, January 18, 2001, ZY201249534.

Eli Lilly (2001b) M. Bandick, Zyprexa Primary Care Presentation, March 13, 2001, ZY100041630.

Eli Lilly (2002a) 2002 Zyprexa EOPs Issues Management Overview, ZY200393285/ ZY200393294.

Eli Lilly (2002b) Re: Potential contractors, June 26–27, 2002, ZY201584949/ ZY201584950.

Eli Lilly (2002c) Janssen meeting feedback, August 8, 2002, ZY200399436/ ZY200399437/ ZY200399438.

Eli Lilly (2002d) Re: Barcelona air traffic control, October 14, 2002, ZY200393552/ ZY200393553.

Eli Lilly (2002e) Your Input Please!, October 16, 2002, ZY200393550.

Eli Lilly (2004) Preparation for After Action Review, February 11, 2004, ZY201588416/ ZY201588417.

Farrar, S. (2000) 'GMC's research fraud backlog', *Times Higher Education Supplement (THES)*, [online] (Last updated 31st March 2000) Available at: www.timeshighereducation.co.uk/story.asp?storyCode=150912&sectioncode=26 [Accessed 29 October 2010].

Ferris Wayne, G. and Connolly, G.N. (2002) 'How cigarette design can affect youth initiation into smoking: Camel cigarettes 1983–93', *Tobacco Control*, 11(Suppl.): i32–i39.

Goldstein, B. (2007) 'How Lilly sells Zyprexa', *Slate*, [online] (Last updated 15th February 2010) Available at: www.slate.com/articles/news_and_politics/hot_document/features/2007/how_lilly_sells_zyprexa/_2.html [Accessed 20 June 2010].

Goodman, B. (2001) 'Do drug company promotions influence physician behaviour?' *The Western Journal of Medicine*, 174(4): 232–233.

Guo, J.J., Keck, P.E., Corey-Lisle, P.K., Li, H., Jiang, D.M., Jang, R. and L'Italien, G.J. (2006) 'Risk of diabetes mellitus associated with atypical antipsychotic use among patients with bipolar disorder: A retrospective, population-based, case – control study', *Journal of Clinical Psychiatry*, 67: 1055–1061.

Guo, J.J., Keck, P.E., Li, H., Corey-Lisle, P.K., Jiang, D.M., Jang, R. and L'Italien, G.J. (2007) 'Diabetes associated with antipsychotic use among Medicaid patients with bipolar disorders: A nested case – control study', *Pharmacotherapy*, 27(1): 27–35.

House of Commons (HoC) (2005) 'The Influence of the Pharmaceutical Industry'. [pdf] London: The Health Committee. Available at: www.publications.parliament.uk/pa/cm200405/cmselect/cmhealth/42/42.pdf [Accessed 10 November 2009].

Illich, I. (1975) *Medical Nemesis: The Expropriation of Health*. London: Calder & Boyars.

Kassirer, J.P. (2005) *On the Take: How Medicine's Complicity with Big Business Can Endanger Your Health*. New York: Oxford University Press.

Krimsky, S. (2004) *Science in the Private Interest: Has the Lure of Profits Corrupted Biomedical Research?* Oxford: Rowman & Littlewood Publishers Inc.

Lader, M. (1999) 'Some adverse effects of antipsychotics: Prevention and treatment', *Journal of Clinical Psychiatry*, 60(12): 18–21.

Lewis, G. and Abraham, J. (2001) 'The creation of neo-liberal corporate bias in transnational medicines control: The industrial shaping and interest dynamics of the European regulatory state', *European Journal of Political Research*, 39: 53–80.

McGoey, L. and Jackson, E. (2009) 'Seroxat and the suppression of clinical trial data: Regulatory failure and the uses of legal ambiguity', *Journal of Medical Ethics*, 35(2): 107–112.

McHenry, L. (2010) 'Of Sophists and Spin-Doctors: Industry-Sponsored Ghostwriting and the Crisis of Academic Medicine', in A.R. Singh and S.A. Singh (eds) *Psychopharmacology Today: Some Issues*. Mumbai: MSM, pp.129–145.

Middlemas, K. (1979) *Politics in Industrial Society*. London: Andre Deutsch.

Miller, D. and de Andrade, M. (2010) 'The Social Issues Research Centre', *British Medical Journal*, [online]. Available at: <www.bmj.com/content/340/bmj.c484.extract> [Accessed 29 December 2010].

Moynihan, R. and Cassels, A. (2005) *Selling Sickness: How the World's Biggest Pharmaceutical Companies are Turning Us All into Patients*. New York: Nation Books.

Robinson, D.G., Woerner, M.G., Napolitano, B., Patel, R.C., Sevy, S.M., Gunduz-Bruce, H. (2006) 'Randomized comparison of olanzapine versus risperidone for the treatment of first-episode schizophrenia: 4-month outcomes', *American Journal of Psychiatry*, 163: 2096–2102.

Sismondo, S. (2008) 'How pharmaceutical industry funding affects trial outcomes: Causal structures and responses', *Social Science and Medicine*, 66(9): 1909–1914.

Smith, R. (2005) 'Curbing the influence of the drug industry: A British review', *PLoS Medicine*, 2(9): e241.

Spielmans, G.I. (2009) 'The promotion of olanzapine in primary care: An examination of internal industry documents', *Social Science and Medicine*, 69(1): 14–20.

Spielmans, G.I. and Parry, P.I. (2010) 'From evidence-based medicine to marketing-based medicine: Evidence from internal industry documents', *Journal of Bioethical Inquiry*, 7(1): 13–29.

Stanton, C.R., Chu, A., Collin, J. and Glantz, S.A. (2010) 'Promoting tobacco through the international language of dance music: British American Tobacco and the Ministry of Sound', *European Journal of Public Health*, 21(1): 21–28.

United States Department of Justice (USDJ) (2009) *Eli Lilly and Company Agrees to Pay $1.415 Billion to Resolve Allegations of Off-label Promotion of Zyprexa*. [press release], 15 January 2009. Available at: <www.justice.gov/opa/pr/2009/January/09-civ–038.html> [Accessed 8 August 2010].

Case study questions

1. Which stakeholders collaborate with the pharmaceutical industry during the promotion of licensed drugs?

2. How may drug companies attempt to stop competitors from promoting their products?

3. Which important stakeholders do not always play a part in pharmaceutical regulatory processes?

4. How may transnational drug companies be subsuming and undermining regulatory systems and, consequently, turning them into a marketing enterprise?

Case Study **8**

Promoting female condoms among female sex workers in India

Sameer Deshpande, Purvi Shah and Sharad Agarwal

PROBLEM DEFINITION AND COMPETITIVE ANALYSIS

India ranks third in the world in terms of the number of people living with HIV/ AIDS (0.3 per cent of its population) (International Institute for Population Sciences (IIPS) and Macro International 2007). This social problem is largely restricted to core groups. In North East India, needle exchange is the primary cause of HIV/AIDS. However, in the Southern states of Maharashtra, Tamil Nadu, Karnataka, and Andhra Pradesh, the virus spreads because of sexual interactions between female sex workers (FSWs) and their male clients. In the past 20 years, the Government of India and a large network of social marketing agencies have undertaken several initiatives to promote the use of male condoms among both FSWs and Indian men. The male condoms have been manufactured to be of good quality, offered at a reasonable price, distributed widely, and promoted persuasively. Despite these extensive efforts, usage of male condoms remains low. One of the primary reasons for this low occurrence lies in the existence of patriarchy in the Indian society. Male clients may insist that FSWs have sex without condoms and be willing to pay more for this service. Fearing the loss of clients, these already marginalized women may succumb to pressure and knowingly take huge risks with their health and lives. They may also unknowingly spread the HIV virus to their uncooperative male clients.

To overcome these barriers, empower women, and increase the incidence of protected sex, in recent years, the social marketing sector has diverted some of its attention to promoting female condoms. A study conducted by Singh and Deshpande (forthcoming) among FSWs in the states of Karnataka, Tamil Nadu, Andhra Pradesh, Maharashtra, and West Bengal showed that FSWs indeed find female condoms superior to male condoms in regards to providing control over practising safe sex and evoking support from male clients, colleagues, and brothel owners. The study also reported few barriers to using female condoms. This case describes the *Swayam* ('self' in Sanskrit) campaign (see Figure CS8.1), which was initiated by Hindustan Latex Family Planning Promotion Trust (HLFPPT), a social marketing organization, in partnership with the Ministry of Health and Family Welfare and the National AIDS Control Organization (NACO), to promote female condoms in the states of Andhra Pradesh, Maharashtra, Tamil Nadu, and West Bengal.

CAMPAIGN OBJECTIVES AND STRATEGY

In 2006, the female condom social marketing programme was introduced in India among FSWs to address their vulnerability and empower them to protect themselves against HIV and other sexually transmitted infections. Within this larger programme, HLFPPT, following NACO guidelines, played a major role in supporting

Figure CS8.1 *Swayam* campaign logo

targeted interventions among FSWs and promoting female condoms implemented by the grassroots-level nongovernmental organizations (NGOs). HLFPPT efforts focused on addressing inconsistent male condom usage and reinforcing risk perceptions relating to using condoms with a regular partner. By integrating female condoms into the existing sexual and reproductive health services, HLFPPT aimed to increase condom usage among FSWs.

HLFPPT worked towards capacitating the NGOs and community-based organizations by integrating female condom messages into their structured outreach activities. These messages promoted female condoms by highlighting their benefits, providing education on correct usage, and addressing pre-existing myths and misconceptions. Since FSWs work in secluded environments, such as brothels and clubs, and are hard to reach, peer educators from the FSW community already volunteering in the targeted interventions were further motivated to serve as sales persons to distribute and promote the product.

SWAYAM AND COMMUNITY EVENTS: AN INNOVATIVE BEHAVIOUR CHANGE COMMUNICATION STRATEGY AND DEMAND GENERATION

In the initial years, HLFPPT faced the challenge of inconsistent reach of peer educators among the FSWs they were catering to. The organization realized that, if FSWs were to accept and adopt female condoms in their regular practice, (1) it would be necessary to continually reinforce product-related messages among users; and (2) it would be critical to ensure interpersonal interaction between the user and the service provider, backed by regular demonstration and counselling. Strong advocacy with NGOs and outreach workers was thus recognized as important. In the second phase, to address these challenges, the *Swayam* campaign was launched in January 2010.

Swayam primarily focused on raising awareness and generating product demand. At regular intervals, grassroots-level NGOs and community-based organizations organized events and set up branded kiosks (canopies) at 'hotspots' (i.e. areas of solicitation) and NGO-based drop-in centres. The events included interactive sessions and games about safe sex and female condoms. Infotainment such as folk shows, quizzes, educational games, and group exercises were used to demonstrate female condom usage. The events also facilitated interactions between trained counsellors and FSWs, allowing the latter to provide feedback on campaign activities (see Figures CS8.2, CS8.3 and CS8.4).

In relation to these events, two additional demand generation features are worth noting. First, *Swayam* carried out felicitations of 'champion female condom users' or 'role models' among FSWs and their male clients to influence their peers to accept and adopt female condoms. Second, *Swayam* events encouraged participation of male partners through various activity-based communication strategies. This largely addressed inconsistent male condom usage and reinforced the perception of risk with a regular partner.

Figure CS8.2 *Swayam* event stall for providing information, counselling, and female condom demonstration and sales

Figure CS8.3 A street play on the usage and benefits of female condoms, performed in Pune, Maharashtra

In terms of a place strategy, female condoms were distributed through a three-step process (see Figure CS8.5); in terms of a price strategy, the condoms promoted were subsidized by the Government of India, and, as a sales promotion strategy, motivational gifts were given to participants and peer educators to elicit behaviour change.

In summary, *Swayam* events turned out to be a unique, lively, attractive forum for directly reaching FSWs, relaying information on the use of female condoms, enabling this community to openly participate in discussions that mattered to them, and for generating demand.

Figure CS8.4 Informative materials on female condom usage provided as takeaways for FSWs along with counsellors providing counselling in the *Swayam* programme

| HLFPPT to NGO at `2 | NGO to Peer Educator at `2.50 | Peer Educator to FSW at `3.50 |

Figure CS8.5 Supply chain of female condoms

RESEARCH AND OUTCOMES

Six months after launch, the campaign had effectively reached and persuaded large number of FSWs to use female condoms, although more needs to be done (see Table CS8.1).

Table CS8.1 Campaign Performance

State	# NGOs	# Events conducted	# FSWs	# FSWs covered	# Purchasers	% Purchasers	Female condoms sold	Average FSWs reached per event
Andhra Pradesh	129	585	147,167	26,749	19,150	71.59	646,195	67
Maharashtra	47	244	50,350	12,954	6,321	48.80	153,811	66
Tamil Nadu	45	228	49,589	9,938	6,674	67.16	160,592	58
West Bengal	40	226	35,711	8,971	5,244	58.46	100,128	50
Total	261	1,283	282,817	58,612	37,389	63.79	1,060,726	62

Source: National AIDS Control Organization (2010)

Further, *Swayam* events were successfully conducted until December 2012 across four states of India, covering more than 300,000 FSWs and substantially contributing to creating awareness and generating demand for female condoms among all FSW categories.

ACCEPTABILITY STUDY

An acceptability study was conducted by HLFPPT among FSWs in June 2010 in all four states to understand the extent of accessibility, awareness, knowledge of usage, and acceptance of female condoms (HLFPPT 2012). The study employed a multi-stage sampling method and gathered data from 4,940 FSWs. Results reflected that 82 per cent of the respondents had seen or heard about the product and that 50 per cent (2,458 FSWs) had used female condoms. Among users:

- 81 per cent had repurchased female condoms;
- 39 per cent reported the female condom to be an effective tool for self-protection;
- 25 per cent reported the female condom to be beneficial in increasing their earnings, since they did not have to refuse clients;
- 51 per cent reported empowerment as the most important reason for using the female condom;
- 93 per cent preferred to purchase from a peer educator;
- FSWs reported that, of 24 sexual encounters over the course of a month with 18 partners, 14 had been protected with male condoms and four with female condoms; and
- FSWs reported that, of the last five female condoms they had used, three had been used with paid clients and one had been used with her regular partner. The final condom was assumed to be still in her possession.

In addition, 309 peer educators were interviewed, of whom 91 per cent had repurchased female condoms.

FSWs reported positive feedback on the usage of female condoms. To give the reader an idea of their responses to female condoms, we provide exemplar quotes:

Since I have started using [the] female condom, I don't lose any clients and I protect myself from infections. I also use it with my regular partner.

(FSW, Maharashtra)

Like the policemen have a gun in their hand to protect the people, I have a female condom as a weapon to protect myself and all my clients and partners.

(FSW, Andhra Pradesh)

It has given me a choice. I sometimes use it without the knowledge of my clients as I can wear it before the encounter.

(FSW, West Bengal)

References

HLFPPT (2012) *Female Condom Social Marketing Program Data 2010–11*. Delhi: Author.

International Institute for Population Sciences (IIPS) and Macro International (2007) *National Family Health Survey (NFHS–3), 2005–06: India*. Mumbai: IIPS.

National AIDS Control Organization (2010) *Female Condom Acceptability Study: HLFPPT*. Delhi: Author.

Singh, A. and Deshpande, S. (forthcoming) 'Perceived superiority of female condoms among female sex workers in India,' *International Journal of Nonprofit & Voluntary Sector Marketing*.

Case study questions

1. In what four Indian states is the *Swayam* campaign being implemented?

2. Why are female condoms considered effective in preventing HIV/AIDS in India?

3. So far, peer educators have reached only 20 per cent of FSWs, but, once reached, the conversion rate is impressive (64 per cent). In other words, peer educators effectively persuade FSWs to purchase female condoms, but they have not reached large numbers. How can the *Swayam* campaign reach larger numbers so that the manager is able to achieve her 100 per cent goal?

Case Study **9**

'Get Your Life in Gear'

Sinead Duane and Christine Domegan

INTRODUCTION

Background to Get Your Life in Gear (GYLIG)

Sophie sits at her desk on the second day of her new job as the Behavioural Change Director at safefood, the promotional body responsible for food safety and healthy eating on the island of Ireland (IOI) (safefood 2011). One of safefood's priorities is to address the complex issue of obesity, which is continuing to increase at a population level. In the past when addressing this wicked[1] problem on the IOI, safefood have adopted mass media approaches to raise awareness of the obesity epidemic within the adult population. Safefood have also adopted a collaborative approach to change. For example, the organization partnered with the Health Service Executive (HSE) in the development and implementation of Little Steps[2] and with the Irish Nutrition and Dietetic Institute (INDI) on Weigh2Live.[3] More recently, safefood adopted the social marketing framework to develop a pilot initiative, Get Your Life in Gear (GYLIG), which focused on the issue of male obesity in truck drivers on the IOI.

Against this background, Sophie's first task is to audit the GYLIG social marketing pilot initiative and present her assessment to safefood's Board of Directors. She needs to know what worked and what did not work within the pilot initiative. She also needs to know what could be improved upon if she is to secure a budget to roll out the programme nationally. Latest developments in social marketing and an ever-evolving social and economic environment also prompt her to reconsider the wider, long-term picture, challenging her to find methods of utilizing her behavioural change expertise in new and innovative ways. In recognition of the substantial task ahead of her, she begins by tackling the various reports, documents and files on her desk compiled over three years. Having gained an overview of the general obesity problem, she decides to narrow her focus by reviewing male obesity in particular.

Contextualizing the issue of male obesity

As identified in the unpublished GYLIG evaluation report (2010), in 2001, 39 per cent of adults on the IOI were classified as being overweight with 18 per cent deemed obese. On further analysis, a higher percentage of men are thought to be overweight or obese than their female counterparts (46 per cent males and 33 per cent females overweight; 20 per cent males and 16 per cent of females obese) (Irish Universities Nutrition Alliance 2001). This is a worrying trend, particularly given that the prevalence of overweight males in the Republic of Ireland (ROI) alone has increased by 3 per cent in less than a decade (1998–2007) (Morgan *et al.* 2008). This problem is further exacerbated by the fact that obese men are at greater risk than women of developing obesity-related illnesses as they are more prone to accumulating excess weight in the abdominal region (De Souza and Ciclitiva 2005; Morgan *et al.* 2008).

Developing interventions to reverse these trends is an increasingly difficult task as many interrelated factors need to be considered. For example, at a basic level, males often do not realize they have a weight problem (Wardle and Johnson 2002). Add to this the fact that males view weight loss differently from females, use less weight-loss services and are less concerned about their weight (De Souza and Ciclitiva 2005; White *et al.* 2008; Gray *et al.* 2009) and the problem intensifies. Men also choose to seek help, if at all, indirectly (Smith *et al.* 2006), and, generally, remain resistant to education strategies (Rumm 2005). It is also now realized that past strategies that relied on gender-neutral messages have failed to catalyse the necessary change. When analysed together, this insight suggests that segmentation of messaging could be a key success factor in the fight against male obesity. This makes creative approaches all the more vital when promoting overweight/obesity-related messages to men (Richardson 2009).

Tackling the issue of male obesity

In parallel with the individual characteristics that are impacting on weight-loss strategies, experts now believe that the obesity epidemic goes beyond individual responsibility and can also be attributed to cultural and societal influences on choice

(Deacon 2007). This means that another layer of combined factors affect the development of obesity. For instance, many elements motivate food choice: as well as the emergence of micro-environments, such as school, workplace and home settings. Wider macro-environments, such as the food industry, governments, together with social attitudes and beliefs, also play a part (Swinburn and Egger 2004; Deacon 2007). Shifts in social constructs, such as work practices, have also impacted on dietary choices, with people striving for convenience, opting for pre-packed, prepared foods that are energy dense (Butland *et al.* 2007). Ready-to-eat foods are also increasingly accessible in a variety of outlets from fast-food counters in petrol station forecourts to convenience stores (Butland *et al.* 2007). Thus, making unhealthy food choices has become much easier (Swinburn and Egger 2004). In effect, all these interrelated factors complicate choice and eating behaviour, with health not always arising as the main motivator for purchase or consumption (Fleming *et al.* 1997).

This contextualization of the problem highlights only a small proportion of the considerations facing those trying to tackle the issue of obesity. Additional indicators include gender and socio-economic status (Butland *et al.* 2007). In response, this case study adopted a systems-based approach when analysing the many direct and indirect factors impacting on change (Butland *et al.* 2007). Figure CS9.1 endeavours to simplify the task by presenting the interrelated elements in visual format. Published in the Foresight Report (2007), Figure CS9.1 provides a generic map of

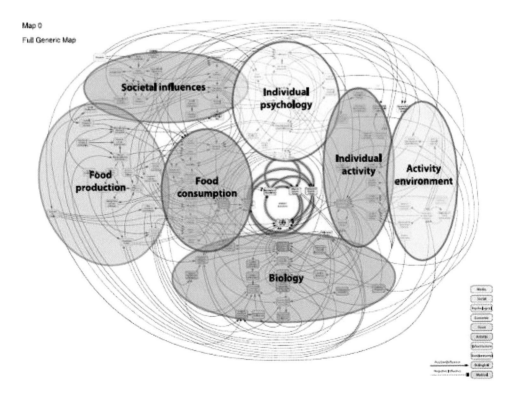

Figure CS9.1 Generic map of influencers of obesity

the contributors to the obesity issue. Each category of influence encompasses a plethora of networks that represent both direct and indirect forces. The map also highlights the deep-seated nature of the problem, making it increasingly difficult to identify cause and solution (Bye 2000). From this perspective, an audit of the relevant stakeholders was crucial in coming to grips with all the elements of the problem, followed by the adoption of a multi-disciplinary partnership approach to facilitate social change.

This broad synopsis of the obesity issue suggests that a multi-level approach should be adopted so that individual, organizational, community- and population-level strategies work simultaneously (Wilson *et al.* 1996; Makrides *et al.* 2006). Reflecting on the systems-based approach (illustrated in Figure CS9.1), programme planners were aware that the pilot would not solve this wicked problem. However, the development of a social marketing partnership pilot initiative could examine multiple layers of the system, resulting in penetrating insights. In this way, contextualization of the obesity issue made Sophie realize the need for innovation in the effort to tackle wicked problems on the IOI. This background summary confirms how, despite the many points of contact with the audience, other direct and indirect factors impact on decision-making processes.

As a next step, Sophie stipulated the boundaries of the pilot initiative – to segment the male population and determine what could or could not be achieved. She saw a situational analysis as the starting point to the planning process.

SITUATIONAL ANALYSIS

The first component of the situation analysis involved conducting extensive desk research in a number of relevant areas, e.g. male obesity and male health-seeking behaviour, as discussed above. This preliminary analysis identified many types of environments, which, when utilized, could maximize the potential for behavioural change strategies. For instance, the workplace has been identified as one setting that can influence the health status of the workforce (World Health Organization 1986, 1997, 2005). Those in employment are thought to spend a third of their lives at work, a factor that can also impact on leisure time (Deacon 2007). As well as influencing physical activity patterns of employees, the workplace setting can also affect employees' eating behaviours, as often one meal, at least, is consumed there (Fleming *et al.* 1997). This gives the workplace the potential to improve health (Brownwell *et al.* 2004), via the promotion of weight-gain-prevention messages and reinforcement of positive lifestyle behaviours (Kwak *et al.* 2006). The decision to segment the target audience by workplace meant that interventions could be tailored to the specific needs of employees, making it easier for the social marketer to profile their value system in the exchange process. Using existing literature and databases, male-dominated occupations were evaluated for suitability. Examples of workforces profiled included truck drivers, taxi drivers, bus drivers and construction workers.

Segmenting the male population

At first glance, the construction industry was identified as a workforce dominated by male employees. However, the economic downturn on the IOI had a detrimental effect on the industry which made it less feasible to pilot the initiative with this workforce. Attention then turned to the truck- and taxi-driving industries. After some preliminary research, professional truck drivers on the IOI were selected as target citizens because, as a workforce, they had been largely neglected from the point of view of healthy eating and physical activity interventions. A summary of some of the results from this research is shown in Table CS9.1.

By making the search more industry-specific, the project planners could grasp what worked and didn't work for similar projects. The initiative benefited by learning from previous mistakes, while also ensuring that duplication of effort did not occur – an important consideration in the current challenging economic climate. This was

Table CS9.1 Preliminary research with taxi and truck drivers: Healthy-eating issues

Taxi drivers	Commonalities	Truck drivers
	No breakfast	
	No proper meals during the day	Dinner in the evening- meat, potato, 2 veg
		Diet better when based at home rather than doing overnights elsewhere
	Want energy quick fixes (anything to get them through the day – some smoke) Unhealthy snacking throughout day in place of meals (jambons, croissants, breakfast rolls), lots of fizzy drinks and energy drinks, chocolate bars, crisps, coffee	
	Eat on the go due to time pressures	
They routinely stop in places that they see as good value	Easy to stop at shop and grab something quick	Lack of parking facilities at eateries
		Roads they travel don't have facilities, i.e. limited truck stops on bypasses
	Know what they should be doing but can't do it	
Like portable food that they can eat at a time which is convenient to them		

also an opportunity to identify the range of direct and indirect stakeholders who could potentially impact on the project's success.

Literature review – the health status of truck drivers

There has been minimal research on the health status of truck drivers on the IOI. However, similarities can be drawn between the limited Ireland-based studies available and international research. Truck drivers can be classified as a high-risk group due to their poor eating habits, which are a composite of constant snacking and irregular meal patterns. Due to irregular shift patterns, they tend to eat at times that are convenient and consume food available in transit rather than bring a packed meal to work (Jack *et al.* 1998). Their erratic schedules and constant driving contribute not only to an isolated lifestyle, but also to sedentary behaviour given the lack of opportunities for exercise. All these factors combined, therefore, make truck drivers a much harder group to reach (Jack *et al.* 1998; Gill and Wijk 2004; Krugar *et al.* 2007; Whitefield Jacobson *et al.* 2007). These issues illustrate the many interrelated factors negatively affecting drivers' health status, which necessitates a broadening of the stakeholder grouping and partnership selection pool.

The literature review was key in forming a preliminary profile of the target audience. To assist in the decision-making process, other techniques such as PESTEL and SWOT analysis were employed, which helped to specifically profile the macro industry factors on the IOI.

PESTEL analysis

The PESTEL analysis considered all the factors that could affect the success of any initiatives developed. This was conducted prior to the selection of the workplace and therefore was subject to change throughout the formative stages of the pilot.

After reflecting on the PESTEL analysis (CS9.2), Sophie considered what else she could have included for presentation to the board.

A SWOT analysis followed.

Strengths:

- The aim of this all-island initiative, an approach recommended in several reports and strategies on IOI, is to tackle the issue of overweight and obesity among men in the workplace;
- The workplace can provide peer support for weight-loss/maintenance activities;
- Initiatives such as 'Gut Busters' in the ROI received media attention and support;
- The initiative, which centres on men's values, adopts a social marketing approach in which a needs assessment and exchange theory are fundamental;
- Work with employers to improve the weight status of their employees, with additional benefits such as improved health and productivity.

Table CS9.2 PESTEL analysis

PESTEL analysis factors		Discussion
Political	All-Island Initiative	Study must incorporate participants from the North and South
	Workplace Health Promotion has been recommended by a number of international bodies	1986 Ottawa Charter for Health Promotion, Jakarta Declaration on Leading Health Promotion into the 21st Century, 2005 Bangkok Charter for Health Promotion in a Globalized World Europe: Luxembourg Declaration on Workplace Health Promotion in the EU, The Lisbon Statement on Workplace Health in Small and Medium-Sized Enterprises and the Barcelona Declaration on Developing Good Workplace Practice in Europe. WHO DPAS
Economic	Current 'credit crunch' and associated job losses	Need to persuade employers that they will receive something of value in return for implementation Return on Investment was important to *safe*food in terms of achieved behavioural change
	Cost of implementing initiative	Need company to invest their own money in the project or, at least, other valuable intangible resources
Social	Social norms of masculinity Social norms of industry	Have the potential to affect employees and management's perception of the initiative Weight gain 'occupational hazard'
	Perceived barriers to change	Need to identify how change can happen easily
	Consumer buying patterns	Consider their employees' purchase decisions regarding food and why they make these choices/where they shop

(Continued overleaf)

Table CS9.2 (Continued)

PESTEL analysis factors		Discussion
	Leisure activities	Need to understand how participants interact outside the workplace, so we can implement initiatives that can be adopted across every aspect of their lives
	Social class of target market	Will lead to the formation of certain attitudes, i.e. purchase decisions, education level concerning health
	Ethnicity	Origins of the workforce and who they interact with will affect their attitude towards initiative
	Attitudes to doing certain jobs	Stereotypes, e.g. 'It's OK to be overweight if you are not dealing with the public'
	Occupations	This will determine the amount of free time that employees will have after work. Other factors to consider include manual versus office jobs
	Management attitude	Will determine how the initiative is supported, implemented and sustained
	Interaction in the home environment	What are the structures of family life?
	Employee attitude towards company	Are they developing a career versus 'just a job' attitude?
Technical	Facilities	Company may not have the facilities to adopt all changes desired, i.e. canteen, gym, healthy vending machine, space
	Cost	Costs incurred in facilitating changes may be over that allocated to initiative
	Platforms of communication	Do companies use email, intranet and/or management to communicate, company newsletter?
	Transportation	How do employees get to work?
Environmental	Obesogenic environment	The number of overweight people in the organization

	Organization culture	This will determine the relationship with the workforce
	Organization size	Will determine the appropriateness of the interventions suggested
	Staff turnover rate	Determine the attitude staff will have to the initiative
	Staff engagement	Working relationship could determine the number of individuals who participate (peer approval and support)
	Support systems	Are there already employee assistance programmes or occupational health and safety initiatives in force?
	Living environment	Will determine who makes purchase decisions; how long they have to travel to work, etc.
Legal	Debate over the need for weight-loss initiative	Some companies may see it as a priority, while some may not
	Employment law	Could determine time off and amount of time allocated to breaks
	Industry-specific regulations	

Weaknesses:

- Does not target men who are not employed as truck drivers;
- Male-orientated workplace weight-loss strategies have not been tried or rigorously evaluated. Evidence is therefore lacking to support the development of the initiative;
- Despite being around since the 1970s, social marketing on the IOI is a relatively new concept and is still developing;
- May target 'health-conscious' employees who would be more likely to get involved in such initiatives, while failing to reach those who are most at risk;
- What about females in the workplace and those who don't need to lose weight (if focus is weight loss)?

Opportunities:

- Partnerships with NGOs who are currently involved within this setting and this target group;

- Collaborate with established men's health networks on the island – Men's Health Forum;
- Pilot study for future template of long-term initiative;
- This programme could be adapted for use with men in other workplaces;
- Workplace programmes that incorporate healthy eating and physical activity have been shown to be effective in the short term. Nevertheless, further studies are needed to prove long-term effectiveness.

Threats:

- Competition for advertising in terms of choices/behaviours that support unhealthy weight, e.g. alcohol, unhealthy food choices, sedentary behaviours;
- Lack of support structures in the workplaces, e.g. lack of employer buy-in threatens the sustainability of any initiative;
- Short-term behaviour change initiatives will not work on a long-term basis;
- Focus on socio-economically disadvantaged men may pose a threat to any initiative as the industries in which they are employed have a high turnover;
- Current economic climate, job instability and industry pressure may mean that employee health is not regarded as a main concern;
- Long working hours in some occupations and long travel distance to work (e.g. construction);
- Sub-contracted staff;
- Social norms of masculinity;
- Men are a 'hard-to-reach' group;
- Unhealthy gut is 'acceptable' for men compared with women.

STAKEHOLDER ANALYSIS

The extensive situational analysis also identified a variety of types of stakeholders who could potentially add value to the GYLIG pilot initiative. These stakeholders ranged from nurses who had worked with truck drivers to men's health policy writers. It also included advocates as well as representatives of the truck-driving industry. In addition to supplying advice on strategy, partnership development and the design of the pilot initiative, stakeholders also provided insight into the type of support needed to implement this kind of project. Although stakeholders did not heavily invest resources in the pilot initiative, they played a key role in facilitating access, while also acting as a network of indirect supporters of the initiative (e.g. friends, employees, policymakers). Analysis of the truck-driving industry revealed the diverse range, layers and networks of direct and indirect stakeholders that would, potentially, be interested in engaging with this pilot initiative. As it was neither possible nor practical to mobilize all stakeholders into partnership, prioritization was crucial. This awareness was also balanced with an understanding that not every potential stakeholder or would-be partner perceived value in participating in the project. The stakeholder analysis continued throughout the project as the network of influencers grew and the project planners became more aware of key gatekeepers and other similar initiatives. An additional outcome of the situational and stakeholder analysis was the development of the formative research plan, including participant profile and the topics for discussion.

RESEARCH

Formative research was used to gain an in-depth understanding of the specific issues that impacted on the truck drivers' lifestyles, with an emphasis on issues that were associated with weight gain. This consisted of 14 in-depth interviews with truck drivers in a distribution depot in Northern Ireland (NI). Six focus groups across the IOI were also conducted as part of a needs assessment; a summary of the primary research profile is included in Table CS9.3.

The research objectives were:

- To gain an in-depth understanding of the **current lifestyles, attitudes and behaviours** of truck drivers and to identify key needs and areas of concern in relation to their general health and wellbeing;
- To investigate levels of interest among truck drivers in a **workplace-facilitated health & lifestyle programme**, with a view to:
  - o determine the feasibility of such a programme;
  - o understand its likely impact on current attitudes and behaviours;
  - o identify the key drivers of success; and
  - o identify potential barriers to success.

Table CS9.3 Primary research profile

Type	Location	Recruitment
14 in-depth interviews	Depot of the pilot company in Belfast	Drivers were interviewed intermittently throughout their working day
6 focus groups	Belfast (2 groups); Dublin (2 groups); Cork (1 group); Sligo (1 group)	Free-find basis according to criteria: Male, different levels of driving experience, mix of ages, drive 20 hours per week, direct employees and short-haul drivers

Key findings included:

- Drivers indicated it was hard to live a healthy lifestyle in their current occupation;
- In response to doctors' advice, some older drivers indicated they had begun to make changes to their lifestyles;
- Drivers who had made the choice to 'become more healthy' in recent years proved that this is possible and felt that wisdom had come with age, experience and, in some cases, from a health scare that had happened – either to themselves or to a close friend/family member;
- Unpredictability of shifts made it difficult to control food consumption during shifts. This was also inhibited by lack of services, fatigue and digestive difficulties;
- Belief that their work prevented them from leading a healthy lifestyle;
- Boredom, fatigue and lack of adequate services on the IOI were major negatives of their occupation; this fed into their perceptions of, attitudes towards and relationship with food;
- Some of the barriers to healthy eating for drivers were lack of education, lack of services, convenience and cost;
- The majority of drivers who were living with a partner/wife felt strongly influenced by the behaviour of their partner/wife, and claimed that they (their partners/wives) were encouraging them to eat more healthily;
- Eating patterns tended to be quite sporadic in nature and many were unsure as to when they were going to get an opportunity to stop and take their breaks. Consequently, they tended to fill up on unhealthy, sugar-filled snacks;
- Most of those who consumed unhealthy snacks were aware that these were not good for them, citing convenience, boredom, seeking energy from 'sugar rush', comfort eating or a 'sweet tooth' as the main reasons for this behaviour;
- Drivers need to see and experience tangible benefits from weight-loss attempts. They also need constant motivation (either from themselves/others) until it becomes a part of their lives;
- Many drivers were using their profession as an excuse not to be 'healthy' as they felt that the nature of their work did not allow them to lead a healthy lifestyle;
- Education around positive changes that can be made should form a key part of the programme, especially given that many drivers feel that their occupation precludes a healthy lifestyle;
- The first step in the process involves motivation and empowerment: helping drivers to realize that it is possible for them to implement positive lifestyle changes;

- Education around healthy eating, food for energy and how small changes can affect their lives positively is of paramount importance for drivers;

- Many of them are eating the wrong foods (increasing levels of fatigue) and for the wrong reasons (e.g. to combat boredom), and have thus developed an unhealthy relationship with, and misguided attitudes towards, food, vis-à-vis what they believe they should be consuming for energy purposes or in order to adhere to the 'stereotypical' image of a truck driver.

The campaign name, 'Get Your Life in Gear' (GYLIG), emerged from the focus group research. The tagline resonated with the male truck drivers who wanted to make changes to their weight and enjoy quality time with their partners and children.

The creation of value exchanges (i.e. highlighting the benefits of the proposed change over the consequences of not adopting the proposed change) with the target audience was key in developing the GYLIG pilot initiative. This meant that an in-depth understanding of the barriers and precursors of change were identified and used to inform development. This social marketing approach precipitated a shift in attitude – moving drivers from intention to implementation mode, so that they actively and voluntarily made changes to their behaviour. The pilot initiative had an inbuilt flexible design so it could be easily adapted to the diverse situations in which drivers found themselves on a daily basis.

The findings of the formative research prompted Sophie to consider other prospective questions for focus groups and individual interviews. She also deliberated on other research strategies that could have been adopted within this pilot initiative. Then she turned her attention to the programme goals and strategy.

GYLIG AIMS AND OBJECTIVES

The research findings were subsequently used to inform and develop a number of initiative objectives to address the needs of the middle-aged male driver profile.

Operationally, 'Get Your Life in Gear' aimed to:

1. Increase truck drivers' physical activity levels to at least 30 minutes per day, 5 days per week by the end of the 12-week period;

2. Reduce truck drivers' consumption of fatty and sugary foods and drinks by 10 per cent over the course of the 12 weeks;

3. Increase truck drivers' fruit and vegetable consumption by at least 1 portion per day over the 12 weeks;

4. Maintain a healthy weight in truck drivers and/or reduce weight by 10 per cent in truck drivers with a BMI over 25.

FORMULATION OF STRATEGY

The marketing mix

The formation of the initiative's strategy, particularly the marketing mix which has been described extensively in a previous case study (Duane and Domegan 2012), identified that there were many interrelated barriers to change, which challenged the implementation of the pilot initiative. These barriers included lack of time and energy, job uncertainty, unsociable hours and lack of roadside facilities. These insights placed restrictions on the design of the marketing mix for this project – e.g. the organization of group activities, such as soccer tournaments, were rejected given the peripatetic nature of the job of truck driver. Focus groups not only indicated diverse levels of fitness among drivers, but also suggested a need for drivers to prioritize quality time with their families. Distrust of industry regulators contrasted with drivers' enthusiasm for health checks. While the importance of making health checks available at a convenient time and location was deemed crucial, the necessity for confidentiality was emphasized particularly, given drivers' fears around the possible implications of health results on driving licences.

In addition, the formative research underlined the value of 'packaging' the pilot initiative as a lifestyle programme as opposed to a weight-loss initiative, the latter having connotations of dieting and hard work. To ensure participation, the drivers deemed it essential that the behavioural changes proposed be small and manageable and relate both to healthy eating and physical activity. By emphasizing behaviours the truck drivers could control, such as how to make healthier choices in service stations and suggesting ways to build physical activity into their daily routines, it was hoped that knowledge and behaviour change would be facilitated.

Product

Research shows that men often use health issues as a motivation for trying to lose weight (De Souza and Ciclitiva 2005). The core product, a 12-week lifestyle programme, offered two free professional health checks, which acted as a hook to garner drivers' interest. Two were offered so that changes in results could be measured pre- and post-initiative – this was in line with drivers' interest in being able to track changes over time. It must be noted, however, that changes in health check results over the 12-week period was not part of the evaluation of this pilot initiative, but used purely as a way to motivate drivers. With travel and long work hours often preventing drivers from accessing health services for routine check-ups, the health check results proved important to them, acting as a benchmark for change, which would also have a knock-on effect on their weight. Indicators included waist measurement, as well as cholesterol and blood pressure checks. The nurses gave the drivers free, confidential and impartial advice, and introduced them to the GYLIG programme to provide information on how to make healthier food

Figure CS9.2 Healthy lifestyle toolkit

choices and become more physically active on the road. A toolkit was also included to aid drivers in making healthy lifestyle changes (Figure CS9.2).

The toolkit

This product consisted of a cool bag, booklet, pedometer, tape measure, *safe*food pen, bottle of water and information on how to sign up for free motivational SMS text messages (nurses also told them how to do this).

The information booklet met the specific needs of truck drivers and contained information about how to deal with particular problematic issues highlighted in the formative stages. Sections included 'eat well', 'be active', 're-think your drink', 'mind your back', 'fight fatigue' and 'beat stress'. Other materials were also used in the development of the information booklet (e.g. 'Tommy the Trucker' and 'Pitstop'), which informed its style, design and presentation to make it as engaging as possible for the target audience. The tone adopted was succinct, yet humorous. Pre-testing of the booklet and recruitment leaflet with both target audience and relevant stakeholders was essential for ensuring drivers' engagement.

As well as providing guidance, the drivers were challenged to set their own goals for the 12 weeks and fill in a food diary for 2 to 3 days so they became aware of what they ate, how much, when and why. A pedometer was also provided to encourage physical activity. This was in line with the formative research, which revealed drivers' clear reluctance to engage in rigorous activity, while emphasizing their awareness of their ability, at least, to walk! The resource was adapted, with kind permission, from one recently developed by the Irish Heart Foundation. To stay healthy, adults are encouraged to walk 10,000 steps a day. The pedometer, therefore, was another tool used to make clear drivers' current levels of activity and to motivate them to build on this level each day.

Prompts such as a cool bag to keep snacks fresh and a bottle of water were also provided to remind the drivers to bring healthier snacks on the road.

After 12 weeks and as the final product offering, drivers were invited to return for a second health check to review their progress.

Place

The place element of the marketing mix needed careful consideration. All the formative research indicated that truck drivers did not form a static workforce and were behaviourally highly unpredictable. To access this cohort, the project planners needed to ensure that health checks were available at a convenient time. Location became another factor key to the success of this initiative: Where were the points of contact? How long would they be there? And could health checks be facilitated at key access points? Three pilot sites were selected that suited the needs of the project planners. Profiles are provided in Table CS9.3.

Pilot site 1 (PS1) was a distribution depot in NI with management who were interested in driver health. Two other pilot sites were chosen based on findings of the formative research. Sites 2 and 3 (PS2 and PS3) both had a positive reputation for catering for the needs of drivers in terms of parking and services provided. Trailers were hired to facilitate the checks on PS2, while the other two had available rooms to accommodate the service. In all three locations, site managers were given the task of informing the drivers of the times for the health checks as these individuals were more cognizant of drivers' 'routines'. By choosing the right location, the project leaders also benefited from the assistance of a key gatekeeper or health champion. This employee had the ability to lead by example and assisted in persuading the drivers in a non-coercive manner. The development of peer trust played a valuable role in recruitment.

Promotion

Given the relatively small funding available for this pilot project mass media promotion was not feasible. Internal communications and word-of-mouth were utilized, where possible, to build support. In both instances, these types of commu-

Table CS9.4 Characteristics of pilot sites

	Type of site and location	Time of health checks	Key characteristics
PS1	Logistical distribution centre, docklands area of Belfast (NI)	Mon–Tues 5am–10am	Access to approximately 100 drivers through direct and indirect employees; Health checks: Took place in two on-site boardrooms
PS2	Service station, docklands area of Belfast (NI)	Wed–Fri 6am–3pm	Docklands-area parking for up to 20 trucks popular with drivers travelling to and from ferries; area also part of industrial estate, therefore popular with 'local' drivers who worked there Health checks: Mobile units rented and placed within 100 yards of truck park due to space restrictions inside service station
PS3	Service station and restaurant, outside of Dublin, ROI	Tues–Thurs 5pm–10pm	Parking for up to 50 trucks, showering facilities for drivers, large variety of foods; hot dinners offered in restaurant, together with extensive deli-counter range Health checks: One large function room in restaurant premises rented and two 'rooms' created using rented partitions

nication increased the legitimacy of the pilot initiative. The onsite recruiters were invaluable in persuading drivers to participate and were arguably more effective than the printed promotional material designed to support the campaign. The pre-testing of these materials ensured that the relevant information was available – drivers wanted this to be humorous, not patronizing. The formative research indicated that, although men didn't diet, they did use their clothes as an indicator of weight gain. Thus, this became the tagline for recruitment. Trust was a big issue for the drivers and, therefore, they did not want the programme endorsed by any industry bodies as recent changes in legislation were eroding this relationship. A sample of the poster campaign for the pilot initiative is shown in Figure CS9.3. Like other products in the toolkit they were used as prompts to remind the drivers to make the changes. Site managers were responsible for displaying the posters. On one occasion, this obligation was not fulfilled, reducing the level of trust between them and project planners.

Other promotional materials associated with ongoing support were also built into the campaign. This was achieved through the extensive use of reminders, text, letter and phone calls. The words of John, a 45-year-old separated truck driver, working 6 days a week to pay the mortgage and support his daughter through her

Figure CS9.3 (i, ii, iii) Samples of Get Your Life in Gear promotional material

final year of school, confirm the value of this aspect of the initiative: 'Just for once, it's so nice to think that someone out there cares about us.'

Peer support, especially evident in one NI site, greatly influenced the drivers, giving them the confidence to participate and allowing them to discuss their results. The power of word-of-mouth, and peer support versus ridicule, should not be underestimated, as the following extract from the evaluation report shows:

John is about 40; he stands outside having a smoke with a few other men who don't seem to have any interest in the programme. They spend a long time talking to recruiters, joking with them and telling them that they are fine and have no interest in a health check. The recruiters reassure them and make it clear that the choice is theirs, and they move on to chatting about other things. They give them leaflets anyway, which the men take out of politeness before leaving to go back to work. That afternoon John comes back to have a health check. He looks a little embarrassed but is determined to go through with it. An hour later, one of his friends follows suit.

Referrals from other drivers became more common as the week went on, which assisted in improving the level of credibility of and trust in the programme. This behaviour was not mirrored in ROI where the majority of the drivers were recruited on their own and could be characterized as longer-distance drivers.

Price

Every element of this programme was voluntary. However, there was an initial cost in terms of time and commitment to take the health check. Participants were also required to adhere to the programme and make the necessary small, manageable changes, e.g. taking a walk, which could equate to spending less time watching TV. In some cases, drivers also admitted to feeling too embarrassed to participate, indicating that an additional confidence booster was necessary. It was hypothesized that the long-term potential benefits of weight loss, however, should offset the costs for drivers, in terms of quality time spent with their families, increased energy, peace of mind gained from taking control and, of course, the feel-good factor of being healthier.

Partnerships

Framing the problem of male obesity as wicked from the outset of the pilot initiative meant that strategic (experts in the area of men's health and obesity) and operational (employers, management, service providers) partnerships were instantly recognized as vital to the programme's success. As with similar projects, the funding agency (*safe*food) did not have the requisite expertise in every area (nutrition, physical activity, workplace health promotion). Without a coordinated partnership effort, the initiative plan or the marketing mix could not have been implemented in such an unconventional workplace setting. The advantages of engaging with key partners included gaining access to the drivers through the pilot sites and the ability to produce an information booklet on topics that mattered to the drivers.

The different types of partners that participated in the GYLIG pilot initiative are illustrated in Figure CS9.4. *safe*food acted as a 'boundary spanner', i.e. they managed the coordination of all partnership activities from planning through to implementation. From Figure CS9.4, it is apparent that different partnership categories did not formally interact with each other, the exception being organizations that were represented in more than one category of partner. This approach ensured that the partnership management process was as smooth as possible for project leaders, and that a single but reciprocal (two-way) line of communication was maintained.

The partnerships developed through the GYLIG pilot initiative contributed to the success of the campaign. However, throughout the planning and implementation process, it proved difficult to engage with any truck-driving industry representatives. As the truck-driving industry is not regulated, no unions exist to speak on behalf of drivers, and, as a consequence of the turbulent economic circumstances, the associations that did exist were unavailable to participate in consultation. Engagement with the major service providers also proved difficult.

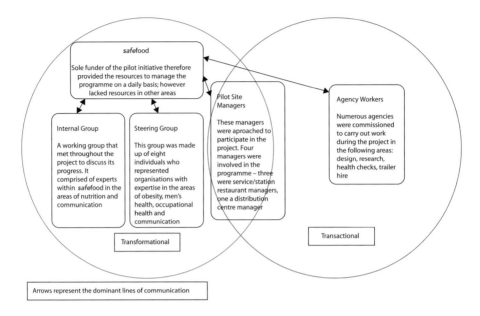

Figure CS9.4 Summary of partners engaged in the Get Your Life in Gear Pilot Initiative

SUMMARY

Figure CS9.5 presents an overview of the practicalities of the Get Your Life in Gear social marketing pilot initiative. The figure outlines a programme that is appealing, accessible, available and appreciated, and actively guided by research (Hastings 2007).

Once the pilot initiative had concluded and the process and outcome evaluations were discussed the project planners took stock of its merits and weaknesses. What were its strengths and drawbacks, its unexpected outcomes? While the pilot initiative began as a weight-loss initiative, it would not have been as successful had it focused solely on one piece of the puzzle. Nevertheless, by 'packaging' it as a lifestyle programme, were the project planners able to fit all the pieces together? Unfortunately not, given the pilot was relatively small in scope. Yet, the pilot project did unearth some disturbing truths related to the mental health of those within the industry. These are highlighted in the following example:

Paul is a cheerful man in his late fifties who promised a recruiter that he would come for a health check. He returned the next day and chatted with recruiters before going into the nurse. Upon filling out the questionnaire, it transpired that he drinks heavily most nights of the week. He had a long chat with the nurse who found him to be severely dehydrated due to the amount of alcohol he consumed the night before. He came out after his health check saying,

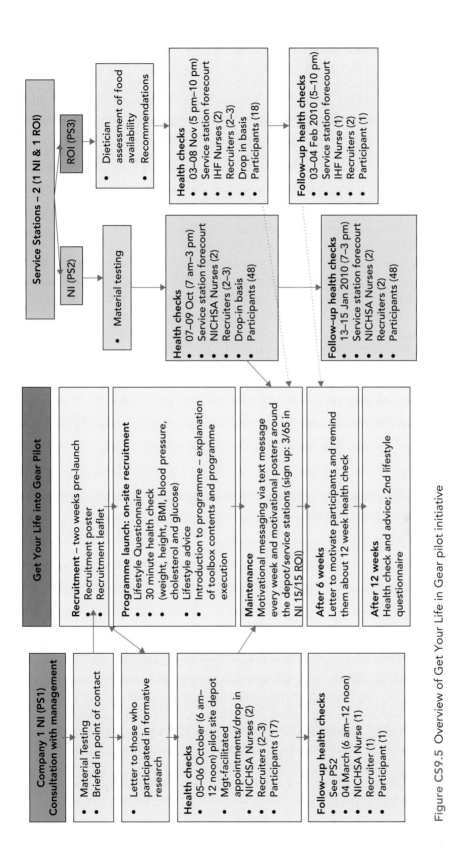

Figure CS9.5 Overview of Get Your Life in Gear pilot initiative

'That's me now; I'm going to get myself sorted out. I have a friend already in the AA and next chance I get I am going to go with him.' The nurse advised that he eat something and drink plenty of fluids before considering driving again, so he bought some hot food at the service station, and, as he said his good-byes to the recruiters, triumphantly produced two bananas from his overcoat, waved them around with a smile on his face, and went on his way.

The project planners had anticipated that stress would be a recurring factor and had included it in their information booklet. However, discussion between the recruiters and the drivers highlighted issues that went beyond stress, such as depression and alcoholism. These outcomes underline the importance of involving interdisciplinary teams in the development of such campaigns, as well as the value of synergizing change. Only when this total market approach is adopted can holistic social change take place. Nevertheless, there is evidence of a shift towards this perspective. For example, as a final outcome of the pilot initiative, more partnership work has been planned in the area of service provision, particularly in 'making the healthier choice the easier choice'. This pilot initiative has also assisted in raising the profile of the health status of truck drivers on the IOI, as well as raising awareness about men's health in general.

Notes

1   Wicked problems are extremely challenging and complex in nature fraught with conflict and tension.
2   Little Steps (2008–10) was an-all island campaign tasked with addressing the issue of childhood obesity (www.littlesteps.eu).
3   Weigh2Live (2008–present) is an online tool that offers free and independent advice and support for individuals seeking to lose weight (www.safefood.eu/weigh2live).

References

Brownwell, K.D., Cohen, R.Y., Stunkard, A.J., Felix, M.R. and Cooley, N.B. (1984) 'Weight loss competition at the work site: Impact on weight, morale and cost-effectiveness', *American Journal of Public Health*, 74(11): 1283–1285.

Butland, B., Jebb, S., Jebb, S., Kopelman, P., MacPherson, K., Thomas, S., Mardell, J. and Parry, V. (2007) Tackling Obesities: Future Choices – Project Report, Foresight – Government Office for Science.

Bye, L. (2000) 'Toward an integrated social change methodology', *Social Marketing Quarterly*, 6(3): 58–62.

De Souza, P. and Ciclitiva, K.E. (2005) 'Men and dieting: A qualitative analysis', *Journal of Health Psychology*, 10(6): 794–804.

Deacon, S. (2007) 'Tackling Weight Problems in Men in the Workplace', in A. White and M. Pettifer (eds) *Hazardous Waist – Tackling Male Weight Problems*. Oxford: Radcliffe Publishing, pp.103–111.

Duane, S. and Domegan, C. (2012) 'Get Your Life in Gear Case Study', in H. Alves and J. Vazquez (eds) *Best Practices in Marketing and Quality-of-Life Research*. Springer XIV.

Fleming, S., Kelleher, C., and O'Connor, M. (1997) 'Eating patterns and factors influencing likely change in the workplace in Ireland', *Health Promotion International*, 12(3): 187–196.

Gill, P.E. and Wijk, K. (2004) 'Case study of healthy eating interventions for Swedish lorry drivers', *Health Education Research: Theory and Practice*, 19(3): 306–315.

Gray, C.M., Anderson, A.S., Clarke, A., Dalziel, A., Hunt, K., Leishman, J. and Wyke, S. (2009) 'Addressing male obesity: An evaluation of a group based weight management intervention for Scottish men', *Journal of Men's Health*, 6(1): 70–81.

Hastings, G. (2007) *Social Marketing: Why Should the Devil Have all the Best Tunes?*, Butterworth-Heinemann. Oxford: Elsevier.

Irish Universities Nutrition Alliance (2001) North/South Ireland Food Consumption Survey: Food and Nutrient Intake, Anthropometry, Attitudinal Data and Physical Activity Patterns. Dublin, *safe*food.

Jack, F.R., Piacentini, M.G., and Schroder, M. (1998) 'Perception and role of fruit in the workday of Scottish lorry drivers', *Appetite*, 30: 139–149.

Krugar, G.P., Brewster, R.M., Dick, V., Inderbitzen, R. and Staplin, L. (2007) Health and Wellness Programs for Commercial Drivers- A Synthesis of Safety Practice, Federation motor carrier safety administration. Washington, DC: Transport Research Board.

Kwak, L., Kremers, S.P.J., Werkman, A., Visscher, T.L.S., van Baak, M.A. and Brug, J. (2006) 'The NHF-NRG in balance – Project: The Application of Intervention Mapping in the Development, Implementation and Evaluation of Weight Gain Prevention at the Worksite', *Obesity Reviews*, 8: 347–361.

Makrides, L., Heath, S., Farquharson, J. and Veinot, P.L. (2006) 'Perceptions of workplace health: Building community partnerships', *Clinical Governance: An International Journal*, 12(3): 178–187.

Morgan, K., McGee, H., Watson, D., Perry, I., Barry, M., Shelley, E., Harrington, J., Molcho, M., Layte, R., Tully, N., van Lente, E., Ward, M., Lutomski, J., Conroy, R., and Brugha, R. (2008) SLAN 2007: Survey of Lifestyle, Attitudes and Nutrition in Ireland – Main Report. Dublin, Department of Health and Children.

Richardson, N. (2009) 'Getting Inside Men's Health', Health Promotion Unit South Eastern Health Board, Kilkenny, Ireland.

Rumm, P.D. (2005) 'Mass communication and social marketing – strategies to improve men's health', *Journal of Men's Health and Gender*, 2(1): 121–123.

Smith, J.A., Braunack-Mayer, A., and Wittert, G. (2006) 'What do we know about men's help-seeking and health service use?' *Medical Journal of Australia*, 184(2): 81–83.

Swinburn, B. and Egger, G. (2004) 'The runaway weight gain train: Too many accelerators, not enough braking', *British Medical Journal*, 329: 736–739.

Wardle, J. and Johnson, F. (2002) 'Weight and diets: Examining levels of weight concern in British adults', *International Journal of Obesity*, 26: 1144–1149.

White, A., Conrad, D., and Branney, P. (2008) 'Targeting men's weight in the workplace', *Journal of Men's Health*, 5(2): 133–140.

Whitefield Jacobson, P. J., Prawitz, A. D., *et al.* (2007) 'Long-haul truck drivers want healthful meal options at truck-stop restaurants', *American Dietetic Association*, 107(12): 2125–2129.

Wilson, M., Holman, P., and Hammock, A. (1996) 'A comprehensive review of the effects of worksite health promotion on health-related outcomes', *American Journal of Health Promotion*, 10: 429–435.

World Health Organization (1986) The Ottawa Charter for Health Promotion. Geneva, WHO.

World Health Organization (1997) The Jakarta Declaration on Leading Health Promotion into the 21st Century. Geneva, WHO.

World Health Organization (2005) The Bankok Charter for Health Promotion in a Globalised World. Geneva, WHO.

Acknowledgements

The authors and *safe*food would like to thank the following individuals and organizations for their participation in the development of Get Your Life in Gear:

- Marita Hennessey, Lead Get Your Life in Gear project planner and contributor;
- Dr Birgit Greiner, Senior Lecturer, Department of Epidemiology and Public Health, University College Cork, Ireland;
- Gerry McElwee, Head of Cancer Prevention, Ulster Cancer Foundation, UK;
- Maureen Mulvihill, Health Promotion Manager and Janis Morrissey, Dietician Irish Heart Foundation, Ireland;
- Finian Murray, Health Service Executive North East, HSE and Member of Men's Health Forum in Ireland;
- Dr Noel Richardson, Director, Centre for Men's Health, Carlow IT, Ireland.

In addition, *safe*food acknowledges the support of the following organizations:

- The Chest Heart and Stroke Association, Northern Ireland;
- The service stations and work sites participating in this pilot programme.

*Safe*food thank the Irish Heart Foundation for allowing their Walking Challenge and other information resources to be adapted for this intervention.

*Safe*food would especially like to thank the many truck drivers interviewed during the development of this programme, as without their valuable input this initiative would not have been possible.

Case study questions

Finally, after weeks of report readings, conversations with colleagues and experts outside the organization, Sophie completed her audit report, and the morning had come to present it to the safefood Board of Directors. Put yourself in Sophie's shoes and ask yourself the following questions:

1. What would your audit analysis, findings, conclusions and recommendations look like?

2. To what extent do you feel that the resulting intervention reflected and addressed all the issues arising from the situational analysis and consumer insight? What else could have been done in terms of segmentation/community/upstream?

3. What are the strengths and weaknesses/limitations in how *safe*food used social marketing?

4. What would you include and exclude from your 30-minute presentation based on the theory and practice of social marketing as presented in this book?

5. How would you progress with a national roll-out of Get Your Life in Gear based on social marketing for behavioural and social change?

Case Study **10**

The National League Against Cancer's 'You Kill, You Pay' campaign: How to fight the tobacco industry

Karine Gallopel-Morvan and Christophe Leroux

INTRODUCTION

The tobacco industry generates massive profits ($900 million turnover daily from the world's four main tobacco industries) (Callard 2010) from a commercialized poison that kills millions (Tobacco kills 15,000 people every day, WHO 2009). The National League Against Cancer, a non-governmental organization, launched a campaign in 2011 called 'You Kill, You Pay', whose aim was to demand that a compulsory levy be imposed on the tobacco industry companies. The funds collected would contribute to managing the costs of the social and healthcare consequences of tobacco consumerism.

The National League Against Cancer is a French NGO whose resources depend on the public's generosity. With more than 727,000 members and 12,000 volunteers, the League is present throughout France, with 103 county committees. Its missions are to carry out research to cure cancer, to prevent and protect from cancer, and to be there for cancer patients in France.

DEFINING THE PROBLEM

The number of smokers increased in France between 2005 and 2010 (27.1 per cent of people smoked in 2005, and 29.1 per cent in 2010). In comparison, 21 per cent of adults smoke in the UK and 13 per cent in California. The number of estimated deaths linked to tobacco in France today is 73,000 (it is the main avoidable cause of death) and the social cost is €772.49 per person (taking into account health expenses, prevention campaigns, loss of productivity, etc.) which is 30 per cent of the GDP. In light of this, in 2011, the National League Against Cancer launched a lobbying campaign: 'You Kill, You Pay'. The objective was to lean on public opinion and influence the opinion of local leaders (through the League's 103 county committees) to get politics moving on the problem of tobacco and against the tobacco industry. Unlike the usual campaigns, where the approach was to show tobacco as a health problem, this time the economic angle was emphasized (with an activist element).

COMPETITIVE ANALYSIS

1. The French government – tobacco sale taxes make up €13 billion of the French government's budget. Nicolas Sarkozy, the president of France from 2007 to 2012, has often acted favorably towards the tobacco industry, which partly explains the increase in the number of smokers in France during this period. To illustrate:

   • strict anti-tobacco laws that exist in France (*The Evin Law*: A ban on all publicity for tobacco products, a ban on smoking in public places) are ineffective because there is little – or indeed no – enforcement of them;

   • anti-tobacco associations have seen a big drop in subsidies over the past few years;

   • little money is dedicated to the fight against tobacco (€0.08 per person in France as opposed to €1.1 in the UK);

   • decisions favorable to the tobacco industry have been made (the 6 per cent price increase on tobacco products is not enough to significantly bring down the number of smokers, but enough to improve tobacco manufacturers' profits. Thus, the cigarette manufacturers' profits have increased by 19 per cent in France in 2011);

   • the Ministry of Health's suggestions for the fight against tobacco are largely ignored.

2. The tobacco industry – lobbies strongly in France and is strengthened by its closeness to MPs, the presence of some of the industry's lobbyists within the

heart of the previous government,[1] the financing of public events (cultural events, exhibitions, etc.) and the frequent disregard of anti-tobacco laws. According to an NGO that is an expert on this subject, the National Committee Against Nicotine Addiction, 75 per cent of tobacconists (very close to the tobacco industry) sell tobacco to people under the age of 18 despite the fact that it is illegal to do so, and 80 per cent of tobacconists do not respect the laws on advertising in their points of sale. This NGO has won 240 lawsuits against the tobacco industry for disregarding laws currently in force.

3. French culture – strongly revolves around the idea of freedom and some opinion leaders are hostile to anti-tobacco politics because they view it as over-hygienist and destructive to personal freedom.

STAKEHOLDER ANALYSIS

Table CS10.1 Stakeholder analysis

Stakeholders	Needs	Benefits from demanding a compulsory levy that would be imposed on the tobacco industry companies	Potential role in the 'You Kill, You Pay' campaign
Politicians	• Approving policies • Adopting measures which the public will approve of • Taking into account general interest and protection of the French citizens	• Reducing the government's budget in the context of the financial crisis • Increasing the government's budget • Image improvement (for considering people's health and not the profits of multinational companies)	• Making sure current laws are respected • Putting new laws into place
Media	• Publicizing an 'event'	• Talking about tobacco differently, from an economic angle, which will please the public (manipulation by multinational companies)	• Talking about the 'You Kill, You Pay' campaign in newspapers, magazines, on TV channels, radio stations, etc.
General Public	• Not feeling manipulated by big multinational companies or industries such as the tobacco industry • Reducing the risk of cancer	• Knowing the cost of nicotine addiction for society	• Influencing politicians and the media through petitions • Strengthening perceptions that the tobacco industry is highly manipulative

103 county committees of the National League Against Cancer	• Getting people talking about the League on a local level (useful for fundraising) and recruiting volunteers • Establishing links with local opinion leaders (such as mayors and deputies) • Getting people talking about tobacco from a local to an international level	• Reducing the number of tobacco-related deaths • Mobilizing the public and finding new sources of opinions and activists • Rejuvenating the League's image and establishing it as an integral part of the fight against cancer risk factors such as tobacco • Being identified as an independent and determined force	• Talking about the 'You Kill, You Pay' campaign in a local context • Influencing local politicians through a petition
Other NGOs	• Having a government that enforces its anti-tobacco laws and votes in new ones, which favor public health	• Reducing the number of tobacco-related deaths • Having more public subsidies to be able to act more effectively	• Strengthening the impact of the campaign
The tobacco industry	• Producing, increasing sales and advertising tobacco products in a restricted context • Influencing governments (so that laws which favor the industry are passed)	• None	• Being against lobbying: Releasing press statements to criticize the idea of taxing on profits

AIMS

Following meetings with politicians, a national campaign was launched on May 31, 2011 (World No Tobacco Day) to the general public. Working on the same principle as the 'You pollute, you pay' taxes which exist for the environment, the campaign slogan was 'You Kill, You Pay'.

OBJECTIVES

The **short-term** objectives of the campaign were:

• that the public and local leaders support this idea by signing a petition, thus creating political pressure;

• that politicians present the idea of taxing tobacco industry profits at important political events;

- that the public be made aware of the profits made by tobacco manufacturers at the cost of 73,000 French lives yearly.

The **long-term** objectives were:

- putting into place a compulsory levy on tobacco at an international level, directly on the manufacturers' profits. This tax would help implement more effective action in the fight against tobacco;
- a drop in the number of smokers in France and associated deaths;
- a drop in the means of action available to the industry, in particular, marketing strategies and/or lobbying.

STRATEGY DESCRIPTION

A social marketing strategy (4Ps) was launched to meet the objectives.

The campaign cost approximately €350,000. Free publicity was also given by some media agencies. In addition, the National League Against Cancer's publicity agency (Reflex) agreed to work on the campaign at a reduced price.

OUTCOMES

1. As of April 19, 2012, more than 30,000 petitions have been signed in support of the 'You Kill, You Pay' campaign (including signatures from opinion leaders such as mayors and deputies).
2. More than 10 million points of contact were reached through the media distribution campaign.
3. 24,000 visits to the website www.tueurs-payeurs.fr.
4. More than 110,000 hits on the 'You Kill, You Pay' videos on the Internet (YouTube, Daily Motion, etc.).
5. Approximately 8000 'shares' on the Facebook campaign.
6. Approximately 250 spin-off articles in the local, national and international press.
7. 63 county committees ordered the 'products' to launch their own local campaigns.
8. The campaign also got people talking on an international level, in the *British Medical Journal* and at the second meeting of the Francophone and Mediterranean League Alliance (in Monastir, Tunisia).
9. At the United Nations Summit on non-transmittable diseases in New York on September 20–21, 2011, the French Health Minister, Xavier Bertrand, spoke on the taxing of tobacco manufacturers' profits during a plenary session.
10. In October 2011, Yves Bur and Jean-Marc Nesme, French MPs who support the fight against nicotine addiction, proposed an amendment to tax the tobacco industry on its turnover. The amendment was rejected.

11. Together with campaigns led by other French NGOs for the fight against tobacco,[2] a working group has been set up by the MP Yves Bur, which is supported by the Ministry of Health, France.

12. The candidate for President of the Republic (elected President of the Republic of France in May 2012: François Hollande) has ruled in favor of the tax 'You Kill, You Pay.'

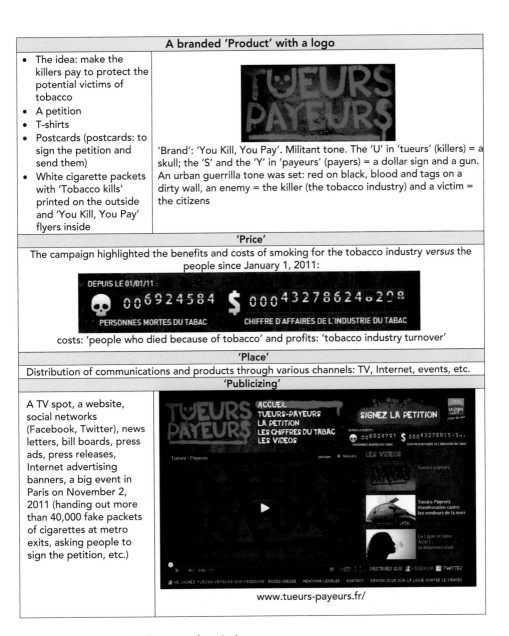

A branded 'Product' with a logo

- The idea: make the killers pay to protect the potential victims of tobacco
- A petition
- T-shirts
- Postcards (postcards: to sign the petition and send them)
- White cigarette packets with 'Tobacco kills' printed on the outside and 'You Kill, You Pay' flyers inside

'Brand': 'You Kill, You Pay'. Militant tone. The 'U' in 'tueurs' (killers) = a skull; the 'S' and the 'Y' in 'payeurs' (payers) = a dollar sign and a gun. An urban guerrilla tone was set: red on black, blood and tags on a dirty wall, an enemy = the killer (the tobacco industry) and a victim = the citizens

'Price'

The campaign highlighted the benefits and costs of smoking for the tobacco industry *versus* the people since January 1, 2011:

DEPUIS LE 01/01/11 :

☠ 006924584 $ 00043278624·208

PERSONNES MORTES DU TABAC   CHIFFRE D'AFFAIRES DE L'INDUSTRIE DU TABAC

costs: 'people who died because of tobacco' and profits: 'tobacco industry turnover'

'Place'

Distribution of communications and products through various channels: TV, Internet, events, etc.

'Publicizing'

A TV spot, a website, social networks (Facebook, Twitter), news letters, bill boards, press ads, press releases, Internet advertising banners, a big event in Paris on November 2, 2011 (handing out more than 40,000 fake packets of cigarettes at metro exits, asking people to sign the petition, etc.)

www.tueurs-payeurs.fr/

Figure CS10.1 (i, ii, iii) Strategy description

DISCUSSION

1. Presenting tobacco from a different angle, separate to health reasons, has prompted a strong reaction and an involvement from the general public.

2. Campaigns lobbying against a powerful adversary such as the tobacco industry must be active over a long period and have significant public support (it is not realistic to hope for a quick result on this).

Notes

1 www.gouvernement.fr/gouvernement/thierry-mariani/cabinet/.
2 e.g. www.CNCT.fr.

References

Callard, C. (2010) 'Follow the money: How the billions of dollars that flow from smokers in poor nations to companies in rich nations greatly exceed funding for global tobacco control and what might be done about it', *Tobacco Control*, 19: 285–290.

WHO (2009) 'Report on global tobacco epidemic: Implementing smokefree environments', Online: www.who.int/tobacco/mpower/2009/gtcr_download/en/index.html (accessed 09/08/2013).

Case study questions

1. Why was a public opinion campaign launched?

2. Why play on the economic implications of tobacco consumption?

3. What important communication tools were used for this campaign?

11

'Cold and Flu Affects More than You': A social marketing campaign targeting influenza transmission on a university campus

Sandra C. Jones, Lyn Phillipson, Karen Larsen-Truong and Lance Barrie

INTRODUCTION

Seasonal influenza and the common cold are common illnesses that can have serious implications for a person's health as well as their ability to carry out work and study. Many university students are among the age groups (18–24) reporting high numbers of notifications of influenza (laboratory confirmed) in Australia

(Department of Health and Ageing 2011). Universities host a large number of students and staff daily who use shared facilities and spend time indoors together. As such, it is expected that transmission risks in universities are similar to those in closed communities (such as healthcare settings and schools). This presents a serious public health issue for universities. In 2011, the University of Wollongong (UOW) funded the Centre for Health Initiatives (CHI) to implement the UOW Cold and Flu Campaign; a campus-based social marketing intervention, to reduce the spread of cold and flu among the UOW population.

PROBLEM DEFINITION

Each year, seasonal influenza in Australia causes an estimated 18,000 hospitalizations, 300,000 general practitioner consultations, and 1,500–3,500 deaths (Newall *et al.* 2007). Influenza and other viral infections are commonly spread person-to-person by inhaling infectious droplets transmitted when talking, coughing or sneezing (NSW Ministry of Health 2011). Viruses can survive for an hour or more in the air of closed environments (Weber and Stilianakis 2008); transmission of the virus from tissues to hands is possible for up to 15 minutes, and from surfaces to hands for up to 5 minutes (Bean *et al.* 1982).

Individuals in closed communities, such as schools, hospitals and aged care facilities, are at high risk of contracting an infectious illness as the spread of the virus is aided by humidity and diminished ventilation (Collignon and Carnie 2006). Transmission risks in universities are similar to those in other closed communities as they host a large number of students and staff daily; these students and staff use shared facilities and spend time indoors in classrooms, libraries and offices. This presents a serious public health issue for universities (Beaton *et al.* 2007).

Promotion of infection control messages and practices is recommended in community settings (Collignon and Carnie 2006). Behaviours that reduce the spread of, or protect against infection from, contagious illness include washing hands regularly, covering the nose and mouth when coughing or sneezing, avoiding close contact with others, regularly cleaning surfaces and not sharing personal items (Department of Health and Ageing 2011). Evidence suggests that university students are not aware of, or not following, these basic procedures to reduce the transmission of these illnesses even in situations of heightened alert and anxiety, such as a pandemic (Van *et al.* 2010). Perhaps most notable is the tendency to cough or sneeze directly into the air, or into their hands (which then touch communal surfaces such as computers and door handles), rather than into their sleeve/armpit or a disposable tissue.

COMPETITIVE ANALYSIS

Campaigns to reduce the spread of colds and flu have tended to focus on the provision of education material that provides little practical information regarding effective interventions to reduce individual risk of infection and transmission, 'leaving the public "warned" but not well armed to respond to the usual "cold and flu" season' (Larson 2006: 49). A social marketing approach was adopted in this project because: behaviours were being sold; the behaviour change was voluntary; the beneficiary was the individual, group or society; an exchange with the consumer was sought; and a consumer orientation was needed (Kotler and Lee 2008, Donovan and Henley 2010). Importantly, an effective strategy to engage the population in the appropriate responses to reduce the transmission of infection requires a careful consideration of the 4Ps, not just 'promotion'.

Formative research (see below) found that university staff tend to 'soldier on' when they are sick, especially younger staff, as they are concerned about letting down their workmates/supervisors by staying home. While staff perceive that it is acceptable (and even expected) for them to 'soldier on', they perceived that 'others' were not doing the right thing by attending the university when they had colds or flu and placing others at risk of infection. There was particular disdain for being coughed or sneezed on, and high perceived susceptibility for those staff who dealt face-to-face with students at reception or service desks.

Students, like staff, said they would still come to university when they are sick because they feel they can't be absent from classes; and that going through the special consideration process is too much trouble, with no guarantee that the matter will be resolved. Overall, (particularly male) students did not perceive cold or flu as a particularly important issue – it was something you 'coped with' but was not perceived as having severe consequences.

STAKEHOLDER ANALYSIS

In regard to a university-funded campaign, staff said they did not want to be 'babied'. They wanted to know that the university cares and looks after them by presenting helpful and useful information and resources. Staff also wanted to see a targeted campaign for students about being socially responsible as this was seen as having a big impact on the spread of colds and flu on campus. They felt that useful strategies for preventing the spread of colds and flu on campus would be to provide hand sanitizer and tissues at reception and service counters.

Likewise, students felt that a campus-based campaign needed to be informative and not patronizing; it should reinforce good behaviours such as hand washing and staying at home when you are sick. Thus, it was evidence that to address student disinterest (due to the lack of perceived severity for cold and flu) the delivery of the campaign messages would require some 'novelty'. Students also discussed practical and environmental changes that could be made in common areas such as the library or computer labs to facilitate a cleaner work area. These included hand wash stations at the front of each venue that people could use before and after using the venue (major lecture theatres, library, computer labs) and disinfectant wipes to use on computer keypads.

AIMS AND OBJECTIVES

In 2011, UOW funded the development and implementation of a campus-based social marketing intervention, to reduce the spread of cold and flu among the university population. The campaign consisted of six stages including a review of previous campaigns, formative research with university staff and students, development of campaign materials, pre-testing materials with the target audience, campaign implementation and a comprehensive evaluation. The key objectives of the campaign were to raise awareness of the importance of preventing the spread of colds and flu and provide clear messages to students and staff concerning actions they could take to reduce their risk of contracting or spreading colds and flu.

RESEARCH

A series of four focus groups were conducted with UOW students (both domestic and international) and staff to discuss knowledge, attitudes and behaviours related to the prevention of transmission of colds and flu. The groups had a particular focus on perceived benefits of, and barriers to, behaviours that would prevent the transmission of colds or flu. The focus groups used a predefined discussion guide and were facilitated by an experienced qualitative researcher. The focus groups also reviewed and discussed some of the existing materials (identified in the materials review) and explored responses to the different messages and images. This step in the research process was crucial as it guided the intervention development and also allowed the research team to gain a deeper understanding of the target group's motivations, intentions and behaviours.

FORMULATION OF STRATEGY

The research team worked with graphic design students to develop a series of creative concepts for use in the social marketing campaign – focusing on social responsibility and highlighting the most effective ways of preventing the spread of colds and flu. A further four focus groups were conducted with students to test the creative concepts.

As a result of the formative research and pre-testing of concepts and messages, the UOW Cold and Flu Campaign was developed. Final creative executions for students had a fun tone to attract people to them but had a serious and consistent message. The key campaign message 'Cold and Flu Affects More than You' addressed the issue of social responsibility, while the three recommended behaviours provided the target audience with simple strategies for carrying this out. The creative executions for staff had a more serious tone and emphasized the impact on others of being sick in the workplace. The images used were of professional people and clearly showed the cough and sneeze into your sleeve behaviour as well as an image that depicted a sick woman at work and her colleagues clearly unimpressed that she did not stay home.

Figure CS11.1 (i, ii, iii) Creative concepts used in the social marketing campaign

Implementation of the campaign occurred over a three-month period in the peak cold and flu season of 2011 (July to September 2011). A core element of the campaign was a set of recommendations on behaviours that individuals can adopt to reduce the spread of colds and flu on campus. These were: wash your hands; cough and sneeze into your sleeve; and stay at home if you are sick.

As well as a communication campaign (print and digital posters, a website, promotion via university media, etc.), the campaign addressed the barriers to behaviour change identified in the formative research (the 'other 3Ps'). These strategies included: desktop hygiene centres distributed across campus to enable easy access to tissues and alcohol hand rub; flu booths with branded merchandise, information resources and 'flu geek' actors to engage passers-by; and ongoing activities for staff and students.

OUTCOMES

The results of the evaluation show that the campaign was highly visible, memorable and effective.

Knowledge: Unprompted recall of the Cold and Flu Campaign was high, with the majority of students (70.3 per cent) and staff (82.6 per cent) reporting they had seen campaign messages.

Attitudes: The campaign reinforced the established beliefs that washing hands frequently and staying at home if you are sick were effective strategies for preventing the spread of colds and flu. Beliefs about the efficacy of the 'cough and sneeze into your sleeve' behaviour improved significantly after the campaign, with both staff and students more likely to believe that the behaviour would reduce their risk of contracting or spreading colds and flu after the campaign.

Behaviour: Pre- and post-analysis showed statistically significant and meaningful increases in the number of staff and students reporting coughing and sneezing into

Figure CS11.2 Desktop hygiene centre

Figure CS11.3 Flu booth

their sleeve; the number of staff staying home if they are sick; and the number of students washing their hands regularly while on campus.

DISCUSSION

Change occurred, not only attitudes and beliefs, but actual prevention behaviours. The campaign reinforced the 'wash your hands' behaviour, promoted discussion of the 'stay at home if you are sick' behaviour, and convinced many to adopt a new behaviour ('cough and sneeze into your sleeve'). The latter two are particularly notable given the existing social norms which are contrary to the promoted behaviour – the 'soldier on' and come to work norm and the 'ick factor' of coughing and sneezing into your sleeve (rather than the socially acceptable but disease-transmitting 'cover your mouth with your hand'). The intervention clearly communicated the key messages to the target audience, with high unprompted recall, and even higher prompted recall.

These changes were achieved despite several limitations inherent in the pilot project – most notably the very short period between the decision to fund the project and the launch of the campaign. Key to the success of this intervention was the use of multiple strategies – addressing all of the 4Ps rather than a single-strategy communication campaign. In addition, the use of a 'settings-based' intervention ensured high levels of awareness and exposure to campaign messages and resources to support knowledge, attitude and awareness change, all of which are sometimes difficult to achieve in small-scale community-based campaigns.

References

Bean, B., Moore, B.M., Sterner, B., Peterson, L.R., Gerding, D.N., Balfour, H.H. (1982) 'Survival of influenza viruses on environmental surfaces', *Journal of Infectious Diseases*, 146(1): 47–51.

Beaton, R., Stergachis, A., Thompson, J., Osaki, C., Johnson, C., Charvat, S.J. and Marsden-Haug, N. (2007) 'Pandemic policy and planning considerations for universities: Findings from a tabletop exercise', *Biosecurity and Bioterrorism: Biodefense Strategy, Practice, and Science*, 5(4): 327–334.

Collignon, P.J. and Carnie, J.A. (2006) 'Infection control and pandemic influenza', *Medical Journal of Australia*, 185: s54–S57.

Department of Health and Ageing (2011) 'Protecting yourself and others'. Retrieved February 9, 2012, from www.health.gov.au/internet/panflu/publishing.nsf/Content/protecting-1/.

Donovan, R. and Henley, N. (2010) *Principles and Practice of Social Marketing: An International Perspective*. NY: Cambridge University Press.

Kotler, P. and Lee, N.R. (2008) *Social Marketing: Influencing Behaviors for Good*. 3rd Ed. Thousand Oaks, CA: Sage Publications.

Larson, E. (2006) 'Warned, but not well armed: Preventing viral upper respiratory infections in households', *Public Health Nursing*, 24(1): 48–59.

NSW Ministry of Health (2011) Influenza Factsheet. Retrieved February 9, 2012, from www.health.nsw.gov.au/factsheets/infectious/influenza.html.

Newall, A.T., Scuffham, P.A. and Hodgkinson, B. (2007) 'Economic report into the cost of influenza to the Australian health system'. Retrieved February 9, 2012, from www.influenzaspecialistgroup.org.au.

Van, D., McLaws, M.L., Crimmins, J., MacIntyre, C. R., and Seale, H. (2010) 'University life and pandemic influenza: Attitudes and intended behaviour of staff and students towards pandemic (H1N1) 2009', *BMC Public Health*, 10(1): 130.

Weber, T.P. and Stilianakis, N.I. (2008) 'Inactivation of influenza A viruses in the environment and modes of transmission: A critical review', *Journal of Infection*, 57(5): 361–373.

Case study questions

1. Identify three reasons why a university campus is an appropriate 'setting' to conduct a cold and flu campaign.

2. What other audiences might also require targeting on a university campus? From the formative research (or otherwise) are you able to identify any other possible market segments for tailoring the 4Ps?

3. This university, like many other universities, has a large international student population. How would you go about identifying the different needs of the various cultural and language groups? Do you think that the 'exchange' would be the same for international students as for domestic students, and how might the campaign components differ for different groups?

12

Quebec's 'Help Them Grow'

François Lagarde and Marie Gendron

INTRODUCTION

Raising a child is one of our most complex undertakings as human beings (Westley *et al.* 2007). This case, which involved the identification of possible interventions and evaluation methodologies to monitor progress toward the focused objectives of early childhood initiatives, proved similarly challenging. This complexity made all the more acute the need for formative research and regular evaluation activities in connection with the Lucie and André Chagnon Foundation's multi-year social advertising campaign to promote early childhood development in the province of Quebec, in Canada.

PROBLEM DEFINITION

The province of Quebec is considered to be one of the most generous jurisdictions in terms of childcare and family-friendly policies. In spite of this favourable context, however, significant challenges remain in the areas of school readiness, academic achievement and school completion.

STAKEHOLDER ANALYSIS

The Lucie and André Chagnon Foundation is Canada's largest family foundation. Its mission is to prevent poverty by focusing on the educational success of young Quebecers: helping them to develop their full potential from conception to age 17, and helping to create environments that meet their needs as well as those of their families. The Foundation supports early, sustained interventions to ensure that children get off to a good start at school, and supports their parents in their role as educators.

The Foundation's intervention strategy entails mobilizing local communities and raising societal awareness in a number of areas by promoting optimal childhood development (physical, psychological, cognitive and social).

AIMS AND OBJECTIVES

The 'Help Them Grow' social advertising campaign was launched in 2009 as part of a comprehensive, multi-level approach to social change. The objective of the campaign was to encourage and support parents in providing appropriate stimulation for their children under six years of age.

FORMULATION OF STRATEGY

The campaign consisted of three waves of television advertising, ongoing Web-based activities (website and social media) as well as events, public relations and partnership activities.

A number of key decisions had to be made at each step of the campaign for which research and evaluation methodologies were adopted. Formative steps took approximately a year to complete. The campaign was launched in the fall of 2009 and monitored three times during 27 months of implementation (February 2010, 2011 and 2012). Additional formative research activities were conducted during the implementation period in order to adjust and further develop certain elements of the campaign.

RESEARCH AND EVALUATION

Research and evaluation questions and methodologies are summarized in the Table CS12.1.

KEY INSIGHTS AND OUTCOMES

The range of methodologies allowed the gathering of key insights during the formative steps, to check on progress and to make incremental adjustments based on what was learnt (Lagarde and Gendron 2011; Léger Marketing 2012).

Table CS12.1 Research and evaluation questions and methodologies

Steps (years)	Questions/Decisions	Methodologies
Problem definition (2008)	The campaign: specific role, objectives, target groups and segments	Secondary: review of literature and theoretical frameworks, population statistics and similar campaigns; consultation of major philanthropic organizations; consultation of some 70 stakeholders, experts, government officials and ethics consultants; discussion papers from five Canadian and international experts
Formative and pre-testing (2009)	Audience perspective Message framing Brief to suppliers Concept testing and refinement Media placement strategy	Secondary: industry data (e.g. media habits) Qualitative: focus groups (adults in general, mothers, fathers, lower SES) Quantitative: survey on the positioning of key terms among adults (development, learning, academic achievement), perceived importance of early childhood and perceived impact of parental behaviours
Evaluation (2010, 2011, 2012)	Campaign awareness and audience appreciation, understanding of key messages and attitude/behavioural changes	Quantitative: pre- and post-wave/campaign surveys
Further formative (2010)	Potential role of social media Further analysis of unique challenges among mothers and lower SES parents	Secondary: industry databases, popular bloggers, social media experts Qualitative: one-to-one interviews Quantitative: survey
Problem definition – Phase 2 (2012)	The campaign: renewed objectives, target groups and segments	Consultations of stakeholders and experts based on Phase 1 results Qualitative: focus groups

Initial insights

- Parents do not respond well to risk communication, but respond positively to opportunities to be in control of some aspects of their lives;
- Their fundamental motivation is universal: a healthy and happy child;
- They are focused on the present, not the future;
- They do not feel incompetent, miserable or helpless. In fact, they may be over-confident: they want to be valued and supported;
- Barriers are costs, lack of time (challenges to life/work balance), lack of access to services, fatigue and stress;

- Parents see the act of talking to their children about ordinary things as the most feasible and beneficial behaviour;
- Words are important: in people's minds, 'academic achievement' is related to the high school years, while 'learning' suggests the primary school years, and 'development' is related to early childhood.

Selected outcomes

- Campaign awareness increased from 29 per cent unaided awareness among parents after the first three-month wave, to 59 per cent after two years of implementation (from 61 per cent to 73 per cent for aided awareness);
- Appreciation of advertising was extremely high (above 90 per cent for all waves);
- Significant attitude changes were observed among parents (between 5 per cent and 22 per cent) on the perceived importance, effectiveness and desirability of the behaviours promoting early child development, such as:
  - Reading a book to your child;
  - Describing everything you do while you are doing it;
  - Telling a story every day;
  - Realizing that everything you say has an impact on your child's development, even before he or she can talk;
  - Realizing that it is never too early to begin working on language development (starting right at birth).
- Although the campaign resulted in a slight decrease in parents' sense of self-efficacy, it was followed by an increase in information-seeking, participation in blogs and forums, etc.;
- The campaign had a significant impact on the self-reported adoption of specific behaviours such as 'having a face-to-face conversation with your child/children at mealtimes, while changing diapers, during bath time, etc.'

EXAMPLES OF PROGRESSIVE LEARNING:

- The pre-testing focus groups and post-wave evaluations showed that parents respond literally to messages and images, such as reading and speaking to a child or telling stories. It is therefore crucial to focus on specific calls to action and pay attention to execution details, such as realistic casting (e.g. babies instead of two-year-olds) and voice-over content;
- In terms of positioning and message framing, it was decided to focus initially on the parents themselves (rather than their children) by positioning them as their children's greatest star (being valued);
- In order to address some of the barriers, the focus was on realistic calls to action that could easily be integrated into daily life, with the child's immediate positive response as the benefit (babbling, laughing or smiling);

- Lower socio-economic segments responded positively, but only after the campaign had been underway for a year. A long-term approach to the campaign and partnership activities is therefore essential;
- The most recent evaluation shows that a plateau has been reached in terms of attitude and behavioural outcomes among parents. This gives an opportunity to renew the objectives and reaffirms the need for more synergy with partners in order to leverage the campaign to address other components of the social marketing mix, including downstream and midstream audiences (grandparents, extended family, neighbours) as well as upstream audiences and issues (e.g. time and work/life balance issues).

Systematic research and evaluation is the ultimate demonstration of an organization's commitment to client orientation, one of the most fundamental social marketing principles. Given the complex nature of childhood development, factoring in the audience's perspective in all steps of the 'Help Them Grow' campaign was vital to making critical decisions. It also helped to stay focused on the objective to make a significant difference to the lives of children in Quebec.

References

Lagarde, F. and Gendron, M. (2011) 'Reaching the hard-to-reach with hope and help', *Social Marketing Quarterly*, 17(2): 98–101.

Léger Marketing (2012) *Campagne sociétale 2011–2012 de promotion de l'intervention précoce auprès des enfants : post-test de la campagne 'Naître et grandir'*. Quebec City: Léger Marketing, February 21, 2012.

Westley, F., Zimmerman, B. and Patton, M.Q. (2007) *Getting to Maybe: How the World is Changed*. Toronto, Canada: Vintage Canada.

Case study questions

1. What combination of research methodologies was used in the problem definition, formative, and evaluation steps?

2. Which questions were addressed through further formative research during the implementation period (in 2010)?

Case Study

13

Using social marketing to improve breastfeeding rates in a low socio-economic area

Ray Lowry, Julia Austin and Molly Patterson

INTRODUCTION

There is clear evidence that breastfeeding has positive health benefits for both mother and baby in the short and longer term in relation to obesity, blood pressure, cholesterol, and cancer. Exclusive breastfeeding is recommended by the World Health Organization for six months, with supplemental breastfeeding recommended to continue for two years and beyond (Hoddinott *et al.* 2008).

The UK millennium cohort survey of 15,890 infants demonstrated that six months of exclusive breastfeeding was associated with a 53 per cent decrease in hospital admissions for diarrhoea and a 27 per cent decrease in respiratory tract infections each month. Partial breastfeeding was associated with 31 per cent and 25 per cent decreases respectively (Quigley *et al.* 2007).

Young mothers and mothers from lower socio-economic groups appear to be the least likely to breastfeed (Infant Feeding Survey 2005). As part of the government's commitment to reducing health inequalities, a target was set to increase breastfeeding initiation by 2 per cent per annum through the NHS Priorities and Planning Framework 2003–2006, focusing especially on women from disadvantaged groups.

PROBLEM DEFINITION

Leicester, Leicestershire and Rutland (LLR) is a large health district in the UK National Health Service where breastfeeding initiation rates were 60.8 per cent compared to the United Kingdom breastfeeding initiation rates of 76 per cent. The greatest decline in breastfeeding occurs during the first four days after birth, resulting in 12 per cent of women in the UK stopping, with 22 per cent stopping by two weeks and 37 per cent stopping by six weeks (Bolling *et al.* 2007). LLR reflects the national picture with an equivalent decline in the first few days after birth, compounding the existing low initiation rates.

In Leicester, between March 2009 and May 2009 inclusive (three months before starting the project), the overall breastfeeding intention rate (expressing an intention to breastfeed) was 69 per cent and the breastfeeding rate at hospital discharge was 58 per cent. The intervention team chosen comprised of women from deprived areas, social classes C2DE (blue-collar workers/unemployed, low socio-economic status) with a breastfeeding intention rate of 55 per cent and a breastfeeding rate at hospital discharge of 46 per cent in the same three months prior to starting the project.

AIMS AND OBJECTIVES

1. To target a socially deprived area of Leicester with low breastfeeding rates and apply a cultural-specific designed programme of interventions to improve these rates by exploring with Leicester women who were unsuccessful with breast-feeding what factors had influenced their decision to discontinue.

2. To use these experiences to inform the development of a breastfeeding programme which was consumer-orientated.

3. To evaluate whether or not there was any benefit from delivering this programme to increase promotion, rates and duration of breastfeeding.

4. To develop an opportunity for midwives to 'upskill' in breastfeeding and gain transferable social marketing skills in developing the public health role of the midwife. By making the professional staff more effective (changing the behaviour of midwives), the behaviour of the target audience (potential breastfeeding mothers) could be influenced.

RESEARCH AND EVALUATION

From a national policy context the limitations of old-style 'mission and message'-based interventions were acknowledged (National Social Marketing Centre, www.nsmcentre.org.uk). There was a much stronger focus on how to develop effective behavioural interventions. The emphasis of the project was on gaining a deep understanding of the women and using this insight to effect a change in behaviour not just in attitude (National Social Marketing Centre).

METHODS

1. Two focus groups were undertaken, which used the body of intelligence and the subsequent social marketing outcomes from previous interventions to pre-test possible intervention strands.

2. Leicester women who had wanted to breastfeed but were unsuccessful were recruited for the study (previous intelligence had been gathered from women who had breastfed and professionals involved in breastfeeding). In previous successful interventions, these 'tipping targets' (i.e. target audience members who might be easily persuaded: at their tipping point) were chosen as the key intervention group as this approach has been more successful than targeting more segments in the first instance.

3. Women were identified by using a targeted recruitment tool in February 2009. A total of 18 women were interviewed who were comparable to the intervention population (same social class, lived in same area, same age band, same marital/family status). There were nine women in each focus group.

4. Participants were informed that the discussion would focus on their experiences, views and frustrations with breastfeeding. The group moderator ensured that the aims of the research were covered. A pre-designed discussion guide and stimulus material (magazines, pictures, confidential storytelling methods, DVDs) were used to promote discussion and to ensure the research aims were covered.

There are six features and concepts that underpin social marketing. These were applied to the results of the focus group identification and to direct the breastfeeding project (Table CS13.1):

Table CS13.1 Social marketing concepts used in the project

	Concept	How used in intervention
1.	Customer orientation	The focus group work gained deep insight and understanding about the consumers, their knowledge, attitudes and beliefs
2.	Behaviour	Understanding existing behaviour and key influences on it, the project team was able to devise an intervention to effect a change

3.	Intervention mix	A range of methods were used to address issues women had voiced
4.	Audience segmentation	The women were identified, using the targeted recruitment tool, to be comparable to the intervention population
5.	Exchange	The focus groups gave the project team an understanding of the real costs of breastfeeding for women and the project team was able to influence women by helping them address some of those issues, e.g. less time with partners, time for themselves
6.	Competition	The project team recognized that there would be competition in terms of lifestyle. External and internal influences were competing for the audience's time (e.g. easier and less time-consuming to bottle feed)

COMPETITIVE ANALYSIS

Three key barriers were identified from the Focus Groups:

1. Relationships

   A one-to-one relationship with healthcare professionals was seen as crucial for successful breastfeeding. The focus group feedback on NHS staff (midwives, primary care staff, health promotion professionals) was that they were 'too pro-breast', and this deterred the women from breastfeeding. Women wanted options on how to feed their babies, but received conflicting advice from professionals and family.

2. Attitudes

   The women were very aware of the benefits of breastfeeding. However, the bombardment of breastfeeding information they received from health professionals during pregnancy made them feel pressured and overwhelmed. Once their babies were born, the women found it difficult to apply this knowledge to practice.

3. Knowledge

   The women recognized that breastfeeding was a skill that needed to be learned and practised. The market research identified further barriers mothers face in relation to breastfeeding their babies, including:

   - lack of help and support to continue;
   - physical discomfort suffered from breastfeeding;
   - time-consuming, competing with current lifestyles;
   - anxiety as partners were unable to help and had less time to bond with their babies; and
   - women who were unsuccessful felt immense pressure and guilt; pressure came from midwives, health visitors and partners to continue to breastfeed for longer.

INTERVENTION

It was obvious from the focus groups (and from previous interventions) that it was not *what* was done by professionals (technical details of support, advice, when advice given), but more *how* the support was given (i.e. attitude of the staff, communication skills, an empathic approach). This lay the foundation for the intervention (see Table CS13.2).

The project team along with parent education and infant feeding specialists prepared an hour-long programme promoting breastfeeding called 'bonding with your baby through infant feeding', which was delivered by community midwives. The programme was open to all pregnant women in the intervention catchment area from 34 weeks pregnant, irrespective of their intended feeding method or feeding methods previously used, and offered an incentive of a gift (small value toiletry) to attend. The sessions were marketed as a new scheme encouraging women to help midwives develop new ways of working. The aim was to avoid social exclusion and to encourage women who may be unsure or undecided of their method of feeding.

The sessions were held in local children's centres to be easily accessible to the women, and they offered a familiar, informal environment with crèche facilities to attract the widest audience. It was envisaged that by holding sessions here key relationships would be forged with midwives, children's centre staff and the women to build on the foundation of the intervention and support breastfeeding following on from the project.

The community midwives who were going to deliver the one-hour programme had a briefing and skills update day organized by the project team, with the aim of engaging the midwives in communication skills to facilitate recruitment and to assist them with delivering the intervention programme. A role player was employed to help midwives to develop in-depth communication skills that embraced the subtleties of the new delivery mechanisms (for example, empathic listening, seeing problems from the point of view of the target audience, and understanding how to

Table CS13.2 The intervention

Product	A customer-focused breastfeeding support service
Price	Ease of access for the target population at low/no cost
Place	Target population-preferred locations
Promotion	Enthuse and 'skill up' health professionals in contact with the target audience
Testing	Materials and approach in groups
Specific channels	Concentrating on front-line clinical staff to both sell the intervention and provide the service
Paid and voluntary agents	Clinicians and supporters of target population
Incentives	Providing the support required by the target audience (especially emotional), with some physical reward for attending sessions

support women appropriate for their personal style). The project team also ensured the midwives were 'upskilled' in breastfeeding to give them confidence in delivering the programme. Infant feeding advisers visited the midwives sharing their top tips and knowledge transference.

All the women within the geographical area who were 34 weeks pregnant received a 'chat magazine' *Take 5* and a DVD 'Best Beginnings Breastfeeding'. The chat magazine subtly addressed other issues that women had brought up at the focus groups. There was a problem page, which addressed issues around new dads, sex after a baby, pressure of being a new mum, followed by articles on how to make decisions for your baby and top tips on feeding in public. There were stories about how women challenged their own social norms and popular cultures of bottle-feeding. There were quotes from mums having difficulties breastfeeding and how they overcame them. It was important that the women recognized the client group as their own and the pictures and stories were of white women, some of whom were single and others with partners not employed, which reflected the composition of the client group.

OUTCOMES

All of the 250 women in the antenatal system during the time of the intervention received the specially produced *Take 5* magazine. All had antenatal care delivered by midwives who were updated on the philosophy of the project. A total of 98 women participated in the one-hour session to promote bonding through infant feeding, which ran over three months from June to August 2009 inclusive. Breastfeeding uptake rates were recorded for all women in the University Hospitals Leicester (UHL) maternity system, which differentiated between all women and those exposed to the intervention. The results are shown in Table CS13.3:

Table CS13.3 Results of intervention

Breastfeeding intention rates for the Intervention Group and the remaining hospital catchment area prior to and following delivery of the intervention

Intention	Before (%)	After (%)	Difference(%)
Intervention	55	60	+5
All teams	68	69	+1

Breastfeeding discharge from hospital rates Intervention Group vs. remaining UHL catchment area prior to and following delivery of the intervention

Discharge from hospital	Before (%)	After (%)	Difference(%)
Intervention	46	51	+5
All teams	58	58	0

Breastfeeding discharge from community care rates for the Intervention Group prior to and following delivery of the intervention

Discharge from community	Before (%)	After (%)	Difference(%)
Intervention	37	42	+5

DISCUSSION

A social marketing approach was adopted in this intervention, unlike previous interventions which had limited success. By taking account of the clinical and social factors that determined breastfeeding behaviour and the help needed to change, this approach was attractive to the local National Health Service, as it was to build on existing strengths and be clinician initiated using insight into the target population's circumstances.

The midwives who covered the area were updated and trained, and they had raised awareness of breastfeeding. Their views were actively sought as the project needed to understand current thinking around breastfeeding. On evaluating their experiences, they told the project team that participating in the project had facilitated discussion between colleagues and that they had become more focused on delivering breastfeeding advice. The preparation to deliver interventions had enabled them to focus on their communication skills with women, developing more subtle approaches to methods of engagement.

The women who had attended the session completed an evaluation form, which gave insight into their experiences – the women had enjoyed the social inclusion, listening to each other and learning from the other women who differed in terms of age, number of children, methods of feeding and level of experience.

References

Bolling, K., Grant, C., Hamlyn, B. and Thornton, A. (2007) *Infant Feeding Survey 2005*, London: The Information Centre.

Hoddinott, P., Tappin, D. and Wright, C. (2008) 'Breast feeding: A Clinical Review', *British Medical Journal*, 336: 881–887.

Quigley, M.A, Kelly, Y.J. and Sacker, A. (2007) 'Breastfeeding and hospitalization for diarrheal and respiratory infection in the United Kingdom Millennium Cohort Study', *Pediatrics*, 119(4): e837–842.

Case study questions

1. What were the characteristics of the 'bonding with your baby through infant feeding' antenatal classes that contributed to this successful intervention?

2. Describe the chat magazine used.

3. From the market research, what were the barriers to breastfeeding the mothers reported?

4. What were the measures of success and how did the intervention do across the population studied?

Case Study

14

Relationship marketing involves parents in drug prevention, but how easy is it?

Susana Marques

INTRODUCTION

Drug problems do not exist in isolation so prevention should not be pursued independently of wider issues relating to parenting, family life and other social issues. While parenting behaviours are very important in preventing substance use, parents tend to underestimate their own influence on children and are not confident about their own role. Studies emphasize the importance of involving parents and families in drug prevention work as a way of reinforcing and ensuring consistency with drug prevention messages delivered through other channels. However, serious difficulties have been found in recruiting and retaining families (Velleman *et al.* 2000). Involving parents in drugs prevention is a time- and resource-intensive process. Transactional thinking is incapable of dealing with such a complex and challenging process.

PROBLEM DEFINITION

In theory, relational thinking can improve social marketing initiatives, but what about in practice? How can relationship marketing help to involve parents in drug education programmes?

Answers can be found in developing a process evaluation of a real-live drug prevention programme using a relationship marketing framework. Process evaluation is appropriate because it examines the 'black box' of programmes, with the emphasis on how programmes operate rather than on behaviour change outcomes.

COMPETITIVE ANALYSIS

Involving parents is difficult and challenging. The evaluation framework tried to make this complexity very explicit, namely the importance of understanding the needs, values and the broader context of parents' lives.

STAKEHOLDER ANALYSIS

To develop the evaluation framework, considerable background work was done, not only with other researchers of the evaluation team, but also with the funders, designers and deliverers of the drugs education programme.

AIMS AND OBJECTIVES

The aim of the evaluation was to understand the potential of relationship marketing in the context of a real-live drug prevention programme.

The objectives were:

- To examine whether the presence of the principles, processes and constructs of relationship marketing helps or whether their absence hinders drug education programmes;
- To examine which aspects of relationship marketing are easier to apply and which are more challenging;
- To explain how relationship marketing affects the assumptions, the design and implementation of drug prevention programmes.

FORMULATION OF THE STRATEGY

The programme: Blueprint (BP)

Blueprint was a major research programme designed to examine the effectiveness of a multi-component approach to drug education. It was the first attempt to design, deliver and evaluate a multi-component programme on such a large scale in

England, and it was intended that the results of the study would guide and inform the development of future drug education. BP was a partnership of three government departments – the Home Office, the Department for Education and Skills (DfES) and the Department of Health (DH). In addition to classroom-based lessons, the BP programme involved work with parents, media, community and policy work. Twenty-nine schools in four LEAs – Cheshire, Derby City, Derbyshire and Lancashire – took part in the programme, including twenty-three intervention schools and six comparison schools.

The design of the parent programme drew on the literature concerning the involvement of families in drug education, with the work of Velleman *et al.* (2000) being particularly influential. The aims of the parent component were threefold:

- To complement and reinforce the classroom component;
- To involve parents in the drug education of their children; and
- To increase parent–child communication about substance use and prevention.

The BP parent component comprised a range of different elements, including the following:

- *Drug Facts for Parents* – an information booklet aimed at raising awareness of drugs facts among parents, distributed to parents during spring 2004;
- *Talking about Drugs* – two issues, one each year, of a magazine containing activities and quizzes that parents could do with their children, with the aim of reinforcing the learning from BP lessons. These were distributed to parents during spring 2004 and 2005;
- *Classroom presentation* – parents were to be invited to attend a presentation given by their child's class, produced as part of the BP lessons;
- *Launch event* – parents were invited to attend a launch event, which included presentations and exercises on drugs and parenting issues, and which introduced the parenting skills workshops;
- *Parenting skills workshops* – parents were invited to attend a series of six parenting skills workshops. The workshops involved a range of approaches including group work, role plays and quizzes.

The parent materials were developed by Dixon Collier Consultancies Limited (DCCL), the School Component Contractor. It was the responsibility of schools to invite parents to attend BP classroom presentations. Launch events and parenting workshops, the core of the Parent component, were developed and implemented by the Parent Trust (The Parent Contractor), a consortium comprising the Community Education Development Centre (CEDC), the Parenting Education and Support Forum and Adfam (family drug support).

This research has greatly benefited from a rich empirical context. BP was the largest and most rigorous evaluation done to date of a multi-component drug prevention programme in the United Kingdom (Baker 2006; Stead *et al.* 2007). This provided not only valuable complementary secondary data (both qualitative and quantitative) but also, and more fundamentally, a sense both of the whole and of context.

The research design used a mix of qualitative methods, enabling triangulation:

- Interviews (approximately 20 hours of interviews with parents, PT coordinator, workshop leaders);
- Observation (approximately 40 hours of observation of launches and workshops);
- Document research (entailed materials targeted at parents; Home Office Document with the Requirements Specification (for a potential contractor); Parent Trust Proposal/Plan; Workshop Leaders Training Manuals; launch evaluation forms; Regular Reports from Parent Trust; Meetings minutes – from meetings between the Home Office and Parent Trust).

PROCESS EVALUATION – A RELATIONSHIP MARKETING FRAMEWORK

A process evaluation was designed using a specific framework that incorporates and reflects relationship marketing principles, processes and constructs.

Saunders *et al.* (2005) suggest a set of components, which constitute what they consider the minimum requirements for a process evaluation:

- Fidelity (quality) – the extent to which intervention was implemented as planned;
- Reach (participation rate) – proportion of the intended priority audience that participates in the intervention;
- Dose delivered (completeness) – number of intended units of the component delivered or provided by interventionists;
- Dose received (exposure) – extent to which participants actively engage with, interact with, are receptive to and use recommended materials or resources;
- Participant satisfaction with the programme;
- Recruitment – procedures used to approach and attract participants at individual and organizational levels;
- Context – aspects of the environment that may influence intervention implementation or study impacts and outcomes.

The evaluation framework for BP does not exclude those components but approaches them from a relationship marketing perspective. This has profound implications. For example, the very concept of 'dose delivered and dose received',

Table CS14.1 Evaluation components and research questions

Evaluation components	Research questions
Key principles of relationship marketing: Consumers seen as the main drivers of the value creation process, Service logic, Process management	What were the main assumptions of the programme? To what extent did the programme assess parents' needs and values? What were the main resources of the programme? How was the programme managed (process versus functionalistic)?
Partnerships and networks	To what extent were partnerships developed?
Key processes: Communication, Dialogue, Interaction and value	To what extent were the key processes explored? To what extent were the programme components and sub-components integrated and linked? To what extent were opportunities for value creation developed and/or explored? How did parents experience the programme?
Key constructs: Trust, Commitment, Satisfaction, Identification, Perceived value and cooperation	To what extent were trust, commitment, satisfaction, identification, perceived value and cooperation developed?
	What were the main strengths and weaknesses of the programme? How critical were these strengths and weaknesses to the programme? What were the key contextual factors and how did the programme deal with them?

to some extent, contradicts the idea of co-creation and value transformation through dialogue and interaction – key processes of a relationship marketing strategy. In terms of recruitment and delivery, these are examined as value creation processes rather than as straightforward and/or isolated processes. Moreover, rather than simply examining satisfaction and treating it as a 'dose received' issue, examining satisfaction as well as five other relational constructs as evaluation components in themselves is important. Therefore, the nature of the evaluation components and specific evaluation questions is different from that suggested in the literature on process evaluation. The specific evaluation components and questions are described in the Table CS14.1.

DISCUSSION

The analysis is structured according to the strengths and weaknesses around the principles, processes and constructs of relationship marketing to demonstrate whether and how these were applied by the programme (Table CS14.2). The

Table CS14.2 Strengths and weaknesses of the programme

Strengths	Weaknesses
The multi-component nature of the programme Communication process: BP parent materials and their relational approach	Parents seen as targets rather than partners: • assumptions of experience and expertise; • no needs and values assessment; • single delivery model
Interaction process: launches and workshops delivered in a relational style Value process: • parents enjoyed participating in the launch and workshops; • parents learned important skills; • parents experienced relational benefits Key relational constructs: parents who attended the workshops trusted the workshop leaders, they were satisfied and they perceived value in the launches and workshops	Product-logic: limited resources (time, knowledge, people) Weak partnerships and networks with potential key partners Functionalistic management of the programme and sub-optimization: • workshops and launches, BP materials and school component seen as specialized functions: sum of isolated parts rather than a whole; • low synchronicity between the parent and the school components Persuasion, not dialogue process: missed opportunities to learn with parents about their needs and values Interaction process as a sum of isolated parts: • missed opportunities to link the launches with the workshops; • missed opportunities to link the workshops with the BP parent materials and the school component; • poor and inconsistent delivery of BP key messages Value process and missed opportunities to create value: • no follow-up on parents and no feedback; • continuity and progression routes were not addressed Relational constructs: their full potential was not explored

relationship marketing principles were particularly challenging to explore and this seriously undermined the programme. For instance, parents were treated as targets rather than partners; the programme was managed according to a functionalistic perspective; it worked upon a product logic, with very limited resources; and true partnerships did not develop with potential key partners such as schools and local agencies. The processes were only partially applied. The BP parent materials did have relational potential; delivery of launches and workshops worked according to a relational style; and parents enjoyed participating in the launches and workshops. However, recruitment and delivery were not managed as integrated processes. Several opportunities for dialogue were missed and the links between the launches, the workshops, the BP parent materials and the school component were weak, causing sub-optimization. Relational constructs were not fully explored. While parents who attended the workshops trusted workshop leaders, perceived value, were satisfied and felt committed, for the great majority of BP parents, workshop leaders, schools and drug school advisers, the constructs were not applied – an omission which yielded negative consequences.

The process evaluation allowed the identification of the vision that shaped the programme and an understanding of how that vision affected its assumptions, design and implementation. The findings suggest that the programme was oriented and shaped by a transactional approach which affected its assumptions and undermined its design and implementation.

Assumptions are very important because they influence the way we understand and see things and the way we act. BP is a very good illustration of that. It was assumed that the Parent Trust's expertise and experience would be sufficient to make the programme work. This led to the assumption that the launch and workshops would be appealing to parents and that parents would simply need to be persuaded to participate.

Assumptions influenced the design and the implementation. The assumption of success made the design overly technical and weak from a strategic point of view. Issues such as key resources, the appropriate management perspective and the need to establish partnerships were not addressed in the PT's proposal. Moreover, the design of that proposal lacked a vision of the whole, clarity and explanatory power. It was not explicit about the link between the launch, the workshops, the parent materials and the school component. Furthermore, the design did not explain why things were the way they were. This is especially important if we take into consideration that the design of BP materials, the launch and workshops, the recruitment, and the project delivery were all in the hands of different people. In such a context, a clear design is critical so that funders, designers, deliverers and implementers share the vision of the programme. In BP, the relationship between design and implementation is evident: the problems with implementation seem to reflect the lack of vision and strategic thinking of the design.

CONCLUSIONS

Relationship marketing raises critical challenges to social marketers. As a new foundation for thinking, relationship marketing is radically different from transactional marketing. The principles, processes and constructs of relationship marketing have a lot of potential. Nevertheless, as this case shows, the transference of relationship marketing to social marketing raises critical challenges and requires deep changes in social marketing thinking and practice.

Relationship marketing is much more than a technique. Relationship marketing is a rigorous methodology and it is important to see beyond its technical potentialities. This implies that recruitment and delivery must be reconceptualized as dialogue, interaction and value-creating processes, which, in turn, will maximize the integrative potential of relationship marketing. In sum, relationship marketing requires strategic vision and a sense of the whole.

Relationship marketing demands critical thinking. This case demonstrates that relationship marketing has major implications in the assumptions, design, implementation and evaluation of social marketing programmes. It also demonstrates that evaluation can be used as a critical exercise of de-construction, making things explicit, visible and open for discussion.

References

Baker, P.J. (2006) 'Developing a Blueprint for evidence-based drug prevention in England', *Drugs: Education, Prevention and Policy*, 13: 17–32.

Saunders, R.P., Evans, M.H. and Joshi, P. (2005) 'Developing a process evaluation plan for assessing health promotion program implementation: A how-to guide', *Health Promotion Practice*, 6(2): 134–147.

Stead, M., Stradling, R., MacNeil, M., Mackintosh, A.M. and Minty, S. (2007), 'Implementation evaluation of the Blueprint multi-component drug prevention programme: Fidelity of school component delivery', *Drug and Alcohol Review*, November, 26: 653–664.

Velleman, R., Mistral, W. and Sanderling, L. (2000) *Taking the message home: Involving parents in drugs prevention*, Drugs Prevention Advisory Service, Home Office.

Case study questions

1. Identify the RM challenges faced by the BP parent programme?

2. How can relational thinking improve the design of complex and multi-component drug prevention programmes?

3. Can the learning from this case be transferred to other social marketing areas/problems? Discuss and explain.

4. Other possible questions to consider – does RM have stronger potential:

   (a) Where the objective is prevention?

   (b) Where the programmes are complex and multi-component?

   (c) In terms of encouraging long-lasting changes in lifestyle behaviours?

15

'Turn it Off'

Doug McKenzie-Mohr

INTRODUCTION

The *Turn it Off* project involved a unique multi-sectoral partnership, initiated by Environment Canada, Ontario Region and developed in conjunction with McKenzie-Mohr Associates and the Ministry of the Environment. Project funders included the Federal Government's Climate Change Action Fund, the City of Toronto (Toronto Atmospheric Fund), the Ontario Ministry of Environment's Drive Clean Office, and Environment Canada, Ontario Region. This case study is a condensed version of the final report from this project.

PROBLEM DEFINITION

While a wide array of public activities contribute to greenhouse gas emissions, one stands out for the potential ease with which it can be altered. This activity involves having motorists turn their engines off while parked and waiting in their vehicle. In Canada, vehicle engine idling is ubiquitous. During the peak of Canadian winters, vehicles are idled approximately eight minutes a day. Natural Resources Canada reported that, in one day alone, Canadian motorists collectively idle their vehicles for a total of 75 million minutes. In aggregate, this idling uses 2.2 million litres of fuel and results in the release into the atmosphere of over 5 million kilograms of greenhouse gases.

The *Turn it Off* project used the unique methodologies of community-based social marketing (CBSM) to encourage members of the public to avoid idling their engines while waiting in their vehicles. CBSM is an innovative approach to facilitating behavior change, emphasizing personal contact and communications, and provides an attractive alternative to traditional information-intensive public environmental outreach campaigns. It involves identifying the barriers to an activity, designing a strategy to overcome these barriers using knowledge from the social sciences, piloting the strategy to ensure that it is successful, and then implementing it on a broader scale.

COMPETITOR ANALYSIS

This project followed a series of sequential steps in developing and applying CBSM strategies at community locations (schools and Toronto Transit Commission 'Kiss-n-Ride' parking lots[1]) in the City of Toronto.

Barrier identification: Existing research on barriers and motivations relating to the behavior of engine idling while waiting in a vehicle was reviewed and consolidated. This research indicated that an effective social marketing strategy would need to:

- remind drivers to turn off their engines;
- clarify the brief length of time that a vehicle should be idled for before being turned off (10 seconds);
- develop community norms that support turning off an engine as the 'right thing to do'; and
- be delivered during warmer months, as comfort and safety are important reasons why idling occurs seasonally.

FORMULATION OF STRATEGY

Two CBSM techniques were considered to encourage motorists to avoid idling their vehicle engines while waiting:

1. **Strategy design:** Visual prompts, signs or auditory aids that remind people to carry out an activity that they might otherwise forget. It was envisioned that signs would be placed in close proximity to where motorists idle their vehicles to remind them to turn their vehicle engines off.

2. **Commitment strategies:** Gaining a commitment to turn off a vehicle engine could potentially be a powerful factor in reducing idling, especially if these pledges were public. Further, making these commitments public might assist in

the development of community norms that turning off an engine is 'the right thing to do.'

Focus groups: Three focus groups were conducted to seek feedback on the proposed strategies. Two of these sessions involved drivers who drop off/pick up children from schools, and one involved drivers who drop off/pick up passengers at a TTC 'Kiss-n-Ride' area. The primary purpose of these sessions was to obtain feedback from typical drivers on the proposed strategies and communications materials for the pilot. The participants made a variety of suggestions regarding the graphics and communications that had been proposed. One of the most significant contributions regarded the anti-idling pledge card that had been prepared. Participants expressed concerns that drivers may feel uncomfortable about signing the pledge cards due to privacy issues.

Based on the feedback from the focus groups, the following communications approaches were developed:

- 'No Idling' signs – A minimum of four temporary signs were prepared for each location to encourage drivers to turn their engines off while waiting. These signs were mounted on concrete bases in order that they could be placed in highly visible locations at each site.
- 'No Idling' window stickers – Commitments in this project were obtained and made public by asking motorists to place a sticker in their window that said 'For Our Air: I Turn my Engine Off When Parked'.
- Information card – Motorists from whom commitments were sought were also provided with an information card that indicated that reducing idling would save money, reduce air pollution and decrease greenhouse gas emissions.

All measurements in this project were made between the last two weeks of May (late spring) and third week of July (mid-summer). The testing of the CBSM techniques involved three stages: baseline data collection; implementing the interventions; and collecting follow-up data:

1. **Baseline data collection:** Baseline measures were taken for 10 days to determine the *frequency* with which motorists idle their vehicle engines while waiting at 12 locations (six schools and six TTC Kiss-n-Ride Sites). The *duration* of idling was also measured. These measurements were taken using *random time sampling*. Random time sampling involves selecting at random small time intervals (e.g. 30 minutes) during which the behavior of motorists at parking lots is observed. In identifying time periods for measurements, consideration

was given to times when motorists were most likely to idle their vehicles (e.g. end of the school day; end of work, etc.). During the baseline period, 53 percent of motorists were observed idling, suggesting that significant opportunity existed to reduce idling through the application of community-based social marketing.

2. **Strategy implementation:** Following these baseline measurements, the CBSM techniques were tested by randomly assigning the six sites in each category (school and TTC) into three groups of two:

   - Two schools and two TTC sites had signs prominently placed in locations where motorists frequently idle (signs only condition).
   - Two schools and two TTC sites also received the signs but, in addition, commitments were sought from motorists. These motorists also received the information card.
   - Finally, two schools and two TTC sites received neither the signs, commitments nor information cards. These four sites served as a control against which changes in the other conditions could be compared.

3. **Collecting follow-up data:** Once the strategies had been implemented, follow-up measurements were obtained for 10 days, again using random time sampling. The intervention was delivered first at the schools and then at the TTC locations. A small team of 'project monitors' was hired to collect baseline data, implement the interventions, and conduct the follow-up measurements. These monitors were carefully trained to collect and record data, and to properly identify idling vehicles (e.g. look for exhaust; vibrating tail-pipe or antenna; vehicle noise, etc.). Data recording forms and 'tip sheets' were prepared to assist monitors and ensure a consistent approach to data collection.

OUTCOMES

Overall, in the course of this project, 8,435 observations of motorists' idling behavior were made. Given the large number of observations made, these findings are indicative of what could occur if this project were implemented on a larger scale.

Pilot results:

- The combination of commitment and signs reduced idling by 32 percent and idling duration by a staggering 73 percent.
- The signs by themselves did not reduce idling incidence or duration.
- Analysis by site location (school or TTC) revealed that the combination of signs and commitment was particularly effective in school settings. In total, 2,377 observations were made of motorists' idling behavior at the school sites. At school sites, the combination of signs and commitment reduced engine idling by 51 percent and duration by 72 percent.
- In total, 6,058 observations were made of motorists' idling behavior at the TTC sites. As with the schools, the combination of signs and commitment was the

most effective strategy in reducing both idling incidence and duration. At TTC Kiss-n-Ride sites, the combination of signs and commitment reduced engine idling by 27 percent and duration by 78 percent.

The combination of signs and commitment had a significant and consistent impact upon idling incidence and duration. Since baseline observations revealed that over 50 per cent of motorists idled their vehicle, this strategy has considerable potential for reducing emissions from idling.

Questions on Case Study

1. Why might the community-based social marketing strategy have been more effective at the schools than at the TTC Kiss-n-and Ride sites?

2. If you were analyzing the results from this case study what might you do differently?

3. How could you know what elements of the anti-idling strategy were responsible for the reductions in idling observed?

Note

1   'Kiss-n-Ride' passenger drop-off/pick-up facility at transit stations – the area has a round indoor waiting area for passengers, with about 20 temporary parking spaces circularly surrounding the structure.

Case Study **16**

Hospital emergency department overcrowding: A social marketing approach

Juan M. Rey, José Montero and Rafael Araque

INTRODUCTION

This case study examines the measures taken by the Andalusian Health Service (SAS) in an attempt to solve the problem of emergency department (ED) overcrowding, and how, following the poor results achieved by the SAS, the Universities of Granada and Cordoba have made alternative proposals to address this issue in a more systematic manner from a social marketing approach.

PROBLEM DEFINITION

The overcrowding of EDs in the public hospitals of Andalusia has become a chronic problem in recent years, largely due to the inappropriate use of emergency care by the population. EDs are designed to provide highly professional medical treatment, with special resources that are readily available to patients who require urgent care at any time of the day or night. However, these services, which should be used only in exceptional circumstances, have now become an all too frequently demanded service within the health system of Andalusia for various reasons.

More than 580 of every 1,000 Andalusians visit EDs each year, double the European average. It is assumed that, given a life expectancy of 80 years, Andalusians will visit EDs 40 times over the course of their lives (Office of the Andalusian Government Spokesperson 2010). These data are even more disconcerting bearing in mind that the health system of Spain offers universal and accessible coverage of internationally recognized quality.

In Andalusia, as in the rest of Spain, the health system is essentially organized as follows:

1. There is a first level of care, generally called 'primary care', which is delivered by general practitioners. The facilities where such care is provided are known as healthcare centres. At this level, general practitioners can refer patients to a specialist if required.
2. A second level, called 'specialized care', is delivered in hospitals and specialized centres. It is at this second level that hospital EDs are located. Some healthcare centres, only those that are strategically located in city centres, provide a limited number of emergency services.

No other healthcare departments have evolved so intensely in the last 20 years. Structural improvements have been undertaken in EDs in terms of space and resources, organizational changes or by increasing the number of staff and specialists. As these departments are highly accessible (in economic, administrative, physical and temporal terms), very efficient, and provide quality care, they have earned wide acceptance and prestige among the general population. These factors have resulted in a clear improvement in both the quality and quantity of the care delivered as well as a steady increase in demand, thus exacerbating the chronic problems affecting EDs: saturation, overcrowding, and excessively long waits for initial care and diagnostic tests, among others.

The growing demand for emergency care can be attributed to population growth, ageing and the increasing prevalence of chronic medical conditions, but also increasingly to the use of EDs as an alternative source of care for non-urgent problems that could be treated on an out-patient basis. This is evidenced by the fact that, while the use of ED services has increased in frequency, the percentage of critically ill patients has not.

This increase in demand for ED services has important implications for healthcare:

1. EDs perform tasks that are typical of primary and other non-urgent levels of care, but cannot provide patients the continuity of care that is required to properly address health problems or the preventive practices that the primary care level offers.

2. It is difficult to treat patients with serious conditions in an effective manner as ED overcrowding impacts on the quality of care. Moreover, such overcrowding leads to increased healthcare costs. It is estimated that the cost of treating a non-urgent condition at an ED is between 2.5 and 3 times higher than if treated in a non-urgent consultation (Pasarín *et al.* 2006).

In response, the SAS adopted a series of measures in an attempt to alleviate overcrowding in emergency departments. Specifically, the SAS has gradually implemented the following strategies:

- Increased waiting times by classifying users according to type (from users with trivial problems who are given very long waiting times to very urgent users who have not undergone triage).
- Improved classification in triage. Often it is difficult to implement the established guidelines, especially when there may be young doctors or nurses in triage.
- Inform/advise users during triage regarding the appropriate steps to be taken in the event of future ailments or problems of a similar character. This strategy is probably the least aggressive and the one that causes staff the fewest problems.
- Referral of users to primary healthcare centres or not attend to trivial cases. This strategy is problematic for two reasons: first, by law, EDs are required to provide care; and, second, because users could suffer a problem that is unrelated to the initial reason for their visit and resort to the media to accuse the ED of denying care to a person in need.
- Publication of brochures with information on the proper utilization of healthcare services, their functions and roles, the exact location of healthcare centres, website addresses, opening hours as well as the hours of EDs in primary healthcare centres that have such departments.

However, the results of the above measures were not as successful as hoped. In Andalusia, about 40 per cent of all hospital emergencies attended to in 2010 could have been dealt with during scheduled visits to a primary care facility, either due to their being trivial or because they did not require urgent care. About another 20 per cent could have been resolved at the EDs of primary care facilities.

All of the above highlighted the need to approach the problem of ED overcrowding in a different manner. With this aim, a research group from the University of

Granada and the University of Cordoba began working on a solution from a social marketing perspective. In what follows, some of the conclusions reached and proposals made as a result of the research are summarized.

AIMS AND OBJECTIVES

The aims of the social marketing approach were to:

1. gain a better understanding of the behaviour of ED users in Andalusia;
2. based on objective (1), segment the population and establish different strategies according to type of user; and
3. reduce ED overcrowding in Andalusia.

COMPETITIVE ANALYSIS

Although social agents do not explicitly encourage behaviour contrary to the proper utilization of EDs, certain aspects that are at times well intentioned could contribute to the inappropriate behaviour of ED users:

- The medical staff themselves can be a source of contradictory messages that eventually have an adverse effect on patients' behaviour. Physicians often contribute to a certain level of social dependence among their patients. Messages such as 'see your doctor if you have any questions' or 'do not self-medicate' may unwittingly encourage the overusage of health resources, thus leading to problems of ED overcrowding and even deadlocks.
- The political irresponsibility of neighbouring countries that prompt their citizens to take advantage of Spain's and, by extension, Andalusia's wider healthcare coverage compared to that of their country of origin has encouraged health tourism.
- Legislative changes are currently being proposed by politicians to revoke the right of illegal immigrants to receive treatment in healthcare centres and permit them to only receive medical care in EDs. Clearly, this will further exacerbate the chronic problem of excess demand for emergency medical services.

STAKEHOLDER ANALYSIS

Table CS16.1 shows the needs, benefits and potential roles of some of the major stakeholders involved in promoting appropriate behaviours among users of public hospital EDs.

RESEARCH

To understand the behaviour of ED users with a view to segmenting this particular population and targeting proposals for change, both the providers of these services

Table CS16.1 Stakeholder analysis

Stakeholders	Needs	Benefits	Potential Role
Citizens	• Quality healthcare	• Reduced waiting times for treatment in the ED • Provide resources that can be invested in improving the services delivered	• Do not take advantage of ED services for non-urgent cases
Governments	• Improve efficiency of health services • Promote effective awareness campaigns • Design effective policies for social action • Balanced public budgets	• Reduce ED overcrowding • Improve government's social reputation • Lower healthcare costs	• Support the design of awareness campaigns on ED utilization • Invest in improving primary care services (professionalization, times, processes, etc.) • Regulation of the health service
Healthcare community	• Deliver effective services • Avoid diagnostic errors	• More time available for urgent care as trivial cases are diverted • Provide more resources (rooms, beds, staff, etc.) • Improved accuracy of diagnoses	• Educate the public on the proper utilization of health resources • Deliver quality care at different points of the health circuit
Media	• Commercial success • Good stories	• Contribute to the common good (efficient healthcare system)	• Dissemination of good ED use practices • Crusading journalism on ED overuse

(healthcare personnel) and the users of two hospitals in Andalusia were studied. To do so, four qualitative research methodologies were used:

1. an analysis of internal ED documents and a review of the relevant literature;
2. in-depth interviews with users;
3. ethnographic interviews with ED staff; and
4. ethnography of both ED staff and users. In the first hospital, a pre-test over a period of two weeks was performed to determine the appropriateness of the methodology and subsequently conducted the fieldwork over a period of six months in the second hospital.

The notes and transcripts of the material obtained were used for the subsequent semantic analysis, to establish categories and meanings, and to obtain the resulting segments. To carry out this process – the fieldwork and the subsequent analysis – experts were used in these methods; specifically, Hammersley and Atkinson (1995), Kvale (1996) and Hagen (1992).

OUTCOMES: SEGMENTATION AND BARRIERS

Segmentation

The study provided valuable information that permitted the researchers to segment users who frequent hospital EDs:

1. **Urgent users**: These are users who are considered to be in need of immediate care due to the severity of their condition or because they are in a life-threatening situation (cardiac arrest, altered level of consciousness, signs of severe gastrointestinal bleeding, severe dyspnoea, etc.).
2. **Non-urgent users** (trivial): These are users who present to the ED with a non-urgent condition of little or no clinical severity and of minimum diagnostic and therapeutic complexity that may be treated effectively in a primary care facility and are therefore most likely to be discharged from the ED. These are also the most problematic ED users. Based on the findings obtained through the fieldwork, these users were further classified into three segments:
   - **Perceived urgency**: These users fear that their condition may be severe, thus prompting them to visit the ED to alleviate their anxiety. This type of user truly believes his or her problem is urgent and therefore seeks treatment at the ED.
   - **Users who do not know where to seek treatment**: This category includes users who know their problem is not urgent but do not know where to seek medical care. This is especially true when healthcare centres are not open, or, in the case of non-residents in urban areas, it is easier to go directly to an ED due

to their high visibility than to find out which type of healthcare facility may be more appropriate for their condition or situation.

- **Overusers:** Overusers are fully aware that their condition does not require urgent care and know where they must go to seek treatment, but find it faster and easier to visit the ED. This segment includes users with mild respiratory infections, or the elderly who come to the ED to have their blood pressure taken.

Barriers

The research also revealed a number of barriers to changing the behaviour of trivial users:

- EDs are perceived as a way to avoid waiting lists or to receive care more quickly.
- The lack of flexible hours at healthcare centres makes it difficult for those who are working to seek care at these facilities.
- Fear that the condition will worsen or that suffering will increase while waiting to be attended.
- Belief that EDs have a greater capacity than healthcare centres for solving problems.
- Beliefs or perceptions instilled by the medical profession regarding patients' lack of autonomy or ability to cope with their condition on their own.
- The social structure of a culture based on the consumption of public resources. The free-rider problem is common in healthcare resource consumption.

FORMULATION OF STRATEGY

In view of the analysis, a series of strategies were proposed based on marketing mix variables, bearing in mind that the desired behaviour needs to be practised, repeated and sustained over a long period of time. Moreover, such behaviour leads to high costs and intangible benefits.

The segmentation of trivial users is summarized according to the 4Ps in Table CS16.2.

DISCUSSION

The limited success of the policies implemented by the SAS does not mean that they are not valid when considered in isolation. However, they did lack a coordinated and more holistic or systemic vision. It is in this sense that a social marketing approach could enhance and complement the effect of such policies to eliminate or alleviate ED overcrowding.

Table CS16.2 Segmentation of trivial users

SEGMENTATION OF TRIVIAL USERS			
	Perceived urgency	Do not know where to seek treatment	Overusers
Product		Use of primary care consultations	
	Visit EDs at healthcare centres		
		Prevent chronic conditions from going unattended. Visit a healthcare centre when they start	
		Ask pharmacists for advice for minor ailments	
Promotion	Publicize the existence of EDs in healthcare centres		
			Publicize the advantages of being treated for non-urgent conditions in healthcare centres
			Publicize the improvements or achievements of primary care in Andalusia
		Present pharmacists as professionals trained to give medical advice	
	Raise awareness of longer waiting times for non-urgent cases		
	Raise awareness of the implications of devoting resources to attend to non-urgent cases		
Place		More flexible hours at primary care facilities	
			Reduce waiting lists to perform diagnostic tests
		Strengthen family physicians' capacity to resolve problems. Provide them with the necessary resources and incentives to attend to cases that saturate hospital EDs	
	Increase the number of healthcare centres with EDs		

(Continued overleaf)

Table CS16.2 Continued

SEGMENTATION OF TRIVIAL USERS		
Perceived urgency	Do not know where to seek treatment	Overusers
	Avoid sensationalistic messages in the mass media on primary care. Encourage messages about improvements in primary care	
	Improve the established circuits in the Andalusian public health system	
Train emergency personnel in social skills to cope with stressful situations		
Improve the tangible elements of EDs		

Specifically, three key contributions are identified as follows:

1. Distinguishing segments according to type of user may permit adapting strategies for action in a more effective manner, provide insight on the reasons that prompt users to use EDs inappropriately, and drive the search for solutions by approaching the problem from the user's perspective rather than that of medical professionals.
2. A multi-stakeholder approach extends the field of vision of social planners by highlighting the importance of modifying the behaviour of both users and other groups in an attempt to eliminate ED overcrowding.
3. The analysis of the primary roles of each stakeholder favours self-criticism among medical practitioners, not so much, or exclusively, in terms of their role as technicians who cure diseases, but also as prescribers of appropriate behaviour among users of medical services.

References

Hammersley, M. and Atkinson, P. (1995) *Ethnography. Principles in Practice.* London: Routledge.
Hagen, I. (1992) 'News viewing ideals and everyday practices: The ambivalences of watching Dagsrevyen' (Doctoral Dissertation). Bergen: University of Bergen.
Kvale, S. (1996) *Interviews,* London: Sage Publications Ltd.
Montero-Simó, M.J. (2003) *El Marketing en las ONGD. La gestión del cambio social,* ed. Desclée de Brower: Bilbao.
Oficina del Portavoz del Gobierno Andaluz (2010) Entrevista a Francisco Murillo, director del Plan Andaluz de Urgencias y Emergencias, Entrevista a Francisco Murillo, director del Plan Andaluz de Urgencias y Emergencias, www.

juntadeandalucia.es/presidencia/portavoz/055972/entrevista/francisco/murillo/director/plan/andaluz/urgencias/emergencias.

Pasarín, M.I., de Sanmamedb, M.J.F., Calafella, J., Borrella, C., Rodrígueza, D., Campasolc, S., Tornéd, E., Torrase, M.G., Guargad, A. and Plasènciaa, A. (2006) 'Razones para acudir a los servicios de urgencias hospitalarios. La población opina', *Gaceta Sanitaria*, 20(2) 91–100.

Case study questions

1. What conclusions can be drawn from the adaptation of strategies to the different segments of trivial users?

2. From the multi-stakeholder perspective, what other stakeholders should be primarily targeted for change?

3. Explain which barrier or barriers impede changing the behaviour of the segment of 'overusers'.

Case Study **17**

Saathiya youth-friendly network innovative Behaviour Change Communication for family planning services in India

Sanjeev Vyas

INTRODUCTION

In general, people in North India tend to marry young.[1] Despite the government-run family planning (FP) programme available through the health care system, most young married couples are either unable or reluctant to seek FP services and products due to behavioural, cultural and gender barriers. This, along with the socio-cultural trend of early marriages, early childbearing and closely spaced births among young married women, leads to significant missed opportunities for provision of FP services and messages.

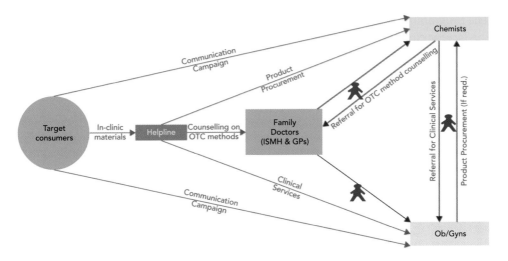

Figure CS17.1 Saathiya programme model

Saathiya ('Trusted Partner' in Hindi)[2] is a social marketing initiative, set up under the USAID-funded Market-based Partnerships for Health Project,[3] to address the underuse of FP services by urban, low-income couples. The Saathiya network is based on an innovative model consisting of 3,000 private sector healthcare providers, i.e. traditional doctors (Indigenous Systems of Medicine and Homeopathy or ISMH doctors), family doctors (GPs), specialists (OB/GYNS) and retail pharmacists. This cadre of professionals deliver high-quality FP information, services and products in selected cities of Uttar Pradesh and Uttarakhand. As well as selecting, training and promoting the providers, the network offers its users a dedicated gender-specific toll-free helpline, which has received more than half a million calls since its inception.

A Saathiya sign displayed prominently outside the clinic informs the target group about the facility's youth-friendly FP and reproductive health services (Figure CS17.2).

Figure CS17.2 Saathiya clinic sign

The programme was successfully piloted in Lucknow (October 2007 to April 2009), the largest city in Uttar Pradesh with a population of 2.5 million, and scaled up in mid–2010 to include six more cities in the North Indian states of Uttar Pradesh and Uttarakhand.

The programme leverages commercial (Pfizer, JK Ansell, GSK and Win-Medicare) and social marketing companies (DKT and PHSI) to promote contraceptives. The Saathiya basket includes condoms, oral contraceptive pills, injectable contraceptives, intra-uterine contraceptive devices and emergency contraception to offer a wide range of FP choices, strengthen product linkages and create demand.

PROBLEM DEFINITION

There is an underuse of FP services among disadvantaged city-dwellers in the states of Uttar Pradesh and Uttarakhand. Married couples with unmet FP needs have little awareness of and minimal access to the Saathiya network of doctors and chemists. This includes couples who regularly visit the neighbourhood Saathiya network ISMH providers for advice and treatment for other concerns, but who miss the opportunity to avail themselves of the high-quality FP services. This could also be because, although most people in lower-income households thought of ISMH doctors as a trusted and affordable healthcare source, they did not consider them as FP providers.[4]

STAKEHOLDER AND COMPETITIVE ANALYSIS

Most couples use FP methods inconsistently, which results in unwanted pregnancies or abortions. It takes time for users to become accustomed to any FP method. What works for one person may not work for another, and, thus, professional counselling is the key to ensuring method uptake and sustained usage. However, couples usually begin a method on the advice of close relatives or friends, and without knowing about side effects and how to deal with them. In the event the method does not suit them, they stop without consulting anyone, as they don't know who to go to. Consulting doctors for FP is simply not standard practice.

Hence, couples take FP advice only from those whom they trust (such as sisters-in-law or friends), and whom they regard as sufficiently close. However, the advice of 'trusted sources' may not always turn out to be the correct advice for them because the advice is often based on personal experience rather than on comprehensive knowledge of FP issues.

AIMS AND OBJECTIVES

The communication focused on young married couples with a need for FP to space their children. Understanding FP-seeking behaviours and related barriers guided programme design and implementation. The communication tasks were fourfold:

- To lead couples, who are consciously seeking FP, to their nearest Saathiya network provider.
- To build confidence among service users so they can ask the provider about FP and make the most of access.
- To enable network providers (particularly positioning ISMH providers as FP experts) to engage with couples to help them adopt the most suitable method.
- To direct couples to the helpline for post-method adoption counselling, if need be.

FORMULATION OF STRATEGY

A multi-pronged strategy was utilized involving the use of different media opportunities, ranging from mass media to local and in-clinic, to drive home the intended messages in a manner that would ensure the desired action from the target audiences. The communication campaign for Saathiya was developed by JWT – Thompson Social, while the media planning was managed by GroupM and Hanmer MSL Public Relations respectively.

The programme logo

The strategic benefits of Saathiya were communicated through the expression: 'Khaas Aapke liye' or 'Especially for you' with the existing programme logo modified to create synergy with the new campaign idea. A base line, 'parivar niyojan sewayen, jo aapke liye sahi' (Family Planning services that are just right for you), was added to clarify the meaning of the word 'Saathiya'. The logo now also serves as the campaign logo (Figure CS17.3).

Radio

Since the programme was limited to seven cities, radio rather than television was identified as the lead mass medium for this campaign. Two radio spots, as well as a radio programme with seven episodes, were produced to position the Saathiya providers as trained FP experts in the neighbourhood, who could be trusted by young married couples for custom-made advice on FP.

The two radio jingles creatively emphasized the important campaign messages:

- Always seek custom-made FP advice and services.
- Your neighbourhood family doctor may also be a trained Saathiya who can provide you with expert advice on all your FP matters.

Figure CS17.3 Programme logo

The radio programme took the communication further by providing information on other aspects of the programme, such as different FP methods suiting each life stage. Following the 'enter-educate' format, the radio programme integrated important messages into storylines and narratives regarding the need to adopt FP for a happy and successful married life.

In-clinic materials

An important part of the strategy was to instil confidence in young couples who visit the Saathiya doctors for other health-related services so they can freely ask for FP services and advice. In this way, the clinics became an important setting for communicating the essential message – via posters, flyers and leaflets. These materials provided a call to action, encouraging couples to seize the opportunity to seek custom-made advice from the trusted expert, Saathiya, who awaits them (Figures CS17.4 and CS17.5). The helpline for follow-up advice was mentioned as well.

A series of additional campaign materials to generate visibility were created, based on situations and characters that encapsulated the core campaign messages.

Mahila gosthi and FP camp invites

The programme designed a new outreach activity in the form of *mahila gosthies* (women's community group meetings) and FP health camps (Figure CS17.6).

Figure CS17.4 (i, ii) In-clinic materials

Figure CS17.4 iii (*Continued*)

Figure CS17.5 (i, ii) Billboard designs

Figure CS17.6 FP outreach camp

Women of reproductive age were identified in low-income areas with the help of health workers and other key opinion leaders (KOLs) in the locality. About 20 such areas of low-income populations were identified in large towns and ten in smaller Saathiya towns.

Women were invited in groups of 20 or 25, and the female field representatives of the Market-based Partnerships for Health Project provided FP counselling using job aids such as flip charts and videos. The meetings had ice-breakers in the form of fun and games in an effort to involve all participants present at the venue. Women who showed an interest in over-the-counter FP methods (condoms, oral contraceptives, etc.) were invited to an FP camp, organized at an ISMH network clinic close by after a gap of a couple of days. Those who wished to know more about a clinical method (injectable contraceptive or IUCD) were similarly invited to a network clinic for counselling by a doctor and for method uptake.

RESEARCH AND EVALUATION

Provider and consumer tracking studies, e.g. mystery client surveys,[5] were conducted in the last quarter of 2011 and the key findings, in the context both of providers and consumers, are separately outlined in Table CS17.1.

Table CS17.1 Results of providers and consumers tracking study

Indicator	Value	Benchmark	Remark
% of providers proactively broaching the subject of FP	26.7%	20%	Significantly above the benchmark
% of providers mentioning side effects spontaneously	76.9%	60%	Significantly above the benchmark

Key findings:

- 26.7 per cent of network ISMH providers proactively broached the subject of FP (above the 20 per cent benchmark).
- 68.3 per cent of network providers discussed at least two modern temporary FP methods and 74.3 per cent asked clients to choose a method.
- The benchmark of 60 per cent was met with network providers screening clients by asking questions about number of children, intention to have a child and age of youngest child.
- The network ISMH providers imparting informed choice of FP methods was significantly above the benchmark of 60 per cent.
- Most providers discussed oral contraceptives with service users in detail, as well as explaining the advantages and disadvantages of the IUCD and condoms.
- A significant proportion of providers gave personal assurances that were found to be above the benchmark.
- Most providers displayed Saathiya signage and made FP information material available at the clinic.

The positive results could be attributed to the fact that the ISMH network providers proactively broached the subject of FP and that it was found to be above the benchmark. They screened clients appropriately before discussing FP methods and provided them with an informed choice. The main FP methods which were spontaneously discussed included oral pills (90 per cent), IUD (48 per cent) and injectable contraceptives (38 per cent). Most network providers discussed key advantages, disadvantages, usage information and side effects of oral contraceptives. They also offered personal assurances and ensured that the Saathiya signage and FP information materials were displayed at their clinic at the time of study.

Consumers

A different sampling design was followed in Lucknow compared to the six expansion cities. The main findings are given below.

Lucknow:

- Awareness and correct knowledge of Saathiya network increased significantly from baseline to endline.
- The proportion of the target population who trusted providers as a source of information for FP and consider them an influencer for FP choices increased from baseline to endline.
- There was an increase in the proportion of the target population who discussed FP with a provider during the last three months from 3.8 per cent at baseline to 6.1 per cent at endline.
- Current use of any FP method increased from 45.7 per cent at baseline to 56.7 per cent at endline.
- The proportion of the target population currently using FP was greater among those exposed to programme communication activities than among controls, indicating that programme communication activities contributed to an increase in current use of contraception over time.

Six expansion cities:

- Awareness and correct knowledge of the Saathiya network increased significantly from baseline to endline.
- The majority of the target population who interacted with the providers trusted them and the information they gave on FP.
- The proportion of the target population who visited health facilities for FP during the last three months increased from 0.4 per cent at baseline to 4.7 per cent at endline.
- 34.1 per cent of the target population were exposed to programme activities; 32.6 per cent to mass media; 32.6 per cent and 11.7 per cent were exposed to on-the-ground activities six months prior to the study. The proportion of the target population who visited a provider for FP in the last three months was greater among those exposed than unexposed.
- Current use of any FP method increased from 39.6 per cent at baseline to 46.6 per cent at endline. Current use among those exposed and unexposed was significantly higher than baseline. Among those exposed to programme activities, current use of FP methods was 52.9 per cent, while among the unexposed the proportion was 45.1 per cent.

DISCUSSION

There was a significant increase in awareness and accurate knowledge of the Saathiya network from baseline to endline as a direct result of the campaign. The acceptance of providers as an FP source improved among target population over time. The proportion of the target population who trusted providers (doctor/

chemist/para-medical staff) as an FP source, and those who regarded FP information as useful, significantly increased between baseline and endline. Regular
provider visits to health facilities in both Lucknow and the six other expansion
cities also ensured that the programme contributed to an increase in discussion
about FP methods. The escalation in use of all FP methods among women in
Lucknow provides further evidence of the effectiveness of the Saathiya network,
which has reaped life-changing benefits for target groups.

Notes

1 As per NFHS–3 (National Family Health Survey 2005), about 60 per cent of
   women and 51 per cent men in Uttar Pradesh get married before the legal age
   of 18 and 21 respectively; 37.8 per cent of women begin childbearing by age 19.
   There is significant unmet need for spacing (25 per cent) among young married
   women (15–24 years); TFR (Total Fertility Rate or children per woman) in
   Uttar Pradesh is 3.82 with 4.13 in rural areas and 2.95 in urban areas.
2 www.saathiyaindia.com/.
3 www.mbph.in/.
4 Saathiya Formative Research, IMRB – PQR, May 2007.
5 Mystery client or mystery shopping is a tool used externally by market research
   companies or watchdog organizations or internally by companies themselves to
   measure quality of service or compliance to regulation, or to gather specific
   information about products and services. The mystery client's specific identity
   is generally not known by the establishment being evaluated. Mystery clients
   perform specific tasks such as purchasing a product, asking questions, regis-
   tering complaints or behaving in a certain way, and then provide detailed
   reports or feedback about their experiences. After the visit the client submits
   the data collected to the research company, which reviews and analyses the
   information, completing quantitative or qualitative statistical analysis reports
   on the data for the client company. This allows for a comparison on how the
   clinics or stores are doing against previously defined criteria.

Bibliography

Agha, S. (2002) 'A quasi-experimental study to assess the impact of four adoles-
   cent sexual health interventions in Sub-Saharan Africa', *International Family
   Planning Perspectives*, 28(2): 67–70 and 113–118.
Arur, A., El-Khoury, M. and Banke, K. (2009) 'Saathiya youth-friendly initiative
   evaluation report', 6 November, Bethesda, MD. Private Sector Partnerships-One
   Project, Abt Associates, Inc.
McCauley, A. P. and Salter, C. (1995) 'Meeting the needs of young adults',
   Population Reports, Series J, No. 41. Baltimore: Johns Hopkins School of Public
   Health, Population Information Programme.

Ram, F., Sinha, R.K., Mohanty, S.K., Lakhani, A., Haberland, N. and Santhya, K.G. (2006) 'Marriage and motherhood: An exploratory study of the social and reproductive health status of married young women in Gujarat and West Bengal, India', New Delhi: Population Council.

Van Rossem, R. and Meekers, D. (2000) 'An evaluation of the effectiveness of targeted social marketing to promote adolescent and young adult reproductive health in Cameroon', *AIDS Education and Prevention*, 12(5): 383–404.

Wolfe, K. (2005) 'Youth friendly pharmacies and partnerships: The CMS-CELSAM experience', Bethesda, MD. Private Sector Partnerships-One Project, Abt Associates, Inc.

Case study questions

1. What role can Behaviour Change Communication (BCC) play in bringing about the necessary changes, i.e. increased uptake of FP and reproductive health services?

2. What strategies can social marketing programmes adopt to strengthen the supply of, and demand for, FP/RH services for the urban poor?

3. Using the Saathiya case study to outline and analyse the existing behaviour of young married couples towards FP in India, what strategies would you recommend in promoting behaviour change using local resources?

4. Are there any interesting and relevant lessons from advertising and communication campaigns for goods and services, such as mobile phones or life insurance, that can be used to develop a communication campaign for FP?

Case Study

18

Internal social marketing: Encouraging pro-environmental behaviour in the workplace

Anne M. Smith

INTRODUCTION

Most applications of social marketing focus on health-related behaviours. However, there is considerable potential for social marketing principles and techniques to contribute to environmental sustainability. Additionally, programmes typically focus on the behaviour of individuals and households. Yet it is organizations that have the greatest negative environmental impact (Stern 2000). This case describes how an 'internal' social marketing programme changed workplace behaviours, creating sustainable working practices and reducing the organization's carbon emissions.

PROBLEM DEFINITION

The increasing level of CO2 emissions and consequent problems of climate change are of growing concern, confronting society at all levels (Senge *et al.* 2008). It is of particular concern to those organizations that face pressure from a wide range of stakeholders, including governments, customers and employees, to reduce their negative environmental impact. This case study focuses on company A, a large UK organization with carbon emissions several multiples of 3,000 tonnes per year. (The figure of 3,000 tonnes was the level set by the Carbon Reduction Commitment scheme on which the UK's DEFRA was consulting at the time of the research (see Carbon Trust 2011).) The key problem for company A was how to engage employees in developing and adopting pro-environmental workplace behaviours so as to reduce carbon emissions. Initially, management decided to implement a social marketing programme to achieve this behavioural change within one department. This involved a group of approximately 100 employees.

COMPETING BEHAVIOURS

There are many competing forces potentially impacting on the individual's or team's adoption of pro-environmental behaviours. Direct competition includes:

Competing behaviours: For example, relating to excessive, or preferred, consumption, such as employees' choice of transport to work; energy usage through failing to turn off equipment or lights and wastage of materials. These were the current behaviours in which people were engaging and which were the focus of the social marketing programme.

Competing benefits and motivation: These include the internal factors, i.e. the physiological, psychological and other personal factors that people experience through engaging in the 'negative behaviours' described above. For example, individuals valued the prestige and freedom as well as the convenience of driving their own car rather than using public transport. Pro-environmental behaviours such as recycling often involve expenditures of energy and effort.

Personal influences: Some work colleagues and managers were dismissive of, or derogatory about, those who engaged in pro-environmental behaviour describing them as 'eco-warriors' or worse.

Wider influences: In the organizational setting, these included senior management, other departments and suppliers. They also included local authorities as providers of public transport and recycling facilities. All of these can potentially contribute to positive behaviours. However, their policies and actions could also create problems for engaging in pro-environmental behaviour in the workplace.

Indirect competition included:

Other social marketing messages: There was evidence throughout the programme that many employees were generally 'fed up' with consistently being told what to do and there was a resistance to constant requests to stop behaving in their chosen way.

Everyday life: Busy lifestyles and multiple commitments underpin much behaviour. Many people complained about the problems involved in being pro-environmental. For example, if you used public transport, how would you pick the children up from school on the way home?

Wider environmental forces: Many employees were not convinced by the whole issue of climate change. They pointed, in particular, to conflicting reports in the media.

STAKEHOLDER ANALYSIS

Internal stakeholders included the group of employees involved in the programme and their line managers; the department tasked with improving the organization's negative environmental impact and its chief environmental officer; other departments, for example, purchasing, engineering and maintenance, and senior management.

External stakeholders included customers, local and central government, and the local community and suppliers. Ostensibly, all stakeholders could share a common goal in reducing carbon emissions and negative environmental impact. However, as the programme developed, a number of competing interests became apparent as discussed below.

AIMS AND OBJECTIVES

The main aim was to develop and implement a social marketing programme that would change negative (or sustain positive) workplace behaviour, resulting in a reduction in carbon emissions. The objectives were:

- To identify the nature of current and potential pro-environmental behaviours
- To identify the drivers and barriers to change
- To design and implement a programme that would facilitate change by increasing drivers and reducing barriers.

FORMULATION OF STRATEGY

Research was conducted over a six-month period with employees, line managers, the chief environmental officer and his team. Multiple research methods were adopted. These included in-depth interviews, focus group discussions, participant observation and a survey. Large group interviews, or workshops, were conducted with approximately 16 employees. Subsequently, focus group interviews were held with smaller groups. An environmental expert estimated the carbon emissions attributable to the department prior to and on completion of the programme.

At the end of the six months, the independent environmental expert estimated a total reduction in carbon emissions of 12 per cent attributable to the department. This had been achieved through behavioural changes relating to energy efficiency and reduced wastage in methods and procedures. The main elements of the programme and findings from the research are shown in Figure CS18.1 and discussed below.

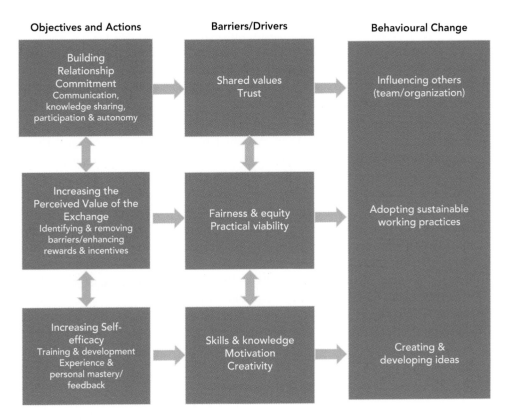

Figure CS18.1 The three elements of internal social marketing and their impact on pro-environmental workplace behaviours

Figure CS18.1 (Column 1) illustrates the three major characteristics of the internal social marketing programme together with a summary of the main actions involved. Collectively, these worked to reduce the barriers and/or enhance the drivers for change shown in Column 2, thus leading to the adoption of new behaviours listed in Column 3. The following is an explanation of the three main objectives and related actions outlined in Column 1:

1. Building relationship commitment

   Internal marketing aims to build relationship commitment based on shared vision and values (Foreman and Money 1995). There were a few employees who were not interested in environmental issues. These often highlighted the competing forces described above. They talked about the conflicting newspaper reports and disagreed with the idea that the individual can make a difference. Some became quite angry at the whole initiative and heated debates developed. There were other employees who did care about the environment but did not trust management. They believed that the initiative was paying 'lip service' to the environmental agenda. They highlighted how people had made suggestions and been involved in initiatives before but believed these had been a waste of time as nothing had been done. Others who had never met the chief environmental officer or his team were very interested, however. Yet, the only avenue for their ideas was through their direct line managers who typically failed to take an interest in employees' suggestions.

   Key relationships had to be established before any initiatives could be progressed, in particular between the chief environmental officer and those most interested in getting involved. In turn this generated other relationships, for example, between those who could provide facilities for site transport and even financial support for projects as well as expert advice. Although senior and middle line management were supportive of environmental initiatives in principle, the bureaucratic management structure discouraged information sharing, participation and autonomy. Communication was also a key problem at this site. There is now an active dialogue between employees and the environment team. Similarly, a high degree of knowledge transfer is taking place between the environment team and various groups of employees. One employee is now the official environmental representative and is a member of the organization-wide 'environmental board' (which reports directly to the managing director). This also emphasizes the important relationships that have been developed.

2. Increasing the perceived value of the exchange

   The concept of exchange is fundamental to internal marketing (Gronroos 1997) and social marketing (Hastings 2007) relationships. An appreciation of exchange and equity theory is also essential to understanding relationships between employee trust, commitment and cooperation. To be successful, relational exchange implies that each party involved sees the exchange as fair and equitable and therefore of value. Barriers identified in the case study included: internal barriers, such as distrust of management's willingness to implement ideas; unsupportive management behaviours; situational factors, such as transport alternatives; obsolete facilities such as heating and lighting systems; lack of an effective energy management system (including metering); perceived lack of finance available for projects; and lack of knowledge and (an often related) belief that new behaviours are not possible (discussed in the next section with respect to 'efficacy'). The chief environmental officer has played a vital role in either reducing or circumventing these barriers. In addition, a need to reward existing practices as well as new initiatives has been recognized.

3. Increasing self-efficacy

An organizational climate that discouraged autonomy and information sharing meant that, while there were a significant number of ideas among employees, the skills and knowledge (for example, technical knowledge) necessary to take the ideas through to development were lacking. In addition, there was no time allocated to working on ideas. Consequently, employees were de-motivated and frustrated, as they simply did not know what to do. Self-efficacy, that is, 'beliefs in one's capabilities to organize and execute the courses of action required to produce given attainments' (Bandura 1997: 3) is central to the social cognitive theory of human behaviour (Bandura 1986). Efficacy (both individual and collective) has been shown to determine the level of opportunity, recognition and task performance related to environmental innovation (Hostager *et al.* 1998). As a response to the insight generated, the environmental manager has organized workshops for key employees who have expressed an interest in taking ideas forward. These are specifically tailored to the policies and processes of company A. They include training as to how to attract funding for projects of varying sizes and how to assess payback, benefits and risks. It should be noted that this was at the request of employees, not the suggestion of management. Learning, through training and development (and in particular personal mastery) has a key role in increasing self- (and collective) efficacy.

Behavioural change (Column 3)

The internal social marketing approach generated the following types of workplace behavioural change.

The research highlighted that pro-environmental workplace behaviour change can involve both direct behaviours, such as adopting and/or creating sustainable working practices, and/or indirect, such as positively influencing others within the organization. A number of employees were already adopting pro-environmental workplace behaviour, for example, through engaging with recycling and car share schemes. Often, these reflected domestic behaviours. A few were also trying to influence others, even though they were sometimes subjected to ridicule. Very few, however, engaged in creating and developing new ideas, even though when asked in the workshops a whole range of ideas were suggested.

DISCUSSION

The case study demonstrates that an internal social marketing approach can achieve pro-environmental goals through behavioural change within an organizational context. Key to success is the identification of 'target audiences' of employees including 'change champions' selected for their positive attitudes towards environmental issues and willingness to become involved in organizational initiatives. New behaviours included the creation and adoption of sustainable working practices that directly resulted in a reduction in carbon emissions. Additionally, the individuals involved are now in a position to influence others across the organization. However, behavioural change required the development of a range of internal products, for example, relating to training and development as well as communication of existing products. Knowledge creation and sharing have a crucial role both in increasing self-efficacy as well as in building relationships and reducing perceived barriers to new behaviours. Consequently, by aligning values, developing trust and commitment, and putting the necessary resources and support mechanisms in place, internal social marketing can achieve pro-environmental behavioural change in the workplace.

References

Bandura, A. (1986) *Social Foundations of Thought and Action: A Social Cognitive Approach*. Englewood Cliffs, New Jersey: Prentice Hall.

Bandura, A (1997) *Self-Efficacy: The Exercise of Control*. New York: W.H. Freeman and Company.

Carbon Trust (2011) Carbon Reduction Commitment Energy Efficiency Scheme (CRC) [online], London: Carbon Trust. Available at: www.carbontrust.co.uk/policy-legislation/business-public-sector/pages/carbon-reduction-commitment.aspx [Accessed 29 June 2011].

Foreman, S.K. and Money, A.H. (1995) 'Internal marketing: Concepts, measurement and application', *Journal of Marketing Management*, 11(8): 755–768.

Gronroos, C. (1997) 'Value-driven relational marketing: From products to resources and competencies', *Journal of Marketing Management*, 13(5): 407–419.

Hastings, G. (2007) *Social Marketing: Why Should the Devil have all the Best Tunes?* Butterworth-Heinemann. Oxford: Elsevier.

Hostager, T.J., Neil, T.C., Decker, R.L. and Lorentz, R.D. (1998) 'Seeing environmental opportunities: Effects of intrapreneurial ability, efficacy, motivation and desirability', *Journal of Organisational Change Management*, 11(1): 11–25.

Senge, P., Smith, B., Kruschwitz, N., Laur, J. and Schley, S. (2008) *The Necessary Revolution: How Individuals and Organisations Are Working Together to Create a Sustainable World*. London: Nicholas Brealey.

Smith, A.M. and O'Sullivan, T.J. (2012) 'Environmentally responsible behaviour in the workplace: An internal social marketing approach', *Journal of Marketing Management*, 28(3–4): 469–494.

Stern, P.C. (2000) 'Toward a coherent theory of environmentally significant behaviour', *Journal of Social Issues*, 56(3): 407–424.

Case study questions

1. List the main barriers to and drivers of behavioural change identified in the case study.

2. The case study illustrates three major characteristics, or objectives, of a successful internal social marketing approach to encouraging pro-environmental behaviour. The focus is on employees. Do you consider that these are equally relevant to a domestic context, i.e. for individuals and households?

3. Focus on an organization with which you are familiar, for example, related to your work, education or leisure activities. Would the internal social marketing programme outlined above be effective in achieving behavioural change in that organization?

   (a) Explain why you think it would or would not; and

   (b) Recommend the main objectives and characteristics of an internal social marketing programme which would achieve behavioural change.

19

Healthy Heroes, Magic Meals and a visiting alien: Community-led assets-based social marketing

Martine Stead

INTRODUCTION

Actively involving the community in developing and implementing social marketing interventions has a number of benefits (Bryant *et al.* 2007). It increases the likelihood of interventions being culturally appropriate, keeps costs down, and is consistent with and contributes to community development and community capacity building. Thus, community involvement can be seen both as a means to an end and as a beneficial outcome in its own right. Recent years have also seen growing interest in the **assets-based** or **community capacities** approach (El-Askari *et al.* 1998; Kretzman and McKnight 1996; Assets Alliance Scotland 2010), which focuses on the resources, skills, talents and ideas within communities for generating change, rather than on their needs and deficits. The assets-based approach to community development can be seen as consistent with social marketing in its emphasis on starting where people are (Lindsey *et al.* 2001) and in the concept of exchange, which envisages both partners in the marketing relationship as contributing something of value (Bagozzi 1975). This case study examines the feasibility and value of a community-led, assets-based social marketing approach in two communities in Edinburgh, Scotland.

THE EDINBURGH PROJECTS

The Community Healthy Lifestyles pilot programme was a joint initiative of City of Edinburgh Council and NHS (National Health Service) Lothian. It was set up to explore the feasibility and value of using social marketing within a community development context, and sought to engage local communities in activities contributing to the prevention of obesity among children and families, the priority target group for the initiative. Projects were funded in Muirhouse in North Edinburgh and Moredun in the south (approximate populations 7,000 and 9,000 respectively). Both communities have higher than national average levels of income disadvantage and ill health (NHS ScotPHO 2010). Initial funding covered the salaries of two part-time project workers (LA, ED) for 18 months, plus a very modest activities and materials budget of approximately £2,000 (€2,382/$3,161).

Given the programme's pilot status, relatively modest budget and timescale, outcomes focused on the feasibility of developing and implementing the projects and on their potential to engage community residents and others.

DEVELOPING THE PROJECTS

Community asset mapping

An asset mapping exercise sought to identify assets within and near the communities that could be harnessed to support the projects. These include **social** assets (statutory organizations, voluntary groups, businesses); **cultural** assets (schools, colleges, libraries, creative individuals who were invited to donate time to the projects); **material** assets (community facilities, potential funding or sponsorship sources, the physical environment); and **individual** assets (the skills, time and enthusiasm of local residents, volunteers and partner organization employees). To strengthen these assets further, social marketing training days were held at the start of each project for all interested residents and local organizations.

Community needs assessment

A needs assessment elicited residents' views of what they liked and disliked about the communities, the barriers to healthy lifestyles, focusing particularly on healthy eating and physical activity, and their suggested solutions. Low-cost and creative methods were used to gather input from 535 residents, including visits to community groups, suggestion boxes, post-it note graffiti walls and questionnaires at the library, food stores, community centres and hairdressers. Project workers compiled the findings and discussed them with small groups of local residents, who then decided on priorities and activities.

Guiding principles

From the asset mapping and needs assessment, four themes and principles emerged to guide the selection of project activities:

1. *Validation and celebration*. The projects would not focus on what the communities were doing 'wrong' but on what they were already doing 'right'. This meant helping people to recognize both their own achievements and skills, and the assets of the communities around them. For example, the needs assessment revealed that many residents walked a great deal, yet they tended not to regard this as 'proper' exercise because it was done out of simple necessity rather than to keep fit. This insight led to a key project decision, that existing healthy behaviours in the communities should be validated rather than focusing on behaviours that people were not yet achieving. Both communities contained what project workers identified as 'healthy heroes' – people who, despite limited resources and without realizing it, were quietly doing remarkable things in terms of healthy living. Examples included individuals who were inventive at cooking on a low income or who had come together to offer support to each other, such as the North Edinburgh 'Buggy Brigade', a group of young mothers who walked regularly together and provided social support to each other.

2. *Speaking to and sharing with one another*. The needs assessment and asset mapping highlighted the power of local voices and role models. Residents spoke of the value of a 'buddy' or 'chum' who could motivate them to exercise, and their suggested solutions for encouraging healthy cooking focused on both giving and receiving peer support: 'go out with them [other residents]and help them buy fruit and veg', 'show me how to eat and use different foods', 'invite you for a meal and taste what I make'. The guiding principle was that information, advice and encouragement should come not from experts but from residents themselves.

3. *Fun*. Project activities should generate a buzz that people wanted to be part of and that made them feel positive about the communities and themselves. The needs assessment indicated that people felt the communities could be apathetic and lacking in 'community spirit'. Any health messages should be light touch and secondary to key benefits such as enjoyment, achievement and participation. This focus on fun was compatible with Smith's (1999) social marketing mantra of making behaviour change 'fun, easy and popular'.

4. *Creativity*. Both projects identified the potential of **creativity** as a strategy for engaging people's interest, generating project activities and materials, and building feelings of pride and achievement. Creativity was recognized in particular as a means of challenging and reshaping residents' vision of their communities.

Across the two projects, the desired *behaviour change* was defined as engagement with healthy lifestyle activities, in *exchange* for enjoyable, sociable experiences. *Target* groups, such as children or low-income parents, were defined for some specific project activities, while other activities were aimed more broadly at all community residents. *Competition* was defined as the perceptual and practical barriers identified in the needs assessment. The key *product* offering was defined as enjoyable participation, while the main *place* strategy was to offer activities on people's doorsteps and to encourage them to see the places around them with fresh eyes. The *price* strategy was to minimize the financial costs associated with healthy eating and physical activity and to address the psychosocial costs by emphasizing sociability and mutual support. Finally, *promotional* messages and content should be upbeat, fun and creative, and generated by local residents themselves.

Project activities

Informed by the insights and principles above, each project came up with a long list of potential activities which was discussed with local residents, resulting in the following:

Muirhouse Million Steps (N Edinburgh). A one-day event to encourage walking and appreciation of local green spaces. Residents were invited to achieve a collective million steps by taking part in a community walk and pooling their 'steps', as recorded by a waistband pedometer, at the end. To cater for different abilities, a shorter and a longer route were offered. All participants received a Certificate of Achievement and a 'goody bag' at the end of the walk containing a 'Passport to Health' (a set of discount vouchers for the local leisure centre and other local amenities), plus fruit, water and other items. The overall tone was celebratory, with stalls and music and local celebrities participating in the walk.

It's Yummy Mummy (N Edinburgh). A cooking competition and accompanying recipe book, which invited local residents to share their creativity and expertise in cooking. Based on the format of popular television shows such as *Masterchef*, entrants were invited to submit a healthy recipe that could feed a family of five for under £5, and to cook it in front of a panel of judges. Successful recipes were included in a colourful cookbook which was launched on Mothers' Day 2011.

Healthy Heroes (N Edinburgh). A billboard and bus-stop poster campaign featuring photographs of groups of local people being 'healthy heroes', with the strapline

'We are becoming healthy heroes. You can too'. The groups included a men's football club, a women's fitness group, and a chair-based exercise class for elderly and frail people.

Mmm . . . Moredun Makes Magic Meals! (S Edinburgh). A six-month partnership with a local food store, part of a Scottish food retail group, to promote healthy home cooking. Each month focused on a favourite recipe of a local resident or group of residents, with the recipe being featured on attractive recipe cards that were distributed within the store and displayed on a billboard outside the store. The local store contributed graphic design and production of the materials, and also promoted each month's recipe ingredients in-store. The aim of encouraging people to try home cooking rather than rely on processed foods was emphasized in the strapline *'Tastier than a ready meal, healthier than a ready meal and cheaper than a ready meal'*.

'Liam and the Alien' Children's picture storybook (S Edinburgh). A picture storybook for pre-school and P1 (age 3–6) children to encourage them to feel proud of living in Moredun and to normalize healthy activities such as outdoor play and eating fruit and vegetables by featuring them in a story. The character and story were developed by local P6 (age 10–11) children during workshops at the local library and school, with guidance from a published children's author who donated her time for free. Illustrations were provided by Edinburgh College of Art students, who were invited to meet and submit sample illustrations to the P6 children, from which the children selected a shortlist of three images. The P6 children in turn showed these images to a class of P1 children, who chose their favourite. The winning student then worked with the P6 children to develop a complete set of illustrations, which were bright, friendly and recognizable as Moredun.

Beautiful Moredun photography competiton (S Edinburgh). A photography competition which aimed to encourage people to visit and appreciate the area's green spaces.

The South Edinburgh project also included a project newsletter, co-written by local people, and other materials. Several of the materials were pre-tested with local residents to refine them before production.

EVALUATION

A low-cost mixed methods case study approach was used to describe the projects' development and implementation processes and to assess the extent to which they engaged community residents in activities designed to promote healthier eating and physical activity. Project workers conducted focus groups, interviews and brief surveys with community residents and local partners to explore their experiences and views of participating in the projects. Quarterly monitoring reports recorded project inputs and outputs, regular interviews were conducted with project workers throughout the programme, and anecdotal feedback was gathered throughout. This kind of mixed methods approach is valuable for evaluating interventions which are not pre-specified and where it is important to capture processes and activities as they develop (Keen and Packwood 1995; Baum 1998), and is also a practical approach where initiatives are operating on a modest budget, as it maximizes the value of both routinely gathered data and opportunistic feedback (Baum 1991; Bamberger *et al.* 2010; Bamberger *et al.* 2012).

Implementation

All activities were successfully implemented within the 18-month project lifecycle. Successful implementation depended on three key factors: utilizing in-house and donated creativity and expertise rather than buying it in; financial and in-kind sponsorship and support from local businesses and organizations; and, most importantly, active participation of the community. In North Edinburgh, action groups, comprising residents and representatives of local organizations, were formed to develop and implement the main activities. The *It's Yummy Mummy* action group was particularly effective in terms of engagement and empowerment, with four local residents in the group taking the lead in designing the rules for the competition, writing letters to celebrity chefs and potential sponsors asking for support, publicizing the initiative by writing an article for the local freesheet newspaper, and helping to compile the final book. In South Edinburgh, a particularly successful example of engagement in intervention development was the children's storybook *Liam and the Alien,* where local children assumed profound ownership of the task and acquired a range of skills, including creative writing, understanding the book production process, conducting research with younger children, briefing the illustrator and working with adults.

Community perceptions and experiences of the project activities

In North Edinburgh, 262 residents, with a range of fitness and ability levels, participated in *Muirhouse Million Steps*. Walkers greatly exceeded the target, taking a combined total of 1,901,625 steps, an average of over 7,000 each. A brief survey conducted with a quarter of the participants found high levels of enjoyment and intentions to walk more in the future, with comments reflecting feelings of pride and appreciation of the local area and of themselves: 'It made me realize how lucky I am to have such a nice walk and views on my doorstep'; 'It's the furthest I've walked for over two years. I've been practising for a month now and have been managing to go quite far but not as far as I did on the day. It was a great achievement for me and I'm really proud of myself'. Responses made in a bus-stop survey to the *Healthy Heroes* campaign reflected themes of pride and motivation, with residents describing the local people featured as 'an inspiration' and suggesting that the community should be 'flooded with these images' rather than 'commercial stuff'.

In South Edinburgh, 3,000 *Moredun Makes Magic Meals* recipe cards (500 each month) were distributed via the food store, library and primary school. A hands-up survey at a local school found high levels of awareness of the campaign, and a quarter of households had made one of the featured meals. Two thousand copies of the story-book *Liam and the Alien* were printed, with some given free to all participating children and local groups, and the remainder sold through local schools and stores and on Amazon.[1] For the children involved in creating *Liam and the Alien*, feelings of pride and achievement were evident. One child said 'it makes me proud to be from Moredun', and a P1 boy said of the finished book, 'I think it's beautiful'. The primary school headteacher told the local newspaper that it 'was the most inspiring project that my team have ever been involved in'.

Project 'legacies'

Although the projects were originally established only as an 18-month pilot, additional funding was later granted for two further 12-month periods. At the time of writing, action groups of local residents in North Edinburgh had been formed to develop *It's Yummy Mummy* into a *Community Food Festival*. In South Edinburgh, the project is taking a more policy-oriented approach, aiming to improve the quality of the local green space. An Action Group has consulted residents on their wishes for the space, and is working with architects on detailed plans. Both projects are seeking to create more sustainable change by skilling up local residents and creating structures for change that have the potential to continue beyond the funding period.

DISCUSSION

This case study illustrates how, on a modest budget, social marketing and community development approaches were combined in two innovative and creative community-led projects encouraging engagement in healthy eating and physical activity-based activities. Community residents were integrally involved, not just as research participants and project beneficiaries, but as decision-makers, creative contributors and implementers. They helped to conduct the needs assessment, decided on project activities, developed skills in research and social marketing, planned and helped to run events, produced materials, and contributed their creativity in storytelling, cooking, recipe creation, photography, writing and organization. A key learning point from this paper is that social marketing is not an expensive club available only to those with large budgets (Stead and Hastings 1997). Communities have skills and assets within themselves that they can bring to bear in a social marketing framework (Middlestadt et al. 1997). Working with communities as 'co-producers' may unlock creative and alternative solutions that are not always available to experts (Smith and Henry 2009). Furthermore, interventions that originate within communities and are owned by them are likely to be more culturally appropriate (Brookes et al. 2010) and more effective in encouraging engagement (Monaghan *et al.* 2008), and may lead to more positive health outcomes (NICE 2009), than those imposed from outside. In other words, approaches that genuinely involve communities in development and implementation make financial, practical and philosophical sense.

Social marketing gave project workers a new perspective and enhanced their existing skills. Three ideas proved to be of particular interest and value: the concept of consumer orientation, the idea that behaviour change should be 'fun, easy and popular' (Smith 1999), and the concept of mutually beneficial exchange. Taken together, these concepts encouraged project workers and residents to foreground throughout the question of why people should engage with the projects and what the projects would offer in return. This perspective informed all their interactions with potential supporters and sponsors, which emphasized mutual win-wins, and the content and tone of all the project activities, which emphasized first and foremost fun and joining in. Addressing health issues in a light touch way, where the main focus is not on health but on creating a shared experience or resource, has been shown to be both a valuable means of engaging local people and beneficial in its own right in terms of esteem, confidence and feelings of connectedness (e.g. Barlow *et al.* 1999).

Note

1   www.amazon.co.uk/Liam-Alien-Various/dp/0956136850/.

References

Assets Alliance Scotland (2010) *Assets Alliance Scotland.* Scotland: Scottish Government/Scottish Community Development Centre (SCDC)/Long-Term Conditions Alliance Scotland (LTCAS). www.scdc.org.uk/news/article/Assets-alliance-scotland-report/.

Bagozzi, R. (1975) 'Marketing and exchange', *Journal of Marketing*, 39: 32–39.

Bamberger, M., Rao, V., and Woolcock, M. (2010) *Using Mixed Methods in Monitoring and Evaluation Experiences from International Development – Policy Research Working Paper 5245.* The World Bank: Washington, DC.

Bamberger, M., Rugh, J., and Mabry, L. (2012) *RealWorld Evaluation: Working Under Budget, Time, Data, and Political Constraints. Second Edition.* Thousand Oaks, CA: Sage Publications, ISBN: 9781412979627.

Barlow, J., Gaunt-Richardson, P., Amos, A. and McKie, L., (1999) 'Addressing smoking and health among women living on low income II. TAPS Tiree: A dance and drama group for rural community development', *Health Education Journal*, 58(4): 321–328.

Baum, F. (1991) *Planning healthy communities: A guide to doing needs assessment.* South Australian Health Commission, Southern Community Health Research Unit. ISSN/ISBN 0724340149.

Baum, F. (1998) 'Measuring effectiveness in community-based health promotion', in K. Davies and G. MacDonald (eds) *Quality, Evidence and Effectiveness in Health Promotion – Striving for Certainties*. London: Routledge.

Brookes, R., Lehman, T.C., Maguire, S., Mitchell, P., Mejia, V.A., Johnson-Aramaki, T. and Raboni, E.M. (2010) '*Real Life. Real Talk.(r)*: Creating engagement in sexual and reproductive health among parents, teens, families and communities', *Social Marketing Quarterly*, XVI(1): 52–69.

Bryant, C.A., McCormack Brown, K.R., McDermott, R.J., Forthofer, E.C., and Bumpus, S.A. (2007) 'Community-based prevention marketing: Organizing a community for health behavior intervention', *Health Promotion Practice*, 8: 154–163.

El-Askari, G., Freestone, J., Irizarry, C., Kraut, K.L., Mashiyama, S.T., Morgan, M.A., and Walton, S. (1998) 'The Healthy Neighborhoods Project: A local health department's role in catalyzing community development', *Health Education and Behavior*, 25(2): 146–159.

Keen, J., and Packwood, T. (1995) 'Case study evaluation', *British Medical Journal*, 311: 444–446.

Lindsey, E., Stjduhar, K. and McGuiness, L. (2001) 'Examining the process of community development', *Journal of Advanced Nursing*, 33: 828–835.

Middlestadt, S.E., Schechter, C., Peyton, C. and Tjugum, B. (1997) 'Community involvement in health planning: Lessons learned from practicing social marketing in a context of community control, participation and ownership', in M.E. Goldberg, M. Fishbein and S.E. Middlestadt (eds) *Social Marketing – Theoretical and Practical Perspectives*. Mahwah, New Jersey: Lawrence Erlbaum Associates.

Monaghan, P.F., Bryant, C.A., Baldwin, J.A., Zhu, Y., Ibrahimou, B., Lind, J.D., Contreras, R.B., Tovar, A., Moreno, T., and McDermott, R.J. (2008) 'Using community-based prevention marketing to improve farm worker safety', *Social Marketing Quarterly*, XIV(4): 71–87.

NHS ScotPHO (2010) Health and Wellbeing Profiles 2010 – Spine Pack: Edinburgh. NHS National Services Scotland, ScotPHO.

NICE (National Institute for Health and Clinical Excellence) (2009) *Community engagement to improve health*. NICE public health guidance 9. Issue Date: February 2008. London: NICE. www.nice.org.uk/PH009/.

Smith, A.J., and Henry, L. (2009) ' "Setting the guinea pigs free": Towards a new model of community-led social marketing', *Public Health*, 123: e1–e5.

Smith, B. (1999) 'Marketing with no budget', *Social Marketing Quarterly*, 5(2): 6–11.

Stead, M., and Hastings, G. (1997) 'Advertising in the social marketing mix: Getting the balance right', in M.E. Goldberg, M. Fishbein and S.E. Middlestadt (eds) *Social Marketing – Theoretical and Practical Perspectives*. Mahwah, New Jersey: Lawrence Erlbaum Associates.

Acknowledgement

The project was funded by the Edinburgh Health Inequalities Standing Group (initially Fairer Scotland Fund now City of Edinburgh Council). Guidance and support were provided throughout by the project steering group which included

City of Edinburgh Council, NHS Lothian, Pilton Community Health Project, South Edinburgh Healthy Living Initiative and the Institute for Social Marketing, University of Stirling.

Case study questions

1. What are the potential benefits in actively involving communities in developing and implementing social marketing activities?

2. And what are the challenges and risks for social marketers in actively involving communities in developing and implementing social marketing activities?

Case Study **20**

National Health Service Corps: Putting members first drives enrollment

Melissa Otero and John Strand

INTRODUCTION

The National Health Service Corps (NHSC) was started in 1972 in response to the healthcare crisis that emerged in the United States in the 1950s and 1960s. Older physicians were retiring, and young doctors started to choose specialization over general practice, leaving many areas of the country without primary care medical services.

The NHSC attracts medical students and recent graduates who are committed to helping those with limited access to primary healthcare. It offers scholarships and student loan repayment to providers for their commitment to work at least two years in an NHSC-approved health center or clinic in an underserved community. NHSC clinicians – primary care doctors, dentists, nurses, physician assistants, mental health professionals – also earn a salary from their sites. In 2009, 3,600 healthcare providers were members of the NHSC.

In 2009, the Health Resources and Services Administration (HRSA), the government agency that runs the NHSC, funded FHI 360, a nonprofit social marketing and health promotion organization, to rebrand and market the program to increase its national visibility and recruit 3,300 primary healthcare providers into the program.

PROBLEM DEFINITION

Historically, demand for the NHSC exceeded available funding. More recently, with increased attention on the issue of healthcare and a growing primary care workforce shortage, the American Recovery and Reinvestment Act of 2009 provided $300 million to support 4,000 new NHSC providers by 2011. With an influx of funding, this program – which had never much needed to market itself – was suddenly faced with having to more than double its size in just two years.

MARKET ANALYSIS

FHI 360 first conducted a market analysis to better understand the NHSC program, including internal operations, available resources and audiences. The inquiry also sought to examine what HRSA was currently doing to promote, manage and support the program, as well as to learn about the external market environment, including target audiences and NHSC competitors. Activities included intercept interviews with new members; observation and attendance at key NHSC events; key informant interviews with NHSC program staff, partners, Ambassadors, alumni and advisors (e.g. National Advisory Council members); a review of background documents and data; an audit of existing NHSC promotional materials; and a consumer experience innovation workshop. These activities were designed to illuminate the current NHSC program's key strengths and successes, weaknesses and gaps, and opportunities.

The analysis revealed that the NHSC was primarily being positioned as a government-run financial program. This positioning was diminishing the value of the NHSC among its most important consumers – its own members and the healthcare providers it was seeking to attract. In addition to the impersonal and bureaucratic way the program was being defined, the 'Corps' in the NHSC did not exist. Once providers learned they were accepted into the program, most said they never heard from the program again, or anyone else in it.

Students haven't heard of [the NHSC]. When they do, they think it's like uniformed service. They might just equate it with another branch of the government.

NHSC [is] not [a] key recognizable phrase. If I went to the new physician reception in my town they would say 'what is that?' But they would know the loan repayment program.

The 'product' being sold – membership in the NHSC – was confusing, required navigating a complex application process, and had no values associated with it other than money. Yet, the analysis also showed that, for most current and potential NHSC members, money was just one part of the attraction of the program. Many NHSC members were already working in underserved communities before they applied for the program and most continued to serve beyond their two-year commitment – and had powerful stories to share. Furthermore, the personal values of providers who were most likely to work in communities with a shortage of health professionals had little to do with money. They valued service and social equity, as well as other benefits such as work/life balance, flexibility, meaningful patient relationships, and the opportunity to learn and practice different skills.

In terms of an emotional connection with the brand, input from members and others involved with the program suggested that the NHSC had a split-personality. Many contradictory words were mentioned to describe the NHSC (e.g. 'cold', 'faceless' and 'demanding' vs. 'dedicated', 'genuine' and 'caring'). A varied picture emerged of the NHSC depending on participants' association with the program and their length of involvement in it. This contradiction may have been attributed to participants feeling one way about their commitment to the social mission of the program, and the fact that they are able to do this work, in part, because of the NHSC, and feeling another way about the impersonal way the program was being run.

Some promotional materials did exist, including a website and a wide social media presence, but their effectiveness was undermined by an overall lack of focus, clear benefits, visual interest and an emotional connection.

The findings also revealed an incredible opportunity to capitalize on the considerable assets that HRSA had in place for a revitalized marketing effort, including a commitment to program success at the highest levels, experienced and committed staff, and extensive relationships and resources throughout HRSA – including regional offices, and internal and external partners – that could be leveraged to market the program and its benefits. These assets, coupled with the significant goodwill that existed around the social mission of the program, primed it for success.

AIMS AND OBJECTIVES

In order to help the NHSC recruit the large number of providers it needed to bring into the program quickly, and lay a foundation for future marketing of the program, the product needed to be repositioned in a way that:

1. was responsive to member needs and values; and
2. communicated NHSC members' core values to the target audience in a clear, consistent and authentic way. FHI 360 created and helped implement a rebranding effort and marketing campaign to:
   - Reframe the NHSC – through the voice of its current members – as relevant, responsive, compelling, exciting and more personal
   - Begin to build the 'Corps' in the NHSC and position this network of like-minded, dedicated professionals as a member benefit

- Develop a suite of NHSC identity products and promotional tools and materials that communicate a revived NHSC brand – both for current and prospective members
- Drive prospective members to register on the NHSC website – the first step to completing the required application (and re-engage those already registered who had not yet applied).

FHI 360 also reinforced with program staff that the current application process was going to be a choke-point for the influx of new applicants expected as a result of a marketing campaign. The process needed to continue to be improved to allow for a smoother entry into the program.

FORMATIVE RESEARCH

Building on the market analysis, brand elements, messages and materials were developed to achieve the objectives. These brand and materials concepts were tested through focus group discussions with potential members – soon-to-be, and current, primary healthcare providers in NHSC-eligible disciplines – all of whom were either accumulating or still repaying student loans. The research revealed a very low awareness of the program among prospective members, as well as preferences for and questions surrounding various brand elements and messages.

After brand elements and materials were tweaked, FHI 360 fielded an online survey (n=201) with secondary audiences already involved in the NHSC, which aimed to confirm the brand and materials testing outcomes from prospective members; get buy-in for the new brand and materials; and elicit any previously unidentified concerns with the new brand and materials.

STRATEGY

The resulting strategy focused on defining and segmenting the target audiences and a '4Ps' approach to marketing the program.

Audience segmentation: Audience segments were driven by HRSA data that identified the specific clinician disciplines in greatest demand by the NHSC healthcare centers and clinics. Target audiences included physicians, physician assistants, nurse practitioners, dentists and dental hygienists. The marketing strategy focused on those current and soon-to-be clinicians, in these disciplines, with a desire to help those with limited access to healthcare. These audiences had to be found and engaged in a way that clearly communicated the NHSC brand and benefits of membership (Table CS20.1):

Product: The NHSC brand was repositioned to feature the program's clinician members and their personal stories about the benefits of their service. The refreshed value proposition offers clinicians the opportunity for rewarding service and professional development – with loan repayment and scholarships to boot (see Figure CS20.1). Key program benefits and messages that had not

Table CS20.1 Audience segmentation

Priority audience ranking	Rationale for ranking, value of audience to the NHSC	What does the NHSC offer them?	What do they want from the NHSC?
Potential Members	Need to meet current and future recruitment goals Actual providers of care	Meaningful and rewarding careers that speak to their values of providing patient-focused care to, and making a difference for, those who need it most	• Financial incentives • Professional growth opportunities • Flexibility – geographically and professionally • Easy application and ongoing paperwork • Connection to the community in which they're placed and a sense of belonging to the Corps
Current Members	Key to recruitment of new members Their satisfaction and retention can improve the reputation/branding of NHSC	Assistance and support to help them make the most of their NHSC experience	• Financial incentives • Flexibility – geographically and professionally • Connection to the community in which they're placed and a sense of belonging to the Corps • Professional growth opportunities • Simple paperwork/requirements

been communicated until now include: flexibility and choice in where members provide services; access to educational, training and networking opportunities; a sense of belonging to a community of providers with a shared desire to serve patients with limited access to healthcare; and the opportunity to pay off all student loans with continued service.

Price: HRSA focused on addressing the three major barriers expressed about the program:

1) its impersonal, bureaucratic personality;
2) its cumbersome application process with unresponsive customer support; and
3) the sense of isolation and abandonment members felt once accepted into the program.

The pricing strategy aimed to humanize the brand, streamline the application process, and foster a sense of community among members serving in diverse settings throughout the country.

Figure CS20.1 Example of advertising poster

Place: HRSA sought to engage its many partners, stakeholders and resources in a coordinated outreach and support effort. FHI 360 redesigned the NHSC website to feature members, highlight the 'Corps Experience,' provide relevant resources and content for members and prospective members, and offer a platform for engagement (Figure CS20.2). The NHSC Facebook page was transformed into an effective customer service tool and became a growing online community for current and prospective members. Orientation conferences were retooled to reflect the new brand and to add more networking time. The NHSC Ambassador program was reconfigured to more directly support and promote the program. Plans for an alumni program were in the works.

Promotion: FHI 360 updated the NHSC logo and all program materials to reflect the new brand personality (Figure CS20.3). Brief video stories were produced that expressed the brand values through the voices of its members. Earned media efforts focused on a radio media tour and pitching local newspapers in members' communities. FHI 360 also employed targeted direct mail and paid advertising campaigns to micro-target the priority clinician segments.

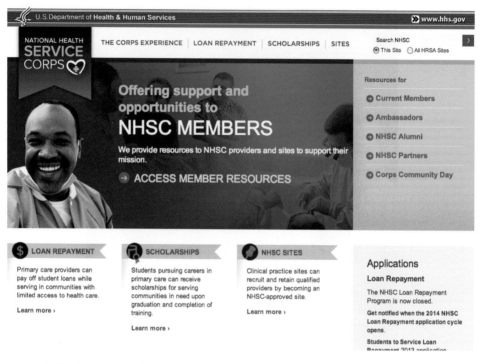

Figure CS20.2 New website

Figure CS20.3 Redesigned NHSC logo

OUTCOMES

On October 13, 2011, a US Department of Health and Human Services press release announced that the largest number of NHSC providers in history – more than 10,000 – are providing healthcare to communities across the country. This is nearly three times the number of NHSC providers there were three years ago, and nearly double the number of providers FHI 360 was tasked with helping to recruit.[1]

Specific outcomes included:

- A 208 per cent increase in the number of visits to the NHSC website homepage (456,836 more visits) from February to July 2011, when compared to the same time period in 2010
- A 2–3 per cent response rate on the tailored direct mail campaign, higher than the industry average of 1–2 per cent, which resulted in 800 to 1,200 new loan repayment program registrants
- An average click-through rate nearly twice the national average (0.15 per cent vs. 0.08 per cent) for the banner advertisement portion of the paid media campaign
- A 72 percentage-point shift from negative to positive online sentiment expressed about the NHSC online (from 18 per cent to 90 per cent), primarily via the NHSC Facebook page and Twitter, from September 2010 to September 2011.

DISCUSSION

1. The key factor in the success of the NHSC marketing campaign was HRSA's commitment to fix the product, namely the NHSC brand, program and features. Too often, social marketers are asked to promote poorly designed programs or poorly delivered services. Once HRSA began to address the major barriers of NHSC personality, entry and engagement, the program almost sold itself.

2. Focusing on the 'consumer experience' – that is, what did the NHSC look like from the clinicians' perspective – helped reframe the marketing challenge for HRSA managers.

3. NHSC clinician members proved to be the best sales force. They simply needed a venue to express their passion, commitment and enthusiasm about the life-changing opportunity offered by the program.

Note

1   The NHSC received new funding from the Affordable Care Act in 2010 to support additional providers.

Case study questions

1. What were the major barriers that had to be addressed?

2. What contributed to the higher-than-average response rates and the final results of the marketing effort?

3. How can social marketers support government program managers to make their programs more consumer-oriented?

21

FAN – Famiglia, Attività fisica, Nutrizione: Ticino, Switzerland's campaign for healthy weight

L. Suzanne Suggs, Natalie Rangelov, Mallely Rangel Garcia and Lucía Aguirre Sánchez

INTRODUCTION

Obesity and being above ideal weight have become increasing problems among both adults and children over the last two decades in many countries. With the rhythm of life becoming more hectic, there is often a perceived lack of time to take care of oneself and meet the basic needs of the body. In order to keep up with this busy world health promoters can adapt and develop innovative and effective strategies to foster healthy weight. The project FAN – Famiglia, Attività fisica, Nutrizione[1] was created with the aim of addressing healthy weight by improving physical activity and dietary habits of families (parents with children attending elementary or first two classes of middle school) living in Canton Ticino,[2]

Switzerland. This project is an innovation in Ticino, since it makes use of new technologies (web, email, and SMS) for disseminating tailored communication about diet and physical activity, in a region that is characterized by a preference for face-to-face communication.[3]

PROBLEM DEFINITION

As in many other countries, the rates of overweight and obesity have increased in Switzerland (Schopper and Promotion Santé Suisse (PSS) 2005; Ufficio federale della sanità pubblica (UFSP) and Dipartimento federale dell'interno DFI 2008; Ufficio federale dello sport (UFSPO) *et al.* 2009). These problems affect both genders in all age groups, including children. In 1992, 31.3 percent of the Swiss population was overweight or obese, and this increased to 38.8 percent in 2002 and to 39.5 percent in 2011 (Monitoraggio della strategia a lungo termine di Promozione Salute Svizzera 2012).

In the region of Canton Ticino, Switzerland's most southern Canton, data are not promising. In 2007, Ticino overweight and obesity rates exceeded those of Switzerland for both men (47 percent in Ticino versus 46.3 percent in Switzerland) and women (30.6 percent in Ticino versus 28.6 percent in Switzerland) (Repubblica e Cantone Ticino, DSS, sezione sanitaria 2009a). Despite the positive trend of physical activity across Switzerland, Ticino has the lowest rates of all the Cantons (Lamprecht and Stamm 2006; Repubblica e Cantone Ticino, DSS, sezione sanitaria 2009b). Indeed, in 2007, 20.1 percent of Ticino men and 34.5 percent of Ticino women were never or rarely active, while in Switzerland fewer residents were inactive: 13.8 percent for men and 17.9 percent for women (Repubblica e Cantone Ticino, DSS, sezione sanitaria 2009b).

COMPETITIVE ANALYSIS

Sedentary occupations (computer use, television watching, etc.), convenience meals, as well as competing time demands are major barriers towards attaining and maintaining a healthy weight. The promotion of unhealthy food (in grocery shops, but also on TV, billboards, packages for children, etc.) constituted a barrier towards promoting healthy diet, in particular to children. Moreover, prices of healthy food, sport facilities and public transportation fees were perceived to be high, and thus represented another barrier. This went hand in hand with the growth of sedentary behaviors. In addition, implementing a new technology-based program in a country where face-to-face communication is standard and often preferred constitutes a challenge. Finally, one of the frequently reported difficulties that health promotion programs face when providing community interventions is reaching the population in need.

STAKEHOLDER ANALYSIS

Actors at many levels (administration, healthcare providers, researchers, families, etc.) are affected by the burden of an overweight and obese population. During the development of FAN, many stakeholders were involved. Table CS21.1 presents the stakeholders, as well as their interests and missions, and roles in FAN.

Table CS21.1 Stakeholder analysis

Stakeholders	Mission and Interests	Role in FAN
Target audience: families living in Ticino, with children in elementary or first two classes of middle school	• Interested in reaching a healthy weight without too much effort	• Participants, but also helped during the planning and pre-testing phase
Funders: Canton Ticino, Service of Health Promotion and Evaluation (SPVS), Dept. of Health and Social Services (DSS) and Health Promotion Switzerland (PSS)	• SPVS and DSS are responsible for the planning and implementation of cantonal health programs • PSS is responsible for the funding of health programs at cantonal level	• Collaborated with the FAN team and supervised the development of FAN and its content, in order to guarantee a continuum with the rest of the cantonal program 'Peso Corporeo Sano', quality and accuracy of content, and program's longevity • PSS funded the program, and supervised and assured an optimal exploitation of existing resources and materials on diet and physical activity
Gatekeepers: Canton officials; Department of Education, Culture and Sport (DECS); elementary and middle school teachers and directors (principals); doctors and dieticians	• Canton officials: assure that only a selection of people access the schools for promoting their projects to avoid overloading and inappropriateness • Teachers and directors: interested in the health of their students • Doctors and dieticians: promote health and treat diseases	• Canton officials (including DECS) provided permission to promote FAN in schools • Teachers and directors: promoted FAN to their students and students' families • Doctors and dieticians: promoted FAN to the target audience
Researchers: BeCHANGE research group of the Institute for Public Communication at the Università della Svizzera italiana	• Its primary interest is research coupled with health promotion	• Planned, developed and implemented FAN • Promoted FAN and conducted all formative research with stakeholders • Conducted assessment and analyzed the results
Media: newspapers and radio	• Disseminate news	• Promoted FAN reaching the population in Ticino through different channels

Note: DECS: Dipartimento dell'educazione, della cultura e dello sport.

AIMS AND OBJECTIVES

The overarching aim of FAN was to promote healthy weight of families in Ticino. The process objectives were to:

- recruit a minimum of 250 families;
- follow the social marketing framework throughout the project;
- collaborate with stakeholders;
- engage the community;
- understand the satisfaction with the program;
- retain participants throughout the program and surveys; and
- implement the campaign as planned.

The cumulative objectives were to:

- improve dietary behaviors and physical activity levels; and
- improve attitudes, knowledge, intention and perceived behavioral difficulty.

RESEARCH

FAN was tested using a randomized controlled trial with three study groups. Participants were allocated randomly to one of the following study groups:

1. web group – parents received information only by visiting the FAN website
2. email group – parents received a tailored weekly email, in addition to access to the website or
3. SMS group – parents received a tailored weekly SMS, in addition to access to the website.

The children of all study groups received a weekly tailored letter via mail. As this was a publicly funded cantonal program, no eligible families were excluded from participation. This meant that all families were allowed access to the program, and thus no control group was included.

Participants also completed three assessment surveys at three different times: baseline, immediate post-intervention and three months post-intervention. In order to capture children's dietary and physical activity habits, two weekly logs (at baseline and first follow-up) were administered to all children.

FORMULATION OF STRATEGY

Following the social marketing framework, FAN aimed at suiting the best needs of the target audience. Hence, FAN was developed with the voluntary involvement of Ticino community. From the promotional materials to the branding, from the weekly content themes to the content timing, design and wording, and the assessment surveys, all the materials were developed and pre-tested with the target audience.

FAN content was delivered across eight weeks through communication technologies. Parents received the information through a weekly updated website, email and short message service (SMS), while children received a weekly printed letter. Communication was tailored on behavioral perceived difficulty (diet or physical activity), and demographic participants' characteristics (age, gender of parents and children, number of children, and class in school).

The communication content was based on existing content, used by the Canton and PSS in other health promoting initiatives and resource outlets, and repackaged for FAN. On the website, three sections were provided to parents: Family, Physical Activity and Nutrition. In order to meet participants' needs, the content was tailored. The first page of the website was tailored to each family's behavioral difficulty and they could access all the general content (e.g. videos, forum, tips, information, etc.). Moreover, children received letters adapted to their gender and age. All participant communication was personalized by addressing each person by name (e.g. 'Ciao Maria!'). The content for parents was designed to reinforce their knowledge, while still providing them with new information. Parents were encouraged to talk with their children, and participate in a forum where they could exchange ideas and chat with a dietician. Children's content was designed to teach knowledge, give new ideas, and improve attitudes towards fruit and vegetables and healthy physical activity. Children were asked to talk with their parents about the weekly topics of FAN. Finally, videos and visually appealing illustrations/caricatures were developed to teach knowledge, model behavior and give faces to the FAN team through a comic-like family (parents, two young kids and a dog).

In Table CS21.2, FAN activities are shown according to the eight social marketing benchmark criteria (The National Social Marketing Centre [NSMC] 2006).

Table CS21.2 FAN activities according to the eight social marketing benchmark criteria

Benchmarks	Strengths – How FAN met them
Customer orientation	Conducted formative research and adapted the project to families' needs and to Ticino's context. Audience involvement
Behavior	Goals: improving physical activity and healthy diet
Theory	Theory-driven approach, using Theory of Planned Behavior
Insight	Formative research was conducted to understand Ticino families' beliefs, motivations, needs and wants
Value exchange	Final lottery for participants that completed all assessment surveys. The prizes were FAN branded materials

Competition	Referred to the competitive analysis in order to create appropriate content and facilitate overcoming barriers
Segmentation	Segmented parents: mothers and fathers of children in elementary school or the first two classes of middle school Children: girls, boys, class 1–2, class x, y, z). Tailored content to both parents and children
Methods mix	Formative research, marketing mix, exchange, assessments and evaluation were conducted using a mix of methods (surveys, focus groups, interviews)

OUTCOMES

The recruitment objective was to enroll at least 250 families and FAN reached far more. Almost 700 families showed interest in FAN, of which 555 enrolled in the project (completed the baseline and were eligible). This translated to 556 parents (one family subscribed with both parents) and 750 children. Retention rate was very high: 72.07 percent at first follow-up and 71.42 percent at second follow-up.

The main findings are:

- Among adults, there were mainly mothers (86.5 percent); among children, boys and girls were almost equally represented with 51.7 percent girls.
- Among adults, the mean age was 41 (range 27–61), while for children 8.5 years of age. The majority of children (83.7 percent) were attending elementary school.
- Participants were mainly Swiss (85.1 percent), and reported a 'good' or 'very good' health status (more than 65.5 percent).
- At baseline, the main difficulty for parents was getting regular physical activity (59 percent of parents), while for children it was to eat healthily (82 percent). Despite some changes in percentages, the trend stayed the same also after the intervention.
- After participating in FAN, 44 percent of parents stated that they changed something in their physical activity and nutrition-related behaviors. They mentioned various activities that were promoted during the intervention, such as walking to school/work even when it rains, or preparing a weekly menu.
- Regarding parents' dietary habits, there was an increase in fruit and vegetable consumption, and a decrease in fat consumption in all three study groups. Also children increased their consumption of fruit in all meals.
- Regarding parents' physical activity level, there was an increase in both moderate and physical activity.

- FAN was globally evaluated as 'positive' or 'very positive' by 83 percent of participants. Criticisms were very few, and addressed to specific features of the intervention. For example, the use of cursive font for children's letters or the length of the surveys.

- Parents stated that FAN acted as a reminder and reinforcement, taking the burden from them. They said that FAN was teaching the children to eat veggies and so the parents did not have to constantly nag. Parents were also happy because FAN advice highlighted that they knew what they should be doing to achieve a healthy body weight for them and their children.

DISCUSSION

By following the social marketing framework, a deep understanding of the needs and wants of the target audience and other stakeholders was gained. FAN was responsive to the community, but also evidence-based. This facilitated the high involvement of families during the development of the intervention, high participation and high retention rates. Indeed, one of FAN's strengths is that it addressed families, instead of parents or children separately. This created a synergy between parents, children and FAN, and stimulated not only reflection, but also behavior change.

Some improvements still need to be done regarding the administration of the surveys, which were perceived as a burden to complete, despite the pre-testing, especially in large families. Moreover, a deeper pre-test of the final contents should be done in order to avoid small criticisms, which can, however, impact participants' satisfaction and involvement in the project. Finally, a major limitation consisted in the limited budget, which determined some choices.

The use of new technologies for this intervention was well perceived overall among the Ticino population. These technologies therefore have the potential to become an important channel for communicating about health, in particular about nutrition and physical activity. Hence, FAN represents a successful attempt in promoting physical activity and healthy diet in an innovative way, to an innovative target audience.

Notes

1   www.fanticino.ch/.
2   Cantons are member states of Switzerland.
3   FAN was developed by the BeCHANGE research group of the Institute for Public Communication at the Università della Svizzera italiana in collaboration with Canton Ticino's Service of Health Promotion and Evaluation (SPVS), Dept of Health and Social Services (DSS), and Health Promotion Switzerland (PSS), within the cantonal program 'Peso Corporeo Sano' ('Healthy Body Weight').

References

Lamprecht, M., and Stamm, H. (2006) *Activité physique, sport et santé – Faits et tendances se dégageant des Enquêtes suisses sur la santé de 1992, 1997 et 2002*. Statistique de la Suisse. Neuchâtel: Office fédéral de la statistique (OFS).

Monitoraggio della strategia a lungo termine di Promozione Salute Svizzera (2012) Indicatori del settore 'peso corporeo sano' – Indice di massa corporea della popolazione residente in Svizzera. Retrieved July 27, 2012, from www.gesundheitsfoerderung.ch/pdf_doc_xls/i/gesundes_koerpergewicht/Grundlagen/Monitoring/Indikatoren/IND_2A_it.pdf.

Repubblica e Cantone Ticino, DSS, sezione sanitaria (2009a) Indicatori sulla salute dei Ticinesi – scheda 2.1 BMI. Retrieved March 4, 2011, from www4.ti.ch/fileadmin/DSS/DSP/UPVS/PDF/Indicatori/INDICATORI/2_Stili_di_vita/2_1_BMI.pd).

Repubblica e Cantone Ticino, DSS, sezione sanitaria (2009b) Indicatori sulla salute dei Ticinesi – scheda 2.2 Attività-fisica. Retrieved March 4, 2011, from www4.ti.ch/fileadmin/DSS/DSP/UPVS/PDF/Indicatori/INDICATORI/2_Stili_di_vita/2_2_Attività-fisica.pdf.

Schopper, D. and Promotion Santé Suisse (PSS) (2005) Poids corporel sain: comment enrayer l'épidémie de surcharge pondérale? Bases scientifiques en vue de l'élaboration d'une stratégie pour la Suisse. Version abrégée. Retrieved March 4, 2011, from www.suissebalance.ch/logicio/client/suissebalance/file/Grundlagen/GesundesKoerpergewicht_fr.pdf.

Ufficio federale della sanità pubblica (UFSP), and Dipartimento federale dell'interno DFI (2008) *Programma nazionale alimentazione e attività fisica 2008–2012*. Bern: Ufficio federale della sanità pubblica (UFSP).

Ufficio federale dello sport (UFSPO), Ufficio federale della sanità pubblica (UFSP) and Promozione Salute Svizzera (PSS) (2009) *Rete svizzera Salute e Movimento. Movimento efficace per la salute. Documento base*. Macolin: UFSPO. Retrieved from www.hepa.ch/internet/hepa/it/home/dokumentation/grundlagendokumente.parsys.65984.downloadList.62638.DownloadFile.tmp/hepaiscreen.pdf.

The National Social Marketing Centre (NSMC) (2006) Social Marketing National Benchmark criteria. Retrieved June 15, 2011, from www.snh.org.uk/pdfs/sgp/A328466.pdf.

Case study questions

1. Briefly describe why FAN was implemented and what outcomes it obtained.

2. Conduct a SWOT analysis on FAN.

3. Given the research aspect of the population-based project, one can assume that survey respondent burden might potentially hinder participant satisfaction and involvement to the program. How would you balance the trade-off between research requirements and social marketing intervention goals?

Case Study **22**

Empower and engage: Tackling the social determinants of risky drinking in two deprived communities

Katie Collins and Lindsay Manning

INTRODUCTION

High-profile issues like drug abuse and smoking can overshadow the issue of drinking, which is often perceived as a harmless and enjoyable social activity. People with alcohol problems are thought to be in a minority. However, according to the World Health Organization, just as much of the global burden of disease is attributable to alcohol as to tobacco.

Drinking too much can cause problems for individuals, families and whole communities. Consequences include accidents, violence, sexual and mental health problems, chronic liver disease, increased risk of other chronic diseases and, ultimately, avoidable deaths.

We wanted to co-create solutions with people rather than design clever messages or products for them because we felt that this would be a more realistic and effective way of supporting them through a change in their behaviour. We also believed that co-created solutions developed in collaboration with local people and stakeholders were more likely to be sustainable in the long term.

PROBLEM DEFINITION

A Primary Care Trust (PCT) in England asked us to work with two communities, which, according to the Index of Multiple Deprivation,[1] are within the 5 per cent most deprived communities in the country. The PCT wanted us to try to understand why many people drank more than the recommended limits and to work with local people to co-create strategies that would help them cut down.

We started the project with a hunch – and it is important to recognize that this was simply our assumption – that the answer would prove more complicated than just providing information about safe drinking levels or attempting to educate people about the dangers of heavy drinking. Instead, we hypothesized that many factors in the social, economic and physical environment would influence drinking behaviour, based on social ecology theory. Consequently, we believed that, even if people wanted to cut down, they might not be able to do so without some changes to their physical and social circumstances.

STAKEHOLDER ANALYSIS

Stakeholders – typically service providers and community leaders, by our definition – were involved in the project from the beginning and were vital to us in getting introduced to both communities. To launch the project, we held a workshop for stakeholders from the police, council, community organizations and charities. We asked these stakeholders to identify and prioritize what they thought the goals of the project should be. Overwhelmingly, stakeholders felt that improving self-esteem, feelings of competence and increasing engagement in the community needed to come before objectives related specifically to drinking.

Through the workshop and subsequent visits to community leaders, we began to build relationships with key stakeholders, including the youth centre manager (a formidable lady with significant influence in the community) and the reverend of the local church. Both these stakeholders had witnessed the effects of risky drinking on local families and they were very engaged from the start, offering us a vast store of local knowledge, access to venues and introductions to other groups. We also formed links with the children's centre's family workers, the employment hub, tenants and residents associations, other churches and faith groups, service providers and housing associations. In one of the communities, we were fortunate to gain the support of a respected city councillor (another formidable personality) who became a very strong advocate of our work and opened many doors that would otherwise have been closed to us.

An awareness of local power structures and politics was vital. In most cases, stakeholders were open about their agendas (as we were about our own) but in others we found ourselves with privileged information that we knew was affecting decision making. In one instance, a stakeholder took a personal dislike to a representative of another project and attempted to use their considerable influence in favour of our work. Our experiences demonstrate not only the importance of effective stakeholder analysis, but also how vital good relationships and trust, built up over time, are to the success or failure of co-created initiatives.

AIMS AND OBJECTIVES

The goals of the project were to:

1. Understand the underlying causes of risky drinking in two deprived communities and

2. Co-create value propositions with the communities that would reduce the levels of risky drinking and that would be sustainable in the long term.

FORMULATION OF STRATEGY

We took inspiration from a methodology called Participatory Action Research. Rather than describing situations as they are or seeking out general rules and principles, researchers following this tradition seek to improve human welfare using methods of reflection and action. With this method, people participate in the inquiry at all stages, including design, data collection, analysis, application and dissemination of research findings (Ozanne and Saatcioglu 2008).

Value co-discovery

We began co-sensing the problem by setting up 'methods stations' in a community centre, which encouraged people to experiment with different ways of expressing themselves about risky drinking. We persuaded people to try out visual methods such as making collages or writing on large boards. We also tried out simple games and more traditional qualitative techniques such as semi-structured interviews. We found that people were willing to share some very personal stories with us in this informal situation. However, we noticed that literacy problems were common, so many people felt anxious about any method that asked them to read or write because they were worried about making mistakes in public. Many people we spoke to were concerned that they would lose control of their stories – that what they told us would become public knowledge or be passed to Social Services. People didn't seem to have much confidence in authority or outsiders and, while we had endeavoured to reduce their level of concern by spending a good deal of time in the community, the trust we had built did not extend beyond the research team.

In the end, we found that co-creating the methods merged seamlessly into the data collection phase. In fact, the approach that seemed to work best with our communities was closer to ethnography than anything else, with one of the authors helping at community events (the youth club bowling outing and a pantomime for example) and making endless cups of tea. Spending so much time with people informally gave us the chance to chat to numerous individuals, some for a few minutes, but others for an hour or more. In this way, becoming part of the community gave us a deep understanding of the problems that people face and the role alcohol plays in their lives.

Participatory Action Research starts with small groups of collaborators, but, as the research progresses, the community of co-researchers should expand to include more and more people. It can take considerable time to get to know people and encourage those with less confidence or who are disengaged to take part. It took several months to build up enough trust to really start to work with 'ordinary' people (rather than the confident community leaders we were introduced to at the start of the project). In total, Lindsay conducted 64 semi-structured depth interviews with 23 males and 41 females in Community 1 and 58 semi-structured depth interviews with 19 males and 39 females in Community 2.

We found that we were correct in our initial assumptions that drinking was often a consequence of other factors rather than a problem in and of itself, though, once people started drinking to excess, this did make their other problems worse. People wanted us to know that there was good community spirit but that they were tired of outsiders pointing out the negatives. We were told that alcohol was readily available and cheap to buy. Even in instances where it was not, we found people would make cutbacks so they could keep drinking. There was a general feeling that the NHS, in particular, and people from other areas, in general, do not understand what people's lives are like and should not presume they know what changes must be made. In summary, seven broad themes emerged from our analysis of the field notes:

1. **Family** can be a trigger (e.g. childhood experiences) and be part of the consequences of risky drinking. But family could also help people cut down and cope with less alcohol.
2. People feel **trapped** in many ways: by their responsibilities, because they can't move away, by their financial situation and by what's available locally.
3. People **worry** about the practical and the social consequences of seeking help: losing children, friends or benefits, and the humiliation of others knowing about their problems.
4. People feel **powerless**, stuck in a rut. They may be suffering mental health or mood problems or simply be bored, de-motivated and feel they have no reason to get up in the morning.

5. People feel physically, emotionally and socially **isolated**: others are at work and they are stuck at home, no one else understands.

6. Men feel **shame** about admitting weakness and losing masculinity; women feel ashamed about not fulfilling caring duties. Consequently, people hide their problems.

7. People are **confused** by conflicting advice, what happens if they ask for help and what is 'normal'.

While people living in both communities had similar life experiences and reasons for drinking, the structures of the communities were quite different. Community 1 had many more facilities and services that 'belonged' to the community, i.e. they were located within the geographical area community members defined as theirs. However, there were some territorial issues, which meant that, if a service or facility were located at one end, people from the other would feel unwelcome there and vice versa. On the other hand, people in Community 2 felt that there was a severe lack of services, activities and facilities. In particular, they told us that they needed a local doctor, dentist and better-quality shops. While such services were accessible in the past, these had all closed down due to lack of funding. Consequently, people in Community 2 were much more difficult to reach and to engage in co-creation activities because not only did they not like having to leave their own territory (which may be as limiting as their home or street), but they also already felt let down and forgotten.

Value co-design

In partnership with social change agency 'Uscreates',[2] the next stage was to organize the value design process. In Community 1, we held a workshop where more than 40 ideas were suggested. Some ideas were quite specific to a particular age and life-stage (e.g. extreme sports could help divert groups of young men from organizing all their social activity around alcohol) but with general principles that apply to all (e.g. provision of activities that people will value, while also reducing isolation and making people feel better, but which do not revolve around drinking). Ideas were both preventative and geared to help people already struggling with their drinking.

We asked the participants to visualize the idea that they felt was the most likely to make a difference. They created a vision for a 'Community Hub', located in the centre of the community (to mitigate the territorial issues). The Hub would host a range of services for all ages as well as being a venue for 'positive' (not stigma-tizing) reasons to visit, such as a café, evening social club and venue for short courses. The Hub would be promoted and supported by 'Community Champions', who would signpost residents and reassure them about what to expect from any services they might access there. Because the philosophy of our approach is collaborative, it is not possible to describe exactly how the Hub will develop; the people involved will shape it over the next few years.

As we knew that people would be very unlikely to come to a workshop in Community 2, we attended two community events, again helped by 'Uscreates', to try to engage people in mini co-design activities. We spoke to 33 people about our research findings and what ideas they had to make things better. Once more, a variety of suggestions were made and many fell under the broad themes of combating isolation and breaking down barriers. Specific suggestions included befriending or mentoring schemes and a community bus to allow people to access services and facilities more easily.

We connected ideas from the value co-design with the feedback we had received in the research about the lack of services and facilities to create the idea of a Mobile 'Hub' that would work hard to engage people street-by-street. The advantage of this approach is that, once established, the Mobile Hub can be used to deliver any intervention, service or enterprise. At its most basic level, we are attempting to get people out of their houses and talking to one another, even just for a few minutes. This Mobile Hub is currently being piloted with the support of a range of local residents and stakeholders, offering a street café, products from a local bakery and greengrocer, health and wellbeing services, youth and family support, and 'Have Your Say' engagement events.

DISCUSSION

We would like to be able to tell you about the difference these two initiatives have made in both communities, with statistics to back up our claims about increased community engagement, reduced isolation and better health. Unfortunately, projects that attempt to tackle the social determinants of health take years to evolve and the value of co-delivery work is ongoing.

Baseline data were collected at the start of the project using a survey designed to gauge the level of:

- awareness and recall of any health and alcohol interventions;
- engagement with the community;
- knowledge of government guidelines about safe drinking and units in drinks;
- claimed alcohol consumption;
- attitude to health in general and socially desirable response.

The survey is being repeated in August 2012 and again in 2013. Even then, we suspect that the changes detected will be relatively minor, which can pose a significant challenge for social marketers advocating this approach in an age of short-term funding and political change.

A second challenge with this approach is the lack of generalizability of the findings, which runs contrary to the traditional 'test and roll out' approach common to many social marketing communications and health promotion initiatives. This means that, technically, every time a social marketer wants to co-create with a different community, they can't assume that the same solutions will have the same results; they need to start the process again from scratch. This takes time and costs money. Consequently, there is the temptation to engage in co-creation 'lite' (an approach that jokingly we sometimes call 'faux-creation' among colleagues in our research centre). Taking this approach, social marketers would work towards outcomes that are somewhat predetermined, taking communities along for the ride and allowing them only limited input to decision-making. There may be a pragmatic middle ground between the two extremes of co-creation projects that take years and those that offer pretend participation. Our friends and colleagues at 'Uscreates' experiment with toolkits and shortcuts that can help to transfer learning from one project to another and this may be a way forward for this method for pragmatic social marketers.

Finally, we note that, while participatory methods like co-creation offer a promising way to empower people to change, they have attracted some criticism as well. Particularly worrying is the accusation that they have not really shown that they can achieve meaningful change (e.g. see Cooke and Kothari 2001). Critics worry that, if we assume the superiority of any form of participation over more traditional approaches without being sensitive to power dynamics and political issues, then we run the risk that people or organizations with disempowering agendas might divert the work in a way that suits their purposes rather than those of the community. This problem adds an interesting dimension to the ongoing debate about the role of commercial organizations in social change initiatives because of their power and profit-making agenda. Would it have been appropriate to give Diageo a role in our project for instance?

Notes

1   The index is a measure that combines over 30 indicators such as income, employment, social and housing issues into a single deprivation score for each area.
2   www.uscreates.com/.

References

Cooke, B. and Kothari, U. (2001) *Participation: The New Tyranny?* London: Zed Books.
Ozanne, J.L. and Saatcioglu, B. (2008) 'Participatory Action Research', *Journal of Consumer Research*, 35: 423–439.

Case study questions

1. What rationale did the researchers have in declining to provide information about the government's recommended alcohol intake?

2. What types of participation do you think were involved in the project? Did levels of participation vary between the two communities or change as the researchers went through the process?

3. In what ways do you think that our process and methods might need to be adapted if instead of people in deprived communities we wanted to work with university students to co-create strategies to reduce drinking?

Case Study **23**

Ethical issues in pro-social advertising: The Australian 2006 White Ribbon Day campaign

Robert John Donovan, Geoffrey Jalleh, Lynda Fielder and Robyn Ouschan

INTRODUCTION

Violence against women is a major public health problem around the globe. The economic costs of violence against women – including medical and counselling costs, lost productivity, women's refuges and justice system costs – run into the billions of dollars (WHO 2002), while the emotional, psychological and quality of life costs for women and children exposed to such violence are immeasurable.

Along with criminal justice system interventions, and counselling and welfare support for victims, in the past decade, there has been considerable use of mass media advertising campaigns in various countries to promote the cause of ending violence against women and to support women victims. Two features of these campaigns are the increasing involvement of men's groups advocating an end to violence against women and the increasing use of male celebrities in the advertising or as ambassadors for such campaigns. One example of the latter is the White Ribbon Day (WRD) media campaign around 25th November each year, the United Nations International Day for the Elimination of Violence Against Women (UNIFEM). The campaign encourages men to speak out about violence against women and to wear a White Ribbon on 25th November to demonstrate their opposition to violence against women.

In Australia, the 2006 WRD campaign was overseen by a National Leadership Group (NLG), supported and coordinated primarily by UNIFEM Australia in partnership with various individuals, government and non-government organizations, and the Saatchi & Saatchi advertising agency.

This case study, based on Donovan *et al.* (2008, 2009), sets out the results of an evaluation to assess reactions to this particularly controversial campaign, which raised a number of ethical issues for pro-social organizations when dealing with sensitive issues and using execution techniques that may impact negatively on vulnerable audiences.

PROBLEM DEFINITION

In 2006, Saatchi & Saatchi developed *pro bono* a media campaign based on the theme of what fathers say colloquially they would do for their daughters (e.g. 'give my right arm'; 'swim through shark-infested waters'; 'go to hell and back'; etc.). See examples in Figure CS23.1.

The materials included a television advertisement to be aired as a community service announcement (CSA), a radio advertisement CSA, 'postcards', web banner ads and, briefly, a viral electronic postcard (e-card). All materials were available for downloading from the WRD website and all visual components of the campaign displayed graphic scenes of, or copy referring to, self-harm or suicide. The 60-second television advertisement showed a young girl about 12 years of age watching her father in four scenes in the following sequence: walking in front of and being run over by a bus; swimming fully clothed out towards, and being taken by a shark; crawling over broken glass leaving a trail of blood; and in a hospital operating theatre being prepared for surgery to have his right arm amputated. The advertisement ended with the following copy on a blank screen:

If there's nothing you wouldn't do for your daughter . . . [fades & replaced by] . . . start by wearing a white ribbon on November 25, UN Day for the Elimination of Violence Against Women.

The suicidal and self-harm imagery in the television advertisement and related materials was severely criticized by mental health and suicide prevention organizations, domestic violence groups, marketing academics and journalists (Hagan 2006;

Maguire 2006; Winter 2006). Professionals in the family and domestic violence sectors' concerns included that the message in the campaign materials was confounded by the use of gratuitous violence in a campaign that was supposedly against violence, and hence could be counter-productive. Marketing communications experts questioned the logic of the message execution and the need for such graphic scenes.

Substantial evidence suggests that media depictions of suicide can encourage vulnerable viewers to undertake suicide and self-harm attempts, particularly where the suicide method is clearly shown (as in the WRD television advertisement), and particularly among people similar to those shown in the media depiction (Pirkis

Figure CS23.1 (i) Promotional materials on the White Ribbon Day website

Figure CS23.1 (ii and iii) Continued

and Blood 2001; Hawton and Williams 2002). Many countries, including Australia, have ethical guidelines or professional codes of conduct for the reporting of suicide and suicide depictions in media entertainment vehicles.

There is also the issue of exposing disturbing images such as those in the WRD campaign to children and young teens, and perhaps particularly in situations of parental disharmony. In Australia, the Australian Commercial Television Code of Practice (CTCP) covers all areas of programming. While the WRD television advertisement's classification did not permit scheduling in children's programming times, there was no way to ensure that large numbers of children would not be exposed to the advertisement. Furthermore, the advertising materials, including the television ad, were freely available on the website without any age restrictions imposed.

Despite the concerns of mental health and suicide prevention professionals (e.g. Crisis Support Services, Sane Australia and the Mental Health Council of Australia – the peak umbrella group for mental health organizations throughout Australia), Saatchi & Saatchi, UNIFEM Australia and WRD defended the campaign materials, claiming that such imagery was necessary to attract men's attention and to motivate men to take action about violence against women and wear a white ribbon on 25th November. They also claimed that their own pre-testing (which they refused to release) did not support any such concerns about the campaign materials.

AIMS AND OBJECTIVES

Given the above concerns and the refusal of the WRD NLG to release the results of their claimed pre-testing of the advertisement, the authors conducted an assessment of men's and women's reactions to the television advertisement to determine whether or not the concerns of mental health and violence against women professionals were justified.

In particular, they wished to assess:

1. The extent to which viewers interpreted the scenes as depicting suicide, and hence contravened the guidelines about media depictions of suicide.
2. The communication efficacy of the advertisement in terms of whether the imagery distracted from the primary intended messages and whether viewers saw a contradiction in using violence in a campaign against violence.

It was the authors' intention to provide the data to the WRD NLG to assist them in determining whether or not to proceed with these campaign materials.

RESEARCH AND EVALUATION

Methodology followed that of standard commercial pre-testing procedures (e.g. Haley and Baldinger 2000) adapted to pro-social advertising (Donovan *et al.* 1999a;

Donovan *et al.* 1999b; Donovan *et al.* 2000). The sample participants were recruited from the Centre for Behavioural Research in Cancer Control's database of members of the general public who had previously indicated a willingness to take part in research projects. It was intended to expose the television advertisement to 50 persons: 25 males and 25 females, half of whom had a daughter around the age of the young girl in the ad. Provisional ethics approval was obtained subject to monitoring of people's reactions to the materials.

Procedure

The research was conducted in a small, nondescript meeting room at Curtin University's Shenton Park Health Research Campus. The advertisement was displayed on a 34cm television monitor with the viewer seated approximately 1m from the screen. Participants viewed the advertisement individually or in groups of two or three. Following Krugman (1972), participants were shown the television advertisement twice with a five-second gap between exposures. The advertisement is exposed twice to allow respondents adequate opportunity to understand the ad. After viewing the television advertisement, participants were asked to complete a self-administered questionnaire containing open and closed-ended questions. They were then asked to look at colour hard copies of the website materials and answer a further smaller set of questions.

The questionnaire items were based on standard commercial copy testing items adapted for social research topics. The main questions of interest for this report were:

- the perceived intended message(s) of the television advertisement;
- the perceived undesirable messages in the advertisement;
- the perceptions of various images as relating to suicide;
- the attitude to the advertisement;
- the likes, dislikes and confusions in the advertisement; and
- two questions that assessed respondents' beliefs about the efficacy of the imagery in the campaign materials.

The authors also included a question as to whether respondents considered that the question wording indicated any bias in favour of or that was critical of the campaign materials.

RESULTS

Distress resulting from exposure

After ad exposure two male respondents demonstrated visible distress (one experienced considerable distress and could not continue), the university's ethics officer concluded that exposure to the advertisement could cause participants unnecessary distress, and ruled that the study could only proceed after full ethics approval and with satisfactory safeguards in place. Hence, interviewing was terminated and all future appointments cancelled. Given that the WRD launch was imminent, and given that the data appeared sufficiently conclusive with respect to the ethical issues involved, no further interviews were conducted. Of the 24 participants who completed the testing, 13 were males and 11 were female. Five persons were aged 30–39 years, nine were aged 40–49 years, and ten were aged 50 years or over. Twelve respondents had children of both sexes, two had only male and two had only female children. Two respondents did not have children.

Perceived intended messages in the advertisement

Respondents were asked: 'What was the main message or messages the ad makers were trying to get across in this ad?' Space was allowed for three responses. The intended main message perceived by 17 of the 24 respondents (71 per cent) was literally consistent with the creative execution idea that 'fathers were prepared to do anything/everything for their daughters'. This was also the most frequently mentioned first response (42 per cent of respondents). Although prompted to provide up to three responses, only seven (29 per cent) specifically referred to wearing a white ribbon for its intended purpose, while eight (33 per cent) referred to violence against women in general or in relation to the white ribbon.

Overall then, the creative idea dominated the intended message perceptions rather than the specific message of wearing a white ribbon and the general message about violence against women.

Perceived undesirable messages in the advertisement

Respondents were then asked: 'Regardless of messages the ad maker was trying to get across, did you see any undesirable messages in the ad?' Half of the respondents (n=12) answered 'yes' to this question, with half of these (n=6) referring specifically to 'the shocking graphic images'. Other responses queried the 'connection' between the violent scenes and the message about violence against women or wearing a white ribbon, and four referred to the (inappropriate) depictions of violence in the advertisement (e.g. 'a message that pain and violence has positive outcomes'). Without any prompting, two respondents spontaneously mentioned 'suicide': 'suggests or promotes suicide'; and 'didn't get the suicide connection.'

Even with these small numbers, these results suggested that, from a purely communication efficacy criterion, one would question the potential effectiveness of this advertisement.

Attitude towards the advertisement

Liking of an advertisement can facilitate acceptance of an advertisement's message – and vice versa – disliking of an advertisement can hinder acceptance of or distract attention from the intended message (Petty *et al.* 1983; MacKenzie *et al.* 1986). Hence, respondents were asked to indicate how much they liked or disliked the advertisement.

Just under half of the respondents (n=10; 42 per cent) indicated that they liked the advertisement, but only one chose the 'a lot' top box response with nine nominating 'quite a bit'. Seven (29 per cent) stated they neither liked nor disliked the ad; and seven (29 per cent) stated they disliked the advertisement, with four selecting the 'a lot' top box response and three the 'quite a bit' response.

That is, although numbers are small, it appears that disliking of the advertisement tended to be more intense than liking of the ad, which was consistent with other data below.

Regardless of their overall like/dislike rating, all respondents were then asked 'what, if anything, they liked about the ad' and 'what, if anything, they disliked about the ad'. With respect to likes, two major themes emerged:

1. the advertisement had a 'powerful','emotive', 'thought provoking impact' (n=8);
2. they liked the father's expression of love/devotion for his daughter (n=5).

Two men liked that the advertisement 'made them feel brave/strong' and one that the advertisement was *'scary'*. Almost a third (n=7) did not like anything about the advertisement.

With respect to dislikes, several themes emerged:

1. the ad's scenes were 'overdramatized/gory/too confronting' (n=5);
2. the ad's message was 'confusing/ not clear' (n=5), such as 'there was no reason for the father's actions' (n=2);
3. undesirable subtexts, such as 'depicted women as helpless' (n=1) and 'used violence in a message against violence' (n=1), the advertisement targeted only men with daughters.

Overall, the likes and dislikes data, in conjunction with the perceived messages in the ad, suggested that, while the advertisement would have a positive or neutral impact on many people, it would be ineffective if not counter-productive with a substantial proportion of the intended target audience. At the very least, the data suggest that the advertiser should look for ways to improve the ad's performance.

Confusions in the advertisement

A common pre-test diagnostic measure is to ask respondents: 'Was there anything about the advertisement that you found confusing?' and, if so, 'what in the advertising did you find confusing?' Advertisers can then make any necessary changes before airing the advertisement. Nearly two-thirds of this sample answered 'yes' to this question: n=15 (63 per cent), a level of confusion that no commercial advertiser would accept.

Mentions of confusions included five main interrelated themes:

1. the message not being clear or made known until the end (n=9);
2. the opening scenes (the man/bus scene in particular) not being clearly linked to the message about violence against women (n=4);
3. respondents not understanding why the father was being put or was putting himself at risk (n=4);
4. a perceived similarity to anti-smoking advertisements (the hospital scene in particular) (n=2); and
5. no explanation of WRD in the advertisement (n=2). One respondent's comment was that he 'thought the guy was committing suicide in front of his daughter just for fun (i.e. for no reason).'

Do the scenes in the advertisement focus attention on or distract attention from the message about violence against women?

A frequent concern with advertising that uses bizarre or unusual execution techniques is that the attention-getting imagery per se might distract from the advertisement's message (Sutherland 1993). Hence, the question was asked: 'Some people say the scenes in the advertisement make men really think about the issue of violence against women. Others say that the scenes in the advertisement make people think about these scenes rather than the issue of violence against women. Which statement do you agree more with?' Respondents were also given a 'neither' option.

Of the 24 respondents, 16 considered that the scenes distracted attention from the intended message about violence against women. Two respondents stated 'neither'.

Suicide perceptions

One of the main issues of concern to mental health professionals was that the advertisement's scenes depicted self-harm and that the scene of the man stepping in front of a bus clearly depicted suicide. Hence, towards the end of the questionnaire, specific questions about perceptions of suicide and self-harm in the imagery were asked. For the bus and swimming scenes separately, respondents were asked: 'While you were watching the scene where the man [steps in front of a bus]/[the man swims out towards a shark] did you think the man was deliberately trying to kill himself?' The responses provided were yes, no and unsure.

For the bus scene, seven respondents (29 per cent) said 'yes' and two (8 per cent) said 'unsure'; for the swimming scene, two said 'yes' and one said 'unsure'. While the majority of respondents answered 'no' for both scenes, these results nevertheless suggested that sufficient numbers of television viewers would interpret the bus scene in particular as depicting suicide, and, hence, for ethical reasons and code compliance, should be removed from the advertisement. In fact mental health professionals could justifiably have argued that even the small number reporting suicide interpretations in the swimming scene would warrant the ethically prudent response of removing that scene also.

Overall, in conjunction with the spontaneous mentions of 'suicide' in the perceived undesirable messages in the ad, the above findings clearly indicated that a substantial proportion of this sample perceived suicide to be depicted or implied in the ad.

DISCUSSION

Ethical issue: first do no harm

The first law of ethics when intervening in sensitive areas should be to ensure that the intervention will do no harm, particularly to known vulnerable groups (Andreasen 2001; Baron 1996; Donovan and Henley 2010; Mclean 2006). The obligation is arguably stronger where the interveners have little control over who is and who is not exposed to their intervention as in this mass media campaign and where materials were easily accessible on the website. Substantial evidence suggests that media depictions of suicide can encourage vulnerable viewers to make suicide and self-harm attempts. These effects appear greatest where the suicide method is clearly shown (as in this television advertisement) and appear to most influence persons similar to those shown in the media depiction.

Mental health professionals considered that the suicide depictions in the advertisement contravened the Australian Government-endorsed media guidelines regarding depictions of suicide in the media. The research data supported those concerns. The pre-testing results confirmed that some men could suffer considerable distress from viewing the advertisement.

A second vulnerable group is that of children in general being exposed to the self-harm violence, but particularly children separated from one or other parent.

Although the television advertisement was excluded from children's programming times, recent research cited earlier shows that many children watch television after the cut-off point where adult material and advertising is permitted (Fielder *et al.* 2009; King *et al.* 2005; Winter *et al.* 2008).

Given these fairly obvious potentially vulnerable groups and the obligation to first do no harm, the authors believed it was incumbent on the WRD NLG to pre-test the ads against these groups. It appears that they did not – or did not do so adequately. Ethical considerations would require the advertisement be tested against not just members of the public in general, but also against men suffering depression, children in general, children of victims of violence and suicide, and women victims of violence.

Communication efficacy

Commercial advertisers commonly pre-test their advertising executions to ensure that intended messages are perceived as such by the target audience, and that undesirable and distracting elements can be identified and removed. Pre-testing ensures that funds expended on the advertising are not wasted or counter-productive. In the case of the WRD television advertisement, the authors' pre-testing data suggest that this advertisement would not be particularly effective and could even be counter-productive.

In summary: the literal execution concept appeared to overshadow the intended messages about wearing a white ribbon and affirming a stance against men's violence towards women. Any reasonable commercial advertiser faced with these data would take steps to eliminate the confusions and distractions as well as avoiding alienating a significant proportion of their target audience.

Apart from the objectives of motivating men to wear a white ribbon on 25 November and to support the broad message of being against violence towards women, a major aim of the WRD campaign was to support professionals in the field who deal with the consequences of violence against women. However, in this case, due to a lack of adequate consultation and pre-testing with this target audience, it appears to have had the opposite effect of alienating many of them (Winter 2006).

CONCLUSION

Interventions in sensitive areas require more than just good intentions. Not only is there a need to understand the 'do no harm' rule, but one must also have the expertise and resources to meet the obligations demanded by this rule.

Pro-social organizations who do not have or who choose not to consult relevant expertise or allocate necessary resources should redirect their efforts to less sensitive areas where their ethical obligations are within their capabilities.

References

Andreasen, A. (2001) *Ethics in Social Marketing*. Washington, DC: Georgetown University Press.

Australian Bureau of Statistics (2008) Causes of Death Australia, 2006-Catalogue No. 3303.0. Canberra.

Baron J. (1996) 'Do no harm', in D.M. Messick and A.E. Tenbrunsel (eds) *Codes of Conduct: Behavioral Research into Business Ethics*. New York: Russell Sage Foundation, pp.197–213.

Bradley M. (2003) 'Honda's new ad goes off deep end', *Sydney Morning Herald* 23 September. www.smh.com.au/articles/2003/09/17/1063625097375.html [Accessed 13 August 2008].

Dahl, D., Frankenberger, K. and Manchanda, R. (2003) 'Does it pay to shock? Reactions to shocking and nonshocking advertising content among university students', *Journal of Advertising Research*, 43: 268–280.

Donovan, R.J. and Henley, N. (2010) *Social Marketing Principles and Practices. An International Perspective*. Cambridge: Cambridge University Press.

Donovan, R.J. and Vlais, R. (2005) 'Review of Communication Components of Social Marketing/Public Education Campaigns Focusing on Violence Against Women', Victorian Health Promotion Foundation, Melbourne. Available: www.vichealth.vic.gov.au/Publications/Freedom-from-violence/Review-of-Public-Education-Campaigns-Focusing-on-Violence-Against-Women.aspx.

Donovan, R.J., Leivers, S. and Hannaby, L. (1999a) 'Smokers' responses to anti-smoking advertisements by stage of change', *Social Marketing Quarterly*, 5:56–65.

Donovan, R.J., Jalleh, G. and Henley, N. (1999b) 'Executing effective road safety advertising: Are big production budgets necessary?, *Accident Analysis and Prevention*, 31: 243–252.

Donovan, R.J., Francas, M., Paterson, D. and Zappelli, R. (2000) 'Formative research for mass media-based campaigns: Western Australia's Freedom From Fear campaign targeting male perpetrators of intimate partner violence', *Health Promotion Journal of Australia*, 10: 78–83.

Donovan, R.J., Jalleh, G., Fielder, L. and Ouschan, R. (2008) 'When confrontational images may be counterproductive: Reinforcing the case for pre-testing communications in sensitive areas', *Health Promotion Journal of Australia*, 19: 132–136.

Donovan, R.J., Jalleh, G., Fielder, L. and Ouschan, R. (2009) 'Ethical issues in pro-social advertising: The Australian White Ribbon Day campaign', *Journal of Public Affairs*, 9: 5–19.

Drumwright, M.E. and Murphy, P.E. (2004) 'How advertising practitioners view ethics: Moral muteness, moral myopia, and moral imagination', *Journal of Advertising*, 33: 7–24.

Fielder, L., Donovan, R.J. and Ouschan, R. (2009) 'Exposure of children and adolescents to alcohol advertising on Australian commercial free-to-air television', *Addiction*, 104(7), 1157–1165.

Hagan K. (2006) 'Grisly TV ad branded "sick" ', *The Age*, November 5.

Haley, R.I. and Baldinger, A.L. (2000) 'The ARF copy research validity project', *Journal of Advertising Research*, November/December: 114–135.

Hawton, K. and Williams, K. (2002) 'Influences of the media on suicide', *British Medical Journal*, 325: 1374–1375.

Jones, S.C. (2007) 'Fast cars, fast food and fast fixes: Industry responses to current ethical dilemmas for Australian advertisers', *Journal of Public Affairs*, 7: 148–163.

Jones, S.C., Hall, D. and Munro, G. (2008) 'How effective is the revised regulatory code for alcohol advertising in Australia?' *Drug and Alcohol Review*, 27: 27–38.

King, L., Taylor, J. and Carroll, T. (2005) 'Consumer perceptions of alcohol advertising and the revised alcohol beverages advertising code', Research and Marketing Group Department of Health and Ageing: Australia.

Krugman, H. (1972) 'Why three exposures may be enough', *Journal of Advertising Research*, 12: 11–14.

MacKenzie, S.B., Lutz, R.J. and Belch, G.E. (1986) 'The role of attitude toward the ad as a mediator of advertising effectiveness: A test of competing explanations', *Journal of Marketing Research*, 23: 130–143.

Mclean, S.A.M. (ed.) (2006) *First Do No Harm: Law, Ethics and Healthcare*. Aldershot: Ashgate Publishing.

Maguire, E. (2006) 'It's the non-abusers who must listen', *Sydney Morning Herald*, 23 November.

Murphy, P. (1998) 'Ethics in advertising: Review, analysis and suggestions', *Journal of Public Policy and Marketing*, 17: 316–319.

Petty, R.E., Cacioppo, J.T. and Schumann, D. (1983) 'Central and peripheral routes to advertising effectiveness: The moderating role of involvement', *The Journal of Consumer Research*, 10: 135–146.

Pirkis, J. and Blood, R. (2001) 'Suicide and the media. Part II: Portrayal in fictional media', *Crisis*, 22: 155–162.

Sutherland, M. (1993) *Advertising and the Mind of the Consumer*. St. Leonards, NSW: Allen & Unwin.

Winter, B. (2006) 'Women see red on White Ribbon Day', in On Line Opinion, 27 November. Accessed: www.onlineopinion.com.au/view.asp?article1/45212 [13 August 2008].

Winter, M., Donovan, R. and Fielder, L. (2008) 'Exposure of children and adolescents to alcohol advertising on television in Australia', *Journal of Alcohol and Drug Studies*, 69: 679–683.

World Health Organization (2002) *World Report on Violence and Health*. WHO: Geneva.

Case study questions

1. What would have prevented this situation occurring in the first place? That is, what should the WRD group have done before developing their communication materials?

2. Was the university ethics officer right to stop the research process or should the researchers have been allowed to gather a larger sample to increase the reliability of the results?

3. When given the results of the research, what should the WRD group have done? Why?

4. The WRD group proceeded with the campaign in spite of protests from a variety of sectors and in spite of the research showing not only ineffectiveness but also counter-productive effects. Why do you think they ignored all the protests and evidence?

Case Study **24**

Applying social marketing to the H1N1 2009 pandemic flu and the promotion of vaccines

Paulo Moreira

INTRODUCTION

During 2009, the H1N1 pandemic flu hit the world and generated global media coverage. The efforts to promote the adoption of the different types of H1N1 flu vaccines produced, meanwhile, were confronted by different types of reactions from the diverse national audiences.

During the second half of 2009, the pandemic (H1N1) 2009 influenza vaccine was made available to adults and children aged 10 years and over all over the world. Acceptance of a novel vaccine being influenced by mass media projections of risk, including risk of infection, risk of death or severe illness, and risk of serious vaccine side effects, demanded professional health communication and social marketing analysis to ascertain the audience's risk perception, attitudes and willingness to accept the pandemic (H1N1) 2009 influenza vaccine.

PROBLEM DEFINITION

Overall, the 2009 influenza A(H1N1) vaccine uptake was considerably lower than seasonal flu vaccine uptake, with the exception of a small number of countries. While 2009 influenza A(H1N1) was presented by mass media news as more serious than seasonal influenza, the pandemic vaccine was perceived to be less safe than seasonal vaccines. Vaccine uptake and related attitudes were, therefore, quite diverse among different segments of the adult population.

The information campaign launched by the World Health Organization (WHO) during the 2009 pandemic generated high media attention on both types of influenza but, apparently, also higher levels of concern about the safety of the pandemic vaccine. Differences in perceived safety are an important factor behind the lower uptake of pandemic vaccine when compared to previous levels of seasonal flu vaccine.

The lack of efficient vaccination coverage assessment mechanisms to measure vaccination coverage in risk groups during the course of the pandemic prevented some countries from having accurate monitoring of their governments' interventions. An exception identified in related studies were the systems in the United States, which enabled the ongoing monitoring of public concerns, attitudes and other difficulties with vaccination coverage. In Europe, there was hardly any such data concerning monitored attitudes during the pandemic and therefore supporting governmental decisions and interventions was difficult.

STAKEHOLDER ANALYSIS

Governments, pharmaceutical industry, health professionals, public health-related NGOs, patient groups and associations, business organizations, the media and the scientific community all had a contribution to this process and are fundamental stakeholders in the promotional process (Moreira 2007a, 2007b). However, their role, involvement and attitude towards the issue display a large variety of positions which need special social marketing efforts to balance.

COMPETITIVE ANALYSIS

What can be competing with the uptake of a free vaccine as was the case of H1N1 in most countries? Health communication factors are central to explore the competitive environment in this context, including credibility both of the product and the sources of the appeals for vaccine intake. Time and effort demanded to take the vaccine as well as the planning and management of the distribution channels also play a central role.

Additionally, health professionals and their interpersonal communication with adult citizens targeted, being a key element of influence over the final user, also turn out to be a central factor in this analysis.

RESEARCH AND EVALUATION

Findings of the few studies (Seale *et al.* 2010; Smith *et al.* 2009; Sypsa *et al.* 2009) carried out on health communication dimensions affecting this case suggested the intention to decline vaccination against pandemic influenza A(H1N1) showed increasing trends during late 2009. The most frequently reported barrier against the vaccination uptake was the fear that the vaccine might not be safe. The intention to decline among individuals belonging to vaccination target groups as supported by perceptions of low likelihood of getting infected or of low risk associated with it, absence of household members suffering from chronic illnesses and low trust in the available vaccines. Perceptions concerning the risk associated with infection were consistently found to affect the intention to accept or decline vaccination and the fear of side effects resulting from vaccine intake were reported barriers.

Overall, in spite of possibly different levels of acceptance in different countries, attitudinal barriers could be used to explain negative intentions towards vaccine uptake in all countries.

INTERVENTION

Governments' implementation of the pandemic vaccination programs broadly followed both the EU/WHO recommendations issued during the summer of 2009. A large majority of national governments worldwide recommended vaccination of those over six months of age with chronic conditions, pregnant women and health-care workers, these being the 'risk groups' identified as priority targets for the A(H1N1) vaccine intake.

OUTCOMES

The international public health community reported particular problems on how to measure success of the national pandemic vaccination programs. It was argued that it may be misleading to analyze whole population coverage since some countries aimed to vaccinate the entire population rather than the high-risk segments (chronic elderly patients, pregnant women). Some countries, however, adopted a risk group approach.

In comparison to the European outcomes, the estimated population coverage for the United States was 27 per cent and 41 per cent in Canada. This was lower than in European Nordic countries and the Netherlands, similar to Spain and Hungary and higher than in the remaining EU/EEA countries.

DISCUSSION

A high variability in national vaccination coverage rates has been identified. Multiple reasons for these discrepancies include the complexity of the communications environment and the responsive capacity of governments on what concerns health communication and social marketing, public perceptions and attitudes but also vaccine availability and distribution strategies. Overall, available data (Mereckiene *et al.* 2012) suggest that national governments and public health authorities responded to and changed their vaccination policies and recommendations in response to the opinion of expert groups and the specific epidemiology of the disease.

References

Mereckiene, J., Cotter, S., Weber, J.T., Nicoll, A., D'Ancona, F., Lopalco, P.L., Johansen, K., Wasley, A.M., Jorgensen, P., Levy-Bruhl, D., Giambi, C., Stefanoff, P., Dematte, L., O'Flanagan, D., and the VENICE project gatekeepers group (2012) 'Influenza A(H1N1) vaccination policies and coverage in Europe', *Eurosurveillance*, 17(4).

Moreira, J.P.K. (2007a) *Public Health Policy in Action: A Framework for a New Rhetoric of Persuasion*, Charleston, SC: Book Surge Publishing. ISBN:1–4196–8224–5 / ISBN–13: 978–1419682247.

Moreira, J.P.K. (2007b) 'A framework for responsive health policy and corporate communication', *Corporate Communications: An International Journal*, 12(1): 8–24.

Seale, H., Heywood, A.E., McLaws, M.-L., Ward, K.F, Lowbridge, C.P., Van, D. and MacIntyre, C.R (2010) 'Why do I need it? I am not at risk! Public perceptions towards the pandemic (H1N1) 2009 vaccine', *BMC Infectious Diseases*, 10: 99.

Smith, B.W., Kay, V.S., Hoyt, T.V. and Bernard, M.L. (2009) 'Predicting the anticipated emotional and behavioral responses to an avian flu outbreak', *American Journal of Infection Control*, 37: 371–380.

Sypsa, V., Livanios, T., Psichogiou, M., Malliori, M., Tsiodras, S., Nikolakopoulos, I, and Hatzakis, A. (2009) 'Public perceptions in relation to intention to receive pandemic influenza vaccination in a random population sample: Evidence from a cross-sectional telephone survey', *Eurosurveillance*, 14: 19437.

Case study questions

1. Discuss the phenomena that could have influenced the attitude of different audiences towards the uptake of the vaccine.

2. Discuss the key elements of a plan and actions within the social marketing framework to enhance the levels of adoption of future pandemic flu vaccines.

Index

Note: Page numbers in **bold** refer to tables and in *italic* to figures. These are only included where there is no narrative text on the same page.